PUBLICATIONS OF THE NEW CHAUCER SOCIETY

# THE NEW CHAUCER SOCIETY

*Studies in the Age of Chaucer*, the yearbook of The New Chaucer Society, is published annually. Each issue contains a limited number of substantial articles, reviews of books on Chaucer and related topics, and an annotated Chaucer bibliography. Articles explore such concerns as the efficacy of various critical approaches to the art of Chaucer and his contemporaries, their literary relationships and reputations, and the artistic, economic, intellectual, religious, scientific, and social and historical backgrounds to their work.

Manuscripts, in duplicate, accompanied by return postage, should follow the *Chicago Manual of Style*, fourteenth edition. Unsolicited reviews are not accepted. Authors receive free twenty offprints of articles and ten of reviews. All correspondence concerning manuscript submissions for Volume 20 of *Studies in the Age of Chaucer* should be directed to the Editor, Larry Scanlon, Department of English, Rutgers University, New Brunswick, NJ 08903-5054. Subscriptions to The New Chaucer Society and information about the Society's activities should be directed to Susan Crane, Department of English, Rutgers University, New Brunswick, NJ 08903-5054. Back issues of the journal may be ordered from Ohio State University Press, 180 Pressey Hall, 1070 Carmack Rd., Columbus, OH 43210; phone, 614-292-6930, FAX 614-292-2065.

# Studies in the Age of Chaucer

# Studies in the Age of Chaucer

Volume 19
1997

EDITOR

LISA J. KISER

PUBLISHED ANNUALLY BY THE NEW CHAUCER SOCIETY
THE OHIO STATE UNIVERSITY, COLUMBUS

The frontispiece design, showing the Pilgrims at the Tabard Inn, is adapted from the woodcut in Caxton's second edition of *The Canterbury Tales*.

Copyright © 1997 by The New Chaucer Society, The Ohio State University, Columbus. First edition. Published by The Ohio State University Press for The New Chaucer Society.

ISBN 0-933784-21-X

ISSN 0190-2407

# CONTENTS

**AN ANNOTATED CHAUCER BIBLIOGRAPHY, 1995**

Studies in the Age of Chaucer

# THE PRESIDENTIAL ADDRESS
The New Chaucer Society
Tenth International Congress
July 26–29, 1996
University of California
Los Angeles

# The Presidential Address

## God-Denying Fools and the Medieval 'Religion of Love'

V. A. Kolve
*University of California, Los Angeles*

At the 1994 congress of this society, hosted by Trinity College, Dublin, Jill Mann delivered her Presidential Address under the provocative title "Chaucer and Atheism"—the atheism in question being, of course, not Chaucer's but her own. "I am uncomfortable," she said, "with the implicit notion that we in the twentieth century can somehow free ourselves from our own historic moment and read texts in their own terms in a way that earlier centuries could not manage." Marxism, Lacanian psychology, deconstructionism, feminism, all engage critically with the medieval text and the culture that produced it. But with respect to religious faith, historicism reigns. Medieval Christianity is a given, to be thought about only from within, and those of us who do not share its beliefs—whether atheist, agnostic, Asian or Jew—mostly suppress that fact. "It is as if religion, unlike feminism, is not an issue"—as if, on a global scale, religious faith had no continuing relevance, no (often appalling) political consequence. We settle for the pleasure of thinking in terms other than our own—a real pleasure, not to be disdained—only occasionally wondering at just what it is we are doing. "Sometimes," Jill Mann said, "I frighten myself with the power of my Christian apologetics."[1]

---

[1] Jill Mann, "Chaucer and Atheism," *SAC* 17 (1995): 11, 14. Seen in the global context, "feminism looks like a parochial concern. It is not gender but religion that is at the center of the present-day conflicts in Ireland, Yugoslavia, Lebanon, Palestine, Egypt, Algeria. Religion, that is, *matters*, and it matters because it has a political function. And it is because it matters that we should be prepared to evaluate and debate it, rather than treating it as something too personal or too sacred to be discussed" (p. 14).

I suspect many in her audience might confess the same, sharing her concern that we do so as an act of secular bad faith, misleading to our students and troubling to ourselves. Casting a skeptical eye on our habit of thinking chiefly "from within" the religious assumptions of the original culture, she offered some striking examples of how a non-believer openly in dialogue with a Christian text might enrich its historical as well as contemporary significance.

Charles Muscatine, himself a former President of this society, just two years earlier in an essay entitled "Chaucer's religion and the Chaucer religion," offered an equally pointed critique of "the religious, almost puritanical Chaucer who emerges powerfully and suddenly at mid-century and is with us still," an idea of Chaucer that seems to him essentially new in the Chaucer tradition. Like Jill Mann, he finds this religious Chaucer "peculiarly difficult to connect to late twentieth-century sensibility"—by which I take him to mean, hard to relate to the way we actually live, the things we actually believe in.[2]

Whether or not a "religious" Chaucer emerges legitimately from the Chaucer texts is too large a question to pursue here. (I feel both honored and chagrined to be named among its chief proponents.) But like Professors Muscatine and Mann and perhaps no small number of you, I sometimes wonder at the fact that so much of my professional life, in the classroom, the library, and at the word-processor, should be spent attempting to recover the intellectual and emotional force of religious beliefs I do not share. In this lecture, I want to take this "emerging topic of presidential discourse" a step or two further, not only to correct an imbalance in my own critical practice, but to introduce to you a figure generally assumed never to have existed at all—the medieval non-believer—and to say a few words on his behalf. I cannot, it is true, produce an atheist who would have been recognizable to the Age of Enlightenment—an age when the universe became entirely rational and God an unnecessary hypothesis. But I can bring forward someone at

---

[2] Muscatine, "Chaucer's religion and the Chaucer religion," in *Chaucer Traditions: Studies in Honour of Derek Brewer*, ed. Ruth Morse and Barry Windeatt (Cambridge: Cambridge University Press, 1990), p. 250. What Muscatine would deny is not Chaucer's orthodoxy, but "the nature, range, depth, and intensity of his religious feeling itself. It is the latter, his enveloping religiosity, that seems to me to be a late twentieth-century discovery or preoccupation." (Ibid.) He rightly deems Ralph Baldwin's monograph, *The Unity of the Canterbury Tales*, published in 1955, the ur–text of readings that allow for genuine religious feeling, at least on occasion, on Chaucer's part. And he is right to judge that monograph "remarkable."

least as interesting, if only because he was so difficult for medieval culture to conceive: the fool of Psalms 13 and 52[3] who says in his heart, There is no God. [*Dixit insipiens in corde suo: non est Deus.*]

Medieval ideas of non-belief can be found, to some extent, in patristic commentary on those psalms, but more telling by far in illustrations to the second of them—Psalm 52—in psalters dating from the thirteenth through the early fifteenth centuries. Since that psalm was illustrated, for liturgical convenience, in virtually every deluxe psalter—the most important class of book produced in the thirteenth century, central to monastic and lay devotion alike—there are many pictures to show us what a God-denying fool looked like in the medieval imagination.

The commentators, we must note, do their best to avoid any confrontation with what we would call the atheistic sense of his claim. In the words of St. Hilary of Poitiers, commenting upon Psalm 52 in the fourth century, such words are said in the heart by those who don't want to be known as fools: "Who can look at the world and not perceive there is a God."[4] St. Augustine, commenting upon Psalm 13, affirmed the same: "Not even those philosophers whose impiety and false and perverse theories concerning the Godhead are to be detested have dared to say: 'There is no God.' This assertion is therefore made merely *in his heart*; even if he dare to think such a thing, he dares not proclaim it."[5] Eusebius,

---

[3] 13 and 52, Vulgate numbering; in Hebrew and post-Reformation Bibles, 14 and 53. Since 13 includes most of 52, modern scholars think them originally a single psalm, entering the collection via independent textual traditions.

[4] "Quis enim mundum contuens, Deum esse non sentiat?" Hilary of Poitiers, *Tractatus in Psalmos*, P.L. 9: 325d.

[5] Augustine, *Enarrationes in Psalmos*, XIII 2, *Corpus Christianorum: Series Latina* (Turnholt: Brepols, 1956), vol. 38, p. 86: "Nec ipsi enim sacrilegi et detestandi quidam philosophi, qui peruersa et falsa de Deo sentiunt, ausi sunt dicere: Non es Deus. Ideo ergo dixit in corde suo, quia hoc nemo audet dicere, etiam si ausus fuerit cogitare." I quote the translation by Dame Scholastica Hebgin and Dame Felicitas Corrigan, *St. Augustine on the Psalms*, in *Ancient Christian Writers: The Works of the Fathers in Translation,* ed. Johannes Quasten and Walter J. Burghardt, S.J., No. 29 (New York: Newman Press, 1960), I. 154; only 2 volumes have been published so far, extending through Psalm 37. In this commentary, Augustine was no doubt thinking of Epicurus and his followers, who taught that the soul dies with the body, that the physical world can be explained by natural causes, and that the gods do not interfere in what happens here on earth. To do so would detract from the perfect bliss they enjoy in intercosmic space, where they live only for themselves. Even philosophers as benighted as this, Augustine reminds us, did not deny the existence of God(s). For a brief explication of Epicurean beliefs, see *The Oxford Classical Dictionary*, 2d ed., pp. 390–92, or *The Encyclopedia of Philosophy*, ed. Paul Edwards (New York: Macmillan, 1967), 2.2–5. Augustine had written commentaries on the first 32 psalms by 392; on the rest by 420 (see Peter Brown, *Augustine of Hippo: A Biography* (Berkeley: University of California Press, 1967), p. 74.

writing in Greek in the fourth century, and already using the word *átheos* for such a person, had explained why such persons must be rare indeed: a "knowledge of God is instilled in all of us by nature."[6] Not until the seventeenth century and after was it possible to respond to "There is no God" as a credible proposition, for which a rational case might be made.[7]

Before then the idea could be stated in only in the most minimal terms—seldom more than a repetition of the formula *non est deus*—and only within a larger text that worked its way to a statement of faith or offered logical counter-proof. The psalm itself offers reassurance in its closing verses: "When God shall bring back the captivity of his people, Jacob shall rejoice, and Israel shall be glad" (52:7). And philosophic texts demonstrating the counter-truth were provided across the medieval centuries, most notably by St. Augustine in his Treatise on Free Will, *De libero arbitrio voluntatis*, completed around 395; by St. Anselm in his *Proslogion*, in 1077–78; and by St. Thomas Aquinas in his *Summa Theologiae*, ca. 1265–68, where the Second Question—"whether there is a God"—is answered by five magisterial proofs of His existence. All three of these texts—each of them enormously influential—address their argument explicitly to the psalter fool. But he is brought forward as a straw man, a striking way to launch the proof, nothing more.[8] The Middle Ages

---

[6] Eusebius, *Commentaries on Psalms*, Patrologia Graeca, ed. Migne, 23:144, on Psalm 13; col. 143 offers a Latin translation: "Etsi vero, quia omnibus a natura insita est Dei notitia." Eusebius allows for a variety of atheists, including some who say God is only an empty name and does not exist at all, some who reject the true God to fabricate others who do not exist, and some who claim merely that he does not concern himself with earthly matters. He emphasizes hypocrisy: they confess many Gods with their mouths alone, while holding no sound belief about God in their heart. The Greek *átheos* can mean "without God" as well as "denying God." Augustine, too, affirmed that the soul by its very nature participates in eternal Truth, reflecting the Trinity in its faculties of memory, understanding, and will. The idea became a commonplace throughout the medieval centuries.

[7] Even in that century, "atheist" served chiefly as a term of abuse, without theological precision. The extensive article on "Atheism" in *Encyclopaedia of Religion and Ethics*, ed. James Hastings et al. (Edinburgh: T. and T. Clark, 1908–26), 2:173–90, remains helpful, esp. p. 176 ff. on atheism in England and France: "what was simply neutral materialism in London became often positive atheism in Paris," though markedly so only in the eighteenth century. The *OED* first records "atheist" in 1571, in Golding's dedicatory epistle to Calvin on the Psalms: "The Atheistes which say . . . there is no God." "Atheism" as a noun first occurs in 1587, in a passage defining it instead as "utter Godlessness." "Theist," interestingly enough, is not recorded until 1662, and "theism" not until 1678. These constitute a secondary formation, invented to oppose "atheism," not vice versa. Atheism, as Derrida might say, is always already there.

[8] See Augustine, *On Free Choice of the Will*, trans. Anna S. Benjamin and L. H. Hackstaff, *The Library of Liberal Arts* (Indianapolis and New York: Bobbs–Merrill, 1964),

otherwise preferred to see *non est deus* as an irrational statement, useful at best in teaching the nature of false logic in the schools. A collection of six *Impossibilia* composed by Siger of Brabant between 1266 and 1276— witty explorations of propositions self-evidently untrue—suitably begins with *Primum impossibile fuit deum non esse* ("The first impossibility [is] that God does not exist").[9] The perceived absurdity of such an idea can be deduced from another example explored by Siger, "The Trojan War is still in progress," or from propositions in other collections, such as "Things infinite are finite," and "A man's foot is greater than the world." Like these, the notion that God might not exist seemed absurd, worth thinking on only as a way of developing logical skill. In Siger's examples, indeed, the refutations form the major part of the text.[10]

In short, the Middle Ages could not make sense of the proposition *non est deus*, and we should not imagine anyone then really wishing to do so. To believe that the order and beauty of the universe did not imply a Creator/Governor/Supreme Being would have involved a paradigm shift as profound as imagining that the earth was not the center of the universe, with psychological consequences even more unsettling. For us, of course, it is different. Christianity is but one religion among many, and there is—in the West at least—no social or moral obligation to choose any at all. We decide for ourselves. But, as Lucien Febvre has demonstrated in a landmark book, *The Problem of Unbelief in the Sixteenth Century*, even in the early modern period Christianity "happened somehow automatically, inevitably, independently of any express wish to be a believer, to be a Catholic, to accept one's religion or to practice it . . . ." "One found oneself immersed from birth in a bath of Christianity from which one did not emerge even at death," for the Church not only baptized one before one had any say in the matter, but buried one when one's say was gone. It provided "rituals that no one could escape"—no

---

p. 38; *St. Anselm's 'Proslogion' with 'A Reply on Behalf of the Fool' by Gaunilo and 'The Author's Reply to Gaunilo,'* trans. M.J. Charlesworth (1965; repr. Notre Dame: University of Notre Dame Press, 1979), pp. 116–17; and Thomas Aquinas, *Summa Theologiae* Ia.2.1, ed. Thomas Gilby, O.P., Blackfriars trans. (London: Eyre & Spottiswoode, 1964), pp. 63–64.

[9] Siger of Brabant, *Die Impossibilia des Siger von Brabant: Eine Philosophische Streitschrift aus dem XIII. Jahrhundert*, ed. Clemens Baeumker, 2.6, *Beiträge zur Geschichte der Philosophie des Mittelalters* (Münster: Aschendorf, 1898), p.1.

[10] For the other examples, and a brief introduction to the genre—a sub-species of the genus *sophismata*—see Roy J. Pearcy, "Chaucer's 'An Impossible' ('Summoner's Tale' III, 2231)," *Notes & Queries* 212 (1967): 322–23.

matter what the mood of one's participation, not even if one sometimes mocked and scoffed. Between birth and death every aspect of human life, educational, marital, economic, political was stamped by religion—so much so that even "the most intelligent of men, the most learned, and the most daring were truly incapable of finding any support either in philosophy or science against a religion whose domination was universal."[11] If the case for atheism could not be made in the sixteenth century, as Febvre decisively demonstrates—his focus is on the bold and brilliant circle of Rabelais—how much slighter the chance of it during centuries too simply but not inappropriately styled an Age of Faith?

Small chance, it would seem, indeed. Medieval commentators on these psalms chiefly make *non est deus* mean *something other* than "there is no God" and modern scholars have mostly followed their lead. But for a long time now, as other duties and projects have permitted, I have been doubting that proposition, and for the simplest of all possible reasons. Some 30 years ago I came upon the image of a non-believer in the pages of a medieval psalter (fig. 1)—or so it seemed to me—and like those zealous folk among us who claim to have seen UFO's, I found myself unwilling to abandon the possibility, at least not without further testing. In fact I soon came upon another such; eventually upon dozens; by now, I would guess, somewhere near two hundred. And there were parallel sightings, equally difficult to explain. I started encountering these enigmatic figures elsewhere, carrying with them (it struck me as possible) the proposition *non est deus* into other pictorial sites and other iconographic traditions—most especially those concerned with the Passion of Christ and the persecution of saints. I started finding fools there, sometimes in the role of temptor or tormentor, sometimes simply as spectator, a face in the crowd looking on. I started thinking seriously about what all these pictures might mean.

But let me return to the first such image I ever encountered—the picture before you, from the Psalter of Jean, Duc de Berry, painted by Jacquemart de Hesdin ca. 1386, after a model by Jean Pucelle.[12] What struck me about it, above all, was its almost shocking modernity: its

---

[11] Lucien Febvre, *The Problem of Unbelief in the Sixteenth Century: The Religion of Rabelais*, trans. Beatrice Gottlieb (Cambridge, MA: Harvard University Press, 1982), pp. 336, 353. The pages between, as well as his concluding chapter, "A Century That Wanted to Believe," are of particular relevance.

[12] Figure 1: reproduced in color by Millard Meiss, *French Painting in the Time of Jean de Berry: The Late Fourteenth Century and the Patronage of the Duke*, 2 vols. (London: Phaidon, 1967), vol. 2, fig. 78, and discussed in vol. 1: 153–54 and 331–32; on

Figure 1: Paris, Bibl. Natl. MS. fr. 13901, fol. 106. Duc de Berry Psalter (Paris, ca. 1386).

pitiless rendering of human suffering, alienation, emptiness, and despair. I had never seen a medieval painting so austere, so unanchored in any meaning external to, or larger than, itself. I saw in it a picture of secular man—or as much as the age could imagine of such a person—half-naked, frail, inhabiting an emptied universe. His clothing is like that worn by Job in his afflictions, with undergarments torn, and a hospital-cloth or winding sheet about his back and head. There is no God to look down on him. Though his figure is not without grace, the draperies not without beauty, the club shapely and of some potential menace, it is a tragic picture for all that—for those details are as nothing when set against the misery of the face (fig. 2), the death in the eyes, the gnawing at something that seems unlikely to yield nourishment of any kind. What the fool is shown eating admits of a variety of interpretations. It may be a cake, a cheese, a loaf. But I first thought it a stone—a possibility I can now verify as authentically medieval. The picture seemed to be above all about hunger, and I saw in it a likeness—how shall I say?—embarrassingly personal. I made some notes on the picture, not because it reminded me of anything in Chaucer—the research I was in fact beginning—nor as a seed for the major research project it would become—it was years before I recognized that—but because I did not want to lose the details of this image. I wanted to know what the fool was eating. I wanted to know what *his* denial of God entailed.

The book I am completing on this subject, expanding a series of four lectures already given at the University of Toronto and Trinity College, Cambridge, will reproduce a great many fools of this kind, and introduce them with appropriate care.[13] Here a few must stand in for

---

Jacquemart see also pp. 151–52, 169–76, and *passim*. For the Pucellian model, as evidenced in the *Bréviaire de Jeanne d'Évreux*, see vol. 2, fig. 605; its fool is wilder in mood, more full of mischief.

[13] The titles of those lectures will give some idea of their content: (I) "The Fool and His Hunger"; (II) "Typologies of the Psalter Fool"; (III) "The Fool as Killer of Christ"; and (IV) "The Feast of Fools Revisited." I gave them first as the Alexander Lectures at Toronto University in late 1993, and then (with the permission of both sponsors) in revised form as the Clark Lectures at Trinity College, Cambridge in early 1994. They are being expanded into a book under contract to Stanford University Press. The NCS Address printed here begins by summarizing some of the material from the second of these lectures, though from a different perspective—its relation to agnostic pedagogy—and then moves on to the subject of a fifth chapter, "The Fool in Love," its material here essayed for the first time. In publishing this NCS address, I have preserved its essential shape and brevity, reserving for the book the full range of idea, evidence, and pictorial representation it requires.

Figure 2: (detail, Figure 1).

many—in all their strangeness, without accompanying explanation—
to establish a minimum visual matrix for this talk. But I have chosen
them to represent the dominant tradition in the thirteenth and early
fourteenth centuries. As you will see, it virtually never depicts the fool
as someone capable of rationality. He is shown instead as feeble-minded
or insane (fig. 3).

There was no textually inevitable reason for that choice. As the text
itself in its third and fourth verses makes clear, the psalmist had a
much broader human reference in mind: "God looked down from
heaven on the children of men: to see if there were any that did understand or did seek God. / All have gone aside, they are become un-
profitable together: there is *none* that doth good, *no not one*" [emphasis
mine].

St. Augustine's commentary on the Psalms, the most influential ever
written, acknowledges the need to transform the unthinkable text into
some more general kind of folly, lest the psalm seem to pertain to "very
few." "A difficult thing it is to meet with a man who says in his heart,

Figure 3: Cambridge, Fitzwilliam Museum MS. 300, fol. 57. Isabella Psalter (Paris, ca. 1255–65).

'There is no God.'"[14] Augustine found one sort of larger relevance by noting that the fool's denial is not spoken aloud but said in the heart, secretly. Surely, he wrote, this concerns that multitude of folk who live

[14] "[E]t difficile est ut incurramus in hominem qui dicat in corde suo: Non est Deus." Augustine makes the point over and over: "non multos . . . perpauci sunt . . . sic pauci sunt. . . . uix inuenitur; rarum hominum genus est qui dicant in corde suo. . . ." *Enarr.*

in sin shamelessly, as a matter of daily habit. Because God has not punished them, they carry on as though he condoned their way of living—
as though, indeed, he were pleased by it. But, continues Augustine, in
a voice of thunder, "he who thinks to please God with evil deeds, thinks
God not to be God. For *if* God *is*, He is just; if He is just, injustice displeases Him, iniquity displeases Him. When you think, God does not
care about my sins, you say nothing else but 'There is no God.'"[15]
Augustine's explanation is both ethical and abstract: to deny God's
Justice is to deny God's existence, inconceivable without it. And to live
as though something were true is to say it in your heart. (We should
note that the so-called "African" psalter used by Augustine translated
*nabal*—the Hebrew word for fool in these psalms—as *imprudens*, not
*insipiens*.)

But one virtually never sees persons of this kind—capable of reason,
however imprudent or unwise—illustrating this psalm. Instead, in a
cycle of 8 psalter illustrations invented in Paris ca. 1205–1230 and soon
standard across Europe,[16] he is shown as a madman or congenital idiot
(fig. 4)—even though in Christian theology reason must consent to sin

---

*In Ps.* 52.2, ed. cit., p. 638. The old 6-volume Oxford translation of Augustine's
Commentary on Psalms was reprinted (in slightly abridged form) in *The Nicene and Post-
Nicene Fathers*, 1st series, vol. 8, first published in 1888. Though its prose style is man-
nered and archaic, it remains useful until the new translation (see n. 5 above) is completed. (It translates Psalm 13, pp. 46–47, and Psalm 52, pp. 202–05, numbering them
14 and 53; see p. 202 for the passage under discussion.) Michael P. Kuczynski, *Prophetic
Song: The Psalms as Moral Discourse in Late Medieval England* (Philadelphia: University of
Pennsylvania Press, 1995) is a useful study of the Psalter's importance to medieval culture at large, and to late medieval English writing in particular; Part I offers a brief history of psalm interpretation, with p. 21 demonstrating Augustine's prominence within
this tradition, an importance he deems "impossible to overstate."

[15] "qui putat Deo placere facta mala, non eum putat Deum. Si enim Deus est, iustus
est; si iustus est displicet ei iniustitia, displicet iniquitas. Tu autem cum putas ei placere
iniquitatem, negas Deum" (ed. cit., p. 639).

[16] Günther Haseloff, *Die Psalterillustration im 13. Jahrhundert: Studien zur Geschichte der
Buchmalerei in England, Frankreich und den Niederlanden* (Kiel, 1938), remains the standard study, linking the development of an 8-picture cycle to the introduction of the Paris
University Bible, and tracing its influence across northern Europe. The novelty of this
tradition consisted in taking its subject (in most cases) from just the first verse of the
psalm. Haseloff notes that Psalm 52 was unusual in showing further development and
variation after 1230 (p. 29)—testifying, I would say, to the cultural volatility of *non est
deus* as a text. An earlier tradition, popular in England and Germany, had divided the
150 psalms into 3 equal groups (at Psalms 1, 51, 101), each with its own picture. This
was sometimes joined to the Paris cycle to create a 10-picture cycle (Psalm 1 being common to both). This permitted an even richer decoration of deluxe Bibles and psalters and
became fashionable throughout Europe.

Figure 4: London, Brit. Lib. MS. Royal 17 E VII, fol. 241. *Bible historiale* (Paris, 1357).

before sin becomes deadly. The choice is striking, of course, and was suggested by the semantic valence of several words used (in psalter Latin and its vernacular translations) for "fool." But its relation to the text makes less and less sense the longer one looks. Where the text speaks of human folly, these images present a radical dysfunction or deficiency of mind.

These versions of the God-denyer are interesting therefore not just as

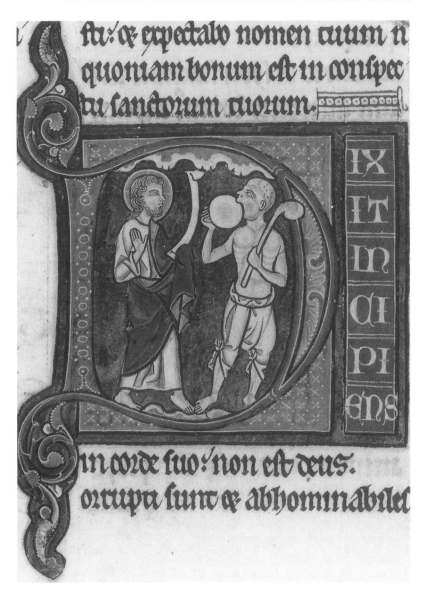

Figure 5: London, Brit. Lib. MS. Add. 30045, fol. 28. Guines Psalter (Paris, after 1228, ?ca. 1240).

a medieval freak show, enticing to the voyeur in us all (fig. 5), but because they so obviously swerve from, and seek to evade, the text's most culturally destructive meaning, the possibility of *no God*. (This is true, with a difference, even for those court fools and jesters who in the mid-fourteenth century begin to replace the feebleminded and the insane.)[17] For to answer the question "Who among us does not believe in the existence of God?" by pointing to a moron, an idiot, a madman (fig. 6), is on the face of it absurd. Such persons are as credulous as any— if, indeed they are able to form any such idea at all—and as little likely to deny the existence of God.[18] Nor will such creatures serve to answer the question "Who among us is an enemy of God's people?" (the psalm's own internal gloss on the fool). Confused in mind, peculiar in behavior, socially outcast, such men pose no threat to kingly rule, or to things as they are, or to anyone's religious faith. They lack cultural standing. The moron's bauble is no more than a soft toy—a bladder filled with air, or stuffed with hair or feathers—incapable of causing harm. Even the madman's club (fig. 7), though it could be swung in anger or self-defense,[19] most often simply rests on his shoulder. In the most anguished and ineffectual of these images, he uses it to threaten God in the sky (fig. 8). What the psalmist has to say of "the children of men"— "there is none that doth good, no, not one"—has been shrunk and narrowed, to implicate only the most marginal of creatures: madmen who have lost their wits, and morons who never had any to begin with.

---

[17] Images of jesters and court fools "swerve" from the atheistic meaning of the text in a different way, substituting instead professional foolery and indecorum, at worst another kind of "carelessness" about God. It is hard to imagine court fools uttering "There is no God" as part of the entertainment they offered.

[18] In some cultures, the idiot was thought to bring good luck and to enjoy God's special protection; his incoherent utterances were sometimes treated as inspired by God. The English word "silly" (ME "sely," akin to German *selig*) originally meant innocent, blessed, and happy. On this see Edwin Radford, *Encyclopaedia of Superstitions*, ed. and rev. by Christina Hole (London: Hutchinson, 1961), "Afflicted Persons," p. 14; Muriel Laharie, *La Folie au Moyen Age XIᵉ–XIIIᵉ siècles* (Paris: Le Léopard d'Or, 1991), pp. 81–83, 87–107; and for a magisterial study, Michael W. Dols, *'Majnūn:' The Madman in Medieval Islamic Society*, ed. Diana E. Immisch (Oxford: Clarendon Press, 1992), esp. chap. 13 on "The Holy Fool."

[19] See, e.g., "Robert of Sicily," in Walter Hoyt French and Charles Brockway Hale, eds., *Middle English Metrical Romances* (New York: Prentice-Hall, 1930), p. 937 (121–28), in which the fool/king strikes the gate porter so fiercely that his nose and mouth bleed. Tristan's entry into Mark's castle, in *La Folie de Tristan*, discussed below, offers another example.

Figure 6: London, Brit. Lib. MS. Stowe 12, fol. 180. Breviary (East Anglian, 1322–1325).

Images of lunacy and mental frenzy uncouple the devastating text (*non est deus*) not only from any possible connection with truth but from any connection with mental processes at all (fig. 9). It cannot even be contemplated as error.

In a rare example that shows both a fool and a proper man wagging his finger at God (fig. 10), we are probably meant to read the fool

Figure 7: Oxford, Bodley MS. Can. Lit. 378, fol. 59v. Psalter (Milan, beginning of the fifteenth century).

symbolically, as a sign for the hidden nature of the other.[20] But pictures of a fool alone, or looked on only by God, or rebuked by a king (fig. 11) frustrate the symbolic transfer. Their signification is stubbornly literal, their only logic unacknowledged anxiety and fear. At their most powerful, I suggest, they tell us that the Middle Ages *was able* to imagine something like atheism—if by that we are willing to mean what it would be like to live in a world without God, or within a mind unable to conceive the idea of God. If medieval man could not think such an idea through,

---

[20] Figure 10: conceivably the proper man is to be seen as rebuking the fool, but his gaze and his wagging finger seem to be pointed upward toward God.

18

Figure 8: Paris, MS. Arsenal 5059, fol. 237v. *Bible historiale* of Jean de Papeleu (Paris, 1317). Photo: Paris, Bibliothèque Nationale.

he could at least give it body and gesture. The opening initial to Psalm 52 thus became a site of existential danger, hospitable only to the most radically other. Within its ornate frame religious nonbelief was made identical with the suffering and alienation experienced—for wholly un-related reasons—by the medieval madman/moron/fool (fig. 12).

So it was not in fact a portrait of a non-believer I met so long ago in the pages of the Duc de Berry's psalter—that has been just a way of talk-ing—but rather an apotropaic image of one—an image meant to do ide-ological work. Just as gargoyles on the cathedrals were designed to ward off evil spirits from without, so these psalter fools were meant to ward off the unbeliever—that part of us capable of existential doubt—always

Figure 9: The Hague, Museum van het Boek/Museum Meermanno-Westreenianum MS. 10B23, fol. 293. *Bible historiale* of Jean de Vaudetar presented to Charles V (Paris, 1372).

potential within. Because the Divine Office required the Book of Psalms to be recited in its entirety every week of the liturgical year, monastic communities *in their own voices* chanted the words of the fool aloud, twice weekly across the medieval centuries. (The iconography of the *insipiens* has a performative dimension.) The text denying divinity— *non est deus*—could not itself be denied or suppressed. But it could be made safe by attributing it solely to the senseless or insane (fig. 13). Scarecrows of the mind, these fools return us to ground zero: to the ter-

Figure 10: London, Brit. Lib. MS. Add. 38116, fol. 60v. Huth Psalter (Lincoln, ca. 1280).

ror, confusion, and vulnerability out of which religious belief is born,[21] and to the fear by which, in moments of greatest stress or doubt, it is sustained. They illustrate the anxiety induced by the text rather than the text itself.

There is about this whole tradition, in fact, a terrible incoherence, a telling pile-up of cultural and religious self-contradiction that can take us deeper into the otherwise unrecorded history of medieval non-belief. As we know from many sources, medieval madmen and idiots were in real life often treated harshly. Europe was still an agrarian, underpopulated society in which few traveled far from their birthplace, inbreeding was inevitable, and born fools not uncommon, though never per-

---

[21] Such pictures might be said to confirm a proverb well attested in both classical and medieval texts: "Timor invenit deos" ["Fear first created the gods;" "We invent the gods out of our fear"]. Chaucer translated it so: "Drede fond first goddes, I suppose" (*TC* 4. 1408; all citations of Chaucer's works are taken from Larry D. Benson, gen. ed., *The Riverside Chaucer*, 3rd ed. [Boston: Houghton Mifflin, 1987]). See *The Riverside Chaucer*, p. 1049, for many other examples. In fuller form the proverb reads "Primus in orbe deos fecit timor" ["Fear first made gods in the world"]. John V. Fleming, *Classical Imitation and Interpretation in Chaucer's* Troilus (Lincoln: University of Nebraska Press, 1990), p. 83 ff., shows it to originate with Statius, not Petronius.

Figure 11: Oxford, All Souls MS. lat. 7, fol. 49v. Psalter (East Anglia, ca. 1310–1320).

fectly assimilated or understood. They could be mocked, knocked about, driven from town to town, stoned by children and set upon by dogs (fig. 14), all in celebration of the normal, the healthy, the whole. It must have seemed appropriate in its way. Mental illness is the most puzzling of human conditions, and was understood then largely in Biblical terms, as a punishment from God for sin.[22] Feeblemindedness too offered fair game, for if reason represents God's image within us, the fool's natural deficiency reveals him less than fully human, in ways mor-

---

[22] Penelope B.R. Doob, *Nebuchadnezzar's Children: Conventions of Madness in Middle English Literature* (New Haven: Yale University Press, 1974), chapter 1, offers an elegant survey of medieval attitudes toward madness, including medical theory concerning its natural causes. Laharie, *La Folie*, significantly extends that investigation and adds a careful study of the treatment of the mad and the simple within a feudal society. Angelika Gross, *'La Folie': Wahnsinn und Narrheit im spätmittelalterlichen Text und Bild* (Heidelberg: Carl Winter Universitätsverlag, 1990), likewise devotes considerable space to the medical explanation.

Figure 12: Oxford, Bodley MS. Douce 118, fol. 60v. Psalter (Artois, end of the thirteenth century).

dantly embodied in the manikin or homunculus psalter fool (fig. 15). Rough treatment for such creatures must have seemed to reflect in some careless, almost carnival way the mystery of God's inscrutable justice—though even the Middle Ages sometimes judged that justice harsh indeed.[23]

[23] This ambivalence can be found within the Old Testament itself, most clearly in the Book of Jonah (4:11) when God changes his mind about destroying Nineveh: "And shall not I spare Ninive, that great city, in which there are more than a hundred and twenty thousand persons that know not how to distinguish between their right hand and their left, and many beasts?" The late fourteenth-century poem called *Patience* amplifies that pardon to include "sottez formadde" who cannot distinguish between the upright of a ladder and its rung, babes in arms who have never done harm, women "unwitty" who can't tell one hand from another, as well as dumb beasts who cannot sin and thus cause themselves grief. God's last-minute decision to extend mercy to all these offends only Jonah, the most irritable of prophets. (See Malcolm Andrew and Ronald Waldron, eds., *The Poems of the Pearl Manuscript*: Pearl, Cleanness, Patience, Sir Gawain and the Green Knight [Berkeley: University of California Press, 1979], p. 205, ll. 509–23.)

Figure 13: London, Brit. Lib. MS. Add. 29253, fol. 41v. Breviary (near Ghent, early fourteenth century).

For there is another part to this story. In more thoughtful contexts and by more thoughtful minds, the mad and simple-minded were also seen to be in need of protection, deserving of pity and compassion. Canon and secular law alike recognized that such persons could not be held responsible for their actions, for the vagaries of what they might do or say.[24] Common sense dictated as much, as did the example of

[24] See R. Colin Pickett, *Mental Affliction and Church Law* (Ottawa: University of Ottawa Press, 1952), *passim*.

Figure 14: Vienna, Öst. Nationalbibliothek MS. 1921, fol. 65v. Prayerbook of Queen Joanna (Naples, third quarter of the fourteenth century).

Figure 15: Paris, Bibl. Sainte-Geneviève MS. 1181, fol. 184v. Aurifaber Bible (Paris, end of the thirteenth century).

Christ, who cast out devils to cure the tortured in mind, and who is recorded as loving the simple and the afflicted with particular devotion. The history of his Passion complicated the matter even more, for in other medieval commentary on these psalms the Jews bring Christ to trial explicitly as a God-denyer—a carpenter's son who by claiming God as his Father denies the divinity that distinguishes God from man. In a notable exchange vividly staged in plays of the Passion, Herod, enraged by Christ's silence, deems him an idiot/mute and sends him back to Pilate in the white coat of a natural fool.[25]

The dressing of Christ as a fool goes well beyond insult, though Herod intends nothing more. It makes visible a deeper truth, first expressed by St. Paul when he described the crucifixion (along with his preaching on it) as "foolishness"—a version of the Passion at once resistant to theological system and trivialized by comforting exegesis. Whereas the Jews seek a sign, he wrote, and the Greeks wisdom, "we preach Christ crucified; unto the Jews indeed a stumbling-block and unto the Gentiles foolishness." Since God has "made foolish the wisdom of this world" (1 Cor. 1:18–25), those who follow Christ must imitate his example in this respect also, as Paul and the apostles have done: "We are made a spectacle to the world and to angels and to men. / We are fools for Christ's sake. . . . / Even unto this hour we both hunger and thirst and are naked and are buffeted and have no fixed abode" (1 Cor. 4:9–10). In a prayer full of paradox he pleads "Take me as one foolish that I also may glory a little" (2 Cor. 11:16–23).[26] For this reason too, images of Christ as the Man of Sorrows are sometimes reminiscent of the psalter fool, for those

[25] In Play 16 of the Chester cycle, Herod says: "Methinkes this man is wonders throo,/ dombe and deafe as a doted doo,/ or frenticke, in good faye . . . Cloth him in white, for in this case/ to Pilate hit may be solace,/ for Jewes custome before was/ to cloth men that were wood/ or madd, as nowe hee him mase,/ as well seemes by his face;/ for him that hase lost his grace/ this garment is full good." (R.M. Lumiansky and David Mills, eds., *The Chester Mystery Cycle*, EETS s.s. 3 [London: Oxford University Press, 1974, 1986], vol. 1, 293, ll. 187–202.) The editors trace the robe from Luke 23:11 (*indutum veste alba*), via Peter Comestor's *Historia Scholastica* and the *Legenda Aurea* which interpret it as a sign of ridicule or mockery, to several other late medieval English texts that unequivocally declare it a fool's garment (ibid., 2. 233n), well supported by the iconographic tradition of Psalm 52.

[26] Cf. St. Bernard's commentary on "Play the mountebank I will" (2 Kings 6:22), quoted by Caroline Walker Bynum, *Jesus as Mother: Studies in the Spirituality of the High Middle Ages* (Berkeley: University of California Press, 1982), pp. 127–28. For the larger topic, see John Saward, *Perfect Fools: Folly for Christ's Sake in Catholic and Orthodox Spirituality* (Oxford: Oxford University Press, 1980), and on early examples in the Eastern Orthodox church, Alexander Y. Syrkin, "On the Behavior of the 'Fool for Christ's Sake,'" *History of Religions* 22 (1982): 150–71. Such an inversion of wisdom/foolishness underlies the account of "What the Lord Jesus Did from His Twelfth to the Beginning of His Thirtieth Year" in the immensely influential *Meditations on the Life of Christ*, ascribed to St. Bonaventure. It tells us that during these eighteen years, unnoted in the Gospels, Christ stayed at home, apparently avoiding all conversation and showing no prowess or valor, causing the people to scoff at him, saying "He is a useless man, an idiot, a good-for-nothing, foolish, bad." At the age of twelve he had proved himself "in advance of his years in wisdom" before the Doctors in the Temple, but afterward he chose to be mistaken for a simpleton, "abject and foolish in the eyes of men so that He would be thought of as devout"—i.e., innocent and unworldly—without making any claim to special understanding. (*Meditations on the Life of Christ*, chap. 25, trans. Isa Ragusa and Rosalie B. Green [Princeton: Princeton University Press, 1961], pp. 94–96.)

images, meant to stir our compassion, similarly trade upon nakedness, abjection, humiliation, and abandonment.[27] The most terrible moment on the cross, after all, occurs when Jesus "with a loud voice" cries out at the ninth hour, "My God, My God, Why hast thou forsaken me?" (Mark 15:34). For Christ too, in this moment of alienation and existential crisis, there was no God. In this respect, the lolling head and death in the eyes of the Duc de Berry fool (fig. 2) might almost have been copied from a painting of Christ crucified. Absent the Resurrection, His passion would read like the fool's. Augustine embraced the paradox in its full power: "We were trapped by the wisdom of the serpent; we are freed by the foolishness of God."[28]

But illustrations to Psalm 52, such as that from the Psalter of Bonne of Luxembourg (fig. 16) forbid compassion and admit no complexity.[29] Instead, the mysterious place of madness and simple-mindedness in God's provision for the human race is brought to bear upon a text too destructive to be confronted directly, leaving both as unintelligible as before. The madman/idiot/fool is a bearer of surplus, inchoate meaning, testifying to an anxiety otherwise unacknowledgeable within the *imperium* of the medieval Church.

I used to think the point of historical research was to reconstruct the logic and coherence of the past, especially for cultures unlike our own. I still think that the first of our professional tasks, the one that teaches us most and best keeps us human. But cultural apologetics—reading "from within"—can take us only so far. I have traced a few of the con-

---

[27] For an example that Millard Meiss (*French Painting: The Late XIVth Century*, vol. 1, pp. 169–71) would attribute to Jacquemart himself, see the Annunciation page with its Man of Sorrows overhead from the *Petites Heures du duc de Berry*, ca. 1375, reproduced in color in Meiss, vol. 2, fig. 94. See also Charles Sterling, *La peinture médiévale à Paris 1300–1500*, vol. 1 (Paris: Bibliothèque des Arts, 1987), p. 124, discussing fig. 63. For my purpose it is enough that these MSS. are nearly contemporary, employ some of the same models, and were made for essentially the same courtly milieu.

[28] "Serpentis sapientia decepti sumus, dei stultitia liberamur;" Augustine, *De Doctrina Christiana* 1.14 (16), *Corpus Christianorum Series Latina* 32 (Turnholt: Brepols, 1962), p. 14; *On Christian Doctrine*, trans. D.W. Robertson, Jr. (Indianapolis: Bobbs-Merrill, 1958), p. 15.

[29] Figure 16: reproduced in color by François Avril, *Manuscript Painting at the Court of France: The Fourteenth Century (1310–1380)* (New York: George Braziller, 1978), pl. 18A, who comments "an anti–Semitic inspiration is evident in the image showing a figure beating and pulling at the hood of a Jew who seems to be drinking from something resembling a chalice" (p. 74). In my forthcoming book I discuss this illustration in a chapter called "The Fool as Killer of Christ."

Figure 16: New York, The Metropolitan Museum of Art, Cloisters Collection, 1969 (MS. 69.86, fol. 83v). The Psalter of Bonne de Luxembourg (Paris, before 1349). All rights reserved, The Metropolitan Museum of Art.

tradictions latent in medieval attitudes toward the mentally impaired, along with others arising from the illuminators' translation of psalter fool into halfwit or madman in order to account for the power of such an image. (Clarity is not the only source of what stirs us most deeply.) But I have done so as well to free myself from complicity in its purpose, coerced by a creed and ideology I do not share.

I want now to go further, to suggest as well a *resistant* reading—a reading "against the grain"—that might speak on behalf of such imagery, according it a dignity and importance wholly unintended by those who first imagined mental deficiency or madness as suitable illustration to this text. We have reached an *aporia*, a breakdown in common sense and logic normally sufficient to signal the end of a discourse. Let us see if it can also begin one, now in the character of that rarest of all psalter fools (fig. 17)—a philosophical man, downcast but clearly rational, capable of *thinking* the thought that denies God.[30]

A resistant reading might run something like this. For those of us agnostic by temperament and intellectual conviction, there must always be an honored place for that which refuses assimilation or incorporation, for those eruptions and fissures that belie otherwise totalizing claims to cultural authority and explanatory truth. The medieval churchmen who first commissioned these images of madman/simpleton/fool testify, almost against their will, to his relevance: to the urgency of our human need for significance beyond ourselves, and to the terror with which we experience the possibility of its absence. And so one may claim for the psalter fool this dignity at least: he presents us with an image instead of an answer to the deepest of all human questions, the question of what life means, and whence such meaning derives? If, in truth, there is no transcendental answer, or if it must include *without transcendence* all that is most abject and unaccommodated in our nature, then we had best learn to acknowledge without flinching—as we have learned to do with *King Lear* or the works of Samuel Beckett—our kinship with this image, produced by a medieval system otherwise not particularly prescient in imagining *us*. The psalter fool is a nightmare, designedly so, but also the relevant nightmare. Better than any other image during the medieval centuries, he kept the possibility of non-meaning open, the questions too confidently answered by faith alive.

Commentary on Psalms 13 and 52 has relatively little to do with the madman/moron tradition. It is born of existential fear and cultural scapegoating, and found its natural expression in the visual arts, where logical explanation is not necessary. The commentators, as I have said,

---

[30] Figure 17: From a Bible made at the beginning of the thirteenth century, and possibly the earliest type of "fool" in the Paris tradition. Haseloff, *Die Psalterillustration*, pls. 5 and 6, reproduces the full cycle of psalter images from this MS., and notes, pp. 24–25, that this type of fool—thoughtful but somewhat sad—was soon replaced by the idiot-madman, a choice that seemed to Haseloff easier to understand.

Figure 17: Florence, Bibl. Laurenziana MS. Plut. 15.11, fol. 286v. Bible (?Paris, beginning of the thirteenth century).

did their best to avoid the atheistic sense of *non est deus* altogether, swerving from it in a number of ways. Across the medieval centuries, they discovered the fool in ordinary sinners who behave as though God were not offended by their sin (the Augustinian reading referred to above). They found him in those who love earthly things and branded them in a generalized way as followers of Antichrist. Or they found him, more confidently still, in the Jew of history—whom they charged with the death of Christ—and in contemporary Jews, whom they saw as perversely denying Christ's divinity still. (The fool as Jew, and the historical consequence of that identification, will furnish me the other major subject of my book; it will not be noticed further in this lecture.)[31] Certain other groups are stigmatized as well: pagans, heretics, and idolators are all sometimes named, usually without elaboration, as versions of the psalter fool.

A motley, ill-sorted crew, linked together (it is essential to note) by a single remarkable fact: none of them can reasonably be said to doubt the existence of God. They may indeed, from the Christian point of view, worship the wrong God, or hold false opinions about His nature, or live less than well. But they do not imagine themselves living in a universe unanchored in divine intelligence and purpose. We might call them God-forgetters well enough—those who live complacently in sin—or God-supplanters—those who prefer a false or inappropriate God—or God-mistakers—those who hold heretical beliefs. But not God-denyers. These weaker versions of the fool of Psalms 13 and 52 are culturally less revealing than the psalter madmen and idiots we have been examining. But they nevertheless allow him one further move, an unexpected underground migration into medieval literary "courts of love." That move—and some praise for his role there—will be my further topic in this lecture. In two great poems of that kind, the *Folie de Tristan*, and Chaucer's *Troilus and Criseyde*—one from early thirteenth-century France, the other from late fourteenth-century England—themes and images related to the psalter *insipiens* once again break open a topic that Christian orthodoxy preferred to think of as settled and closed. In a song from *Stop the World! I Want to Get Off*, Anthony Newley used to ask of love "What kind of fool am I?"—

---

[31] This other interpretation was made current in the West by Augustine, from whence it infects the commentary tradition as a whole. It depends upon reconstruing "non est deus" to mean "He is not God," and making knowledge of the Passion part of David's prophetic wisdom. "The Fool as Killer of Christ" was the subject of my Presidential Address to the Medieval Academy of America in 1993, as well as the third of my Alexander/Clark lectures. Because of the number of pictures its argument requires, I have reserved its publication for my forthcoming book.

a question I once intended to ask on behalf of Tristan and Troilus in the title of this address. But the question I have in mind might be better put so: What did the fool of Psalm 52 bring to "love *paramours*," the medieval "religion of love?"

The larger story of Tristan and Yseult's adulterous love, fueled by a love-potion they drink unaware, is well known to this audience, but possibly not so well the *Folie de Tristan* in its most relevant detail. Let me retell it briefly, from the version preserved in Berne, using a French ivory casket (fig. 18), made ca. 1325, to make clear the iconographic dimension of its meaning.[32] The first panel, far left, is irrelevant to my

[32] Figure 18: reproduced from Roger Sherman Loomis and Laura Hibbard Loomis, *Arthurian Legends in Medieval Art* (New York: Modern Language Association, 1938), fig. 91, discussed on p. 56. Loomis recognized that the second panel might be indebted to *Dixit insipiens* iconography: "The figure of Tristan with his club in hand and the attitude of the king on his throne were probably inspired by some such miniature in a Psalter" (p. 56). But he thinks no further on it. Tristan's haircut, a kind of cruciform tonsure in which two hairlines intersect each other, is commonplace in many Psalm 52 illustrations and may be the sort of shearing "en croiz" Tristan gives himself in the Oxford *Folie*. But see Ruth Mellinkoff, *Outcasts: Signs of Otherness in the Northern European Art of the Late Middle Ages*, California Studies in the History of Art, vol. 32 (Berkeley: University of California Press, 1993), 1: 186–88, for another possibility, the rough checkerboard haircut also sometimes shown in late medieval representations of the fool. Julia Walworth, "Tristan in Medieval Art," in *Tristan and Isolde: A Casebook*, ed. Joan Tasker Grimbert (New York: Garland, 1995), pp. 255–99, Stephanie Cain Van D'Elden, "Reading Illustrations of Tristan," in *Literary Aspects of Courtly Culture*, ed. Donald Maddox and Sara Sturm-Maddox (Cambridge: D.S. Brewer, 1994), pp. 343–51, and Michael Curschmann, "Images of Tristan," in *Gottfried von Strassburg and the Medieval Tristan Legend*, ed. Adrian Stevens and Roy Wisbey (Cambridge: D.S. Brewer, 1990), pp. 1–17, are valuable guides to the larger tradition, but none of them comment on Tristan as fool. Merritt R. Blakeslee, *Love's Masks: Identity, Intertextuality, and Meaning in the Old French Tristan Poems* (Cambridge: D.S. Brewer, 1989), a learned and sensitive study of the Old French Tristan poems, includes a long section on "Tristan's Disguises" (pp. 59–95), including "Tristan *Fou*"—"the most frequently retold of the disguise episodes in the medieval Tristan corpus" (p. 72, with sources listed in n.19). Blakeslee studies the fool disguise as a punishment for sin, as a consequence of grief and guilt in love, and as a version of ungoverned passion; he derives it from the witty fool (both *ménestral* and *jongleur*); and sets it alongside the medieval wild man (a kinship developed with particular care in the Oxford *Folie*.) It is a richly comprehensive account, but does not touch on Tristan's relation to the psalter fool. Jacqueline Schaefer has looked at madness in these poems in several essays: "Tristan's Folly: Feigned or Real?," *Tristania* 3 (1977): 4–16; "Specularity in the Mediaeval *Folie Tristan* Poems or Madness as Metadiscourse," *Neophilologus* 77 (1993): esp. p. 365 and 367n.6; and in a collaboration with Angelika Gross, "Tristan, Robert le Diable und die Ikonographie des *Insipiens*: der Hund als Neues Motiv in Einem Alten Kontext," in *Schelme und Narren in den Literaturen des Mittelalters*, Wodan: Tagungsbände und Sammelschriften (Greifswald: Reineke-Verlag, 1994), where Schaefer relates Tristan's disguise to the type of the psalter *insipiens*, interpreting the features they have in common as negative with regard to the psalm, but positive with regard to the love-affair (p. 64), and studying them as an example of inversion, the world–upside–down, in which folly in one sphere becomes truth in another (p. 66). Laharie, *La Folie*, had earlier (in 1991) noted that the symptoms of certain mad

Figure 18: Leningrad, The Hermitage, Tristan Casket II (Paris, ca. 1325).

present topic: it illustrates an earlier episode in which King Mark, uncle to Tristan and husband to Yseult, hides in a tree to spy upon the lovers, who see him reflected in the water of a spring. But the other three panels illustrate the story of Tristan's "folly," an episode common to French, German, and English versions from the twelfth through the fifteenth centuries, but never more powerfully told than in the Norman poem I shall summarize here.[33]

As the poem begins, Tristan, long exiled from King Mark's court, decides he must return to Tintagel, no matter how great the danger, to see again the woman he loves. "Alas," he laments, "what shall I do if I cannot see her? . . . I am in great agitation at every moment of the night and day. When I do not see her I nearly go out of my mind. Alas, what shall I do? . . . She might think me a coward if threats were enough to stop me; for I could always go to her in secret or dressed like some pitiable madman. For her sake I am willing to be shaven and shorn if I cannot disguise myself any other way."[34] The idea captures his imagination, and so he sets out at once for the distant sea, carrying no armor, and suffering so greatly that the poet describes him as being already a madman. When he reaches Cornwall, to prevent anyone thinking him sane, "he tore his clothes and scratched his face. He struck any man who crossed his path. He had his fair hair shorn off. Nobody on the seashore thought he was anything but mad, for they did not know what was in his mind."[35] He walks like this

---

lovers (Yvain, Lancelot, Tristan and Amadas) correlated with the madmen of psalter illustration; see pp. 145–52, and for their cure, pp. 224–32. So far as I know, these studies from the 1990s are the first to connect the *Folie* poems with the *insipiens* tradition.

[33] See M. Domenica Legge, *Anglo-Norman Literature and its Background* (Oxford: Clarendon Press, 1963), pp. 121–28, on the two versions. She thinks the *Folie Tristan d'Oxford* written in Anglo–Norman probably the later, with both deriving from some lost common source. Blakeslee, *Love's Masks*, pp. 133–37, offers a bibliographic guide to the many versions of the episode, including the standard editions by Ernest Hoepffner of the two *Folie* poems. They are conveniently published together, along with other Tristan poems, and translations into modern French, by Jean Charles Payen in *Les Tristan en vers* (Paris: Garniers, 1974), pp. 247–97, which I follow here. All translations I cite of the *Folie Tristan* are by Alan S. Fedrick, from *The Romance of Tristan by Beroul and the Tale of Tristan's Madness* (Harmondsworth, Penguin Books, 1970), pp. 151–64. I wish to thank Penguin Books for permission to quote from this translation. I have changed its "Yseut" to "Yseult" for uniformity with my other texts.

[34] "Las! que ferai, quant ne la voi?/ Que por li sui en grant efroi/ Et nuit et jor et tot lo terme:/ Quant ne la voi, a po ne deve./ Las! que ferai? Ne sai que faire. . . . / Tenir me porroit por mauvais,/ Se por nule menace lais/ Que je n'i aille en tanpinaje/ O en abit de fol onbraje./ Por li me ferai rere et tondre,/ S'autremant ne me puis repondre" (ll. 90–94, 104–109).

[35] "Ses dras deront, sa chere grate;/ Ne voit home cui il ne bate;/ Tondrë a fait sa bloie crine./ N'i a un sol en la marine/ Qu'il ne croie que ce soit rage,/ Mais ne sevent pas son corage" (ll. 130–36).

for days, though people shout at him and throw stones at his head, think-ing all this suffering good, for soon he would achieve his desire: "he would make himself appear to be a fool, for he wanted to speak to Yseult."[36]

Because no door is closed to a fool, Tristan enters the court and im-mediately commands the attention of the king, who sees in him some possible entertainment. "Fool," he says, "what is your name?" "My name is Picous." "Who was your father?" "A walrus." "By whom did he have you?" "A whale. I have a sister I will bring to you. The girl is called Bruneheut: you shall have her and I will have Yseult."[37] But soon this fool's patter, so aggressively rude and sexual, gives way to something imaginatively finer: "Listen to this!" said Tristan. "Between the clouds and the sky, where there is no frost, I shall build a house of flowers and roses and there she and I will enjoy ourselves."[38] Yseult listens to all this with ever mounting alarm, thinking that Tristan must be dead and their secrets made known to this ugly fool, who recounts the story of their love in riddling ways. His narration begins with reference to the love po-tion—"she and I drank it—ask her!"[39]—and reaches its climax as he raves on: "I have leaped and thrown reeds and balanced sharpened twigs, I have lived on roots in a wood and I have held a queen in my arms. I shall say more if I have a mind to."[40] The king, suddenly uncomfortable, tries to end the *récit*: "Rest yourself now, Picolet. I am sorry you have done so many things. Leave your jesting for today."[41] But Tristan, ever more daring, presses on, reminding the king that he once found the lovers asleep in the forest with a naked sword between them—an ad-venture that only the king and Yseult and Tristan (and somehow this fool) could know. Mark looks to the queen, who has bowed her head and covered her face with her cloak, and hears her say: "Fool, a curse on the

[36] "Et se fera por fol sanbler,/ Quë a Ysiaut viaut il parler./ Droit a la cort en est venuz,/ Oncques huis ne li fu tenuz" (ll. 148–51).

[37] "Fox, com a non? —G'é non Picous./—Qui t'angendra?—Uns valerox./ —De que t'ot il?—D'une balaine./ Une suer ai que vos amoine:/ La meschine a non Bruneheut:/ Vos l'avroiz, jë avrai Ysiaut" (ll. 158–63). The exchange of females, here wittily proposed, links Brangain's name to Yseult in a further onomastic derangement—Bruneheut—recollecting the wedding night in which Brangain replaced the no-longer virginal Yseult in the bed of her husband the king.

[38] "Et dit Tristanz: 'O bee tu?/ Entre les nues et lo ciel,/ De flors et de roses, sans giel,/ Iluec ferai une maison/ O moi et li nos deduison'" (ll. 165–69).

[39] "Moi et Ysiaut, que je voi ci,/ En beümes: demandez li . . ." (ll. 176–77).

[40] "Jë ai sailli et lanciez jons,/ Et sostenu dolez bastons,/ Et en bois vescu de racine,/ Entre mes braz tenu raïne./ Plus diré, se m'an entremet" (ll. 184–88).

[41] "Or te repose, Picolet./ Ce poise moi que tant fait as:/ Lai or huimais ester tes gas" (ll. 189–91).

sailors who brought you across the sea and did not throw you into the water."[42] But Tristan deflects that insult onto one he thinks a greater fool, her cuckolded husband: "My lady," he answers, "a curse on your *cocu*."[43] Brangain later brings him to Yseult's chamber, where the dog Husdant and a certain gold ring finally convince Yseult that the fool is indeed her lover. And so the poem is able to end happily: "Tristan slipped under the sheets without another word and held the queen in his arms."[44]

But even in that final embrace their love is inseparable from suffering, alienation, offense, and danger. In disguising himself as a fool, Tristan symbolically enacts the *real* nature of his passion as it would have been understood in the literature of wisdom: a passion sustained in defiance of the king and all feudal obligation, in opposition to God's laws against adultery, and in denial of the true celestial Jerusalem to which all Christian souls must aspire. The only happy place Tristan can imagine— a house of flowers and roses between the clouds and the sky, where there is never frost—is quite literally a fool's paradise, a fantasy born of love that seeks its heaven on earth, in contempt of Christian eternity. In the Oxford version of this poem, Tristan invents an even more fantastic setting for their transfigured love, "a hall which I visit . . . large and beautiful and made of glass, pierced through with sunbeams. It hangs in the clouds high in the air but the wind does not rock nor shake it. Within the hall is a room made of crystal and fine panelling and when the sun rises in the morning it is filled with light."[45]

---

[42] "Fol, mal aient li marinel/ Qui ça outre vos amenerent,/ Qant en la mer ne vos giterent" (ll. 213–15).

[43] "Dame, cil cox ait mal dahé!" (l. 217). In translating this as "My Lady, a curse on your fool" (p. 156), Fedrick misses Tristan's attack on Mark.

[44] "Entre Tristanz soz la cortine:/ Entre ses braz tient la raïne" (ll. 573–74).

[45] *Folie d' Oxford*, ll. 299–308, as translated by Lynette R. Muir, *Literature and Society in Medieval France: The Mirror and the Image, 1100–1500* (New York: St. Martin's Press, 1985), p. 104, in her discussion of the theme of "the world upside down." Jean–Charles Payen, "The Glass Palace in the *Folie d'Oxford*: From Metaphorical to Literal Madness, or the Dream of the Desert Island at the Moment of Exile—Notes on the Erotic Dimension of the Tristans," in *Tristan and Isolde: A Casebook*, ed. Joan Tasker Grimbert (New York: Garland, 1995), writes suggestively about the poetic implications of this version of a lover's paradise: "Up there, they will be able to love in the light, no longer in the shadows. . . . As fear is forever abolished, so also will be guilt, hence the transparency"—and on its compensatory nature—"But Tristan is too lucid not to know that the luminous home beyond the clouds is simply a projection of a desperate desire" (p. 121). Payen sees well the profound opposition of this fantasy to feudal ideology: in the twelfth century "there is no salvation to be found outside of society, no matter how intense one's ardor" (p. 118). But he does not touch on its destructive relation to Christian ideas of salvation. Blakeslee, *Love's Masks*, pp. 53–54, 82, 92, thinks it a disguised reference to the wood of

Medieval medicine thought erotic love a pathology capable of driving a lover literally mad, whether through excessive desire, overwhelming despair, or grief over some failure to be faithful. Gawain and Lancelot both undergo madness of this kind elsewhere in the Arthurian story. Figure 19, for instance, shows Lancelot indistinguishable from an idiot, in the company of King Arthur and Queen Guinevere.[46] But Tristan's "folly," in its willed embrace of the signs of madness and its disdain for conventional moral wisdom, draws to itself ideas more complex by far. By moving Tristan into iconographic register with the psalter fool, the poet suggests that one who loves in this fashion, making a mortal woman his highest good and seeking his only heaven in her arms, becomes, in Christian terms, a God-denying fool.[47] The real madness of Lancelot and Gawain can be cured. The "feigned" madness of Tristan is of a different pathology altogether.[48]

---

the Morois in which the two lovers for a time escape civilization and its moral codes, and to Yseult's bed chamber, where they find their greatest happiness together. That is to read it well in terms of Tristan's intention; but the specific terms of his invention turn it into a (false) celestial paradise, in ways Blakeslee acknowledges only in passing, p. 53 n.62.

[46] Figure 19: On this MS. see Loomis, *Arthurian Legends in Medieval Art*, p. 94 and fig. 222 (folio number incorrectly cited). Mary Frances Wack, *Lovesickness in the Middle Ages: The* Viaticum *and Its Commentaries* (Philadelphia: University of Pennsylvania Press, 1990), offers a learned guide to the medical tradition. Judith Silverman Neaman, *The Distracted Knight: A Study of Insanity in the Arthurian Romances* (Ph.D. diss; Ann Arbor: University Microfilms, 1968), studies the literary tradition.

[47] Eilhart von Oberge's *Tristant*, written between 1170 and 1190, includes the story several decades before the Parisian cycle of psalter illustration took form—which means the kind of madman Tristan pretends to be is drawn originally from the ordinary world of wandering fools, madmen and idiots, just as the psalter fool would be. See the trans. by J. W. Thomas (Lincoln: University of Nebraska Press, 1978), pp. 145–50. But the *Folie* poems sound a deeper note by juxtaposing Tristan's fool disguise with a fool's vision on eternity—unknown in earlier versions—thus evoking that reading of Psalm 52 which interpreted idolatry—the worship of false gods—as a denial of God's existence. When Parisian psalter illustration installed a madman/moron in the Psalm 52 initial, it conferred iconographic authority upon an understanding of Tristan's folly already implicit in those texts. The Hermitage Casket (ca. 1325) reproduced above (figure 18) makes clear how readily that new iconography was assimilated, for its Tristan, with his heavy club and cross-tonsured haircut, is unmistakably derived from a Parisian typology of the psalter fool. As I shall demonstrate in my book, madness and idiocy had been converging upon the text of the psalm ever since Jerome first rendered the Hebrew word *nahal* as *insipiens* rather than as *imprudens* or *stultus*. But so far as I know, the Tristan legend is the first to overlay the figure of lover and fool in a way that carries serious religious implication.

[48] For this reason I would not link Tristan together with Yvain, Lancelot, and Amadas, as though their love–madness were of a single kind (*pace* Laharie, *La Folie*, pp. 145–51). Concerning the other three, Neaman puts it well (*The Distracted Knight*, p. 173): "The love madness in fiction comes not from love but from the hopelessness of love. It is not incurable, and the cure is always related to the cause; furthermore, the cures are never

Figure 19: Bonn, Universitätsbibliothek MS. 526, fol. 404v. Prose Lancelot (Amiens, 1286).

Elsewhere in the legend, Tristan presents himself to Yseult in other forms of significant disguise, most notably as a pilgrim and as a leper. In those instances too he transforms himself into an "image" with iconographic resonance, a disguise both false and true. But his disguise as a

---

purely medical. They come either from some sign of mercy from the lady—i.e., her care of him, her forgiveness—or her repetition of some magic incantation like the linking of their two names."

fool is the last in the series, subsuming all the rest. In that guise, before the king and queen and court, he tells again the full story of their love—a tale told by an idiot, in fragments and riddles, evading sense, precluding ordinary judgment.[49] And it is in the guise of a madman/fool that Tristan takes Yseult in his arms for the last time.[50] They never meet again alive.

One would expect such imagery—Panofsky called the technique "concealed symbolism"—to clarify the moral intention of the poem. But the magic potion, and the lovers' struggle to resist its power, prevent the fool disguise from functioning so simply. All that is compelled and unchosen in their relationship prevents any confident dismissal of them. When they call upon God for help against their enemies, as they often do, they generally receive his protection, even in circumstances as equivocal as Yseult's ordeal by fire.[51] And so it is in the *Folie*. The weird illogic that could see in an idiot or madman a God-denying fool is carried over, unresolved and entire, into a narrative of erotic love, leaving us uncertain whether Tristan's madness is feigned or real—and if real, whether it is a precondition or a punishment for this kind of loving. As with the fool in the psalter illustrations, we once again reach an *aporia*, a breakdown in sense that takes us beyond the certainties of cultural systems and deeper into the mystery of being human. The love of Tristan

[49] This act of renarration has been much discussed; see Matilda Tomaryn Bruckner, *Shaping Romance: Interpretation, Truth, and Closure in Twelfth-Century French Fictions* (Philadelphia: University of Pennsylvania Press, 1993), chap. 1, for a particularly thoughtful account focused on the *Folie d'Oxford*.

[50] In the Berne *Folie*, Brangain advises her lady, "Go and find clothes for him. He is Tristan and you are Yseult . . . do all you can to please him until Mark comes back from the river." In response Yseult becomes a witty jester too: "May he find so many fish that he does not come back for a week!" (Fedrick trans., p. 163). In the anonymous thirteenth-century prose version (Paris, Bibl. Natl. MS. fr. 103) the queen gives Tristan costly robes and linen to wear on secret visits in her chamber. But he must revert daily to his disguise as a fool, sleeping under the stairs, in order to remain in Tintagel. When he is discovered two months later he has to flee. See *The Romance of Tristan and Isolt*, trans. Norman B. Spector (Evanston: Northwestern University Press, 1973), p. 71.

[51] For an elegant essay on Gottfried von Strassburg's presentation of this love as "beyond human judgment," see Esther C. Quinn, "Beyond Courtly Love: Religious Elements in *Tristan* and *La Queste del Saint Graal*," in *In Pursuit of Perfection: Courtly Love in Medieval Literature*, ed. Joan M. Ferrante and George D. Economou (Port Washington, N.Y.: Kennikat Press, 1975), pp. 179–219. Quinn writes of the ordeal by fire: "Gottfried presents the exoneration of Isot before the highest tribunal by the direct intervention of the Deity. This is, of course, a fictitious Deity, indifferent to His own laws, but it is a daring stroke on Gottfried's part—to involve the Lord Himself in the web of deceptions which the subtle Queen weaves—to present Him as deceived or as willing to aid her in deceiving" (p. 187).

Figure 20: Oxford, Bodley MS. Laud. Lat. 114, fol. 71. Psalter (English, illuminated third quarter of the fifteenth century).

and Yseult refuses to be reduced to simple madness, or foolishness, or Christian adultery. Grander and more awesome than any of those alone, it is folly of the God-denying kind.

None of this much looks like, or sounds like, Chaucer's *Troilus and Criseyde*. That must be admitted. In the two hundred years (more or less) that separate the Norman and the English poems, the "courtliness" of court literature has greatly increased, and a court fool or jester has begun to replace the madman/idiot in psalter illumination to Psalm 52 (fig. 20). But Chaucer too draws deeply upon the language of religion to give tragic stature to a story of unsanctioned erotic love. At the conceptual center of his poem, as this audience well knows, an identification is made between Criseyde, a young Trojan widow, and a statue of the goddess Pallas Athena—a religious idol called the Palladion—

whose continued presence (and worship) in Troy guarantees the safety of the city. (In the course of time, both will be removed, and Troilus/ Troy destroyed.) By this means, as D. W. Robertson, Jr. suggested a long time ago, and as John Fleming more recently has shown in careful detail,[52] Judaeo-Christian ideas of idolatry interpenetrate the pagan ethos of the poem, in which a beautiful woman is loved and worshipped in ways Christianity deemed appropriate only to God. In its first three Books, Troilus is *converted* to the *service* of love; he *worships* the idea (the idol) of Criseyde; he is *initiated* into the mysteries of sexual experience, as into the mysteries of a sacred *rite*; and he finds *heaven* in her arms (the timeworn metaphor renewed in some of the most sublime love poetry ever written), a heaven he declares worth even the price of his soul. In Books 4 and 5 he experiences the loss of that love with the shattering intensity of someone losing his religious faith—a loss that ultimately destroys him, though his soul is rewarded after death in certain carefully delimited ways.[53] Ideas of idolatry generate much of the poem's religious language and ritualized devotion, while simultaneously alerting us to the possibility of transgression, contamination, and category error.

But idolatry cannot fully account for the ethos of the poem. A discourse of folly is operative as well, varying in force from the ordinary foolishness of lovers, scoffed at by Troilus before he first sees Criseyde, to the God-denying folly—including frenzy and despair—intrinsic to the way he finally loves her. The Tristan legend explores the power of love, symbolized by a magic potion, to set itself up against God and feudal society in ways that refuse all compromise and resolution. Chaucer's *Troilus*, in contrast, explores the power of love to become a religion of its own, founded on illusion and tragically incomplete. This maximum version of love's folly—in which sexual love is asked to express and fulfill our deepest spiritual needs—brings something distinctive to the medieval discourse of love, extending its range from the comic to the tragic, the trivial to the sublime, without ever losing touch with the carnal and obscene.

[52] See Fleming, *Classical Imitation*, particularly chapter 3, "Idols of the Prince." Michael Camille, *The Gothic Idol: Ideology and Image-making in Medieval Art* (Cambridge: Cambridge University Press, 1989), offers a brilliant study of the theme of idol worship in medieval art. His final chapter, "Idols in the Mind," focuses on the topos of woman on a pedestal, both as an object of courtly-love desire and an idol of perverse devotion.

[53] See Barry Windeatt, *Oxford Guides to Chaucer: Troilus and Criseyde* (Oxford: Clarendon Press, 1992), pp. 231–40, on "Love and Religion," for a thorough presentation of the textual evidence behind such a reading.

Patristic commentary, as I have said, made the fool's *non est deus* remarkably inclusive by attributing it, in its weakened form, to pagans, heretics, and idolators as well as sinners who just don't give a damn, and think God doesn't either. None of these turn up often in initials to the psalm, but two exceptions (each supported by a sister manuscript or two) are perhaps worth thinking about in relation to Chaucer's poem. In a late twelfth-century Bible illuminated by Manerius of Canterbury, working as an itinerant painter probably in Troyes (fig. 21), the *insipiens* kneels before an altar worshipping an idol in the form of a goat.[54] The image communicates a sense of transgression and category-error very powerful still, and may (just possibly) be intended as a form of devil-worship.[55] But another, probably better, reading suggests itself as well, since the goat is a common medieval symbol of lechery,[56] and lechery (both adultery and fornication) had been closely linked with idola-

[54] On this MS. see Walter Cahn, *Romanesque Bible Illumination* (Ithaca, NY: Cornell University Press, 1982), pp. 221–22, and his more recent *Romanesque Manuscripts: The Twelfth Century*, 2 vols., *A Survey of Manuscripts Illuminated in France,* ed. François Avril and J.J.G. Alexander (London: Harvey Miller, 1996), 2:#81. Though an Englishman, Manerius is thought to have been working in France when he made this Bible.

[55] In medieval iconography, the devil often has goat-like features (hairy skin, a beard, caprine horns, cloven hooves, a tail, etc.) which scholars trace back to antique representations of the nature god Pan. But his face is generally human; I know of no instance where he is shown simply as a goat. Confessions of devil worship exacted by the Inquisition describe him appearing in the form of a toad, a giant black cat, a great disembodied head, or an unusually pale ice-cold man. Beryl Rowland cites two instances in which heretics were accused of worshipping or fornicating with the devil in the form of a goat, but *in vilissimi hirci forma* may simply mean (as above) a devil with goat-like features. See her *Animals with Human Faces: A Guide to Animal Symbolism* (Knoxville: University of Tennessee Press, 1973), p. 83.

[56] For instance, a late thirteenth-century relief, carved on a porch of the Cathedral of Freiburg im Bresgau shows Sensuality (Voluptas) as a beautiful naked woman draped in the flayed skin of a goat, its head covering her sexual parts—reproduced as fig. 7 in *Woman Defamed and Woman Defended: An Anthology of Medieval Texts,* ed. Alcuin Blamires (Oxford: Clarendon Press, 1992). A sequence of Sins and Virtues illustrating Chaucer's *Parson's Tale,* ca. 1450–60 (Cambridge, Univ. Lib. MS. Gg.4.27) personify Lechery as an elegantly-gowned woman riding upon a goat (fol. 233). See Roger Sherman Loomis, *A Mirror of Chaucer's World* (Princeton: Princeton University Press, 1965), fig. 179. There is nothing arcane about this tradition. Medieval bestiary lore describes the male goat (*hircus*) as "a lascivious and butting animal who is always burning for coition. His eyes are transverse slits because he is so randy. . . . The nature of goats is so extremely hot that a stone of adamant, which neither fire nor iron implement can alter, is dissolved merely by the blood of one of these creatures." See *The Book of Beasts: Being a Translation from a Latin Bestiary of the Twelfth Century,* trans. T.H. White (London: Jonathan Cape, 1954), pp. 74–75. For a full account see Rowland, *Animals With Human Faces,* pp. 80–86. Chaucer's discussion of Lechery in the *Parson's Tale* links the sin explicitly with idolatry: "Certes, be it wyf, be it child, or any worldly thyng that [a man] loveth biforn God, it is his mawmet, and he is an ydolastre" (10.859).

Figure 21: Paris, Bibl. Sainte-Geneviève MS. 9, fol. 209. Manerius of Canterbury Bible (?Troyes, late twelfth century).

try from earliest Biblical times. In the Old Testament Yaweh characteristically thinks of Himself as married to Israel, even though she is often unfaithful, "whoring after strange gods."[57]

An alternative iconography for Psalm 52 that not only focuses upon erotic love but stands closer to Chaucer's *Troilus* in both provenance and date provides intriguing visual evidence to support such a claim. I know of just three examples, but their interest is considerable, particularly the one we shall look at first—from a great display Bible made in England

---

[57] For a closely related illustration see Paris, Bibl. Natl. MS. lat. 11535, fol. 30v, where the *insipiens* (standing before the altar with a goat-idol) wears a kind of pointed beret, indicating that he is a learned man. (Reproduced in Haseloff, *Die Psalterillustration*, pl. 3). On this MS., a partial copy of the Manerius Bible (or a hypothetical sister MS.), see Cahn, *Romanesque Manuscripts*, 2:#92.

Figure 22: London, Brit. Lib. MS. Royal I E. IX, fol. 148. Bible (English, ca. 1405–1415).

that may have been owned and treasured (more on this later) by Henry IV and Henry V. In its *insipiens* initial (fig. 22) three kinds of folly are represented.[58] The first shows God mocked by a jester or court fool, wearing a professional costume of long pointed hood, dagged tunic, and bells. He points to his mouth to indicate speech, and wags his index finger against God, signifying argument, contention, or presumption. A

---

[58] Figure 22: Kathleen L. Scott generously allowed me to see in galley-proof her descriptions of this MS. (and the sister MS. in Turin discussed below) from her *Later Gothic Manuscripts 1390–1490*, 2 vols., *A Survey of Manuscripts Illuminated in the British Isles*, ed. J.J.G. Alexander (London: Harvey Miller, 1996), where they are numbered #26 and #27 respectively. She dates the Big Bible ca. 1405–15, thinks it probably a London production, and identifies its dominant illustrator (Hand A, setting the style for several other hands) as the Carmelite–Lapworth Master, the "learner hand" of the Carmelite Missal. Scott raises serious doubts about Margaret Rickert's attribution of some of the work to Herman Scheerre.

second kind is represented by the frivolity and carelessness of the courtly group on the left—a casual, complacent forgetfulness of God, as though justice were no part of his nature. This company gazes at, points to, and smiles upon an elegant young couple who stand in their midst in passionate embrace—a love that in English moral writing of the time was called "fol-delit," just as prostitutes were called "fol-wommen," and sexual love outside marriage the doing of "folye."[59] God looking down from the heavens sees no one doing well. To allow this picture into our analysis of love *paramours* requires a certain iconographic shift. In the *Folie de Tristan*, Yseult's task was to recognize her lover beneath the appearance of a God-denying fool. In *Troilus*, the task is reversed. We are asked to recognize a God-denying fool in the form of a courtly lover.

This image from an English show Bible is capacious in the manner of the commentaries, ready to include almost anyone except a credible non-believer, someone actually engaged in thinking "there is no God." But it is serious in its own highly *mondaine* way. A courtly milieu of this sort, marked by ease, urbanity, and sexual sophistication, illustrates very well not only the ethos of *Troilus and Criseyde* but, more strictly speaking, the Augustinian interpretation of *non est deus* noted earlier: to cease to fear God's Justice is effectively to deny His existence.[60] The embracing couple makes another point as well, emphasizing the carnal basis of this love, however "courtly" in manner. Despite the public nature of

---

[59] See *MED*, s.v. *fol* (adj. 3), p. 675, and *folie* (noun 2b), p. 682; Chaucer frequently uses the words in this sense in his Parson's Tale discussion of Lechery (10. 852–55, 884). For *fole femme* meaning "whore" in medieval French, see Adolf Toblers and Erhard Lommatzsch, eds., *Altfranzösisches Wörterbuch* (Wiesbaden: Steiner, 1954), cols. 1999–2000. In both languages more is meant than "foolish woman," "stupid woman," "mad woman." *Fol'amors*, coined as an antonym to *fin'amors*, could also serve as a synonym.

[60] It would narrow the meaning of the picture too much to see the lascivious couple as representing fornication merely. All sin, of course, was understood to deny God one way or other—to deny His supremacy, His authority, His commandments—and "sinners" (unspecified) occasionally appear in the inventories of commentators trying to identify a plausible *insipiens*. But the connection is no stronger than that. The text illustrated has more to do with the First Commandment ("Thou shalt have no other Gods before me") than with the Sixth (against Adultery); it tells us specifically these are God-denying fools, and suggests that certain sophisticated ways of thinking about love similarly exceed traditional moral categories altogether. Cf. the Rohan Book of Hours (Paris, Bibl. Natl. MS. lat. 9471, made ca. 1419–27), which shows on fol. 235 a crowd of Israelites adoring a naked male idol while a similar couple embraces voluptuously in their midst. Reproduced in facsimile by Millard Meiss and Marcel Thomas, *The Rohan Master: A Book of Hours*, trans. Katharine W. Carson (New York: George Braziller, 1973), pl. 123, with helpful commentary.

Figure 23: Turin, Bibl. Nazionale, Universitaria di Torino MS. I. 1. 9, fol. 16. Psalter (English, ca. 1405–1415).

the occasion, the lover manages to press his leg forward, ever so delicately, between his lady's thighs. In a closely related English psalter now in Turin (fig. 23),[61] the company is (if anything) more courtly still in dress and behavior, and the parallel gesture even more shocking: the lover has his hand up his lady's dress. In this picture, either the model

---

[61] Figure 23: photo courtesy of Kathleen Scott. This MS. too is of enormous size, one of the seven largest Psalters that survive from the fifteenth century. For a full description see Scott, *Later Gothic Manuscripts*, 2: #27.

for or a copy of the picture we have been examining, someone I take to be a "natural" fool—the bald head, vacant manner, and shoeless stockings suggest as much—stands smiling vacuously at God, as though nothing here were to be taken seriously. Figure 24, from a French *Bible moralisée*, continues the tradition into the late fifteenth century.[62]

An early connection of the Bible version with the English court is a real possibility, a court for which, some two decades before, Chaucer's *Troilus* had been written, a court in which it remained well known. The Bible entered the British Library as part of the Royal collection of manuscripts and was thought by earlier scholars to have belonged to Richard II. They saw in it stylistic affinities with the school of Bohemian illumination introduced to England at the time of Richard's marriage to Anne of Bohemia. Art historians these days date it more conservatively, to the reign of Henry IV, ca. 1405–15, and remind us that royal association can be no more than conjecture, since the MS. lacks marks of ownership of any kind. But Jenny Stratford has recently reopened the question, suggesting that this manuscript—so huge one person can scarcely lift it—may well be the "Great Bible" mentioned by Henry V in his last will and its codicils (1421–22). King Henry V there bequeathed to the nuns of Syon Abbey (which he had founded) all the books he had lent them, except for the *magna Biblia*, described as having belonged to his father, Henry IV, and now left as a legacy to his unborn son.[63] The size and sumptuous decoration of MS. Royal I. E. IX

---

[62] Figure 24: the MS. was commissioned by Philippe le Hardi of Burgundy and illustrates an abbreviated text of Psalm 52 (in both French and Latin) with a double image, as is customary in moralized Bibles. This one shows a court fool spinning with distaff and spindle—reversing traditional male and female roles—beneath the words "Sans nombre," a comment wittily relevant to fools, but also the motto of the royal house of Anjou. The picture below shows two erotic couples in a landscape, one in a standing embrace, the other seated. The standing man is a monk, the other, youthful and sporting a rich fur hat, holds his lady on his lap, her skirt pushed high with his hand between her legs. The text tells us that this psalm is spoken against worldly persons (*les mundains*) and sinners who give themselves up to sin as though there were no God (*si ne fust point de dieu*). This MS., splendidly begun by the Brothers Limbourg, ca. 1402–1404, was completed much later by an inferior imitator, whose work includes the illustration of the Psalms. See Millard Meiss, *French Painting in the Time of Jean de Berry: The Limbourgs and their Contemporaries*, 2 vols. (London: Thames and Hudson, 1974), pp. 67–68, 81–84. The mid fourteenth-century MS. used as a model survives as Paris, Bibl. Natl. MS. fr. 167; its equivalent illustration shows a madman above, with four men playing dice below—a pastime in which chance or Fortune is reverenced in place of the deity.

[63] See Jenny Stratford, "The Royal Library in England before the Reign of Edward IV," in *England in the Fifteenth Century: Proceedings of the 1992 Harlaxton Symposium*, ed. Nicholas Rogers, Harlaxton Medieval Studies IV (Stamford: Paul Watkins, 1994), 193–94, with a full bibliography on the question.

ıt ın ſıpıeııs ın coᶝce ſuo
n eſt ɒeus·

æ eſt ceſt le pſeaume ɒᵒ
ınaleth.

ul a ɒıt en ſon cuer quı
t poınt ɒe ɒıen·

oſalıno ᵃᵖᵃechenɒuntur
aın et pᵃatıs ɒeɒıtı quı
atıs uacant ac ſı no ellet
ınnıa coᵃum aɒ pᵃecatu
et ɒeus confunɒet eos ·
bıt conuerſos aɒ ſe.

pſeaume ſont ᵃepᵃıs les
ıtɒaıns et le pecheurs q̇ ſe
a pecher comme ſı ne fuſt
ıeu et quı toute leur eſtu
tıſſent a pecher ⁊ ɒıeu les
a ſe ıl ne ſe conuertıſſeȶ.
uertıᵹ a ſoy eſlerſceᵃa :

Figure 24: Paris, Bibl. Natl. MS. fr. 166, fol. 120. *Bible moralisée* (Paris, ca. 1470–80).

make it an entirely plausible candidate for the Bible Henry V treasured so. His father had been briefly Chaucer's patron, in the year before Chaucer's death, and Henry himself clearly admired the poet's work, acquiring one of the earliest and best copies of Chaucer's *Troilus* (now Pierpont Morgan MS. M. 817) sometime during the same years in which scholars would now date the huge Bible, i.e., between 1403 and the year he became king, 1413; the Morgan copy bears Henry's coat of arms as prince on the first leaf.[64] (If the Bible did in fact belong to Henry IV, and was passed on to Henry V, others before me may have used this image to think about Chaucer's *Troilus*.)[65]

But my argument is thematic, not documentary. I have called attention to the blatantly sexual gestures in these pictures because Chaucer's *Troilus* explores the idealization of erotic love with a comparable double vision. It plays Troilus's idealized view of Criseyde against all that Pandarus more cynically knows of her and of her sex; it conducts the love affair through a number of awkward and embarrassing events; and it explores the most sublime moments of this love—both happy and tragic—in sexually allusive language so bold as to leave many readers resistant still to its implications. When Pandarus, for instance, in a brief moment of conscience, needs reassurance that he is doing nothing dishonorable, Troilus offers to procure in exchange any of his sisters that Pandarus might desire. Similarly destructive of love's idealized self-

---

[64] See A.I. Doyle, "English Books In and Out of Court from Edward III to Henry VII," in *English Court Culture in the Later Middle Ages*, ed. V.J. Scattergood and J.W. Sherborne (New York: St. Martin's Press, 1983), p. 172. Doyle suggests Henry V may also have commissioned Corpus Christi College, Cambridge MS. 61 of that poem, with its famous frontispiece of Chaucer reciting to courtiers; Henry's unexpected death could account for its program of illustrations being left unfinished (p. 175).

[65] Lee Patterson's profound study of this poem, "Ambiguity and Interpretation: A Fifteenth-Century Reading of *Troilus and Criseyde*," in his *Negotiating the Past: The Historical Understanding of Medieval Literature* (Madison: University of Wisconsin Press, 1987), pp. 115–53, focuses on the uses made of it for the nuns of Syon Abbey. In a treatise concerned to show how "flesshly love hideth and coloureth him undre love spirituel" (p. 121), the author quotes Troilus's song (p. 124) and ends by offering this advice regarding carnal love's "sweet poison": "Of which poison if ye lust more to rede,/ Seeth the storie of Troilus, Creseide and Dyomede" (p. 127)—which suggests a copy of that poem may have been available in the Abbey library. Part III of Patterson's chapter, called "*Troilus and Criseyde* in the Nunnery," is of great interest here, not only in its allowance for textual ambiguity, but in its demonstration that all interpretation is partial and partitive, as in this case of a monastic author writing for nuns. "Disambiguating is always, and properly, a process of deciding not what a text means but what we want it to mean. . . . One of the great achievements of Augustinian hermeneutics is to make the preemptive nature of interpretation explicit" (pp. 150–51). If the Psalm 52 illustration studied above was for a time available to at least some of those nuns, the Syon Abbey connection is rich indeed.

image is the way Criseyde is brought to Pandarus's house, not knowing Pandarus intends to deliver her to Troilus there. Troilus, in hiding, watches her arrival through the window of a "stewe"—a word used in a private house (like Pandarus's) to mean simply a "bath," but elsewhere and more commonly "public brothel." Pandarus indeed unlocks "the stuwe door" to usher Troilus into his first experience of "heaven": "Make thee redy right anon, / For thow shalt into hevene blisse wende" (3.703). To reach that room where he will make love to Criseyde for the first time, Troilus must creep through a gutter, a "privy wente," that sounds as if it were part of the palace's sanitation system (3.787). And after her departure from Troy, he and Pandarus will visit her empty house, comparing it not only to a reliquary robbed of its holy relic—its "seynt"— but to a lantern whose light has been quenched (extinguished). Here too the language chosen has a double meaning: "queynte [cunt] is the lyghte" (5.553, 543). The pun on "queynt" is not locker room humor, but punning notation of a profoundly serious kind, more subtle and understated than the sexual gestures in the two psalter pictures just examined, and in service of a double truth.[66] Troilus is at once a young man experiencing sexual love for the first time, and an idealist whose capacity for "trouthe" (fidelity in that love) separates him as decisively from Pandarus as from Diomede the Greek, the rival who eventually replaces him in Criseyde's heart. Like a Tuscan tray made ca. 1400 depicting a radiant Venus (fig. 25), in which "queynte" is quite literally "the lyghte," puns of this sort remind us that "courtly" ways of thinking about love both dignify and disguise ordinary sexual desire.[67]

---

[66] Cf. the lament in which Troilus asks his eyes why they don't "wepen out youre sighte;/ Syn she is queynt, that wont was yow to lighte?" (4. 312–13). (See also 4. 1429–31, where "the grete furie of his penaunce/ Was queynt with hope, and therwith hem bitwene/ Bigan for joie th'amorouse daunce.") Fleming's chapter "Quaint Light in Troy," in *Classical Imitation*, offers a witty history of modern criticism's frequent squeamishness concerning these puns—an anachronistic decorum that invades even *The Riverside Chaucer*, p. 1051 n.543, which comments: "Frost rightly argues against reading a pun in *queynt*, Yale Rev. 66, 1977, 551–61." But Frost's essay is belle–lettristic at best. It testifies to interpretive discomfort without producing scholarly evidence of any substantial kind.

[67] Figure 25: Tristan is second from the left; Troilus last on the right. Such trays, commissioned to present sweetmeats or other offerings to a bride or mother, often depict subjects from secular poems. See John Pope–Hennessy and Keith Christiansen, *Secular Painting in 15th–Century Tuscany: Birth Trays, Cassone Panels, and Portraits*, Metropolitan Museum of Art Bulletin, Summer 1980 (New York: Metropolitan Museum of Art, 1980), pp. 4–11. One of their examples, showing a mother receiving presents in her bedroom as the baby is tended by women below, has an inscribed prayer: "May God grant health to every woman who gives birth and to their father . . . may [the child] be born without fatigue or peril," etc. (figs. 4 and 5). On the tray reproduced here, see Loomis, *Arthurian Legends in Medieval Art*, fig. 135 and p. 70; and esp. Paul F. Watson, *The Garden of Love*

Figure 25: Paris, Louvre, RF 2089. Birth tray or salver (Tuscan, ca. 1400). Photo: Musées Nationaux, Paris.

---

*in Tuscan Art of the Early Renaissance* (Philadelphia, The Art Alliance Press, 1979), pl. 67 and pp. 80–84. He derives its compositional formula from that developed for the Assumption of the Virgin, notices that Venus extends her arms in the fashion of the Man of Sorrows displaying his wounds (an *Ostentatio Veneris*), and names its theme unequivocally as "the power of sex," "the power of Venus," and its subject "Our Lady of Pleasures." Granted the tray's dynastic occasion, it seems unlikely this Venus was thought of as being opposed to respectable, married love. As Watson notes, the apple trees and lush garden symbolize fecundity, creating a paradise "sacred to a deity but open to virtuous mortals"; "Venus [here] ideally replaces these worthies' consorts." Michael Foss, *Chivalry* (London: Michael Joseph, 1975), p. 96, reproduces the tray in color.

Rhetorically speaking, the religious temple of Chaucer's Book 1 and the "stewe" of Book 3 are two versions of the same—an erotically charged space in which Troilus looks with longing on Criseyde—each revealing a different aspect of that desire. The Tuscan tray likewise creates a time-less space whose goddess represents something constant in human ex-perience. Making no distinction between lovers who lived before Christ (Samson, Achilles, Paris, Troilus) and those who lived after (Tristan and Lancelot), the tray spiritualizes carnal love, presenting it as something glorious and ennobling, transcending history. (The fact such trays were commissioned to commemorate a marriage or a birth virtually pre-cludes ironic interpretation.) The erotic illustrations to Psalm 52 we have examined do otherwise: their passionate couples embrace beneath the gaze of an offended God.

But Chaucer has it both ways, in a manner these images can help us chart more precisely. For it is only with regard to the final thirty-five lines of the *Troilus* (the so-called Palinode to a poem 8239 lines long) that these psalter illustrations become fully relevant to its ethos. There Chaucer speaks at last in his own unmediated voice, to an audience ad-dressed for the first time as Christian, of a love that will not "falsen" or betray:

> O yonge, fresshe folkes, he or she,
> In which that love up groweth with youre age,
> Repeyreth hom fro worldly vanyte,
> And of youre herte up casteth the visage
> To thilke God that after his ymage
> Yow made, and thynketh al nys but a faire,
> This world that passeth soone as floures faire.
>
> And loveth hym the which that right for love
> Upon a crois, oure soules for to beye,
> First starf, and roos, and sit in hevene above;
> For he nyl falsen no wight, dar I seye,
> That wol his herte al holly on hym leye.
> And syn he best to love is, and most meke,
> What nedeth feynede loves for to seke? (5. 1835–48)

Chaucer tells us here, in verse of the gravest beauty, that what Troilus sought in loving Criseyde can be found only in the love of Christ. But

Chaucer does not imagine, here or anywhere else in the poem, that loving Christ was an option available in Troy.[68]

Until those final stanzas, Chaucer employs the language of worship and idolatry not to judge Troilus as though he were Christian—that would be absurd—but to explore human experience on that far shore where "love celestial" and "love of kind" overlap, blurring their difference, obscuring their true relation. For Eros too promises transcendence, creates its own Gods, and is powerful enough to destroy even its most faithful servants. This is why "pagan love" remained relevant to medieval Christian audiences, and why it is capable of moving us (and teaching us) still.

But the poem is also about something culturally more specific: the relation of Christian humanism to all that was most noble in the pagan past, to all that aspired to honor and truth before the Incarnation. It was necessary to believe, on Christ's own authority, that except through Him no one comes to God the Father. And so one had to believe as well in the damnation of all who lived before His birth—give or take a few Old Testament Jews—including even the just who had no access to His salvation. This response to the problem of the "good pagan," at once totalizing, inhumane, and theologically essential, constituted for the Middle Ages another great *aporia*—another breakdown in logic and sense—that proved troubling to many, including (most famously) Pope Gregory the Great in his prayers for the Emperor Trajan, William Langland in his anguished quest in *Piers Plowman* to understand the terms of salvation, and Julian of Norwich, hinting at a Great Event to come, in which all who ever lived will be saved. I would add to this list—which could easily be extended—the name of Geoffrey Chaucer.

For *Troilus and Criseyde* seems to me more than a poem about erotic love. It is also, in its highest ambitions, a poem about the tragedy of paganism, written out of a humanist sympathy that determines both its tone and its proportions. Until Christ is named in its final lines, the

---

[68] In an interpretive move more tactful than D.W. Robertson's, Fleming, in *Classical Imitation*, measures Troilus against the highest ideals of paganism rather than of Christianity—as though he were a pagan philosopher or statesman, whose proper study is wisdom. But Troilus is a young warrior, experiencing romantic love for the first time, and he aims at something quite different—whatever can be known of heaven within his lady's arms. I think we are meant to allow him a young man's folly, even as he seeks to make spiritual sense of it. (Philosophy is certainly not his calling. Whenever he tries to think through a Boethian question, he gets the answer wrong.)

poem's deepest longings are expressed in terms of erotic love, and its wisdom can reach no further than the fact that such love, like all our worldly bliss, will end in woe. The Palinode could not move us so deeply—even those of us who are not Christian—were it not for the pressure generated by all that has gone before.

The relation between "love of God" and "love of kind" (love of creatures of *our own kind*) is the great unresolved mystery of the poem. Both are fired by the same "love's hete" (1.978) and are explored within a pagan ethos valuable in no small part because it keeps the question open, acknowledging all that Troilus's love for Criseyde has in common with idolatry and fornication, but refusing to see it only in those terms. St. Augustine himself might have understood that, up to a point, for in his theology, there is nothing disparaging in the admission that desire occupies so dominating a place in our life. It is, in his view, only an expression of the fact that we have life from God, and not, like God, in ourselves and from ourselves. In desire, therefore, there is nothing reprehensible or evil. In so far as it gives expression to the actual condition of man as a created being, it is, on the contrary, praiseworthy in the highest degree. If we were to cease to desire, it would be as though we possessed our "good" in ourselves, with no need to seek it anywhere else—appropriating to ourselves something of the divine independence and self-sufficiency.[69]

This, of course, describes only the foundation of Augustine's theology of desire: ultimately, he tells us, we must seek its fulfillment in love of God, rather than in things (or creatures) of this world. But Augustine wrote after the Incarnation, when Christ had redefined the goals and possibilities of such devotion. To my mind Augustine's generalized understanding of desire, summarized above, resonates more deeply with the confused idealism of Troilus's love than does the full theology of *The City of God*, or those modern readings that would use the Palinode to erase everything that has gone before, leaving only a hymn to the love of Christ—the love that will not fail. Until the Palinode Chaucer uses religious language in a way that very carefully keeps the Christian God out of the picture: He does not look down upon Troilus and Criseyde, as He does upon the lovers in the psalter illustrations just examined. By freeing the poem of that scrutiny until its story has come to an end,

---

[69] I paraphrase here the powerful analysis by Anders Nygren, *Agape and Eros*, trans. Philip S. Watson (Philadelphia: Westminster Press, 1953), pp. 478–80.

Chaucer is able to imagine paganism in its fullest reach while taking an exact measure of its limitations.

Troilus's love for Criseyde is foolish in several senses, not excluding the comically naive, and it has much in common with psalter folly, especially of the kind shown in these two nearly contemporary English initials. But it is also a quest for transcendence, and in that, lays claim to tragic stature, enacting a higher form of "trouthe" than anyone else in the poem attempts or achieves. It earns him at the end a certain reward: a soul-journey to the eighth sphere, where he hears ravishing music and is granted a moment of total ethical clarity. Looking down on "this litel spot of erthe that with the se / Embraced is," Troilus declares all earthly joy mere "vanite / To respect of the pleyn felicite / That is in hevene above" (5.1815–19). Learning at last contempt for the world, he laughs at the sorrow of those who weep for his death, and curses "al oure werk that foloweth so / The blynde lust, the which that may nat laste, / And sholden al oure herte on heven caste" (5.1818–20).

For pagans and Christians alike, Heaven, by definition, is eternal and unchanging—what always has been and always will be. But human history is otherwise, the offspring of time, a progress the Middle Ages thought of as divided into Seven Ages (the Sixth inaugurated by the birth of Christ) or a sequence of Three Laws (Natural Law, the Written Law of Moses, and the Christian Law of Grace). And so Troilus, loving and dying long before the birth of Christ, can be allowed only a glimpse of this heaven and then the decent obscurity of a pagan afterlife: "And forth he wente, shortly for to telle,/ Ther as Mercurye sorted hym to dwelle"—wherever Mercury determined he should remain (5.1826–27). If Elysium is implied, it is not named, nor is there any mention of Hell. In that imprecision and obscurity the tragedy of Troilus merges with the general tragedy of the world before Christ: there is no Christian God in that sky, and nothing of what follows death is known. The truth that Troilus's soul sees with such perfect vision from the eighth sphere is the truth about human love, not the redemptive love of Christ.

In this poem, then, the destiny of the honorable pagan dead remains a mystery—an *aporia*—fully as much as the spiritual value of erotic love. (The gods Troilus supplants in worshipping Criseyde are nothing more than pagan "rascaille," dismissed as such in the poem's closing lines. His moment in history allows him access to no worthier kind.) Though the Palinode can put the question about paganism, here rendered as a question about love, into new historical perspective, the poem cannot resolve either question from within the boundaries of the narrative proper. As Augustine wrote, commenting on the verse "There is none that doth good, no, not one" in Psalm 13, "No man has really practiced virtue until the coming of Christ, because unless Christ has first instructed him, no man is able to practice virtue."[70] Chaucer's poem has to separate itself from itself in order to offer more.

For those of us who do not share the Christian belief, Chaucer's carefully nuanced respect for the pagan past offers a valuable model for our own response to his poem—a way of participating even in its concluding truths without denying our own. It comes down to something like this. If, as we believe, "love of kynde" (our love for one another) is the best there is, then that is what there is, and we might as well accept it, in all its limitations, without despair. For us, the "correction" proposed so eloquently in the Palinode becomes a way of describing the fragility, instability, and incompleteness of human love, without in fact replacing it with some higher kind that is eternal, unchanging, and ever true. To name something is not to demonstrate its existence; to lack something is not to call it into being. For non-believers too the need to posit such a love from within the poem becomes almost unbearably moving, and we acknowledge the simple beauty with which it is announced, when its moment comes, as part of the poem's grandeur of design and nobility of spirit. But from outside the Palinode's system of belief—the place from which the rest of us read the poem—the redemptive love of Christ as an answer to all that limits and denies us here must seem a fantasy fully as tenuous—and every bit as human—as the love of Troilus for Criseyde. For us the Palinode reads differently, but not ignobly. We honor it as yet another "soul journey" into the unknowable unknown.

Jill Mann proposed a kind of dialogism as a way of resolving the argument between her own atheism and the Christianity of the poems she teaches and serves. There is much to be said for that sort of conversation, and I try to practice it too. But we need not—nor does she—conceive of it solely as a dialogue across the ages. Psalm 52 illuminations of the kind

---

[70] Augustine, *Enarrationes in Psalmos*, Ps. 13:2: "[N]emo intellegatur fecisse bonitatem usque ad Christum; quia non potest quisquam hominum facere bonitatem, nisi ipse monstrauerit" (ed. cit., 38:86); *St. Augustine on the Psalms*, trans. Hebgin and Corrigan, 1.154.

with which we began are already in dialogue with the great images of theological order that dominate the iconography of the age—Doomsday images, for instance, that show Christ in the heavens, displaying his wounds as he separates the saved from the damned. We have only to give these psalter fools their full voice to right the balance. We can even, if we wish, reaffirm Christ's kinship with them as "holy fool" to clear again the threshing floor, to free his memory from all the horror that Church and State have perpetrated in His name.

So let us reclaim, for our own study of the Middle Ages, the dignity and seriousness of God-denying folly—as St. Paul did for Christian folly, in dialogue with Greek ideas of wisdom, and as Erasmus did for Renaissance Humanism at large. Even Aquinas granted it a certain priority, adducing the psalter fool as proof "That God exists is therefore not self-evident."[71]

That has surely always been so, though Aquinas, like other medieval thinkers, could admit it only as preface to a counter-proof, in his case a *Summa Theologiae*. For an unmediated image of non-belief we may look to the madmen, idiots, and jesters of Psalm 52 illustration, as avatars and embodiments of that which Christian orthodoxy could least explain: the fact of madness and imbecility per se, the undercurrent of existential fear even within religious faith, the category confusions intrinsic to erotic love, the destiny of the virtuous pre-Christian dead, and not least, as it was then understood, the necessary role of the Jews in crucifying Christ so that mankind as a whole might be redeemed. God-denying folly is made to explain it all. There is literature that celebrates the system—Dante and Aquinas are its great masters—and literature that testifies to our unease within it, attentive to all that remains excluded and obscure. Out of the real but puzzling existence of idiots

---

[71] "Ergo Deum esse non est per se notum." Aquinas, *Summa Theologiae*, 1a.2, I (ed. cit., pp. 6–7).

The author and publisher would like to express their gratitude to the following institutions who kindly provided photographs and permission to reproduce them in this volume: BONN: Universitätsbibliothek, Fig. 19; CAMBRIDGE: Fitzwilliam Museum, Fig. 3; FLORENCE: Biblioteca Laurenziana, Fig. 17; THE HAGUE: Museum van het Boek/ Museum Meermanno-Westreenianum, Fig. 9; LONDON: British Library, Figs. 4, 5, 6, 10, 13, 22; NEW YORK: The Metropolitan Museum of Art, Fig. 16; OXFORD: All Souls College, Fig. 11; OXFORD: Bodleian Library, Figs. 7, 12, 20; PARIS: Bibliothèque de l'Arsenal, Fig. 8 (Photo: Bibliothèque Nationale); PARIS: Bibliothèque Nationale, Figs. 1, 2, 24; PARIS: Bibliothèque Sainte-Geneviève, Figs. 15, 21; PARIS: Musée du Louvre, Fig. 25 (Photo: Musées Nationaux); TURIN: Biblioteca Nazionale, Fig. 23 (Photo: Kathleen L. Scott); VIENNA: Österreichische Nationalbibliothek, Fig. 14.

and madmen the Middle Ages constructed a symbolic iconography of the fool, using what it could not well explain to explain almost every-thing else it could not well explain. It is in many ways a horrendous story, with painful human consequence. But this much at least can be said. Wherever God-denying folly is found, the deepest questions re-main open, establishing the relevance of the medieval experience to our own. It is possible to embrace all that is most abject in the psalter fool and reject the stigma he is intended to carry.

# THE BIENNIAL CHAUCER LECTURE
The New Chaucer Society
Tenth International Congress
July 26–29, 1996
University of California
Los Angeles

# The Biennial Chaucer Lecture

# In Flaundres

David Wallace
*University of Pennsylvania*

*for Miri Rubin*

> Social anxiety . . . is just maladjustment to change. But who has
> anticipated, or adjusted to, the scale of change in Southern
> California over the last fifteen years? . . . the urban galaxy domi-
> nated by Los Angeles is the fastest growing metropolis in the ad-
> vanced industrial world.
>
> Mike Davis, *City of Quartz*

The space of Chaucer studies is still preeminently England:
ostensibly fourteenth-century England, but often the England of those
Victorian founding fathers honored by one of our sessions.[1] The time of
Chaucer studies has been closely complicit with that of regnal history;
recent interest in the Lancastrians may confirm the habit of situating
Chaucer along the timeline of emergent English nationalism. But

---

This text represents "In Flaundres," a talk given at the Huntington Library on 27 July
1996. Some substantiating details, sacrificed to the fifty-minute format, have been restored. I have reprieved one paragraph (cut for the talk) on Sir Thopas as a Flemish tapestry; I have added one crucial sentence on the discovery of Flanders, as recorded by
Bavaria Herald, as "dat woeste land" ("the waste land").

[1] "Foundational Moments: England"; Derek Brewer, presiding, with Sigmund
Eisner, Charlotte Brewer, and Steve Ellis. Ellis, in his unpublished paper "Chaucer's
England, England's Chaucer," discusses fascinating and egregious Victorian attempts to
endow Chaucer with essential Englishness. F. D. Maurice, for example, wrote in 1866
that Chaucer "has been called a Wycliffite. He is not that. He is simply an Englishman.
He hates friars, because they are not English and not manly. He loves the poor parson,
because he is English and manly" (qtd. in Ellis, p. 2).

fourteenth-century Chaucer is not, in these senses, a poet of England: his native ground—the place where he spent most of his time—is not "England," but rather the eastern quadrant of a territory immediately abutting continental Europe. In strict political terms, this territory extended into the continental landmass, after 1347, with Edward III's colonizing of Calais; Flanders was hence to be seen as a border country.[2] In simple economic terms, hence in the practice of everyday life—the myriad exchanges of language, manufacturing, foodstuffs, *tydinges*, and merchandise—England and Flanders had long been interdependent.[3]

It would be difficult to isolate a discourse of England in Chaucer, but there is a discourse of Flanders.[4] As a discourse, this bears some relation to a territory called Flanders, has consequences for those tagged as Flemish, but speaks most eloquently of the anxieties and desires of its English authors. "Flaundres" plays in Chaucer like certain names that reverberate through our own cultures: Belfast and East LA; Brixton, Brooklyn, and Berkeley—we may never have been to these places, but we know

[2] I follow May McKisack in speaking of colonization: ". . . on 4 August 1347," McKisack writes, Edward III "entered the town and proceeded to evacuate almost all the inhabitants, in order to people it with English colonists whose descendants were to hold it for another two hundred years"; *The Fourteenth Century, 1307–1399* (Oxford: Clarendon Press, 1959), p. 137.

[3] It is important to note that exchanges between England and the Low Countries included both luxury items and the staples of everyday life. "Londoners," Vanessa Harding writes, "drank Dutch beer and perhaps some Rhenish wine, and ate imported apples, pears, onion, and garlic"; "Cross-Channel Trade and Cultural Contacts: London and the Low Countries in the Later Fourteenth Century," in Caroline Barron and Nigel Saul, eds., *England and the Low Countries in the Late Middle Ages* (New York: St. Martin's Press, 1995), p. 163. On the extraordinary mixing of Middle Dutch and Middle English terms that occurs in select fifteenth-century business documents, see Laura Wright, "Trade between England and the Low Countries: Evidence from Historical Linguistics," in ibid, pp. 169–79. Dutch terms for activities associated with beer-brewing and boatbuilding proved especially influential.

[4] Citation of "Flaundres" in Chaucer hence works in ways comparable to the naming of "Lombardy." "Lumbardye" evokes both the historical territory ruled by northern Italian despots, or tyrants—an imaginative terrain explored by Fragment 4 of *The Canterbury Tales*—and an alarming set of possibilities for English polity under Richard II. See David Wallace, *Chaucerian Polity: Absolutist Lineages and Associational Forms in England and Italy* (Stanford: Stanford University Press, 1997), pp. 31–54, 261–387.

The terms "Flaunders," "Flaundryssh," and "Flemyng," like "Lumbardye," are used somewhat loosely by Chaucer (as by his contemporaries). Flemings and Brabantines were keen to distinguish themselves from one another. In London, Fleming and Brabantine weavers organized themselves into separate guilds; there is no evidence that such separation saved alien workers from the massacre at St. Martin Vintry in June 1381. Chaucer refers ten times to Flanders or things Flemish, makes no reference to Brabant, and speaks once of "Pipers of the Duche tonge" (*The House of Fame* 1234).

what goes on there. In the first part of my talk, everything leads to the Pardoner, whose tale begins "In Flaundres . . . ." The second part, a six-minute coda, recognizes that every discourse has its afterlife.

"Flaundres," of course, means something now to each one of us. For my grandparents' generation, Flanders betokened mud, death, poppies, and a postwar shortage of eligible men. Closer to our own time, the narrator of Alan Hollinghurst's novel *The Folding Star* enters an "austere Town Museum," somewhere in Flanders: "I felt a little out of step," he says, "among those chaste northern saints and inward-looking Virgins— there wasn't one of them that welcomed you or held your gaze as the dark eyed Italian gods and holy men so often did."[5] The narrator's experience in this museum is colored by his own loneliness and channeled by a polarizing of northern and southern styles effected by nineteenth-century European art history. Such assumptions concerning the division of the Italian from the Flemish are continuously disrupted in Flanders. Those who visited Bruges during the 1990 Congress may remember being surprised to discover Michelangelo's *Virgin and Child*, framed by the baroque interior of the early gothic Onze Lieve Vrouwekerk. This statue forms part of Flemish culture: it was commissioned by Jan van Moescroen, merchant of Bruges, in 1505.[6]

Flanders and Italy form two angles of a trading triangle that flourished for centuries during the Middle Ages; the third corner is England, or that eastern quadrant of England running from Hull in the north to Southampton in the south. This triangle is peculiarly the space of Chaucer's business and professional life.[7] It is not *the* international space

---

[5] Alan Hollinghurst, *The Folding Star* (London: Chatto and Windus, 1994), p. 9. For Hollinghurst's narrator, the "austere Town Museum" functions as a gay pickup joint.

[6] See Bernard McDonagh, *Belgium and Luxembourg*, Blue Guide (New York: Norton, 1993), pp. 167–68.

[7] Violent, class-interested aspects of this particular space are admirably evoked by Paul Strohm, "Trade, Treason, and the Murder of Janus Imperial," *Journal of British Studies* 35 (January 1996): 1–23 (esp. p. 22). The 1379 revolts of the Flemish weavers drew Imperial to England in search of new trading concessions. According to Walsingham, this Genoese merchant (representing the Duke and Commonalty of Genoa) intended to turn Southampton into the preeminent port of western Europe. On August 26, 1379, however, he was murdered outside his London residence in St. Nicholas Acton Lane. "Principal responsibility for this murder," Strohm writes, "must indeed rest with an inner circle of wool merchants. But civic support for the crime seems to have extended well beyond the members of this small circle" (p. 15). Such harnessing of xenophobic sentiment to purposes of economic self-interest, countenanced here by the highest echelons of London society, was soon to be repeated, at a lower social level, through the massacre of Flemings (discussed below).

of late medieval England: the places traveled in *The Book of Margery Kempe*, particularly those of the second book, are typically reached from Lynn, a town that looks northward and eastward toward Prussia, the Hanseatic ports, and the Baltic.[8] Whereas Margery sails to Danzig, Chaucer crosses to Calais.

At about the time Chaucer was born, in 1343, his father John received a royal permit allowing him to ship merchandise from his hometown of Ipswich to Flanders.[9] Ipswich is on the estuary of the Orwell, a key reference point for the Merchant of *The General Prologue*, who "wolde the see were kept for any thyng / Bitwixe Middelburgh and Orewelle" (lines 276–77).[10] Middelburgh, in Zeeland, was home to the English wool staple between 1384 and 1389.[11] Chaucer's Merchant "wolde the see were kept" because piracy was rife (and the French, in 1386, had commandeered the Flemish fleet with a view to invading England).[12] This Merchant, said to be expert at exchanging *sheeldes*, a fictional money of account sold at London and redeemed at Bruges, wears "a Flaundryssh bever hat" upon his head (line 272).[13]

When the Chaucers of Ipswich became vintners of London, their links with Flanders persisted.[14] Our Geoffrey had occasion to travel "versus partes Flandrie" as a diplomat or messenger on royal service, involved with Anglo-French peace negotiations, Anglo-French marriage

---

[8] The northward and eastward orientation of Lynn is in part determined by the peculiar geography of the Wash. The basic Baedeker for Margery is hence T. H. Lloyd, *England and the German Hanse, 1157–1611* (Cambridge: Cambridge University Press, 1991), rather than (as for Chaucer) T. H. Lloyd, *The English Wool Trade in the Middle Ages* (Cambridge: Cambridge University Press, 1977).

[9] This same permit warned him against attempting to smuggle any wools, hides, or wool-fells out of the country without paying customs duties. See Martin M. Crow and Clair C. Olson, eds., *Chaucer Life-Records* (Austin: University of Texas Press, 1966), p. 4.

[10] The Orwell is a river and not, as *The Riverside Chaucer* suggests, a coastal town. All references to Chaucer follow *The Riverside Chaucer*, ed. Larry D. Benson (Boston: Houghton Mifflin, 1987).

[11] West Flanders was under French control at this point, rendering access to Calais from Bruges difficult.

[12] "In three successive years from 1385 to 1387," J. J. N. Palmer writes, "England was faced with invasion from massive armadas concentrated at Sluys"; "English Foreign Policy 1388–99," in F. R. H. Du Boulay and Caroline Barron, eds., *The Reign of Richard II* (London: Athlone Press, 1971), p. 82.

[13] "English bills for Bruges in Flanders," Kenneth S. Cahn writes, "were quoted in English sterling against the shield or *ecu* (*scudo*) which did not exist as a coin, but which signified 24 (silver) groats, Flemish currency"; "Chaucer's Merchants and the Foreign Exchange: An Introduction to Medieval Finance," *SAC* 2(1980):85.

[14] Rhenish wine "could only pass to England through the markets or ports of the Low Countries" (Harding, "Cross-Channel Trade," p. 156); the ships transporting this wine were often piloted by Flemish masters.

plans, and reparation for war damage suffered by Flemish cities.[15] But even from the vantage point of Calais, which was at the northern tip of Artois (hence "closely nudging the weaving towns of Flanders"),[16] Chaucer could see how Flemings were caught between the rock of France and the hard place of the invading English. In 1363, the staple for English wool was transferred from Bruges to Calais, since Edward III wished to make the garrison at Calais self-financing: the wool will pay for the war; the warriors will protect the merchants.[17] This policy was sealed in 1363 with the foundation of the Calais mint; Flemings were now expected to travel to English territory to buy English wool with English-minted coin to finance the war that was their ruin.

The wool business had made the economies of Flanders and England interdependent for more than two centuries before Chaucer took up his position as Controller of Wool Custom at the port of London in 1374, a post he held until 1386.[18] Before 1270, Flemings dominated the business of exporting wool from England; after this date, however, Italians gradually displaced Flemings in shipping and financing.[19] Such arrangements continued to work well for the Flemings so long as they could obtain a steady supply of high-grade English wool, convert it into cloth, and send it on for export.

---

[15] See Crow and Olson, eds., *Life-Records*, pp. 29–66 (quotation from p. 44); Walter Prevenier, "Les perturbations dans les relations commerciales anglo-flamandes entre 1379 et 1407: Causes de désaccord et raisons d'une réconciliation," *Studia Historica Gandensia* 182 (1973): 477–97; and Pierre Chaplais, *Some Documents Regarding the Fulfilment and Interpretation of the Treaty of Bretigny, 1361–1369*, Camden Miscellany, vol. 19 (London: Royal Historical Society, 1952), esp. pp. 6–8 (on Article 12, dropped from the ratified treaty, which proposed that the King of England should renounce claims to the sovereignty of, inter alia, Flanders). The return trip from England to Bruges has been calculated as taking twelve days in Chaucer's time. The return trip to Paris took thirty-one days, Cologne thirty-nine, and Lombardy seventy-one. See Crow and Olson, eds., *Life-Records*, p. 30 n. 5.

[16] Caroline Barron, "Introduction: England and the Low Countries, 1327–1477," in Barron and Saul, eds., *Low Countries*, p. 2.

[17] See Lloyd, *Wool Trade*, pp. 209–10, and David Nicholas, *Medieval Flanders* (New York: Longman, 1992), p. 290.

[18] By 1127, traffic between the two regions was speedy enough for news of the murder of the Flemish count to reach London within two days; by the end of the thirteenth century, English wool was essential to the Flemish economy. See Lloyd, *Wool Trade*, p. 6. On Chaucer as Controller, see Crow and Olson, eds., *Life-Records*, pp. 148–270.

[19] When Chaucer took office, Italians were still preeminent; the bulk of Italian exports was handled by Florentines. See Wendy Childs, "Anglo-Italian Contacts in the Fourteenth Century," in Piero Boitani, ed., *Chaucer and the Italian Trecento* (Cambridge: Cambridge University Press, 1983), pp. 65–87; Lloyd, *Wool Trade*, p. 255; Kathleen Biddick, *The Other Economy: Pastoral Husbandry on a Medieval Estate* (Berkeley: University of California Press, 1989), p. 3.

The Flemish textile industry was dominated by three major cities: Ypres, Ghent, and Bruges. Flanders and Holland, plus the cities of northern Italy, were the most intensively and precociously urbanized cities in Europe. Flemings were proud of having created so much out of so little. They knew their natural resources to be poor: local polders, loam, or sand plain—fit only for a light scratch plough—could not sustain much of a population; inferior grassland yielded scrawny sheep.[20] Urban ingenuity hence substituted for natural plenty: corn was imported from France, wool from England, and labor from the rural hinterland; water, vital for the textile industry, was channeled through the digging of canals. Textile manufacture dominated all other industries: at Ghent in 1356–58, it occupied some 63 percent of the professionally active population.[21] Weavers and fullers were the two largest textile guilds. Division of labor was highly complex: 53 nontextile guilds have been discovered at Ghent, plus no fewer than 146 other nontextile trades denied rights of organization.[22]

The guild-governed cities of Flanders present a peculiar evolutionary variant in political form, in that they strive toward the independence achieved by German and Tuscan cities while owing allegiance to the count of Flanders, himself a fief of the French crown. All but the last of these counts spoke French but not Flemish; they presided loosely and often distantly over what we might term a bastard bastard feudalism.[23] These guild-governed cities have much in common with their Italian counterparts.[24] Urbane values of improvisation and quick wit were as admired in Reynard the Fox as in Boccaccio's *Decameron*. Urban specta-

[20] See Nicholas, *Medieval Flanders*, pp. 259–65; Wim Blockmans, "The Economic Expansion of Holland and Zeeland in the Fourteenth–Sixteenth Centuries," in A. Aerts, B. Henau, P. Janssens, R. Van Uytven, eds., *Studia Historica Œconomica: Liber Amicorum Herman Van der Wee* (Leuven: Leuven University Press, 1993), pp. 48–50.

[21] See Wim P. Blockmans, "Urban Space in the Low Countries, 13th–16th Centuries," in *Spazio urbano e organizzazione economica nell'Europa medievale*, Annali della Facoltà di Scienze Politiche, no. 29 (1993–94), p. 165. Equivalent figures for Ypres are 52 percent (in 1431) and for Bruges 25 percent (during the fourteenth century. As we shall see, different, capital-intensive enterprises occupied a large percentage—perhaps 50 percent—of the professionally active population of Bruges).

[22] See David Nicholas, *The Metamorphosis of a Medieval City: Ghent in the Age of the Arteveldes, 1302–1390* (Lincoln: University of Nebraska Press, 1987), p. 20; Nicholas, *Medieval Flanders*, p. 309.

[23] The four oldest money exchanges of Bruges, for example, were hereditary fiefs of the count. See Nicholas, *Medieval Flanders*, pp. 231, 301.

[24] There was considerable expenditure on public works, and city dwellers owed a fierce primary allegiance to their cities (rather than to any larger territorial unit, such as "Flanders" or "Tuscany"). A delegation of Flemings, "de singulis villis Flandriae, qui

cle and drama were precociously developed; it is no coincidence that most surviving Middle English drama is found in towns and districts linked by trade with Holland and Flanders.[25]

The urban culture of Flanders was, and knew itself to be, precocious and precarious. It is always a precarious undertaking in Catholic cultures to propose improving upon nature: the Vatican was nervous of gas lighting in the nineteenth century and fears contraception in the twentieth. Intensive urbanization subjected the constitutive parts of the urban body politic, in Flanders as in Italy, to severe new pressures. One source of relief for the city was to unify all social classes by beating up on the countryside.[26] The "White Hoods of Ghent" spent much time terrorizing rural populations.[27] An antipeasant song mocks peasant lineage, peasant dress, peasant labor, weaponry, and dancing (to pipers). Its chorus singles out peasant diet and peasant gluttony for repeated ridicule: "broot ende caes," "bread and cheese."[28]

The most precarious aspect of Flemish polity concerned its balancing of allegiances between England and France, suppliers of wool and grain.

---

majoris reputationis essent et fame," showed up at the English parliament in 1382, offering Richard II kingship of their country (the count of Flanders having run off to France); see Thomas Walsingham, *Historia Anglicana*, ed. H. T. Riley, 2 vols., Rolls Series, 28.1 (London: Longmans, 1863–64), 2: 70–71. To judge from Walsingham, they met with a somewhat puzzled reception: could they be said to represent Flanders, or just its constituent cities?

[25] See Alexandra F. Johnston, "Traders and Playmakers: English Guildsmen and the Low Countries," in Barron and Saul, eds., *Low Countries*, p. 100. For a fine account of the involvement of London mercantile companies in dramatic performance, see Carol M. Meale, "*The Libelle of Englyshe Polycye* and Mercantile Literary Culture in Late-Medieval London," in Julia Boffey and Pamela King, eds., *London and Europe in the Later Middle Ages* (London: Center for Medieval and Renaissance Studies, Queen Mary and Westfield College, University of London, 1995), pp. 192–98.

[26] See Wallace, *Chaucerian Polity*, pp. 125–81.

[27] See David Nicholas, *Town and Countryside: Social, Economic and Political Tensions in Fourteenth-Century Flanders*, University of Ghent, Publications of the Arts Faculty, no. 152 (Bruges: De Tempel, 1971), pp. 138–41, and Nicholas, *Medieval Flanders*, p. 228.

[28] The text of the song, which opens by announcing "our" desire to sing of the churls—"Wi willen van den Kerels zinghen"—follows Louis de Baecker, *Chants historiques de la Flandre, 400–1650* (Lille: Ernest Vanackere, 1855), pp. 173–77. For a partial translation of this seven-stanza poem, see Nicholas, *Medieval Flanders*, pp. 253–54. The poem dates from ca. 1323–28—a period in which rebellious peasants were staging their own public spectacles by forcing nobles to execute their own relatives (Nicholas, ibid, p. 215). Another such poem was composed at court, appealed to urban interests, and was housed in a monastery; see Walter Prevenier, "Court and City Culture in the Low Countries, 1100–1530," in Erik Kooper, ed., *Medieval Dutch Literature in Its European Context* (Cambridge: Cambridge University Press, 1994), p. 23.

Generally speaking, the cloth-producing cities inclined toward the English, and the counts favored France; but there were many factional variations.[29] At the beginning of the Hundred Years' War, the Flemish count, Louis of Nevers, followed a pro-French policy that infuriated Edward III of England and, following English reprisals, plunged the Flemish textile industry into depression. Jacob van Artevelde, a Ghentian broker and merchant, developed an alliance with England: in January 1340, Edward III entered Ghent and was proclaimed King of France; his son, John of Ghent—John of Gaunt—was born just a few months later.[30] Bruges and Ypres resented the new preeminence of Ghent, and Ghentian weavers fought Ghentian fullers in a bloody battle on the Friday market; Jacob van Artevelde was killed soon after. Louis of Male, the new count of Flanders, invaded Flanders in September 1348. Weavers were banned from assembly and government in all Flemish cities, provoking a steady stream of emigration that added a timely boost to the emergent English textile industry.

This buoyant native industry was clearly in the ascendant during Chaucer's years at the Customs House, years that saw its long-established counterparts in Florence and Flanders in catastrophic decline. In 1378, while Chaucer—financed by the War Funds—was courting despots and mercenaries in Lombardy, the government of Florence was overthrown by the Ciompi, woolworkers in an industry made desperate by the lack of English wool. In 1379, Flanders was engulfed by civil war. The century in Flanders between 1270 and 1385 has been summarized as "a

---

[29] Including, as in London, persistent division between victualling and nonvictualling trades; see Nicholas, *Medieval Flanders*, p. 224. Such balancing has, of course, long been a specialty of the Low Countries: the EEC is based in Brussels, rather than in Paris or Berlin. Two days before Hitler came to power, Johan Huizinga—the most influential of apologists for Flemish culture; see Margaret Aston, "Huizinga's Harvest: England and *The Waning of the Middle Ages*," in Aston, *Faith and Fire: Popular and Unpopular Religion, 1350–1600* (London: Hambledon Press, 1993), pp. 133–54—was in Berlin, lecturing on the virtues of the Netherlands as cultural mediator between greater powers. See Bert F. Hoselitz, introduction to Johan Huizinga, *Men and Ideas: History, the Middle Ages, the Renaissance*, trans. James S. Holmes and Hans van Marle (London: Eyre and Spottiswoode, 1960), p. 10. As in 1933, so in the Middle Ages, such mediatory skills were annulled when the great powers went to war with one another. Indeed, Flemings were often punished by one great power for showing allegiance to another; see Lloyd, *Wool Trade*, p. 99.

[30] Lionel of Antwerp, Earl of Ulster, Duke of Clarence (and Chaucer's first master) had been born at Antwerp on November 29, 1338. Philippa, mother of John and Lionel, was daughter of the count and countess of Hainault (whose territory was located immediately to the south of Brabant and to the east of Artois). See T. F. Tout, "Lionel of Antwerp," in *Dictionary of National Biography*, ed. Sir Leslie Stephen and Sir Sidney Lee, 63 vols. (London: Smith, Elder, 1885–1900), 33:335–38.

numbing list of virtually annual foreign attacks or serious internal violence"; the six-year civil war at the end of this period has been assessed
"a total disaster."[31] In December 1381, Philip van Artevelde (son of
Jacob, and pensioner of the English crown) took power at Ghent, took
control of the city records, and hunted down the eldest male relative of
anyone implicated in his father's death.[32] Ghent seized Bruges in May
1382; in November, the French slaughtered van Artevelde and his army
in a swamp. In the summer of 1383, Richard II sent a "Crusade" to
Flanders under the Bishop of Norwich; having destroyed the unfortified
suburbs of Ypres, the English returned safely home. Weavers from Ypres,
who worked in these suburbs, soon joined the trail of emigrants to
England.[33]

There is no doubt that English textiles, deemed by Walter Prevenier
"sans tradition de réputation" before 1350,[34] benefited on international
markets from difficulties suffered by Florentines in 1378 and by
Flemings after 1379. Two pilgrims in *The General Prologue* may be directly associated with this upturn in English fortunes; here is the first
who comes to mind:

> A good WIF was there OF biside BATHE,
> But she was somdel deef, and that was scathe.
> Of clooth-makyng she hadde swich an haunt
> She passed hem of Ypres and of Gaunt. (lines 445–48)

It is notable here how the name of the English city (the place the Wife
is wedded to) bumps up against the names of the two most famous weaving towns of Flanders;[35] naming is power, as the Shipman's merchant

---

[31] See Nicholas, *Medieval Flanders*, p. 209, and Lloyd, *Wool Trade*, p. 225.

[32] See David Nicholas, *The van Arteveldes of Ghent: The Varieties of Vendetta and the Hero in History* (Ithaca, N.Y.: Cornell University Press, 1988), pp. 120–59. This use of archives offers some instructive parallels with the English 1381.

[33] See Nicholas, *Medieval Flanders*, p. 307. Some Flemish textile workers emigrated to Brabant.

[34] Prevenier, "Perturbations," p. 494. In treaty negotiations of 1389, the Flemish ambassadors stated that if English cloths were to enter Flanders, "it would mean the de-
struction of our country" (qtd. in John H. Munro, "Industrial Protectionism in Medieval Flanders: Urban or National?" in Harry A. Miskimin, David Herlihy, and A. L. Udovitch, eds., *The Medieval City* (New Haven, Conn.: Yale University Press, 1977), p. 239.

[35] The authority of these Flemish names could not be dispersed overnight: fifty years
later, another English poet would complain "of cloth of Ipre, that *named* is better than
oures" (emphasis mine); see *The Libelle of Englyshe Polycye: A Poem (Attributed to A.
Molyneux) on the Use of Sea-Power, 1436*, ed. Sir George Frederic Warner (Oxford:
Clarendon Press, 1926), line 74.

says.[36] The English name that mattered most in Flanders before 1350 was "Cottswold," designating the first-grade raw material from which Flemish textiles were made. Cotswold wool, in the 1380s, was more likely to support native English industry than the fullers and weavers of Flanders; Bath (who knows) might be the coming name to drown out talk "of Ypres and of Gaunt."

The Wife's riding posture is at once comfortable and militant: she ambles, but wears sharp spurs; she laughs and carps (beneath a hat of shieldlike dimensions). The second pilgrim in *The General Prologue* set in hostile relation to Flemish territory is similarly characterized through a mix of militant and companionable registers: the Squire, who

> . . . hadde been somtyme in chyvachie
> In Flaundres, in Artoys, and Pycardie. (lines 85–86)

The discovery of "Flaunders" here, round the corner of the couplet, surely aims to raise a snicker from Chaucer's first audience. Flanders, Artois, and Picardy—those continental regions lying closest to the English mainland—form a sorry complement to the vast litany of distant battles and campaigns attributed to the Knight. Mention of "Flanders," in the 1380s, would stir memories of the recent and humiliating[37] bishop's "Crusade" to Ypres; mention of "chyvachie" would draw attention to the distinctive mode of combat employed by the English in this and other campaigns. The aim of *chevauchee* was *not* to engage the enemy in battle, but rather to cut a wide swathe of havoc, damage, and destruction.[38] Lovers of "chivalrie, / Trouthe and honour,"

---

[36] Without a name, *creauncing*, credit-worthiness, is next to impossible: "We may creaunce whil we have a name, / But goldlees for to be, it is no game" (*ShT* 289–90).

[37] See Margaret Aston, "The Impeachment of Bishop Despenser," *Bulletin of the Institute of Historical Research* 38 (1965):127–48. Aston assesses the failed Crusade and its aftermath as "the turning point in the foreign politics of the reign" (p. 127). In 1382, the English government was divided over which of "deux noble chymyns" to follow: intervention in Flanders or in Portugal. After the bishop's impeachment, the "way of Flanders" was effectively closed; Gaunt chose to pursue the "chemin de Portyngale" (*Rotuli Parliamentorum: Ut et petitiones, et placita in Parliamento 1278–1503*, ed. John Strachey et al., 6 vols. [London, 1783], 3:133; Aston, "Bishop Despenser," pp. 132, 135).

[38] My understanding of *chevauchee* is indebted to Lachlan Mead, "Beating Ploughshares into Swords: Fourteenth-Century English Warfare and the *Canterbury Tales*," a paper written for the 8220 Chaucer seminar, University of Minnesota, spring 1996. See further Christopher Allmand, *The Hundred Years' War: England and France at War, 1300–1450* (Cambridge: Cambridge University Press, 1989), p. 55; Herbert Hewitt, *The Organization of War under Edward III, 1338–1362* (Manchester: Manchester University Press, 1966), p. 100.

like the Squire's father (*GP* 45–46), were uneasy about these distinctively English tactics, which saw the lower echelons of military society—squires, yeomen, and below—do most of the decisive fighting.

Our second citation of "In Flaundres," like the first, evokes suggestions of chivalric lineage compromised by considerations of Flemish provenance: the father of Sir Thopas is said to be

> Yborn . . . in fer contree,
> In Flaundres, al biyonde the see,
> At Poperyng, in the place. (*Th* 718–20)

Again, the uncovering of "In Flaundres" sounds a retreat from epic register: "al biyonde the see," "In Flaundres"—forty miles from Dover. Critics have argued that "Poperyng," too, conduces to mirth, since it sounds funny.[39] Ypres and Ghent certainly do not belong in *Sir Thopas*, since they were powerful names with unfunny associations. Poperinge, however, was a *respectable* name: the town headed up the secondary tier of Flemish cloth-producers. It could never be more than middling since it was landlocked and lay too close to Ypres: when Poperinge got ideas above its station, Ypres sent out the militia to smash up its machinery.[40]

The middling status of Poperinge befits Sir Thopas, a middling kind of knight and a distinctively Flemish one. I have yet to find a Flemish Sir Thopas: the closest I've come so far (not very close) is Simon Saphir of Ghent, demesne wool-merchant of the King of England.[41] It is worth noting, however, that Chaucer's Sir Thopas wears Flemish-fabricated (Flemish-speaking)[42] stockings (lines 733–35):

> Of Brugges were his hosen broun,
> His robe was of syklatoun,
> That coste many a jane.

[39] Poperinge was "no doubt selected by Chaucer," the *Riverside Chaucer* argues, "for its comic-sounding name and commonplace associations" (p. 918, n. to line 720). See further William Witherle Lawrence, "Satire in *Sir Thopas*," *PMLA* 50 (1935):81–91.

[40] See Nicholas, *Medieval Flanders*, pp. 280–83. Poperinge, ten kilometres west of Ypres, was home to the largest textile industry in Flanders outside the Three Cities.

[41] See Lloyd, *Wool Trade*, p. 12.

[42] My contention here is that all Chaucerian deployments of "Brugges" require—for reasons of meter—a particular disyllabic articulation suggestive of Flemish rather than of French (or modern English) usage.

"Brugges" is much more than a middling name, although it was famed not for its textiles, but as the greatest money market of late medieval Europe. The Genoese were prominent in such business at Bruges, although the "jane" was not one of their more sought-after coins: it was worth about one English halfpenny. Collocation of Bruges and the "jane" serves to remind us, however, of the Flemish–Italian–English trade/finance/war triangle so familiar to Chaucer. John de Mari, citizen of Genoa, was employed by Edward III to hire Genoese mercenaries and made payments at Bruges in 1373; in this same year this same John de Mari led Chaucer and company to Genoa on the king's "secret business."[43]

The middlingness of *Sir Thopas* is most eloquently suggested by its "drasty" tail-rhyme "rymyng" (line 930), which offered lower to middling audiences economical accounts of great Anglo-Norman ancestral heroes (such as "Beves and sir Gy [of Warwick]" [line 899]). Evocation of Flanders accords with all this just perfectly: for it suggests, to Chaucer's audience, the vigorous imitation of nobility in the land of the non-noble. The fundamental non-nobility of the Flemish may be readily deduced from their buildings: for "in contrast to Italy," Wim Blockmans notes, "the nobility of these regions did not dwell in the cities and thus did not impose its magnificent architecture in the urban space."[44] Most urbanized space in Flanders serves the needs of merchants and artisans. Whereas Italian aristocrats built high, nonfunctional towers to the glory of their family name, Flemings built belfries. Adapted from the feudal *donjons* of Picardy, Flemish belfries assumed purely civic functions in accommodating the watch, housing the city archives, and sounding the hours of the working day.[45]

At the battle of Courtrai on July 11, 1302, the craftsmen of Bruges had defeated the army of France. This was the first major battle in which

[43] See Crow and Olson, eds., *Life-Records*, pp. 32–40, esp. p. 38 n. 1. John de Mari's payments were made, apparently in March 1373, to Francis de Mari (possibly a relative), a leader of Genoese crossbowmen.

[44] Blockmans, "Urban Space," p. 166. Blockmans is speaking of Flanders and Brabant. Flemish non-nobility is further celebrated by the thirteenth-century *Prise de Nuevile* (in French, but spiced with Flemish borrowings), which describes how a large group of Flemings assembles in the industrial quarter of Arras and goes off to assault a castle. For excellent discussion of this burlesque poem, and of its possible bearing on *Sir Thopas*, see J. A. Burrow, "Chaucer's *Sir Thopas* and *La Prise de Nuevile*," *The Yearbook of English Studies* 14 (1984):44–55.

[45] See Blockmans, "Urban Space," p. 174; Nicholas, *Medieval Flanders*, p. 257; Herman Liebaers et al., eds., *Flemish Art: From the Beginning Until Now* (New York: Arch Cape Press, 1988), pp. 61–63.

urban infantry had defeated cavalry commanded by nobles; some 500 pairs of golden spurs were taken from fallen French aristocrats and housed in a Flemish church.[46] This legendary triumph did not, however, dispel the allure of French culture in Flanders. In the Middle Dutch *Reinaert*, the Flemish bourgeoisie were invited to laugh at the obsessive cultivation of French by Flemish nobles: the little dog Courtois, "Courtier," speaks French "in and out of season."[47] But these same Flemish urbanites were themselves avid consumers of French or French-derived chivalric adventures; such "romances of prys" (as *Sir Thopas* terms their English equivalents [line 897]) became the favored form of fantasy literature, in Bruges as in London, for the town-bound business and mercantile classes.

J. M. Manly has surmised that the English audience of Chaucer's *Sir Thopas* was accustomed "to poke fun, not without a little resentment, at the efforts of the Flemish *bourgeoisie* to ape the manners of the English and French aristocracy, and with their newfound wealth to compete in dress, in manners, and in exploits on the battlefield with the ancient chivalry of France and England."[48] Manly was not English, but there is no doubt here that disciplinary loyalty leads him to unite French and English culture against that of the upstart Flemish. It is true that English royal blood was not willing to ally itself, in the twelfth, thirteenth, or fourteenth centuries, with that of Flanders or its counts.[49] It is also true that throughout this period, England was much indebted to industrial and money-making technologies pioneered by the Flemish; was, as Caroline Barron says, "the junior partner" in such ventures.[50] In the field of vernacular literature, however, Flemish and English were as peas in a pod: retarded, west Germanic country cousins in the kingdom of the French. Chaucer, in assigning himself *Sir Thopas*, embraces that which Manly cannot contemplate.

The territories of the Chaucer triangle—Florence, Flanders, and London—hosted emergent vernacular traditions attempting to make their way forward, out from under French domination. Italy, following Brunetto Latini's transplanting of the *Rose* in the 1260s, had made significant progress by the mid-Trecento; Flemish and English, by contrast,

---

[46] See Nicholas, *Medieval Flanders*, pp. 192–94.

[47] Prevenier, "Court and City Culture," p. 18.

[48] J. M. Manly, "*Sir Thopas*, a Satire," *Essays and Studies by Members of the English Association* 13 (1928): 59–60.

[49] With French-leaning Hainault, yes, but not with Flanders.

[50] Caroline Barron, "Introduction: England and the Low Countries," p. 21.

were still in thrall to their lordly lingua franca.[51] Italian is closely related to the pedigreed languages of Latin and French; Flemish and English, by contrast, are hybridized languages lying along the shifting borderline of Romance and Germanic tradition. In this sense, to write in English in the 1380s is broadly equivalent to writing "in Flaundres"; by insisting that Flemish "sounds funny," the English can distance themselves from the realization that, to the rest of the world, it was difficult to distinguish Flemings from Englishmen.

It is worth noting, perhaps, that Chaucer's grandfather was known as "Robert Malin le Chaucer." The original family name of the Chaucers, according to Derek Pearsall, "is likely to have been Malyn"; "Malines" is the French name for the Flemish Mechelen, a town acquired by the Count of Flanders ca. 1333 and said to be "strongly Flemish in character."[52]

Before moving on to *The Shipman's Tale*, I'd like to take one more pass at Sir Thopas, specifically at his socks—those "hosen broun" of "Brugges" (*Th* 733). Periodically, by way of encouraging the emergent English textile industry, common or middling people would be forbidden to wear alien cloth.[53] At the same time, their social superiors were all too keen to lay their hands on foreign textiles, especially "arras" or tapestries. Richard II, in particular, was a tapestry junkie, boosting the royal collection from seven in 1377 to no fewer than fifty by 1399. Magnates, such as the earl of Warwick, were also keen to acquire sets (depicting, for example, the adventures of Guy of Warwick).[54] Such luxury items, Scott McKendrick has argued, "served a prominent role in the king's general projection of his great personal wealth and power"; they often accompanied the king across the Channel to surround him at events involving continental rivals.[55] There is a clean disassociation here between the exigencies of kingly status-projection and any sense of loyalty to native (English) industry. Why should kingly power wish to

---

[51] See David Wallace, "Chaucer and the European *Rose*," in Paul Strohm and T. J. Heffernan, eds., *Studies in the Age of Chaucer: Proceedings*, no. 1 (1984): pp. 61–67, and Kooper, ed., *Medieval Dutch Literature*, passim.

[52] See Crow and Olson, eds., *Life-Records*, p. 2; Derek Pearsall, *The Life of Geoffrey Chaucer: A Critical Biography* (Oxford: Blackwell, 1992), p. 16; and McDonagh, *Belgium and Luxembourg*, p. 220.

[53] See Lloyd, *Wool Trade*, pp. 116, 121.

[54] See Scott McKendrick, "Tapestries from the Low Countries in England during the Fifteenth Century," in Barron and Saul, eds., *Low Countries*, pp. 49, 51.

[55] McKendrick, "Tapestries," p. 50. Julius Caesar, Ann Kuttner informs me, traveled through Gaul with *tessellata* (mosaic) and *sectilia* (intarsia) floors, to be reassembled for his *convivia* (dinners); see Suetonius, *Divus Julius*, ch. 46–48.

stage itself surrounded by the fruits of foreign, artisanal labor? *Sir Thopas* lifts the lid on such paradoxes, honoring "roial chivalry" (line 902) while acknowledging the workaday exigencies of small foreign coins and hungry horses needing "good forage" (line 783). Its themes are precisely those favored by royal and magnate purchasers of *arras*: scenes from romances, hunting, and courtly "love-likynge."[56] *Sir Thopas* is, in short, a genuine Flemish tapestry.

Flanders looms large in *The Shipman's Tale*. We spend just five lines securely *in* Flanders, but much energy and calculation is dedicated to the business of getting there: "whan youre housbonde is to Flaundres fare" (line 199); "To Flaundres wol I go" (line 239); "wel I see to Brugges wol ye go" (line 258); then, finally (lines 299–301):

> The morwe cam, and forth this marchant rideth
> To Flaundres-ward; his prentys wel hym gydeth
> Til he came into Brugges murily.

Flanders, and specifically Bruges, figures in this account as a vortex inexorably sucking in the merchant-protagonist and, following a brief and hectic interval, propelling him out again. Time within Bruges, described as "the commercial emporium of western Europe," as "*the* commercial metropolis of the west,"[57] is spent as follows (lines 302–6):

> Now gooth this marchant faste and bisily
> Aboute his nede, and byeth and creaunceth.
> He neither pleyeth at the dees ne daunceth,
> But as a marchaunt, shortly for to telle,
> He let his lyf, and there I lete hym dwelle.

Foreign merchants had plenty of opportunity for dicing and dancing at Bruges: taverns, bathhouses, brothels, and gambling houses lay within easy reach of their lodgings along *Vlamingstraat*, just north of the market square.[58] The Shipman's merchant ignores such temptations: yet he

---

[56] *Sir Thopas* 850; McKendrick, "Tapestries," p. 49.

[57] Bryce Lyon, "Flanders," in *Dictionary of the Middle Ages*, ed. Joseph R. Strayer, 13 vols. (New York: Scribner, 1982–89), 5:80; Wim Blockmans, "The Social and Economic Context of Investment in Art in Flanders around 1400," in Maurits Smeyers and Bert Cardon, eds., *Flanders in a European Perspective: Manuscript Illumination around 1400 in Flanders and Abroad*, Proceedings of the International Colloquium, Leuven, September 7–10, 1993 (Leuven: Uitgeverij Peeters, 1995), p. 718.

[58] See Blockmans, "Urban Space," p. 174, and Nicholas, *Medieval Flanders*, p. 296.

is, of course, consumed by a greater gambling game, since (as the Man of Law suggests) merchants are professional rollers of the dice, medieval crapshooters hoping for a six-and-five (and fearing one-and-one).[59] English and other foreign merchants at Bruges held their meetings at the Carmelite monastery, a convenient site for "creauncing"; but commercial exchanges of the kind essayed in *The Shipman's Tale* maintain precarious relations to Christian doctrine, since they entail mysterious vanishings of value that border on usury.[60] At Bruges they are conducted with "sheeldes," that imaginary unit of exchange: to redeem the loan of 20,000 "sheeldes" extended to him by the Italian bankers at Bruges, the merchant must scare up real coin from his associates and pay the Italians at their Paris branch.[61]

Bruges of *The Shipman's Tale* can be seen, then, as the eye or aporia of a vortex where agreements escape, for a moment, secure material referents (although, on the home front, the husband's vanishing into Flanders cues more material forms of exchange, of "frankes" for "flankes" [lines 199–203]).[62] The trajectory traveled by the Shipman's

[59] See *MLT* 122–25. The gambling intrinsic to merchant trade concerns not just the risky attempted business of buying cheap, traveling, and selling dear (see *Decameron* 2.4), but all dealings with exchange of monies; see Raymond de Roover, "The Bruges Money Market around 1400," *Verhandelingen van de Koninklijke Vlaamse Academie voor Wetenschappen, Letteren en Schone Kunsten van België, Klasse der Letteren*, 63 (1968):32–37. Those of noble or royal blood should not feel the impulse to roll the dice, since they could hardly better the lot of their lineage. When "the kyng Demetrius" succumbed to gambling, "The kyng of Parthes, as the book seith us, / Sente him a paire of dees of gold in scorn, / For he hadde used hasard ther-biforn" (*PardT* 621–24).

[60] See Blockmans, "Urban Space," p. 174; de Roover, "Money Market," pp. 11–14; Curtin, "Cross-Cultural Trade," p. 6; and Jacques Le Goff, *Your Money or Your Life: Economy and Religion in the Middle Ages* (New York: Zone Books, 1988). There is nothing specifically Christian about "creauncing," since those of pagan "creaunce" (such as the Man of Law's Syrian guild of drapers and spicers) may also be reputed credible, creditworthy, "sadde and trewe" (*MLT* 135).

[61] For more exhaustive, technical description of these complex processes, see Cahn, "Chaucer's Merchants," pp. 85–90; see also John M. Ganim, "Double Entry in Chaucer's *Shipman's Tale*: Double Entry before Pacioli," *ChauR* 30 (1996):294–305.

[62] The simultaneity of these exchanging processes—those of Bruges and of Seint-Denys—encourages us to consider all three protagonists—merchant, monk, and wife—as essential players in this complex commercial enterprise. The wife, we might think, is joining a famous Flemish occupation: Flemish women traveled the trade routes with the cloth and were prominent as prostitutes in both Florence and London. But this wife has a rationale for her urgent need for capital accumulation: she needs must spend "on myn array, / And nat on wast" (*ShT* 418–19) since her primary social function is to image forth the status of a husband "That riche was" (line 2), but unpedigreed. Italian merchant wives showed a precocious grasp of their new symbolic role in the new commercial economy, leaving Italian merchant husbands—like chronicler Giovanni Villani—to recycle old forms of misogynistic lament. See Wallace, *Chaucerian Polity*, pp. 18–19; on prostitution,

monk and merchant forms a strongly articulated triangle: Seint-Denys, Bruges, Paris. Such triangles, involving the shifting of credit notes, coin, and merchandise, were often traveled by those in the wool business eager to avoid customs dues and brokerage fees, or to buy on leveraged capital; Chaucer, as customs officer, was expert in such matters. A merchant might buy English wool in the Cotswolds on credit, sell it at Venice for cash, loan the cash in Flanders at high interest, and then (finally) pay off the Cotswold wool. England, Italy, and Flanders—the Chaucer triangle—form the classic configuration for such enterprise, although there were variants.[63] An Exchequer enquiry of 1383 revealed that one Hugelin Gerard had bought wool at Westminster, faked a sale at Calais, then sent on the merchandise to Bruges.[64] *The Shipman's Tale*, then, is French and Flemish in its setting, Italian in its *modus agendi* (as Lee Patterson observes), and, in its professional concerns, peculiarly Chaucerian English.[65]

And so we come to our third, final, and most enigmatic citation of "in Flaundres." This phrase, "In Flaundres," opens *The Pardoner's Tale*; but after this opening, no reference is made to anything specifically

---

see Ruth Mazo Karras, *Common Women: Prostitution and Sexuality in Medieval England* (New York: Oxford University Press, 1996).

Monks, particularly English monks, had long proved indispensable to the economy that cycled its money through Bruges. The ransom value of Richard I, King of England, had been assessed at one year of the Cistercian wooldip (plus that of two minor orders); English monasteries were household names in Flanders (see Lloyd, *Wool Trade*, pp. 288–90). Monkish woolgrowers had pioneered many of the business techniques—such as double-entry bookkeeping—that established preconditions for later capitalist expansion; visitors to Fountains Abbey, during the 1984 Congress, may have been surprised to discover a wool factory staffed by hundreds of men (with a clearly delineated class system). But perhaps most crucially, established religion lent emergent commerce a language and framework for transacting business, so that a merchant (as in *The Shipman's Tale*) might *creaunce* or, in monklike seclusion, "rekene with hymself" (line 78). Such discursive borrowing proved particularly crucial for Flemings and Florentines, whose urban class structures were effectively severed from subservience to nobility (and hence from nobility's monopolistic hold over ethical discourse). The Shipman's merchant in Bruges is said to live neither nobly nor churlishly, but "as a marchaunt"—a phrase of uncertain ethical valence that demands immediate qualification through a listing of practical activities.

[63] See *Libelle*, ed. Warner, p. xxvi. Italian merchants were allowed to transport English wool from London to Calais, but were not supposed to seek direct access to Flemish markets.

[64] See Lloyd, *Wool Trade*, p. 256.

[65] Patterson perceptively describes *The Shipman's Tale* as "the most Boccaccian of the *Canterbury Tales*"; *Chaucer and the Subject of History* (Madison: University of Wisconsin Press, 1991), p. 361.

Flemish. In *The Shipman's Tale*, the merchant asks *"Quy la?"* (line 214) and the monk swears "by Seint Denys of Fraunce" (line 151), reminding us that the tale indeed opens at Seint Denys in France; but in *The Pardoner's Tale*, nothing. We can hunt for localizing details: the land is plague-ridden; Flanders suffered most acutely from plague *after* the European pandemic of 1348–49.[66] Flemings were famous drunks: Ghentians invaded Bruges during the procession of the Holy Blood in 1362 because they counted on "the wholesale inebriation" of the population. Tavern life was dangerous: a man sitting in a pub in Eeklo in 1373 was hit in the head with a battleaxe; fortunately, he was wearing an iron helmet at the time.[67] Such anecdotes, while usefully exemplifying discourses of Flanders, actually lead us away from what happens "in Flaundres," as the Pardoner tells it; for whereas anecdotes bring the assurances of familiar literary form, the Pardoner's narrative at once disintegrates into listing and troping (*PardT* 463–71):

> In Flaundres whilom was a compaignye
> Of yonge folk that haunteden folye,
> As riot, hasard, stywes, and tavernes,
> Where as with harpes, lutes, and gyternes,
> They daunce and pleyen at dees bothe day and nyght,
> And eten also and drynken over hir myght,
> Thurgh which they doon the devel sacrifise
> Withinne that develes temple in cursed wise
> By superfluytee abhomynable.

It is not clear whether "that develes temple" is to be imagined as a tavern, or as the human body itself. Perhaps both at once: Hieronymus Bosch can imagine a tavern within the giant body of a man (see fig. 1).[68] Bosch also isolates and amplifies many of the objects found in the Pardoner's opening passage to create fantastic new landscapes of damnation: dice and gaming tables; naked people impaled on stringed instruments; wind instruments protruding from every human orifice. Bosch provides us with important clues as to what is going on "in

---

[66] See Nicholas, *Medieval Flanders*, pp. 305–7. Ghent numbered about 50,000 people in 1357, but half that by 1385.

[67] See Nicholas, *Medieval Flanders*, pp. 230, 313.

[68] See further *Le jardin des délices*, in Roger H. Marijnissen, with Peter Ruyffelaere, *Jérôme Bosch: Tout l'œuvre peint et dessiné* (Anvers: Fonds Mercator, 1987), pp. 84–153, esp. pp. 134, 139, 141.

Fig. 1. Hieronymus Bosch, *Garden of Earthly Delights*, triptych (Prado, Madrid), detail, right wing.

Flaundres": he projects a landscape where natural cycles are arrested, where nature is used up, compromised, or destroyed; where human beings, at once crowded together and isolated from one another, are tortured by artifacts of their own devising.

As in Bosch, so we encounter in *The Pardoner's Tale* both the disintegration of symbolic representation and the reconstitution of shattered discursive form through the employment of the most traditional religious schemata: the Seven Deadly Sins, the exemplum, the Biblical

81

citation, the oath. In the Pardoner's hands, this process is both satisfying and suspect, as religious narrative is reduced to its most basic elements and then reconstituted through a brilliant tour de force of storytelling. Such brilliance cannot be denied, but the Pardoner can finally be repudiated as a purveyor of counterfeits: shitty trousers proffered as "a relyk of a seint" (*PardT* 949); the shoulder bone of "an hooly Jewes sheep" sold to cure "pokkes," "scabbe," and animal diseases (*PardP* 350–60). The Pardoner speaks of counterfeiting just before launching into his tale—"I wol noon of the apostles countrefete" (*PardP* 447), he says; talk of counterfeiting offers another precarious historicizing toehold for the Flemish setting of his tale. In 1385, the first Burgundian count of Flanders, Philip the Bold, forced Flemings to renounce alliance with England; in 1388 he backed the minting of counterfeit English nobles. These debased Flemish coins were so skillfully manufactured that they circulated in England as legal tender, thereby undermining the English economy while insulting, *disparaging*, the honor system that English nobles supposedly imaged forth.[69]

Discussion of the natural and the counterfeit, meshed with anxieties about nativeness and passing-as-native, bring us to questions of sexuality. Recent engagements with the Pardoner's sexuality have been shadowed by the recognition (unconscious, or unspoken) that the figure of the Pardoner is, historically speaking, marked for extinction.[70] Other pilgrim types will disappear during the Henrician revolution; monks, nuns, and friars will walk the Shakespearean stage (if not, at least not openly, the streets of London). Pardoners, however, will become the *particular* target of anti-Catholic polemic. Chaucer's representation of the Pardoner certainly helped sustain this sixteenth-century discourse of ridicule, vilification, and homophobia. But what were the wellsprings of such a discourse for Chaucer in the fourteenth century, and of what anxieties do they speak?

[69] See J. H. A. Munro, *Wool, Cloth, and Gold: The Struggle for Bullion in Anglo-Burgundian Trade, 1340–1478* (Toronto: University of Toronto Press, 1972), pp. 47, 53, 58; Lloyd, *Wool Trade*, pp. 244–45; and Nicholas, *Medieval Flanders*, p. 321.

[70] See Glenn Burger, "Kissing the Pardoner," *PMLA* 107 (1992):1143–56; Burger, "Queer Chaucer," *English Studies in Canada* 20.2 ( June 1994):153–70 (esp. pp. 161–62); Burger, "Doing What Comes Naturally in *The Physician's and Pardoner's Tales*," in Peter Beidler, ed., *Chaucerian Masculinities* (forthcoming); and Steven F. Kruger, "Claiming the Pardoner: Toward a Gay Reading of Chaucer's *Pardoner's Tale*," *Exemplaria* 6, no. 1 (spring 1994). For a strikingly unshadowed reading of the Pardoner, see Carolyn Dinshaw, "Chaucer's Queer Touches / A Queer Touches Chaucer," *Exemplaria* 7, no. 1 (spring 1995).

In the fifteenth canto of his *Inferno*, Dante meets Brunetto Latini, his sometime teacher, at a place where fire rains from the skies, the earth is barren, and nature runs backwards: the circle of the sodomites. This circle is delimited by a series of walls; its architect is said to build

> Quali Fiamminghi tra Guizzante e Bruggia
> temendo 'l fiotto che 'nver' lor s'avventa,
> fanno lo schermo perché 'l mar si fuggia. . . . (15.4–6)[71]

> [Just as, between Wissant and Bruges, the Flemings,
> fearing the tide that rushes in on them,
> make the bulwark to drive back the sea. . . .]

Hell's builder is actually said to be less ambitious than the Flemings: his walls are said to be "né sí alti né sí grossi," "neither so high nor so thick" (15.11). The Flemings, we have noted, were proud of having built such great urban cultures upon land recovered from marshland and sea, employing ingenuity and technical cunning where nature proved deficient. They were pressured by the knowledge, passed on by Dante's *Inferno*, that the business of improving upon nature is perilous for those seeking salvation within Catholic cultures. They were further pressured by suggestions that the marshy desolation of Flemish landscapes bespoke unnatural resistance to the claims of noble blood: for Bavaria Herald (who had traveled to the English court in 1390), the waste land ("dat woeste lant") of Flanders could only be redeemed by the healing touch of knightly rule.[72] And yet, as the Flemish cities told their count,

---

[71] Dante Alighieri, *La commedia secondo l'antica vulgata*, ed. Giorgio Petrocchi (Turin: Einaudi, 1975). Durling and Martinez point out, following Parodi (1920), that the Italian forms of the names in line 4 of canto 15 sound like the words for "flaming" (*fiammeggia*), "wriggling" (*guizzante*), and "burning" (*brucia*); puns and equivocal language are a striking feature of this canto. See *The Divine Comedy of Dante Alighieri*, vol. 1, *Inferno*, ed. and trans. Robert M. Durling, with introduction and notes by Ronald L. Martinez (New York: Oxford University Press, 1996), p. 238.

[72] As Gelre Herald, Claes Haynenzoon accompanied William I of Guelders to England in 1390; he bought heraldic flags for the fleet and (while in England) bought bells to attach to these flags. Later, as Bavaria Herald (herald-in-chief to Duke Albert of Bavaria at the court of Holland), he wrote a *Wereldkroniek* (Chronicle of the world, 1405–9); see Frits Pieter van Oostrom, *Court and Culture: Dutch Literature, 1350–1450* (Berkeley: University of California Press, 1992), pp. 129–30, 134. On folio 75 r–v he tells of "een stout ridder," Liedrijcke by name, who "was armed with gold and azure and bore a shield of gules. This knight," the Herald continues, "beheld that Flanders was very desolate and little inhabited, and was a wild forest, marsh, and wasteland. . . . But God, from whom all virtue flows, gave him the grace to conquer and settle the desolate land

Flanders could not and would not be different: "Flanders *is* a sterile country, infertile in itself, completely founded on the fact and course of merchandise, densely populated with foreigners, merchants, and others."[73]

Chaucer's Pardoner, assumed incapable of natural reproduction, also proves skilled in generating wealth from sterile conditions: where his genitals should be, "in his lappe," he carries a wallet full of pardons. There is convergence here between that which the Pardoner embodies, or unembodies, and the land of which he speaks. And of course, inasmuch as anti-Semitic discourse is not *about* Jews, so this discourse of "in Flaundres" is not about Flemings (or those whose sexuality is considered sterile). Although *The Pardoner's Tale*, following its opening phrase, finds not a single Flemish referent, it does touch down in London: once in Fish Street, and twice in "Chepe." It was in Cheapside that the dizzying effects of a highly complex division of labor, serving local and international markets, was most acutely registered. The "fumositee" of Spanish wine drunk in "Chepe" (with the Pardoner) transports us to "Spaigne" (lines 565–72), to similarly phantasmagoric scenes in Bosch, but most directly to Langland, Cheapside's poet laureate, whose B Prologue dissolves in street cries and a roll call of specialized employment: wool weavers and weavers of linen, tailors and tinkers and toll collectors, and so on (lines 220–23).[74] This litany is amplified five passus later, when Glutton enters a tavern (not a million miles from *The Pardoner's Tale*) to find Pernele of Flanders, a Cheapside scavenger, and more than two dozen other people pursuing highly specialist trades.

Langland's unease in pursuing vernacular poetics as part of this newly complex division of labor has, thanks to Anne Middleton and others, be-

---

so that from him sprang as many rulers as from David, who was a shepherd and later became a great mighty king in the land of the Jews"; van Oostrom, *Court and Culture*, p. 144. The suggestion here is that Flemings, like Jews, will only find salvation for their "woeste land" by recognizing the redemptive power of ancient and noble bloodlines.

[73] Cited by David Nicholas, "Of Poverty and Primacy: Demand, Liquidity, and the Flemish Economic Miracle, 1050–1200," *American Historical Review* 96 (1991):41 (emphasis added); the Four Members of Flanders are addressing their count in 1473. Peter Stallybrass, in the course of a generously detailed response to this talk, points out that "much of what you say about the 'unnaturalness' of Flanders is also true of Venice: a city built on water, with no agriculture (on the actual island), dedicated to commerce and the luxury market" (private correspondence). Venice, as conceived through centuries of European drama, writing, and film, extends imaginative possibilities, adumbrated by, or projected upon, medieval Flanders: sodomy, sterility, usury, artfulness, and death.

[74] See William Langland, *The Vision of Piers Plowman: A Critical Edition of the B-Text*, ed. A. V. C. Schmidt (London: Dent, 1978).

come more widely recognized. Chaucer shares Langland's anxieties. In *The General Prologue*, which is *about* the division of labor, Chaucer puts himself in the Pardoner's company as part of a group Derek Pearsall calls "miscellaneous predators."[75] As such, he writes "in Flaundres" in two senses: first, as purveyor of a funny-sounding mother tongue that would command little respect in Florence, Avignon, Paris (or even, as yet, parts of Westminster); second, as a poet struggling to assess the possibilities of a complex, commercial, urbanizing, aggressive, post–bastard feudal society pioneered by those cities north of Calais. Through his Pardoner, he tastes the exhilaration and the terror of a world that, finding nature deficient, exhausted, or all used up, dares to improve upon nature. It is here that historicist and psychoanalytic approaches, often set apart in Chaucer studies, might unite to explore prehistoric traces of "the ego's era."[76] Technological innovation, craft specialization, and increasing urbanization will open new social and economic possibilities *and* incubate new forms of psychic disturbance, fragmentation, and disequilibrium *while* identifying newly projected threats to personal and social well-being.[77] New senses of spatial constriction will fuel the drive to outward-bound territorialization, nation making, and empire building, while at the same time, paradoxically, demanding fixed boundaries of selfhood, nationality, and sexuality.

The denatured, or ambiguously natured, character of the Pardoner is insisted upon at his first appearance, in *The General Prologue*, and reasserted through the threat of castration at the end of his speaking. This

---

[75] *The Canterbury Tales* (London: George Allen and Unwin, 1985), p. 58.

[76] On the notion of "the ego's era," which "begins before the advent of capital, [but] is accelerated by it," see Teresa Brennan, *History after Lacan* (New York: Routledge, 1993), p. 3. My own understanding of how historicist and psychoanalytic approaches might talk to one another owes much to the remarkable Cambridge (UK) Alternative Medieval Seminar: thanks in particular are due to core members Simon Gaunt, Jane Gilbert, Sarah Kay, and Nicolette Zeeman and to satellite members Chris Cannon, Rita Copeland, Louise Fradenburg, and Paul Strohm. For a pioneering attempt to map some interconnections between the ego and social topography, see Peter Stallybrass and Allon White, *The Politics and Poetics of Transgression* (Ithaca, N.Y.: Cornell University Press, 1986), esp. pp. 125–48.

[77] In Flanders, as in many other parts of Europe, such developments are accompanied or symptomatized by increasing use of judicial torture; see Raoul C. van Caenegem, "La preuve dans l'ancien droit Belge des origines à la fin du XVIIIᵉ siècle," in *La Preuve*, 2, *Môyen Age et Temps Modernes*, Recueils de la Société Jean Bodin, no. 17 (1965), pp. 399–403. First recorded at Bruges in 1258–60, the use of torture spread rapidly in Flanders in the course of the fourteenth century. "Avec le temps," van Caenegem observes, "la primauté de l'aveu dans le procès criminel est devenue telle qu'on en est arrivé à déclarer indispensable pour toute condamnation à mort" (pp. 401–2).

last attack on the Pardoner's personhood concedes that his language *is* beguiling: so very like our own, and yet—not. The urge to isolate the Pardoner from the social collectivity at the end of his verbal performance "in Flaundres" again returns us to that uneasy English/Flemish border-line. Interest in differentiating discourses at permeable linguistic or ter-ritorial boundaries is rarely benign: witness Bosnia. Trevisa, in his fa-mous survey of languages, speaks of Flemings "in Þe west syde of Wales" moderating "here strange speche."[78] Chaucer's Cook, the most disorderly of lowlife Londoners, shows himself familiar with the sayings and in-flections of Flemings ("'sooth pley, quaad pley,' as the Flemyng seith" [*CkP* 4357]); his fellow Londoner and drinking companion, the Manciple, has "the Flemyng" say that little talking causes less trouble.[79] In 1381, some thirty or forty Flemings were massacred in London at the Church of St. Martin, Vintry. All chronicles note this massacre; one of them reports that linguistic inflection proved crucial in isolating Flemings: "And many fflemmynges loste hir heedes at that tyme, and namely they that koude nat say Breede and Chese, but Case and Brode."[80]

Caroline Barron has said that "no-one was executed by mob violence or lynch law on the streets of London between 1381 and Cade's Revolt in 1450."[81] This remarkable assertion cannot dispel unease about those lines in *The Nun's Priest's Tale* that would compare the chasing of a fox to the shrill shouts let out by "Jakke Straw and his meynee," when "they wolden any Flemyng kille" (lines 3394–96). It is the complacency of these lines that makes them so disturbing; their accommodating of tar-geted homicide within the familiar confines of classroom exercise or barnyard fable. Their effect compares with that of Chaucer's most dan-gerously freighted anti-Semitic line, spoken within the comfortable confines of a saint's legend: "Whoso that troweth *nat* this [namely,

---

[78] Text of Trevisa's 1387 rendering of Ranulph of Higden, monk of Chester, follows Basil Cottle, *The Triumph of English, 1350–1400* (London: Blandford Press, 1969), p. 18. Trevisa's translation concedes that these Flemings speak "Saxonlych ynow"; other lin-guistic groups in England are said to employ "strange wlaffyng, chyteryng, harryng, and garryng grisbittyng," amounting to "apeyryng of þe burþtonge" (p. 19).

[79] "The Flemyng seith, and lerne it if thee leste, / That litel janglyng causeth muchel reste" (*ManT* 349–50).

[80] MS Cotton, Julius B.II, as edited by C. L. Kingsford in *Chronicles of London* (Ox-ford: Oxford University Press, 1905), p. 15. Kingsford dates this manuscript 1435 (pp. viii–ix).

[81] Barron, "Introduction: England and the Low Countries," p. 12. Barron prefaces this statement by noting that "London, and indeed other English towns, were at times tur-bulent, but . . . ."

Christian revelation; my emphasis], a beest he is" (*The Second Nun's Tale* 288). A vicious discourse may not kill, for a specified number of years, but it remains a discourse-in-waiting.

As years pass, however, there remains the hope that such a discourse might disclose its secret: that it speaks not of Jews, Pardoners, Flemings, or of the ambiguously gendered, but of the anxieties of its authors. Of the anxieties, but also of the fantasies, hopes, and desires. The Pardoner, characterized by Carolyn Dinshaw as that "paradoxical figure of wily cynicism and plangent desire,"[82] is at once the most extinct of Chaucer's personages and, for modern subjects, our most authentic ancestor.

In 1435, Philip Duke of Burgundy abandoned his alliance with England, sided with the French, and (in the summer of 1436) joined the siege of Calais. The town was relieved by Humphrey, Duke of Gloucester, who then raided west Flanders and burned Poperinge; in London, houses of Flemish merchants were sacked by the mob. Shortly after this, someone in London or Westminster, close to the inner circles of power, wrote a poem called *The Libelle of Englyshe Polycye*.[83] Lydgate wrote of Humphrey's triumph at Calais,[84] but the *Libelle*-poet—superior to Lydgate in technique and intellect—drew inspiration directly from Chaucer; he devotes much space to beating up on Flemings. Some of this simply recycles commonplaces glimpsed in *The Pardoner's Tale*: "ye have herde," he says, that Flemings go nowhere without first drinking beer

---

[82] Carolyn Dinshaw, *Chaucer's Sexual Poetics* (Madison: University of Wisconsin Press, 1989), p. 160.

[83] Authorship of the *Libelle* is not at present known. Warner argues for Adam Moleyns, clerk of the Council (*Libelle*, pp. xl–xlv). Carol Meale suggests that John Carpenter, common clerk of the city (1417–38) and a close associate of mayor and mercer Richard Whittington, "is a plausible candidate to be investigated as the work's patron" ("Mercantile Literary Culture," p. 219). The poem survives in two editions (nineteen manuscripts), dated 1436–38 and 1437–41 (with further revised versions of the second edition); see *Libelle*, ed. Warner, pp. lii–lvi, as updated, corrected, and augmented by Meale, pp. 206–8, 219–26, and appendix (listing all known manuscripts, pp. 226–28).

[84] See *The Debate of the Horse, Goose, and Sheep*, in John Lydgate, *The Minor Poems of John Lydgate*, pt. 2 of *Secular Poems*, ed. Henry Noble MacCracken and Merriam Sherwood, Early English Text Society [hereafter EETS], o.s., 192 (London: Oxford University Press for EETS, 1934). When Philip "Cam before Caleis with Flemynges nat a fewe," he was beaten back and "vnethe escapid with the liff" (lines 414–19). Further anti-Fleming rhetoric is essayed by the poem edited as "A Ballade, in Despyte of the Flemynges" (a title derived from MS Lambeth 84, fol. 201v.: "And in despyte of þe Flemyng[es], an Englissh man made this English yn baladdys"; see Lydgate, *Minor Poems*, pp. 600–601. On the frustrated romancing of Duke Humphrey through Lydgate's *Fall of Princes*, see Wallace, *Chaucerian Polity*, pp. 332–34.

(lines 282–87), and then (he says) "Undre the borde they pissen as they sitte" (line 288); the English, he says, made them shit in their breeches when they ran home from Calais (lines 290–92).[85] Elsewhere, the influence of Chaucer (and specifically of *The Pardoner's Tale*) is heard more directly. Flanders trades with Spain: why not territorialize this sea, keep it under English control, and stop the commons of Flanders, that sterile land, from living off our superior native product?

> Thus, if the see be kepte, then herkene hedere,
> Yf these ij. londes comene not togedere,
> So that the flete of Flaundres passe nought,
> That in the narowe see it be not brought
> Into the Rochelle to feche the fumose wyne,
> Nere into Britoune bay for salt so fyne,
> What is than Spayne, what is Flaundres also?
> As who seyth, nought; there thryfte is alle ago.
> For the lytell londe of Flaundres is
> But a staple to other londes iwys,
> And all that groweth in Flaundres, greyn and sede,
> May not a moneth fynde hem mete of brede.
> What hath thenne Flaundres, be Flemmynges leffe or lothe,
> But a lytell madere[86] and Flemmyshe cloothe?
> By draperinge of oure wolle in substaunce
> Lyvene here comons, this is here governaunce. . . . (lines 108–23)

The *Libelle*-poet argues that the English should pursue their expansionist ambitions by following the logic of their coin: the noble, which images forth "kyng, shype and swerde and pouer of the see" (line 35). Such ambitions are thwarted, however, chiefly by Flemings, who continue to counterfeit our coin and contest our naval superiority. The *Libelle*-poet deploys his inherited anti-Fleming rhetoric to energetic effect (spiced with some homophobic anti-Italianism):[87] but Flanders can

---

[85] On Flanders' supposed exemplifying of "the evils of drinking and of cupidity," see Dorothy M. Norris, "Chaucer's *Pardoner's Tale* and Flanders," *PMLA* 48 (1933):636–41 (quote from p. 636).

[86] Or *rubia tinctoria*, used for dyeing cloth.

[87] That might almost have been penned by C. S. Lewis, in defense of *Beowulf*: "What Chaucer Really Did to *Il Filostrato*," *Essays and Studies by Members of the English Association* 17 (1932):56–75. (What Lewis was really saying in this article was later veiled from public view by judicious cuts made in the anthologized versions.) The long-lived tradition of deducing national character from qualities associated with a nation's exports is already

no longer be rolled over quite so easily, since it forms part of Burgundy, allied with France. What to do? In the second half of the poem, attention drifts westward. Ireland is "fertyle": things there grow and multiply and are so "comodyouse" that it is "straunge and merveylouse" (lines 682–85). Gold and silver ores are found in abundance there, quite wasted on "the wylde Yrische," since "they are rude and can thereone no skylle" (lines 686–88). "In wylde Yrishe," the poet concludes, "myght we find the cure" (line 691). This "cure" is, of course, counterfeited from Flanders: just as the Flemish have done to us—take a raw native product, export it, transform it through superior technology— so we will do to the Irish. The poet concludes with a modest proposal: just one year's expenses sustained in the war with France "Myght wynne Yrelond to a fynall conquest" (line 770).

The *Libelle* proved popular with powerful people: manuscript owners included Lord Burghley (chief minister to Elizabeth I) and Samuel Pepys (Secretary to the Admiralty); in one manuscript, presented as a gift in 1471 by a William Caston, the poem is renamed "The *byble* of Englyshe polecie."[88] The *Libelle*-poet had promised to write another "lytell boke," detailing how the Irish "cure" might be effected (line 775). This book does not survive, but its imaginative enterprise is carried forward in the next phase of English westward expansion by Richard Hakluyt. The Americas, for Hakluyt, like Ireland for the *Libelle*-poet, are imagined as a fabulous repository of natural resource. English merchant adventurers are struggling to revive their continental trade in unfinished cloth; the queen is disturbed by the "pitifull outecryes" of unemployed cappers, knitters, and spinners.[89] What, then, if instead of bringing to England finished commodities, "as wee

---

well underway in the *Libelle.* Italian ships bring "Apes and japes and marmusettes taylede, / Nifles, trifles, that litell have availed, / And thynges wyth whiche they fetely blere oure eye, / Wyth thynges not endurynge" (lines 348– 51); "oure best chaffare," by contrast, is the more straightforward "Clothe, woll and tyne" (lines 375–76). For an account of relationships between commodity values, volumes of export, and emergent political structures, see Hendrik Spruyt, *The Sovereign State and Its Competitors* (Princeton: Princeton University Press, 1994).

[88] *Libelle*, ed. Warner, p. lv; my emphasis. This manuscript, formerly at Keswick Hall, Norwich, was sold in 1936 and is now Boston Public Library MS 1519. The William Caston who gave the book in 1471 to William Sonnyng was once thought to be the celebrated William Caxton, governor of the Merchant Adventurers at Bruges; but see now Meale, "Mercantile Literary Culture," p. 220.

[89] Richard Hakluyt, *Discourse of Western Planting*, ed. David B. Quinn and Alison M. Quinn, Hakluyt Society, e.s., 45 (London: Hakluyt Society, 1993), pp. xxiii, 32.

bringe nowe the commodities of Fraunce and Flaundres," we were to bring "substaunces vnwroughte" [from the Americas] "to the ymployment of a wonderfull multitude of the poore subiectes of this Realme"? England again, in short, might do to wild and primitive peoples what Flanders has done to England.[90]

The Libelle of Englyshe Polycye does not appear in the first, 1589 edition of Hakluyt's Principall Navigations, Voiages and Discoveries of the English Nation. In the second edition, however, Mandeville's Travels and Pliny are out,[91] and the Libelle is in—and so too is that "cunning Cosmographer," Geoffrey Chaucer.[92] I am not suggesting that "the

[90] "Above all," write the Quinns of Hakluyt, "he was completely ignorant of the way of life of North American Indians" (Discourse, p. xxii).

[91] See Richard Hakluyt, Principal Navigations (1589), photo-lithographic facsimile, with introduction by David Beers Quinn and Raleigh Ashlin Shelton, 2 vols., Hakluyt Society, e.s., 39 (Cambridge, Mass.: Hakluyt Society and Peabody Museum of Salem, 1965), vol. 1, pp. xxv–xxvii, l–lii.

[92] In Hakluyt's "A preface to the Reader," Chaucer appears immediately after discussion of Henry of Derby's journeys "into Prussia & Lithuania, with a briefe remembrance of his valiant exploits against the Infidels there," and of Thomas of Woodstock's "trauel into Pruis, and of his returne home. And lastly, our old English father Ennius, I meane, the learned, wittie, and profound Geffrey Chaucer, vnder the person of his knight, doeth full iudicially and like a cunning Cosmographer, make report of the long voiages and woorthy exploits of our English Nobles, Knights, & Gentlemen, to the Northren, and to other partes of the world in his dayes"; "A preface to the Reader," Voyages, Navigations, Traffiques, and Discoueries of the English Nation, 3 vols. (London: George Bishop, Ralfe Newberie, and Robert Barker, 1598–1600), 1:8 (my pagination). At vol. 1, p. 124, Hakluyt prints "verses of Geofrey Chaucer in the knights Prologue," dated 1402 (as Chaucer "writeth himself in his Epistle of Cupide"). This account of exploits against the pagan, ending with the line "ayenst another Heathen in Turkie," is immediately followed by a switch from military to mercantile registers, announced by the following title: "The original, proceedings and successe of the Northren domestical and forren trades and traffiques of this Isle of Britain from the time of Nero the Emperour . . . vntil this present time" (1:124). The Libelle of Englyshe Polycye appears in this section (1:187–208). Some topical (post-Armada) marginal glosses have been added. For example, by "For aliance of Scotland and of Spaine" we find: "This is now to be greatly feared" (1:200; Libelle, ed. Warner, line 732).

Scholars in Belgium and Holland proved to be extraordinarily hospitable, helpful, and stimulating in the planning and thinking through of this project. Thanks, in particular, are due to Raoul and Pat van Caenegem, Ludo Milis, Walter Prevenier, and Hilde de Ridder-Symoens. Michael Main, doctoral candidate at Columbia University, guided me through the streets of Bruges; Wim Blockmans escorted me through Leiden and spent the better part of a day answering my questions. Rita Copeland, Paul Strohm, and Marjorie Curry Woods read drafts of the talk at a very late stage and offered crucial, convergent critiques. Miri Rubin, whose European and global vision is a constant source of inspiration, helped me navigate this project from Cambridge and London to Ghent and Leiden; to her, this talk is dedicated.

learned, wittie, and profound Geffrey Chaucer" honored by Hakluyt be made accountable for the westward turn and the conquest of the New World. I am suggesting, however, that there are lines of filiation in the history of Chaucer that keep track with our movement, in the study of Chaucer, from Canterbury to Bruges, from Dublin to Los Angeles. And if this Chaucerian discourse of "Flaundres" speaks to the anxieties, and to the pleasures, of improving upon nature, then Los Angeles is our "Jerusalem celestial"; LA is "in Flaundres," only more so.

Studies in the Age of Chaucer

# Anne of Bohemia and the Making of Chaucer

Andrew Taylor
*University of Saskatchewan*

In 1382 the young Anne of Bohemia arrived in England to marry King Richard II as part of an alliance designed to promote his imperial ambitions.[1] Poor—she brought no dowry and was accompanied by an impecunious train of courtiers who probably spoke as little English as she did—and by many accounts not beautiful, she was the object of scorn. As the Westminster chronicler remarked:

De ista regina sic quidam scripsit metrice:
Digna frui manna datur Anglis nobilis Anna;
set scrutantibus verum videbatur non dari set pocius emi, nam non modicam pecuniam refundebat rex Anglie pro tantilla carnis porcione.

[About this Queen somebody wrote the verse:
Worthy to enjoy manna,
To Englishmen is given the noble Anna;
but to those with an eye for the facts it seemed that she represented a purchase rather than a gift, since the English king laid out no small sum for such a small piece of flesh.][2]

From this unpromising beginning, Anne went on to exercise a notable influence in the kingdom, interceding with the king on numerous occasions and gaining a reputation for prudence, charity, and the devout

---

[1] Constantin Höfler discusses the diplomatic negotiations behind the marriage; "Anna von Luxemburg," *Denkschriften der kaiserlichen Akademie der Wissenschaften,* Philosophisch-Historischen Classe, 20 (Vienna, 1871), pp. 89–240, esp. pp. 123–38.

[2] L. C. Hector and Barbara F. Harvey, eds., *The Westminster Chronicle, 1381–1394* (Oxford: Clarendon Press, 1982), pp. 24–25. I have used their translation except for the last line, which they soften to "to secure this tiny scrap of humanity."

reading of Scripture. She is one of the women Susan Bell terms "arbiters of lay piety and ambassadors of culture," while Agnes Strickland, in her history *Queens of England,* goes so far as to call Anne the first of "the nursing-mothers of the Reformation."[3] This influential queen, Anne the Good or Anne the Wise as the chroniclers eventually called her, was also allegedly a patron of Chaucer's and is widely held responsible for imposing upon him the task of writing *The Legend of Good Women* as an amends for his depiction of Criseyde. It is the intersection of these two figures, the historical queen and the censorious patron figured in Alceste, the consort of the God of Love, that is my topic. I wish to advance two arguments: first, that although we cannot have anything approaching direct access to Anne, and although she herself could only exert her cultural influence indirectly and through heavily predetermined social narratives, at the point of triangulation of these various formations there lay a real woman of significant cultural authority. The second is that the repudiation of Anne and her authority has been closely tied to the construction of Chaucer as a self-sufficient author. Since my second argument claims that the literary tradition denies the social conditions of its inception, I wish to begin by considering what we can know of the historical Anne of Bohemia before turning to Chaucer's poems.

One possible means of recapturing the cultural power of the historical Anne, or indeed of many other medieval women, would be to look for traces of the books they owned or commissioned. Thus Bell argues that while women writers in the Middle Ages are few and hard to find, "as readers of vernacular literature, as mothers in charge of childhood education, as literary patrons who commissioned books and translations, and as wives who married across cultural and geographical boundaries, women had a specific and unique influence."[4] Recognizing this influence is not just a matter of doing fresh research; as Mary Erler and Maryanne Kowaleski argue, it requires a reassessment of cultural authority itself along the lines of recent feminist scholarship, "which broadens the conventional understanding of power to include new forms of power and

---

[3] Agnes Strickland, *Lives of the Queens of England,* 2d ed., 6 vols. (London, 1880), 1:416.

[4] Susan G. Bell, "Medieval Women Book Owners: Arbiters of Lay Piety and Ambassadors of Culture," *Signs* 7 (1982): 742–68, rpt. in Mary Erler and Maryanne Kowaleski, eds., *Women and Power in the Middle Ages* (Athens and London: University of Georgia Press, 1988), pp. 149–87. The actual quotation appears on p.743 of the article.

[5] Erler and Kowaleski, eds., *Women and Power,* p. 1. See also Julia Boffey, "Women Authors and Women's Literacy in Fourteenth- and Fifteenth-Century England," in Carol M. Meale, ed., *Women and Literature in Britain, 1150–1500* (Cambridge: Cambridge University Press, 1993), pp. 159–82, esp. p. 159 and n. 2.

new areas for its exercise."[5] Similarly, Bell's study contributes to recent efforts to look beyond the conventional category of authorship, with its emphasis on the autonomy of the artist and his ability to create *ex nihilo*, toward other, more collaborative forms of cultural production.[6]

There are difficulties, however. We cannot assume that because a book belonged to someone, that person necessarily read it.[7] Buying a book, particularly by commissioning it, would seem a surer indication of interest, but even here caution is in order. Poets may claim a connection in the hopes of acquiring patronage or flatter a patron whose interest in their work is nominal, and men sometimes commission works on behalf of women or children whom they wish to be instructed. As Madeline Caviness observes, apropos of the Hours of Jeanne d'Evreux, "we should not assume the female owner/reader exercised the control we normally ascribe to a patron; the term 'matron,' symmetric in gender but asymmetric in meaning, fits the role assigned to Jeanne."[8] The problem, therefore, is not just one of the paucity of surviving evidence of book ownership. Even if we could track down many of the books Anne owned and commissioned they would not provide objective or unproblematic witnesses to her cultural authority. Instead the books must be regarded as a separate category of witnesses, who, while not necessarily more reliable or straightforward in their testimony than the fictions of poets, at least offer a unique perspective.

The list, which I offer in the hopes that others may expand it, is in many ways disappointing. Anne must have owned a number of religious books, but only one has survived, an illuminated Book of Hours, Oxford, Bodleian Library, MS Lat. liturg. f. 3.[9] Anne was also the patron

[6] For a range of approaches to the question, see Lesley Smith and Jane H. M. Taylor, eds., *Women, the Book and the Godly* and *Women, the Book and the Worldly*, Selected Proceedings of the Saint Hilda's Conference, 1993, 2 vols. (Cambridge: D. S. Brewer, 1995).

[7] The books of King Richard II are a case in point. His large collection of romances and *chansons de geste* has sometimes been taken as evidence of his old-fashioned tastes, but in fact he inherited these books and sold many of them. See Richard Firth Green, "King Richard II's Books Revisited," *The Library*, 5th ser., 31 (1976): 235–39.

[8] Madeline H. Caviness, "Patron or Matron? A Capetian Bride and a Vade Mecum for Her Marriage Bed," *Speculum* 68 (1993): 356. In her discussion of the phallic marginalia in Jeanne's personal Book of Hours, Caviness, who finds the marginalia threatening rather than titillating, draws attention to "the mediating role of Jeanne's husband as the real patron of the work," arguing that he may have used the book as a means of regulating the young queen's sexual desire (p. 357 n. 121).

[9] Lucy F. Sandler, *Gothic Manuscripts, 1285–1385*, 2 vols. (Oxford: Oxford University Press, 1986), 1:21,53. The illuminations, which may have been added later, were discussed by Sandra Penketh in her paper "Women and Books of Hours," delivered at the conference "Women and the Book," St. Hilda's College, Oxford, 1993.

of a number of religious or learned institutions, including Coventry Charterhouse, Eye Priory, and Queen's College, Oxford.[10] There is no record of her receiving books from these institutions, although she might have, for this was a standard form of cultural exchange. It was once widely believed that Anne's train included a number of Bohemian artists, whose influence could be seen in such works as the Latin Bible MS Royal I.E.ix, which was probably executed for Richard; the Carmelite Missal, which survives only as scraps, now collected in London, BL Additional MSS 29704, 29705, and 44892; and the *Liber regalis*, the Westminster manuscript on the coronation, which contains a picture of Anne and Richard.[11] However, as Amanda Simpson has shown, many of the most lavish Bohemian manuscripts were not in fact executed until the 1390s, well after Anne's arrival in England and in many cases probably not until after her death in 1394.[12] Lucy Freeman Sandler, reviewing the evidence, concludes that Richard's marriage to Anne "does not appear to have been accompanied by a significant wave of Bohemian or German influence on the art of England."[13] This does not diminish the influence of the English court as a center of artistic patronage, but it significantly weakens the case for Anne's influence within the court in this particular area.

Anne had contact with numerous writers, including Sir John Clanvowe, who dedicates his *Booke of Cupide* to her by having the contesting birds decide to refer their debate to the Queen's judgment.[14]

---

[10] The Coventry Charterhouse, which was dedicated to Saint Anne, had been inadequately endowed, and in 1385 Richard came to Coventry to lay the stone of a new church and promise his continuing support. See J. Anthony Tuck, "Carthusian Monks and Lollard Knights: Religious Attitude at the Court of Richard II," *SAC*, Proceedings, no. 1 (1984): 156. A charter granted to Eye for £60 is "at the special request of the queen, who is their patron"; *Calendar Patent Rolls, 1381–85*, p. 491.

[11] George F. Warner and Julius P. Gilson, eds., *Catalogue of Western Manuscripts in the Old Royal and King's Collections in the British Museum*, 4 vols. (London: Trustees of the British Museum, 1921), 1:22; Margaret Rickert, "The Reconstruction of an English Carmelite Missal," *Speculum* 16 (1941): 92–102, and *The Reconstructed Carmelite Missal: An English Manuscript of the Late XIV Century in the British Museum (Additional 29704–5, 44892)* (Chicago: University of Chicago Press, 1952), pp. 51 and n. 5, 76–80.

[12] Amanda Simpson, *The Connections Between English and Bohemian Painting during the Second Half of the Fourteenth Century* (New York: Garland, 1984).

[13] Sandler, *Gothic Manuscripts*, 1:51; see also 1:19–21, and on the *Liber regalis*, 2:177–78.

[14] As V. J. Scattergood notes, this "ornate compliment . . . makes it almost certain that it was intended for the royal court"; Scattergood, ed., *The Works of Sir John Clanvowe* (Cambridge: Brewer, 1965; Totowa, N.J.: Rowman and Littlefield, 1975), pp. 9–10. If the poem is indeed by Clanvowe, who died in 1391, then the queen in question is Anne.

Leaving aside for the moment the question of *The Legend of Good Women*, however, I have been able to locate only one surviving work known to have been specifically *commissioned* by Anne: a Latin treatise on heraldry composed by one Master Johannis de Bado Aureo, which is preserved in at least five fifteenth-century manuscripts.[15] It is a short work that deals for the most part with the technicalities of heraldry. John says that he composed the treatise "at the request of certain women and especially Lady Anne, formerly Queen of England" [ad instanciam quarumdam personarum et specialiter domine Anne, quondam regine Anglie] "because it is difficult to discern and describe heraldic emblems." The work was probably originally in French.[16] John's claim that Anne commissioned the work cannot be accepted unquestioningly, but it is both plausible and suggestive. For a young queen feeling her way through the protocol of a foreign country and playing a major role in its chivalric rituals, a knowledge of heraldry was a professional necessity. She had come, after all, to the court where Lord Chandos and the earl of Oxford almost came to blows over the right to be the first to drink from the king's cup. As queen of England she would need to know her quarterings. The relatively straightforward introduction to the subject offered by this short treatise would have filled a real need. We might even go so far as to infer from this alleged commission that Anne played an active role in court ritual, that she was not just a beauty queen handing out the prizes that the judges passed to her, but a master of ceremonies that were not without political significance. Perhaps this is to see spring in a single swallow, but in her numerous acts of intercession Anne appears to have followed an analogous pattern, achieving a degree of freedom and self-expression within the social constraints of chivalric culture.

Even before she had arrived in England, Anne had been assigned the role of queen as merciful intercessor, a role with strong Marian overtones played most famously by Queen Philippa on behalf of the burghers of

[15] See "Tractatus magistri Johannis de Bado Aureo cum Francisco de Foveis in distinctionibus armorum," in the fifteenth-century heraldic miscellany London, British Library, MS Add. 29901, fols. 60 ff; and for commentary, Maude V. Clarke, *Fourteenth Century Studies*, ed. L. S. Sutherland and M. McKisack (Oxford: Clarendon Press, 1937; rpt. 1968), p. 278.

[16] As Felicity Riddy has pointed out to me, the word "formerly," which occurs in at least two of the surviving manuscripts, casts grave doubts on the suggestion that the text was written for Anne in its current form, i.e., in Latin. Even if we were to credit Anne with good reading knowledge of Latin, it is unlikely that this would have been the case with the "certain ladies," or for that matter with most other gentlemen, who might have been interested in the topic.

Calais. Anne interceded with Richard on behalf of the rebels in 1381; she interceded in 1388 with the earl of Arundel on behalf of Simon Burley and with the archbishop of Canterbury for six others; and in 1392 she interceded on behalf of the City of London in an elaborate public ceremony. There is even a legend that Anne interceded on behalf of Wycliffe.[17] Lesser figures also attracted her mercy, and the Calendars of Patent Rolls are filled with references to pardons granted "at the supplication of the queen" or at "the request of Queen Anne." On several occasions, Anne's cultural patronage also took the form of intercession, as when she pleaded on behalf of Queen's College in 1384.[18]

There is probably an element of historical truth within these heavily conventional accounts of Good Queen Anne. We have no hard evidence that Anne was calm and sensible and otherwise fitted the stereotype assigned to her, but we have abundant evidence that Richard was short-tempered, extravagant, and of little political judgment, and also that he was strongly attached to her. On her death, Richard, never stable at the best of times, appears to have been driven wild by grief, burning the queen's palace at Sheen to the ground.[19] Not surprisingly, many historians have seen Anne as a moderating influence, almost as a Dame Prudence, tempering the extravagances of a young and foolish king. These associations also appear to have occurred to Chaucer. His translation of the *Livre de Melibée et de Dame Prudence* omits the reference to the

[17] Anthony Steel, whose interpretation of Anne seems motivated by an animosity against Strickland, credits the story, although only to diminish it; *Richard II* (Cambridge: Cambridge University Press, 1941), p. 110. The ultimate source for this legend would appear to be Strickland (*Lives of the Queens*, 1:416), who claims to have based it upon some comments in Harris Nicolas's *History of the Order of the Garter*.

[18] A copy of her letter survives in an eighteenth-century transcription in the college archives; John R. Magrath, *The Queen's College*, 2 vols. (Oxford: Oxford University Press, 1921), 1:18. Richard responded on May 16, 1384, with a letter patent taking the college into his care. In light of Anne's association with Bible reading, it is perhaps worth noting that Queen's College had been a hotbed of Lollardy throughout the 1370s, starting in 1369 when Nicholas Hereford, who may have assisted in the translation of the Wycliffite Bible, arrived at Queen's along with John Trevisa. See David C. Fowler, "John Trevisa and the English Bible," *MP* 58 (1960): 88–89.

[19] It is sometimes suggested that Richard gave further signs of hysteria by immediately launching a campaign into Ireland and then returning to suppress the Lollard uprising brutally. See, for example, Herbert B. Workman, *John Wyclif: A Study of the English Medieval Church*, 2 vols. (Oxford: Clarendon Press, 1926), 2:390. Adam of Usk, for one, claims that "the king, clad, with his train, in weeds of mourning, straightway passed over into Ireland"; *Chronicon Adæ de Usk, A.D. 1377–1421*, ed. and trans. Edward Maunde Thompson, 2d ed. (London: Henry Frowde, 1904), p. 151. In fact, the campaign was delayed for some time.

woes of a land ruled by a boy, presumably lest the parallels became too apparent.[20]

While they are not totally without referential content, however, the accounts of Anne's intercession certainly cannot be taken as straightforward reporting. As Paul Strohm demonstrates so well in *Hochon's Arrow*, the role of the queen as intercessor was shaped by preexisting interpretive structures grouped around certain images of how a manly king and a womanly queen should behave.[21] The queen is the humble supplicant, placating her husband's wrath and mitigating his stern resolve with words of caution and tenderness or with tears. It is in these terms that Froissart describes Queen Philippa, pregnant and weeping, kneeling at the feet of Edward to plead for the lives of the burghers of Calais.[22] Strohm's investigation of the circumstances of this event in a sense diminishes the queen's agency, showing how far both the public rituals of intercession and their subsequent descriptions were fictions—Philippa cannot have been pregnant at the time.[23] In particular, the claim that the queen just happens to be there, joining the implacable king belatedly and by accident—which is a standard element in the accounts of both Philippa's and Anne's acts of intercession—must be questioned. These scenes bear every indication of having been at least partially contrived, political dramas that gave the king an opportunity to change his mind and exercise clemency (often the politically astute move) without appearing unmanly. Strohm still believes, however, that within these

---

[20] John S. P. Tatlock, *The Development and Chronology of Chaucer's Works*, Chaucer Society, 2d ser., vol. 37 (London, 1907), p. 192; see also *Melibee*, line 1199. The line appears to have been in wide circulation at the time. Adam of Usk also applies it to Richard in his chronicle (p. 140), and Walsingham makes reference to it in his objection to Richard's extravagant taxes; *Thomæ Walsingham, Historia Anglicana*, vol. 2 (A.D. 1381–1422, ed. H. T. Riley, Rolls Series, vol. 28 (London, 1864), p. 97.

[21] Paul Strohm, *Hochon's Arrow: The Social Imagination of Fourteenth-Century Texts* (Princeton, N.J.: Princeton University Press, 1992), esp. ch. 5.

[22] Jean Froissart, *Oeuvres*, ed. Kervyn de Lettenhove, vol. 5 (Brussels, 1868), p. 215.

[23] Strohm, *Hochon's Arrow*, p. 102 n. 6, citing the work of John Carmi Parsons. See also Parsons, "The Pregnant Queen as Counsellor and the Medieval Construction of Motherhood," in John Carmi Parsons and Bonnie Wheeler, eds., *Medieval Mothering* (New York: Garland, 1996), pp. 39–61; "Ritual and Symbol in the English Medieval Queenship to 1500," in Louise Olga Fradenburg, ed., *Women and Sovereignty, Cosmos* 7 (Edinburgh: Edinburgh University Press, 1992), pp. 60–77; and "The Queen's Intercession in Thirteenth-Century England," in Jennifer Carpenter and Sally-Beth MacLean, eds., *Power of the Weak: Studies on Medieval Women* (Urbana and Chicago: University of Illinois Press, 1995), pp. 147–77; and Lois L. Huneycutt, "Intercession and the High-Medieval Queen: The Esther Topos," in Carpenter and MacLean, eds., *Power of the Weak*, pp. 126–46.

interpretive structures a determined woman such as Anne could at least partially invent herself, a position with which I would concur. That contemporary chroniclers ultimately chose to write Anne as Prudence rather than as Luxury suggests that Anne was an astute player.

The role of the foreign queen was perilous; as an alien and a woman, she could all too easily become a scapegoat for the extravagance of the feudal court.[24] The French queen Isabeau de Bavarre, for example, was vilified for her alleged extravagance and promiscuity. The depiction was not entirely arbitrary: even if the accusation that Isabeau had an affair with the duke of Orleans is mere slander, her mistreatment of her mad husband King Charles seems well established, and it was this, as much as anything else, that confirmed her unpopularity. It is worth noting, however, how much Good Queen Anne shared in common with the she-wolf Isabeau. There is every indication that despite her worldly reputation, Isabeau was a pious reader. A special collection that she commissioned in 1398, containing only the Office of the Virgin and the Hours of Our Lady, had to be cleaned and repaired the following year—Isabeau appears to have been reading her Book of Hours to pieces.[25] Good Queen Anne, on the other hand, was open to charges of extravagance very much like those brought against Isabeau, as indeed was any feudal queen. Both women allegedly held courts of love of some kind, and both enjoyed the splendors and luxuries of court life.[26] Walsingham, for one, comes very close to blaming Anne for the heavy taxes this required, but then shifts the blame at least partially to her courtiers.[27] In short, while the part of Anne the Good was no doubt in large measure provided for

[24] On the role of the adulterous queen as scapegoat, see Peggy McCracken, "The Body Politic and the Queen's Adulterous Body in French Romance," in Linda Lomperis and Sarah Stanbury, eds., *Feminist Approaches to the Body in Medieval Literature* (Philadelphia: University of Pennsylvania Press, 1993), pp. 38–64; Chantal Thomas, *La Reine scélérate: Marie-Antoinette dans les pamphlets* (Paris: Editions du Seuil, 1989); and Lynn Hunt, "The Many Bodies of Marie Antoinette: Political Pornography and the Problem of the Feminine in the French Revolution," in Lynn Hunt, ed., *Eroticism and the Body Politic* (Baltimore: Johns Hopkins University Press, 1991), pp. 108–30.

[25] Jean Verdon, *Isabeau de Bavière* (Paris: Tallandier, 1981), pp. 92–94.

[26] Richard Firth Green, "The *Familia Regis* and the *Familia Cupidinis*," in V. J. Scattergood and J. W. Sherborne, eds., *English Court Culture in the Later Middle Ages* (London: Duckworth, 1983), pp. 87–108. While skeptical of the existence of a more formal structure, Green notes that an informal *cour amoreuse* "sprang into being wherever members of the *familia regis* fell to discussing love poetry" (p. 106).

[27] "Non enim Regi magna donaria suffecerunt, nisi et Reginæ æqualia præberentur; nec, cum populo grave visum fuisset ejus honoris intuitu exhibuisse perampla donaria, si ad usum eorum prudenter conservata fuissent. Sed quicquid hausit eorum manus avida, mox alienigenis de gente Reginæ, scilicet Boemiis, prodigaliter erogavit, unde

the queen, I think we must credit her with the political skill that en-
sured that she finally got the good part, particularly when all the indications were that she was initially on her way to getting the bad.

Nor were Anne's merciful intercessions always mere charades. When
the Merciless Parliament of 1388 sought the life of Simon Burley,
Richard's tutor and the man who had brought Anne over to England,
she spent three hours kneeling before the earl of Arundel begging for
his life, but in vain. Arundel's reply, "Mamie priez pour vous et pour
vostre mary il le vault mieulx," has a grim ring to it, and Judson Allen
might even be right when he describes Anne's pleading on this occasion
as "presumptuous to the point of mortal danger."[28] The game of merciful queen was one that was easy to lose; to win it must have taken more
than acquiescence.

Anne had another role to play, that of a pious reader of vernacular
scripture. There is a legend that she had in her possession a copy of one
of the early Wycliffite Bibles, complete with glosses. This is the basis
for Strickland's claim that Anne was among "the nursing-mothers of the
Reformation." Those who credit the story include Herbert Workman,
who claims that Purvey presented the book to her, and Margaret
Deanesly, who says that "[t]hrough the instrumentality probably of
some Lollard at court, these 'doctors of the gospels' were presented to
the queen."[29] Bell takes the story from Deanesly, bringing it into wider
circulation.

Here, once again, we must proceed with caution. The belief that
Anne was a major supporter of Bible reading and translation is based
on two sources. The first is a passage in which Wycliffe claims that
Anne could have owned the four gospels in Latin, Bohemian (i.e.,

---

contigit ut, post regni circuitionem, magis inopes reverterentur quam egressi fuerant; ut
cunctis verum esse constaret illud proverbium Sapientis; 'Væ terræ, cujus rex puer est'"
[Nor indeed were great gifts for the King sufficient, unless they were matched by equal
gifts for the Queen. Nor would it have seemed a burden to the people to have offered,
out of respect for the King, even more lavish gifts if they had then been wisely safe-
guarded. But whatever property of theirs was greedily collected, the foreigners in the
Queen's retinue, i.e., the Bohemians, soon wastefully demanded, so that as a result after
the circuit of the realm they returned more needy than when they set out, so that all
might see the truth of that proverb of Solomon "Woe to the land that has a boy for its
king"]; Walsingham, *Historia Anglicana*, 2:97.

[28] Judson B. Allen, *The Ethical Poetry of the Later Middle Ages* (Toronto: University of
Toronto Press, 1982), p. 267.

[29] Workman, *John Wyclif*, 2:165; Margaret Deanesly, *The Lollard Bible and other
Medieval Biblical Versions* (Cambridge: Cambridge University Press, 1920), p. 278.

Czech), and German and that nobody would have dared to accuse her of heresy: "Nam possibile est quod nobilis regina soror Cesaris habeat evangelium in lingwa triplici exaratum, scilicet in lingwa boemica, in lingwa teutonica, et latina, et hereticare ipsam propterea implicite foret luceferina superbia" [For it is possible that the noble Queen, sister of the Emperor, might have had the Gospels set out in three languages, namely in Bohemian (Czech), German, and Latin, and to call her a heretic on that account would indeed be diabolical pride].[30] Now, "might have had" is not "had"—and of course Wycliffe might be lying—but as a purely hypothetical example, a trilingual Bible would be both overly ingenious and superfluous. To make his polemical point, Wycliffe need only have said that Anne possessed a Bible in her mother tongue. Nor is there any improbability in Anne's owning a trilingual Bible. Anne's father, Wenceslas, had a beautifully illuminated German Bible, and her eldest sister, Marguerite, who married Louis, king of Hungary and Poland, had a Psalter in Latin, Polish, and German.[31] The story of Anne's trilingual Bible is therefore at least credible. More importantly, perhaps, whether true or not, it shows that within a year or two of her arrival in England, Anne's authority was being used to sanction Bible reading.

We come to a second, and more problematic, source, that which claims Anne had an *English* Bible. According to an anonymous Lollard tract on Biblical translation, Archbishop Arundel praised Anne at her funeral for reading the Bible in English, saying,

it was more joie of hir þan of any woman þat euere he knewe ffor, not-wiþstanding þat sche was an alien borne, sche hadde on Engliche al þe foure Gospeleris wiþ þe doctoris vpon hem.[32]

Before scrutinizing this story, it is worth thinking for a moment of its implications. On the one hand, there is nothing that outrageous in an aristocrat merely owning an English Bible. Lollard Bibles may have begun to circulate within Anne's lifetime; and Thomas of Woodstock—duke of Gloucester, the youngest son of Edward III—who was mur-

---

[30] R. Buddensieg, ed., *John Wiclif's Polemical Works in Latin*, 2 vols. (London, 1883), 1:168.

[31] Deanesly, *Lollard Bible*, p. 20.

[32] C. F. Bühler, "A Lollard Tract: On Translating the Bible into English," *MÆ* 7 (1938): 178.

dered at Calais in 1397, had an illuminated copy of the Early Version, now in the British Library.[33] At a slightly later period, Wycliffite Bibles were in the possession of aristocrats of unimpeachable orthodoxy, most famously Henry VI.[34] On the other hand, the royal acquisition of any book often became a symbolic gesture of approbation. Anne might have owned an English Bible discreetly without making a political gesture, but if she not only owned a copy of the Wycliffite Bible but also let this be widely known, it would have been patronage of the most powerful order. Indeed, if she had done so, there would be considerable grounds to consider her the most influential patron of English Biblical translation in her day.

Unfortunately, the story is not reliable. As Anne Hudson has argued, "the story itself cannot be dated earlier than 1401, and may have been concocted within Lollard circles to give authority to the *Glossed Gospels*."[35] Hudson notes that the Lollard tract that contains the story is based for the most part on a determination produced in 1401 by the orthodox Richard Ullerston, but that "the story of Anne's funeral does not appear in that source."[36] This story must have been added by the anonymous Lollard compiler or translator at a later date, sometime between 1401 and 1414, and is in many ways implausible.[37] If Arundel had examined these Glossed Gospels he would have found much that was objectionable, even in the shorter version.[38] If the anonymous Lollard is distorting the archbishop's remarks, however, this does not necessarily

---

[33] Gloucester had a huge two-volume English Bible valued at 40 s., of which half survives (British Library MSS Egerton 617 and 618, which originally formed one of two volumes), and also "vn liure dengleis de les euangelies" valued at 6s. 8d. as well as "vn nouvel liure des Evangelies glosez en Engleis" valued at 10 s., neither of which survive. On the ownership of Egerton, see Jeanne Krochalis, "The Books and Reading of Henry V and His Circle," *ChauR* 23 (1988): 51, and Sven L. Fristedt, "A Weird Manuscript Enigma in the British Museum," *Stockholm Studies in Modern Philology*, n.s., 2 (1964): 115–21. Given the confidence with which he identifies the heraldic arms in the Egerton MSS as those of Gloucester, Fristedt's conclusion that the evidence "very strongly suggests" that they once belonged to Gloucester (p. 121) seems if anything unduly cautious.

[34] Anne Hudson, *Lollards and Their Books* (London: Hambledon, 1985), p. 182.

[35] Anne Hudson, *The Premature Reformation: Wycliffite Texts and Lollard History* (Oxford: Clarendon Press, 1988), p. 248.

[36] Ibid, p. 248 n. 106.

[37] Hudson, *Lollards*, p. 81. It is also now generally recognized that Purvey was not the author of the *Later Version*—although this is a separate question. See Hudson, *Lollards*, pp. 101–8.

[38] Anne Hudson, ed., *Selections from English Wycliffite Writings* (Cambridge: Cambridge University Press, 1978), p. 167.

mean that he is cutting them from whole cloth. It seems unlikely that he would simply have chosen Anne at random or that he would have specified the Glossed Gospels unless Anne at the very least had something of a reputation for piety and learning, although the claim might just have been based on Wyclif's earlier reference to Anne's Bible in German, Bohemian, and Latin. Even if we are to dismiss the report of Arundel's funeral oration as a Lollard fabrication, it shows, as does the earlier reference to her trilingual but non-English Bible, that Anne's contemporaries thought of her as a Bible reader and that Lollard writers were anxious to appropriate this reputation to validate lay reading and vernacular translation. Why Anne was acquiring this reputation and whether this use of her authority to legitimate Biblical translation was one that she had in any way encouraged remain open questions. As with her role as merciful intercessor, it is impossible to determine where the fictions end and her own actions begin.

The claim that Anne was one of the "nursing-mothers of the Reformation" must be moderated. We do not have enough information to make such confident judgments, and what we can know suggests that Anne, even if she had wished to foster reformist tendencies, would have perforce been far more circumspect than Strickland or Bell allows. We are left with something rather different: glimpses of a courageous and astute woman maneuvering to find a modicum of freedom in a perilous situation; a cultural maker, but one who worked through indirections. Tentative as this portrait is, however, it stands in sharp contrast to that offered by the poets. While contemporary religious commentators and eventually even contemporary chroniclers took Anne seriously, poets and literary critics have tended either to dismiss her as a shallow misreader incapable of understanding Chaucer's sophistication or to ignore her altogether.

The legend that Anne considered Chaucer's depiction of the treacherous Criseyde a slander against women and commanded him to write *The Legend of Good Women* begins with the F version of the Prologue to the *Legend* itself.[39] The narrator describes how he awoke one fine May morning and, leaving his books behind, went out to do his devotion to

---

[39] On the dating of the F and G Prologues, see William A. Quinn, *Chaucer's Rehersynges: The Performability of* The Legend of Good Women (Washington, D.C.: Catholic University of America Press, 1994), pp. 23–26, summarizing the general consensus that F is earlier, and Sheila Delany, *The Naked Text: Chaucer's* Legend of Good Women (Berkeley: University of California Press, 1994), pp. 34–43, challenging it.

the Daisy, whom he praises with elaborate idolatry as the "emperice and flour of floures alle" (*LGWP* F 185).[40] He mentions in passing that he is not taking sides as to the relative merits of the flower or the leaf (191–92):

> For, as to me, nys lever noon ne lother.
> I nam withholden yit with never nother.

The lines would appear to refer to some kind of court game of love centering around a mock debate, but at this juncture the reference is both cryptic and gratuitous. It is here, in this elaborate expression of respectful disinterest, that Chaucer for the first time in the poem alludes to his relation to the court, insinuating that its interests weary him.

Returning to his home, the narrator falls asleep, and in his sleep he sees the God of Love walking with his court. The courtiers kneel in worship of the daisy; the narrator kneels as well; when they rise he is discovered and his identity as an author is revealed. The God of Love is on the point of condemning Chaucer for slandering love, particularly through his translation of the *Roman de la Rose* and his portrayal of Criseyde, when his queen, Alceste, intervenes, launching into a disquisition on the duties of a prudent and merciful monarch. The God of Love cedes to her plea for mercy, surrendering Chaucer into her custody, and she specifies more fully what he is to do (479–89):

> "Now wol I seyn what penance thou shalt do
> For thy trespas. Understonde yt here:
> Thow shalt, while that thou lyvest, yer by yere,
> The moste partye of thy tyme spende
> In makyng of a glorious legende
> Of goode wymmen, maydenes and wyves,
> That weren trewe in lovyng al hire lyves;
> And telle of false men that hem bytraien,
> That al hir lyf ne don nat but assayen
> How many women they may doon a shame;
> For in youre world that is now holde a game."

---

[40]All citations of Chaucer's works are from Larry D. Benson, gen. ed., *The Riverside Chaucer*, 3d ed. (Boston: Houghton Mifflin, 1987). Further references to *The Legend of Good Women* are cited parenthetically in the text.

This depiction of Alceste as an intercessor, placating an irate king and warning him against tyranny, echoes the advice of Prudence in the *Melibeus* and offers a possible link to Queen Anne, but it is only upon Alceste's final instruction that any connection is made directly: "And whan this book ys maad, yive it the quene, / On my byhalf, at Eltham or at Sheene" (496–97). Of course these lines complicate any suggestion that Alceste may simply be *equated* with Anne, but on their basis it will be widely assumed that Alceste is the queen's mouthpiece, that the queen's displeasure is real, and that a genuine royal command lies behind *The Legend of Good Women*.[41]

The question of how we are to read the poem's nested ironies and whether they ultimately tend against Alceste remains hotly disputed.[42] On the one hand, Alceste is in many ways a strong figure, especially in contrast to her husband. Sheila Delany, for example, notes, "We are given a male deity who is narrow-minded, selfish, and temperamental, with a female adviser who is balanced, objective, and controlled"; she argues that this reversal of gender stereotypes "has the effect of exculpating the poet even as he is charged with misogyny."[43] On the other

---

[41] A further parallel is that Alceste is called an "emperice" and comes, like Anne, out of "the hous of Cesar." See David Wallace, "'Whan She Translated Was': A Chaucerian Critique of the Petrarchan Academy," in Lee Patterson, ed., *Literary Practice and Social Change in Britain, 1380–1530* (Berkeley: University of California Press, 1990), p. 210.

[42] The controversy can be traced back to the claim of Harold C. Goddard ("Chaucer's *Legend of Good Women*," *JEGP* 7, no. 4 [1907–8]: 101) that the *Legend* was "a most unmerciful satire upon women," a claim countered by John L. Lowes in "Is Chaucer's *Legend of Good Women* a Travesty?" *JEGP* 8 (1909): 513–69. Eleanor Leach reopened the possibility of a comic reading in "The Sources and Rhetoric of Chaucer's 'Legend of Good Women' and Ovid's 'Heroides'" (Ph.D. diss., Yale University, 1963). The 1980s saw several readings that detected feminist sympathies in the *Legend*'s comedy. Ann McMillan ("'Fayre Sisters Al': *The Flower and the Leaf* and *The Assembly of Ladies*," *Tulsa Studies in Women's Literature* 1 [1982]: 27–42) argues that Chaucer mocks the conventions of the alleged "defences" of women, which she judges "profeminist in claims but antifeminist in assumptions" (p. 30). Ruth Ames ("The Feminist Connections of Chaucer's *Legend of Good Women*," in Julian N. Wasserman and Robert J. Blanch, eds., *Chaucer in the Eighties* [Syracuse: Syracuse University Press, 1986], pp. 57–74) sees the poem as a mockery of "the romantic ideas of these 'saints' of Cupid" and of "the 'folye' of those who trust the God of Love" (p. 58). Elaine Tuttle Hansen ("Irony and the Antifeminist Narrator in Chaucer's *Legend of Good Women*," *JEGP* 82 [1983]: 11–31) similarly claims that "Chaucer's irony is directed not, indeed, at women but at Cupid, at the narrator of the *Legend of Good Women*, and at the antifeminist tradition" (p. 12). In *Chaucer and the Fictions of Gender* (Berkeley: University of California Press, 1992), however, Hansen rejects this earlier view, and the desire to find in Chaucer a protofeminist, finding the *Legend* "a poem about men, not women" (p. 3). Similarly, Carolyn Dinshaw, in *Chaucer's Sexual Poetics* (Madison: University of Wisconsin Press, 1989), sees in the tales "the appropriative and exclusionary processes of masculine literary tradition in its entirety" (p. 75).

[43] Delany, *Naked Text*, p. 105.

hand, Alceste is ultimately no less reductive a reader than the God of Love: her intercession is an act of queenly mercy, not of higher understanding; and the defense she offers, that the poet is a fool and not responsible for his actions (362–64), makes her a dubious ally. Her directions for the new commission are as simplistic as her reading of his previous work, and significantly, it is she, not the God of Love, who issues them. Both Alceste and the God of Love want propaganda, but it is Alceste who directs the poet to write it.[44]

Even if we take the more generous reading and stress Alceste's role as wise counselor and peacemaker, the Prologue still depicts her role as at best intercessory and as confined to matters of literary policy. She is in effect acting as the queen of a court of love, and the earlier dismissive reference to the debate between the flower and the leaf gives some indication of the ultimate triviality of such matters in the poet's eyes. By implying that her only role was to act as a judge in matters of courtly love, Chaucer, like Clanvowe, effectively diminishes the queen's cultural and political influence, reducing sexual politics to a matter of pleasing the ladies.

In any case, the subtleties are soon lost. The legend of Anne the censor gathers strength with Lydgate's remarks in his *Fall of Princes*:

> This poete wrot, at request off the queen,
> A legende off parfit hoolynesse,
> Off Goode Women to fynde out nynteen
> That dede excelle in bounte and fairnesse;
> But for his labour and [his] bisynesse
> Was inportable his wittis to encoumbre,
> In al this world to fynde so gret a noumbre.[45]

By this point Anne's role as the instigator of the legend has become both an established fact and a misogynistic joke. Lydgate solidifies the image of Anne as a demanding but shallow patron, one prone to meddling in matters she did not properly understand.

The ease with which Lydgate's version of the story has been accepted and Anne blamed for imposing upon Chaucer a tedious duty he ultimately abandoned appears most clearly in the early critical commentary on the *Legend*. According to J. B. Bilderbeck, "it may be urged that

[44] Ibid, p. 114.
[45] Henry Bergen, ed., *Lydgate's* Fall of Princes, Early English Text Society, e.s., 121 (London, 1924), p. 10, lines 330–36.

the scheme of the legend as a whole, was one which could hardly have commended itself to the author's artistic temperament, and which it is improbable he would have voluntarily undertaken, in view of the burdensome monotony incidental to the treatment of such a subject."[46] John Tatlock observes that here "Chaucer expresses far more sense of haste and weariness than in any other of his works."[47] Even F. N. Robinson, while calling attention to the literary tradition of the apologetic palinode and thus problematizing the assumption that Alceste's speech is a clear and direct reference to a royal command, nonetheless suggests that the *Legend* "may have been called forth by actual condemnation of his *Troilus*," and concedes the work is unhappy and, for the modern reader, "tiresome."[48]

It is only comparatively recently that the *Legend* has attracted more sympathetic attention. For many of the critics who have participated in this recuperation, however, the possibility of salvaging the poem seems dependent on severing the connection with the queen. For Robert Frank, Jr., the command of Alceste is a fiction Chaucer has contrived that "lends an illusion of orthodoxy to the new kind of story he is introducing."[49] Sheila Delany largely dismisses the question of the dedication to Anne and its historicity as one that need not "affect my (or any other) interpretation."[50] Donald Rowe is prepared to accept that the F Prologue was "written immediately for the royal circle," but is quick to assure us that this is not to "assign to Anne and Richard the status of patrons in a vital, symbiotic relationship with the poet."[51] In much the same way, Lisa Kiser does not so much deny the possibility of a royal commission as diminish it:

And if the poem was originally commissioned by Queen Anne (as many believe) merely to amuse or placate the ladies at court who wanted to read love stories that corrected the antifeminist clerical tradition, then Chaucer has cer-

[46] J. B. Bilderbeck, ed., *Chaucer's* Legend of Good Women (London: Hazell, Watson and Viney, 1902), pp. 88–89.

[47] Tatlock, *Development and Chronology*, p. 112.

[48] F. N. Robinson, ed., *The Works of Geoffrey Chaucer*, 2d ed. (Boston: Houghton Mifflin, 1957), p. 481.

[49] Robert Worth Frank, Jr., *Chaucer and* The Legend of Good Women (Cambridge, Mass.: Harvard University Press, 1972), p. 35. Frank stresses that "We know nothing about specific censorship or a royal directive or a queen's request" (p. 27).

[50] Delany, *Naked Text*, p. 238.

[51] Donald W. Rowe, *Through Nature to Eternity: Chaucer's* Legend of Good Women (Lincoln and London: University of Nebraska Press, 1988), pp. 152–53.

tainly managed to convey more significant themes than one might ever think possible in a poem with such an undistinguished origin.[52]

It would seem that as long as the poem remains a command performance, it cannot easily be regarded as anything more than an unfortunate burden which Chaucer wisely abandoned.[53] Literary excellence presupposes a higher degree of independence. Given this view, it is scarcely surprising that Anne's patronage has received little serious consideration from Chaucerians and that her other accomplishments have been swallowed by a great silence.

What is so frustrating about the simplistic objections raised by Alceste and the God of Love to *Troilus and Criseyde* is that more telling objections might so easily be made, objections that were almost certainly in circulation in Chaucer's day. While the God of Love objects first to Chaucer's translation of the *Roman de la Rose*, which he terms "an heresye ayeins my lawe" (*LGWP* F 330), presumably because of its delineation of all the mechanisms of seduction, many would regard *Troilus and Criseyde* as more corrupting for its glamorization of *fin' amor*. Taken together, the two books provide a primer for a man who wishes to conduct a courtly love affair. The complex amatory negotiations of the medieval court required an extensive familiarity with the current literary conventions.[54] When Chaucer expresses the hope that the *Troilus* "may don gladnesse / Unto any lovere, and his cause availle" (*TC* 1.19–20) there is no reason to suppose that the remark is merely a literary formula. A thorough knowledge of *Troilus and Criseyde* would have availed a male lover in the pursuit of worldly vanity and "thise wrecched worldes appetites" (5.1851), all at the expense of the women at the court. The code of love was not just a harmless aristocratic

[52] Lisa J. Kiser, *Telling Classical Tales: Chaucer and the* Legend of Good Women (Ithaca, N.Y.: Cornell University Press, 1983), pp. 151–52.

[53] One of the few to explicitly reject such assumptions is Jill Mann; in *Geoffrey Chaucer* (Atlantic Highlands, New Jersey: Humanities Press, 1991), pp. 32–47, Mann notes that we cannot be sure that Chaucer did leave the *Legend* unfinished. See further N. F. Blake, who suggests that part of the *Legend* may have been lost; "Geoffrey Chaucer: The Critics and the Canon," *Archiv für das Studium der neueren Sprachen und Literaturen* 221 (1984): 71–74.

[54] Richard F. Green, *Poets and Princepleasers: Literature and the English Court in the Late Middle Ages* (Toronto: University of Toronto Press, 1980), esp. pp. 114–27; Raymond Southall, *The Courtly Maker: An Essay on the Poetry of Wyatt and His Contemporaries*, ch. 4, "The Public World of Courtly Love" (New York: Barnes and Noble, 1964), and John Stevens, *Music and Poetry in the Early Tudor Court* (London: Methuen, 1961).

fantasy but a social discourse of coercive power, and it was recognized as such in Chaucer's day, perhaps most clearly by Christine de Pizan.[55]

Of course, none of this proves that Anne necessarily disapproved of *Troilus and Criseyde*. As a vulnerable alien herself, certain aspects of Criseyde's situation would have been familiar to her, not least of them the need to manage a reckless and far less mature partner. The tradition of depicting Richard as a second Troilus (an important one in court ceremonies) might have even encouraged the association of Criseyde with Anne, in her mind or in others.[56] But whether Anne disapproved of the poem or not, it is unlikely that her judgment was superficial, least of all as superficial as that attributed to the God of Love and Alceste.

Chaucer's association of Anne and Alceste is a powerful example of the painting of lions, a rewriting of history so successful that we can now recapture only traces of what it may have overwritten. To the extent that Alceste is taken to speak for Anne, represent her interests, or share her tastes, the poem does her a gross injustice, transforming a woman of considerable political and cultural authority into a shallow censor and trivializing any potential moral critique of *Troilus and Criseyde*. Carolyn Dinshaw is right, I think, when she describes the *Legend* as a masculine fantasy of control, in which the narrator "both represents the independent, forceful woman so troubling in *Troilus and Criseyde*, and neutralizes her power."[57] I would extend this reading to the social order, in which Chaucer's masculine fantasy of control, as

---

[55] For Christine's objections see, in particular, the letter of Sebille de Monthault, Dame de la Tour, in her *Livre du duc des vrais amants* (and repeated in the *Livre des trois vertus*), which shows a powerful recognition of the ways in which amatory rhetoric entraps women; *Oeuvres poétiques de Christine de Pisan*, ed. Maurice Roy, 3 vols. (Paris: 1886–96), 3:163–65, and *The Book of the Duke of True Lovers*, trans. Thelma S. Fenster and Nadia Margolis (New York: Persea, 1991), pp. 115–17. Modern critiques of the code are numerous. See, for example, Toril Moi, "Desire in Language: Andreas Capellanus and the Controversy of Courtly Love," in David Aers, ed., *Medieval Literature: Criticism, Ideology and History* (New York: St. Martins, 1986), pp. 11–33. Readings of *Troilus and Criseyde* that draw attention to the role of *fin' amor* in patriarchal ideology as exemplified in the poem remain divided on the final effect. Cf. David Aers, *Community, Gender, and Individual Identity: English Writing, 1360–1430* (London and New York: Routledge, 1988), esp. pp. 118–134; Carolyn Dinshaw, *Chaucer's Sexual Poetics*, pp. 28–64; and Allen J. Frantzen, *Troilus and Criseyde: The Poem and the Frame* (New York: Twayne, 1993), esp. pp. 88, 112, all generally supportive of the poem as a critical exploration of patriarchy (although with significant differences), to Elaine Hansen, *Chaucer and the Fictions of Gender*, esp. 186–87.

[56] See, for example, the *Concordia* of Richard Maidstone, celebrating Richard's reconciliation with the City of London, discussed by A. G. Rigg, *A History of Anglo-Latin Literature, 1066–1422* (Cambridge: Cambridge University Press, 1992), pp. 285–86, and Strohm, *Hochon's Arrow*, p. 107.

[57] Dinshaw, *Chaucer's Sexual Poetics*, p. 72.

expressed through his narrator, neutralizes the disturbing power of *actual* women, particularly, although not exclusively, Anne. Chaucer, through his poem, thus places Anne, the real woman, in the position described so well by Luce Irigaray: ". . . off stage, outside representation, out of play, and beyond subjectivity and identity."[58]

This leaves us, of course, with a methodological dilemma. Granted that we will never be able to know very much about Anne, or about her relation to Chaucer, which way does our duty to the past lie? Given the current urge to recover something of women's cultural activities in the past and the dearth of surviving evidence, there is a strong temptation to make bricks without straw and to construct Anne's story from the scantiest evidence. Derek Pearsall alludes to a similar problem in his recent life of Chaucer: "The danger . . . is that a semi-fictional biography will be fabricated which will then be used to endorse views of the poems that the biographer has arrived at by no other means than the usual one of reading them."[59] Thus, in regards to Chaucer's relation to the historical Anne of Bohemia, I want to stress that I am not arguing that Alceste *is* Anne, or even that she consistently acts as a figure for Anne, only that she is associated with Anne to some degree. Nor am I arguing that the story of Anne's commission of the *Legend* should be taken as an established historical fact; still less that if it were, this would resolve the poem's complexities. But just because Anne's relation to the poem, or almost any other cultural artifact, is problematic does not mean that by ignoring it we can avoid all the dangers of speculative historiography. Almost inevitably, as modern readers of medieval poetry, we will trace out an implied historical narrative to link the textual fragments that have survived. When Pearsall confidently asserts that it is "very doubtful" that Anne "either commissioned or received the work," he effectively claims not that the queen's role is unknowable, but that it was negligible.[60] Others are not so sure.[61] Certainly, our image of Chaucer

---

[58] "Hors scène, hors représentation, hors jeu, hors je." I draw on the discussion of Jane E. Burns and on her translation in *Bodytalk: When Women Speak in Old French Literature* (Philadelphia: University of Pennsylvania Press, 1993), p. 1.

[59] Derek Pearsall, *The Life of Geoffrey Chaucer: A Critical Biography* (Oxford: Blackwell, 1992), p. 2.

[60] Pearsall, *Chaucer*, p. 191.

[61] Critics who accept that the story of the commission has some basis in fact include James I. Wimsatt, *Chaucer and His French Contemporaries: Natural Music in the Fourteenth Century* (Toronto: University of Toronto Press, 1991), pp. 161–62, and Quinn, *Chaucer's Rehersynges*, p. 11. Wimsatt draws attention to the equally hostile reception of Machaut's *Jugement du roy de Behaigne*; however, this example might equally be taken as evidence that Alceste's objection to *Troilus and Criseyde* was based only in a literary convention.

as a regular reader before a group of noble men and women such as those in the famous Corpus Christi frontispiece has been significantly modified.[62] It still seems unlikely, however, that a poet who worked in court circles would have entirely fabricated the story of the queen's command, which would then have seemed both a joke without a point and an act of *lèse-majesté*.[63] The balance of probability seems to favor there being some historical basis for the legend of Anne's command, however much this command may then have been fictionalized, just as it seems more likely that Anne did receive the poem at some point than that she did not.[64]

---

See also Jack B. Oruch, "St. Valentine, Chaucer, and Spring in February," *Speculum* 56 (1981): 534–65, who argues that Chaucer, rather than reflecting actual court entertainments, was "the original mythmaker" in the case of St. Valentine's day festivities (p. 565), a position shared by Henry A. Kelly, *Chaucer and the Cult of St. Valentine* (Leiden: E. J. Brill, 1986).

[62] Major statements on Chaucer's audience include Dieter Mehl, "The Audience of Chaucer's *Troilus and Criseyde*," in Beryl Rowland, ed., *Chaucer and Middle English Studies in Honour of Rossell Hope Robbins* (London: George Allen & Unwin, 1974), pp. 173–89; Derek Pearsall, "The *Troilus* Frontispiece and Chaucer's Audience," *YES* 7 (1977): 68–74; Paul Strohm, "Chaucer's Audience," *Literature and History* 5 (1977): 26–41, and *Social Chaucer* (Cambridge, Mass.: Harvard University Press, 1989), esp. 47–83; V. J. Scattergood, "Literary Culture at the Court of Richard II," in Scattergood and Sherborne, eds., *English Court Culture*, pp. 29–44; Richard Firth Green, "Women in Chaucer's Audience," *ChauR* 18 (1983): 146–54; and Felicity Riddy, "'Women Talking about the Things of God': A Late Medieval Sub-culture," in Meale, ed., *Women and Literature in Britain*, pp. 104–27.

[63] Furthermore, Donald R. Howard argues that if we accept that Chaucer began the *Legend* in 1386 (a date for which there is no firm proof, but one that Pearsall himself accepts), and if Alceste's command that he compose the legend "yer by yere" is taken to mean "one story each year," then Chaucer would have composed nine stories, the number that survive, by Anne's death in 1394; *Chaucer: His Life, His Works, His World* (New York: Dutton, 1987), p. 395. This is, at the least, a curious coincidence. Howard argues that this explanation would reconcile the apparent contradiction that the poet is to compose the legend as long as he lives but also bring it to the queen when it is finished, noting in support that Chaucer generally uses the phrase "year by year" in the sense of "one year after another." The Prologue mentions that the God of Love is accompanied by nineteen ladies (F 249), and this too may be explained by a court connection. Bernard Witlieb notes that by 1386 there were nineteen ladies in the order of the Garter; cited in Howard, ibid, p. 396.

[64] The extent to which such games and court debates actually existed as staged rituals is difficult to determine. Richard Green's caution is very much to the point: "[I]t is easy to understand how a handful of courtiers engaged in a casual discussion of love poetry might have been regarded, and have regarded themselves, as constituting a judicial *cour amoureuse*, and how a poet whose work had met with some kind of disapproval in court circles might have maintained the fiction of its having been officially proscribed by a formal court of love"; *Poets and Princepleasers*, p. 123. Such a reading does not, however, minimize the social pressures on the poet from the court.

Perhaps we can advance one step further. The denial of the possibility of Anne's cultural authority by both Chaucer and Chaucerians seems too persistent to be attributed exclusively to an empiricist urge to avoid the untidiness of historical speculation. Instead, this dehistoricization might be seen as one aspect of the authorial construction of Chaucer, first as a poet rather than just a princepleaser, then as a voice of male detachment, humane wisdom, and down-to-earth English common sense; and finally as the forefather of the canon of English literature.

The construction of Chaucer has taken many forms, by no means all of them hostile to his royal connections. Seth Lerer, for example, finds in Chaucer's fifteenth-century disciples a nostalgia for "a past world in which kings govern, courts patronize, and poets live as 'laureates' under their munificent rule."[65] But at several crucial junctures, there has been a firm effort to elevate Chaucer's art from political pressure and the taint of the Ricardian court. The effort to present Chaucer as a national poet whose works would enhance the prestige of the language and the legitimacy of the Lancastrian order, while casting him ever more firmly in the role of adviser to princes, obviously required that his Ricardian connections be minimized.[66] It is not until much later, however, in the wake of Dryden's famous praise that Chaucer "follow'd Nature every where," that Chaucer's impatience with courtly conventions becomes a measure of his poetic genius. An early instance comes in an anonymous biographical note of 1766, which praises Chaucer because he "discovered nature in all her appearances, and stripped off every disguise with which the Gothic writers had clothed her."[67] A century later, James R. Lowell echoes the point: "Chaucer is the first who broke away from the

---

[65] Seth Lerer, *Chaucer and His Readers: Imagining the Author in Late-Medieval England* (Princeton, N.J.: Princeton University Press, 1993), p. 15.

[66] On the Lancastrian construction of Chaucer, see John H. Fisher, *The Importance of Chaucer* (Carbondale and Edwardsville: Southern Illinois University Press, 1992), pp. 143–46, and "A Language Policy for Lancastrian England," *PMLA* 107 (1992): 1170; John M. Bowers, ed., *The Canterbury Tales: Fifteenth-Century Continuations and Additions* (Kalamazoo, Mich.: Medieval Institute Publications, 1992), p. 3; Larry Scanlon, "The King's Two Voices: Narrative and Power in Hoccleve's *Regement of Princes*," in Patterson, ed., *Literary Practice and Social Change*, pp. 216–47, esp. p. 226; Derek Pearsall, "Hoccleve's *Regement of Princes*: The Poetics of Royal Self-Representation," *Speculum* 69 (1994): 386–410, esp. pp. 397–99; and Lerer, *Chaucer and His Readers*, p. 49 and n. 57. For cautions against Fisher, see Pearsall, "Hoccleve's *Regement*," p. 399 n. 45, and Joseph A. Dane, "The Importance of Importance," *Huntington Library Quarterly* 56 (1993): 307–17.

[67] Quoted in Caroline F. E. Spurgeon, ed., *Five Hundred Years of Chaucer Criticism and Allusion, 1357–1900* (New York: Russell & Russell, 1960), 1:429.

dreary traditional style, and gave not merely stories, but lively *pictures* of real life as the ever-renewed substance of poetry."[68] For Frederick Furnivall, Chaucer was "the most genial and humourful healthy-souled man that England had ever seen," in part because he kept "his eye open to all the beauties of the world around him," and while "studying books, and, more still, woman's nature," he was "clear of all nonsense of Courts of Love, etc."[69]

Arguably, this dismissal of the "nonsense of Courts of Love, etc." simply fulfills a poetic agenda that Chaucer coded into his own works. While the attitude toward court patronage in his poems is characteristically allusive, many have read in them an increasingly defiant rejection of the limitations imposed upon a court poet by a frequently insensitive audience.[70] John Gardner attributes the changes to the Prologue to Chaucer's desire "to revise out references to Queen Anne and her poetastering court."[71] Robert Worth Frank, Jr., sees in *The Legend of Good Women* a critical transition in Chaucer's art toward a poetry "more of the world and less of the garden."[72] Lee Patterson similarly finds that the *Legend* "registers Chaucer's desire to escape from subjection to a court, and to aristocratic values generally, that are felt as increasingly tyrannical."[73] For Patterson, the disparagement of the court through the figures of Alceste and the God of Love is a crucial step in the poet's emancipation: ". . . subject to the intransigent and uncomprehending demands of a *gentil* audience, the poet in turn subjects *gentillesse* itself to relentless critique."[74] What is disparaged, however, whether by the poet, the critic, or the tradition they form together, is not merely courtliness but a feminine courtliness, a world in which men are at the beck and call of women and must devote themselves to the

---

[68] Quoted in Spurgeon, *Chaucer Criticism*, 2.3:109; italics in original.

[69] Quoted in Spurgeon, *Chaucer Criticism*, 2.3:114, and, for the last phrase, 113.

[70] Cf. Glending Olson's characterization of Chaucer as "a maker who became a poet," in "Making and Poetry in the Age of Chaucer," *Comparative Literature* 31 (1979): 288.

[71] John Gardner, *The Poetry of Chaucer* (Carbondale and Edwardsville: Southern Illinois University Press, 1977), p. 203.

[72] Frank, *Chaucer and* The Legend of Good Women, p. 36.

[73] Lee Patterson, *Chaucer and the Subject of History* (Madison: University of Wisconsin Press, 1991), p. 237.

[74] Ibid., p. 238. Cf. his "Court Politics and the Invention of Literature: The Case of Sir John Clanvowe," in David Aers, ed., *Culture and History, 1350–1600: Essays on English Communities, Identities, and Writing* (Detroit: Wayne State University Press, 1992), pp. 7–41. Although intent on reclaiming the court as "a site where literature is produced," Patterson still maintains that for Chaucer it was also "a historical origin to be transcended" (p. 9).

inanities of the debate over the merits of the flower and the leaf. Gentility is feminized that poetry may be masculinized.

And if any poet has been masculinized, it is Chaucer. To quote one revealing formulation, Chaucer "was a man before he was a poet, and among men essentially an Englishman."[75] Donald Howard speaks for many Chaucerians when he claims that "in his best poems we *feel* him as a 'man speaking to men.'"[76] Of all the winning qualities of manly "Dan Chaucer," the one stressed again and again is his good humor, what Coleridge called his "manly cheerfulness."[77] The tolerant and gently ironic voice of the Canterbury narrator has been accepted as the true voice of the author. Any suggestion that Chaucer wrote in bitterness of spirit or under duress would undermine an image of his tolerant humanity and manly equanimity—and that image has become a matter of strong identification for many of his readers, myself, I confess, among them.[78] That male critics, like male poets, suffer genuine anxiety at following such unmanly and cloistered pursuits as reading and writing, may help explain why Chaucer's displacement of Anne, and other acts of clerical domination such as those in *The Nun's Priest's Tale*, have been for so long readily accepted as examples of Chaucer's genial nature and masterful irony and why so little thought has been paid to what may have provoked them.[79] The exigencies of courtly patronage and the indignity of having a woman boss must be purged from the text so that it may claim the stable order of detached, masculine self-control and artistic independence.

This authorial construction has been built so well that Chaucerians have still not managed to break from it entirely. Certainly the reading of Alceste and the *Legend* has shifted dramatically, and where we once

[75] Henry Dwight Sedgwick, *Dan Chaucer: An Introduction to the Poet, His Poetry and His Times* (Indianapolis: Bobbs-Merrill, 1934), p. x.

[76] Donald R. Howard, "Chaucer the Man," *PMLA* 80 (1965): 337; italics in original.

[77] Quoted in Spurgeon, *Chaucer Criticism*, 2.3:190. Cf. her own list of what attracts readers to Chaucer, which includes his "delightful humour" and "toleration and broad-mindedness" (1:liii).

[78] See, for example, Pearsall's frank acknowledgment of his interest in finding Chaucer "a decent sort of fellow" and his provocative suggestion that it might be equally possible to imagine Chaucer to have been "a time-serving opportunist and placeman, who pictured his own pliability in all that he saw"; *Life of Chaucer*, p. 8.

[79] Hansen, *Fictions of Gender*, p. 288, alludes to this possibility among Chaucerians. Cf. the claim of Sandra M. Gilbert and Susan Gubar ("The Man on the Dump versus the United Dames of North America; or What Does Frank Lentricchia Want?" *Critical Inquiry* 14 [1988]: 405) that "American literary men have tried to prove that they are not prisoners of sex but macho soldiers in the armies of the night."

saw a poet who was bored, we are now more likely to see a poet who was either ironic or uneasy and conflicted. But few Chaucerians have yet turned their attention to the historical Anne. The work of Strickland, Deanesly, and Bell is, as far as I have read, scarcely ever mentioned in the criticism on the *Legend*, old or new.[80]

This silence seems symptomatic of a more general failure in literary studies to recover those traces of human activity that vex poetic formulations. While the possibility that critical/textual play will end up denying human agency or the lived experience of real women is a recurring concern in feminist scholarship, avoiding this danger is not easy.[81] As David Aers has recently argued, current disciplinary divisions do not merely encourage us to confine our work to certain predetermined canons; they make it very difficult for us to do anything else.[82] Even those who would be prepared to assign Anne or Richard a vital symbiotic role in discursive production are not necessarily in any position to do so. We remain trapped within the confines of canonical editions, such as Robinson III, even when we wish to embark on historicizing projects.[83] In our readings the chaos of the political moment recedes, and the cries of the Peasants' Revolt or the Merciless Parliament come to us only as distant echoes. No less muted is the conversa-

---

[80] A major exception is David Wallace, who examines the role of Queen Anne and the Bohemian court extensively in chapter 12 of *Chaucerian Polity: Absolutist Lineages and Associational Forms in England and Italy* (Stanford: Stanford University Press, 1997). I would like to thank him for allowing me to consult this work in draft. See also Alfred Thomas, *Anne's Bohemia* (Minnesota: University of Minnesota Press, forthcoming).

[81] For a particularly charged example, see the objections raised to R. Howard Bloch's "Medieval Misogyny: Woman as Riot," *Representations* 20 (1987): 1–24, in *Medieval Feminist Newsletter* 6 (1988), and Jane Burns, *Bodytalk*, p. 13; the review of *Bodytalk* by Nancy A. Jones in *Bryn Mawr Medieval Review* (bmmr1@cc.brynmawr.edu), November 24, 1994, praising Burns for challenging "the semiosis (read erasure)" of women in the work of Bloch and the others; and the response by Bloch on December 4, 1994. The issue is frequently couched in terms of the conflict between historicism and poststructuralism.

[82] See David Aers, "A Whisper in the Ear of Early Modernists; or, Reflections on Literary Critics Writing the 'History of the Subject,'" in Aers, ed., *Culture and History*, p. 195.

[83] The quest for origins underlying much historicist criticism has been the subject of theoretical scrutiny. In the field of Chaucer studies, see in particular Louise O. Fradenburg, "'Voice Memorial': Loss and Reparation in Chaucer's Poetry," *Exemplaria* 2 (1990): 169–202, and Gayle Margherita, "Originary Fantasies and Chaucer's *Book of the Duchess*," in Lomperis and Stanbury, eds., *Feminist Approaches to the Body*, pp. 116–41. But the drive to exclude the historical also requires scrutiny. Margherita's comment on *The Book of the Duchess* seems applicable: "Founded in absence or loss of reference, the text must nonetheless affirm its own plenitude and unity by reconstituting the presence/absence dyad within the diegesis proper. The text's authority thus comes to depend on an affirmation of the boundaries separating inside and outside, that is, on its ability to relegate woman, and thus lack, to the interior of narrative space" (pp. 127–28).

tion of the courtiers or the commands of the queen. Without an alternative, we succumb all too easily to the images of his social condition that the poet provides for us.

Of course we can have no direct access to a "real" Anne outside textuality. What we know of her we know through stories and what she did she did through stories. But not all textual orders are homologous.[84] This is why the relation between Alceste and Anne or between Anne and Chaucer should not be formulated exclusively within the textual tradition that is Chaucer's legacy. This is particularly true to the extent that the Chaucer tradition is founded on the denial or minimization of female patronage.

We have made Chaucer well, constructing him, along lines that he and his immediate followers set out for us, as the father of English literature. We have adopted vernacular literature as our secular scripture, crediting it with the perduring aesthetic stability that Chaucer ascribes to Virgil, Lucan, and Statius, a stability removed from all forms of political pressure and any taint of careerism, just as we have accepted Chaucer's self-presentation as the calm and humane voice of masculine commonsense. Together we have made him so well that we are in no position to consider the role that Anne, arguably a more important figure in her day, may have played in making him for us.[85]

[84] See Fredric Jameson's critique of "the mirage of immanence," in *The Political Unconscious: Narrative as a Socially Symbolic Act* (Ithaca, N.Y.: Cornell University Press, 1981), pp. 282–83 n. 2.

[85] I would like to thank Alcuin Blamires, Anne Hudson, Ann Matter, John Parsons, Felicity Riddy, Paul Strohm, David Wallace, and Nicholas Watson for their valuable suggestions. Earlier versions of this paper were delivered at the conference "The Women and the Book," organized by Lesley Smith and Jane Taylor at St. Hilda's College, Oxford, 1993, and at a session organized by Glending Olson at the 1993 meeting of the Modern Language Association of America in Toronto. I benefited greatly from the comments of the participants on both occasions.

# A Fourteenth-Century Erotics of Politics: London as a Feminine New Troy

Sylvia Federico
*Washington State University*

Nicholas Brembre, former mayor of London and associate of Richard II, was hanged in 1388 after being charged with treason by the anti-Ricardian Lords Appellant. Rumored among his purported crimes, as recorded by Thomas Walsingham in the *Historia Anglicana*, was that he had entertained the idea of renaming London "Little Troy" and thought to style himself "Duke" of the city.[1] Another London text from the late 1380s, the alliterative poem *Saint Erkenwald*, uses the name "New Troy" to describe the city's current status as a center of moral virtue and economic success. Unlike in Saxon times, when the city was the seat of Satan, the anonymous author boasts, "Now þat London is neuenyd hatte þe New Troie, / þe metropol and þe mayster toun hit euermore has bene."[2] On the one hand a mark of a citizen's capital treason, and on the other a mark of the capital's civic progress, London's Trojan precedent had an extremely ambivalent political currency in the last twenty years of the fourteenth century.[3]

---

[1] Thomas Walsingham, *Historia Anglicana*, ed. Henry Thomas Riley, 2 vols., Rolls Series, vol. 28 (London: Longmans, 1863), 2:174. Henry Knighton similarly records the belief that, had Brembre lived, "he would have had himself made duke of Troy by the king, for in ancient times London was called the second Troy ("Troia minor"), and so he would have been the duke of London, the name of London being changed to Troy"; *Knighton's Chronicle, 1337–1396*, ed. and trans. G. H. Martin (Oxford: Clarendon Press, 1995), pp. 500–501.

[2] *Saint Erkenwald*, ed. Ruth Morse (Cambridge: D. S. Brewer, 1975), lines 25–26.

[3] The significance of London's Trojan past is further suggested by the appearance of Troy in two late-fourteenth-century books commissioned by London citizens. Thomas Carleton, a wealthy embroiderer and one-time supporter of Brembre's rival, John Northampton, commissioned a collection of statutes relating to the government of England and the city of London. Prominent in this collection (which was probably compiled in early 1383) is a section entitled "De Londonie fama," which narrates the city's

Largely because of Geoffrey of Monmouth's interested treatment of English legendary history in his *Historia Regum Britanniae*, London was thought to have ancestral ties to old Troy. According to Geoffrey, Diana appeared to Brutus, a descendant of Aeneas, and explained that the *translatio imperii* from the ancient world to the modern one would be achieved through him and his heirs:

Brute, past the realms of Gaul, beneath the sunset lieth an island, girt about by ocean . . . Seek it! For there is thine abode for ever. There by thy sons again shall Troy be builded; there of thy blood shall Kings be born, hereafter Sovran in every land the wide world over.[4]

After searching the entire island, Brutus selected the site for the main city of the prophesied place and named it after Troy:

When he came to the river Thames, he walked along the banks till he found the very spot best fitted to his purpose. He therefore founded his city there and called it New Troy, and by this name was it known for many ages thereafter, until at last, by corruption of the word, it came to be called Trinovantum.[5]

Destined to replicate and perhaps even surpass the glory of Troy, London could be associated with the ancient city for the political profit of the English. The *Saint Erkenwald* poet's use of Trojan precedent to

---

legendary history and its founding by Brutus (British Library Additional MSS 38, 131, fol. 83). A second book, thought to have been produced in 1395 for a London fishmonger, consists almost exclusively of ordinances related to the fishmongering trade, with a curious exception. The two paragraphs from Geoffrey of Monmouth's *Historia Regum Britanniae* that recount London's foundation by Brutus and the city's legendary name, "Troia nova" (which I discuss below), are emphasized in this manuscript by marginal drawings of a finger pointing to the relevant text (BL Egerton 2885, fol. 8b). I am especially grateful to Sheila Lindenbaum for calling my attention to these documents, and to Hannes Kleineke for sharing with me his paper on the topic, "Carleton's Book: The Political Philosophy of a Fourteenth-Century London Embroiderer."

[4] Geoffrey of Monmouth, *History of the Kings of Britain*, trans. Sebastian Evans, rev. Charles W. Dunn (New York: Dutton, 1958), p. 18.

[5] Geoffrey of Monmouth, *History*, p. 27. The historian continues that the name Trinovantum was lost as a result of the political corruption of King Lud: "But afterward, Lud . . . possessed him of the helm of the kingdom, and surrounded the city with right noble walls, as well as with towers builded with marvelous art, commanding that it should be called Kaerlud, that is, City of Lud, after his own name." In an interesting precursor to Brembre's "crime," Lud's desire to rename the city provoked dissent within London's ruling circle: "Whence afterward a contention arose betwixt him and his brother Nennius, who took it ill that he should be minded to do away the name of Troy in his own country" (pp. 27–28).

justify his claim that London is a "metropol" and a "mayster toun" exemplifies the kind of motivated comparison between the two realms spawned by Geoffrey's political myth-making.[6]

But London's mythic attachment to Trojan precedent was complicated by treachery, specifically the sexual treachery that permeated the history of Troy. As D. W. Robertson noted some time ago, England's Trojan origins provided inspiration, but also served as a warning for the English. Along with the precedent of a grand empire, "it was remembered that Old Troy was burned by the Greeks, having first weakened itself through lust."[7] The Trojans were noble war heroes, but they were also defeated war heroes, men whose military prowess was stained and ultimately limited by unnatural desires. Rape, bigamy, secret affairs, betrayal, adultery, temporary marriages, and perhaps even incest were part of the legacy of the ruling families of Troy.[8] The dangerous implication of this aspect of the Trojan legacy was that London, too, was full of unnatural, deviant rulers whose passions would lead to the destruction of the city. The Appellants' charge that Nicholas Brembre had thought to destroy the name of the Londoners ("nomen Londoniarum delevisse meditatus fuerat") by calling the city "Little Troy" ("Parva Troia") can be seen as a capitalization on this other, unsavory association of Troy with destructive passion, and a mobilization of this association for political gain.[9] While it is impossible to say

---

[6] See Francis Ingledew, "The Book of Troy and the Genealogical Construction of History: The Case of Geoffrey of Monmouth's *Historia regum Britanniae*," *Speculum* 69 (1994): 681–88, for how the Trojan myth was appropriated (via Geoffrey's text) by late twelfth-century aristocratic discourse to justify the Norman invasion. For an overview of English historiographers' dissemination of the myth, see John Clark, "Trinovantum—the evolution of a legend," *Journal of Medieval History* 7 (1981): 135–51.

[7] D. W. Robertson, *Chaucer's London* (New York: Wiley, 1968), p. 3.

[8] Medieval redactors of the story of the Trojan war often pointed to Paris's abduction of Helen (and usually blamed Helen's lust, not Paris's) as the root cause of the trouble. Criseyde's betrayal of her lover, Troilus, was similarly seen as a direct cause of the fall of Troy, since Troilus's survival was thought necessary for the survival of the city. And a few commentators have suggested a possible incestuous, not to mention adulterous, relationship between Helen and her brother-in-law, Deiphoebus. These originary acts of sexual deviance were transferred to the post-Trojan world via Aeneas, who (according to Ovidian versions of the story) married Dido only to renounce her afterward. See for example Guido delle Colonne, *Historia Destructionis Troiae*, ed. Nathaniel Edward Green (Cambridge: Medieval Academy of America, 1936), pp. 70–74; Servius's commentary on the *Aeneid*, *Servianorum in Vergilii Carmina Commentariorum*, ed. E. K. Rand (Lancaster: American Philosophical Society, 1946), 2: 316–17 [cited in Lee Patterson, *Chaucer and the Subject of History* (Madison: University of Wisconsin Press, 1991), p. 110 n. 71]; and Chaucer's *Troilus and Criseyde* (2.1702–8) and *House of Fame* (lines 293–95), both in Larry D. Benson, gen. ed., *The Riverside Chaucer* (Boston: Houghton Mifflin, 1987).

[9] Walsingham, *Historia Anglicana*, 2:174.

just what the former mayor had hoped to achieve for himself or his king by using the name "Little Troy," or even, for that matter, if he really said it, the volatile signifying power with which the idea of Troy was invested made it possible for Trojan deviance and destruction to adhere to him, and not the glory of Trojan empire.[10] What was, on one level of interpretation, a presumably imperial impulse on Brembre's part was simultaneously available at another level to be interpreted as an unnatural, destructive impulse.[11]

These two principal Trojan determinations reiterate the split, noted recently by Elizabeth Bellamy, in which the European idea of the *translatio imperii* "represses and flees from the destruction of Troy, even as it nostalgically yearns to recuperate the tragic *Troiana fortuna* into a narcissistic revision of imperial 'wholeness.'"[12] The fantasy of imperial wholeness is both permitted and threatened by Trojan precedent, an interpretive impasse that leads to what Bellamy calls the "neurosis" of the latter-day empires self-fashioned in the image of ancient Troy: European imperial identity is forged through the process of struggling to reject the same Trojan heritage it rests on. Whether we call this post-Trojan European identity narcissistic, neurotic, or anything else, it springs retroactively from the myriad images of the destroyed ancient city. Unnatural desire, and especially unnatural sexual desire, not only caused Troy's fall, but was also the fortunate flaw that permitted the establishment of later empires. To put this from an English perspective, the fall of Troy is productive, leading to Brutus's voyage and the founding of the British empire. But so, too, is unregulated Trojan desire productive of English political identity. In this case, "the desire for a city

[10] Sheila Lindenbaum, "The Smithfield Tournament of 1390," *Journal of Medieval and Renaissance Studies* 20 (1990): 10–15, discusses Richard II's use of the term "New Troy" and the political resonance it had for Londoners in 1390. While one cannot know for certain exactly what Richard had hoped to achieve, Lindenbaum argues, his use of the term was an "alienating gesture" (p. 10) that underscored the exclusion of the London citizenry from the tournament and from the social order it represented. Michael Hanrahan, "Traitors and Lovers: The Politics of Love in Chaucer, Gower, and Usk" (Ph.D. dissertation, Indiana University, 1995), pp. 102–8, traces the name "New Troy" as a Ricardian indicator during the period and argues that the Appellants seized on Brembre's use of the term as an especially effective way to further associate him with Richard II.

[11] Jean Laplanche and Jean-Bertrand Pontalis, *The Language of Psychoanalysis*, trans. Donald Nicholson-Smith (New York: Norton, 1973), p. 292, define an overdetermined formation as one "related to a multiplicity of unconscious elements which may be organised in different meaningful sequences, each having its own specific coherence at a particular level of interpretation."

[12] Elizabeth J. Bellamy, *Translations of Power* (Ithaca, N.Y.: Cornell University Press, 1992), p. 34.

not seen"[13] opens up a space of imaginary activity, within which mutually exclusive possibilities may coexist. The best example of the multiple identities capable of being constructed out of the ruins of Troy is, again, the case of Nicholas Brembre. Constituting himself in the image of imperialism as the Duke of New Troy, the former mayor was then constituted in turn as a deviant traitor to the realm.

The specter of a grand Trojan empire ruined by passion—an image invoked in the name "New Troy"—was not just a convenient and easily controlled tool used for the construction of exemplary identities for some and deviant identities for others; it could and often did exceed the realm of its designated use, producing associations of empire and ruination outside of their intended targets. What Troy meant for London was split between prophesied glory of empire and doomed destruction by lust. Similarly, how Troy made meaning in London was split between the strategic, controlled uses of its associations and the uncontrollable excesses of these associations.

The volatility of the significance of Troy stems from its liminal location somewhere between history and fantasy. The ultimate unreal city, Troy is (and was) always already obliterated, always only a word and never a place. In this way Troy can be seen as a textual phenomenon, a voided signifier open for multiple reinscriptions. But at the same time, the ancient city is also designated as a historically and geographically "once real" place. Hovering somewhere between historical truth and utter fiction, Troy "exists only retroactively in the imaginations of belated observers."[14] Similar to the status of recovered memories of the primal scene in the context of psychoanalysis, the idea of Troy is more significant for the way that it operates than for its actual truthfulness; the reconstructed primal scene is an occasion for interpretation that, regardless of its veracity, produces the truth of and for the subject in analysis.[15] Likewise, "memories" of Troy are really not memories at all, but rather interpretive acts disguised as (and functioning as) history. Interpretations or readings of an "unreal" event or text like Troy are, like all interpretive acts, based on motivated constructions and willful expressions of allegiance or disavowal. But the always empty, open space

---

[13] Bellamy, ibid., p. 50.

[14] Ibid.

[15] Ned Lukacher, *Primal Scenes: Literature, Philosophy, Psychoanalysis* (Ithaca, N.Y.: Cornell University Press, 1986), p. 24, writes that the primal scene is "situated in the differential space between historical memory and imaginative construction, between archival verification and interpretive free play."

of what Troy can mean is particularly suitable for excessive significations—linguistic and emotional associations that spill over their ideological containers and flood the interstices of the Trojan fantasy text.

Invoking London's mythical past by calling the city "New Troy,"
John Gower's *Vox Clamantis* and Richard Maidstone's *Concordia Facta
inter Regem Riccardum II et Civitatem Londonie* construct a space that is
neither London nor Troy. It is in this fantasy place, where historical
memory and imaginative construction vie with one another for interpretive ascendancy, that translations of identity can occur. Some of the
identities constructed and destroyed in Gower's and Maidstone's interpretive texts are obviously motivated and traceable to certain specific
political aims, but many identities (both exemplary and deviant) produced in the texts are contrary to their own presumed intentions. What
makes these "failures" of intended Trojan association productive is that
they permit new possibilities of identity which—although presenting
a challenge to Gower's and Maidstone's stated ideologies—promise and
deliver a release from the writers' otherwise restricted positions. London
in disguise as New Troy is a realm that frees political thought to envision the city in ways that had not been possible before.

Both poems specifically address moments of great crisis in London's
semblance of civic order. Gower, who lived right across the river in
Southwark, added book 1 as a preface to his already completed *Vox
Clamantis* shortly after the armed risings in and around London in June
of 1381. Over the course of several days, thousands of armed men primarily from Kent and Essex were joined by even greater numbers of
like-minded Londoners in a violent siege of the city. They burned
houses to the ground and beheaded their enemies, including the
Archbishop of Canterbury. London officials were seemingly paralyzed
by this invasion and mysteriously offered little or no resistance to the
rebels, until the dramatic events at Smithfield, featuring the young
Richard II in a heroic role, brought the rebellion in London to a close.[16]

---

[16] See Andrew Prescott's "The Judicial Records of the Rising of 1381" (Ph.D. dissertation, University of London, 1984). R. B. Dobson, *The Peasants' Revolt of 1381* (London:
Macmillan, 1983), provides edited and translated chronicle accounts that trace the
events leading up to the revolt and record its consequences. Recent interpretations of the
social composition of the rebels include Christopher Dyer, "The Social and Economic
Background to the Rural Revolt of 1381," in R. H. Hilton and T. H. Aston, eds., *The
English Rising of 1381* (Cambridge: Cambridge University Press, 1984), pp. 9–42; and
Andrew Prescott, "London in the Peasants' Revolt: A Portrait Gallery," *London Journal* 7
(1981): 125–43.

Maidstone, a Carmelite friar about whom little else is known,[17] wrote his *Concordia* after witnessing the August 1392 street pageant that celebrated the reconciliation of Richard II with the citizens of London after their so-called "quarrel." This quarrel, which probably started over the citizens' refusal to lend money to the crown, culminated in the king's taking away the liberties of the city, arresting the mayor and other city officials, and removing the royal bench from London to York.[18]

At issue in both the rising of 1381 and the quarrel between London's citizens and the king is a compromising of London's cohesive corporate identity. The rebels' physical entrance into the city and the king's abrogation of its freedoms eleven years later were invasions from without that provoked questions about the city's physical and legal integrity. Furthermore, these invasions highlighted the degree of internal cohesiveness, or lack thereof, that characterized the space called "London" in the late fourteenth century.[19] In the case of the rebels' invasion, London's integrity was able to be violated from without because of pervasive divisions within the city walls. The king's invasion in 1392 was prompted by the Londoners' exclusion of him from their benefit, manifested in their unusual show of unity in joining together to refuse Richard a loan. The potential conflicts and strange alliances contributing to the crises of 1381 and 1392 include those between rival mayoral parties, citizen and noncitizen merchants, freemen and disenfranchised workers, competing guild and trade interests, the royal court and the citizens, as well as factions within the court.

---

[17] Maidstone (d. 1396) was a Doctor of Theology who wrote tracts against the Wycliffites and defenses of begging friars (for example, the 1380 *Protectorium Pauperis*). Born in Kent and ordained in 1376, he was a member of the Carmelite house at Aylesford. See the biographical notes in the introduction to the text, *Concordia Facta inter Regem Riccardum II et Civitatem Londonie*, ed. and trans. Charles Roger Smith (Ph.D. dissertation, Princeton University, 1972), pp. 1–10.

[18] See Caroline M. Barron, "The Quarrel of Richard II with London: 1392–97," in F. R. H. Du Boulay and Caroline M. Barron, eds., *The Reign of Richard II* (London: Athlone, 1971), pp. 173–201.

[19] London's internal conflicts prompt David Wallace, "Chaucer and the Absent City," in Barbara Hanawalt, ed., *Chaucer's England: Literature in Historical Context* (Minneapolis: University of Minnesota Press, 1992) to speak of the impossibility of representing the city as a unified whole. London is an "absent city" in Chaucer's poetry because: "[T]here is no idea of a city for all the inhabitants of a space called London to pay allegiance to; there are only conflicts of associational, hierarchical, and anti-associational discourses, acted out within and across the boundaries of a city wall or the fragments of a text called *The Canterbury Tales* (p. 84)".

Clearly, talking about London as a unified city-subject is impossible—as impossible as talking about seamless and whole human subjects.

But even though the idea of a unified city or a unified psychic identity is a fantasy, that does not mean that people will stop trying to pretend it is true. Indeed, according to Jacques Lacan, the fantasy of psychic wholeness is the very thing upon which "real" identity is constructed. In particular, Lacan's understanding of the gendered dynamics at work in the construction of identity asserts that the idea of woman exists to bolster the idea of man as a unified entity:

As negative to the man, woman becomes a total object of fantasy (or an object of total fantasy), elevated into the place of the Other and made to stand for its truth. . . . The absolute "Otherness" of the woman, therefore, serves to secure for the man his own self-knowledge and truth.[20]

Constructed in language as different, and set up as that which man is not, "she" becomes the defining counterpoint for masculine identity and in this way can be said to produce what man is.

But masculine identity, from the point of view of Lacan's work, is always in danger of being exposed as a construction by woman's excessive *jouissance*. The possibility of something outside of the signifying system undermines that system itself and everything constructed in and by it.[21] Like the idea of Troy, the idea of woman is an always voided signifier, one that simultaneously supports and threatens to destroy masculine identity.

Gower's and Maidstone's poems can be seen as engaging the very issue of the fantasy of London as an integrated whole. Tellingly, the vehicle that permits fantasies of integration and disintegration is a woman, or rather, an idea of a woman: Gower's New Troy is a widow, and Maid-

---

[20] *Feminine Sexuality: Jacques Lacan and the école freudienne*, eds. Juliet Mitchell and Jacqueline Rose, trans. Jacqueline Rose (New York: Norton, 1982), p. 50.

[21] The controllable, manageable position of "woman" as sexual difference, or lack, and the uncontrollable, unmanageable position of "woman" as *jouissance*, or excess, are impossible to keep separate. The *petit autre* inscribed as difference in the phallic order, and the Other whose mysterious *jouissance* threatens and promises to exceed the boundaries of that order, collapse together in Lacan's formulation to become the tenuous fantasy upon which man's identity is constructed. The danger of being annihilated, however, is also the pleasure of being released. According to Lacan, the fantasy of woman is like the fantasy of God: "she" offers the promise of an escape from the restricted and always inadequate positions of identity available in signification. In this way, the fantasy of woman's extrasymbolic position threatens, but also promises, to release man from the system of self-identification he conjured through "her." See *Feminine Sexuality*, pp. 138–48.

stone's is a wife. London's corporate identity is represented as a woman's corporeal identity; the city is a fantasy feminine body capable of being open or closed, invaded or protected, chaste or common. This city-as-woman offers numerous possibilities for political commentary on the men who are inside or outside of "her." The men who enter into London—the rebels in 1381 and the king in 1392—are portrayed in these poems as occupying gendered positions of identity that correspond to the licit or illicit sexual behavior of the city-as-woman. By allegorizing his city as a chaste and vulnerable widow, Gower attempts to smooth over London's internal conflicts in a mirage of completion, construct cohesive boundaries, and explain and blame away violations of those boundaries in terms of the sexual impropriety of outsiders. Maidstone's portrayal of London as a penitent spouse attempts to gloss the king as an ideal ruler and stabilize a political fiasco by translating it into a domestic rift, thereby allowing the relationship between sovereign and city to continue for the benefit of both parties. When these two London writers called their city a feminine New Troy, they were constructing an idea of the city and of the men in it—an ideology of masculine "self-knowledge and truth" based on feminine Otherness—which, when controlled, could produce politically motivated exemplary or deviant identities.

But the slippages that accumulate in the process of trying to construct masculine identity in the feminine city generate a host of excessive associations and identities that literally have no place in the ordered schemes favored by Gower and Maidstone. These placeless political associations, generated by the necessarily unstable eroticization of city space, represent utopian possibilities for new forms of civic behavior and identity—a kind of political *jouissance*. Only in the fantasy space of a feminine New Troy, with the multitudes of erotic and political associations embedded within it, could these alternative visions of an Other London arise.

## I. Rebels, Rulers, and Gower's Vision of the Future

The first book of Gower's *Vox Clamantis* is a space particularly suited to the entertainment of fantasies and alternative identities. First, Gower's own name is written in a riddle:

If you should ask the name of the writer, look, the word lies hidden and entangled within three verses about it. Take the first feet from "Godfrey" and add them to "John," and let "Wales" join its initial to them. Leaving off its head, let "Ter" furnish the other parts; and after such a line is arranged, the right sequence of the name is clear.[22]

This rather precious obfuscation of the identity of the poet sets the stage for the more serious confusions of generic identity found in book 1 of *Vox*: Gower claims to have had dreams which will "furnish memorable tokens of a certain occurrence" (p. 50), but then proceeds to narrate some of the events of the 1381 rising as though he had witnessed them personally. Along the way, he invokes elements of classical myth, pastoral idyll, apocalyptic prophecy, beast fable, travelogue, and moral exemplum. Furthermore, he refuses to identify exactly what kind of dream, or vision, or waking nightmare he is having: "In this dream I did not spend the hours which sleep requires, although I do imagine seeing this calamity in my dreams" (p. 95) ["Non dedimus sompno quas sompnus postulat horas, / Tale licet sompnis fingo videre malum"].[23]

These confusions of identity, genre, and levels of consciousness contribute to the general sense of nightmarish instability that Gower is trying to invoke, and have been discussed as aspects of the author's poetic achievement.[24] But the sheer elusiveness of the terminology at work in book 1 places both the poem and the poet in a chaotic zone of shape-changes, a place where Gower's stated project frequently gets away from him. Between and across the boundaries of the several established genres, as well as between the boundaries of competing authorial personae, are gaps and openings and revealing links in which something other than what Gower says he means gets said.

Gower's first fantasy[25] is that England was a paradise before the revolt. The land was fertile, meadows grew with flowers, birds sang with untutored throats, and fountains flowed from brooks, just like the gardens of Paradise (p. 52):

[22] John Gower, *The Major Latin Works of John Gower*, trans. Eric W. Stockton (Seattle: University of Washington Press, 1962), p. 50. Subsequent quotations of *Vox Clamantis* in English translation will be cited parenthetically in the text according to page numbers in Stockton's edition.

[23] John Gower, *The Complete Works of John Gower*, ed. G. C. Macaulay, 4 vols. (Oxford: Clarendon Press, 1902), vol. 4, 1:2139–40. Subsequent quotations of Gower's Latin will be cited parenthetically according to line numbers in Macaulay's edition.

[24] See John H. Fisher, *John Gower: Moral Philosopher and Friend of Chaucer* (New York: New York University Press, 1964), pp. 170–73.

[25] Here and throughout, I mean by the word "fantasy" a heavily invested alternative to reality that may or may not be consciously constructed. There is a debate in psychoanalytic discourse as to whether fantasy (or "phantasy") properly denotes a conscious desire, like daydreaming, or an aspect of the unconscious process, like the dreamwork. Freud

This sole region laid claim to all that land, air and sea fostered and held good. Here was the ornament of the globe, the flower of the world, the crowning glory of things, containing every delight that enjoyment seeks. It was planted with trees, sown with greenery, and surpassing in every gift which man asks for himself.

Exemplifying the perfect accord between man and nature, England is described here as a Cockaynian realm of plenty. The bountiful, open paradise provided its citizens with all they could possibly desire.

Moving from a mode of exaggerated pastoral topography to the explicitly fantastic generic structure of a dream vision, Gower begins his discussion of the revolt itself by transforming the rebels into animals. The already-unsettled vision narrative is augmented by a perverse catalog of animals in which the rebellious bands are depicted as nightmarish mobs of asses, oxen, swine, dogs, cats, foxes, birds, flies, and frogs. These unnatural beings, neither fully human nor fully beast, trample over the English countryside and ruin everything in their path.

In the course of this generic shift, London is transformed into a feminine New Troy:

On my right I then thought I saw New Troy, which was powerless as a widow. Ordinarily surrounded by walls, it lay exposed without any wall, and the city gate could not shut its bars. (p. 69)

> [A dextrisque nouam me tunc vidisse putabam
> Troiam, que vidue languida more fuit:
> Que solet ex muris cingi patuit sine muro,
> Nec potuit seras claudere porta suas.] [lines 879–82]

The vulnerable, open widow is caught unawares; "stunned at the coming of such a strange calamity" (p. 70) ["stupet ignotum tale venire malum" (line 894)], she is defenseless and eligible for the rebels' bestial plunder.

The fantasy of the city as an utterly powerless widow turns the invading rebels into rapists: ". . . the savage throngs approached the

---

himself was unable to distinguish between the two types, since he found that the contents of both conscious and unconscious fantasies "often coincide with one another even down to their details"; *The Standard Edition of the Complete Psychological Works of Sigmund Freud*, trans. and ed. James Strachey et al., 24 vols. (London: Hogarth, 1953–74), 7:165 n. 2. What Freud *was* able to say definitively about fantasies is that they always seek to express themselves (they will out), and they always reflect a desire on the part of the subject—regardless of his or her awareness of this desire. See Laplanche and Pontalis, *Language of Psychoanalysis*, pp. 314–19.

city . . . and entered it by violence" (p. 70) ["adeunt vrbem turbe violenter agrestes, / Et . . . ingrediuntur eam" (lines 911–12)]. The previous description of the rebels as generally brutish is extended here into a realm of ferociously masculine sexuality as the physical bounty of the feminine city is plundered by the animals; the madness "plunged into any—and everything forbidden" (p. 70) ["in vetitum quodlibet ipse ruit" (line 900)]. The initial shape-change of the rebels into animals is revised again as the invaders take on a human, criminal form to correspond with the city's transformation into a vulnerable woman.

This description in *Vox* of the hypermasculine rebels forms part of a contemporary discursive network linking deviant political behavior with deviant sexual behavior, and is in accord with a similar tactic used by Walsingham to describe the rebels' entrance into the private apartments of the king:

Who would believe that peasants, and not just regular peasants, but the lowliest kind, not only in groups, but even individually, would dare to plunge into the bedroom of the King, and that of his mother, with the nastiest of sticks, . . . and that when they had done all of these things (both, like we said, in crowds as well as individually having gone into the rooms), they grew haughty and started sitting, lying, and joking around on the King's bed; then, on top of this, they propositioned the mother of the King with kisses.[26]

The sexual depravity ascribed to the rebels, represented here poking their nasty sticks into places they do not belong, is in keeping with other contemporary opinions that asserted the debauchery of the rustics. Walsingham reports that some people, in trying to determine the causes of the revolt, held the peasantry morally responsible as a whole because of their generally dissolute ways of life. They are said to spend their nights drinking and swearing false oaths ("noctes insomnes in potationibus, ebrietatibus, et perjuriis transigentes"), and their days fighting with each other ("rixando, litigando, cum proximis con-

---

[26] My translation of Walsingham, *Historia Anglicana*, 1:459. The Latin reads: "Nam quis unquam credidisset, non solum rusticos, sed rusticorum abjectissimos, non plures, sed singulos, audere thalamum Regis, vel matris eius, cum baculis subintrare vilissimis, . . . Et cum haec omnia facerent, et, ut diximus, plerique soli in cameras concessissent, et sedendo, jacendo, jocando, super lectum Regis insolescerent; et insuper, matrem Regis ad oscula invitarent quidam."

tendendo"). They are given to wantonness, accustomed to fornication, stained with adultery ("libidini dediti, fornicationibus assueti, adulteriis maculati"), and finally, their sexuality is bestial. In a significant twist on an old phrase, Walsingham reports that every single one of them "whinnied after" his neighbor's wife: ". . . unusquisque post uxorem proximi sui hinniebat."[27] The chronicler's assertion that people generally had a low opinion of the peasants, and that they associated them particularly with sexual wrongdoings, places Gower's suggestion that the rebels were animalistic rapists of the chaste city in a tradition of innuendo-laden political discourse.

But the peasants were not the only ones blamed for the revolt. Walsingham also reports that some people thought the rebellion was due to the moral failures of the lords, who provided a bad example for those under them by living in incest and violating the sacrament of marriage: "Alii peccatis dominorum ascribebant causam malorum, qui in Deum erant fictae fidei . . . vivendo incesti, violatores conjugii."[28] That sexually immoral behavior could be blamed for contributing to the rising of 1381 indicates not only how intertwined the two discourses of erotics and politics were, but also the extent to which these discourses were widely available for appropriation within and across social boundaries. That is, despite his notorious hostility toward the rebels, Walsingham concedes via these reports that what happened in 1381 may have been the result of the misgovernment of the upper tiers of society, and not necessarily solely attributable to the generally sinful nature of the lower tiers.

Similarly, Gower's attempts to link political behavior to sexual behavior show the wide availability of sexual metaphors for political uses. But his attempts, precisely because of the easy availability and mobile signifying power of the metaphors, also slide around and end up pointing toward something other than what the poet claims he means. Although Gower explicitly blames the revolt on the innate grossness of the rabble in book 1 of Vox, he also frequently admits to other causes and thus contradicts the blame he places on the peasants elsewhere in the poem. For example, in the midst of his description of how perfect England was before the revolt, when all kinds of birds sang wonderful songs, he notes that

[27] Walsingham, ibid., 2:12.
[28] Ibid.

Philomena recovered her lost property of speech and by her notes proclaimed what had been done. And Procne sang too of her sister's lost virginity—for so great are the tricks in love. (p. 53)

As a demonstration of the triumph of good over evil, no doubt the example of Philomena and Procne is meant to suggest the free-flowing nature of truth before the revolt muddied everything. But it is a particularly unfortunate example, suggesting as it does that reports of vicious rape and mutilation were declared throughout the supposed paradise. Gower's artificial "before and after" scenario, dictated by his narrative stance of telling an already fulfilled prophecy, requires him to ignore England's prerevolt imperfections even as he discloses them.

The portrayal late in book 1 of the postlapsarian England, after the idyllic "second paradise" was ruined by the rebels, further reveals that the country had been imperfect long before the revolt. Gower's presumed point is that the rising bereft England and its citizens of the free-flowing natural bounty of the realm and corrupted its "natural" hierarchies of political, social, and religious order. The rebels single-handedly destroyed England to such a degree that the narrator does not even recognize his homeland. He asks an old man, "Tell me, what island is this?" The man answers by describing the ravaged land, but with a special emphasis on the historical division of the English people:

This once used to be called the Island of Brut, an exile. Diana gave it to him out of pity. The people of this land are wild. Their way of life involves far more quarreling than love. Because this people sprang from different tribes, it has faults of a varied nature. . . . This land, which bloodshed and slaughters and wars always control, was born of mixed stock. The unsightly fields bring forth bitter wormwood, and by this fruit the land shows how harsh it is. (p. 92)

> [Exulis hec dici nuper solet Insula Bruti,
> Quam sibi compaciens ipsa Diana dabat.
> Huius enim terre gens hec est inchola, ritus
> Cuius amore procul dissona plura tenet.
> Nam quia gens variis hec est de gentibus orta,
> Errores varie condicionis habet
>
> . . . . . . . . . . . . . . . . . . . .
> Hec humus est illa vario de germine nata,
> Quam cruor et cedes bellaque semper habent:
> Tristia deformes pariunt absinthia campi,
> Terraque de fructu quam sit amara docet.] (lines 1963–68, 1977–80)

The language here suggests that England's problems are historical, per-petual, and perhaps even genetic. So it is not that Gower's England is a place transformed by the rebellion, but that the country was never in accord to begin with. Even Geoffrey of Monmouth's founding myth has a revised emphasis: no longer divinely prophesied as the place that will surpass Troy, now England has been given to the loser out of pity.

Not only is England shown to have been imperfect well before the re-volt, but the rebels themselves come in for less and less of the blame for their rising in the mutating strangeness of Gower's fantasy space. The supposed rapists of New Troy are not simply the hypermasculine crim-inals Gower claims them to be; their misdeeds are instead attributable to deviant feminine sexuality:

And time and time again the cruel Coppa, following on foot, urged her cock on toward various things which she had an idea were mischievous. The chat-terer made up in talk for what she could not do in deeds, and she alone incited a thousand to general wickedness. And when the gander coupled with her, he deserted his own goose and aspired to new game everywhere. (p. 62)[29]

> [Multociensque suum fera Coppa pedisseca gallum
> Prouocat ad varia que putat esse mala;
> Quod nequit in factis ex dictis garrula suplet,
> Ad commune nephas milleque sola mouet.
> Ancer et ipse suam, cum qua se miscuit, aucam
> Linquit, et in predam spirat vbique nouam.] (lines 545–50)

The terrible rapists turn out to be the henpecked dupes of a monstrous feminine symbol of misrule.[30]

---

[29] Macaulay's note (Gower, *Complete Works*, p. 374 n. 545) reads "*Coppa*: used as a fa-miliar name for a hen in the *Speculum Stultorum*, pp. 55, 58, and evidently connected with 'Coppen' or 'Coppe,' which is the name of one of Chantecleer's daughters in the Low-German and English *Reynard*."

[30] Symbols of feminine misrule were plentiful in Gower's era, and they were often linked to political misrule. Pointing out the several similarities between Chaucer's Wife of Bath and the rebels of 1381 (inferior social status, exclusion from and consequent hos-tility toward haute literate circles), Susan Crane argues that the Wife's *Prologue* is per-haps Chaucer's most overlooked response to the rebellion. Alison "identifies herself as the voice of a maligned group," and her tearing out the page of Jankyn's Book of Wicked Wives is seen by Crane as analogous to the rebels' famed violence against texts; "The Writing Lesson of 1381," in Barbara Hanawalt, ed., *Chaucer's England: Literature in Historical Context* (Minneapolis: University of Minnesota Press, 1992), p. 215. Moreover, the Wife's *Prologue* and Gower's earlier French poem, *Mirour de l'Omme* (trans. William Burton Wilson [East Lansing, Mich.: Colleagues, 1992], pp. 347–48), provide a com-bined contribution to the relationship between unruly commons and unruly women in

Likewise, Gower's metaphor for London—a widow—underscores the instability of the commonplace association of political and sexual misbehavior. On the one hand, widows were an especially vulnerable group and were acknowledged as such in late medieval London with special city customs relating to their financial protection. But widows were also an important part of the city's economic structure, and were not given their dead husbands' property and goods simply out of charity, but were expected to participate in the economy of the city by continuing their husbands' businesses, often even becoming members of the guilds to which their deceased husbands had belonged.[31] The image of an economically independent widow was frequently conflated during the period with the image of a sexually voracious woman (witness Alison of Bath)—an ambivalence that Gower himself had helped to reinforce in his *Mirour de l'Omme*:

But those merry widows—wearing green with little flowers of pearls and embroidery to attract new love affairs to their bedrooms—do not at all resemble the turtledove. . . . I distrust the old hag who is prettified when her breasts are dried up.[32]

It is this image of the deceitful, sexually consuming widow to which Gower reverts in book 1 of *Vox Clamantis*. Just as the monstrous rebels are revised and turned into victims of feminine misrule, so too is the victimized chaste city—the widow New Troy—transformed into a sex-

---

nearly parallel passages that describe the three evils that can beset a man. Gower writes: "There are three things with a single behavior that ravage mercilessly when they get the mastery. One is flood waters. Another is wild fire. The third is the multitude of little people when they are stirred up, for they will not be stopped by reason or by discipline." In *The Wife of Bath's Prologue*, Alison ventriloquizes one of her three old husbands in a way that echoes, with a significant difference, Gower's three evils: "Thow seyst that droppyng houses, and eek smoke, / And chidyng wyves maken men to flee / Out of hir owene houses; a, benedictee!" (lines 278–80). Misbehaving women and rising commons are not only intolerable, they are symbolically interchangeable.

[31] See Caroline M. Barron, "The Widow's World in Later Medieval London," in Caroline M. Barron and Anne F. Sutton, eds., *Medieval London Widows: 1300–1500* (London: Hambledon, 1994), pp. xiii–xxxiv. The degree of economic self-sufficiency afforded to women, and especially to widows, in the late fourteenth century has been seen as evidence of a "golden age" for women during the period. See Caroline M. Barron, "The 'Golden Age' of Women in Medieval London," *Medieval Women in Southern England*, Reading Medieval Studies, vol. 15 (Reading: Graduate Centre for Medieval Studies, University of Reading Press, 1989), pp. 35–58.

[32] Gower, *Mirour*, p. 246.

ually voracious, monstrous woman. London as New Troy is not vulnerable; she is a merry widow who willingly spread her gates open for the rebels: "Everything was surrendered. We unlocked our doors to the enemy and faith was kept only in faithless treason" (p. 70) ["Omnia traduntur, postes reserauimus hosti, / Et fit in infida prodicione fides" (lines 903–4)].[33] The moral blame for the rape/invasion thus lies within the city, the erstwhile victim, herself: "O the degenerate nature of our former city, which allowed the madly raging rabble to take up arms!" (p. 71) ["O denaturans vrbis natura prioris, / Que vulgi furias arma mouere sinis!" (lines 979–80)]. Gower's description of the city opening herself up for the rebels' entrance is not unlike his earlier condemnation of a prostitute plying her trade in Southwark:

Every day of the week, behold, Wantonness leads her life near the stews. Very basely she drags out her life there, where she is every man's companion, caring nought to what class he belongs. . . . Ah, whore, . . . thus you are common in your wantonness as the roads of the country are common, over which all men, both worthy and miserable, great and small, may go at will.[34]

---

[33] Gower's allusion here to faithless Londoners admitting the rebels into the city intersects with several other contemporary opinions regarding how the rebels gained entrance. Dobson records a group of chronicle entries that blame the poor of the city and its environs: *Letter-Book H*, the Anonimalle chronicler, and Walsingham all more or less agree that the "perfidious commoners" of London and its suburb, Southwark, demanded that the bridge be lowered for the rebels to cross into the city; see Dobson, *Peasants' Revolt*, pp. 156, 168–69, 209. Froissart dramatically adds to this consensus by claiming that poor Londoners thought to themselves, "why do we not let these good people enter into the city? they are our fellows, and that that they do is for us"; Dobson, ibid., p. 188. Another grouping of records suggests that the blame lay with a more established and privileged segment of London's population, but does not explicitly articulate this charge. Knighton, *Chronicle*, pp. 210–11, says that the rebels passed over the bridge with no opposition, even though the citizens had long known that they were coming ("et tamen ut dicebatur ciues Londonienses de eorum aduentu longo ante tempore intellexerunt"). *The Westminster Chronicle, 1381–1394*, eds. and trans. L. C. Hector and Barbara Harvey (Oxford: Clarendon Press, 1982) similarly suggests that "the whole of London, the prey of internal confusion and, as many thought, of some degree of internal dissension, was without a clear view of what was to be done" (p. 9). The rumor that several treasonous aldermen conspired to admit the rebels has been discredited because of the "unscrupulously partisan" nature of the supporting documents: the jurors' returns of 1382. These two returns, which accused certain members of the victualling party of treasonously plotting the destruction of the city, had their genesis in the strife between the mayoral factions of Brembre and John Northampton. See B. Wilkinson, "The Peasants' Revolt of 1381," *Speculum* 15 (1940): 12–35, for a discussion and transcription of the jurors' return of November 4, 1382; and Andre Reville, *Le Soulevement des travailleurs d'Angleterre en 1381* (Paris, 1898), pp. 190–96, for the return of November 20.

[34] Gower, *Mirour*, p. 127.

The indiscriminate city is too common, its entrance open to all comers like a prostitute.

But Gower's blaming of the victim for her own rape disguises the ultimate target of his censure. London as a defenseless widow should have been protected, and London as a promiscuous widow should have been controlled. The men charged with these duties utterly failed to perform when the moment came:

No boldness of a Hector or Troilus defeated anything then, but instead those who were defeated suffered the whole affair without courage. Priam did not shine then with his usual honor; instead, the master put up with whatever the servant did to him. (p. 72)

> [Hectoris aut Troili nil tunc audacia vicit,
> Quin magis hii victi rem sine corde sinunt;
> Nec solito Priamus fulsit tunc liber honore,
> Set patitur dominus quid sibi seruus agat.] (lines 993–96)

The London rulership is as effectively absent as the widowed city's dead husband.[35] Gower's insistently martial metaphor, with its pathetic catalog of defeated Trojan war heroes, is not so much a lamentation for the loss of the city as it is a condemnation of London's leading men. The protectors and controllers of the feminine city failed to do their masculine jobs; in essence, they failed to be men. As one of the identities possible in the fantasy space of New Troy, the emasculated man emerges from Gower's uncontrollable metaphors: "The peasant attacked and the knight in the city did not resist" (p. 71) ["Rusticus agreditur, miles nec in vrbe resistit" (line 991)]. The men in charge of London are, at best, not men.[36]

At worst, though, these unmanly men are traitors. Gower's comparison of the London rulers with notorious traitors from Troy crystallizes the suggestive undertones from elsewhere in the poem into blatant criticism of the upper tiers of English society. Not content to merely emas-

---

[35] No doubt Gower would argue that the city's deceased husband is Edward III (d. 1377), the king who was considered a paragon of masculinity before senility and Alice Perrers took their toll on him.

[36] Knighton, *Chronicle*, pp. 212–13, similarly remarks: "The knights who were to accompany [the king] foolishly allowed their ardour to cool, lamentably hiding the boldness of their spirit, and as though struck by some womanish fear (quasi timore femineo), not daring to go out, stayed in the Tower."

culate them, Gower likens the rulers to deceitful Trojans who helped destroy their own city:

Behold, even the old man Calchas, whose wisdom was greater than everyone's, then knew no course of action. Antenor did not know then by what means to arrange peace treaties; instead the great frenzy destroyed all his efforts. (p. 71)

> [Ecce senem Calcas, cuius sapiencia maior
> Omnibus est, nullum tunc sapuisse modum:
> Anthenor ex pactis componere federa pacis
> Tunc nequit, immo furor omne resoluit opus.] (lines 961–64)

Calchas, a prophet who switched sides and joined the Greeks, and Antenor, a self-server who helped the Greeks orchestrate the horse trick, are represented here in surprisingly sympathetic language, as though Gower were unaware of the men's notoriety as traitors.

An even more striking example of the way Gower's Trojan metaphor resists his supposed point is his depiction of the death of Simon Sudbury, Archbishop of Canterbury, at the hands of the rebels. Sudbury is introduced "as if through a symbol" ["quasi per figuram"] as "the high priest Helenus, who served Troy's Palladium at the altar" (p. 72). But Helenus not only served the Palladium, he *sold* it to Antenor and Aeneas in an act widely thought to be instrumental in causing the destruction of the city. The rebels charged Sudbury with treason and executed him for it; Gower, surprisingly, reasserts the rebels' interpretation of treason by figuring Sudbury as Helenus.

The slippage that occurs in Gower's poem in the spaces between established genres makes a phenomenal mess of competing significances and interpretations of the revolt. Troy is a supersaturated symbol with such a wide range of references that it often seems as though Gower sat down to write "Troy style," pulled out at random a bunch of mythological names, and plugged them in as metaphors without considering what those names meant (several times he even lists Greek and Trojan names together and represents them as equally victimized by the invasion of New Troy). Besides this instability of the Trojan overlay, Gower's eroticization of the city's relationship with the rebels likewise eludes his moral grasp and creates masculine identities that are far from what we may assume he intended. The poet is at all points undermining his condemnation of the rebels to such a degree that his "mistakes" might be seen as systematic—perhaps unconscious, but with a consistent logic behind them nevertheless. The logic behind book 1 is the rest of the poem called *Vox Clamantis*, composed before the revolt.

The "mistakes" in book 1 are in keeping with the strategies and motives of the rest of *Vox*, a long-winded poem in which Gower attacks the moral laxity of all social groups and subgroups of England, but with a special emphasis on the rife corruption among the leadership of the two higher estates. Aligning his authorial persona with the lower classes, Gower claims that his *Vox Clamantis*, or "Voice of One Crying," is a representation of the *vox populi*; his is the voice of the little people, crying out against the injustice of the secular and clerical governors of the country. The passages in book 1 that criticize these leaders and indicate that their perversion contributed to the rebellion are thus not mistakes at all, but instead represent a continuation of the moralist's original thesis: that the rulers are primarily responsible for the damage being done to England.

In its call for reform in the upper tiers of society, the bulk of Gower's *Vox* constantly veers toward and draws upon many of the same generative assumptions as the voices of the rebels themselves. Book 1, added as a preface to the poem immediately after the revolt, can be seen as an attempt to address this disquieting similitude by distancing Gower's *vox* from the riotous *vox populi* of the rebels in 1381. Steven Justice, for example, has recently remarked that Gower's depiction of the rebels as beasts in book 1 constitutes a "virtuoso mockery" that keeps Gower's own voice from being too similar to theirs; the characterization of them as "hopelessly undiscursive" successfully "erases any trace of verbal performance on the part of the rebels and disembarrasses Gower's own claim—to represent the popular voice—of a discrediting similarity."[37] But book 1 is a compensatory act in the extreme and, like all compensatory acts, embarrassingly traceable in its intent. The numerous slips and holes in Gower's attempts to color the rebels bad do more than thoroughly compromise his project to discredit them; they also reveal his strategy of self-justification as a social critic.[38]

---

[37] Steven Justice, *Writing and Rebellion: England in 1381* (Berkeley: University of California Press, 1994), pp. 212, 213.

[38] Justice makes a very similar point (ibid., p. 209). The difference in my view is that Gower's strategies of self-reconstruction become visible in light of his *failure* to discredit the rebels, as opposed to his success at doing so.

Until the revolt presented him with an opportunity to speak on the same side as his audience, Gower was squarely on the outside of the London political scene. Not only did he live in Southwark, a place that functioned as "a dumping ground and exclusion zone for early modern London,"[39] but he was ideologically in the suburbs as well. *Mirour de l'Omme* and *Vox Clamantis* often seem like the same poem written in two different languages: they both catalog the sins of the estates, with variants, and examples, and correctives. They both argue that English social life should return to its moral center, obey its time-honored hierarchies, and stop deviating from the old, good ways. The man Chaucer called "moral Gower" was forever repeating the same moral over and over again; there was no currency to his message. But with the outbreak of the revolt, suddenly Gower's message shifts from one of tired, outdated moralism to dangerously relevant social criticism. Depicting himself wandering across the countryside hiding from the violent mob, Gower elaborates on his difficult position:

I was not at liberty to confide secrets to anyone; on the contrary, my silent lips withheld their words. . . . Whenever I was on the point of speaking, I considered myself to be in ambush; and looking upon the ground, I uttered only a few words. When my lot forced me to say something to somebody, I passed the time idly with glib talk. Again and again a soft answer turned away wrath, and my very safety depended upon agreeable words. (p. 82)

> [Non michi libertas cuiquam secreta loquendi
> Tunc fuit, immo silens os sua verba tenet.
> . . . . . . . . . . . . . . . . . . . .
> Memet in insidiis semper locuturus habebam,
> Verbaque sum spectans pauca locutus humum:
> Tempora cum blandis absumpsi vanaque verbis,
> Dum mea sors cuiquam cogerat vlla loqui.
> Iram multociens frangit responsio mollis,
> Dulcibus ex verbis tunc fuit ipsa salus.] (lines 1493–94, 1505–10)

But Gower is not afraid of the rebels here; he is afraid for the reception of his *Vox* after the revolt, when his customary blaming of the two higher estates is no longer a worn-out message but is instead a dangerously

---

[39] Wallace, "Absent City," p. 60. See also Martha Carlin, *Medieval Southwark* (London: Hambledon Press, 1996), for the economic, political, and social marginalization of medieval Southwark.

seditious trope. By publishing *Vox* anyway, with book 1 as a provocative preface, Gower takes the risk of establishing himself as a voice crying out for good reason and as a social critic who is not behind the times, but painfully in tune with them. The revolt permits Gower to speak, for once, with real contemporary relevance.

With a renewed sense of being called, Gower constructs himself as a prophet and a leader at the end of book 1 of *Vox*. Just as Cassandra's unheeded prophecy about Troy came true, so had Gower's own warnings (in his earlier poetry) about the impending doom of New Troy fallen on deaf ears. His prophecy having been fulfilled in the form of the revolt, Gower boldly ventures to offer himself as a political leader: fleeing the burning New Troy in a ship, buffeted by storms "more grievous than Styx" (p. 85), passing by a sea-monster "brother to Scylla, raging more than Charybdis" (p. 87), losing the steersman (p. 87), and finally putting in at an unrecognized but eerily familiar place (p. 92), the poet figures himself as Aeneas.

But just as Aeneas initially met with opposition in Italy, so does Gower's leader-persona see that he has a lot of work to do to renew England. Coming out of his dream, and with a new sense of the importance of his mission, the narrator sets his sights on writing for the sake of the new society:

O wakeful sleep, whose difficult meaning my writings must now tell! . . . Let the task of long standing which is wontedly mine now yield, and let my former care be banished by this new one. (p. 95)

> [O vigiles sompni, quorum sentencia scriptis
> Ammodo difficilis est recitanda meis!
>
> . . . . . . . . . . . . . . . . . . . . . . . . . . .
>
> Quod solet esse michi vetus hoc opus ammodo cedat,
> Sit prior et cura cura repulsa noua.] (lines 2145–46, 2149–50)

Although Gower is not writing anything new (it is still the same old *Vox*, after all), he is reinterpreting how his work should be read: *Vox Clamantis* is, according to the postrevolt Gower, a utopian manual for the postrevolt England. Similarly, Gower's authorial persona is no longer that of a single voice crying (unheeded) in the wilderness of Southwark; his is a London voice bravely crying for obviously necessary social reform.

Gower's social criticism, like the rebels' own demands for change, rests on a backward-looking idealism and imagines a future defined by an illusory golden age of relations between and among the estates. The vision of the future is an idealized fantasy of the past, when kings were kings (and neither besotted old men nor boys) and knights were knights (and not traitors), when the rulers of the country were responsible for and protective of the people under them, and when the clergy was not made up of mercenaries, buying and selling their offices. Gower has not succeeded in erasing any of these retro-radical ideas from his poem; on the contrary, his addition of book 1 to *Vox* reasserts the need for radical reform and ultimately serves to reassert the rebels' grievances.[40] It is in this sense that Gower's political vision is utopian: not despite, but because of the rising of 1381, the retrospective idealism of *Vox Clamantis* becomes a plausible plan for the future.

## II. Ricardian Imperialism Yields to Rome

Eleven years after his manual for the future appeared, political and social conditions had not improved along the lines Gower had called for. The years between 1381 and 1392 saw more violence and discord in London, fierce factional struggles and vindictive squabbles among civic and royal government officials, and, much to Gower's disappointment, the maturation of Richard II from a boy-king with great promise to a willful and unstable tyrant.[41] The best example of Richard's tyranny is the so-called "quarrel" he had with the city of London when the citizens refused to lend him large sums of money. Richard retaliated by sus-

[40] That Gower's moral censure of the upper tiers of English society is akin to the rebels' own views does not mean that Gower "sympathized with" the revolt. No doubt he was horrified by what happened in June of 1381—not just because of the outrageous acts of violence but also because, in his view, the lower tiers of the population had no business in governmental affairs, no right to assert themselves, and no proper voice with which to complain (even if they had a legitimate grievance). The right and responsibility to speak out about social and political problems is one Gower firmly reserves for himself, or men like him. The rebels' violation of their proper place in the tripartite social structure is surely as noxious to Gower as the corruption and treason of the knights and clerics in the upper levels of the hierarchy.

[41] An indication of Gower's changing views about Richard II might be noted in his textual emendations to his English poem, *Confessio Amantis*, in the years leading up to the quarrel: In 1390, he dedicated it to Richard; by 1392, he had removed those parts of the poem praising the king; and in 1393, he rededicated *Confessio* to Henry of Lancaster. See Macaulay's introduction to volume 4, pp. xxviii–xxix.

pending the city's customary freedoms, removing the mayor and the sheriffs of London from their offices and putting them in jail, and replacing them with men hand-picked by himself to act as wardens and keepers of the city. He imposed huge fines on the city for mishandling its affairs, and finally placed the "entire income" of London at his own disposal.[42]

In August of 1392, the citizens of London put on a sumptuous pageant in an effort to convince Richard to relent and restore their customary liberties. The pageant was wildly extravagant: the conduits flowed with white and red wine, the streets were decorated with banners and flowers, and parades of guildsmen and city officers in costume turned out to greet the king. Expensive gifts were lavished on Richard and his wife, Anne of Bohemia, and a tableau of John the Baptist in the wilderness and a chorus of angels were staged for the king's pleasure, all at considerable cost to the Londoners.[43]

Richard Maidstone's *Concordia Facta inter Regem Riccardum II et Civitatem Londonie*, written and dedicated to Richard II in 1393, records the events of the pageant as though the author had witnessed them in person. Unlike Gower, Maidstone claims his poem to be an account of what actually happened; it is not a dream or an explicitly fantastic space. The *Concordia* emphasizes the enthusiasm of the Londoners for their task and Richard's goodness and grace in accepting their apologies. The author's perspective is that of a loyalist to the king, a view announced in his dedication: "O Richard, as you are allied to me by the double bond of name and authority, I am impelled by Friendship and honored to recount for you in meter the splendid sights which I beheld of late in

---

[42] Barron, "Quarrel," p. 189. For the economic and political contexts of the quarrel, see also Ruth Bird, *The Turbulent London of Richard II* (London: Longmans, 1949), pp. 102–9; May McKisack, *The Fourteenth Century* (Oxford: Clarendon Press, 1959), pp. 467–68; and Pamela Nightingale, *A Medieval Mercantile Community* (New Haven, Conn.: Yale University Press, 1995), pp. 326–37, who suggests that the citizens may have refused the king his loan because of a widespread shortage of coin, or a genuine crisis of cash availability. It is still unclear how the Londoners had the money (or for that matter, the time) to stage an elaborately organized and expensive reconciliation ceremony on such short notice and with such limited cash.

[43] Besides Maidstone's poem, the pageant is described in Knighton, *Chronicle*, pp. 547–49; Walsingham, *Historia Anglicana*, 2:207–11; and the *Westminster Chronicle*, pp. 503–9. See also Helen Suggett, "A Letter Describing Richard II's Reconciliation with the City of London, 1392," *English Historical Review* 62 (1947): 209–13, for a record of the pageant apparently written by a member of Richard's party.

Trenovant."[44] Maidstone's poem thus declares itself a celebratory narration of an exemplary moment in the relationship between city and sovereign. The king is "more handsome than Paris," "peace-making, clement, and careful to destroy nothing good" (p. 167); London is decorated in splendid finery as the "entire city unites" (p. 171) ["tota cohors sociatur"][45] to greet its king.

Like Gower before him, Maidstone calls on a sexualized metaphor to describe the relationship between New Troy and the men in the city. In a cross between a wedding ceremony and a renewal of vows, the pageant celebrates the reunion of Richard and London as husband and wife. Richard's is an idealized masculine identity in relation to this city-as-woman, which is portrayed here as a wife who erred against her lord by refusing him services. In keeping with Maidstone's allegiance to Richard, London's misbehavior—and not the king's—caused the "bridegroom to forsake his bridal chamber" (p. 167) ["desereret thalamum sponsus ut ipse suum" (line 24)]. But because of the city's fine display, lavish gifts, and demonstration of utter subjection to Richard, he now desires to come again to his spouse.

When Richard, the groom inclined but not yet committed to forgiveness, enters into his chastened, decorated bride, he is presented with the emblematic sword and keys of London—tokens signifying his right to enter the city, his wife, whether by force or consent, respectively. Upon presenting the king with these patently phallic symbols, the keeper of the city says to him, "Let not the most beautiful walls in the kingdom be rent nor torn, for they are the king's own and whatever is in them" (p. 181) ["Non laceret, non dilaniet pulcherrima regni / Menia, nam sua sunt, quicquid et exstat in hiis" (lines 145–46)]. The keeper's words suggest that the city walls constitute a "vaginal symbol" complementing the phallic tokens of entrance presented to the king, thereby showing Richard that he is entitled to London's goods and services just as a husband is entitled to sex with his wife under the terms of the marital *debitum*. Acknowledging that the king can enter his wife with or without her consent, the city here asks not to be

---

[44] *Concordia*, p. 163. All subsequent quotations of Maidstone's poem in English translation will be cited parenthetically in the text according to the page numbers in Smith's edition.

[45] *Concordia*, line 55. Subsequent quotations of Maidstone's Latin will be cited parenthetically according to the line numbers in Smith's edition.

raped.[46] To reinforce the image of the city's sexual submissiveness, the gifts she gives are announced as signs "that the citizens now yield themselves—bodies, riches, the Trojan citadel, their all" (p. 189) ["dantur in hoc signum quod se reddunt modo cives— / Corpora, divicias, Pergama, queque sua" (lines 213–14)].

Anne of Bohemia's role in the pageant further demonstrates how a good wife ought to behave with her king. The queen models an ideal of civic behavior by throwing herself at the king's feet and begging for the city to be forgiven: "'Beloved,' she says, 'my king, my spouse, my strength, my life . . . who among all kings possesses a city that has honored him like this one this day?'" (p. 217). The king responds to the pleas of his wife and declares himself ready to forgive London her waywardness. The citizens, taking their cue from Anne, then fall to their knees rejoicing and praising Richard: "'Long live the king! May the king live forever!'" (p. 225). The celebratory narrative concludes with the citizens united in posture and in speech, all agreeing that to be subject to Richard is to be fulfilled. Maidstone's poem demonstrates to the king that the citizens accept his authority wholly and that his identity as a masculine ruler is secure—an idea symbolized by the prostration of the Londoners and by their presentation to him of the sword and keys of the city.

But of course the Londoners are not putting on this dramatic display of abjection unprompted. Their liberties having been removed (along with their elected officials and their legal means of redress—the royal court), and under threat of even greater violation and restriction, the citizens are participating in what Louise Fradenburg calls a communitarian experience—a ritual that "helps to obscure constraint" through "a remaking of the subject to enable identification with, and idealization of, an authority experienced as liberating and unifying rather than repressive and divisive."[47] The remaking of the subject of authority is evident in the pageant when throngs of notoriously competitive guildsmen join together in one parade:

Here are the Silversmiths, the Fishmongers, and beside them are the Mercers and the Vintners; here the Apothecaries, the Bakers, the Painters, and the

---

[46] Paul Strohm makes this point in *Hochon's Arrow* (Princeton, N.J.: Princeton University Press, 1992), p. 108.

[47] Louise Fradenburg, *City, Marriage, Tournament* (Madison: University of Wisconsin Press, 1991), p. 74.

Masons; here the Cutlers, Shearers, and Armourers; here the Carpenters, the Tailors, the Menders. . . . Each guild is clearly delineated by its own livery. Whoever should witness these squadrons, I think, would not doubt that he was seeing the forms of an angelic order. (pp. 173–77)

As recorded in the *Letter-Books*, however, guildsmen in the victualling trades were famously opposed to their counterparts in the nonvictualling trades, and vice versa—a relationship symbolized by the fierce competition and often violent strife during the early and mid-1380s between Mayor Brembre, who was a grocer, and his archrival, Mayor John Northampton, a draper. The pageant's collection of bakers and vintners marching alongside painters and masons, and fishmongers alongside mercers, while not impossible to imagine, constitutes an unusual and purposeful alliance.[48]

The guildsmen's unity is matched by other unlikely social and political unions: men and women parade together; leading citizens and aldermen brush shoulders with a criminal from Southwark (pp. 185–87); and "every order" of "the clergy of the entire church" (p. 169) forms in procession. Separate and often hostile bands of Londoners reconstruct themselves here as loving subjects of the king. In this way the pageant does "essential work for sovereign love; it is a way of securing desire for

---

[48] *Letter-Book H* records the skirmishes during the early 1380s between the two dominant trade factions, represented most famously by the mayoralties of Brembre and Northampton. This struggle is seen to continue even as late as 1389, when the legitimacy of the mayoral election of William Venour, a grocer, was contested by the loser, goldsmith Adam Bamme, who then went on to achieve the mayor's seat in 1390 in voting clearly delineated along the established factional lines between victuallers and nonvictuallers; *Calendar of Letter-Book H, 1375–1399*, in *Calendar of Letter-Books of the City of London*, ed. Reginald R. Sharpe (London: Corporation of London, 1907), pp. 348, 359. While there is some consensus that the overt conflict between these two parties died with Brembre in 1388, and that the city of London then proceeded to solidify a relatively unified and stable ruling oligarchy (see Barron, "Quarrel," p. 174, and Bird, *Turbulent London*, p. 119), perhaps the rivalry between the victuallers and nonvictuallers enjoyed a fate more like Northampton's: exiled for a time, only to return when court and city politics required its usefulness. Pamela Nightingale's study, "Capitalists, Crafts and Constitutional Change in Late Fourteenth-Century London," *Past and Present* 124 (1989): 3–35, shows members of the two parties to be surprisingly mobile, often forming alliances across party lines when circumstances could benefit from a unified front. Even more suggestive, Nightingale traces how the political machinations of the king, John of Gaunt, and others frequently depended on the trade groups' differences and exploited these local antagonisms for their own ends. We might then see the apparent unity of the competing guildsmen in the pageant as a symbolic response to this "divide and rule" strategy: a show of allegiance would be the most threatening display possible to a king who had depended on a bitterly divided citizenry for his own political viability.

hierarchy."[49] Richard operates as a source of unifying pressure on the Londoners; his threats to their autonomy impelled them to put aside their differences, however temporarily, and show themselves to the king as his faithful subjects.

At the same time that the Londoners' identities are being transformed by the obligatory *communitas* of the pageant ritual, however, they are also working to transform Richard's identity. Communitarian experience helps shape the *object* of sovereignty as well as its subjects, and should be thought of as a form of interpellation that not only calls the citizens loving subjects but also calls Richard a deserving object of that love. In other words, the apparently spontaneous demonstration of the citizens' love for the king is not so much a record of their love as it is a construction of Richard as a lovable king, and the narrative of this demonstration is likewise not so much a record of the past as it is a prescription for the future. The orderly unity and easy compliance of the once riotous and willful city exerts pressure on the king to respond in a complementary fashion.[50] By playing the role of a wayward but penitent wife, the city invites Richard to play a stern but forgiving husband in language often bordering on a command: "Let not the bridegroom hate the bridal chamber which he has always loved" (p. 181) ["Non oderit thalamum sponsus quem semper amavit" (line 147)]. The pageant constructs an ideal identity for the king through its elaborate insistence that he is not a tyrant: he *will* be forgiving, he *will* give them back their liberties, because, as everyone knows and says, he is just, fair, and good.

In Maidstone's account of the happy ceremony, the feminine space of the city is used to construct an exemplary masculine regnal identity for Richard. He can be all forgiveness and love as long as the city is all culpability and humble remorse. The Londoners' demonstration of their desire, and their entreaties for his forgiveness—mirrored in and augmented by the tableau of Anne on her knees—help to create the king as a paragon of masculine virtue. He loves and respects his wife, and his city, and will forbear. Through the use of the metaphor of sexual relations, Maidstone shows the city applying the gentle pressure of abjec-

[49] Fradenburg, *City*, p. 74.

[50] Gordon Kipling, "Richard II's 'Sumptuous Pageants' and the Idea of the Civic Triumph," in David M. Bergeron, ed., *Pageantry in the Shakespearean Theatre* (Athens, Ga.: University of Georgia Press, 1985), p. 97, suggests this dynamic in his discussion of the religious significance of the pageant: ". . . the king, through his willing acceptance of the Christlike role that the civic triumph thrusts upon him, must *imitate* Christ the King."

tion in an effort to influence the man with the power that no one disputes or resents.[51]

But women and cities could behave in more ways than the choices offered them here in the *Concordia*. As Fradenburg notes, the city is "created" by the king (in the sense that he grants its privileges) and is therefore a dependent in relation to the aristocratic order. But the city is equally defined by its separateness from that order:

The gift given to the city by the king is the gift of difference: the city is demarcated, contained, and inside it special activities are pursued. The creation of the city is thus an act of divisiveness.[52]

The problem with women and cities is that they had an unsettling margin of freedom with which to bestow their goods; they could trade as *femmes sole* without their husbands; buy, sell, and profit on their own; sue and be sued independent of their husbands; train their own apprentices and participate in their own mysteries. As Caroline Barron notes, the balance of power in marriage would correspond to these economic realities.[53]

If we see London, the feminine city, as a successful businesswoman and wife, one who has something Richard wants and needs, the tenor of the pageant is quite changed. It becomes a show of wealth, a display of the wares she could choose to bestow, if *Richard* were to behave properly. Although Barron is careful to distinguish between economic and political power, arguing that the possibilities of increased status for London women "were entirely economic and in no way political,"[54]

[51] The feminine city's display of submissiveness is part of the same form of political vocabulary that Queen Anne uses to persuade her husband. The keeper of the city articulates the logic of this strategy when he prays that Anne will "soften royal severity that the king may be forbearing to his people. A woman mellows a man with love" (p. 191) ["Fleotere regales poterit regina rigores, / Mitis ut in gentem rex velit esse suam. / Mollit amore virum mulier" (lines 229–31)].

[52] Fradenburg, *City*, p. 12. That this "gift of disruption" is specifically feminine becomes clear in Fradenburg's discussion. Included in a system of aristocratic order, that is, when she is behaving herself, the city "may be the 'free maternal city' of plenitude; . . . repudiated, it may be Babylon, the city of earth—site of sexuality, ungovernable women, beautiful clothing, trade, crafts, and, in the end, grief" (p. 12).

[53] Married women in London "were frequently working partners in marriages between economic equals." Moreover, this equality of husband and wife may have resulted in financial advantages for both of them, in the form of "being able to shift goods, or cash, from one partner to another in times of economic pressure"; Barron, " 'Golden Age,' " p. 40.

[54] Ibid.

there is a convincing argument for the conflation of the two. In the narrow context of participating in civic government, holding ward office, or any of the other privileges afforded to freemen of the city, of course Barron is right, women did not participate in London's governance. But as the case of the quarrel between London and Richard shows, economic power is a form of political power. The citizens' refusal to lend money to the crown—money that they had available to lend—was a political act; it was an assertion of their independence from the king.[55]

The parades of impressively organized and outfitted guildsmen, for example, emphasize not only the economic productivity of the city, but also its own internal hierarchical structures that compete with the hierarchy of subject to king, city to sovereign.[56] Moreover, there is a martial quality to the "mighty force" of the guildsmen, arranged in "squadrons," each guild like a "phalanx" (p. 177) ["tam valido" (line 99), "turmas" (line 97), "phalangas" (line 101)]. This language suggests that the guildsmen—with their considerable economic power—are going off to do battle with an enemy, not to meet a husband on their knees. The parade represents a threatening force; as Maidstone acknowledges, the guildsmen are fully capable of destroying what gets in their way:

First one guild and then another wends its way back to the city: the road was scarcely sufficient for such an army. Throng presses on throng—here a man lies thrown to the ground, there one falls, here one collapses. (p. 185)

> [Illa prius, hec posterius ars, tendit ad urbem:
> Vix exercitui sufficiebat iter.
> Turba premit turbam—iacet hic, ruit hic, cadit ille.] (lines 169–71)

The intimidating and even dangerous unity of the guildsmen, finally, is exactly that which threatens Richard, since the problem leading to the

---

[55] As Kipling, "Civic Triumph," p. 95, writes, "in Richard's eyes, London's refusal of a loan had constituted a breach of the city's feudal loyalty."

[56] Benjamin R. McRee, "Unity or Division? The Social Meaning of Guild Ceremony in Urban Communities," in Barbara A. Hanawalt and Kathryn L. Reyerson, eds., *City and Spectacle in Medieval Europe* (Minneapolis: University of Minnesota Press, 1994), p. 195, notes that "guild processions, however simple or elaborate their external trappings, were, at heart, public declarations of autonomy. They announced that the marchers were part of an independent body with its own goals, its own rules, and its own corporate identity. . . . They emphasized not the wholeness of the community, but its division into separate, semiautonomous subgroups."

quarrel in the first place was the "entire city uniting" to refuse the king his loan. The show of unity during the pageant could thus easily be interpreted as a taunt that demonstrates to Richard just how united the citizens can be, whether in acquiescence or opposition to his desires.[57]

Maidstone further reveals that all is not abject and controlled in the city when he comments on a group of royal ladies whose cart turns over during the procession:

When one of the ladies thereupon exposed her womanly thighs, the people scarcely were able to hold back their laughter. And that fall is pleasing; may it come to pass, I pray, what that fall signifies to me: All extravagance and cupidinous love will tumble down. (p. 193)

> [Femina feminea sua dum sic femina nudat,
> Vix poterat risum plebs retinere suum.
> Casus et ille placet; veniat, rogo, quod michi signat:
> Corruat ut luxus et malus omnis amor.] (lines 253–56)

Two seemingly opposed interpretations of the exposure of women's bodies are offered here: that of the people on the street and Maidstone's own. But they really are not all that different, for both ultimately approve of the uncontrollable sexuality represented by the flash of thigh. The Londoners' raucous laughter and Maidstone's remarkably twisted moral both call the fall pleasing. London's unseemly "extra-marital" sexuality continues to thrive in the midst of the official wedding ceremony and suggests that there are a host of alternative arrangements possible between men and women and kings and cities.

Anne's model behavior can likewise be revised into something other than a show of submissiveness. The queen interprets the symbols of the pageant and the behavior of the citizens and tells Richard that they honor him. On her knees, she occupies the position of moral authority over her husband; as the keeper of the city remarks, "What a man does not dare, the woman alone can" (p. 213) ["Quod vir non audet, sola potest mulier" (line 442)]. Paul Strohm is right to point out that "the

---

[57] Glynne Wickham, *Early English Stages, 1300–1660*, 2 vols. (London: Routledge and Kegan Paul, 1959), 1:64, argues a similar point and concludes that the pageant represents the king's capitulation to the merchants, who "were powerful enough through their wealth to call his bluff."

actual thrust of her speech is practical and advisory," and that Anne is "anything but abject"[58] when she suggests to Richard that it is "acceptable now to return the city's ancient rights and to restore its liberties" (p. 219). The queen's important role in the pageant as a successful intercessor discredits the very form of institutionalized subservience in marriage that the pageant is supposed to celebrate and further suggests that, if Anne is a model for the city's behavior, London might similarly advise Richard as to what to do and why.

There is another potentially difficult symbolic association attached to Anne's prominent role as intercessor between Richard and his city/bride, and that is the complicated dynamic of the king's real wife giving him a second one, or even acting as a bawd by arranging another woman's services for him. In a triangulated exchange of procurement, the keeper of the city gives Anne gifts of considerable expense and asks her to be the broker of the new relationship between her husband and another "woman," London. These unsavory sexual undertones (Richard as a bigamist or even a prostitute's john) are the by-products of Maidstone's attempts to construct Richard as a masculine ideal in relation to an imperfect feminine city. Competing with the poem's portrayal of a just and good husband and king is the image of a sexual criminal.

The Trojan metaphors in the *Concordia* similarly exert a destabilizing influence on Maidstone's declared position. For example, he praises Anne's beauty: "Very beautiful herself, she stands surrounded by beautiful maidens; the New Troy conquers under these Amazons" (p.179) ["Pulchra quidem pulchris stat circumcincta puellis; / Vincit Amazonibus Troia novella sub hiis" (lines 123–24)]. Anne as an Amazon allied with New Troy is a figure for, most likely, Penthesilea, the warrior queen who came to the aid of the Trojans. With the introduction of this metaphor, Richard, who is supposed to appear in the poem as a patient and ultimately just ruler, is suddenly on the wrong side of the Trojan war; his intervention in London's autonomy is likened to the Greeks' invasion of Troy. Maidstone produces an upside-down revision of the battle between the Greeks and the Trojans in which Richard comes into New Troy and is conquered, defeated by a woman warrior in league with an impressive civic army.

Maidstone's depiction of a perverse imperialism, defined by the adherence of Ricardian deviance to what is supposed to be an image of New Trojan glory, intersects with and perhaps comments on Richard's

[58] Strohm, *Hochon's Arrow*, p. 111.

desperate attempts to maintain his own sovereign autonomy toward the end of his reign. The king's removal of the freedoms of London came at a time when he was struggling with his regnal persona, fluctuating wildly between abusive tyrant and abused victim. Maidstone delves into this problem when he draws a false comparison between Richard's treatment of New Troy and fair rule in Rome: "Like Rome, London is ruled by these men [the aldermen] in accordance with the senatorial law, and a mayor, whom the people elect, presides over them" (p. 173) ["Iure senatorio urbs hiis regitur quasi Roma, / Hiisque preest maior, quem populus legerit" (lines 73–74)]. But London at this moment was *not* ruled by its elected officials; the king had replaced them with his own men. Maidstone's "comparison" thus serves to contrast the ideal of elected, senatorial rule with the actual practice of Richard's tyranny, and suggests that Ricardian London is presently not enough like Rome— that other locus of civic glory stemming from the fall of Troy.

Far from congratulating Richard for his wisdom and good governance, the *Concordia* is instead warning a deviant king to look to the future of his city and perhaps to that of his own reign. The poem's allusions to post-Trojan history place Richard along a continuum of noble descent which at once compliments his lineage even while anticipating a future without him. The ambivalence of imperial chronology is indicated in the words of the keeper to the king:

Since you take after your father, you have brought to the name "Richard" whatever was honorable. Thus, from excellent kings and noble forebearers noble offspring follow. Destiny gave as was fitting. (p. 209)

> [Prole patrissante, "Ricardi" quod fuit ante
> Nomen, adhuc repetit quicquid honoris erat.
> Regibus ergo probis patribusque bonis bona proles
> Successura fuit; sors dedit ut decuit.] (lines 399–402)

While filling the name "Richard" with idealized content, the keeper simultaneously puts Richard in his (chronological) place; the king with great ancestors will soon enough be a memory himself.

Anxieties over treacherous precedents and usurping rulers underlie the terms of the quarrel between the king and the Londoners. Richard was extraordinarily careful to adhere to protocol and to established legal procedures when he took his steps against the city, suggesting that he was very much aware of the validating function of precedent, and that he knew he might need to call on it to justify his actions.[59] His final speech in Maidstone's poem focuses on his willingness to return to the old ways and further indicates that he had always practiced the ancient customs until the Londoners violated them: "You shall administer this city according to the ancient laws. As long as justice exists in not chang-ing the customary way, let what was lawful before be so now" (p. 225) ["Legibus antiquis hanc regitote plebem. / Antea quod licuit, liceat modo, dum tamen equm / Extiterit solitum non variando modum" (lines 534–36)]. Richard's idealized vision of civic history pretends an ancient absence of conflict between city and sovereign, and obliquely asserts that London's newly deviant behavior, as opposed to his own, is responsible for initiating the quarrel.

Maidstone's account of the king's "primal scene," in which Richard (falsely) remembers London as perpetually obedient, depicts a willful reinterpretation of the past designed to permit the future everyone de-sires. Of course the citizens wanted their liberties restored, but Richard, in turn, needed London in the 1390s, and he especially needed the eco-nomic potential of this profitable spouse at his disposal.[60] The *Concordia* presents an image of how a good city could behave with a good king, and rather generously glosses Richard on his best behavior; but it also shows the full capability of either party to deviate from their mutually beneficial relationship. Through the metaphor of marital roles, Maidstone's text revises civic roles to allow London her independent profit-making abilities "under" the king. This new dynamic for city-sovereign, wife-husband relations is one that puts on a display of tradi-tional feudal and baronial ties in order to achieve a return to modern business as usual—business that is good for everyone.

The *Concordia*, dedicated and presumably presented to the king in 1393, shows Richard how he can relent with his dignity intact, and get his money, too. But by describing the pageant as that which ends the

[59] See Barron, "Quarrel," pp. 185–86, for how carefully Richard applied the statute of 1354, which detailed the procedures to be followed in correcting faults in London's government.

[60] Similarly, men needed the economic potential of women at this moment in London's history. Barron, "'Golden Age,'" pp. 40–41, notes that the theory of conjugal unity, in which the man and the woman become one body in marriage, was eased in London in the fourteenth century to accommodate the desirable practice of women mak-ing money. This was because women's economic potential was good for men; but as soon as their work ceased to be profitable for men, "women were pushed out of the skilled labour market" (p. 48).

quarrel and reconciles the king with his city, Maidstone is engaging in a bit of premature representational closure. The quarrel did not end until 1397, when Richard finally restored the liberties of the city *in perpetuum*, after having kept them predicated upon his own interpretation of the citizens' good behavior for five years. The poem's premature resolution of the quarrel is perhaps an indication of a wishful fantasy closure, but it also functions as a form of symbolic pressure in itself.[61] Reminding Richard of his precarious position along the continuum of imperial history, the poem presents the king with a script of his own best policy already enacted and suggests that he follow it.

"Remembering" the precedent of Troy in both its glory and its deviance, and relying on the similarly split image of woman as both idealized and debased, Gower and Maidstone envision the city of London as its fantastic Other, the feminine New Troy. Their figuration of London in the future perfect constitutes a utopian historiography, one that depends on, even as it condemns, the generative, productive deviance of the past.

---

[61] Paul Strohm, "'Lad with revel to Newegate': Chaucerian Narrative and Historical Meta-Narrative," in Robert R. Edwards, ed., *Art and Context in Late Medieval English Narrative: Essays in Honor of Robert Worth Frank, Jr.* (Cambridge: D. S. Brewer, 1994), p. 170, suggests the socially structuring power of literary representation when he writes that "the most conclusive way to gain control of an unruly but powerful symbol is by employing it in a narration, by assimilating it to an exemplary sequence of events that unfolds in time and that, preferably, ends with a determinate conclusion illustrating or vindicating one's claims."

# Romance, Exemplum, and the Subject of the *Confessio Amantis*

William Robins
*University of Toronto*

T he version of the story of Apollonius of Tyre that John Gower presents in book 8 of the *Confessio Amantis* is an ancient romance construed according to the expectations for an exemplum.[1] Many of the other medieval adaptations of this ancient romance may have been "exemplary" in a wide sense of that term, referring in a loose fashion to any stories that were presented so as to engage the reader morally. Gower's version, however, is the first to be couched in the more precisely defined structure of an exemplum, such as was developed in late thirteenth-century sermons and thence introduced into fourteenth-century narratives as a device for linking a story to a specific moral argument.[2] Employed as one element in a sermon or moral treatise, an exemplum bears both a narrative and a rhetorical burden: through a narrative emplotment it must present a particular case of the operation of some abstract vice or virtue, while at the same time it is also meant to warn

A slightly different version of this paper originally appeared in my "Ancient Romance and Medieval Literary Genres: Apollonius of Tyre" (Ph.D. diss., Princeton University, 1995), pp. 167–200. I wish to thank John V. Fleming, Robert Hollander, Seth Lerer, Thomas Pavel, and the members of the Seminar on Contemporary Critical Theory at Princeton for their comments and advice.

[1] Citations of the *Confessio Amantis* are by book and line number from John Gower, *Confessio Amantis*, ed. G. C. Macaulay, vols. 2–3 of *The Complete Works of John Gower* (Oxford: Clarendon Press, 1899–1902).

[2] "This is the first version . . . in which the story is presented explicitly as a moral exemplum, albeit in a style which owes much to romance conventions"; Elizabeth Archibald, *Apollonius of Tyre: Medieval and Renaissance Themes and Variations* (Cambridge: D. S. Brewer, 1991), p. 192. On the history of the *Historia Apollonii Regis Tyri* and its adaptations see Archibald, *Apollonius of Tyre*; G. A. A. Kortekaas, ed., *Historia Apollonii Regis Tyri* (Groningen: Brouma's Boekhuis, 1984); and Elimar Klebs, *Die Erzählung von Apollonius aus Tyrus: eine geschichtliche Untersuchung über ihre lateinische Urform und ihre späteren Bearbeitungen* (Berlin: G. Reimer, 1889). On the history of the exemplum, the standard work remains J.-Th. Welter, *L'Exemplum dans la littérature religieuse et didactique du moyen âge* (Paris: Guitard, 1927).

listeners from, or exhort them to, a course of behavior through the *moralisatio* following a tale. Gower's "Tale of Apollonius" has such a *moralisatio* and is set within a larger exemplary framework, yet there is a striking dissonance between the emplotment inherited from this ancient romance and the moral attached to it.

For a reader who might be determined to find a moral in every story, the *moralisatio* of this tale will seem no more exceptionable than other tenuously linked conclusions common in medieval literature, and might appear, as it does to A. J. Minnis, "obvious."[3] But for a reader mindful of the way an exemplum ought to match its narrative and exhortatory purposes (*"solum quod facit ad rem est narrandum"*[4]), as is generally the case in the other tales of the *Confessio Amantis*, the relation between this romance and its proffered moral seems, as it does to Charles Runacres, "uninformative and confusing."[5] Dramatically opposed strategies of reading, according to which this moralization of ancient romance can appear as obvious or as confusing, are already present within Gower's poem, voiced respectively by the teller, Genius, and the listener, Amans. This opposition, I will argue, produces the conditions by which ancient romance becomes a tool with which Gower can investigate the nature of exemplarity, both in the "Tale of Apollonius" and in the *Confessio Amantis* as a whole. I will claim that the goal of Gower's strategy to contrast romance and exemplum is to prompt his readers to recognize their situation at the intersection of two discursive modes, a situation which I will describe, in the terms of recent theories of subjectivity, as the subject-position Gower expects of the readers of his text.

---

[3] "The ethical import is obvious"; Alastair Minnis, "'Moral Gower' and Medieval Literary Theory," in A. J. Minnis, ed., *Gower's* Confessio Amantis: *Responses and Reassessments* (Cambridge: D. S. Brewer, 1983), p. 76. The medieval imperative to read literature morally in this fashion is well discussed by Judson Boyce Allen, *The Ethical Poetic of the Middle Ages: A Decorum of Convenient Distinction* (Toronto: University of Toronto Press, 1982).

[4] "Eligenda sunt de multis exempla magis necessaria et utilitatem continencia evidentem et brevia et si fit longa narracio rescidenda sunt inutilia vel minus utilia et solum quod facit ad rem est narrandum"; Humbert de Romans, *De habundancia exemplorum*, cited in Welter, *L'Exemplum*, p. 73.

[5] "Whatever its importance in the context of the whole *Confessio*, 'Apollonius of Tyre' is an uninformative and confusing *narracio* about incest"; Charles Runacres, "Art and Ethics in the *Exempla* of *Confessio Amantis*," in Minnis, ed., *Gower's* Confessio Amantis, p. 124. Runacres notices a key distinction, often overlooked by critics, that to be a successful exemplum and to be an appropriate conclusion to the *Confessio Amantis* are not the same thing. A similar unsuitability of the *moralisationes* to the narrative patterns of other tales in the poem has been suggested by Winthrop Wetherbee, "Genius and Interpretation in the *Confessio Amantis*," in Arthur Groos, ed., *Magister Regis: Studies in Honor of Robert Earl Kaske* (New York: Fordham University Press, 1986), p. 259: ". . . moralization is a foil to the concrete embodiment of Gower's message."

In the array of stories told by Genius to lead Amans out of carnal love and toward moral self-control, this story occupies the rhetorically critical final position. Also the longest of these tales by far, it includes the themes covered by all of the previous books: "'Apollonius' reflects and completes the entire poem as well. The Tale is a kind of 'exemplary summa.'"[6] The story seems to carry the task of setting an interpretive paradigm for the entire collection, yet in its very length, episodicity, and variety it violates the usual categorizations that make an exemplary encapsulation possible. The plot of Gower's version differs little from that of its source in the Latin *Historia Apollonii*:[7] Prince Apollonius flees the wrath of the incestuous king Antiochus, loses his wife and daughter, and is buffeted back and forth across the Mediterranean in a series of unpredictable setbacks and random occurrences; having fallen hopeless and helpless into despair, he is unexpectedly reunited with his daughter and wife and restored to happiness and power. It is a narrative of chance and directionless wandering like the genre of ancient Greek romance it derives from, a genre that Bakhtin has characterized as follows:

This logic is one of *random contingency*, [*sovpadenie*] which is to say, chance *simultaneity* [meetings] and *chance rupture* [nonmeetings], that is, a logic of random *disjunctions* in time as well. In this random contingency, "earlier" and "later" are crucially, even decisively, significant.

And again:

Moments of adventuristic time occur at those points when the normal course of events, the normal, intended or purposeful sequences of life's events is interrupted. These points provide an opening for the intrusion of nonhuman forces—fate, gods, villains—and it is precisely these forces, and not the heroes, who in adventure-time take all the initiative.[8]

[6] R. F. Yeager, *John Gower's Poetic: The Search for the New Arion* (Cambridge: D. S. Brewer, 1990), p. 218. "Within the overall structure of the *Confessio Amantis*, then, the 'Tale of Apollonius' is the capstone"; ibid., p. 229.

[7] Gower cites his source as Godfrey of Viterbo's *Pantheon*, which perhaps served as an important precedent for versification and abridgment of the tale, but his primary source is the prose *Historia Apollonii*. The relation to both the *Pantheon* and the *Historia Apollonii* is set out in Macaulay's notes to his edition of the *Confessio Amantis*.

[8] Mikhail M. Bakhtin, "Forms of Time and of the Chronotope in the Novel: Notes toward a Historical Poetics," in *The Dialogic Imagination: Four Essays*, ed. Michael Holquist (Austin: University of Texas Press, 1981), pp. 92, 95 (emphasis in the original). See also Patricia Parker, *Inescapable Romance: Studies in the Poetics of a Mode* (Princeton, N.J.: Princeton University Press, 1979), for a sustained analysis of romance as a genre of contingency and wandering error.

We need not fully subscribe to Bakhtin's characterization of the Greek romances, nor think that contingency belongs to romance as if according to some idealized notion of generic form, in order to recognize that in relation to other kinds of fictional narrative available to Gower in fourteenth-century England, the story of Apollonius of Tyre provides an extreme instance of a narrative principle of random chance such as Bakhtin describes. This greater degree of narrative contingency was a salient differential that marked the medieval reception and appropriation of the story; to speak here of the genre of the tale of Apollonius is simply to indicate the presence of this distinction within Gower's literary environment.

Against the other tales in the *Confessio Amantis*, this heightened degree of contingency is especially noticeable. R. F. Yeager speaks of the "Tale of Apollonius" as if it establishes a ground to test the moral maxims of the other exemplary stories against "a situation more like 'real life,' in which everything can (and usually does) occur with no warning and in no prescribed order."[9] As a genre encapsulating this sense of experiential confusion, ancient romance shares qualities with the nonnarrative genre that Gower speaks of in the Prologue as "compleignte" (Prol. 516), the mode of blaming one's woes on unseen external forces and so abdicating one's own sense of agency, as Apollonius does in the face of ill fortune. The restoration of the prince's good fortune is what will underpin Genius's exemplary reading of the tale of Apollonius, but even this restoration is brought about by chance and thus emphasizes how this story, especially in comparison with other Middle English traditions of fiction, recounts a random succession of chance-driven events. The challenge this story poses for any exemplary interpretation can be illuminated by Karlheinz Stierle's analysis of how Boccaccio divorced his fictions from exemplary didacticism by acknowledging the contingency of the world: "Contingency is the true poet of the novella."[10] For Gower, contingency drives the poetics of the ancient romance that he turns to for his poem's final tale, and while there are other traditions of medieval romance appearing among the tales of the *Confessio Amantis*,

---

[9] Yeager, *John Gower's Poetic*, p. 218.

[10] Karlheinz Stierle, "Boccaccio, Montaigne and the Crisis of Exemplarity" (a paper delivered at the colloquium "The Renaissance Crisis of Exemplarity," Princeton, N.J., October 1994). The relevant arguments about Boccaccio are put forward in his "L'Histoire comme Exemple, l'Exemple comme Histoire: Contribution à la pragmatique et à la poétique des textes narratifs"; *Poétique* 10 (1972):186–90.

in this essay I will use the terms "romance" and "ancient romance" to designate this outer limit of giving shape to the experience of a chance-driven world.[11]

In the *Confessio Amantis*, the teacher Genius tells the story to the lover Amans, presenting it as an exemplary narrative by overlooking its tone of aimlessness and by focusing instead on the closing episodes of good fortune. His *moralisatio* reiterates an ethical imperative voiced frequently throughout the poem: a person's internal moral disposition will determine the outcome of external events.

> Lo, what it is to be wel grounded:
> For he hath ferst his love founded
> Honestliche as forto wedde,
> Honestliche his love he spedde
> And hadde children with his wif,
> And as him liste he ladde his lif;
> And in ensample his lif was write,

[11] Gower uses the term "romance" once in the poem, in a discussion of love-delicacy. For Amans, "romance" is the genre that articulates his own predicament and that he does not tire of hearing (6.875–84):

> And ek in other wise also
> Fulofte time it falleth so,
> Min Ere with a good pitance
> Is fedd of redinge of romance
> Of Ydoine and of Amadas,
> That whilom weren in mi cas,
> And eke of othre many a score,
> The loveden longe er I was bore.
> For whan I of here loves rede,
> Min Ere with the tale I fede.

Insofar as these romances have a temporal dimension of contingency and incompleteness, they can be understood within my use of the term "romance." They can also be understood thematically as stories about erotic chivalry, as they are by Scanlon, who claims (as I do, albeit with a different field of application) that "Gower's objection to romance is that it insufficiently recognizes its own contingencies"; Larry Scanlon, *Narrative, Authority, and Power: The Medieval Exemplum and the Chaucerian Tradition* (New York: Cambridge University Press, 1994), p. 268. One difficulty with Scanlon's approach is that the "Tale of Apollonius," because it shows a successful containment of erotic drives, is seen not as a romance but as "a story of royal forbearance rewarded" (p. 296)—reiterating past interpretations of the tale and overlooking its place in the story of Amans's nonconversion. I claim that Gower is especially drawn to the "Tale of Apollonius" because with it he can explore the nature of romance even beyond considerations of thematic content, that is, as a temporal and narrative mode, and at its point of greatest thematic overlap with the opposing mode of exemplarity.

That alle lovers myhten wite
How ate laste it schal be sene
Of love what thei wolden mene.
For se now on that other side
Antiochus with al his Pride,
Which sette his love unkindely,
His ende he hadde al sodeinly,
Set ayein kinde upon vengance,
And for his lust hath his penance. (8.1993–2008)

This forced reduction of the narrative does not presume to account either for the continual trials that beset Apollonius or for the way the passing of time is marked by an incessant and undirected series of external buffetings. With his "ferst" and "ate laste," Genius has introduced a temporal format for understanding the story that entails a particular pattern of causality: a character's moral disposition is seen to come first, and his or her good or bad fortune follows inevitably as a consequence. Priority and posteriority are no longer parameters for recounting a series of externally impinging events but instead are accorded an insistent moral directedness. The plot of the romance and Genius's *moralisatio* instantiate different notions of "temporality," if that term is understood in the rich sense given to it by Ricoeur to mean a possible shape of destiny, including not only a particular analytical conception of time but also conditions of narratability, moral valuations, and reflections on agency. In Ricoeur's formulation, narrative forms negotiate between the incommensurable models of temporality available at any period, "ways of inhabiting the world that lie waiting to be taken up by reading."[12] We can use this insight to grasp the degree to which Gower finds in ancient romance an emplotment that leans toward a temporality of contingency, and in exempla a pattern that emphasizes a temporality of moral necessity. What Genius's *moralisatio* accomplishes is a transposition from one pattern to another, where the temporality of romance is taken as a metaphor for, or as evidence of, the moral temporality of an "ensample."

Amans is unmoved by Genius's exhortation. Having always defined himself as subject to the whims of the lady he loves, Amans conceives of the world in romance dimensions, as the playground of unstable fortune, and not in the exemplary and moral terms Genius urges (8.2029–39):

---

[12] Paul Ricoeur, *Time and Narrative*, trans. K. McLaughlin and D. Pellauer, 3 vols. (Chicago: University of Chicago Press, 1984–88), 2:5.

> Mi fader, hou so that it stonde,
> Youre tale is herd and understonde,
> As thing which worthi is to hiere,
> Of gret ensample and gret matiere,
> Wherof, my fader, god you quyte.
> Bot in this point miself aquite
> I mai riht wel, that nevere yit
> I was assoted in my wit,
> Bot only in that worthi place
> Wher alle lust and alle grace
> Is set, if that danger ne were.

He does not see how the example of Antiochus and Apollonius might tie in with his own predicament, and acquits himself of any need to learn from it. It is a "gret ensample," but not for him.

Amans's resistance discloses a paradox that throws into doubt not only Genius's office but also Gower's avowedly exemplary enterprise, and even some basic assumptions in the general use of exempla. This paradox of exemplarity arises from the following logic: if a person's internal makeup determines the outcome of external pressures, and if exemplary persuasion is a pressure external to the listener, then for a disinclined listener no exemplum (or other moral persuasion, for that matter) could achieve the conversion necessary to enable its own proper reception. A melancholy or obstinate listener serves to reveal the hermeneutic circle of exemplary reasoning, where an ideal of internal priority is in conflict with a rhetorical duty to persuade. If the use of exempla by preachers was developed as a way to move hesitant listeners, especially those *"in scientia debiles et in fide rudes,"*[13] to consider questions of morality, then Gower is taking this underlying premise to its next logical step: what if the listener remains unmoved despite such *"exterioribus exemplis"*?[14] Further rhetorical skill presents one possible answer to this problem, and nonverbal compulsion another, harsher one. But Gower's answer is rather to make this problematic obstacle a central theme of his poem, and thus rhetoric—the possibility of engaging the will and reflection of a listener, even while asserting that

---

[13] *Speculum laicorum*, cited in Welter, *L'Exemplum*, p. 75.

[14] "Ad edificacionem rudium et agrestium erudicionem, quibus quasi corporalia et palpabilia et talia que per experienciam norunt frequencius sunt propenda, magis enim moventur exterioribus exemplis quam auctoritatibus vel profundis sentenciis"; Jacques de Vitry, cited in Welter, *L'Exemplum*, p. 68.

listener's self-responsibility—becomes not subsidiary chaff to some moral kernel but a moral issue in its own right.[15]

Gower argues most strongly for the priority of internal morality over the affairs of the world in the narrating persona of the Prologue, as part of an urgent call to listeners and readers to heed his advice (Prol. 544–49):

> For after that we falle and rise,
> The world arist and falth withal,
> So that the man is overal
> His oghne cause of wel and wo.
> That we fortune clepe so
> Out of the man himself it groweth. . . .

Elsewhere, however, the narrating voice avoids such strong claims, or even argues that external pressures determine our scope for moral rectitude. This latter position is also given voice in the rest of the poem by Amans, who does not feel obliged to heed advice to reorder his morals: "The tales sounen in my Ere, / Bot yit myn herte is elleswhere" (7.5411–12). After the "Tale of Apollonius," and after a final analogy showing how he should accept good counsel, Amans rejects Genius's approaches even more soundly (8.2149–61):

> Mi fader, so as I have herd
> Your tale, bot it were ansuerd,
> I were mochel forto blame.
> Mi wo to you is bot a game,
> That fielen noght of that I fiele;
> The fielinge of a mannes Hiele
> Mai noght be likned to the Herte:

---

[15] Olsson describes Gower's paradox well: "Only by an engagement of all its faculties can the mind advance through sense-perception and imagination, through likeness confirming opinion, to wisdom. This course is manifestly closed to the person trapped in the fantasies of melancholy, and that presents a great challenge to the poet"; Kurt Olsson, *John Gower and the Structures of Conversion: A Reading of the "Confessio Amantis"* (Cambridge: D. S. Brewer, 1992), p. 37. The dilemma of exemplarity here differs slightly from what students of the Renaissance speak of as a "crisis of exemplarity"; the Renaissance "crisis" is explained in terms of the impossibility of representing a general truth through a particular, and is thus primarily an issue of representation rather than of rhetoric. See Stierle, "L'Histoire comme Exemple"; and Timothy Hampton, *Writing from History: The Rhetoric of Exemplarity in Renaissance Literature* (Ithaca, N.Y.: Cornell University Press, 1990).

> I mai noght, thogh I wolde, asterte,
> And ye be fre from al the peine
> Of love, wherof I me pleigne.
> It is riht esi to comaunde;
> The hert which fre goth on the launde
> Not of an Oxe what him eileth.

Here Amans is rejecting no particular exemplum, but the very analogical premises of exemplary reasoning. This dismissal, because it is generated by Amans's own self-serving criteria for interpreting stories, will be impossible for Genius to overcome with simply more exempla.[16] Exemplary literature will fulfill its function only for somebody who accepts the premises of the mode of reasoning, for somebody already prepared to receive its teaching. Genius and Amans, however, now stand in "debat and gret perplexete" (8.2190).

Gower's own instructive aims in the *Confessio Amantis* are potentially undercut by the paradox he draws attention to. Rather than discounting this issue, he opens his work up to it and takes the interrogation of the grounds of exemplarity as the theorem of the poem as a whole. Amans's recalcitrance, Genius's varying persuasions, and the authorial persona's contradictions all develop around this task, and all come to a head with Genius's moral reduction of this final exemplary, or rather romance, narrative.

Amans's inability to read Genius's stories as compelling exempla is bound up with his inability to read his own life as a teleological narrative. His desire does not yet grasp "What is my beste, as for an ende" (8.2059), a concluding *telos* around which he might order his account of the course of his life: a "final ende, / The point wherto that I schal holde" (8.2394–95). The Aristotelian terminology of ends here reminds us that, whatever its idiosyncrasies, Gower's discussion of ethical behavior is guided by widespread late medieval attention to the *Nicomachean Ethics*. In the *Nicomachean Ethics*, Aristotle's analysis of

---

[16] For Olsson, the problem of addressing a melancholy listener is overcome in the *Confessio Amantis* through the plain style and the use of exempla, particularly in the combination of many exempla which leads to a "more complex, less inflexibly understood, and truer self-perception"; Olsson, *John Gower and the Structures of Conversion*, p. 36. While I agree that a recognition of the variety of "structures of perception" (p. 14) is of crucial importance for Amans's conversion and for Gower's project, I doubt that the paradox of exemplarity can be effectively resolved by simply multiplying the number and varying the topics of the exempla.

ends already presents the dilemma that comes from bringing into play two ways of understanding experience. Because the good life is based on a habit of virtue which endures throughout one's life, then a truly virtuous disposition could only be proved by a completed life. However,

if it is necessary to see the end and only then call a man blessed, not as currently blessed but as having been so before, how is this not a paradox that, when he is happy, being happy might not be predicated truly of him; because we do not wish to call living men happy on account of their variations, and because we consider happiness to be permanent and by no means easily changeable, whereas fortunes continually wheel around about men. It is clear that if we should follow one's fortunes, we would frequently call the same man happy and then wretched, for they declare a happy man to be a chameleon and give him weak support.[17]

Can we call a living man happy,

or must we add that he must both live thus and die as befits this aim? For the future is not clear to us, but we claim happiness to be an end and entirely complete in every way. If this is the case, we may call blessed (blessed, that is, in

---

[17] "Si enim utique finem videre oportet et tunc beatificare unumquemque non ut existentem beatum, set quoniam prius erat, qualiter non inconveniens, si quando est felix, non vere dicetur de eo existere, propter non velle viventes felicitare propter transmutaciones et propter permanens quidem felicitatem existimare et nequaquam facile transmutabile, fortunas autem multociens recirculari circa eosdem? Manifestum quod si sequamur fortunas, eundem felicem et rursus miserum dicemus multociens, camaleonta quendam felicem nunciantes et debiliter firmant"; Aristotle, *The Nicomachean Ethics*, trans. Robert Grosseteste, in R. A. Gauthier, ed., *Aristoteles Latinus, Ethica Nicomachea*, XXVI-1/3, fasc. 4 (Leiden-Brussels, 1974) p. 389 [1100a32-b7]; the English translation is my own but depends much on Ross's informed translation of the Greek original: Aristotle, *The Nicomachean Ethics*, trans. David Ross, rev. J. L. Ackrill and J. O. Urmson (Oxford: Oxford University Press, 1980). A variety of Latin translations would have been available in fourteenth-century England, as well as numerous commentaries. In 1370, Nicholas Oresme translated the work into French for Charles V, and vernacular adaptations of the Nicomachean Ethics were available through Brunetto Latini's *Tresor* and through the translations of Giles of Rome's *De regimine principum*, including the Middle English version by John of Trevisa. The medieval reception of the *Nicomachean Ethics* is discussed by René Antoine Gauthier, introduction to Aristotle, *L'Éthique à Nicomaque*, ed. R. A. Gauthier and J. Y. Jolif, 2d ed., 4 vols. (Louvain/Paris: Publications Universitaires, 1970), 1:111–46; and by Georg Wieland, "The Reception and Interpretation of Aristotle's *Ethics*," in N. Kretzmann, A. Kenny and J. Pinborg, eds., *The Cambridge History of Later Medieval Philosophy* (Cambridge: Cambridge University Press, 1982), pp. 657–72.

human terms) those among living men for whom the circumstances described do exist and also will exist.[18]

Because true happiness, something "entirely complete in every way," requires the concurrence of moral and biographical circumstances, the habit of virtue always remains in potential conflict with the uncertain future.

The difficulties that Aristotle confronts in the *Nicomachean Ethics* stem largely from bringing into convergence these two incommensurable ways of conceiving the course of life. At issue here is whether happiness comes from an internal ordering of the soul or from external gifts of fortune. While Aristotle tends to favor the former, he admits that happiness "seems to need the external goods as well, as we have said; for it is impossible, or not easy, to perform good acts, if unable to enjoy the use of what exists."[19] The philosopher's unsureness here about whether the convergence of external and internal goods is logically or only practically necessary points to an uncertainty at the heart of the *Nicomachean Ethics*, as Sarah Broadie points out: "Aristotle's discussion swings between the notion of the supreme good as *a certain sort of life*, and the notion of it as *some element within a life* which may dominate that life in the sense of typifying it."[20] For the purposes of this discussion, we can cast this distinction as one between a biographical and a moral framework for conceiving of the good life. In terms of ends, is the good life to be directed toward the achievement of certain external successes or instead toward gaining the knowledge that external successes are insignificant? In terms of the narrative temporality such ends anchor, is the good life to be conceived of according to a biographical account of successive accomplishments and setbacks, or according to a moral account of an enduring habit of virtue? The *Nicomachean Ethics* is marked by this interplay of incommensurable ends, an overlap of competing patterns by which behavior might be understood.

---

[18] "[V]el apponendum et victurum sic et finiturum secundum racionem, quia futurum inmanifestum nobis, felicitatem autem finem et perfectum ponimus omnino omnimode. Si autem ita, beatos dicemus vivencium quibus existunt et existent que dicta sunt, beatos autem ut homines"; Aristotle, *Nicomachean Ethics*, p. 390 [1101a15–22].

[19] "Videtur tamen et eorum que exterius sunt bonorum indigens, quemadmodum diximus. Inpossibile enim vel non facile bona operari, inpotentem tribuere existentem"; Aristotle, *Nicomachean Ethics*, pp. 386–87 [1099a31–32].

[20] Sarah Broadie, *Ethics with Aristotle* (New York: Oxford University Press, 1991), p. 24 (emphasis in original).

Medieval ethical thinking may have been driven largely by accommodating Christianity to such Aristotelian considerations of narrative, as Alasdair MacIntyre has suggestively argued.[21] In the fourteenth century, when priests studying the Aristotelian curriculum and also responsible for the *cura animarum* turned to exempla to give compelling shape to their sermons, the direct link between the *Nicomachean Ethics* and rhetorical experimentation may never have been stronger.[22] The Christian reception of the *Nicomachean Ethics* shows an unambiguous celebration by theologians of the ideals of contemplation and of internal accounts of success, generally seeing external and internal goods as truly irreconcilable and in an obviously hierarchical relationship; such commentators are less interested in the potential conflict between "biographical" and "moral" models than they are in the potential conflict between ethical considerations, which are still concerned with behavior in this temporal world, and theological considerations, according to which all categories of temporality are transcended.[23] Gower's poetry is no doubt shaped by this Christian intimation that external fortune and internal virtue are irreconcilable, but he also, like the philosophical (as opposed to theological) commentators of the fourteenth century, takes seriously Aristotle's starting proposition that ethical considerations can be discussed apart from religious speculation, and that both biographical and moral ends give rise to compelling models for speaking about one's life.

What for Aristotle was treated as a philosophical puzzle about teleologies becomes for Gower a literary issue to be dealt with by experi-

[21] Alasdair C. MacIntyre, *After Virtue: A Study in Moral Theory* (Notre Dame: Notre Dame University Press, 1980), pp. 165–80.

[22] What Gauthier calls "la régne de l'*Éthique à Nicomaque* sur la morale médiévale" stretched beyond pure philosophy, as is evident in the fact that from 1335, the Dominicans of Provence prescribed all members of the order to read the *Nicomachean Ethics*, and after 1366, it was a required work in the Master of Arts curriculum at Paris; Gauthier, "Introduction," p. 135. See also Wieland, "Reception and Interpretation," p. 668. The works of Giles of Rome and Brunetto Latini not only digest the *Ethics* but also are important models in the history of exempla; Welter, *L'Exemplum*, pp. 168–69, 190–91. The connection between study of the Ethics and the writing of literature in the fourteenth-century forms a much-neglected and potentially rich field.

[23] Albertus Magnus, *Super Ethica commentum et quaestiones: Tres libros priores*, ed. W. Kübel (Münster: 1968); St. Thomas Aquinas, *Sententia libri Ethicorum*, vol. 47 of *Opera omnia*, ed. Fratrum Praedicatorum (Rome: Santa Sabina, 1969). See Gauthier, "Introduction"; Wieland, "Reception and Interpretation"; H. V. Jaffa, *Thomism and Aristotelianism: A Study of the Commentary by Thomas Aquinas on the Nicomachean Ethics* (Chicago: University of Chicago Press, 1952); and L. J. Elders, "St. Thomas Aquinas' Commentary on the *Nicomachean Ethics*," in L. J. Elders and K. Hedwig, eds., *The Ethics of St. Thomas Aquinas* (Vatican City: Libreria Editrice Vaticana, 1984), pp. 9–49.

menting with kinds of narrative. Rival "endes" are viewed in terms of the temporal configurations they anchor, and the friction between contingent time and moral time is bodied forth in a counterpoise between romance and exemplary genres. Or, more accurately, ancient romance and exemplarity come to stand less as genres than as two distinct modes—akin to Northrop Frye's pregeneric, archetypal *mythoi*—for casting shapes of destiny in narrative.[24] The two modes are distinguished in their assumptions about temporality, for the contingent time of romance involves a personal sense that one's unfolding biography is subject to the whims of external fortune, while the moral time of exemplarity accounts for behavior according to ethical categories of cause and effect. Throughout the *Confessio Amantis* different literary genres present themselves as hybrids or overlaps of these modes, and so as capable of being interpreted in light of either (the copresence of a third mode, that of history, will be discussed below). The convergence of modes in any one story is thus also a potential conflict, and Gower places as his culminating tale the romance of Apollonius of Tyre where the concurrent invocation of two patterns of temporality is most pointedly awkward.

Bringing these issues to a head within the story is the climactic recognition scene between Apollonius and his daughter Thaise. Called from her position as schoolmistress to cheer up this dejected king, Thaise appeals to Apollonius through several stages of address. Singing is ineffectual, because it remains external: she "lich an Angel sang withal; / Bot he nomore than the wal / Tok hiede of eny thing he herde" (8.1671–73). Switching from music to the "wordes" (8.1675) of tale telling and question posing, verbal engagement elicits some attention: "Wherof sche made his herte change, / And to hire speche his Ere he leide" (8.1678–79); but even such attention involves no responsive reaction, and words do not move him from despair:

> Bot he for no suggestioun
> Which toward him sche couthe stere,
> He wolde noght o word ansuere,

[24] Northrop Frye, *Anatomy of Criticism: Four Essays* (Princeton, N.J.: Princeton University Press, 1957). Frye's notion of romance, which differs significantly from that at stake for Gower, also takes the story of Apollonius of Tyre as a central, nearly pure example of the mode; see Northrop Frye, *The Secular Scripture: A Study of the Structure of Romance* (Cambridge, Mass.: Harvard University Press, 1976), pp. 48–52.

> Bot as a madd man ate laste
> His heved wepende awey he caste,
> And half in wraththe he bad hire go. (8.1684–89)

In despair at the losses he has had to bear, Apollonius is "as a madd man" (8.1687), an epithet that specifies the seriousness of his ethical plight since madness, according to Aquinas, constitutes the only condition in which external misfortune impinges on moral choices: the happy man "will not be changed easily from happiness to unhappiness except by frequent and great changes that deprive him of the use of reason."[25] Thaise's touch then leads Apollonius to strike her, but he "sobreth his corage" (8.1700) at her reprimand, knowing he deserves such a rebuke. After all this, the achievement of Apollonius's recovery comes about for another reason (8.1702–11):

> Bot of hem tuo a man mai liere
> What is to be so sibb of blod:
> Non wiste of other hou it stod,
> And yit the fader ate laste
> His herte upon this maide caste,
> That he hire loveth kindely,
> And yit he wiste nevere why.
> Bot al was knowe er that thei wente:
> For god, which wot here hol entente,
> Here hertes bothe anon descloseth.

Ignorant of Thaise's identity, Apollonius feels a natural love he does not comprehend. As the final stage of appeal he asks her who she is, and Thaise, unaware that this man is her father, is moved by the same overwhelming intuition and tells what she had told no one else (8.1725–31):

> Fro point to point al sche him tolde,
> That sche hath longe in herte holde,
> And nevere dorste make hir mone
> Bot only to this lord al one,
> To whom hire herte can noght hele,

---

[25] St. Thomas Aquinas, *Commentary on the Nicomachean Ethics*, trans. C. I. Litzinger, 2 vols. (Chicago: Regnery, 1964), 1:199 [16,10].

> Torne it to wo, torne it to wele,
> Torne it to good, torne it to harm.

The ensuing recognition of his daughter converts Apollonius from un-responsive despair to a suffusion of joy. In this scene we are presented with "an almost mystical sense of ties of blood."[26] External promptings have failed until they touch this internal predisposition. Thaise's story moves Apollonius not out of intelligence or pity or persuasion, but out of kinship; not because it offers an *analogy* to his own predicament, but because it is a *part of his own story*.

As Kurt Olsson has seen, this episode is central both for interpreting the tale of Apollonius and for making sense of the story of Amans's own con-version, which directly follows in the closing pages of the *Confessio Amantis*. For Olsson, the "wordes" Thaise utters play an instrumental role:

Thaise's "demandes" inspire him to listen and thereby to discover a courtesy that sobers his "corage" and restores his own power to love "kindely," to man-ifest an "honeste" affection that is both natural and ordered.[27]

This decisive role of Thaise's questions to Apollonius is taken to prove that "only an external agent can draw him out of his near despair."[28] By direct analogy, at the level of the frame-tale, Amans is seen to be con-verted by Genius's storytelling: ". . . solace is found in a 'philosophie' generated out of the 'problemes' and 'demandes' represented in and by Genius."[29]

While Olsson defines well the interpretive issues at stake for this episode, some modification of his conclusions is needed to account for the process of recognition as it is presented in the text of the poem. Thaise's "sondri bordes" and "demandes strange" have no lasting effect, are not inspirational, and occasion not courtesy but aggression. The dy-namic between internal preparation and external agent is certainly in focus here, but not in such a way that the efficacy of the external agent

---

[26] Peter Goodall, "John Gower's *Apollonius of Tyre: Confessio Amantis*, Book VIII," *Southern Review* [Australia] 15 (1982): 247.

[27] Olsson, *John Gower and the Structures of Conversion*, pp. 222–23. I register my objec-tions to Olsson's work only to distinguish my reading from his, which is an important and sustained analysis of the entire *Confessio Amantis*, the general approach of which I share.

[28] Olsson, *John Gower and the Structures of Conversion*, p. 223.

[29] Ibid.

can be taken for granted. If this story suggests a prerequisite for effective conversion it is this: exterior promptings have to be commensurate with internal needs. Failing this, the use of "demandes," however engaging superficially, cannot achieve a moment of self-discovery.

This dynamic holds true also at the level of the frame-tale, at the level where the story of Apollonius might become instrumental in Amans's own conversion. Because the themes of kinship and incest remain simply topics of Genius's pedagogy, and because the story is offered as a kind of analogy, Genius's exemplum is ineffectual. If the scene of the recovery of Apollonius is meant to be analogous to the conversion of Amans, they correspond only in suggesting, perplexingly, that instruction by analogy is unpersuasive.

Genius acknowledges that Amans can be converted only by willing it himself (8.2142–48):

> Mi Sone, now thou hast conceived
> Somwhat of that I wolde mene;
> Hierafterward it schal be sene
> If that thou lieve upon mi lore;
> For I can do to thee nomore
> Bot teche thee the rihte weie:
> Now ches if thou wolt live or deie.

But Amans, as seen above, denies any responsibility to heed Genius's teaching, or even to accept the premises that underlie it. Turning then to Venus for help more pertinent to his lover's state, Amans is surprised to find Venus rejecting his petition by claiming that old age disqualifies him from her court of love (8.2426–39):

> Bot mor behoveth to the plowh,
> Wherof the lacketh, as I trowe:
> So sitte it wel that thou beknowe
> Thi fieble astat, er thou beginne
> Thing wher thou miht non ende winne.
> What bargain scholde a man assaie,
> Whan that him lacketh forto paie?
> Mi Sone, if thou be wel bethoght,
> This toucheth thee; foryet it noght:
> The thing is turned into was;
> That which was whilom grene gras,

> Is welked hey at time now.
> Forthi mi conseil is that thou
> Remembre wel hou thou art old.

It is this response from Venus, and not Genius's stories, that succeeds in "touching" Amans: "Tho wiste I wel withoute doute, / That ther was no recoverir" (8.2443–44). Venus's words set in motion a process of self-recognition so individual that Amans now takes on his proper name: "Sche axeth me what is mi name. / 'Ma dame,' I seide, 'John Gower'" (8.2320–21). What dynamic of conversion are we to say is at work here?

A double apprehension of life's course is occasioned by the stage of old age, defined by Augustine as dual in its aspects, and properly characteristic of the sixth and present age of history, "during which time the exterior or 'old' man is wasted by old age while the interior man is from day to day renewed."[30] For Gower "exterior" and "interior" are not so much descriptions of two aspects of life as they are two possible descriptions for a whole life, and he places at the center of his poetic project a dynamic by which a person might move from one of these competing models of self-definition to another. Amans, having always hoped to consummate his carnal desire, had defined himself according to external goods and so according to a conclusion which was always deferred. When the unmasking of his senile impotence provides an unexpected moment of closure, Amans's sense of himself as a lover is belied. The logic of evaluating his life according to external goods breaks down under its own weight: such an external way of thinking is a "thing where thou miht non ende winne" (8.2430), making Amans out to be, in Aristotle's phrase, a chameleon and weakly supported.[31]

As the *Nicomachean Ethics* explains, with a consideration of only external goods and a biographical sense of time it would be impossible to predicate any quality for a living person's life because of the changes the future might bring; a moment of closure marked by ill-success, such as

---

[30] "Sexta, ab adventu Domini usque in finem saeculi speranda est: qua exterior homo tanquam senectute corrumpitur qui etiam vetus dicitur, et interior renovatur de die in diem"; Augustine, *De diversis quaestionibus*, 83.1.58, cited in J. A. Burrow, *The Ages of Man: A Study in Medieval Writing and Thought* (Oxford: Clarendon Press, 1986), pp. 199–200. See pp. 160–61 of Burrow's study for a discussion of the *Confessio Amantis*; also J. A. Burrow, "The Portrayal of Amans in *Confessio Amantis*," in Minnis, ed., *Gower's Confessio Amantis*, pp. 5–24.
[31] Aristotle, *Nicomachean Ethics*, p. 389 [1100b6–7].

Priam's, would require evaluating the entire course of that life as a failure. Within the same parameters, "being a lover" cannot be predicated of Amans. He takes on the name John Gower because he can no longer be called "amans," just as he realizes that he no longer knows what love might be (8.2870–77):

> Venus behield me than and lowh,
> And axeth, as it were in game,
> What love was. And I for schame
> Ne wiste what I scholde ansuere;
> And natheles I gan to swere
> That be my trouthe I knew him noght;
> So ferr it was out of mi thoght,
> Riht as it hadde nevere be.

Thus while the mode of exemplarity had been inadequate for recasting Amans's sense of himself, ancient romance now appears equally inadequate because its temporal *unpredictability* results in its qualitative *unpredicability* (and if no quality can be predicated of a character then a paradigmatic narration ceases to be possible). Brought to a recognition of this limit to his chosen genre of romance, Amans is left to reconstrue the claims of Genius's genre of exemplarity.

As Olsson has acutely observed, questions of temporality are central to Amans's conversion and so to the poem as a whole:

All of Gower's various concerns in this work come together in a statement that reassesses the passage of time. . . . The problem of age and its resolution is centered in a convergence of two senses of time and "ende": old age might betoken physical corruption and mortality on the one hand, or the *telos* of a fulfilled nature, the *perfectio aetatis* on the other. . . . Gower uses a recognition of the one sense to open out into a recognition of the other, through a conversion that must take place in time.[32]

Olsson's insight into the drama between these two senses of time, however, loses some of its strength and applicability when the two temporal categories are treated as if elided; Amans, in his view, is converted from a state in which time was neglected to a state in which time, in all its senses, is acknowledged: "The old becomes new, in Gower's argu-

---

[32] Olsson, *John Gower and the Structures of Conversion*, p. 231.

ment, at the point of entering time, of recognizing the uncertainty and precariousness of life in the 'flesch.'"[33] By stressing a single "point of entering time," Olsson's analysis is in danger of underrating the differences between two conflicting patterns of time. Indeed, attention to the way in which Gower pits one sense of time against another is indispensable for evaluating the role of time in Gower's favored literary technique, which is to make these temporal frameworks manifest in a few competing literary genres.

In the episode of conversion, Amans's previous obsession with gaining the object of his desire yields to a recognition of the discursive modes according to which desire can be conceived. Gower has employed ancient romance as an instrument to interrogate the structure of exemplarity, and vice versa, in order to show his character caught between the two. Amans casts off an exclusively romance conception of his relation to the world, but has not therefore committed himself to an exemplary model. Both narrative modes have their limits: the first lacks meaningful perspective, while the latter is unresponsive to lived experience. Amans/Gower is finally positioned as a subject who has to adjudicate between the competing narrative modes that constitute his ability to think about himself. The tension at the end of the *Confessio Amantis* thus brings into focus the situation of Amans in the work as a whole, having to make his way through the confusion of genres that Genius's tales present—history, hagiography, pagan mythology, fable, astrology, etc. These "structures of perception"[34] are not indeterminate, but show the overlap of basic discursive modes which are the patterns out of which Amans must define his own life, and in their interplay constitute the condition of his own individual moral activity.

By offering the *Confessio Amantis* to his readers, Gower must confront the paradox of exemplarity, this time as potentially disturbing his own aim to convey some message by his poetry. Thus the Prologue to the poem, where a voice of convinced authority urgently instructs the audience how to amend their ways, ought not to be seen as providing a stable set of principles by which to interpret the rest of the work. The Prologue presents a moral conception of causes and effects in the world, and is to be contrasted to other positions. The narrating voice of the

[33] Ibid, pp. 240–41.
[34] Ibid, p. 14.

Prologue takes upon itself the office of instruction vacated by the contemporary clergy, but at moments even that persona acknowledges an obstacle to such a vocation (Prol. 900–5):

> And yet these clerkes alday preche
> And sein, good dede may non be
> Which stant noght upon charite:
> I not hou charite may stonde,
> Wher dedly werre is take on honde.
> Bot al this wo is cause of man.

All woe may be caused by man, and the outcome of all actions may be determined by one's internal charity, but to attempt to teach this truth through strong assertion overlooks the experiential plight of the audience, who lacks the external conditions of peace necessary for the practice of charity. The dynamic of moral "amendement" will have to take ample account of the claims of another conception of the world, a conception in which the contingency of the world is accepted as a pressing psychological problem.[35]

The *Confessio Amantis* does not urge total acceptance of the propositions of the Prologue, but rather a recognition of the genres available for making sense of needs and desires. Indeed, in the Prologue Gower suggests that the reader's relation to society is conditioned by the possibilities of narrative, for a particular temporal conception is ascribed to each of the three estates, implicating different temporalities of discourse, and thus different genres, in the fabric of English society. Rulers are judged against a distant golden age, finding in "Cronique" the genre to which they are held accountable (Prol. 101). The clergy is criticized against the better priests of the past and against their insufficiency as personal models for the present, accountable to a moral sense of time with its exemplary perspective: "For thei ben to the worldes ÿe / the Mirour of ensamplerie" (Prol. 495–96). Those who constitute the commons consider only recent experience, lamenting their contingent subjection to Fortune in "compleignte" (Prol. 516). These three genres— chronicle, exemplum, and complaint—are recognizable patterns for making sense of temporal experience which, because they are seen as complicit with the structures of society, remind us that the issues of

[35] On the "implicated persona" of the Prologue, see Anne Middleton, "The Idea of Public Poetry in the Reign of Richard II," *Speculum* 53 (1978): 94–114.

competing genres and modes raised by Gower are heavily freighted with social and political expectations.

The position of exemplarity occupied by the clergy involves the same moral and rhetorical assumptions as the exemplary mode of narration which we have seen presented by Genius. Complaint against fortune, blaming external causes for ill events, gives voice to the perspectiveless experience of personal suffering and endurance and thus finds its fullest narrative expression in the contingency of ancient romance. Chronicle's universal history offers a different conception of time as an impersonal, regular passage of years, kingdoms, and ages, appearing in Gower's poetry as the mode of Biblical history, as in the Prologue's well-known account of the deteriorating ages of the world and in the opening history of Biblical incest-prohibitions in book 8. Within the framework of the poem, however, universal history appears not as a framework within which personal morality can be understood so much as a text or argument to be heard and interpreted at certain moments in an individual's process of moral reflection. Impersonal historical time is acknowledged, but the plight of Amans is cast in the shape of personal experience; chronicle withdraws from the poem as complaint-romance and exemplarity become the two predominant, incommensurable ways of conceiving such a personal experience of the world.[36] The Prologue hints at differences between these three modes, but no way is given to adjudicate between their various assumptions. Rather, the Prologue serves as a spur (line 1084) to bring readers to an admission that their own predicament of making sense of the world is bound up in competing narrative understandings of temporality.

Aware that the reader's internal disposition will determine the interpretation of his poem, Gower's rhetorical strategy (and his ethical gambit) is to prompt his readers to consider the logic and built-in limits of the patterns by which they conceive experience, offering the possibility that other patterns—in particular an ethical pattern—might be recognized as potentially compelling. The reader might reconceive available frames of perception according to the master modes of chronicle,

---

[36] Ricoeur, in *Time and Narrative*, distinguishes between an Aristotelian "cosmological time" and an Augustinian "personal time," a distinction that constantly needs qualification when applied to narrative forms, but which is helpful to explain why universal chronicle, which follows much of the impersonal sense of cosmological time, falls away in importance from Gower's concern with the personal, first-person experience of the world.

exemplum, and complaint (as in the Prologue), or according to the intersecting claims of exemplum and romance (as in the greater part of the *Confessio Amantis*). This disposition of intersecting, basic modes of self-conception provokes readers to perceive that they cannot think of themselves except through these structures, much as one cannot conceive of the body except as a site of interplay and ineluctable division between the four elements, "of cold, of hot, of moist, of drye" (Prol. 977). One's foundation of moral responsibility is in fact a site of intersection and division, and thus the elemental ground for moral accountability is a kind of "intersected subject."

The subject-position envisaged here is thus not equivalent to a romantic notion of a fully autonomous interior self, for reflection is seen as participation in discursive modes shared by society and preceding the individual. And yet this situation differs from the postmodern, decentered subject for which the self is an illusion created by language, for Gower dearly holds to the belief in an interiority from which to choose between, or at least to feel and endure, competing narrative options. The ground upon which to order one's thoughts, desires, and actions is constituted rather by an activity of first-person enunciation. After Amans has been converted and has accepted the name John Gower, he is charged by Venus to "go ther vertu moral duelleth, / Wher ben thi bokes, as men telleth, / Whiche of long time thou hast write" (8.2925–27). In this instance, Amans/Gower's locus of moral virtue is equated with the place occupied by his writings, both his past writings and the activity of writing down this story about himself as an example to future readers based on the example of the writings of past writers (Prol. 1–11). Able now to review and give shape to the experience of having read his own life through and against available narrative patterns, the character/narrator recognizes that he occupies an individual position of ethical responsiveness, and his readers are spurred to realize that they too can articulate their course of engagement with various models of self-conception. This "withinne" of first-person enunciation, which is also the "wher" from which one can write oneself reading, grounds a person's capabilities of reflection, will, and agency, and describes the position occupied by Gower's intersected subject.

It should be clear that my conclusions about the *Confessio Amantis* differ from those of the recent study by Larry Scanlon, who in his attention to narrative modes, exemplarity, and subjectivity shares many of my basic concerns. For Scanlon, it is well worth noting the striking similarity between [theories of the subject] and the formal logic of the exemplum. For the exemplum's enactment of authority in fact assumes a process of identification on the part of its audience. That is to say, the exemplum expects the members of its audience to be convinced by its *sententia* precisely because it expects them to put themselves in the position of its protagonists, to emulate the protagonist's moral success, or avoid his or her moral failure. It persuades by conveying a sense of communal identity with its moral lesson.[37]

Scanlon discusses the *Confessio Amantis* as if it too expects this subjection of its audience; but it is precisely because the expectations of exemplary authority on this matter cannot be guaranteed that the subject-position imagined by Gower is more complicated; the poem, which is constructed by the logic not of a single narrative mode but of two or more, resists any attempt to reduce its significance (whether rhetorically or politically understood) to the idealized functioning of exemplarity. Gower's "intersected subject" arises from a formal logic that still offers a role to human agency, and it forms a crucial rhetorical premise for the poem's portrayal of the contradictory enactment of various kinds of discursive authority.

Convenient signposts in the history of moral reflection could be invoked for us to make sense of Gower's purposes. The Augustinian description of the soul as an interior source of self-enunciation is a deeply felt inheritance,[38] and Gregory the Great's abiding attention to the way the soul is present in "the shipwreck of this world"[39] through the sufferings and endurance of the body helps explain Gower's emphasis on the genres of complaint and romance (Gregory is the only patristic authority named in the poem).[40] In contrast to these precursors, however, the object of the poet's investigation is not the religious soul but rather the

---

[37] Scanlon, *Narrative, Authority, and Power*, p. 35.

[38] Étienne Gilson, *The Christian Philosophy of Saint Augustine* (London: Gollancz, 1961); Charles Taylor, *Sources of the Self: The Making of the Modern Identity* (Cambridge Mass.: Harvard University Press, 1989), pp. 127–42. Ricoeur speaks of the temporal aspect of this *distentio animi*: ". . . from an Augustinian point of view, the future and the past exist only in relation to a present, that is, to an instant indicated by the utterance designating it. The past is before and the future is after only with respect to this presence possessing the relation of self-reference, attested to by the very act of uttering something"; Ricoeur, *Time and Narrative*, 3:19.

[39] "Vitae huius naufragium"; Gregory the Great, *Moralia in Job*, ed. Robert Gillet (Paris: CERF, 1950), 1:113.

[40] Gregory is named five times: Prol. 284 and 945; 5.1746, 1756, and 1901. Jerome is mentioned as the translator of the Bible at 4.2654.

ethical category of self-responsibility, where decisions are guided not by absolute truths but through a process of negotiating between options which show their truth only "roughly and in outline";[41] this we can speak of as Gower's deep Aristotelianism. But to speak in terms of this intellectual history more specifically might be misleading, couched as that discussion would be in analytical terms eschewed by Gower.[42] The *Confessio Amantis* is poetry rather than philosophy, and draws more on homiletic techniques than expository speculation. Poems and pulpits do more to explain for us this sense of the subject, intersected by competing discursive modes which can be imagined in literary fashion, and constructed through participation in an intersubjective world of responsibility and responsiveness.

The guiding principle of the *Confessio Amantis* is not to *represent* such a subject-position. Within the stories, for instance, the stable identity ultimately achieved by Apollonius runs counter to the instability Gower explores through the *Confessio Amantis* as a whole; such nostalgia is available only within the constraints of a single mode, whether exemplary or romance, and is not adequate to the experience of an intersected subject. Amans/Gower, as the hearer of these various stories, is depicted in a schematic fashion that does not portray how lived experience among shifting discursive claims might be handled in the actual social and material world. Gower thus differs from his friend Chaucer, whose innovative techniques for representing the subjectivity of his characters have been the object of much recent critical attention.[43] Gower is not primarily concerned to *represent* the subjectivity of a char-

---

[41] "Grosse et figuraliter veritatem ostendere"; Aristotle, *Nicomachean Ethics*, p. 376 [1094b20].

[42] One promising domain for analytical explorations of a subject-position similar to that imagined by the *Confessio Amantis* would be fourteenth-century philosophical commentaries on the *Nicomachean Ethics* where Augustinian inwardness and Aristotelian *phronesis* are both centrally present.

[43] See especially H. Marshall Leicester, *The Disenchanted Self: Representing the Subject in the* Canterbury Tales (Berkeley: University of California Press, 1990), and Lee Patterson, *Chaucer and the Subject of History* (Madison: University of Wisconsin Press, 1991). Leicester explains one premise of his study thus: ". . . disenchantment means the perception that what had been thought to be other-originated, the product of transcendent forces not directly susceptible to human tampering and subversion, is in fact humanly originated, the product of human creation. . . . A fully disenchanted perspective constitutes the world as a tissue of institutions rather than natures and therefore tends to see experience and social existence as an encounter between conflicting interpretations rather than the passive reception of preexisting meanings" (pp. 26–27). Whatever its applicability to *The Canterbury Tales*, such a perspective is not foreign to Gower's technique in

acter, but rather to *provoke* the subjectivity of the reader, to create the conditions whereby a reader can come to understand the site he or she occupies at the intersection of incommensurable modes of narrative self-conception. The "Tale of Apollonius," bearing the pattern of ancient romance into the fourteenth-century culture of exemplarity, becomes one of the tools Gower strategically manipulates for implementing that purpose, a purpose which, however, can only be a gambit for Gower, for he knows that he cannot guarantee the success of his strategy of provocation no matter how earnestly he wishes to secure it.

---

the *Confessio Amantis*, except that for Gower this understanding of experience does not entail "disenchantment" but rather constitutes the very ground for ethical, as opposed to theological, considerations. My own analysis of the relation between Gower's treatment of the tale of Apollonius and Chaucer's reference to the same story in the introduction to *The Man of Law's Tale*, presented in its first form as "Romance and the Paradox of Instruction in Gower's *Confessio Amantis* and Chaucer's Introduction to the *Man of Law's Tale*" (paper delivered at Kalamazoo, Mich., May 1995), will be put forward more fully in a future article.

# Sources and Analogues of Chaucer's Canterbury Tales: Reviewing the Work

Helen Cooper
*University College, Oxford*

S*ources and Analogues of Chaucer's* Canterbury Tales, edited by W. F. Bryan and Germaine Dempster, has been a staple resource of Chaucerian scholars for over half a century. It is, however, showing its age: few of its chapters any longer represent the current state of scholarship; and the first chapter in particular, on the literary framework of the tales (that is, sources and analogues for Chaucer's whole conception of the work) is no longer tenable at all.

A full revision of *Sources and Analogues*—a new book to provide an authoritative replacement of Bryan and Dempster's—is now under way under the general editorship of Robert M. Correale, with Mary Hamel as his coeditor. By the invitation of the editor of *Studies in the Age of Chaucer*, and with the encouragement of the New Chaucer Society Board of Trustees, the new first chapter, on the work as a whole, is published here in advance of the rest, to indicate how far our knowledge of Chaucer's sources and literary context has come since the original volume appeared.

## Introduction

*The Canterbury Tales* is a framed story-collection, a form that originated in the East, was adopted with enthusiasm in the medieval West, and reached its peak of popularity in European literature in the fourteenth century. In the *Tales*, the frame takes the form of a pilgrimage with the pilgrims as storytellers, and the tales are told in competition with each other; both these elements have sources and analogues of their own that are independent of the generic nature of the whole work as a collection of tales. In addition, the relationships established between the stories as they pick up related themes and motifs from each other—sometimes from adjacent tales, sometimes from more distant ones—is a process that interlocks with the frame of the work but that also has much in common with debate, itself a widespread literary form but also one found much more widely in medieval culture.

This survey of sources and analogues will attempt to cover all four of these areas—story-collections and how they organize their constituent tales; debate; poetic contests; storytelling pilgrims—to give some idea of the origins of the large structures of the whole work. The problems attendant on such a survey are rather different from those for the individual tales. There are works that we know from other evidence that Chaucer read, and that may have set him thinking—as the articulation of the stories within Ovid's *Metamorphoses*, for instance, may have done—but that do not offer models for the solutions he himself adopted; there are others that offer closer parallels to Chaucer's solutions but where the clinching evidence that would prove direct debt has been in dispute, Boccaccio's *Decameron* being the most striking instance. Specific topics of debate, such as pro- and antifeminism, can be thoroughly documented as they occur in sections of the *Tales*, such as *The Wife of Bath's Prologue*; but Chaucer's informing principle of structuring his story-collection by analogy with a series of dialectical debating positions derives from more general conventions of debate literature, and from the wider usages of disputation in medieval culture, in the law courts, the schools, Parliament, and so on, where specific source texts are beside the point. Some of the evidence for pilgrims' habits of storytelling and for poetic contests is historical rather than literary, so surviving written sources can only poorly represent what may have been Chaucer's direct inspiration.

If any one work can stake a primary claim to being Chaucer's model for the *Tales*, it is the *Decameron*. The possibility of Chaucer's knowledge of the work has been much debated, and the arguments are outlined below. It was rejected as a source by R. A. Pratt and Karl Young in their contribution to Bryan and Dempster's *Sources and Analogues of Chaucer's* Canterbury Tales on the grounds that "its basic conception is that of a succession of aristocratic garden scenes rather than of a moving pilgrimage of diverse and discordant personalities," and they regarded "storytelling in the course of a moving pilgrimage" as "fundamental in the design" of the *Tales*.[1] Furthermore,

---

[1] R. A. Pratt and Karl Young, "The Literary Framework of the Canterbury Tales," in W. F. Bryan and Germaine Dempster, eds., *Sources and Analogues of Chaucer's* Canterbury Tales (1941; rpt. New York: Humanities Press, 1958), pp. 20–21.

we have no decisive evidence that Chaucer was acquainted with it. . . . Chaucer does not mention the *Decameron*, he borrows no stories directly from it, and no copy of it can be traced in England during the period of his life. (p. 20)

They therefore proposed as Chaucer's model the *Novelle* of Giovanni Sercambi, which Chaucer likewise does not mention, from which he borrows no stories directly, and which was barely known in Italy (there is only one surviving manuscript), let alone England; but it does contain a collection of stories told on a journey, by a single first-person narrator.

Sercambi's claims were always tenuous; they were put beyond consideration by more recent research, which has established that the work was not composed until 1400 or later, too late for Chaucer to have known it.[2] Its removal from the scene allows space for the *Decameron* to reenter, and its claims to be reappraised. The shift of critical emphasis that has taken place over the last fifty years allows a new stress on the literary over the literal, the dynamics of articulating a story-collection over the choice of a journey to provide the occasion for the storytelling; and with the shift, Boccaccio's work looks to be an increasingly certain candidate as the inspiration behind the *Tales*. Even Pratt and Young's claim that it never functions as Chaucer's immediate source for individual tales is open to question; and although it does not furnish the model for every aspect of Chaucer's work, such as the pilgrimage and the organization as a competition, those can, as has been indicated, be supplied from other sources more immediately available to Chaucer.

### I.i. Story-collections

Story-collections were in themselves a distinct genre in the Middle Ages, with their own conventions of organization, content, purpose, and audience expectation. They do not, however, constitute a homogenous form.[3] They vary in structure from collections of brief narratives assembled without any kind of introduction or attempt at linking, to collections that are articulated in the most elaborate ways. Most were concerned with giving moral instruction; but exemplary tales are designed to make morals attractive, and the didactic can easily find itself

---

[2] *Giovanni Sercambi: Il novelliere*, ed. Luciano Rossi (Rome: Salerno, 1976), 1:xix–xx. Rossi also disproves the existence of a hypothetical lost short form of the work supposedly dating from ca. 1374.

[3] For a broader survey, see Helen Cooper, *The Structure of the* Canterbury Tales (London: Duckworth, 1983; Athens, Ga.: Georgia University Press, 1984), pp. 8–55.

subsumed by the entertaining. There is a broad correlation between simple structure and moral emphasis at one end of the spectrum of story-collections, and literary complexity and a greater stress on pleasurableness at the other; and it is to this latter variety that *The Canterbury Tales* belongs.

Given this range of models, the distinctiveness of the *Tales*, and with that the likelihood of its having a source identifiable from among the many collections circulating in the fourteenth century, can best be brought out by a rapid survey of the different kinds of story-collections in existence, and in particular those known to Chaucer or those compiled within the sphere of English, Anglo-French, or Anglo-Latin culture. The simplest kind of collection either has no frame at all or just a prologue: Chaucer himself produces examples of the form in *The Legend of Good Women* (though the elaboration of the prologue distinguishes the poem from most such collections) and *The Monk's Tale*. Most commonly, collections of this kind contain stories of a single genre—narratives of abandoned or suffering women in the *Legend*, tragedies in *The Monk's Tale*. Chaucer's source for the *Legend*, Ovid's collection of letters from abandoned women, the *Heroides*, belongs to this category; it also gets a mention in the Man of Law's survey of story-collections in the Introduction to his tale (lines 54–55).[4] Such collections may be secular in nature, especially those that are classical or modeled on the classics—not only the *Legend*, but early humanist works such as the stories of famous women in Boccaccio's *De claris mulieribus*. Even these, however, often have an exemplary function, most explicit in works such as the first-century *Factorum et dictorum memorabilium libri novem* of Valerius Maximus, which the Wife of Bath's Jankin included among his reading (*WBP* 642–49).[5]

There is a handful of secular story-collections of this simple structure that originated in the Middle Ages, such as the *Lais* of Marie de France; but most of those compiled in this period, including the most widely disseminated examples, were religious or didactic, or both. Collections of saints' lives and of beast fables, where each story carries an accompanying *moralitas*, are usually structured in this way. The best-known in-

---

[4] All citations of Chaucer's works are from Larry D. Benson, gen. ed., *The Riverside Chaucer*, 3d ed. (Boston: Houghton Mifflin, 1987); further citations will appear in the text.

[5] *Valerii Maximi factorum et dictorum memorabilium libri novem*, ed. Carolus Kempf, Bibliotheca Teubneriana (1888; rpt. Stuttgart: Teubner, 1966).

stances of the form were collections of exempla for use by preachers. Foremost among these is the *Gesta Romanorum*, a ragbag of assorted stories of which the order and even the contents vary extensively from manuscript to manuscript.[6] It originated early in the fourteenth century, probably in England; both Gower and Hoccleve draw on it, and Chaucer occasionally mentions stories it contains, although he may have derived them from other sources. In preaching collections of this sort, the stories may potentially be of mixed kinds, but the moral or allegorical purpose overrides any development of variety for its own sake.

A rare exception to the single-genre nature of most of these collections with minimal frames is the *Novellino*, an Italian collection of a hundred brief narratives with a prologue dating from around 1300 that was one of Boccaccio's models for the *Decameron*.[7] Mixed in with its short *novelle* (which include one of the closest analogues of *The Merchant's Tale*) are episodes from Arthurian tales, beast fables, and moral tales, including a version of the story that the Pardoner tells about meeting death in the form of a hoard of gold.

There is a further group of story-collections that provides a simple linking mechanism between tales in addition to providing a prologue announcing the nature of the work, though there are not many examples of this kind that appear to have been known to Chaucer; Boccaccio's *De casibus virorum illustrium*, which may have been the inspiration for *The Monk's Tale* (the scribe of the Ellesmere manuscript suggests as much), is the main possible exception. In the *De casibus*, those who have fallen from high estate into misery pass before Boccaccio's eyes to tell their stories and allow the opportunity for moralization; its content, of posthumously recounted biographies, recalls Dante's *Inferno*, though here it is the ghosts of the dead that move past while their recorder stays still. The work decisively entered English culture early in the fifteenth century when Lydgate translated it, by way of an intermediary French translation, as *The Fall of Princes*.[8] Another such loosely linked collection, the

---

[6] See the edition by Hermann Oesterley (Berlin: Weidmann, 1872). A Middle English translation was made early in the fifteenth century; *The Early English Versions of the Gesta Romanorum*, ed. Sidney J. H. Herrtage, Early English Text Society [hereafter EETS], e.s., 33 (1879).

[7] *Il Novellino*, ed. G. Favati (Genoa: Bozzi, 1970). The work is often known by the title given by its first printed edition in 1525, *Le ciento novelle antike*.

[8] *Giovanni Boccaccio: De casibus virorum illustrium*, ed. P. G. Ricci and V. Zaccaria (Milan: Mondadori, 1983); *Lydgate's Fall of Princes*, ed. Henry Bergen, EETS, e.s., 121–24 (1924–27).

*Disciplina clericalis* of Petrus Alfonsi,[9] has its roots in Arabic traditions through its origins in Spain; it may have been written around 1110, when he was working in England as physician to Henry I.[10] The work was widely disseminated throughout Europe, but although this too was translated into English in the fifteenth century,[11] Chaucer probably knew it only at second hand through quotations in Albertanus of Brescia's *Liber consolationis et consilii*, the source of *Melibee*. Its frame is very loose, consisting of little more than statements such as "A father said to his son—" or "A master said to his pupil—," and offers none of the dynamics found in the *Tales*.

More suggestive are works that develop the frame to make a story in its own right. In some works from which Chaucer draws stories or examples, such as histories, the Bible, the *Roman de la rose*, and the *Divina Commedia*, the stories become incidental to the larger frame in the sense that the overarching structure does not exist exclusively for their sake but rather takes precedence over them. Such works turn into story-collections in texts such as William of Waddington's Anglo-Norman *Manuel des Pechiez* and its English adaptation, Robert Mannyng of Bourne's *Handlyng Synne*, where the stories are told to illustrate the major topics of Christian instruction: the Ten Commandments, the seven deadly sins, the seven sacraments, and so on.[12] Mannyng began his version in 1303, so the work belongs with the great fourteenth-century flowering of story-collections. It is paralleled in its structure from the end of the century by Gower's *Confessio amantis* with its architecture of the seven sins against love. This was certainly known to Chaucer; Gower includes a greeting to him, put into the mouth of Venus, at the end of the earliest version of the poem,[13] and Chaucer's

---

[9] *Petrus Alfonsi: Disciplina Clericalis*, ed. Alfons Hilka and W. Söderhjelm (Heidelberg: C. Winter, 1911); *The 'Disciplina Clericalis' of Petrus Alfonsi*, trans. and ed. Eberhard Hermes, trans. into English by P. R. Quarrie (London: Routledge and Kegan Paul, 1977).

[10] See John Tolan, *Petrus Alfonsi and his Medieval Readers* (Gainesville: University of Florida Press, 1993), pp. 10–11. The work is given a more elaborate history by Thomas D. Cooke in *A Manual of the Writings in Middle English, 1050–1500*, vol. 9 (New Haven: Connecticut Academy of Arts and Sciences, 1993), section XXIV: Tales, p. 3326.

[11] *Peter Alphonse's Disciplina Clericalis*, ed. William Henry Hulme, Western Reserve Studies, vol. 1, no. 5 (Cleveland, Ohio: Western Reserve University Press, 1919).

[12] *Robert of Brunne's "Handlyng Synne,"* ed. Frederick J. Furnivall, EETS, o.s., 119, 123 (1901, 1903), gives the Anglo-Norman text in parallel.

[13] *Confessio* 8.2941*–57*, in *The English Works of John Gower*, ed. G. C. Macaulay, EETS, e.s., 81–82 (1900–1901).

own reference to incestuous stories in the Introduction to *The Man of Law's Tale* (lines 77–85) is generally taken as an allusion to the *Confessio*. The early stages of the composition of the *Tales* would have overlapped with the writing of the *Confessio*, but there is no surviving evidence that either poet was inspired to write a story-collection by the example of the other, and they handle the problems and opportunities of the form very differently. Gower's use of a single narrator to offer instruction appears at first glance to be close to Mannyng's *Handlyng Synne*, but Mannyng speaks as narrator in his own voice; Gower's fictional instructor Genius and his first-person interlocutor Amans, who is a fictionalized version of Gower himself, move a step closer to Chaucer's practice in the *Tales* but still offer a very different kind of framing dynamic.

There are in addition some works with multiple narrators who tell tales within more fully autonomous frames. Two by Boccaccio have indeed been proposed as models for the *Tales*: the *Ameto*, in which an assembly of minimally allegorical nymphs recount their sexual histories (one of these, an account of the grotesque lovemaking of a *senex amans*, offers some overlap in subject with *The Merchant's Tale*); and the *Filocolo*, an immensely long retelling of the romance of Floris and Blancheflour that includes an episode in which the characters propose conundrums on the topic of love, *demandes d'amour*, some of which set up the problem at issue by telling stories (one of these, retold in the *Decameron*, constitutes an analogue to *The Franklin's Tale*). Chaucer could have known either, or indeed both; but even for the *Filocolo* the evidence is very weak, and the latest scholarship on the subject does not claim indebtedness on Chaucer's part.[14] Story-collections with autonomous frames originate much earlier than this, however: the *Seven Sages of Rome*, Oriental in origin, was some two millennia old by the time it reached the West in the mid-twelfth century. It was very widely disseminated in many languages, including an English translation made probably in the late thirteenth century.[15] It is included in the Auchinleck manu-

---

[14] See Barry Windeatt, *Oxford Guides to Chaucer: Troilus and Criseyde* (Oxford: Clarendon Press, 1992), pp. 47, 147; he perceives congruence of story rather than "actual textual borrowing." For a broader discussion of "what larger, more abstract concepts and ideas Chaucer might have derived from such a text," see David Wallace, *Chaucer and the Early Writings of Boccaccio*, Chaucer Studies, no. 12 (Woodbridge: D. S. Brewer, 1985), pp. 39–72.

[15] On its history, see Killis Campbell, *The Seven Sages of Rome* (Boston: Ginn & Co., 1907). The various Middle English versions probably all derive from the same translation; see the edition by Karl Brunner, *The Seven Sages of Rome*, EETS, o.s., 191 (1933).

script, which it has been suggested that Chaucer knew;[16] but even if he had read the work, he made little or no use of it (he makes oblique references to one of its stories in *WBP* 231–34 and in *The Manciple's Tale*, but tales of this kind often circulated independently), and none at all in terms of structure. The relation of the frame of the *Seven Sages* to the stories it contains is very different from the *Tales*: a prince is accused of sexual misconduct by his stepmother, and the tales are told to the king by his teachers and his stepmother alternately to preserve or threaten his life. The frame, in fact, could exist without the stories, as the Canterbury pilgrimage could not.

Oriental story-collections[17] developed the most sophisticated methods of articulating their constituent tales, but only isolated examples were known in the medieval West. They offer a highly complex structure in which stories are recessed within stories: the supreme example of the form, the *Thousand and One Nights*, makes the fact that no tale is ever complete before several more are under way into the object of the frame story. This particular work was not known in Europe until much later, but some other examples of the form made their way into Western culture by way of Spain: *Kalila and Dimna*, also known as the *Fables of Bidpai*, entered by this route, becoming known through its Latin translation, the *Directorium vitae humanae*.[18] Although Chaucer does not base his work on collections of this kind, he does use stories of Oriental origin on occasion, most particularly in *The Squire's Tale*; and both there and more largely over the whole work he shows signs of a concern to get away from presenting tales simply as a sequence of autonomous stories, and he too will experiment with techniques of recession and insetting.

Another work that offers a similarly elaborate configuration of its constituent tales and that he most certainly did know is the *Metamorphoses* of Ovid. Chaucer himself appears to suggest a parallel between his

---

[16] See two essays by Laura Hibbard Loomis, "Chaucer and the Breton Lays of the Auchinleck Manuscript" and "Chaucer and the Auchinleck MS: *Thopas* and *Guy of Warwick*," rpt. in her *Adventures in the Middle Ages* (New York: Burt Franklin, 1962), pp. 111–49.

[17] On these see Katherine Slater Gittes, "The *Canterbury Tales* and the Arabic Frame Tradition," *PMLA* 98 (1983): 237–51.

[18] *Johannis de Capua Directorium vitae humanae*, ed. Joseph Derenbourg, Bibliothèque des Hautes Études, no. 72 (Paris: F. Vieweg, 1887–89). The work did not appear in any version in English until the sixteenth century, when Sir Thomas North translated an Italian translation of a Spanish translation of John of Capua's Latin (*The Morall Philosophie of Doni*, 1570; edited by Joseph Jacobs as *The Fables of Bidpai* [London: David Nutt, 1888]).

own work and Ovid's in the Introduction to *The Man of Law's Tale*, where he has the Man of Law claim (lines 91–96),

> "Me were looth be likned, doutelees,
> To Muses that men clepe Pierides—
> *Methamorphosios* woot what I mene;
> But nathelees, I recche noght a bene
> Though I come after hym with hawebake.
> I speke in prose, and lat him rymes make."

The reference appears to be to the daughters of Pierus who challenged the Muses, themselves also known as the Pierides, to a singing contest and were turned into chattering magpies for their presumption.[19] In a typically backhanded way, Chaucer appears to be setting himself up as Muse in comparison to the Man of Law's magpie, even while he is himself the ventriloquist behind the Man of Law. In a very broad sense, the *Metamorphoses* kind of story-collection, which offers a frame that exists to justify the telling of the stories and that both introduces and links the tales, represents the category to which *The Canterbury Tales* itself belongs; but the absence of any plot to its frame (which is constituted as an arrangement rather than a story, starting with the Golden Age and working through to Augustus) and its lack of a distinctive group of narrators telling *all* the stories make it a very different work.[20] It was known in two major forms in the fourteenth-century West, in its original Latin, often accompanied by moralizing commentaries, and in the French *Ovide moralisé*,[21] which incorporated substantial moralities into the poetry. Chaucer will occasionally use material from the Latin glossators, for instance in his descriptions of the pagan gods in *The Knight's Tale*; but in contrast to these medievalized versions of Ovid, his own reading concentrates to a remarkable degree on the stories alone, not on any exemplary or allegorical function they might be made to bear.

---

[19] *Ovid: Metamorphoses*, ed. and trans. Frank Justus Miller, Loeb Classical Library (Cambridge, Mass.: Harvard University Press; London, Heinemann, 1944, 1951), 5.295–345, 669–78.

[20] It has nonetheless been proposed as Chaucer's primary model for the *Tales* by Judson Boyce Allen and Theresa Anne Moritz, *A Distinction of Stories: Chaucer's Fair Chain of Narratives for Canterbury* (Columbus, Ohio: Ohio State University Press, 1981).

[21] Ed. C. de Boer, *Verhandelingen der Koninklijke Akademie van Wettenschappen te Amsterdam: Adfeeling Letterkunde*, Nieuwe Reeks, vols. 15, 21, 30, 37, 43 (1915–38). There is no clear evidence that Chaucer knew the work.

## I.ii. The *Decameron*[22]

Two points emerge from such a survey of generic analogues to *The Canterbury Tales*: first, that Chaucer's own story-collection participates in a widespread current fashion for such works; and second, that it is strikingly different from most in the dynamics offered by its frame story, in the articulation of its tales, and in its refusal to offer any consistent moralization. Very few works offer any detailed resemblance; and of those that do, the *Decameron* is by far the closest, to the point where deliberate imitation becomes more likely than mere coincidence.

The case against Chaucer's knowledge of the work is based on the lack of specific verbal parallels such as are characteristic of his borrowings from other works of Boccaccio, notably the *Filostrato* and the *Teseida*. He never gives the impression of working extensively with a copy in front of him; he often uses a source other than Boccaccio even when he is telling a tale that also appears in the *Decameron*. There are, however, more parallels of both idea and phrasing in the two works than have generally been recognized, and they occur in precisely those areas that are unique to these two collections: in their handling of a frame for their storytelling that includes both multiple tellers and a fictional audience; in the interplay both writers invite between that fictional audience and their implied readers, and between fictional tellers and their self-presentation as authors; in their comments on the nature and function of fiction; and in their articulation of a story-collection that forgoes the more obvious kinds of thematic unity.

There is a big difference between acknowledging that Chaucer was not working with a copy of the *Decameron* on his desk, and denying that he knew it at all. A theory between the two has recurrently been proposed, that Chaucer had read or heard the *Decameron* while in Italy—conceivably even from an Italian merchant in London[23]—but did not have a copy of his own to set in front of him while he was writing.[24]

---

[22] My thanks are due to Nigel Thompson, David Wallace, and Peter Beidler for advice and suggestions on this section.

[23] David Wallace, *Giovanni Boccaccio: Decameron* (Cambridge: Cambridge University Press, 1991), pp. 108–9, notes that as early as 1373 the work was "moving around the European trade routes with the merchant classes who figure so prominently in its pages"; on its links with the *Tales*, see p. 111.

[24] This possibility was put forward by R. K. Root in 1911 ("Chaucer and the *Decameron*," *Englische Studien* 44 [1909]: 1–7) and has been argued since by various other critics, including J. S. P. Tatlock ("Boccaccio and the Plan of Chaucer's *Canterbury Tales*," *Anglia* 37 [1913]: 69–117); occasionally a closer connection has been argued, for instance by

This would explain his tendency to work from different sources for analogous stories, and the freedom of treatment he gives himself where no alternative source is known; but his deployment of similar methods and dynamics in articulating a collection would not require a text of the *Decameron* at hand, and the closest parallels show the kind of creative reinvention that would more plausibly come from thinking about Boccaccian ideas than from reworking his precise words.

The parallels can be summarized as follows:

(1)   The *Decameron* is the only story-collection prior to the *Tales* where the stories are told by a series of narrators who agree to tell tales to each other as a pastime, and where these stories (unlike in the *Filocolo* and *Ameto*) are the *raison d'etre* of the work. In both, the *brigata* or *compaignie* who are to tell the stories are introduced in a naturalistic fashion that gives them an illusion of historical authenticity in contrast to their overtly fictional tales. Both groups are described as meeting up by chance (in the church of Santa Maria Novella, at the Tabard Inn); they agree to spend time together (to leave Florence for a succession of country houses, to travel to Canterbury as a group) and to tell stories under the direction of a master of ceremonies (a sovereign elected for each day in the *Decameron*; the Host in the *Tales*).

(2)   Five of the Canterbury tales—the Reeve's, Clerk's, Merchant's, Franklin's, and Shipman's[25]—have analogues in the *Decameron* (Reeve, Day 9.6; Clerk, 10.10; Merchant, 7.9 (and see also 2.10); Franklin,

---

Donald McGrady ("Chaucer and the *Decameron* Reconsidered," *ChauR* 12 [1977]: 1–26). For a more skeptical survey of the relationship between the works, see Robin Kirkpatrick, "In the Wake of the *Commedia*: Chaucer's *Canterbury Tales* and Boccaccio's *Decameron*," in Piero Boitani, ed., *Chaucer and the Italian Trecento* (Cambridge: Cambridge University Press, 1983), pp. 201–30. Much of the belief that Chaucer did not know the *Decameron* can be traced back to the doubt expressed by Herbert M. Cummings, *The Indebtedness of Chaucer's Works to the Italian Works of Boccaccio: A Review and Summary*, University of Cincinnati Studies, no. 10 (Cincinnati: University of Cincinnati, 1916), pp. 176–97, but his arguments are neither sufficiently detailed nor decisive. Peter G. Beidler provides an extensive review of past scholarship in "Just Say Yes, Chaucer Knew the *Decameron*: or, Bringing the *Shipman's Tale* Out of Limbo," in Leonard Koff and Brenda Schildgen, eds., *The Decameron and the Canterbury Tales* (forthcoming). A detailed survey of the similarities between the two works is made by N. S. Thompson, *Chaucer, Boccaccio and the Debate of Love* (Oxford: Clarendon Press, 1996).

[25] See Peter G. Beidler, "Chaucer's *Merchant's Tale* and the *Decameron*," *Italica* 50 (1976): 266–84, and his "Just Say Yes," for a full discussion of the extent of the work's possible contribution to the *Merchant's* and *Shipman's Tales*.

10.5; Shipman, 8.1). In addition, there is a more distant analogue to *The Man of Law's Tale* (5.2); and both *The Pardoner's Prologue* (6.10) and *The Miller's Tale* (3.4, with more distant links to 8.7 and 7.4) share motifs with the *Decameron*. Two of these tales, the Shipman's and Franklin's, may well be using the *Decameron* as their immediate source; and fully a quarter of the tales in Chaucer's collection have analogues in the work. None of his other known or possible sources, nor any other medieval or classical story-collection, comes near to offering such a high proportion of parallel stories.

The doubt over Chaucer's knowledge of the work results from the fact that in most of these instances either versions closer to Chaucer's are known from other sources, or else the similarities are too loose to prove direct indebtedness. This last is true even of the two *novelle*, 8.1 and 10.5, that provide the closest analogues known for the *Shipman's* and *Franklin's Tales*: in both, the plot outlines are the same but the details are extensively changed. One is therefore faced with a choice between an implausible coincidence in the proportion of analogues, and the indisputable evidence in many instances for rival sources. The theory of memorial reconstruction would resolve this dilemma: Chaucer could have read or heard the *Decameron* (or parts of it: it is striking that the closest connections are with the tales of days 7, 8, 9, and 10, and the *Conclusione*), and then sought out versions of the same stories to retell when he was working on the *Tales*.

(3)   In both works, the author remains as a first-person presence alongside the storytellers, and although this is done in very different ways (Boccaccio retains his separate identity outside the frame, Chaucer puts himself within it as part of his own fiction), they both use their presence to justify their work in strikingly similar terms. Boccaccio reminds his audience of his presence on three occasions: at the start; in an intervention before the Fourth Day's storytelling, when he tells a story of his own, so dissolving some of the distance between himself as author and his fictional narrators in a way that Chaucer takes much further; and in the *Conclusione dell'autore*. In the last of these he presents the most detailed defense of his work, using arguments that reappear in Chaucer's mouth in the *Tales*. Both insist that the broadness of some of their stories is due to the need for true reporting, that "Whoso shal telle a tale after a man, / He moot reherce as ny as evere he kan / Everich a word" (*GP* 731–33), or that "io non pote' né doveva scrivere se non le raccon-

tate" ["I could not and ought not to have written them other than they were told"];[26] and, like Chaucer, Boccaccio denies that he made the stories up himself, being rather a mere transcriber (*Conclusione* 1258.17). Both remind their readers that they may skip offensive tales, and that if they do not it is their fault (lines 3176–86 in *The Miller's Prologue*, which does at least appear before the first of Chaucer's scurrilous stories; Boccaccio mischievously leaves his warning until the end,[27] though, as he also notes, he does provide summaries before each story that indicate something of the content—one could say, not enough). They both thus stress the moral responsibility of the reader over the author: "Blameth nat me if that ye chese amys," as Chaucer puts it (*MilP* 3181).

Both authors also stress from the start the pleasure and profit that their stories may bring. Boccaccio insists several times, from the *Proemio* forward, that his stories are both entertaining and profitable, full of *sollazzevoli cose* and *utile consiglio* (*Proemio* 7.14), pleasurable matters and useful advice; Chaucer puts the same idea into the Host's requirement for *sentence* and *solaas* (*GP* 798), but restores the traditional order of the two (profit first, pleasure second) that Boccaccio inverts. That literature combines the profitable and the pleasant is of course a commonplace of long standing, but the contexts in which both authors use it are closely similar: the association of story-collections with exemplary tales and preaching anthologies means that their inclusion of distinctly immoral stories requires particular justification. Boccaccio explicitly stresses the therapeutic value of such recreation,[28] both by the setting in the Black Death and in the *Conclusione*; the tales of the pilgrimage are told as part of a celebration of recovery from sickness (*GP* 18).

Boccaccio's disingenuous defense of polite language for impolite things is also an issue taken up in the *Tales* (*Conclusione* 1254–55.3–5,

---

[26] *Decameron*, ed. Vittore Branca, 2d ed. (Turin: Einaudi, 1984), *Conclusione* 1258.16; a closely similar remark is made earlier, "Se alcuna cosa in alcuna n'è, la qualità delle novelle l'hanno richiesta . . . se io quelle della lor forma trar non avessi voluto, altramenti raccontar non poterlo" ["if anything in any (of the stories) is (unseemly), the nature of the tales required it . . . if I did not wish to distort their nature, I could not have told them otherwise"] (1255.4). Compare the passage around the quotation given from the *Tales, GP* 725–36, and *MilP* 3173–75.

[27] "Chi va tra queste leggendo, lasci star quelle che pungono e quelle che dilettano legga" ["You who go along reading these tales, leave aside the ones that give offense and read the ones that please"] (*Conclusione* 1259.19); compare Chaucer's invitation to "Turne over the leef and chese another tale" if one finds "harlotrie" offensive (*MilP* 3176–86).

[28] See Glending Olson, *Literature as Recreation in the Later Middle Ages* (Ithaca, N.Y.: Cornell University Press, 1982), especially pp. 155–83.

*GP* 725–42). Boccaccio claims that his use of double-entendres avoids unseemliness, so that nothing he writes is *disonesta*; Chaucer denies *vileynye* on his own part, and blames his fictional pilgrims. Boccaccio attacks objectors who are more concerned with moral words than deeds; Chaucer cites Plato to justify "large" language as "cosyn to the dede." Both, rather startlingly, conclude their apologies with references to Christ: Boccaccio with an appeal to be allowed the same *auttorità* as the painter who represents Christ's maleness (*Conclusione* 1256.6), Chaucer with an appeal to Christ's own example in speaking "ful brode" (*GP* 739). There is another parallel to this passage of Boccaccio's, where he goes on to insist that the difference in representations of the Crucifixion does not affect the underlying truth, in Chaucer-pilgrim's excursus on literary theory in the prologue to *Melibee*, where he argues that the *sentence* of the Gospels is one although the words vary (*Mel* 943–52).

To summarize: in both works, the authors use their presence to offer the same justifications for writing, the same excuses for their stories not all being moral, the same transferring of ethical responsibility to their audience or readers, and similar discussions of the relation of word to meaning.

(4)    Although the *Tales* goes much further than the *Decameron* in its generic and stylistic diversity,[29] which in turn reflects its greater variety of narrators, both offer a wider range of tales than the typical single-genre medieval story-collection, and both stress this diversity through giving varied audience reactions within the work. Although Boccaccio's tales are all assimilated to the *novella* while Chaucer highlights generic difference, he makes the variations within that form explicit: his narrators talk diversely of diverse things ("diverse cose diversamente parlando," Day 4.7, p. 547.5), and occasionally react in different ways (after Lauretta's song at the end of Day 3, "diversamente da diversi fu intesa," p. 456.18; compare Chaucer's "diverse folk diversely they seyde" [*RvP* 3857]).[30]

---

[29] On these qualities in the *Decameron*, see Thompson, *Chaucer, Boccaccio*, pp. 8–19, and Vittore Branca, *Boccaccio Medievale e nuovi studi sul* Decamerone (Florence: Sansoni, 1981), pp. 83–133, where he writes of the "bifrontalità del *Decamerone*, nei 'temi' e negli 'stili'" (p. 133), toward the comic on the one hand and the lyric or tragic on the other; the elegance and elaboration of style is, however, continuous, as he himself demonstrates (pp. 45–82).

[30] The point is developed by Thompson, *Chaucer, Boccaccio*, p. 17.

Boccaccio's tales are stylistically more homogenous than Chaucer's, but both will mix styles for parodic purposes. Interestingly, both *The Merchant's Tale* and its Boccaccian analogue, 7.9, combine a high romance–style opening with bawdy content. Boccaccio further distinguishes his serious, pitiful, and comic stories from each other by audience reaction, of debate (4.4, 10.4, 5, and 10), praise (10.8, 9), compassion (4.2), or laughter (*passim*). Chaucer's wider range of genres is accompanied by a meticulous deployment, or parody, of rhetorical decorum, high-style genres being assigned to the *gentils* and low-style *cherles tales* to the low-born; and like Boccaccio, he sometimes underlines these differences by giving audience reactions: appreciation of the nobility of the Knight's tale, laughter after the Miller's, soberness after the Prioress's. When such a general response is not given, the Host often steps in with a reaction of his own, usually a notably inappropriate or inadequate one, so that the *Decameron* pattern of beginning the link to the next story with a response to the previous one is maintained.

(5)    To counter the risks created by this diversity of the collections flying apart, both Boccaccio and Chaucer develop connections of theme and motif between tales. In the *Decameron* this is done most explicitly through the setting of a specific topic for each day (the first and ninth excepted), though it is often treated with wit or parody. In 2.1, for instance, the very first story told under this regime of prescribed theme, the specified reversal from misfortune to happiness is illustrated by the story of a man who narrowly avoids execution; in 4.2, the prescribed gloomy topic is subverted. Similar processes of parody and subversion occur in the Knight's and Miller's tales, on the pursuit of one woman by two men; in the Monk's and Nun's Priest's treatments of Fortune; and in the "marriage group" and all the other tales on the nature of women. Chaucer does not, in the work as we have it, divide his tales into separate days, though the pilgrimage schema would make such a division possible; but the groups of tales he did leave work on a principle of interrelatedness[31] less explicit than Boccaccio's but otherwise closely similar.

In addition, Boccaccio's tellers will often point out a specific connection with the previous story as a trigger for their own, or sometimes refer back some distance to a common motif (e.g., dreams in 4.5, 6 and 9.7),

---

[31] See Cooper, *Structure*, pp. 108–207.

in ways comparable to Chaucer's picking up of motifs across tales: he too places dreams at significant points in the *Monk's* and *Nun's Priest's Tales*; the Wife of Bath is recalled in the Clerk's Envoy and by Justinus in *The Merchant's Tale*. Boccaccio takes this reappearance of characters much further than Chaucer, but confines them within the *novelle*: the adventures of Calendrino and his companions recur on several occasions (8.3, 6, 9; 9.3, 5). Chaucer by contrast goes further in creating some kind of interplay between the characters of his frame and the characters within the tales—not just with the Wife and the other tales of marriage, but between the Wife and Friar, Friar and Summoner, Miller and Reeve, and Squire and Franklin. Even this has an approximate parallel in the *Decameron*, when the start of the sixth day's storytelling is delayed by the dispute between the servants Licisca and Tindaro over a story strikingly similar to those narrated by their masters and mistresses; and this event in the frame affects the later *novelle* when Dioneo recalls it in the evening in order to prescribe the topic of the storytelling for the seventh day.

Some of the connections between *novelle* are more casual: that two tales of the same day may be set in the same area or town, for instance. 7.3 is a story of fornication between a mother and her child's godfather, set in Siena; in the tenth tale of the day, Dioneo recalls this to introduce his own story with the same plot elements and setting. A similar relationship is found in the *Tales* between the Miller's and Reeve's tales of adultery, with their Oxford and Cambridge settings; Chaucer inherited the Lombard setting of *The Clerk's Tale* from Petrarch, but he changed the location of *The Merchant's Tale* to match, presumably in order to pair with it.

Chaucer's tales are often linked by contrast within a larger similarity—the *Knight's* and *Miller's Tales*, the *Second Nun's* and *Canon's Yeoman's*—and this too is a principle already made explicit in the *Decameron*, where, for instance, stories of tricks played on men by women will be countered by one played by a man on a woman (8.1). Chaucer is also fond of motifs of overgoing, where the aesthetic competition between stories turns into requital or revenge; and here too there are parallels in the *Decameron*, not between tellers—who in contrast to Chaucer's are consistently polite and courteous, more given to denigrating themselves than each other—but in the stories themselves. So 8.7, about a guiler beguiled, is capped by 8.10, in which Dioneo promises to surpass the pleasure already given by such stories by telling of the deception of the greatest deceiver so far. Here the *Tales* offer parallels in such connections between stories as the Reeve's tale of two students' sexual revenge on their deceiver, itself told as revenge against the

Miller's tale of one student's successful adultery, and the Friar's and Summoner's tales of the deception of their venal *alter teipse*.

None of these many and various parallels in Boccaccio offers an indisputable *verbal* source for any of the tales or framing material found in Chaucer. What they do show, over and over again, is a convergence of interpretations as to what a story-collection might be, and of solutions to the problem of how to articulate such a very diverse collection. The most obvious interpretation of this convergence is that it represents Chaucer's own elaboration of a model he recalled from the *Decameron*. The alternative possibility, that Boccaccio and Chaucer independently invented similar connective schemes for their tales and told many of the same stories, appears less and less plausible as the parallels mount up.

## II. Debate

The social and moral variety of Chaucer's pilgrims and the stylistic and generic diversity of their tales are not ends in themselves. They enable Chaucer to set up a series of different and opposed assumptions about human existence and experience, and to present various attitudes to specific issues that were matters of dispute in the larger world. The narrative articulation of the tales works through the Host's calling on one pilgrim to follow another; but the tales are also connected as a series of elements in a debate, or in several debates. The "marriage debate" is the most familiar of these, but it has tended to be treated as an autonomous unit within the larger work; in fact, the whole of *The Canterbury Tales* participates in that fascination with opposites that characterizes the Middle Ages, and that found expression in the debates of the law courts, royal and baronial councils, Parliament, and the schools, in the entire academic method established by works such as Peter Lombard's *Sentences*, and in debate poetry.[32] Debate thus took up a far larger space in the ordinary conduct of life than in the modern age, being the medium of much intellectual activity and of the procedures of administration, and extending beyond serious public life into the realm of entertainment—debate for its own sake. This happened even within the

---

[32] See Thomas L. Reed, Jr., *Middle English Debate Poetry and the Aesthetics of Irresolution* (Columbia: University of Missouri Press, 1990), pp. 41–96, for a study of the institutional context of literary debates. John W. Conlee's introduction to his *Middle English Debate Poetry: A Critical Anthology* (East Lansing, Mich.: Colleagues Press, 1991) notes how a "preoccupation with the interaction of opposites" was a "fundamental habit of mind" (p. xi). For the Latin debate tradition, see Hans Walther, *Das Streitgedicht in der lateinischen Literatur des Mittelalters* (Munich: Beck, 1920).

schools, where positions in a disputation were often assigned, so that whether or not the disputant believed in the thesis he was arguing was irrelevant; it was the quality of the argument that was all-important. So, in 1407, the "Scholar-Errant" John Argentyn of Strasbourg arrived at the University of Cambridge and challenged all comers to dispute with him.[33] That such debates took place in public underlines the fact that they were occasions for enjoyment as well as for the practice of professional skills; exercise and display, indeed, took priority over the discovery of a concluding or conclusive truth.

Such a shift of dialectic toward the aesthetic is taken a large step further in the fashion for debating *demandes d'amour*, and in debate poetry, the popularity of which spans the Middle Ages from the ninth century to the fifteenth. Jean de Meun's continuation of the *Roman de la rose* itself constitutes an extended debate in narrative form. Of formal debate poems, some, such as the *Thrush and the Nightingale*, come to a conclusion: the question disputed by the birds, of whether women are a good thing or not (a perennial favorite, also extensively debated over the *Tales* well beyond the limits of the "marriage group"), is resolved by the Nightingale's appeal to the example of the Virgin. Many others are not resolved: the *Owl and the Nightingale* ends before the judgment is given, and it is hard to see what decision could do justice to the issues set out in the poem. Various specific topics are argued in the course of the birds' dispute, but the overarching issue is an irreconcilable difference of attitudes represented in the poem by the fact that owls are owls and nightingales nightingales, and neither is wrong to be so. Chaucer is highly unlikely to have known the work, but in *The Parliament of Fowls* he offers an analogous scheme, in which a specific *demande d'amour* as to which of the three birds of prey (noble birds, in the medieval hierarchy of species) should win the hand of the formel is hijacked by the array of views on courtship, love, and faithfulness presented and represented by the lower birds. The cuckoo's or the goose's solutions would be wrong for the eagle or the turtledove; but their rightness for a cuckoo or a goose constitutes at least part of the point of the poem. The lack of any answer to the initial *demande* may have some topical reference, but more significant within the text is the natural and continuing irreconcilability of different mind-sets, different assumptions about behavior, beliefs, priorities,

---

[33] Reed, *Debate Poetry*, p. 52.

and the metaphysics of the universe: precisely the same differences that characterize the Canterbury pilgrims and the tales they tell.

The *Parliament* is especially interesting in relation to the *Tales* in that it illustrates how debate can be conducted on both overt and latent levels. Explicit are the rival claims of the birds of prey to have the formel's hand, a debate conducted by all the disputants on the same premises of desert and reward; and also the opposing attitudes to the whole idea of courtship and service, which emerge out of contrasting assumptions about the conduct of life and love. Implicit is the dialectic set up by the structure of the poem, with its opposition between the deathly sensuality of the Temple of Priapus and the regenerative sexuality of the Hill of Nature—though the dialectic is announced by the double inscription over the gate, of the entrance as the way to destruction and death or fertility and bliss. *The Canterbury Tales* takes such a structure much further. The different social estates and their views on the world take the place of the hierarchy of birds. Some specific topics are debated: the "woman question" is unusual in the work for the degree of self-consciousness accorded to it as a debate, with the Wife of Bath directly challenging the orthodox line-up of traditional opponents in her Prologue. Others are recognizable from their familiarity as issues of dispute in broader medieval culture: for instance, the issue of fortune versus fate versus Providence, debated between (among others) the prisoner "Boethius" and Philosophy, or, as the Nun's Priest notes, by Bishop Bradwardine (*NPT* 3242), is discussed as an issue in itself in *The Knight's Tale*, but then pursued more generally through the way in which later tales assume one principle or another in presenting their action: chance in *The Miller's Tale*, Fortune in *The Monk's Tale*, rival principles of fate (in the shape of the stars, lines 190–203, 295–315) and Providence in *The Man of Law's Tale*, the absolute divine control of events in *The Second Nun's Tale*.

This last debate is itself one aspect of a wider issue in the *Tales*, of secular and spiritual attitudes to life, the claims of the world against the claims of God; and here too a tradition of debate poetry encloses the *Tales*, with debates on the subject between the Soul and the Body, or between the Part Sensitive and the Part Intellective.[34] The positions

---

[34] For Middle English debates between body and soul, see Conlee, *Debate Poetry*, pp. xxiv–vii and 3–62; for the *Dialogue between the Part Sensitive and the Part Intellective*, see pp. 193–99.

adopted in such explicit debates within the *Tales* are endorsed by the implicit oppositions set up by the larger dialectic structures of the work that oppose romance to saint's life, saint's life to fabliau. Opposed genres and tellers similarly foreground sublimated love or virginity or amoral animal sexuality or plain lust. The women who come close to embodying the cardinal and theological virtues—Custance's fortitude, Virginia's temperance, Prudence's prudence, Griselda's justice (shown in her rendering of due obedience, which was taken as a primary expression of justice in the Middle Ages), Cecilia's faith, hope, and charity[35]—present a silent dialectic opposition to the Wife's enthusiastic espousal of carnality, insubordination to one's husband, and all the rest of the charges traditionally made by men against women.

These large oppositions of this world against the next, fleshly caricature against spiritual sublimation, Carnival against Lent, have a history that goes deep into medieval culture. Of the debates that express such a dichotomy, one of the most thought-provoking in relation to the *Tales* is the *Dialogue of Solomon and Marcolphus*. This consists of a series of aphorisms delivered by the wise king Solomon and capped—Chaucer's term *quited* would be more accurate—by one-liners from the witty and subversive churl Marcolphus. The *Dialogue* originated in Latin some time before the eleventh century;[36] it was not translated into Middle English until the late fifteenth century, but the work was familiar enough in England for the *Proverbs of Hendyng*, widely known in the fourteenth century, to describe Hendyng as "Marcolves sone," and John Audelay and Lydgate also refer to Marcolphus.[37] There is no firm evidence that Chaucer knew the work, but its method, of juxtaposing "official" and "unofficial" views of the world and everything in it, constitutes an epitome of the structural methods of the *Tales*. Solomon speaks with the sober authority of orthodoxy: the four evangelists uphold the world. Marcolphus responds with a total refusal to be impressed and a measure of cheerful obscenity: four props hold up the latrine to keep men from falling.[38] Solomon's views on women, both in favor and (most

[35] On the secular heroines, see Denise N. Baker, "Chaucer and Moral Philosophy: The Virtuous Women of *The Canterbury Tales*," *Medium Ævum* 60 (1991): 241–56; on Cecilia, see *SNP* 110, 96–97, 118.

[36] *Salomon et Marcolfus*, ed. Walter Benary (Heidelberg: C. Winter, 1914), p. vii.

[37] *The Dialogue or Communing between the Wise King Salomon and Marcolphus*, facsimile of Gerard Leeu's edition of 1492, ed. E. Gordon Duff (London: Lawrence and Bullen, 1892), p. xviii.

[38] *Salomon*, ed. Benary, p. 9 #38.

often) against, were part of the standard antifeminist debates of the Middle Ages, and Chaucer cites the Biblical ones frequently; the *Dialogue* adds others, and counterpoints the king's conventional wisdom with the churl's sardonic streetwiseness. So Solomon's sententious "A good wyf and a fayre is to hir hosbande a pleasure" is quitted by Marcolphus's "A potfull of mylke must be kept wele from the katte."[39] The shift in register from formality to low-style animal imagery, and in focus from ideals of marriage to appetite and availability, is closely analogous to the stylistic and thematic counterpointing of the *Knight's* and *Miller's Tales*. In the more discursive part of the work, Marcolphus brings in a woman to answer Solomon's antifeminism; she points out to him that it makes much better sense to allow women rather than men to have multiple spouses, since a man cannot manage seven wives but a woman with seven husbands would have no trouble.[40] The same thought seems to have crossed Chaucer's mind, with his heptagamous and henpecked Chauntecleer and the Wife of Bath's continuing enthusiasm for finding husband number six.

*Solomon and Marcolphus* is a powerfully suggestive analogue to Chaucer's methods in the *Tales*, but not necessarily more than that. The history of debate poetry, and of debates within poetry, is so dense as to make the identification of specific sources for Chaucer's various procedures near to impossible. Some sources and analogues can be identified for the bird debates of the *Parliament*, but by the time one reaches the *Tales*, the *Parliament* itself is a much closer analogue than any of its own sources. A number of those are nonetheless suggestive in relation to the *Tales*, for the topic that the birds of the source poems debate is the merits of one estate against another, whether knights or clerks make better lovers.[41] Chaucer's Clerk is at odds, not with the Knight, but with the virago Wife of Bath, with her sharp spurs and buckler-sized hat; and it has been suggested that her successive treatments of the lovemaking of a clerk (the sexually adept Jankin) and of a knight (the initially brutal,

---

[39] *Dialogue*, ed. Duff, fol. 4a; *Salomon*, ed. Benary, p. 6 #8; "'Mulier bona et pulchra ornamentum est viro suo': 'Olla plena de lacte debet a catto custodiri.'"

[40] *Salomon*, ed. Benary, p. 39, cap. 15: "Quid faciet, si septem habuerit? Supra vires hominis est istud facere. Melius est enim, ut unaqueque mulier septem habeat maritos."

[41] These texts are collected in translation in *Chaucer's Dream Poetry: Sources and Analogues*, ed. and trans. B. A. Windeatt, Chaucer Studies, no. 7 (Woodbridge: D. S. Brewer, 1982), pp. 85–119; the texts are edited by Charles Oulmont, *Les Débats du clerc et du chevalier dans la littérature populaire du Moyen-Age* (Paris: Champion, 1911). Two of these, *Melior et Ydoine* and *Blancheflour et Florence*, are Anglo-Norman.

later reluctant, protagonist of her tale), and their conversion into compliant and respectful lovers, may owe something to these debates.[42]
Other debate poems use different estates or professions as protagonists—clerk and husbandman, sailor and farmer, courtier and soldier.[43]
Chaucer too sets representatives of the social estates at odds—Miller
and Reeve, Summoner and Friar—but for reasons that have their origins in real-life professional rivalries rather than in literary texts: it is
he himself who turns their prologues and tales into what amounts to
paired debate poems.

Chaucer's avoidance of any conclusion, or any judgment between
them, is itself broadly typical of one major element of the debate genre.
Thomas L. Reed's study has shown how unresolved debates characteristically stress the multiple, the temporal, the mimetic, the ambivalent,
the irreverent, and the recreational.[44] The rival speakers, rival tales, and
rival ideas put forward in the *Tales* replay such a model on a grand scale.

## III. Poetic contests

*The Canterbury Tales* is unique among story-collections in being organized as a competition, with a prize: a *soper at oure aller cost* on the pilgrims' return to the Tabard. This is not an element found in the
*Decameron*, despite the *brigata*'s occasional capping of each other's tales;
its probable sources lie elsewhere, in medieval poetic traditions previously connected with lyrics rather than story-collections, and which are
known through both literary texts and historical records. It may appear
one of the more fanciful elements of the frame, but it has antecedents
in real life as well as literature.

Poetic contests have a long history, stretching back at least as far as
Theocritus and the Greek dramatists. The literary history of medieval
contests takes three major forms. The Virgilian pastoral singing-match,

---

[42] Paule Mertens-Fonck, "Life and Fiction in the *Canterbury Tales*: A New
Perspective," in Piero Boitani and Anna Torti, eds., *Poetics: Theory and Practice in Medieval
English Literature*, J. A. W. Bennett Memorial Lectures, 7th ser. (Woodbridge: D. S.
Brewer, 1991), pp. 105–15; see especially pp. 108–9. John Alford has further suggested
that the Clerk and Wife are presented so as to recall the traditional rivalry between Logic
and Rhetoric: see "The Wife of Bath *versus* the Clerk of Oxford: What Their Rivalry
Means," *ChauR* 21 (1986): 108–32.

[43] Conlee, *Debate Poetry*, pp. xvi, 210–15.

[44] Reed, *Debate Poetry*, pp. 38–39, gives a summary of the opposing qualities of resolved and unresolved debates; he discusses the "aesthetics of irresolution" over the
course of the whole book.

itself derived from Theocritus, converged with debate in the early Middle Ages, so that the rivalry between singers extended both to the quality of song and to the quality of argument.[45] Examples of such classically derived pastoral singing-matches could conceivably have been known to Chaucer (Boccaccio's *Ameto*, for instance, contains one in which rival shepherds sing in support of the worldly versus the ascetic life, or perhaps the active versus the contemplative[46]); but if they were, he did not develop the possibilities they offered. Poetic contests and competitions that owed nothing to classical models were central to Welsh culture in the fourteenth century,[47] though England was generally much less permeable to Welsh culture than it was to French. Provence, France, and England invented their own forms of contest in the *tenso* and the *jeu-parti*, which again combined debate with poetic skill, and the flyting, which stressed the skillful deployment of abusive rhetoric. Such forms were given an acknowledged place in courtly, academic, and even ecclesiastical settings. In the late twelfth century, London schoolboys engaged in verse contests of both the intellectual and vituperative kinds; and a more elaborate flyting between Michael of Cornwall and Henry of Avranches, which took the form of a mock lawsuit in rhyming Latin couplets, was reputedly performed by the poets over the course of three separate occasions in 1254–55 before judges including the Abbot of Westminster, the Dean of St. Paul's, the Chancellor and Masters of the University of Cambridge, and assorted bishops.[48] Later vernacular poets with as high an opinion of their writings as Skelton and Dunbar were as anxious to preserve their flytings as they were their more courtly or polite poetry. Similarly, tales in Chaucer that compete in ill-will and abuse—the Miller's and Reeve's, the Friar's and Summoner's—can do so with no concomitant downgrading of their

[45] Helen Cooper, *Pastoral: Mediaeval into Renaissance* (Ipswich: D. S. Brewer, 1977), pp. 13–15.

[46] *Commedia delle Ninfe Fiorentine (Ameto)*, ed. Antonio Enzo Quaglio (Florence: Sansoni, 1963), pp. 47–52.

[47] See A. O. H. Jarman and Gwilym Rees Hughes, *A Guide to Welsh Literature*, vol. 1 (Swansea: Christopher Davis, 1976), pp. 134, 144, on the competitions (first recorded in 1176); the two winners, one poet and one musician, were rewarded with a chair and a prize. On the contest between Dafydd ap Gwilym and Gruffudd Gryg, see Rachel Bromwich, *Dafydd ap Gwilym*, Writers of Wales (Cardiff: University of Wales Press, 1974), pp. 66–71.

[48] A. G. Rigg, *A History of Anglo-Latin Literature, 1066–1422* (Cambridge: Cambridge University Press, 1992), pp. 188–91, 193–98.

rhetorical skill. The "debate" element is subsumed into the larger idea of the contest.

The close connection of debate with poetic rivalry is most strikingly illustrated in the *jeux-partis*, in which two poets would argue a *demande d'amour*. Most of the surviving French examples come from a single source, the "confrerie des jongleurs et bourgeois d'Arras," a fraternity that existed to promote poetry and song.[49] Such societies, familiar as the *Meistersinger* in Germany and known in French as *puys* (probably because the earliest, dating from 1229, met at Notre Dame du Puy at Valenciennes), were founded in a number of European towns in the thirteenth and fourteenth centuries, including London. The form taken by the London Puy is especially interesting in relation to the *Tales*, for its annual assembly consisted of a competition for the best song, both music and words being judged; and those members who came provided with a song received their dinner free, at the expense of the rest of the *compaignie*—the statutes use the same word for the society as Chaucer does for his association of pilgrims.[50]

These details, together with a great many more about the conduct of the *confrarie*, are known from its surviving statutes, which were twice supplemented[51] to put the financial, poetic, and religious provisions of the society (for it, like devotional and parish guilds,[52] had pious aims too) on a clearer footing. The fraternity and its associated annual assembly, "une feste ke hom apele 'Pui,'" were founded in the late thirteenth century by merchants of the city,

en le honour de Dieu, Madame Seinte Marie, touz Seinz, e toutes Seintes; e en le honour nostre Seignour le Roy e touz les Barons du pais; e por loial amour

---

[49] *Recueil général des jeux-partis français*, ed. Arthur Långfors, Societé des Anciens Textes Français (Paris: Firmin Didot, 1926); he gives biographies of the participants from the Arras *confrerie*, pp. xxvi–lii.

[50] *Liber Custumarum*, in *Monumenta Gildhallae Londoniensis*, vol. 2, pt. 1, ed. Henry Thomas Riley, Rolls Series (London: Longman, 1860), pp. 225, 216. The statutes and supplementary articles run from pp. 216–28; a summary is given on pp. cxxix–xxxi. The later articles express a concern that the contest is turning into a poetry competition, and insist that music is required too (p. 225). For an account of its history and its relation to continental *puys*, see Anne F. Sutton, "Merchants, Music and Social Harmony: the London Puy and its French and London Contexts, circa 1300," *London Journal* 17.1 (1992): 1–17.

[51] There is a new set of articles introduced by a fresh proem, *Liber*, p. 219, but these still speak of the founding of a chapel as a pious hope for the future; by p. 227, the chapel has been founded, and the concern is with its financing.

[52] On the activities of these in the later Middle Ages, see Eamon Duffy, *The Stripping of the Altars* (New Haven, Conn.; and London: Yale University Press, 1992), pp. 141–54.

ensaucier. Et por ceo qe la ville de Lundres soit renomee de touz biens en tuz lieus; et por ceo qe jolietes, pais, honestez, douceur, deboneiretes, e bon amour, sanz infinite, soit maintenue. (*Liber custumarum*, p. 216)

[To the honor of God, our Lady Saint Mary, and all saints male and female; and in honor of our lord the King and all the barons of this land; and for the promotion of loyal friendship. And in order that the city of London may be renowned for all good things in all places; and in order that good fellowship, peace, and sweet and courtly pastimes, and true love, may be maintained without limit.]

Its members and benefactors included the great merchant Henry le Waleys, mayor of the city on numerous occasions (1273–74, 1281–84, 1297–99); he had close connections with continental Europe too—he was also mayor of Bordeaux in 1275—and it may have been such international links that inspired the founding of the fraternity: its statutes make careful provision about the subscriptions of members who are out of the country on the occasion of the *feste*. A prince was appointed each year to head the *confrarie dou Pui* and sort out quarrels between its members. He and his successor, together with selected assessors, would judge the songs; a copy of the best one was hung on the wall of the hall below the prince's blazon, and its composer crowned. One of the winning songs, by one Renaus de Hoiland, survives in the Public Record Office, with a rough crown drawn onto it.[53] At the conclusion of the feast (for which a not-too-expensive menu is prescribed in the later articles, to avoid excessive costs), the winning poet, having enjoyed his free meal, rode through the city between the outgoing and incoming princes to the latter's house, where all the members would dance, drink once, and then return home on foot.

In its broader organization, the London Puy resembled a devotional guild of the kind that Chaucer's Guildsmen belong to: an association for the purposes of piety and mutual benevolence. The fraternity was associated with the building of the chapel of the Guildhall in 1299, and Henry le Waleys gave the Puy an annuity of five marks to maintain a

---

[53] London, PRO E 163/22/I/2. The words and music of the first stanza, which begins "Si tost c'amis entant a bien amer," are printed by Christopher Page in *The Cambridge Guide to the Arts in Britain*, vol. 2, ed. Boris Ford (Cambridge: Cambridge University Press, 1988), p. 237; Page remarks that "the musical notes are messy and seem to have been copied too soon after a feast." See also John Stevens, "Alphabetical check-list of Anglo-Norman Songs c. 1150–c. 1350," *Plainsong and Medieval Music* 3 (1994): 1–22 (15–17).

chaplain there.[54] It did, however, differ from many religious guilds in one particular, in that it did not admit women to its *feste*: although, as the supplementary articles that introduce this rule note, ladies will be the subject of every *chaunt roiale*, and members must be reminded by their absence that they are bound to honor all ladies at all times and in all places, when they are present as well as when they are not.

It is not known how long the Puy continued. Henry le Waleys died in 1301; another early member, the vintner John of Cheshunt, who had been its third prince, was dead by 1310; the last reference to the Puy in the records is from 1304.[55] It may well, however, have been a later generation of members who revised the statutes so as to prevent the excessive expenditure of earlier princes;[56] it could have survived a couple of decades into the fourteenth century, closer to the date when the *Liber Custumarum* was completed, or conceivably even longer. What is clear is that the idea of writing in competition was not only current on the continent in the fourteenth century, but was prominent in England in the generation of Chaucer's London grandparents, and among the same social group of merchants and vintners from which he himself took his origins. His Canterbury pilgrims form a looser fraternity, but of a not dissimilar kind: they agree to associate as a *compaignie* gathered for a mixture of literary and pious purposes; they are headed by a temporary lord who will judge their poetry, and who endeavors to maintain good-

---

[54] *Calendar of Letter-Books preserved among the Archives of the Corporation of the City of London at the Guildhall*, ed. Reginald R. Sharpe, 11 vols. (London: John Edward Francis for the Corporation, 1899–1912), *E* 1–2 (flyleaf).

[55] For a recent summary biography of Henry le Waleys, see Gwyn A. Williams, *Medieval London: From Commune to Capital*, corrected ed. (London: Athlone Press, 1970), pp. 333–35. John of Cheshunt is named as the third prince in the *Liber Custumarum*, p. 219, where it is noted that he instituted the custom of presenting a candle at St. Martin's le Grand. Of three Johns of Cheshunt in the records (a taverner; a feathermonger who moved into the wine trade, which was wide open to entrepreneurs, and who became one of the leading citizens of London; and a weaver who appears rather later), he is almost certainly to be identified with the second. He is described as "late vintner" in a record of 1310 relating to his heir (*Letter-Book B*, p. 254 [fol. 112]). For the record of 1304, see *Letter-Book C*, pp. 138–39 (fol. 84b), when John le Mirouer was ordered to pay 100 shillings to the work of the Chapel of the Blessed Mary of the Pui. This case provides one tenuous link between those associated with the Puy and the Chaucer family: among those who imposed the fine was William de Leyre, who in 1301 claimed rent against a tenement from members of the Heyron family, including Chaucer's step-grandfather; the property eventually passed to Chaucer's father in 1349 (Vincent B. Redstone and Lilian J. Redstone, "The Heyrons of London: A Study in the Social Origins of Geoffrey Chaucer," *Speculum* 12 [1937]: 182–95, esp. pp. 190, 184–85).

[56] *Liber Custumarum*, pp. 225–26.

will between its members (*FrP* 1288); and the climax of their association will be the prize supper.

## IV. Pilgrimages and storytelling

The evidence for pilgrims amusing themselves with storytelling is largely literary but need not therefore be fictional. The scenario offered by the *Tales*, of thirty mounted pilgrims listening to a narration by one of their number, is not naturalistic, but it is probably an exaggeration of a historical practice. One of the references closest to Chaucer occurs in the Prologue to *Piers Plowman*, a work he probably knew. There, the pilgrims are one of the many estates represented on the Field of Folk:

> Pilgrymes and palmeres plighten hem togidere
> For to seken Seint Jame and seintes in Rome;
> Wenten forth in hire wey with many wise tales,
> And hadden leve to lyen al hire lif after.[57]

"Telling tales" here refers first to storytelling on the road and then to tall stories told afterward, travelers' tales of the kind Chaucer also ascribes to pilgrims in *The House of Fame* (lines 2122–23). The casualness of these references indicates that the association of pilgrims and storytelling was a familiar one. Nonpoetic testimony to the dual practice of entertainment on the road and tall stories afterward comes from the Lollard William Thorpe, who describes pilgrims as given to singing "rowtinge songis" and playing bagpipes (both practices that the Archbishop of Canterbury, his interrogator, defended) and afterwards being "greete iangelers, tale tellers and lyeris."[58]

Some of these exaggerations and inventions—not all of which were recognized as such—survive to form a body of pilgrimage literature, in which pilgrims recount their real or, more often, imaginary experiences in exotic places: *Mandeville's Travels* was the runaway success in this field. It was not necessary even to go to Jerusalem to acquire such a fund of travelers' tales: Thorpe and Langland suggest that Galicia, Italy, or even

---

[57] *William Langland: The Vision of Piers Plowman, A Complete Edition of the B-Text*, ed. A. V. C. Schmidt, 2d ed. (London: J. M. Dent, 1995), Prol. 46–49. The passage appears in almost identical form in all three versions of the text.

[58] *The Testimony of William Thorpe, 1407*, in *Two Wycliffite Tracts*, ed. Anne Hudson, EETS, o.s., 301 (1993), pp. 64–65.

England would do just as well. Against this background, *The Canterbury Tales* is most distinctive for its difference from the genre to which at first glance it might seem to belong;[59] but this generic expectation became something of a self-fulfilling prophecy, since by the sixteenth century "canterbury tale" had become a synonym for a cock-and-bull story.[60] Chaucer himself associates his pilgrims' tales with pastimes rather than lies; but he also differentiates the illusory naturalism of the frame from the overt fabulousness of the stories. In telling pilgrims' tales, he is by implication entering a larger debate about the status of fiction, fable, and lying.

[59] Donald R. Howard, *Writers and Pilgrims: Medieval Pilgrimage Narratives and their Posterity* (Berkeley: University of California Press, 1980), pp.77–103.
[60] *OED*, s.v. *Canterbury*, A.1.

# REVIEWS

MARY-Jo ARN, ed. Fortunes Stabilnes: *Charles of Orléans's English Book of Love: A Critical Edition*. Medieval and Renaissance Texts and Studies, vol. 138. Binghamton, N.Y.: Medieval and Renaissance Texts and Studies, 1994. Pp. xiii, 624. $45.00.

Near the end of his quarter century of captivity in England (1415–1440), Duke Charles of Orléans rendered into English a series of recently composed French lyrics and narrative poems, creating a combined work that is longer, more complex, and more coherent than the texts from which it is drawn. While Charles's French poetry has long been available in the excellent edition by Pierre Champion (*Poésies* [Paris: Champion, 1923]), this fascinating English compilation remained largely inaccessible to readers outside of a narrow coterie of Middle English experts because of the difficulties presented by its two previous editions (by George Watson Taylor in 1827, and an Early English Text Society [EETS] diplomatic text by Robert Steele and Mabel Day in 1941–1946). The first version, an inaccurate transcription, appeared only in forty-four copies, and the EETS version, although an improvement upon its predecessor, presents only sparse notes and apparatus and an unpunctuated text. Continuing the mission of the Medieval and Renaissance Texts and Studies series, Mary-Jo Arn has achieved an expert and readable edition that makes Charles d'Orléans's body of English poetry available to a wide readership. This handsome new edition presents the definitive discussion of Charles's social and literary contexts, a clearly organized text, and a thorough, learned commentary. It certainly fulfills the editor's wish to provide a text accessible to "a broad middle range of users: Chaucerians interested in Chauceriana, Middle English scholars with interests in the fifteenth century, in dream visions, in love literature, in courtly literature, in fixed-form verse, in the narrator . . . Old French scholars with interests in . . . the legacy of Machaut and other French writers, codicologists and scholars interested in book production, manuscript layout, transmission history, and reception, historians of the Middle Ages, and many others."

Professor Arn's 129 pages of introduction cover simply everything that extended group of scholars could hope for. The first section, "The

Poem," presents an overview of the argument of the poem, and an explanation of the title for the collection (drawn from lines 4680–4735 of a ballade in which the narrator complains that Fortune is not variable, but rather dependably malign). A detailed biographical sketch on Charles follows, including a fully documented time line of his long sojourn in captivity at the houses of various English nobles (1415–1440). Arn continues with an analysis of Charles's English and a review of past disputes over alternative authorship for his English poetry, a discussion of date and provenance, and the influence of this body of work on later English works. She then turns to literary and formal considerations, examining the poem's English sources and influences, such as Chaucer's *Book of the Duchess* and *Troilus and Criseyde* and John Gower's *Confessio Amantis,* and including French antecedents as well known as Machaut or as obscure as Charles's boyhood friend Jean de Garencières. Arn discusses the Duke's rich library holdings in the course of this inquiry. The poem invokes a wide variety of popular love-poetry conventions, including the heart, lovesickness, Maying, the Flower and the Leaf, St. Valentine's Day, the games of Chess and Post and Pillar, the goddess Venus, and, of course, the influence of Fortune—all of which receive discussion here. Analyses of the poem's form and style (with keen observations on the poet's subtle humor), of Charles's preferred verse forms and of versification, and of the English poems' relation to their French counterparts round out this section. A brief overview of linguistic matters and a detailed paleographical and codicological study, including discussions of the scribe and revision, transmission history, editorial principles, and presentation of the text, conclude the editor's introduction.

The text itself is an exemplary production, combining the attractive original *mise-en-page* (including Gothic initials) with clear numeration of individual poems and lines, references to Charles's parallel French poems, manuscript foliation, and unobtrusive glosses (which usefully provide translations of entire phrases rather than simple English synonyms) at the foot of the page. Arn's text provides modern punctuation not found in the manuscripts, which should prove essential to most readers, but maintains original spelling (including thorn and yogh), and is only emended at places where the editor was confident the reading results from scribal error. Five appendices follow the text, covering such matters as distribution of ballad form, corrections of the earlier editions, and Charles's use of diplomatic forms and epistolary conventions. The editor also provides a thorough bibliography, and indices of first lines, ballade refrains, and French counterparts of English poems.

A complete list of textual variants is followed by 105 pages of explanatory notes, in which the editor displays both a broad erudition and specific mastery of these poems and the commentary they have engendered. A full and painstakingly organized glossary and a list of proper names conclude the volume.

This work is generously and attractively produced and printed, durably bound, and inexpensive for a text of its quality and (relatively) limited audience. Not surprisingly, it bears the Committee on Scholarly Editions seal of approval. Professor Arn's edition of these understudied poems by Charles d'Orléans provides a great service to students of late medieval literature and culture, and also sets a standard of quality for editors and publishing houses, one of which the MARTS series ought to be proud.

MICHAEL G. HANLY
Washington State University

ANNE CLARK BARTLETT with THOMAS BESTUL, JANET GOEBEL, and WILLIAM F. POLLARD, eds. *Vox Mystica: Essays on Medieval Mysticism in Honor of Professor Valerie M. Lagorio*, Cambridge: D. S. Brewer, 1995. Pp. xiv, 235. $71.00.

It is understandable that the editors wanted to honor Valerie Lagorio with a festschrift devoted to medieval mysticism. Her phenomenal energy and tenacity of purpose gave that subject a new, high academic profile. But it is perhaps a pity to have called this volume *Vox Mystica*, since the essays received, while they relate to medieval devotion, do not by any means all deal directly with mysticism; and the editorial framework of headings—method, practice, communities, and texts—under which the papers are arranged does nothing to illuminate them either. It might have been better to allow the offerings by scholars in the field of medieval religious writing to speak for themselves, and pay more attention to mundane editorial duties: ensuring that references are consistently given, sentences syntactically coherent, and words clearly spelled. But would "imagistic and religious patters [*sic*] associated with mystical encounter" (p. 25) then have been relinquished?

Some of the essays are indeed concerned with contemplative matters. Two give accounts of aspects of Augustinian thought transmitted and modified in the medieval period that enrich understanding of mystical texts. Frank Tobin's elegant account of Augustine's investigations of visions in "Medieval Thought on Visions and Its Resonance in Mechtild von Magdeburg's *Flowing Light of the Godhead*" illuminates more than the particular text on which he concentrates. In the context of a complex Augustinian tradition of response to music, Robert Boenig throws new light on Rolle's use of the theme of *Canor*. He suggests a subtle interplay in Rolle's writing between philosophical ideas, metaphor, and a literal musical context in which the delights of *ars nova* were challenging the austerities of plain song. Music's role in structuring spiritual experience at many levels is further demonstrated by Gertrud Jaron Lewis in her investigation of the role of music and dancing in the spiritual lives of fourteenth-century, German-speaking, Dominican women living in community. Contemporary accounts reveal not only the demands of singing the office in choir, but the way in which music penetrated contemplative experience: the nuns heard angels singing (Margery Kempe would have understood that) or themselves danced and sang for joy, even whirling round the altar like spinning tops. Mary Giles examines, thought-provokingly, a related phenomenon, the enacted raptures of Sor Maria of Santo Domingo (her use of the term "dramatic contemplation" begs many questions), by relating it to modern "holy theatre" techniques. Rosemary Drage Hale sets out promisingly to examine the relationship between the outward physical senses and beliefs about the mystical sensorium of the soul but, sidestepping into fashionable questions about culturally constructed gender differences, loses direction in an awareness of a "hermeneutic quicksand of ethnocentric methodologies and a tangle and ahistorical interpretations [*sic*]" (p. 11). Two papers deal directly with texts. Ritamary Bradley, with customary lucidity, shows how the Latin *Vita* of Beatrice of Nazareth imposes an antifeminist stereotype on the emphasis of her contemplative spirituality, thus distorting her own personal vernacular account, *The Seven Experiences of Loving*. Stephen Hayes edits a delightful Middle English meditation on the Annunciation, the paradigm of contemplative experience in "a wele disposed soule."

Other papers explore aspects of the culture associated with contemplatives. Elizabeth Psakis Armstrong executes a neat little gender study of the way Thomas à Kempis and Teresa of Avila use sexual stereotypes only to transcend them: monks are to manifest their manhood in the arts of peace and the ideals of silence; nuns to achieve the strength to achieve the calmness of discretion as lords of their bodies. St. Teresa might well have recognized "a strength that will amaze men" (p. 111) in the recusant Bridgettine sisters, whose experiences are recounted by Ann Hutchison from primary sources. Four offerings have to do with the conventions of spiritual friendship. Anne Clark Bartlett illuminates the way in which the conventions of texts prompted by spiritual friendship suggest that this relationship transcended the dominant culture of sexual segregation. Her broadly based examination provides a wider perspective on Edwin L. Conner's argument that Aelred of Rievaulx's *De spirituali amicitia* is a source for the *Cloud of Unknowing*. It is true that it is "entirely appropriate" to study the *Cloud* in the context of the epistolary genre of spiritual friendship" (p. 97), but any precise debt to Aelred is less apparent. Margot King translates letters from Mechthild of Hackeborn to a laywoman friend taken from *The Book of Special Grace*. She gives no rationale, contextual note, or comment of any kind; however, in the introduction the editors explain, rather unfortunately, that "these letters . . . are dedicated specifically to Valerie Lagorio." Brant Pelphrey's "Afterword: Valerie's Gift" may, perhaps, be read as an exercise of spiritual friendship in a modern idiom.

Two essays concern themselves with the way mystical encounters with God underlie the contexts of overtly secular literature. Both suffer from a lack of intellectual rigor in their use of terminology. Beverly Boyd's unanalytical equation of the language of prayer with mysticism vitiates the analysis of Chaucer's *An ABC* and of *The Prioress's Tale*, in which the complex perspectives provided by narrative voices are finally flattened out into the statement that "the composer is nevertheless Chaucer, writing the language of prayer and hence of mysticism" (p. 103). John Hirsh highlights the depth of the religious cultural issues encoded in *Havelok*, *Lay le Freine*, and *Sir Gawain and the Green Knight* and relates them to the evidence supplied by the mystics as to their sense of the presence of God.

Two essays deal with the complex relationship between cultural moments and the transmission of mystical texts. Alexandra Barratt provides a welcome and entertainingly informative account of the editing of Julian's texts (though Sister Anna Maria Reynold's dissertation was for the University of Leeds, not Liverpool). James Hogg offers a wealth of bibliographical scholarship as he traces the transmission of the texts of the Revelations of St. Bridget of Sweden, which resulted in a Middle Low German Compilation skillfully adapted to more popular devotional needs. The insight thus provided into the amazing pains taken by the "translator" to reorganize his Latin texts in the vernacular enriches our understanding of a significant cross-cultural activity in the medieval period.

MARION GLASSCOE
University of Exeter

CHRISTOPHER BASWELL. *Virgil in Medieval England: Figuring the* Aeneid *from the Twelfth Century to Chaucer*. Cambridge Studies in Medieval Literature, vol. 24. Cambridge: Cambridge University Press, 1995. Pp. xviii, 438. $60.00.

At the heart of this book, perhaps at the heart of its author, are three chapters, each studying a British manuscript of the *Aeneid*, representing readerly activity from the twelfth to the late fourteenth centuries, and a useful appendix called "Manuscripts of Virgil Written or Owned in England during the Middle Ages." The book's first project is to document the multiple ways of reading the *Aeneid* during these centuries, and to group them into three ample clusters: the well-known allegorical tradition; the increasingly familiar romance tradition, in which female characters and vernacular languages challenge a more conservative, masculinist, and imperialist Virgil; and—underappreciated these days—the pedagogical tradition lodged in the schools.

Baswell's first manuscript, Oxford AS 82, bears three sets of annotations spanning three centuries, the three sets together evincing the variety of purpose and intention for which Baswell argues in the pedagogical tradition. Against the line of scholarship that has taken commentary's dominant method to be allegorical and medieval readers "unable or unwilling to understand ancient texts as set in a past which must be imaginatively recaptured" (p. 48), Baswell argues for these commentators' persistent efforts to recover with precision the particularities of language, religion, social order, and geography in Virgil's world.

Baswell's exemplar of the familiar commentary tradition, that of "spiritual allegory" and "platonizing cosmology," is the twelfth-century Cambridge, Peterhouse College MS 158—a manuscript containing, as Baswell discovered, an unexpectedly early transcription of the commentary on Martianus Capella attributed to Bernardus Silvestris. Calling upon such late-antique fabulists as Macrobius and their high-medieval beneficiaries, Baswell traces in P158, with its substantial allegorizing narratives preceding and following the poem, a "codicological move from marginal notes more closely tied to the authorial text, to a separate *commentum* more loosely inspired by that text" (p. 91). Like others, Baswell emphasizes that this kind of reading is generated by a reverence for Virgil's arcane wisdom, with the paradoxical result that Virgil's poem is taken as demanding integumental interpretation and eliciting the ingenuity of a *magister* in ways that the more grammatical pedagogical tradition does not. Baswell follows the geohistorical fortunes of this manuscript, one document in the intellectual life of the English west country in the twelfth century showing that "Chartrian Platonism and humanist interest in the classics" comprised "a major strand in the milieu of English culture," even after "similar interests had begun to die down on the continent" (p. 133).

Finally there is a fourteenth-century Bodleian manuscript, Add. 27304, with its idiosyncratic commentary by a Norwich reader whose need to make of the *Aeneid* a series of hortatory *exempla* links him to moral allegory—a familiar enough tradition, but one emerging here in the effort of one reader as lively, peculiar, and personally urgent. The behavior of Virgil's characters is taken to exemplify social, sexual, and preacherly ideals: "Behold how suitably [Aeneas] answers, and men should answer questions to the point"; "[Virgil] shows how a woman should be given to her husband [i.e., *intacta*]" (p. 151); on Dido's curses against Aeneas, "by so much more strongly is excommunication to be feared" (p. 154); perhaps most wonderfully, "Note, Aeneas flees Dido at the order of Mercury and Jupiter. And mankind does not flee sin at the order of God and the preacher" (p. 153). Warmth of feeling toward this Norwich reader and toward the pedagogical impulse of all commentary is one of Baswell's strengths; in his patient, detailed reconstructions of classroom and clerkly readerships, he vivifies a hunger for utterance and response among teachers, students, and texts. The fruits of these reading dynamics, notwithstanding their male-only institutionalism, deserve the acknowledgment that they receive here: at this time we can do with some positive identification with such reading communities.

With the two final chapters, Baswell moves from codices and commentaries to poems proper—the *Roman d'Eneas*, *The House of Fame*, *The Legend of Good Women*—and their Virgilian intertextuality: second-level engagements with both Virgil and commentary traditions. This second project, linked occasionally to the first by reminders of the three commentary traditions, is dominated by the related thematics of gender and writing, and a critical paradigm in which polarities are frustratingly locked in double binds. Thus the chapter on the *Eneas*, joining a growing body of scholarship on "the romance Virgil," argues that the poem's explorations of women's agency and affect and of eros more generally are poised irresolvably between subversion and containment. "It is this double power of dilation—both to make space for the feminine and erotic, and to contain their effects by making them into artifacts—that most deeply characterizes the 'romance *Aeneid*'" (p. 173). Or again, "much of Lavine's role in the *Eneas* is to function exactly as an *altera Dido*, but in a version rendered safe and containable" (p. 186). On the episode of the temple of Venus from *The House of Fame*, Baswell concurs with Boitani and others that Chaucer there represents the *Aeneid* as a "supreme model of art" but does so "precisely by re-enacting the moment where the 'supreme model' marks out its own and all art's limitations, its inevitable embedding in and unbinding by time and the audience" (p. 246). *The Legend of Good Women* is characterized by "a double, unresolved hermeneutics" (p. 255) in which the model of reading suggested by the *Prologue*'s imagery of seasonal cycle is locked in conflict with the model of reading suggested by the imagery of male voyeurism and the naked text. So, for example, Alceste is "the achieved version of an enhanced, but still limited and always endangered feminine power," and the legends themselves provoke reactions both "sympathetic" and "leering" from the narrator (p. 254).

The power of such binarisms based on subversion-and-containment to generate persuasive readings is undeniable—even when, as in this book, they seem unmoored from any Foucauldian, historicist, or particular feminist theoretical origins (a move that solves some problems with the model but creates others). After Baswell's fine chapters on manuscript commentaries and their varied exchanges with the *Aeneid*, the discussion of the *Eneas* and the Chaucer works seemed strikingly enclosed and univocal; I hankered after readings of the poems along lines suggested by the discussion on commentaries. Don't these works too show, as direct commentaries did in Baswell's manuscripts, how the needs of readers create meaning as assertively as the needs of authors and patrons? Again, if the aim of the chapters on the *Eneas* and the Chaucer poems is to complicate the picture of male readers developed in the chapters on manuscript commentaries, then the chapters might mount some theoretical challenge to, or simply divergence from, the powerfully totalizing, fixed structures of gender polarity and dynastic imperative. A gesture outward from the trap of hierarchies endlessly subverted but contained occurs in Baswell's own discussion of *The House of Fame*, where the diverse Babel of the world of tidings is that "from which new art may be made"; the eventual disorganization of the rich array of literary traditions that had provided an embarrassment of riches at the start of the poem proves a liberation, leaving Geffrey "suddenly buoyant" and the poem filled with energy (p. 248). The subversion/containment model can't do much to account for the new, for change that brings the future, but the poem perhaps can. The Babel of tongues pervades Baswell's account of the explosive variety of versions, forms, and media of antique story after Chaucer, a variety eliciting models of analysis that supplement pairs of cultural binarisms with more complicated models of reader identification—identifications that movingly underwrite Baswell's work on manuscripts.

THERESA M. KRIER
University of Notre Dame

RICHARD BEADLE and A. J. PIPER, eds. *New Science Out of Old Books: Studies in Manuscripts and Early Printed Books in Honour of A. I. Doyle.* London: Scolar Press, 1995. Pp. viii, 455. $109.95.

This unusually handsome volume with its sixty-nine black-and-white plates is a fitting tribute to Ian Doyle, one of the most learned students of medieval manuscripts in this century and one of the most generous of scholars in sharing that learning with colleagues. This is the second such collection to honor Doyle, the first constituted of essays delivered at the sixth York Manuscripts Conference.[1] Both collections reflect the high standard of manuscript studies in England and this country as well as the beneficent effects of Doyle's scholarship in a variety of disciplines.

---

[1] A. J. Minnis, ed., *Late-Medieval Religious Texts and Their Transmission: Essays in Honour of A. I. Doyle*, York Manuscripts Conferences: Proceedings Series, vol. 3 (Cambridge: D. S. Brewer, 1994).

The range of subjects treated in these fifteen essays is extraordinarily diverse, and I make no pretense of being competent to offer an opinion on many of those topics, but I shall rather attempt in a sentence or two to suggest what readers will find in these pages.

The collection begins with "From Flax to Parchment: A Monastic Sermon from Twelfth-Century Durham," by Mary A. and Richard H. Rouse, an edition and translation with introduction and notes. The Rouses refer to biblical commentary traditions to account for apparent disjunctions in the structure of the sermon, which curiously allegorizes both the scribe's writing tools and the linen garment in which he is clothed.

Margaret Laing and Angus McIntosh analyze the linguistic features of the two scribes who copied the *Poema morale* and the *Trinity Homilies* into Trinity College, Cambridge, MS 335. Using computerized transcriptions which, because of their full lexical and grammatical markup, are more sophisticated than those available for the preparation of the *Linguistic Atlas of Late Mediaeval English*, they characterize Scribe A as a careful *literatim* copyist, Scribe B as a dialect translator, and then present the results of their analysis to localize both texts and scribes.

Trinity College, Cambridge, MS B.16.2 is a handsome presentation copy of Wyclif's Latin writings, the most extensive surviving in England of a mixed set of early and late works. Anne Hudson provides an account of the physical structure of the manuscript and summarizes what is known of the nature of its texts and their relations to those in other manuscripts. Done with Hudson's characteristic thoroughness and care, this study, as she warns, in many cases raises rather more occasions for further research than it provides solutions.

Malcolm Parkes, in an important and detailed study of the process of authorial rolling revision in the early manuscripts of John Gower's works, rejects G. C. Macaulay's and John Fisher's arguments that the poet's earliest manuscripts were produced in a scriptorium where his texts were carefully overseen by Gower himself. Their position was based on the rational assumption that "where one finds two or more scribes collaborating in two or more manuscripts, and . . . when their handwriting and other scribal practices exhibit sufficient points of similarity to suggest the existence of a 'house-style,' one may infer the existence of a scriptorium" (p. 81). Examining four manuscripts of the Latin works and one with both Latin and vernacular texts (Bodley's MS Fairfax 3), all with extensive revisions and corrections *reflecting changes made by Gower*, Parkes shows through examination of the patterns of scribal revision among ten different hands that these scribes did not work in a common scriptorium under authorial (or other) supervision. Moreover, there is no evidence that any two scribes collaborated, since "no two scribes appear to have worked simultaneously on any one manuscript" (p. 95). Instead, Parkes argues, individual early owners among Gower's circle independently sought some of the same scribes to correct and bring up to date their copies of his texts. He suggests that similar revisions made in the first-generation copies of Chaucer's texts account for the different textual traditions appearing in the earliest surviving, though already second- and third-generation, manuscripts.

Michael G. Sargent addresses the problem within a manuscript culture of assuring uniformity in the texts of an international community such as the Carthusian houses during the period between the end of the Great Schism (1410) and the solution to the problem embraced by the order early in the sixteenth century in the form of the printed book. Beginning with a thumbnail history of Carthusian book production between the early twelfth century and attempts within the order to guarantee the uniformity of custom and rite among houses, Sargent discusses the aims and effects of Oswald de Corda's *Opus pacis* as well as ordinances made by the chapter in the course of the fifteenth century, arguing that the promise of textual uniformity was at least equal to economic considerations as an incentive for the movement from script to print.

Kathleen L. Scott defines and discusses eleven terms and two symbols appearing in the margins of late fourteenth- and fifteenth-century English manuscripts as instructions to limners on "decorative and general production work" (p. 142). The accompanying set of eighteen black-and-white plates is particularly valuable for showing the range of meanings attached to these terms.

Professor Toshiyuki Takamiya offers an *editio princeps* of a poem he titles "On the Evils of Covetousness," an otherwise unrecorded Middle English poem from a manuscript in his collection. This 300-line meditation on (among other themes) the evils of avarice, the certainty of death, the untrustworthiness of friends, the instability of Fortune, the debate between soul and body, and so forth appears in a structure Takamiya rightly calls associative. The edition is accompanied by a full description of the physical features of the manuscript and a brief discussion of contemporary analogues.

George Keiser extends his codicological work with manuscripts of Lydgate's *Lyf of Our Lady* to inventory the nature and range of textual divisions in other late-medieval medical texts, such as the *Liber de diversis medicinis* and Gilbertus Anglicus's *Compendium medicinae*, in Caxton's edition and the Winchester manuscript of Malory as well as in other early printed texts of Middle English romances, and in Nicholas Love's *Mirror of the Blessed Life of Jesus*. However, the most important contribution here is Keiser's detailed account of the *ordinatio* and apparatus of various manuscript renderings of Lydgate's *Lyf of Our Lady*.

Peter J. Lucas proposes that Eugene Vinaver's distinction between the authorial process of composition and the scribal process of textual reproduction, though it is "desirable and may be useful," is less true to late medieval practice than the assumption that "many texts . . . probably began their life in an author's place of study where they may have not only been revised and altered but also copied by those who had composed them" (p. 227). This article continues Lucas's distinguished series of studies devoted to the author/scribe John Capgrave. Capgrave provides a valuable test case, since of his twelve extant works, eight survive in autograph copies and four others in copies he revised for presentation. Capgrave is, as Lucas argues, "the classic instance of autograph among Middle English authors" (p. 230). Lucas examined three different types of copies, ranging in formality from the author's working copy (not a rough draft, but not for presentation) to superior copies written in a formal, but not the most formal, script for presentation, to luxury copies in Capgrave's most formal hand and designed for presentation to very important people. The rate of authorial self-correction is, not surprisingly, highest in the working copy. Interestingly, the rate of correction over erasure is highest in the luxury manuscript. More interestingly, the rate of uncorrected error was higher in the superior copies than in the working copy, though Lucas rightly suggests that the more relevant correlation is with the relative distance from the original. What we cannot know, because we do not have enough Capgraves and Hoccleves who copied their own works, is whether their behavior as scribes was typical or exceptional.

Roger Marchall (*fl.* 1436–1477), a physician to English kings and fellow at Cambridge's Peterhouse College who collected or annotated a considerable number of medical manuscripts, over forty of which have survived, is the subject of Linda Voigts's fascinating study. She provides an account of his career and family connections, speculating about Marchall's intentions to further medical and astrological/astronomical studies at Cambridge, and provides in the appendices a detailed catalogue of those manuscripts either owned by Marchall or associated with him as well as a baker's dozen reproductions of portions of Marchall manuscripts.

Still another distinguished addition to a series of connected studies of language, manuscripts, and texts of the late medieval dramatic productions of East Anglia is Richard Beadle's "Monk Thomas Hyngham's Hand in the Macro Manuscript." Beadle argues that the texts of *Wisdom* and *Mankind*, though once independent sections of a manuscript now containing the *Castle of Perseverence* as well, were nevertheless both copied by their earliest owner. Using paleographic and codicological evidence, Beadle argues, in my view persuasively, that Hyngham copied both plays, though both paleographic and linguistic evidence requires the passage of several years between his copying *Wisdom* and *Mankind*.

Lotte Hellinga argues for a Dutch rather than Alsatian origin for printer Wynkyn de Worde and discusses connection between his typefaces and woodcuts and the work of printer/designers in Holland, and Mary C. Erler offers further evidence of the roles of women in the circulation and preservation of manuscripts in an account of early sixteenth-century exchanges of books between nuns and laywomen.

When on Mary's accession to the throne in 1553 antiquarian and first Protestant bishop of Ossory John Bale decided to leave his see in haste for the continent, he left behind him "two great wain loads" of books, later listed in the second edition (Basel, 1557) of his *Scriptorum illustrium maioris Brytanniae catalogus usque ad annum hunc 1557*. He never got them back, and O'Sullivan here attempts to match up manuscripts surviving in Trinity College, Dublin, with Bale's list.

J. T. Rhodes surveys the development of devotional attitudes toward the body of Christ in English eucharistic practice in the sixteenth and early seventeenth centuries, arguing that the changes in attitudes and practice owe rather more to literacy and the availability of books than to the more sweeping religious changes and persecutions of that turbulent century. The collection ends with E. Rainey's useful bibliography of Doyle's published scholarship.

HOYT N. DUGGAN
University of Virginia

PETER G. BEIDLER, ed. *Geoffrey Chaucer: The Wife of Bath*. Case Studies in Contemporary Criticism. Boston and New York: Bedford Books of St. Martin's Press, 1996. Pp. xiii, 306. $9.95 paper.

If medievalists have been slow to claim and use newer forms of literary criticism in their scholarship, then they have been even slower to introduce their undergraduate students to forms of criticism. These practices have been more commonly undertaken by scholars in later periods of literary history. Peter Beidler's volume on the Wife of Bath attempts to answer a lack of available materials for the medievalist on an important text in a masterly way. The Case Studies in Contemporary Criticism series specifically targets important texts in British and American literature. The intent is not only to introduce undergraduate students to an authoritative text but also to present them with accessible examples of criticism from New Historicism, Marxism, psychoanalytic studies, deconstruction, and feminism. Beidler and the writers of the essays deserve commendation in their efforts.

In addition to his role as editor of the volume, Beidler prepared the biographical and historical contexts sections as well as the text of the *Prologue* and *Tale*. Writing for the student who has little sense of late medieval history, Beidler addresses central issues of the Chaucer biography and historical events, such as the Black Death and the reign of Richard II, briefly but without the sweeping generalizations that sometimes characterize introductory explorations of scholarly topics for nonspecialist readers. Perhaps most useful in this section are his translations of sources for the *Prologue* and *Tale* along with his comparisons of them with the Chaucerian text. Briefly but with the clarity of a seasoned scholar, he demonstrates Chaucer's artful manipulation of his sources. For this volume, he uses the Hengwrt as the base text, and in doing so, provides readers with some helpful comments on the enterprise of textual editing, medieval and modern. With glosses and explanatory footnotes, the *Prologue* and *Tale* are made quite accessible for readers who have little or no experience with Middle English.

The second part of the volume is devoted to a critical history and to essays demonstrating various approaches to the *Prologue* and *Tale*. In his introductory essay in this section, Beidler traces succinctly the range of approaches to *The Canterbury Tales* in general and to the *Wife of Bath's Prologue and Tale* in particular. He notes many source studies, historical studies, and New Critical studies, in addition to more recent critical strategies that inform our understanding of the tale. Most helpful here is his ability to explain various approaches and their conclusions in "jargon-free" language (p. viii). Readers looking for bibliographical references will not be disappointed here or throughout the volume.

After Beidler's introduction are more general introductions to the critical methodologies provided by Ross C. Murfin as part of the series; then essays devoted to the *Prologue* and *Tale* follow. There are a few spots of redundancy here, but particularly given the audience the volume is attempting to reach, the reinforcement will likely be welcomed. Readers of Chaucer scholarship will recognize the names Lee Patterson, Laurie Finke, Louise O. Fradenburg, H. Marshall Leicester, Jr., and Elaine Tuttle Hansen. Clearly each has contributed to Chaucer scholarship in the last decade, and in many cases, they have shaped the future of Chaucer studies. Thus, introducing students to these scholars is in itself an important activity. The essays are original, rather than excerpted from longer works by the same authors. The essays were written for students, yet they maintain scholarly rigor. Skillful instructors will be able to demonstrate to their students the similarities and differences in Patterson's New Historicist and Finke's Marxist essays. The same activity could be done with Fradenburg's psychoanalytical, Leicester's deconstructionist, and Hansen's feminist essays. More advanced readers of Chaucer will find new insights into the *Prologue* and *Tale* as well.

Whether Beidler's volume is used in a literature survey, an introduction to literary criticism course, or a Chaucer course, it will prove a valuable addition.

DANIEL F. PIGG
University of Tennessee at Martin

ROBERT J. BLANCH and JULIAN N. WASSERMAN. *From* Pearl *to* Gawain: *Forme to Fynisment*. Gainesville: University Press of Florida, 1995. Pp. 207. $39.95.

Robert J. Blanch and Julian N. Wasserman are well known for their publications on the *Gawain*-poet. *From* Pearl *to* Gawain develops their earlier interests (in medieval law and semiotics) and also pursues some new themes, such as the iconography of hands in the text and the manuscript illuminations, and the ways in which the poet positions himself as narrator through the use of personal pronouns. As the authors point out in the introduction, previous criticism on the *Gawain*-poet has tended to treat the poet's works in isolation. Thus, there are many books solely devoted to *Gawain* or *Pearl*, and still more books that discuss all four poems in separate chapters; but we have no detailed study of the common ground that is covered by all four poems and that reveals them, so obviously, to be the oeuvre of a single author. *From* Pearl *to* Gawain aims to fill this gap, and it exemplifies both the possibilities and the pitfalls of a holistic approach to the *Gawain*-poet.

Blanch and Wasserman succeed in establishing interesting connections between the four poems, and in catching some of the peculiar turns of the poet's mind. One chapter, for example, draws attention to the poet's interest in hands, an interest so strong that he can hardly mention God without also imagining the divine "hondes" that make and unmake creation. Another chapter makes interesting comparisons between the poet's legalistic preoccupation with contracts in *Gawain* and the "covenants" made between God and man in *Patience* and *Cleanness*. The argument leads neatly to the best chapter of the book, on the subject of miracles, those moments in which the ordinary laws of nature, the covenants of *kynde*, are briefly suspended. While many other critics have arrived at the idea that all of the *Gawain*-poet's works deal with sudden encounters between a strange order of nature (divine, heavenly, or supernatural) and the world of our ordinary experience, Blanch and Wasserman take this observation as a point of departure for some mutually illuminating analyses of passages from all four poems, spiced with pertinent comments on the nature of miracles by Augustine and Aquinas. As in all other chapters, references to secondary works are plentiful, although the provision of comparative material from primary sources is less generous, and rather limited in range by a marked preference for the Doctors of the Church.

While vindicating some of their claims for common themes in the four poems, Blanch and Wasserman frequently downplay the obvious differences between them. *Patience* indeed threatens the Ninevites with extermination, but the notion that *Sir Gawain* is also centrally about the destruction of cities (including Camelot and the "toun" in which the poet says he has heard the story) would seem absurd. But here it is, in all seriousness: "In an apocalyptic warning appropriate for Jonah preaching at Nineveh, the poet [in *Sir Gawain and the Green Knight*] seems to be saying that, without repentance, the 'toun' of today will share the fate of Camelot, which did not listen, rather than that of

Nineveh, which did heed the danger" (p. 25). The pursuit of similarities also leads the authors astray when they attempt to link God's sympathy with people "who do not know one hand from the other" in *Patience* with Gawain's choice to strike the Green Knight with the axe rather than the holly bob which the Green Knight carried in his other hand: "Presumably, then, Gawain could have wielded the holly sprig as a weapon. Certainly, then, his fetching of a "dunt as [he] hatȝ dalt' . . . would have been a less somber affair" (pp. 105–6). This indeed "challenges accepted interpretations," as the publisher's blurb promises, but whether or not it will dislodge them will depend on our willingness to take seriously the possibility of a romance in which a knight goes in quest of a monster who is armed with a green holly-bob.

Such occasional lapses of judgment by no means invalidate the overall thesis that the works of the *Gawain*-poet intersect in fascinating ways; but they do raise the question of whether the intersection is quite of the kind that the authors imagine.

AD PUTTER<br>
University of Bristol

Robert Boenig. *Chaucer and the Mystics:* The Canterbury Tales *and the Genre of Devotional Prose.* Lewisburg: Bucknell University Press, 1995. Pp. 231. $37.50.

I am not, as a rule, overly fond of exegetical readings of Chaucer, nor of critical approaches that view Chaucer as primarily a religious writer. I was never overly sympathetic to Robertsonianism during its heyday. But every now and then a work comes along that forces me to go back and take a long, hard look at my own critical assumptions about the relationships between secular and religious texts in the Middle Ages. Robert Hanning's 1982 essay on *Sir Gawain and the Green Knight*, "Sir Gawain and The Red Herring: The Perils of Interpretation" (in Mary J. Carruthers and Elizabeth D. Kirk, eds., *Acts of Interpretation: The Text in Its Contexts, 700–1600* [Norman: Pilgrim, 1982]), was one such work; Robert Boenig's *Chaucer and the Mystics* is another. What I found most attractive and persuasive in Boenig's claim that Chaucer drew on mystical writings to shape *The Canterbury Tales* is his refusal to reduce all readings of Chaucer to one mystical reading, as the exegetical critics of the 1960s so often did with patristics. Instead, his introduction doubly contextualizes his readings of *The Canterbury Tales*. He locates them within the interpretive communities available to the contemporary Chaucer scholar (New Criticism, exegesis, reader response, the New Historicism), and he locates Chaucer's own practices of reading and writing within the interpretive communities of which he himself was a member and within which his work circulated. Readings of Chaucer that draw upon mystical writings are made more plausible, for instance, by Chaucer's friendship with John Clanvowe and Lewis Clifford, both known for their interest in mysticism, and by the independent circulation of *The Parson's Tale* in a manuscript anthology of devotional texts (Longleat 29) that included works by Richard Rolle and Walter Hilton.

*Chaucer and the Mystics* argues that *The Canterbury Tales* shares with mystical writing a tendency simultaneously to affirm and deny ideas, language, and even reality. This dynamic of affirmation and denial not only elucidates particular passages or tales, but the peculiar architectonics of *The Canterbury Tales* itself and particularly the failure of control that causes the text to lapse into fragmentation and ultimately silence (p. 11). Boenig bases his claim on theories of language articulated by Pseudo-Dionysius, a fifth- or sixth-century Syrian monk, and reiterated by late medieval mystical writers. The aporia created by this persistent paradox, this affirmation and denial of language, results in increasing fragmentation, until the mystical writer simply falls silent before the inexpressible ineffability of the Godhead. This approach serves Boenig well in dealing with those tales that make explicit use of mystical themes: it provides enough material for two chapters on *The Prioress's Tale*, which are the most illuminating in the book. Equally productive are the discussions of the Parson's relatively straightforward sermon and the parodies of mystical knowledge in the *Miller's*, *Friar's*, and *Summoner's Tales*. I found especially intriguing Boenig's analysis of the ways in which both Margery Kempe and the Wife of Bath model themselves on other texts and even create themselves as texts, though I was disappointed by his curious silence on recent feminist interpretations of *The Book of Margery Kempe*. In the last decade there has been an explosion of feminist writing on medieval women mystics that might have informed this reading, yet absent from the chapter on Margery and Alice was not only any reference to Sheila Delany's 1983 essay on the two, but also (among others) recent books by Karma Lochrie, Lynn Staley Johnson, and Dyan Elliott.

Where Boenig's argument seems more stretched and less persuasive are in the chapters dealing with tales whose contexts seem further removed from mysticism or which draw explicitly on other medieval discourses, such as courtly love. The author's attempt to connect Custance in *The Man of Law's Tale* to mystical women because she wished to avoid her father's efforts to marry her (p. 104) or to tie Dorigen's distraught reaction to Averagus's departure—"she mourneth, waketh, wayleth, fasteth, pleyneth"—with those mystics who practiced fasting or sleep deprivation as part of their devotions (p. 140) seem tenuous and forced. In these readings Boenig seems to forget his own initial insight that mystical writings provide only one intertext among many through which Chaucerian texts circulated (and continue to circulate). In doing so, he misses what I think are important theoretical insights, as, for instance, when he turns to *The Knight's Tale* to illustrate Chaucer's adaptation of Pseudo-Dionysian language theory. Arcite's understanding of Palamon's prison as a blissful "paradys," he argues, drives a "Pseudo-Dionysian wedge between signifier and signified. Palamon and Rolle share a common view of language" (p. 25). But certainly such an elementary use of oxymoron might as easily be explained by any number of familiar literary critical approaches, from New Criticism to Derridean deconstruction, or better yet by the relatively commonplace discourse of courtly love, which is one of the generic conventions of the tale. There is no compelling reason to turn to Pseudo-Dionysius or Richard Rolle to understand this passage. To be sure, medieval scholars have long recognized that courtly love and mysticism share a common vocabulary, perhaps even a common understanding of the oxymoronic nature of love. But Boenig's reading of this passage and others like it do not explore how Chaucer's audiences would have understood this common vocabulary. How did they know when a particular sentiment was being evoked in a mystical context or a courtly one? Would one context necessarily exclude the other or would each retain a trace of the other? Boenig's failure to entertain these questions makes readings such as this one seem forced. But more important, it obscures what may be a more audacious claim lurking within the book's argument. Boenig's major contention—that the mark of Pseudo-Dionysian (and hence mystical) writing is that language constantly undoes itself—does not substantially differentiate the Pseudo-Dionysian aesthetic from a late twentieth-century aesthetic that also privileges language's failure to secure referentiality. Boenig might have argued that our own critical preference in the late twentieth century for language that undoes itself, that drives a wedge between signifier and signified, is ultimately Pseudo-Dionysian in origin. A claim this audacious would require a detailed examination of the historical development of our aesthetic ideals that may be beyond the scope of this investigation, but it strikes me as at least plausible that the repressed that returns in late twentieth-century appreciations of texts like *The Canterbury Tales* is the religious origin of our own aesthetic canon.

LAURIE FINKE
Kenyon College

VERN L. BULLOUGH and JAMES A. BRUNDAGE, eds. *Handbook of Medieval Sexuality*. Garland Reference Library of the Humanities, vol. 1696. New York and London: Garland, 1996. Pp. vi, 441. $68.00.

This useful if uneven volume "aims to address the needs of students (and even faculty members) who are interested in the study of medieval sexuality and who would like a guide to the sources and literature bearing on medieval sex" (p. xv). *Handbook of Medieval Sexuality* comprises, in addition to the editors' introductory history of the study (and neglect) of medieval sexuality, eighteen chapters divided into three sections: "Sexual Norms" features chapters on confessionals, canon law, Western medicine and natural philosophy, gendered sexuality, chaste marriage, and male sexuality; "Variance from Norms," on homosexuality, lesbians, cross-dressing, prostitution, contraception and early abortion, and castration and eunuchism; and "Cultural Issues," on sexuality in religion (Jewish, Muslim, and Eastern Orthodox) and literature (French, Old Norse, and English).

This handbook will certainly guide students toward many fruitful areas of research. While the editors disavow any claim to comprehensiveness, the amount of information and quality of research made readily available here testify to the vitality of the growing fields that constitute "medieval sexual studies." Jacqueline Murray's chapter on lesbians exemplifies the strengths of the interdisciplinary and theoretical approaches that distinguish many of the chapters: it takes the marginalization of lesbians in both medieval culture and modern

230

scholarship as the catalyst for an invigorating survey of how we can learn about medieval lesbians from canon law, the penitentials, medical writings, court records, poetry and letters, and art and music. Equally ambitious is Laurie Finke's chapter on French literature, which uses the critical debates about "courtly love" and the fabliaux to categorize the major theoretical approaches to literature's status as representation of sexuality: the "reflective," which sees these genres as reflections of a prior reality; the "hermeneutic," practiced by both exegetical and New Critical readers, which seeks a "hidden reality" behind the text's ostensible meaning; the "specular," which focuses on the sublimation of sexuality into textuality; and the "dialogic" notion that literary texts "reflect, but also in turn shape, those social conditions [of their creation] in a process that is, finally, dialogic" (p. 353).

Not all the entries, however, are as rigorous and sophisticated as these. Chaucerians in particular will be disappointed by David Lampe's chapter "Sex Roles and the Role of Sex in Medieval English Literature," which quotes the Wife of Bath, for example, at length, but gives no notice whatsoever to the crucial recent work on gender and literature by Carolyn Dinshaw and many others. Lampe instead points out that class and age are the determining factors in Chaucer's portrayals of sexual athletes, concluding by affirming "the truism that 'age and youth are often at debate' and also that aristocratic status . . . can also be a source of restraint (*noblesse oblige*) because of the importance of paternal bloodlines for the inheritance of property and title" (p. 413). Of the rest of the Middle English corpus, Lampe surveys obvious passages from *The Owl and the Nightingale*, the secular lyrics, Dunbar, the romances, the *Gawain*-poet, Malory, Gower, Langland, and drama—a reasonable selection, to be sure, yet one might question the decision to expend half a page on Harrison Birtwistle's 1991 opera *Gawain* (p. 416) while ignoring the erotic mystical writings of Julian of Norwich and Margery Kempe. Finally, this chapter is full of such awkward sentences as "If aristocratic Emilye desires not to marry, . . . she is told that because of her social station she cannot maintain that role, but must marry" (p. 413), and such typographical errors as "handomse" (p. 411), "Chacuer's" (p. 411), *"condioun"* (for ME *condicioun?* [p. 412]), and "drwogh" (for ME *drowgh* [p. 414]).

The more explicitly historical chapters that refer to "literature" for the most part employ the "reflective" approach identified by Finke. Margaret McGlynn and Richard Moll point to Chaucer's *Second Nun's,*

*Parson's,* and *Merchant's Tales*, the N-Town cycle, and Margery Kempe in suggesting that secular literature might be helpful to the scholar of attitudes toward chaste marriage, and Jacqueline Murray cites January to exemplify the notion that "those [elderly men] who indulged in sexual exploits were seen as humorous victims of self-deception" (p. 138). While these are certainly valid and very helpful approaches, a fuller engagement with literature's "dialogic" nature would have enriched the collection. For instance, its readers will not discover that such major medieval works as Alan of Lille's *Plaint of Nature* and Dante's *Comedy* (which appear very briefly in Warren Johansson and William Percy's chapter "Homosexuality" [p. 170]) rely heavily on sexual or erotic metaphors in their constructions of, respectively, grammatical solecism and the spiritual journey.

It is very useful to have an index to such a diverse collection of materials, even if it seems to have been rushed through the editorial process. Peter Damian's two appearances appear separately, under "Peter Damian" and "Damian, Peter"; the important treatise *Women's Secrets*, discussed on pages 52, 89–90, 93, 96, and 264, is listed only as "women's secrets, 264"; the Pauline notion of the "marital debt," surveyed on pages 94–95, 130–31, 335, and 408, does not appear under the entry "marriage"; the sole mention of Dante is not listed; there are separate entries for "birth control" and "contraception;" and the *Piers Plowman* listing does not draw attention to the note on the connection David Greenberg draws between Langland's term "ragamuffin" and the Old Norse term *ragr*, denoting effeminacy (p. 395 n. 62). A similar error, not in the index, is the listing of *The Canterbury Tales* as a secondary source in Murray's chapter on male sexuality (p. 149).

These errors do not detract from *Handbook of Medieval Sexuality*'s valuable function as both a summary of the research of recent decades and a useful guidepost to further work. While the traditional historical emphasis of most of the chapters results in a lack of engagement with the questions many Chaucerians have been asking for the last decade, nevertheless Bullough and Brundage are to be commended for undertaking this project. Its publication will help many of us move well beyond the easy reliance on the Wife of Bath in our teaching of medieval sexuality.

LAWRENCE WARNER
University of Pennsylvania

JACQUELINE DE WEEVER. *Chaucer Name Dictionary: A Guide to Astrological, Biblical, Historical, Literary, and Mythological Names in the Works of Geoffrey Chaucer.* Garland Reference Library of the Humanities, vol. 709. New York and London: Garland, 1996. Pp. xxi, 451. $24.95 paper.

The decision to release a paperback version of this 1987 volume assumes a substantial audience of scholars and students. Presumably the publisher felt that those who otherwise would consult the library's hardbound version will find it convenient to have at hand an annotated listing of each personal name mentioned in Chaucer's works. And this is a hefty volume, offering information about Chaucer's use of classical, biblical, and contemporary sources that careful readers will find helpful. Entries begin with paragraphs on the lives/significance of the named characters—far and away the most useful part of the volume—to which are added paragraphs on Chaucer's references to those characters, followed by (in most cases—de Weever is not entirely consistent) the number of uses, spelling variants, line numbers, and indications of where the different variants appear in a line. Short bibliographic references complete many entries, but these are arbitrary and limited and, nine years after the volume's initial hardbound publication, often out of date.

Regardless of its bulk, a dictionary is only as valuable as it is accurate. As one examines the *CND* it becomes evident that this is a book to be used only with great care. When my review copy arrived, I turned to the entry on Absolon to see what I might find to help a student exploring the possibility of a political significance in Chaucer's use of this name. De Weever's strategy is to include separate listings for each of a name's referents; hence I discovered two entries, "ABSALON, ABSOLON[1]" for David's son, "ABSOLON[2]" for Chaucer's parish clerk. The entry on the biblical character includes the information that blond hair was an "attribute of beauty" from the twelfth century on, but instead of referencing Paul Beichner's article "Absolon's Hair" mistakenly cites his "Chaucer's Hende Nicholas," which does not mention David's son and refers to his Chaucerian namesake only in passing. The entry on Chaucer's clerk belatedly cites "Absolon's Hair," but neglects to mention the color that Chaucer gives to his character's hair (also blond) and places Chaucer's thirty-two references to Absolon (an incorrect count) in *The Knight's Tale* (pp. 4–5)! Such confusion is typical of the volume.

Looking closely at the first four pages, I found errors in almost every entry: "Moses" for "Moises" and "*Mel* 1099" for "*Mel* 1100" (p. 3; de Weever's line references to the prose of *The Parson's Tale* and *The Tale of Melibee* are almost always inaccurate, usually by one line but occasionally by as many as four); "HABRADATES" for "HABRADATE," "Achetofel" for "Achitofel," "*ParsT* 638–40" for "*ParsT* 639–41," and a spurious medial reference to "*KnT* 3657," leading to the miscounting of the thirty-one references to Absolon's name (p. 4); "*Metr* 7.45" for "*Metr* 7.43" and "*Metr* 7.43" for "*Metr* 7.45" (p. 5); "*MLT* 198" for "*MLT* 197–199," "*SqT* 236–240" for "*SqT* 238–242," "*NPT* 3142" for "*NPT* 3141," "*BD* 1067" for "*BD* 1066–71," and "Hector" for "Troilus" (p. 6).

Random checking of later entries confirmed the pattern: "*PardT* 575" for "*PardT* 505" (p. 8); "*LGW* 1927" for "*LGW* 1977" (p. 9); the spelling "Aleyn" for "Alayn" for *RvT* 4089 (p. 12); the cross-reference "John¹" for "John²" (p. 19); *ShipT* 441, *NPT* 3241, *ParsT* 381 and 987 missing, *ParsT* 675 spuriously added, and *ParsT* "690" for "694," "750" for "754," "765" for "768," and "955" for "958" under the listing for Augustine (pp. 48–49); *FranT* "929" for "989" and "989" for "982" under the listing for Aurelius (p. 50); "ELEATICIS" for "ELEATICS" (p. 128); and 3638 omitted under the *MillT* listing for Nicholas (p. 255)—one notes here de Weever's peculiar decision to modify the abbreviations in *The Riverside Chaucer*; "*LGW* 2228–2392" for "*LGW* 2228–2393," "Nicholas" for "Absolon," the personal name "Sir Thopas" for "The pilgrim Chaucer's tale," and "more sweetly than" for "as sweetly as" under the listing for Philomene (p. 287). In short, it was rare to discover an entry without an error. While the *CND* can be helpful in locating a reference, one must assume a name, spelling, or line number to be unreliable unless one has checked it oneself.

I would question, therefore, the publisher's decision to reissue the *CND* without substantial correction, and the author's acquiescence in this decision. It is true that in covering the entire Chaucer canon the *CND* supersedes the less ambitious efforts of Hiram Corson (*Index of Proper Names and Subjects to Chaucer's Canterbury Tales* [1911; rpt. 1967]), Bart Dillon (*A Chaucer Dictionary: Proper Names and Allusions, Excluding Place Names* [1974; erroneously called *Dictionary of Proper Names in the Works of Geoffrey Chaucer* in de Weever's introduction, p. xiii]), and Arthur Finley Scott (*Who's Who in Chaucer* [1974]), but the *CND* has itself been superseded by Larry Benson's *A Glossorial Concordance to the Riverside Chaucer*, which offers accurate references to each word used by Chaucer, including names, and also reprints the complete line in which each reference appears. Unless one needs a Chaucer name dictionary at home, and few of us do, I would see no reason to purchase the *CND*.

DAVID RAYBIN
Eastern Illinois University

MURRAY J. EVANS. *Rereading Middle English Romance: Manuscript Layout, Decoration, and the Rhetoric of Composite Structure.* Montreal and Kingston; London; and Buffalo: McGill-Queen's University Press, 1995. Pp. xx, 203. $44.95.

In the preface to his monograph Murray Evans explains, "The present study focuses on the structural implications of physical layout and decoration in twenty-six manuscript collections that contain romances" (p. xii). However, one page later Evans states that, in fact, he has limited his attention to fifteen of these manuscripts. On this puzzling note begins a very puzzling book.

The first chapter is a discussion of *compilatio* and *ordinatio* (without defining either term or distinguishing clearly between them) and physical layout and decoration (which support *ordinatio*). To illustrate these terms, Evans has very brief discussions of, first, two manuscripts and, then, the presentation of *Guy of Warwick* in the Auchinleck MS (Edinburgh, National Library of Scotland, MS Advocates 19.2.1). Chapter 2—replete with large and unattractive pie charts and other graphs—surveys the use of seventeen manuscript conventions (incipits, explicits, display scripts, etc.); data concerning these conventions have been fed into a computer database for the purpose of comparing their use with romances and other kinds of writings. (The fact that the numbering of the pie charts illustrating distribution of these conventions in the manuscripts does not correspond to the numbering of the sections in which the conventions are discussed presents the reader with a particular challenge.) In the next two chapters Evans looks at individual romances in their manuscript contexts and considers the definition of two subgenres of romance, the homiletic romance and the Middle English (Breton) lay. The concluding chapter discusses the "rhetoric of composite structure":

"a set of relationships that encourages a reading of Middle English romances in their original manuscript contexts" (p. 114).

This monograph is not an insignificant piece of scholarship, and it
ought not be ignored by those undertaking serious study of romances
and romance manuscripts. However, before taking on this monograph,
the reader would be well advised to be in control of a good deal of information about romance manuscripts and to have, as this reader did,
facsimiles and microfilms of the manuscripts at hand. Very little is
explained about the origin and nature of the fifteen manuscripts discussed, and for information about them, particularly their contents, the
reader has to resort to tables at the end of the book (which fill forty-two
pages in all). Using these charts is somewhat trying because, with the
omission of page numbers and running headlines on these forty-two
pages, the reader must hold the book on the vertical and look below the
table proper and above the list of contents to discover which part of
which manuscript is the subject of the table on the page.

In his treatment of the fifteen manuscripts, Evans fails to provide sufficient and necessary information about their original readers, even
though that is well known in several cases and is, potentially, important to his arguments. To take the most obvious and troubling example: Evans's discussion of Oxford, Bodleian Library, MS Douce 261 does
not explore and exploit pertinent information. Evans does report that
the book is dated 1564 and was copied by "E.B." from printed texts.
However, he fails to make clear that this is certainly not a medieval
manuscript, and any comparison of it with medieval manuscripts requires cautious explanation of the fact that the scribe, Edward Banyster,
copied not only the texts, but also the illustrations (and there are seventeen more than the four that Evans's chart indicates), the initials, and
the emblems from printed texts. To put information about this manuscript into a database consisting of information about *medieval* manuscripts is hardly appropriate, for its scribe—a recusant and an antiquarian who owned at least eight pre-1500 manuscripts—surely looked
at the works he copied with very different eyes than earlier scribes who
copied the same works. (Evans cites the article by M. C. Seymour in
which information about Banyster is set forth, but he makes no use of
that information.)

Even in the most interesting portions of the monograph, where Evans
provides useful insights about individual works, his exposition is less
than satisfactory, for it is both spare and cluttered. While Evans gives
lengthy reports of previous criticism of the romances, using abundant

quotations from that criticism, including summaries of the romance plots taken from it, his own comments are lean, spare, skeletal, undeveloped. It is ironic that a book concerned with the layout of texts should have an unhelpful layout itself. Evans divides his text into small blocks and uses several hierarchies of headings to show the relation of the parts. Unfortunately, this presentation, along with a lack of transitional statements, requires that the reader frequently turn backward and forward to understand how an individual section fits into the larger structure of the chapter.

Those with a serious interest in Middle English romances and romance manuscripts would be wise to read this monograph, for it does contain some valuable information and insights, especially about the different versions of romances and the implications of the fact that certain groups of romances frequently occur together in manuscripts. However, the reader should not expect an easy passage through the relatively small number of pages (about 100) of text. Caveat lector: approach with caution and, above all, with patience.

GEORGE R. KEISER
Kansas State University

THELMA FENSTER, ed. *Arthurian Women: A Casebook*. Arthurian Characters and Themes, vol. 3. New York and London: Garland Publishing, 1996. Pp. lxxvii, 344. $35.00.

Of the nineteen essays (excluding the lengthy introduction) that appear in this volume, fifteen are reprints. Two (E. Jane Burns, "Rewriting Men's Stories: Enide's Disruptive Mouths," and Laurence Harf-Lancner, "Fairy Godmothers and Fairy Lovers") are abridged versions of pieces as they originally appeared, and two (Harf-Lancner and Anne Berthelot, "From the Lake to the Fountain: Lancelot and the Fairy Lover") are translations from the original French. Thus, there is little here that one could not find in previously published sources. The primary value of such a book, therefore, is in the assimilation of a group of carefully selected articles into one convenient volume, in keeping with the intent of the Garland casebook series, whose editors have pronounced "the proliferation of research devoted to Arthurian material" to be "daunting" (p. xi) and have set out to simplify the task of researchers and students

237

by assembling collections of notable articles on given themes or characters.

Thelma Fenster, editor of *Arthurian Women: A Casebook*, has done an excellent job of selecting articles to be included in the volume, balancing studies on medieval texts with those of nineteenth- and twentieth-century works, and including articles that focus on French, German, English, and Italian literature. However, inherent in such a collection of reprinted articles are annoying inconsistencies. For example, some essays include bibliographies while others do not, and consequently footnote styles vary among the articles. It is also unfortunate that contributors' notes are not included in the volume. They would be particularly useful in a book of this sort, which covers several disciplines and includes scholars who work in a number of different literary periods.

Fenster's lengthy opening essay is divided into four sections (1) justifying the need for the book, (2) listing and summarizing the roles of Arthurian women, (3) showing how the feminine presence in the Arthurian corpus finds its richest fulfillment in the fairy world (a curious section that evolves into a brief essay on Marie de France's "Lanval"), and (4) setting forth the various sections of the volume: "Resisting Tales," "Story, Gender, and Culture," "Fairies' Tales," "Iseut and Guenevere in the Nineteenth Century," "Another Look," and "Revisionary Tales: Guenevere and Morgan in the Twentieth Century."

The temptation to comment individually on each of the articles is quelled by their sheer number and the space limitations of this review. However, taken together the essays handily demonstrate a variety of approaches to and perspectives on Arthurian texts and underscore the flexibility of the Arthurian legends that have been adapted so variously from age to age and from country to country to the tastes of their receptor audiences. They also suggest some of the difficulties inherent in dealing with characters whose names and roles may vary from text to text, which seems to be even more of a problem with female characters than males.

Gender issues are significant, as one might expect in such a volume, and are broached from the very first essay, Roberta Krueger's "Love, Honor, and the Exchange of Women in *Yvain*: Some Remarks on the Female Reader" (later expanded in her book *Women Readers and the Ideology of Gender in Old French Verse Romance*). Not all the writers agree on the notions of gendered creativity or biologically determined (i.e., gender-based) reader responses. On the one hand, Marilyn Farwell

("Heterosexual Plots and Lesbian Subtexts: Toward a Theory of Lesbian Narrative Space in Marion Zimmer Bradley's *The Mists of Avalon*") argues that Bradley's novel commits a "narrative transgression . . . not in the tension between Avalon and Camelot, or in the idealized feminine world of Avalon," both of which remain fundamentally heterosexual, but "in the momentary revelation of sameness as the core of Avalon" (p. 327), specifically shown in a brief scene between Morgaine and Raven. This she calls "lesbian space," a term that deconstructs the idea of lover and beloved as heterosexual to open a narrative space that underscores not "alterity" but sameness. Perhaps at the opposite end of the spectrum, Constance Hassett and James Richardson ("Looking at Elaine: Keats, Tennyson, and the Directions of the Poetic Gaze"), in one of the few previously unpublished articles in the volume, raise the question of gendered creativity in terms of the female characters of Tennyson and Keats. Seeking in some sense to redress the excesses of feminist criticism against what they [feminist critics] consider to be "gender imbalance" in the "repression of potentially creative women who identify with the silenced and viewed females of traditional art" (p. 289), the authors set forth to demonstrate that it is simplistic to assume that there is a rigidly controlled response to art based on gender, arguing instead that readers respond, as did the poets in question, by identifying with both male and female characters, that "the gaze imagines the gaze back" (p. 297).

Dealing with these same issues in somewhat less provocative but nonetheless interesting ways are the essays of art historians Joanne Lukitsh and Muriel Whitaker, both examining the works of female illustrators of Arthurian works. Lukitsh ("Julia Margaret Cameron's Photographic Illustrations to Alfred Tennyson's *The Idylls of the King*") looks at Cameron's compelling images of Arthurian scenes that underscore "the experiences of the women characters of Camelot" (p. 247). Whitaker, in another of the rare new articles in the collection ("The Woman's Eye: Four Modern Arthurian Illustrators"), reviews the Arthurian illustrations of Eleanor Fortescue Brickdale, Jessie M. King, Dorothea Braby, and Annegret Hunter-Elsenbach and poses the question of whether the "woman's eye" sees differently from man's. She concludes that they reveal "a progressive development of decorative ingenuity" (p. 284): from early manifestations in the works of Brickdale that tended to privilege women while at the same time relying on Pre-Raphaelite images that impeded her originality, to the works of

Hunter-Elsenbach, whose *Morte d'Arthur* Whitaker sees as unaffected "by considerations of the maker's gender or personality," concluding that "it is simply a work of art" (p. 285). Aside from their contributions to the issue of gendered creativity, these articles are refreshing in that they deal with the visual materials in the Arthurian corpus, which are too seldom considered by Arthurian scholars.

Theoretical underpinnings for articles in the volume, such as the works of Luce Irigaray, Jacques Lacan, and Julia Kristeva, often provoke responses. For example, Ann Marie Rasmussen, in her previously unpublished essay " 'Ez Ist ir g'artet von mir': Queen Isolde and Princess Isolde in Gottfried von Strassburg's *Tristan und Isolde*," takes issue with Julia Kristeva's notions of masculine "linear time" versus feminine "monumental time," concluding that such socially constructed categories are unstable and that "monumental time" can have a "linear dimension" capable of interrupting and redirecting "linear time" (p. 51). And in her article ("Female Heroes, Heroines and Counter-Heroes: Images of Women in Arthurian Tradition") Maureen Fries moves beyond Georges Dumézil's male typology to set forth an interesting female typology useful to Arthurian and non-Arthurian scholars alike.

The fourth of the new articles in the volume is that of Regina Psaki ("'Le Donne Antiche e' Cavalieri': Women in the Italian Arthurian Tradition"). Since American scholars are generally less familiar with Italian Arthuriana than they are with the French, German, Welsh, English, and even Scandinavian texts, this essay, which claims to be the first ever published on women in the Italian Arthurian tradition, is indeed a welcome article. Psaki points to the fact that these texts, primarily prose romances and *cantari*, have been usually judged "inferior" even by Italian scholars, but contends that the reputation is undeserved and based primarily on the fact that they do not follow the "ideal model" of Chrétien's "biographical romances" but rather "the second wave of French Arthurian literature" (p. 128), refashioned, as writers of Arthurian works have always done, to suit their receptor audience. Nevertheless, she demonstrates that women in the Italian texts are equally marginalized in a male universe, serving as "objects of desire and . . . exchange, motivating forces, rewards, temptations, distractions, and origins or pretexts of adventure" (p. 127).

Well chosen as the final article in the volume, Raymond Thompson's "The First and Last Love: Morgan Le Fay and Arthur" points to the changing figure of Morgan through the Middle Ages, from a "super-

natural fay" to the "evil witch in later medieval romances" to a rehabil-
itated twentieth-century Morgan who becomes an "admirable oppo-
nent" and "the true love and worthy companion" of Arthur. Thompson
argues that her new role points, primarily among female writers, to the
"recognition that the best hope for a better world lies in cooperation,
rather than competition, between men and women" (p. 342). It is a
hopeful conclusion to a volume that brings together a number of excellent articles, with only an occasional exception. The critic who approaches this volume looking for much new research will be disappointed. However, while there is little that is significantly new in
*Arthurian Women*, the volume will no doubt be a useful addition to the
library of many Arthurian scholars.

JUNE HALL McCASH
Middle Tennessee State University

JOHN H. FISHER. *The Emergence of Standard English*. Lexington:
   University Press of Kentucky, 1996. Pp. 208. $34.95 cloth, $14.95
   paper.

This collection of John H. Fisher's essays on Standard English provides
a welcome and useful arrangement of several related arguments that he
has made over the past twenty years. In it one can see more clearly the
recent (and older) scholarly traditions on which he has drawn, the original contributions that he has made, and the discoveries by others that
have followed from those contributions—from his ideas about the
processes of linguistic standardization, and specifically about the situation in England; from his hypotheses and tentative suggestions along
the way; and from his collaborative archival work.

Fisher's analyses of the emergence of Standard English have made use
of an approach to Middle English dialectology laid out by Angus
McIntosh and M. L. Samuels in a series of programmatic essays during
the 1950s and 1960s. A key element in that approach is the scrutiny of
variations that might seem part of the writing system only and not necessarily indicators of variations in the spoken language. In some of the
early work on that project Samuels noted the importance of the Central
Midlands dialect in the formation of written Standard English and

coined the term "Chancery Standard." With attention to Samuels's findings Fisher has argued the double hypothesis that the rise of Standard English was more separate both from the English of London and from the spoken language of any region (because it was a written language) than the traditional histories of the language have recognized.

A part of Fisher's argument that especially captures the imagination is the idea that a few individuals, particularly the Masters of Chancery in the early fifteenth century, were strategically placed to alter the course of the English language as no individuals have been able to do since. This idea led Malcolm Richardson to investigate the individuals so placed, including Henry V; and it led John Fisher, together with Richardson and Jane L. Fisher, to collect and edit *An Anthology of Chancery English* (1984), a valuable complement to R. W. Chambers and Marjorie Daunt's *Book of London English: 1384–1425* (1931).

Fisher's investigations in sociolinguistics and historical philology have worked well with his skill and learning as an editor and critic of the great Middle English poets to accommodate within his story the evidence from both literary and bureaucratic sources. Three chapters on Chancery English and European chancelleries are followed by two chapters on Chaucer's texts and languages, one chapter on *Piers Plowman*, one on Caxton, and a final chapter on the history of Received Pronunciation. Whereas literary and sociolinguistic approaches to the history of the language are sometimes opposed, Fisher sees the treatment of Chaucerian manuscripts in the early fifteenth century as consistent with the idea of implementing a national language policy. When published in 1988, chapter 5, "Animadversions on the Text of Chaucer," was an essay that focused on the psychology of Chaucer and the reasons why he did not superintend the preservation of a single one of his poems. In the present context, especially in light of chapter 2, "A Language Policy for Lancastrian England" (1992), the essay becomes an implicit "prequel" of sorts, setting up the messy textual situation that Chaucer's son Thomas and the English monarchs inherited. The fifteenth-century revisions in the presentation of *The Canterbury Tales* between the Hengwrt and Ellesmere manuscripts, and the proliferation of literary manuscripts generally, can then be seen as part of a deliberate policy by Henry IV and even more by Henry V. By this view, Chaucer was chosen as the cynosure for a strategy that was both linguistic and political.

Fisher carries out a similar mapping of manuscript features onto the stages of linguistic standardization (again using three stages proposed by Samuels) in chapter 7, "*Piers Plowman* and Chancery Tradition." The sixteen manuscripts of the B-version range in date from the beginning of the fifteenth century into the sixteenth century. Tables display features of script and orthography (the forms of anglicana *a*, single compartment *a*, etc.; yogh versus *gh* in *thoughte, heighe*, etc.) to show movement by the scribes toward Chancery Standard. Chapter 8, on Caxton, carries the story into the age of print and argues that Caxton must be regarded as "a transmitter rather than an innovator." Here Fisher makes most explicit his argument that "a principal characteristic of any standard language is its divorce from regional pronunciation, lexicon, and syntax" and that "the most important development in the writing of English in the fifteenth century was the beginning of its emancipation from speech" (p. 124).

As a coauthor of one of the traditional histories of the English language, I have profited from Fisher's work on standardization and have moved subsequent editions in directions that he has indicated. If I find it difficult to give up altogether the usual ideas about the importance of London English as the basis of Standard English and to divorce the spoken language from the written, it is partly from the evidence that the Fishers and Richardson have assembled—for example, in Signet letters that highlight the London English of Henry V. In resisting the traditional view of impersonal and inexorable forces at work shaping the language, Fisher's summaries seem to downgrade the importance of any variety of London speech, including this one (which in the absence of recording equipment we can never know directly). One might try a thought experiment that imagines the shape of the English language if the royal court, and eventually Chancery, had been located in, say, Edinburgh for three hundred years. The idea that a certain stratum of London speech was the major basis of written standard English is not incompatible with the original, fructifying point that Fisher urges throughout his essays: the intentional direction from the top in imposing forms of the language that may not otherwise have become the familiar forms of international English six centuries later. If the language of Henry V and of the mayor and aldermen of London was as close to Chancery Standard as Fisher and his collaborators have shown, then we are not far, in general outline, from what H. C. Wyld and A. C. Baugh suggested in the 1920s and 1930s.

To that outline Fisher's work (together with the work of scholars preceding and following his) brings hypotheses for making more precise the mechanisms of linguistic change in late Middle English. The process by which northern forms were introduced into Standard English, for example, is a subject of continuing controversy, as is the relative importance of influences from the Central Midlands and from East Anglia.[1] Even when the evidence is, as Fisher acknowledges, circumstantial, the coherence of the story that he traces and the archival materials that he has provided will continue to stimulate scholarly investigation and discovery.

THOMAS CABLE
University of Texas at Austin

PIER MASSIMO FORNI. *Adventures in Speech: Rhetoric and Narration in Boccaccio's* Decameron. Middle Ages Series. Philadelphia: University of Pennsylvania Press, 1996. Pp. xiv, 155. $29.95.

Pier Massimo Forni is already well known as one of the prominent Boccaccio scholars in the United States. *Adventures in Speech* is a significant contribution toward his larger aim of mapping out Boccaccio's "narrative poetics" (p. 114). This book follows close on the heels of *Lessico critico decameroniano* (coedited with Renzo Bragantini), his essay in which he shares an interest in the relation of Boccaccio's famous realism to his patterns of language; it also develops some lines of thought suggested a few years earlier in his *Forme complesse nel Decameron* with regard to "the Boccaccian habit of exploring the narrative potential of rhetorical forms." Hence the title of this new book, with its suggestion that narrative adventures are already implicit in figures of speech. While some parts of the book have appeared previously in Italian, much of it is new or amplified besides being made available in English. Although the chapters can be read independently, they work together coherently to build up Forni's larger view of the relations between rhetoric and narrative in the *Decameron*.

The book is divided both into five chapters (plus an appendix) and into three sections. The first section focuses on the interplay of cornice

---

[1] See, for example, Laura Wright, "About the Evolution of Standard English," in M. J. Toswell and E. M. Tyler, *Studies in English Language and Literature: "Doubt wisely"; Papers in Honour of E. G. Stanley* (London: Routledge, 1996), pp. 99–115.

and tales. Chapter 1 surveys the narrators' comments about why they have chosen to tell particular stories. "There is always reasoning on the choice of topic; there is continuous justification and rationalization among the narrators" (p. 7). Their explanations include the production of new tales in response to previous ones; Forni points out how narrators, in referring to the same previous tale, may sum it up—and thus interpret its point—quite differently. The narrators' repeated and problematic concern about truthfulness is also discussed. Chapter 2 focuses on the production of pleasure for the brigata—and for us—not only from the contents of a tale in itself but also from its structural relations to previous material. The Calandrino cycle is an important example here, as we are shown again how one narrator reopens and reinterprets material seemingly closed and finished by a previous narrator.

Section 2 (chapter 3) analyzes the rhetoric of beginnings in Boccaccio's tales, finding a pattern of polarization between the *novum* and the *notum*: a promise of new and unusual followed by a normalization through phrases that render this particular character, action, or situation typical. We are asked by this formula to evaluate the tale in relation to everyday life. The *syntax* of realism, i.e., the parenthetical comments that establish typicality, are as important as content to the creation of Boccaccio's famous effect of realism.

Section 3 (chapters 4 and 5) returns with a new approach to the first section's question of *inventio*: the how and why of coming up with particular stories. Chapter 4 develops suggestions of chapters 2 and 3, discussing the material realization of metaphorical phrases as a source of narrative. Forni sets this technique into the context of other literary examples, both classical (e.g., Ovid) and modern (e.g., Bontempelli). He adopts as useful Koelb's term *logomimesis* and Bergson's and Freud's observations of its production of comic effects, while resisting Todorov's sweeping claim that all of the fantastic and supernatural derive from rhetorical figures. *Logomimesis* suggests that not only do words imitate reality but that realistic narrative may also be spun out of figures of speech. A number of examples from the *Decameron* are discussed in this light: 7.9 (chopping down the pear tree), 5.10 (a proverbial "asino"), and a number of tales that "realize" sexual metaphors. Chapter 5 explores a variety of rhetorical models for Zima's device (3.5) of speaking for his beloved in a dialogue with himself. This exploration leads to intriguing connections to poetry by Cino da Pistoia and Dante's *Vita nuova*. Analysis of the parodic aspects of Boccaccio's inventions relates this chapter to parts of section 1.

The appendix connects to the rest of the book through its search for Boccaccio's models and its concern for how Boccaccio produces rhetorically the all-encompassing effect often proclaimed by his readers. Here Forni traces verbal connections between the story of Tancredi and Ghismonda and Ovid's tale of Myrrha in the *Metamorphoses*, thus offering strong support to Muscetta, Almansi, and others who have seen in 4.1 hints of incestuous passion. This presence of incest, in turn, albeit implicit rather than explicit, helps to produce the effect of the *Decameron*'s inclusivity of all kinds of love.

I have only one small quibble with Forni's many fine insights and arguments. In chapter 1, with regard to the pot of basil story, he shifts in the course of a page from "wondering" and "entertaining the possibility that the declared creative sequence from story to song must be reversed in order to understand the story's process of inventio" (p. 22) to the firm declaration that "the sequence must be reversed" (p. 23). Although this is plausible, I would like to see some argument for disbelieving Boccaccio's claim before conceding that what was entertained as a possibility suddenly "must be" so.

Forni's work is otherwise clearly laid out, persuasively presented, and very readable. He draws on the whole history of *Decameron* commentary, from fifteenth- and sixteenth-century readers through eighteenth-century scholars to the most recent writings on Boccaccio. He displays as well a deep familiarity with a very wide range of texts, classical, medieval, and modern. The questions he raises help to recast fruitfully and to see the connections among traditional discussions of Boccaccio's realism, artful construction, parody, and fascination with language.

JANET LEVARIE SMARR
University of Illinois

SIMON GAUNT. *Gender and Genre in Medieval French Literature.* Cambridge Studies in French, vol. 53. Cambridge: Cambridge University Press, 1995. Pp. x, 372. $64.95.

Although there is much that is thought-provoking in Dr. Gaunt's study, the reader does come away from it with a slight sense of disappointment that less has been made of the material than might have been hoped. It is not just that the title includes the buzz word *gender*, which still raises some expectations of polemic, but that at the end of the day the genders and the genres that emerge from the book are those that we knew all along. In his introduction, Dr. Gaunt spends considerable time considering the question of genre and its importance to medieval as well as modern studies, and to pointing out that the concept survived the onslaught of the structuralists of the 1960s and 1970s. He is also at pains to indicate that he is concerned with gender as a construct applying to the masculine as well as to the feminine, and that, unlike biological sex, gender is a multiplex and polyvalent construct within each "sex." Finally, as his epigraph (three quotations from the *Oxford English Dictionary* defining "gender," "genre," and "genus") implies, he is aware of the necessary interplay of these terms and their subtending ideologies in generating each other. Disappointment, therefore, arises from the body of the book, which treats in five successive, and hermetic, chapters five genres (*chanson de geste*, *roman courtois*, troubador *canso*, hagiography, fabliaux) drawn from traditional literary history, and deals with gender within them also in a very traditional way: the warrior and his companion; the knight and his lady; the male and female saint; sex, the body, and "obscenity." This aprioristic view that there is an inherent unity between gender and genre is reinforced in the conclusion, in which the major challenges to other (preexisting) gender constructs is seen as coming from other (frequently subsequent) genres. Only marginally (in the cases of the *trobairitz* and Clemence of Barking as hagiographer) is serious concern shown for the ways in which a genre questions itself in terms of its representation of gender. What seems to be missing, then, is any attempt to redefine the traditional boundaries established for Old French literary genres on the basis of the genders constructed.

The stress placed by the introduction on the multiplicity of the socially and culturally constructed gender as a definition of power, prestige, or function is also lost to some extent as the book progresses. The epic (categorized by its chapter title as representing "Monologic Masculinity") is seen as marginalizing not only "women" but also any form of "alterity." Now this is to start the analysis from where it might end. It asserts the uniformly masculine (and by extension French-Christian) discourse of the poems, and relies on an increasingly contested view that *chansons de geste* which give a significant role to feminine characters show "romance influence," and can therefore be excluded from the analysis. On the one hand it rejects a priori any attempt to assess the construction of a feminine persona in songs as diverse as *La Prise d'Orange*, *Fierabras*, and *Aye d'Avignon*;

on the other it excludes from analysis such constructs of masculinity as the magician, the good Saracen, the priest, or the clerk. The only space allowed to the feminine in the chapter is in the tendentiously titled subsection "Women in the Men's Room" in which women are represented as an implicit challenge to, but also an explicit adjunct of, the male heroic order. The view of Guibourc (in *La Chanson de Guillaume*) as merely a prop to a faltering hero, while not devoid of truth, misses many points by not considering her role as nurturer (of Vivien and Gui) and agent of conciliation (between Guillaume and Reneward).

Chapter 2 (on romance: "The Knight Meets his Match") concentrates on the verse romance of the twelfth century and, with the exception of a section dealing with the *Eneas*, specifically Arthurian romance. The analysis of the *Eneas* does look briefly at the question of the companionship of Eneas and Pallas and of Eurialus and Nisus, but apart from a passing remark on the resemblance of the latter pair to Ami and Amile, no attempt is made to draw lessons about the generic affiliations of the *Eneas*, any more than in the slightly more developed discussion of the suppression of difference in *Floire et Blanchflor*. Indeed, most of the section is concerned with analyzing the homophobic diatribe of Lavinia's mother against the hero, which again is not set in the context of similar material, in the *lais* of Marie de France, for example. Although some space is devoted at the end of the chapter to considering the attack on courtly masculinity in the person of Gauvain (notably in *Le Chevalier à l'épée*), most of the chapter deals with Chrétien's *Lancelot*. The thesis that Chrétien pours his irony equally on Lancelot and Guinevere is not wholly new, but the conclusion of the analysis, that Chrétien and his alter ego, Godefroy de Leigni, conspire in a male bonding of clerks to contest that of chivalry (represented by Lancelot and Meleagant) while marginalizing the female presence (Guinevere and Marie de Champagne), has important implications for the future of romance and novel form in French and its handling of the limits of fiction. Gaunt, however, places his emphasis on clerical mistrust of the feminine and disdain of the chivalric.

The chapter on the troubadours and *trobairitz*, while raising some very interesting questions about the gender-sensitive relationships of the different personae to their material (and to the object-subject of their songs), is unfortunately marred by a number of mistranslations of texts at points where the interpretation of the poems matters. So in a poem by Azalais de Porcairagues *seignoreiar* is translated "lord it over" (with negative connotations) rather than "be paramount among" (a positive connotation); the defensible paraphrase of the *lieu commun* "Domna met mot mal s'amor / que ab ric ome plaideia, / ab plus aut de vavasor" ["A lady places her love badly when she deals with too rich (really: "powerful") a man, too powerful a knight" (really: "with anyone higher born than a vavasor")] becomes indefensible in the commentary (p. 168) when the *ric ome* is identified, not contrasted, with the *vavasor*, erroneously called an *aut vavasor*. A similar failure to recognize the standard reference to the lady's husband in the *gelos* of stanza 4 of a song by the Comtessa de Dia (p. 172) vitiates the discussion of that poem. What would be very instructive, but what Gaunt does not do, would be to confront in detail in their context the exploitations of these motifs of Occitan *canso* by *trobairitz* with their use by male singers.

One persistent problem with the book is the tendency to extrapolate conclusions about genre from narrow manuscript evidence. So, on page 45, MS f. fr. 860 of the Bibliothèque Nationale is described as "a book about male bonding," and the presence of *Ami et Amile* in this collection of epics related to Roncevaux provides the paradigm for reading that poem, with no account taken of alternative transgeneric intertextualities provided by other redactions of the Ami and Amile legend. On page 76 the presence of Wace's *Brut*, the *Eneas*, the *Roman de Troie*, and the romances of Chrétien copied together in one manuscript (BN f. fr. 1450) is taken as evidence for reading the first three texts according to the paradigm for romance established by Chrétien's canon, rather than considering that the generic attribution of Chrétien might be questioned by the location of his texts. Finally, in dealing with the fabliaux, Gaunt's thesis that the texts are significantly concerned with mobility (social—in part derived from Rychner's analyses of "courtly" and "non-courtly" redactions of fabliaux—textual, and even gender mobility) is exemplified at length from *La Demoiselle qui ne pooit oïr parler de foutre*, which attributes different social classes to the protagonists in different redactions. Although the argument is bolstered to some extent by the differing emphasis placed on the question of class in variant versions of *De Berengier au long cul*, no account is taken of the large number of fabliaux in which the social status or "order" of the protagonists is determined by the title of the tale, a title attributed by an author who names himself on occasion and who not infrequently cites the authentic source of his tale as a proof of veracity.

Gaunt's book suffers from falling between two stools. It is a highly erudite piece of work supported by extensive scholarship. Each chapter offers some insights, and often instructive insights, into the question of gender in medieval French literature. A lack of space (or time, acknowledged in the introduction), produced perhaps by the pressure on scholars recently to publish at an artificially accelerated rhythm, has produced a simplification of arguments within each chapter, based on a reduced corpus of frequently well known material, and a structure for the study that relies on rather than investigates our received "map" of the corpus of Old French literature.

PHILIP E. BENNETT
University of Edinburgh

M. VICTORIA GUERIN. *The Fall of Kings and Princes: Structure and Destruction in Arthurian Tragedy. Figurae*: Reading Medieval Culture Series. Stanford: Stanford University Press, 1995. Pp. xi, 336. $39.50.

The title of this book suggests a study of the *de casibus* tradition of tragedy in medieval Arthurian literature. But the book, an eclectic series of essays not always related to tragedy, is more idiosyncratic than that title leads us to expect. M. Victoria Guerin offers sometimes careful and sometimes fanciful readings of a series of medieval Arthurian texts.

Accepting Chaucer's definition of tragedy in the Prologue to *The Monk's Tale* and in his *Boece*, Guerin finds it not incompatible with Aristotle:

Many elements of Aristotelian tragedy are common in medieval literature: the concepts of reversal . . . and recognition. . . . Equally common are the means by which, according to Aristotle, this necessary recognition is to be achieved: signs and tokens, suddenly reawakened memories, logical inference, and revelation through the intricacies of plot reunite lost lovers and family members in medieval romance as in classical drama. These reunions most often lead to a happy ending, but they frequently raise at least the specter of incest or kin-slaying along the way, and in some cases these potential disasters are realized in what might legitimately be termed "tragedies" in the Aristotelian as well as the medieval sense. (pp. 6–7)

Guerin does not examine the central features of Aristotle's theory, but focuses on "the specter of incest or kin-slaying," which "adds an element of horror to the act and to the reader's reaction of pity and fear, bringing the tale more closely in line with the Aristotelian paradigm for tragedy. Mordred is the demonic element in the Arthurian corpus, the ideal symbol for that forgotten or repressed action or, at times, aspect of the protagonist which arises unexpectedly to destroy and which is the essence of the tragic flaw" (pp. 7–8). Thus Arthur's "tragic flaw" is, for Guerin, his act of incest, unintentional though it was.

The opening chapter is an interesting and informed reading of the Vulgate Cycle from the perspective of the presence of Mordred, now in the Arthurian tradition the bastard and incestuous son of King Arthur. There are intriguing parallels drawn between Mordred and Lancelot, his "polar opposite" (p. 51): both are raised in ignorance of their true fathers until they have proven themselves as knights; both have an initial virtue that fails; both covet Guenevere; and both betray the king and through this betrayal help to bring about the fall of Camelot. The irony, of course, is that "Lancelot has for many years been guilty in secret of the crime to which Mordred aspires: betrayal of Arthur and adultery with Guinevere" (p. 66). Guerin thus sees Mordred as Lancelot, "reduced to the essence of his crime: betrayal of his lord and 'father'" (p. 67). In the end Lancelot is "displaced by Mordred who embodies, by his birth and in the pattern of his treason, all the implications of illicit love" (p. 65). In this Mordred-centric reading, Mordred is, finally, "the necessary agent of Apocalypse" (p. 65).

Far less successful than Guerin's long opening chapter are the three subsequent and shorter chapters on Chrétien's *The Knight of the Cart*, his *Story of the Grail*, and the anonymous *Sir Gawain and the Green Knight*, selected because they "exemplify the veiled treatment of Arthur's nemesis . . . and deal obliquely with the incest story" (p. 17). Her careful reading of the Vulgate Cycle gives way here to fanciful speculations that find little support in the text and offer even less illumination.

Although Mordred is never mentioned in Chrétien's romances, Guerin goes in search of him. In *The Knight of the Cart*, for example, the funeral cortege that passes by the window where Gawain and Lancelot are standing is also "Arthur's funeral cortege that passes in effigy before the eyes of the watchers in the tower. The episode may be seen as a sort of dramatic *tableau vivant*, a visionary moment belonging to the fatal understratum of the *Charette* and existing for the benefit of those in the tower" (p. 107). But understratum can be critically dangerous when it leads to the fanciful conclusion that the bier with the wounded knight and the tall knight leading a lovely lady function as "a representation of Mordred's usurpation of the queen and Arthur's consequent death" (p. 108). Founded upon such conjecturing, the conclusion is simplistic: "Lancelot/Méléagant (i.e. Mordred), by taking Arthur's place as the queen's lover, will bring about the king's death" (p. 118). Mordred's absence from the romance seems only to confirm his understratum presence, and Chrétien's success rests in transposing "the Mordred story with first Méléagant and then Lancelot in the role of usurper" (p. 145).

In *The Story of the Grail*, Guerin sees Perceval as another Mordred figure, for in the Arthurian tradition "there is only one other character (besides Perceval) whose maternal and paternal lines are so thoroughly and disastrously intermingled: Mordred, for whom Arthur is both father and maternal uncle as a result of the king's incest with his half-sister" (pp. 141–42). The Fisher King is identified with Arthur and "his wound with a sexual mutilation representing Mordred's usurpation of the throne and the queen" (p. 158), the episode at the Grail Castle thus becoming "a second opportunity for Perceval, as Mordred's representative, to examine the mystery of his own lineage" (p. 162).

The reading of *Sir Gawain and the Green Knight* is another relentless search for the Mordred figure: "[T]he Mordred parallel . . . underlies *Sir Gawain and the Green Knight*'s plot. . . . Bertilak and his lady are doubles of Arthur and Guenevere: that is, of Mordred's father and (step) mother, not of Gawain's. By taking Mordred's place in the otherworld, Gawain must try to see the pattern set before him and to avoid enacting the ready-made scenario" (pp. 210; 216). Mordred, the "oedipal everyman" (p. 216), is such an understratum omnipresence—he is never mentioned in the romance—that Guerin's speculations can become silly; for example: "It may not be too far-fetched to suppose that, in addition to the association of the pentangle virtues with Gawain's own, the choice of the *pen*tangle as symbol may have stemmed from the fact that Gawain is a member and, here, an emissary of the house of *Pen*dragon, bearing its honor and its sins with him into the otherworld, where he is to be tested in a pattern that closely implicates his (*tangled*) genealogy as both Arthur's nephew and Morgan's" (p. 221–22).

*The Fall of Kings and Princes* succeeds when its author exercises care and sensitivity, as in her textual examination of the Vulgate Cycle. When she practices much less care, as in the case of the three episodic romances, she sheds no new light.

DAVID STAINES
University of Ottawa

CAROL FALVO HEFFERNAN. *The Melancholy Muse: Chaucer, Shakespeare, and Early Medicine*. Duquesne Language and Literature Series, vol. 19. Pittsburgh: Duquesne University Press, 1995. Pp. xiv, 185. $48.00.

The theory of humors stimulated far-reaching discourses on erotic love and mental disorders, the psychological and social consequences of which are still with us. Although since Ovid, the signs of melancholy and affiliated mania had been widely dispersed in imaginative and moral literature, Carol Falvo Heffernan's book is a reminder that the medical conception of melancholy is both prior and persistent. Still, *The Melancholy Muse* strikes this reader more as an extended essay, along the lines of John Livingston Lowes's 1914 article "The Loveres Maladye of Hereos," rather than a deeply scholarly work or a highly imaginative interdisciplinary study. Heffernan says that her aim "to demonstrate that the two poets and the medieval-Renaissance physicians viewed melancholy in parallel ways" may seem "too modest" (p. 4). Apart from the problems entailed in compressing fourteenth- and sixteenth-century constructions of melancholy, Heffernan's modesty of purpose prevents her from fully developing, for her readers' benefit, relevant issues in medical theory such as the physiology of the body's heat, humors burnt to ashes, the rising of the spirits from the lower body to the brain, brain cell theory, and the like. To know more about the circulation of the doctrine of *adustion* in the sixteenth century might suggest new ways of reading such a line as "Consumed with that which it was nourished by."

After a survey of writings on melancholy from Galen to Bernard of Gordon, Heffernan analyzes Chaucer's narrator of *The Book of the Duchess*, *Troilus and Criseyde*, Shakespeare's Jaques in *As You Like It*, and *Hamlet*. The narrator of *The Book of the Duchess* does not suffer from "a clear-cut case of lovesickness" (p. 41), although he must suffer from some form of *amor hereos*, melancholy, or mania, which causes his insomnia. His attempt to cure himself with reading can be derived from medical remedies for "melancholy care" and "mania" that include listening to songs (Avicenna) and reading aloud (Caelius Aurelianus). Moreover, congenial conversation and pleasant surroundings will cure such patients as the black knight and his interlocutor, according to Caelius Aurelianus, Johannes Afflacius, and Bernard of Gordon. Is Dorigen Chaucer's feminine counterpart to these distraught males?

Furthermore, what does the medical diagnosis of lovesickness have to do with the noble love of literature and the court? In Avicenna, the medical problem and the psychological state belong to two different domains, the former expounded in the *Canon of Medicine*, the latter in the *Treatise on Love*. For relief of the medical ailment of *amor hereos*, Avicenna prescribes *coitus*. Heffernan refuses to pursue this medical remedy for *Troilus and Criseyde* and takes issue with Mary Wack's view (1984) of Criseyde as "a cure for Troilus's lovesickness" on the grounds that "The erotic high point of the consummation in book 3, considered from this perspective, is reduced to 'a night in therapeutic intercourse with Criseyde,'" which situation "would seem to make a love poem captive to—rather than based on—the medical model" (p. 86). But one might ask why we should hesitate to trust this poet to be playing more than one game at once. Despite, or because of, Heffernan's careful mapping of the transformation of Troilus's lovesickness to the "purest form of love," her argument stops short of the possibilities of both the comic aspects of curative sex silently voiced by Criseyde at the end of book 2 and also the religious transcendence of veneal love and earthly death seen in the Troilus of the epilogue.

Whereas Heffernan identifies Jaques's "most humorous sadness" as the *adust* type of melancholy, which derives from the burnt-off excess of humors (pp. 98, 103, 105), Hamlet's melancholy has advanced to the hallucinatory stage by act 3, if his mother is right that the ghost he sees is "the very coinage" of his own brain; for melancholy madness in Andrew Boorde's *The Breviarie of Health* (1547) is, to begin with, "a sickness full of fantasies, thinking to here or to see that thing that is not heard nor seene." As melancholy's intimacy with madness led earlier twentieth-century critics to Freudian and neo-Freudian analyses of Hamlet, Heffernan follows, searching for the best psychological rationalizations for Hamlet's irrational pain in a discourse essentially begun by the Hippocratic writers on humoural theory.

Lea T. Olsan
Northeast Louisiana University

THOMAS HONEGGER. *From Phoenix to Chauntecleer: Medieval English Animal Poetry*. Schweizer Anglistische Arbeiten/Swiss Studies in English, vol. 120. Tübingen, Basil: A. Francke Verlag, 1996. Pp. ix, 288. N.p.

There have been any number of studies of medieval English literature dealing with animals and its Latin, French, or Italian background, but no examination concentrating exclusively on the major functions of the animal figures in the chief examples of medieval English animal poetry. It is such a task that Thomas Honegger has set himself in this dissertation, completed at the University of Zürich. His monograph provides the reader with a wealth of information for understanding the role played by animals in the *Physiologus* tradition in Old and Middle English (chapter 2); in "bird poems" from *The Owl and the Nightingale* to Chaucer's *The Parliament of Fowls* (chapter 3); and in two Middle English beast fables/epics, *The Vox and the Wolf* and Chaucer's *The Nun's Priest's Tale* (chapter 4).

Honegger's extensive study of the Physiologus tradition (pp. 17–100) proceeds along structuralist lines, developing a model of an "ideal" chapter from Latin representatives of the *Physiologus* that serves as a point of reference for his analysis of the Old and Middle English texts in this grouping. Such a typical chapter begins its presentation of an animal with a biblical citation that mentions that animal explicitly, develops "scientific" data about the animal adopted from natural history in a first section, then interprets these characteristics spiritually and allegorically in the next section, and concludes with a brief statement of affirmation ("And so the Physiologus has spoken well concerning . . ."). Honegger's analysis of *The Old English Physiologus* concludes that the structure of its entries recapitulates this model, though generally without the explicit citation of a biblical verse at the beginning and with a more extensive moralizing epilogue. The function of the animals in the Old English text remains that of providing an occasion for the *significatio*: only those characteristics that support a consistent spiritual interpretation of the animal are mentioned in the section of "scientific" data. It is on structural grounds as well that Honegger justifies his analysis of *The Phoenix* here, for the implicit division in this poem between a section of characteristics of the phoenix derived from natural history and one devoted to the eschatological and typological signification of these characteristics parallels the model he has developed of the typical chapter in the *Physiologus* tradition. Unlike its Old English precursor, *The Middle English Physiologus* demonstrates an increased interest in the *sensus moralis* in its interpretation of animal characteristics. As Honegger emphasizes in particular in his analysis of the chapter on the dove in *The Middle English Physiologus* (which has no equivalent in the *Theobaldi "Physiologus"* that served as the Latin source for most of the English work), moral interpretation is the characteristic method of *significatio* in the Middle English text.

Of the uses of animals in secular Middle English literature, Honegger is concerned mainly with two traditions: that which employs the allegorical and symbolic (and generally courtly) dimensions of animal characteristics on the one hand (pp. 103–66), and the genres of the beast epic and beast fable on the other (pp. 169–227). Symbolic qualities of animals are used in a number of Middle English genres, such as political poetry like *Mum and the Sothsegger* (identified here by its outdated title, *Richard the Redeles*, and erroneously attributed to William Langland [p. 10]), but the examples in this tradition analyzed by Honegger, in which animals play a major role, generally involve questions of love and frequently employ the debate form. Although that form regularly presents the question of the animals' usefulness to human beings as the pivotal point of the debate, the author of *The Owl and the Nightingale* initially frustrates this expectation, reminding the reader frequently of the avian nature of the debate's protagonists instead. In Honegger's understanding, the shifting nature of the symbolic reading the birds give of each other—the owl attempts to identify itself with the *nycticorax* tradition, for example, while the nightingale attempts to force it into the *bubo* tradition—supports the open-ended "conclusion" of the poem in which neither bird is declared the winner of the debate. Among the poems of love casuistry, Chaucer's *The Parliament of Fowls* illustrates what Honegger describes as the "entire variety of the different functions of birds" (p. 165) in this type of literature. At first, birds are merely stock poetic figures, part of the background of the *locus amoenus*; then, in the avian catalogue, Chaucer alludes to the allegorical values of birds; and finally, Honegger argues, in the parliamentary debate the fowls are used to express various human attitudes toward love (rather than to represent social classes or historical personages) without becoming mere mouthpieces for these attitudes, such as one finds in the use of bird protagonists in the late thirteenth-century *The Thrush and the Nightingale*. For Honegger, the choice of fowls for the speaking roles allowed Chaucer to confront concepts of high courtly love with those concerned with the futility of amorous desire, the question of *cupiditas*, or even a more biological urge for procreation within one unified context, because the symbolic and natural qualities attributed to birds, rather than any other animal, sanctioned such a wide range of reference.

The same care that Honegger takes in delineating the intellectual context of the functions of animals in the *Physiologus* tradition and in "bird poems" is evident in his treatment of beast fables/epics. Seen against the background of the literature dealt with in the preceding chapters, where the didactic functionality of the animal figures is something the various traditions have in common, Honegger observes that already in the late thirteenth-century English adaptation of the *Roman de Renart*, *The Vox and the Wolf*, animals serve the chief purpose of entertaining and amusing the audience rather than instructing it through their symbolic and allegorical dimensions. *The Nun's Priest's Tale*, as Honegger argues once again in reference to Chaucer, makes use of all the options in the use of animals that are described earlier in his study. On the level of "natura," the starting point for animal literature from the *Physiologus* onward, Chaucer's protagonists are described in clearly defined biological terms; like the beast fable, these animals are also obviously related to types of human beings, though Chaucer never avails himself of the beast fable's closure, instead allowing the ambiguous mixture of animal and human characteristics to play itself out throughout the text. What is peculiar to Chaucer's work, according to Honegger, is that from the myriad possibilities of allegorical and symbolic interpretations of roosters, hens, and foxes, for example, all of which are documented in this chapter from the secondary literature on the tale, there is nothing that is compelling as a restriction on the narrative's polyvalence. Even the particular changes that Chaucer's tale represents in the history of the fable of *The Cock and the Fox* (regardless of whether they are to be attributed to Chaucer himself)—the mock-heroic treatment of the animals, for example, or Chauntecleer's erudition—are not able to be resolved into a reading on only one level. Such an understanding of the tale's uniqueness is not unprecedented in the critical literature on Chaucer, and one would have been interested to see how Honegger might go on to place this narrative in a larger hermeneutic context; but his command of the traditions of animal interpretation allows for a more precise description of the singularity of Chaucer's achievement than has been common up to now.

The physical layout of the book is generally clear, but the graphic illustrations of narrative forms often present the reader with a confusing visual image of dots and diagonal lines that adds nothing to the clarity of the prose descriptions of the texts. One might also suggest that books of the Bible could more easily have been referred to with common abbreviations (e.g., Matt., Ps.) rather than lengthy and sometimes incomplete Latin phrases ("*Secundum Matthaeum*," p. 30; "*Psalmi Iuxta Hebraicum*," p. 119; both forms also appear in the index, p. 286). But these are minor matters in what is generally a competent account of the function of animal protagonists in the chief examples of animal poetry in medieval English literature.

RICHARD NEWHAUSER
Trinity University
(San Antonio, Texas)

STEVEN JUSTICE. *Writing and Rebellion: England in 1381.* The New Historicism Series, vol. 27. Berkeley, Los Angeles, and London: University of California Press, 1994. Pp. xiv, 289. $40.00.

Steven Justice has written an exciting, ruminating account of the gestures of writing in the English Peasants' Rising in 1381. Where other historians and literary scholars have examined the causes and effects of the rebellion during that summer in 1381 or been concerned with the image of the rebellion in canonical literature, Justice wants "to understand the thought of a rural revolt and of the rural communities that produced it; to trace what the English vernacular meant to those who spoke nothing else, and what writing meant to those who were not thought to read; to observe, from a starting angle, the development of vernacular literature, in the more usual and canonical sense of that word" (p. 4). *Writing and Rebellion* mostly dwells on the first goal, understanding the *mentalité* of rural English communities in the late fourteenth century by using not only the chronicle accounts of the Rising and the writings of Langland, Wyclif, Gower, and Chaucer but also work on the social history of fourteenth-century England. Justice argues that the Peasants' Rising was largely a struggle for literate and economic power, which is to say class warfare by other means, although his book also presents a more complex analysis of medieval class relations than the traditional schemes of lords, clergy, and lower laity or lord and tenant allow. Vernacular literacies became the means by which peasants and clerics used the idiom of reform in the writings of intellectuals such as Wyclif to challenge traditional clerical and aristocratic authority and dominance in the name of a better social, economic, and spiritual order. But Justice's book is not really an account of the "development of vernacular literature." *Writing and Rebellion* treats the canonical poetry of Langland, Gower, and Chaucer mostly as skeptical or scornful responses to the vernacular literacy and rural ideology of the Rising or, in the case of the B-text of *Piers Plowman*, as unintentionally providing a vocabulary and idiom for the rebels' discourse.

Chapters 1 ("Insurgent Literacy") and 4 ("The Idiom of Rural Politics"), the core of Justice's argument, make for compelling, provocative reading. These two chapters, describing in detail the historical and cultural situation within which the famous six letters from John Ball and three laymen were composed, juxtapose the official royalist and clerical chronicle versions with an alternative representation from the perspective of the peasants and clergy who made the rebellion. Justice shows how peasants' functional literacy was motivated by economic concerns and documentary culture. Three more chapters ("Wyclif in the Rising," "*Piers Plowman* in the Rising," and "Insurgency Remembered") discuss the importance of Wyclif's writings and Langland's poem in shaping the idiom of the rebellion and the efforts of later Ricardian writers (Langland, Gower, and Chaucer) to dissociate themselves from the rebellion.

The book opens with a brief narrative summary (pp. 1–4) of the events of the Rising. Beginning on May 30, 1381, peasants and some clergy attacked royal and local officials and grammar masters; plundered abbeys; burned charters and other financial documents held by sheriffs and escheators; marched on London and executed Simon Sudbury, the king's chancellor and Archbishop of Canterbury, Robert Hales, the royal treasurer and prior of the Knights Hospitaller in England, and others; suffered losses themselves (Wat Tyler, a leader of the Rising, was mortally wounded by the mayor of London); and forced King Richard to negotiate royal charters of manumission abolishing villeinage and fixing land rents. But by July, Richard had regained control of London and the countryside. John Ball and other rebel leaders were executed, and the royal charters of manumission were revoked.

Who were these peasants and the clerical leaders of the Rising such as John Ball? Justice's important point is that if we want to understand who the rebels were, we have to understand how they used and thought of writing. The Peasants' Rising was motivated and structured by what Justice calls "rural literacy" and "the gestures of writing." Medieval historians, literary scholars, and codicologists, but not many historians of literacy, have for some time now been systematically dismantling the distorted modern view of medieval literacy as primarily a Latin affair controlled by the clergy and intellectual elites. In late fourteenth-century England, literacy and education were more available and desirable among the rural and town people than ever before, and the spread of literate technologies and attitudes had a destabilizing effect in many areas of society. Michael Clanchy's influential *From Memory to Written Record* (first published 1979), Brian Stock's *The Implications of Literacy* (1983), and numerous other studies of the uses of literacy, modes of reading, book ownership, and literate models of cognition in the everyday lives of medieval men and women have accumulated plenty of evidence that literacy was more widespread and writing more dispersed throughout later medieval Europe than the traditional clerical distinction between literate *clerici* and illiterate *laici* suggests. Vernacular literacies and the increased understanding of literate power prompted the lower classes to have access to and to use pragmatic modes of communication or record keeping such as charters, rent agreements, and inventories, spiritual texts such as sermons and penitentials, political tracts, and previously elite forms of literature.

How then to understand "rural literacy"? Using textualist approaches to both literary and historical materials (loosely, New Historicism), Justice argues that Knighton's *Chronicon*, Walsingham's *Chronicon angliae*, and the *Anonimalle* chronicle misunderstood the peasants' behavior and motives and, paradoxically, that the chroniclers' inability to comprehend rural literacy makes them more, not less, reliable because they do not filter out of their accounts details they presume mean something else. In their narratives of the rebellion, Knighton and Walsingham include six Middle English texts ascribed to John Ball, Jack Milner, Jack Carter, and Jack Trewman, texts well known to students of the Peasants' Rising, Langland scholars, and social historians of medieval and early modern England. But Justice launches his argument from what he calls Knighton's "mistake," both a representation and a parapraxis (p. 7). According to Knighton, Ball sent three letters to the leaders of the rebellion, while the three Jacks spoke to the crowds (pp. 15–17). Knighton assumes that Ball and other clerics were the literate leaders of illiterate peasants. *Writing and Rebellion* is a sustained and cogent argument that the chroniclers could not have been more wrong. Justice's analysis depends on a theory of performativity as it problematizes identity categories. The chroniclers identify the rebels as illiterate hooligans while Justice posits that they were literate economic and social reformers. Rather than search for hidden evidence, Justice reveals that the evidence for his claim is right on the surface in the traces of the Rising.

Justice's book effectively begins and ends with the rebels calling out the abbot of the great house of St. Albans and tossing charters and rolls of the house into the flames, while they demanded "a certain ancient charter confirming the liberties of the villeins, with capital letters, one of gold and the other of azure; and without that, they asserted, they would not be satisfied with promises" (pp. 256–57). The simplicity of Justice's question belies the complexity of his answer: If the rebels were rebelling against literate culture, why did they not burn all documents and the libraries as well? More important, if the rebels were illiterates with no experience with writing, how could they know to ask for a specific charter according to what it looked like, presumably because they believed it to be critical support for their economic grievances?

Justice's approach to the history of literacy builds on (and in some cases revises) the important work of medievalists such as Clanchy and Stock and of cultural critics such as Innis, McLuhan, de Certeau, and Bakhtin, whose work has enormous importance for understanding the functions and histories of writing and social relations. Using the term "writing" in a broad, performative sense, Justice argues a strong functional-symbolic approach to literacies keyed to local practices and concerns. He differs sharply from the views of David Cressy, for whom Plantagenet England was a collection of full, partly full, or mostly empty literate glasses, based on a single standard of what it meant to be literate. At the same time, Justice recognizes the importance of oral practices in the construction of medieval literacy, and his functional-symbolic approach to literacies offers a specific critique of the oral/written divide model found in the work of Goody and Ong. Justice convincingly argues that whoever the three Jacks were, the texts ascribed to them were composed in different places using tag phrases and apothegms derived from Wyclif's writings on virtuous poverty and perhaps Ball's own letters (pp. 20–21). In other words, some among the rebels were reading, hearing, and circulating clerical writings and "reaccenting" them, to use Bakhtin's term, in their own idiom and in their own villages for local purposes. Also, the admonition in one of Ball's letters to tell Langland's character Piers Plowman to "go to his werk" suggests how rebels could read Langland's poem more literally than Langland himself imagined: "The kind of reading Ball brought to *Piers Plowman*, and the kind of writing he took from it, can explain how the rebels could appropriate the poem on their own terms and *at the same time* delegate its central character as the embodiment and authorization of their claims to power and how Wit's 'bastards' could become elements in an ideology of rebellion" (p. 106). Langland's vagueness about specific social, economic, and spiritual reforms left open a performative space for peasants to take literate and political action.

Precisely what kind of action the peasants took and what those actions meant is the heart of *Writing and Rebellion*. We aren't used to thinking of burning documents or books as acts of literacy, along with writing, reading, and archiving, but that is just what Justice argues. In towns and rural areas outside of London, "insurgent literacy" included writing and circulating letters which asserted a more literal reading of Wyclif's call for a return to the "trewþe" of political communion, the bond between the monarch and the people, and Langland's criticisms of ecclesiastical power and wealth. The rebels' own writing and the chronicle accounts of the rebellion describe the peasants' utopian identification with the king against the king's advisers, lords, and great clergy (p. 63) and also the rebels' refusal to accept the royal bureaucracy's authority and legitimacy to administer the law. As performance, insurgent literacy included a number of "gestures" of "assertive literacy" (pp. 24–25), conceived of as both technology and ideology, that is, as labor (p. 24): writing, reading, and keeping charters, deeds, and other documents; burning documents; attempting to negotiate a new economic arrangement with the king; publishing broadsides. Unlike other historians of literacy, Justice also maps out important sites of rural communication—the alehouse, mill, and church—and the importance of local festivals, especially Midsummer, in the symbolic action of the Rising. However, Justice carefully distinguishes the idea of annual popular celebrations from the particular ways Midsummer 1381 fueled the Rising (pp. 153–56): "The rebels in 1381 translated the symbolic resistance of midsummer into actual resistance, building their fires not from the underbrush of the manorial forests but from the literate underpinnings of manorial rule. . . . [T]he ideology on which the insurgency drew was concerned not with rebellion but with order and survival" (p. 155).

Justice's narrative of the Rising is at odds with that of the royal chroniclers, for whom the rebellion was a dangerous, irrational, bacchantic spree of looting, killing, and pillaging. He also modifies the Bakhtinian view of carnival as motivated by opposition to official rule but often, as Bakhtin's critics point out, subordinated to it. By rethinking the role of carnival in terms of rural literacy, Justice also revises the views of modern leftist historians such as Rodney Hilton, who believes the rebel peasants did not deny the traditional medieval tripartite social order of lords, clergy, and lower laity and therefore understands the Rising primarily as a "class conflict" between lords and tenants. Rejecting both Bakhtin's and Hilton's views, Justice argues that later medieval English classes were more fluid and literately constructed:

Were the most prosperous peasants more like minor lords than less prosperous peasants? In some ways, yes; but then the minor lords did not rebel. . . . Where we locate class divisions depends on where we look from, how close or distant our perspective and how local or global our questions; but it does not depend only on that. Classes can make themselves by choice.

The rebel letters were a way of making a class. In asserting that literacy existed where it did not belong, they drew the class line, the line that separated the exploited from the exploiters, at exactly the point where writing was controlled. (p. 192)

The chapters on rural and insurgent literacy are the strongest in Justice's book. I found chapter 5 ("Insurgency Remembered") less focused, although still very worthwhile. Some of the most significant nonchronicle representations of the Rising erupt in Gower's *Vox clamantis*, Langland's narrative revisions in the C-text of *Piers Plowman*, and Chaucer's *Canterbury Tales*. Justice reads *The Nun's Priest's Tale* as a complex, sometimes personal joke at Gower's expense after Gower had distanced himself from the rebellion in the prologue to book 2 of *Vox clamantis*. With the same close reading techniques he used when examining the rebels' six letters, Justice hears Gower's verbal idiom and its parody in Chaucer's narrative. *The Nun's Priest's Tale* and the tales connected with it in *The Canterbury Tales* sequence work to contain the literate and political subversion of the rebellion even as the pilgrims are riding through an area where the rebellion was strong and violent.

Justice reads the C-text of *Piers Plowman* as Langland's effort to contain the effects of an alternative vernacular literacy and put some distance between himself as an author and those members of his reading audience for whom the Rising was an empowering moment because they read *Piers Plowman* more literally than Langland wished. In this final chapter, the major writers of fourteenth-century England are read as seeking, in various ways, to contain the subversive effects of the Rising. One of Justice's sidebar arguments is that the late medieval idea of authorship emerges in such anxieties over unintended readings by uncontrolled audiences, that is, in the circulation of texts among various audiences whose frames of reference cannot be prescribed in advance. Where some read democracy, others read promiscuity or corruption. Here, Justice adds new dimensions to our understanding of authorship and the "author function" in the later Middle Ages, different from accounts of medieval authorship that rely on the scholastic tradition or literary nationalism.

Justice, recognizing the ambiguity of materialist criticism, asserts that "We must begin from those texts that are, without question, distorted by interest and ideology, and we must begin from the distortions themselves" (p. 256). But sometimes Justice's ethnomethodology gets the better of his argument. When he suggests that the rebels may have rejected Piers Plowman's pilgrimage and the search for *trewþe* because they "asserted the transparency of terms [*dowel, dobet, dobest*] Langland made mystery of" (p. 130), Justice erases any engagement between the poem and Langland's readers. Instead of not understanding Langland's poetic questioning, some of the rebels may simply have understood Langland's poem and rejected the argument. Also, while Justice shows us the symbolic and performative dimensions of the gestures of writing in the Rising, he remains aloof from questions about the peasants', clerics', and crown's responsibilities for the actions they took. He acknowledges that the Rising did produce its share of "gratuitous or meaningless" acts of violence and pillaging and also acts of revenge and rough public justice, not to mention the possibility that some peasants were simply led along by mob psychology. But in his "thought experiment" Justice posits that the Rising was acted out with a "maximum (rather than the customary minimum) of discipline, consistency, purpose, and information on the part of those who made it . . ." (p. 10). He takes the absence of pillaging at the Savoy and the fact that no libraries were destroyed wholesale as evidence that the rebels were working with a specific agenda for taking control of documentary culture. If so, then we can ask, what part of the agenda was fulfilled when rebels, after beheading the archbishop of Canterbury, forced grammar masters at Bury St. Edmunds to swear never again to teach the *ars grammatica*? Were these literacy teachers attacked because they were connected with priories and bishoprics? Maybe. Or because they were teaching Latin literacy? That seems unlikely. Or because they were teaching literacy? After Justice's argument in chapter 1, hardly. Who was responsible for rural and village literacy education? What were their connections with the priory and cathedral schools and with Latin as well as vernacular literacy? Justice cites important studies by Orme, Moran, and others on medieval and early modern English schooling, but he breezes past the question of education by saying that "training in the alphabet and in pronunciation" was sufficient "to yield some control of the written vernacular; so much only would be needed, and so much could probably have been passed along without any formal instruction at all" (p. 33). Well, yes, some such knowledge could have been disseminated this way, but was it? Peasants' access to desired literacy had to be located somewhere. Parish priests, clerics, and traveling grammar tutors constituted a fragile but critical network of literacy instructors reaching into the rural areas and villages of fourteenth-century England. We know that, as teachers of elementary literacy, all clerics were not suspect. John Ball was a leader of the Rising. So what distinguished one cleric from another—local community identities and associations between rural layfolk and clergy, as Justice briefly suggests? By focusing so closely on writing and the gestures of rebellion in terms of economic clashes, Justice gives us a dense but narrow picture of literacy among rural and tradespeople. Everyday literacy remains very much in the background of *Writing and Rebellion*, but it is the ground upon which Justice's argument is based. Moreover, Justice claims that charters gave peasants experience with documentary (read, "official") culture and a motive for making it their own (p. 35). But when we consider peasant literacy experiences and education, clearly more than charters—*Piers Plowman* for example—are shaping popular reading practices. What else might peasant households have been reading to give literate shape to their experiences?

Questions about literacy education and lay reading suggest other ways in which the Rising resonated with fourteenth-century English textuality. By all accounts, the Rising of 1381 was pretty much a man's world, although an occasional woman does appear in the narratives of the Rising. But women readers and writers are much more visible in other aspects of fourteenth-century English art, spirituality, religious heterodoxy, and education. And literate women were specifically singled out by official culture's interrogation of the unruly laity. Given women's increased activity in other areas of medieval English literate culture, their relative absence from the Rising, which Justice calls a "medieval literacy crisis," opens up a space for further historical and cultural inquiry. What kinds of experiences constituted rural and peasant female literacies? Was female literacy more sequestered than male literacy in the fourteenth century? The extent of literacy education and other reading experiences in the late Middle Ages remains to be explored in the field Justice has turned over.

Justice's *Writing and Rebellion*, which recently won the MLA Prize for a First Book, is an exciting, provocative, and controversial book. Its methods and conclusions should provoke us to rethink the ways we identify official cultures and resistances in the later Middle Ages. By reading historical and literary texts about the Rising within a broader and deeper discursive and performative field—"symbolic action" in response to "cultural psychosis" and economic injustice—Justice concretizes the ambiguity of the term *history*: as what has occurred and also as an account of what has occurred. As Letterman might say, Justice's book is theoretically easy on the eyes, but he is at home with Kenneth Burke, Clifford Geertz, and Michel Foucault. Unlike Foucault, Justice interprets power with more diffuse, less top-down models. But the Lacanian problem of how things become objects underwrites Justice's entire project. *Writing and Rebellion*, rather than blending so-called Old Historicism and New Historicism, shows how historiography is always about re-creating or destabilizing myths, that is, how history is not only saying but doing. The history of medieval literacies is one of the ways we are learning how we got to be modern.

MARK AMSLER
University of Delaware

LAURA D. KELLOGG. *Boccaccio's and Chaucer's Cressida*. Studies in the Humanities, vol. 16. New York: Peter Lang, 1995. Pp. xi, 144. $42.95.

Like a beautiful puzzle with a few pieces missing, Criseyde continues to enthrall and frustrate us. Though Chaucer reveals some of her thoughts, Criseyde's motives remain a mystery, and this enigmatic quality is part of her charm. Laura Kellogg's book sets out to dispel some of the charm. Working against the current practice of reading Criseyde as a victim of her circumstances, Kellogg traces Criseyde's origins back through Boccaccio, Guido, Benoît, and Dares, in an attempt to expose Criseyde in all her incarnations as the embodiment of infidelity who teaches prudence and morality through her negative example.

Kellogg's central claim is that both Boccaccio and Chaucer create narrators who miss the moral lesson Criseyde's example is supposed to teach. The irony created by this blindness to Criseyde's "true" meaning is supposed to make the reader see that each poem is actually a condemnation of excessive desire and inconstancy. Creating a sense of continuity between the various depictions of Criseyde is thus one of Kellogg's main tasks, though it also becomes one of the book's weaknesses. Kellogg explains away the differences in characterization between Boccaccio and Chaucer by establishing a kind of Ur-character (whom she calls Cressida) who is a combination of inconstant women from Virgil, Ovid, Dares, Guido, and Benoît. However, the essentializing drive of such an approach hobbles Kellogg's analysis, because she must forgo any nuanced consideration of the changes in Criseyde that Boccaccio and Chaucer introduce into their versions of the story.

Kellogg devotes her first chapter, "Cressida's Literary History and Her Inheritance from Dido," to the origins of her character in classical sources. She begins with a brief account of the classical sources—the *Iliad*, Dares and Dictys, and Ovid's *Heroides*—and then moves into a more detailed discussion of Benoît de Sainte-Maure's *Roman de Troie*. Here she focuses on Benoît's asides in which he predicts Briseida's future infidelity. Next comes a brief discussion of the more frankly misogynistic portrait of Briseida as a seductress in Guido delle Colonne's *Historia destructionis Troiae*. Kellogg claims, surprisingly, that Guido condemns Briseida more openly than Benoît because he is writing history rather than fiction. She then generalizes that "[m]edieval historiography has determined that Cressida can only epitomize patent inconstancy. Her fickle nature, evil motives, and heinous behavior make Briseida's personal qualities as clear and true, therefore, as the destruction of Troy" (p. 10). Ignoring the fact that such language seems more suited to a serial murderer than an unfaithful lover, how is it that Guido's Briseida has suddenly become the true Cressida? Kellogg makes no mention of contemporaneous historiographic accounts that would confirm Guido's portrait as universal, but rather moves hurriedly on to an entirely new area of inquiry: the influence of various portrayals of Dido on depictions of Criseyde. Kellogg maintains that we cannot understand Cressida without a broader view of her connections to other classical heroines, especially Dido. This is a worthwhile point, and Kellogg notes that medieval poets were often caught between Virgil's condemnation of Dido's behavior and Ovid's more sympathetic portrayal of her as a wronged woman. However, she deals rather awkwardly with Chaucer's clear preference for the Ovidian version of Dido's story by suggesting that Chaucer is somehow denying reality: "A knowledge of Virgil, however, undermines that which Ovid and Chaucer have written" (p. 18). Such a reading rather anachronistically makes Chaucer and Ovid seem like contemporaries, and completely overlooks the possibility that Chaucer may be asking us to read Dido as more complicated than Virgil made her.

Chapter 2, "Boccaccio's Criseida and Her Narrator," starts out more auspiciously with a sustained consideration of the attitude of Boccaccio's narrator toward the *Filostrato*. Kellogg is right to point out the ironies of the situation. The poem begins with a letter from the narrator to his estranged beloved, Filomena, where he explains that he hopes she will come to understand his pain through the story of Troiolo. This is perhaps not the best choice for the lovesick narrator, since his identification with Troiolo predicts his ultimate failure to lure Filomena back into his clutches. Such blindness on the part of the narrator makes him a perfect foil to an ironic reading of the *Filostrato*. Kellogg points out that the lessons on Fortune in Boethius's *Consolation* provide a counterpoint to Troiolo's and the narrator's hopeless pursuit of love. Nevertheless, this is rather well trodden ground: as Kellogg's notes reveal, much of what she says has already been dealt with in the work of Robert Hollander and Janet Smarr. After this section the chapter descends into a needlessly detailed summary of the *Filostrato*, accompanied by occasional interpretive comments reiterating that Boccaccio's Criseida cannot escape the inconstancy assigned to her by literary tradition. When they first spend the night together, Criseida asks Troiolo, "Shall I strip myself?" The newly-married are bashful the first night." Kellogg reads this remark as a sign that Criseida is trying to escape sin by referring to her liaison with Troiolo as a marriage (though the reference to marriage may be intended to arouse rather than excuse). Here Kellogg sees a parallel between Criseida and Dido. True, Virgil's Dido does have moral scruples about her love for Aeneas and thus insists she is married to him; however, Criseida shows no corresponding worries with Troiolo. I think an argument could be made that there are some faint echoes of *Aeneid* 4 here, but, if anything, the comparison with Dido serves to reinforce the differences between the two women; indeed, it is Troiolo who acts more like Dido. Hence, Kellogg's moralizing readings overlook subtleties and at the same time raise questions she fails to address. In the story as a whole, is Boccaccio using Criseida to show us that Troiolo should have read his Boethius more carefully and not pursued the pleasures of the flesh, or that he should have renounced his love for Criseida and found another girlfriend? And if Boccaccio wants us to condemn Criseida, why does he make her so appealing? Kellogg sidesteps these issues and ends the chapter with the rather obvious conclusion that the narrator has succeeded in making Criseida an emblem of infidelity but failed in his efforts at making the book a go-between, thus sealing his own fate as a latterday Troiolo.

Chapter 3, "Chaucer's Criseyde and Her Narrator," begins by setting up some contrasts between the *Filostrato* and *Troilus and Criseyde*. Unhampered by love, "Chaucer's narrator attempts to engage in a relationship not with a lady but with his *auctores*, with history and literature" (p. 61). Kellogg is right to focus on the tension between Chaucer's sources and his vision of Criseyde. Many commentators have noted how Chaucer has transformed Boccaccio's Criseida into a more complex and ultimately more sympathetic character. Kellogg does not disagree with this view; however, she asserts that Chaucer's development both of the entire poem and of Criseyde's character stems from the narrator's need to delay the inevitable revelation of Criseyde's bad faith. While the urge to postpone things does afflict Chaucer's narrator, especially in book 4, it seems excessive to label the love scene in book 3 as mere procrastination: "The love scene . . . fills much of Book III in Chaucer because the narrator prolongs the exchange between Troilus and Criseyde in order to avoid the future issues with which he must inevitably deal" (p. 74).

This approach is very reductive, to say the least, and it allows Kellogg to avoid examining much of the poem.

Illogical connections and discontinuous arguments are chronic problems throughout Kellogg's book, but for some reason they intensify in this final chapter. Thus on page 68 her discussion of the narrator's anxieties over translation in the proem to book 2 leads to the following statements: "For the narrator, the changing nature of language compounds the problems encountered through translations; these linguistic difficulties, in turn, explain to the reader the basis for what is actually the narrator's refusal to admit or to state the truth, to accept responsibility for his words. Criseyde, in specific, exemplifies the narrator's avoidance of responsibility and therefore of truth." No further explanation of this point follows. This reader was left wondering how the narrator can be accused of avoiding the truth about Criseyde (and by "truth" Kellogg appears to mean her infidelity), when he announces at the beginning of the poem that he will tell "how that she forsook hym er she deyde." All of Criseyde's interior battles, the complexity of her response to Troilus and her whole situation at Troy, fall by the wayside as Kellogg encourages us to see Chaucer's Criseyde as a collection of falsehoods.

The three chapters of Kellogg's book are followed by an appendix, "Boccaccio's Dido," which gives brief descriptions of the various texts of Boccaccio in which Dido appears. This is the most interesting section of the book, because it does not try to fit Dido into an overly narrow interpretive paradigm but rather notes how Boccaccio moves back and forth between the Virgilian and Ovidian depictions of Dido in his poetry and prose. There are the seeds of a larger project here. The entire book would have benefited from much more development; here it is a barely touched-up version of a dissertation. The bibliography is thin: for a book that devotes much of its discussion to the *Filostrato*, it is surprising not to find the books of David Wallace or Thomas Stillinger cited. David Aers's essay "Chaucer's Criseyde" and Marilynn Desmond's *Reading Dido* are also absent (though Desmond's book may have appeared too recently for inclusion). Weighing in at under 150 pages (including the bibliography), Kellogg does not give herself the space to analyze the Criseidan character with real depth and nuance.

I had hoped that this book would be an analysis of Criseyde in the context of Boccaccio's and Chaucer's relationships to prior literary traditions. These two authors look back at their literary heritage with a combination of admiration and skepticism. As Boccaccio and Chaucer negotiate their own routes through the hermeneutic forest that surrounds classical poetry, it is often the figures of women who reveal the extent to which these poets have diverged from their models. When Chaucer refuses the obvious misogyny of earlier versions of the tale by creating a Criseyde who is both engaging and enigmatic, it seems to me he is telling us something about his own role as a translator and poet in an emerging Middle English literary tradition. Alas, Kellogg is not interested in discussing such matters as creative imitation and allusion in any depth. She returns repeatedly to the simplistic notion that earlier sources provide a kind of absolute truth about a particular narrative or character. Such an approach cannot account adequately for the transformations that Chaucer wrought upon the *Filostrato*. If Criseyde's only attribute is her inconstancy, then she becomes a stick figure hardly worthy of scrutiny. Surely her staying power over the centuries has proven otherwise.

DISA GAMBERA
Carleton College

LAURA C. LAMBDIN and ROBERT T. LAMBDIN, eds. *Chaucer's Pilgrims: An Historical Guide to the Pilgrims in* The Canterbury Tales. Westport, Conn., and London: Greenwood Press, 1996. Pp. xiv, 398. $79.50.

In this long and ambitiously comprehensive set of chapters on Chaucer's pilgrim company (thirty-two chapters: one per personage), the editors have gathered essays from an equal number of contributors (thirty-two), themselves included. They proceed under the portmanteau premise that a reading of *The Canterbury Tales* will profit from a far more detailed knowledge of occupational data concerning these travelers than a late twentieth-century reader is likely to discover from the allusive information provided by the poet in his own *General Prologue* pilgrim portraits. Despite Muriel Bowden's *Commentary* (1948) and Jill Mann's *Estates Satire* (1973), the editors assert a fundamental difficulty in locating information concerning the vocations of the pilgrims. This book, they claim, will repair a "critical fissure" and fill a "gap" of "some six hundred years" duration by providing these thirty-two essays, each of which proposes to supply "an in-depth entry describing that pilgrim's specific function in fourteenth-century England" (p. xi).

Not surprisingly, the essays—aimed at an audience that includes "all teachers and students of Chaucer, from high school to graduate school" (p. xi), and authored by a company of contributors ranging from seasoned senior scholars to graduate students specializing in technical writing—are uneven in quality. At best, one still must question the *omnium gatherum* attempt to load into one volume a mass of vocational data that, in nearly every instance, is already easily available elsewhere, often no further away than the notes, commentaries, and bibliographies included in the standard Benson edition of *The Canterbury Tales*.[1] There is something problematical, too, about the editorial decision to standardize the format of each essay, so that in thirty-two relentlessly similar excursions, readers find a detailed description of typical daily occupational routine (which may, or may not, have subsequent relevance to the poetry of Chaucer) followed by attempts to revisit the overmapped critical categories of teller-tale connections and *General Prologue* links to the *Tales* that follow.

However salutary (or dubious) one judges the governing premise and the individual entries of this reader's guide, one must unfortunately note that the Lambdins' collection suffers from an array of editorial deficits—some quite serious—that impair the volume's overall credibility and usefulness. These include errors of fact; errors of translation; persistent problems of usage and tone; and bibliographies frequently so outdated, in the main, or so laden with sources of questionable weight, that the foundational assertions derived therefrom are highly problematic. It is not a pleasant, but a necessary, duty to detail some of these typical shortfalls.

In a quoted verse from "The descryuyng of mannes membres" (pp. 30–31), for example, where the poet is metaphorizing "shoulder," "backbone," "fingers," and "arms," the serial cognate "hondes" is improbably translated as "hounds." Chaucer's "mayster-hunte," who "With a gret horn blew thre mot" (*BD* 375–76), becomes a senseless huntmaster who "With a great horn blew three must" (p. 34). The Host's jesting address to the Nun's Priest—"For if thou have corage as thou hast myght" (*NPE* 3452)—translates to "For if you have heart as you might have" (p. 64); later the same line is rendered "For if you have as much heart as you might" (p. 334): in neither case does might make right.

---

[1] All Chaucer citations are from Larry D. Benson, ed., *The Riverside Chaucer* (Boston: Houghton Mifflin, 1987).

The Wife in *The Shipman's Tale* utters a chatty "by golly" in place of the original "pardee" (line 219), while her husband's remark to the monk daun John concerning chapmen—"that hir moneie is hir plogh" (line 288)—suffers an unsuccessful sex-change operation, asserting that "her money is her plow" (pp. 217–18). Meanwhile, the "lusty bacheler" of Arthur's court in *The Wife of Bath's Tale* (line 883) translates to a plain old "lust bachelor" (p. 252).

The *General Prologue* lines that describe the Physician as a diagnostician who employs images and natural magic in his work (lines 415–18) have been unaccountably furnished with a Modern English translation of lines 442–44, which conclude the portrait of the Doctour of Phisik with the familiar observations concerning his pestilential winning, and special loving, of gold. Harry Bailly's wry description of his wife as a shrew whose strong-arm tactics he dares not withstand—"For she is byg in armes, by my feith: / That shal he fynde that hire mysdooth or seith" (*MkP* 1921–23)—is here subjected to a gratuitous shifting of pronouns, "he" to "you" and "hire" to "she." In the skewed translation that ensues, the Host's comically exaggerated warning to other hapless men—who likewise will find this woman a formidable future foe should they ever trespass against her in word or deed—has been collapsed into a garbled prediction of Goodelief's wrongdoings unmasked, or suffered (?), by some anonymous addressee: "That shal you find that she misdid or said" (p. 335).

Blatant errors like those cited in this sampler of faulty work persist throughout the book. They are supplemented by a blundering, ponderous lack of felicity in virtually all translations [editorially (?)] supplied for all Middle English lines. There are even translations supplied for Modern English translations: "One hand in the hopper, the other in the bag, / As the wheel went round, he made his grab . . . [One hand in the hopper, the other in the bag, / As the wheel went round, he made his grab . . .] (p. 274). Very early on, this sort of sloppy, unchecked slippage achieves the status of critical mass, strongly implying an editorial lack of basic familiarity with the very medium of Middle English whose Chaucerian text these essays propose to illuminate.

Errors of fact are frequent as well: we encounter, for example, "such writers as Jovinian" who authored *Adversus Jovinianum* (p. 248); "fighting men who in the later Middle Ages wielded England's long bowman" (p. 28); the "cycle drama" *Everyman* (p. xiv). Among a number of disinformations we are told that the Squire "had not acquitted himself honorably in battle" (p. 19); that "the Merchant is the tenth character to be described" in the *GP* (p. 94); and that "even today . . . procreation is the only truly acceptable reason for sexual activity within the dictates of the Roman Catholic Church" (p. 246). Scholarly sources are at times misquoted (e.g., Owen, p. 276) or appropriated without attribution (cf. Hussey, *Chaucer's World*, ch. 16, for the "two damned souls" of p. 312).

Adding to the lapses of misinformation, misquotation, and mistranslation, there is also a distressing problem of tone in a number of chapters, often straining toward the overcolloquial, sometimes collapsing into outright absurdity in the effort to be cool: the Squire, e.g., is analogized to "R2D2 serving Luke Skywalker" (p. 17); the Doctour of Phisik would not qualify "for the title of Mr. Charity, 1489" (p. 221); the Wife of Bath "liked to shop" (p. 244), and her addiction to the "vagaries of fashion" are carefully documented by recourse to John Mellencamp's redo of Van Morrison's "Wild Nights" (p. 247). Clarence Thomas and Anita Hill are brought in to testify to the perdurance of sexual harassment and "lack of respect for women" (p. 248), while *The Magnificent Seven* (p. 378) makes a walk-on appearance, along with medieval versions of "a kind of goon squad or mini-Mafia" (p. 376). Perhaps the highschoolers envisioned by the editors as an audience for this book have dominated the imaginations of too many of its contributors, but the final result is not one of scholarly responsibility.

Obviously, no book this fulsomely capacious will prove entirely worthless. Chapters by contributors like John H. Fisher (the Maunciple), Constance Hieatt (the Cook), John Conlee (the Yeoman), and Julian Wasserman [with Marc Guidry] (the Carpenter) provide welcome relief. Christine Chism's chapter (the Chanoun) also supplies a useful and critically productive base of information for understanding the imaginatively wrought connections between canons, alchemists, and poets.

In the final analysis, however, the volume of essays, taken as a whole, is marred by so many serious flaws that it is not possible to recommend it to any readership. Scholars will not need or use this book and high school or undergraduate students making use of it will often be misled or seriously misinformed, at least as often as they will be assisted, in understanding Chaucer's poetry.

At nearly 400 pages of small type, and with a killer price tag of nearly $80, this is not a "must have"; in fact, it's a definite "don't buy."

DOLORES WARWICK FRESE
University of Notre Dame

A.J. Minnis with V.J. Scattergood and J. J. Smith. *Oxford Guides to Chaucer: The Shorter Poems*. Oxford: Clarendon Press, 1995. Pp. xiv, 578. $72.00.

Compared to its predecessors (Helen Cooper, *The Canterbury Tales* [1989]; Barry Windeatt, *Troilus and Criseyde* [1992]), this third and last volume of the *Oxford Guides to Chaucer* (*OGC*) is heftier (578 pages, vs. 437 for the *Tales* and 414 for the *Troilus*), and, more significantly, it brings the series very much into the 1990s in critical style as well as date. A. J. Minnis's discussions of *The Book of the Duchess* (*BD*), *The House of Fame* (*HF*), *The Parliament of Fowls* (*PF*), and *The Legend of Good Women* (*LGW*) adopt a personal, often tendentious voice and undertake to engage aggressively many of the critical issues and perspectives that have entered, and to a great extent transformed, Chaucer criticism during the last 20 years. (By contrast, the appended survey of the lyrics by V. J. Scattergood does not overtly manifest Minnis's concern "to consider the ideological implications of various readings" of Chaucer's poetry [p. 1].)

Responding positively (if not without some ambivalence) to the evolution of the "New Historicism," Minnis offers his "readings of Chaucer's love-visions within an anthropology of courtly didacticism and play and as inscriptions of aristocratic ideals of conduct and processes of cultural fashioning" (p. 4), while resisting the notion that Chaucer is to be understood exclusively "as occupying the position of sophisticated princepleaser"—an understanding that runs counter to Minnis's "identifications of certain prospects of dissidence in Chaucerian fiction," specifically with respect to "aristocratic mores, traditional misogyny, [or] authoritarian literary theory" (p. 5).

Overall, Minnis rejects attempts to read the dream-poems in ways that he regards as anachronistic or overly generalized. He has no patience with the Robertsonian, allegorizing school (Chaucer, to him, is clearly a secular poet who avoids opportunities to allegorize, as when he borrows details for his version of the Ceyx and Alcyone story in *BD* from the *Ovide moralisé*, but avoids its *moralitas*). And in at least partial opposition to feminist critiques of the representation of women in the dream poems, he aims at "a historicized gender criticism which attempts to respect the room for dissent which the culture of Chaucer's day allowed, in so far as that can be recuperated by recourse to such evidence as is available to us" (p. 5). (To this end, Minnis distinguishes between the "structural antifeminism" of late medieval European civilization, by which Chaucer could not avoid being somewhat affected, and "phobic antifeminism," that special animosity most characteristic of clerics, from which he largely absolves the poet [see pp. 427–32].)

Two introductory chapters locate the dream-poems with respect to vernacular literary traditions and the social ideologies of Chaucer's audience. "The Shorter Poems: Social and Cultural Contexts" offers an excellent summary of recent theorizing about Chaucer's social and professional placement and its impact on his poetic development. Minnis argues for the crucial influence of the "international [i.e., French-based] court culture," promoted by Edward III and Richard II, both on Chaucer's poetic formation and on the "receptive company of courtiers who shared an interest in poetry and a highly personal and earnest piety" (p. 19)—the so-called "Lollard Knights" who collectively establish a "horizontal axis [on which] may be sought the audience of Chaucer's courtly poetry" (p. 22).

"Chaucer and the Love-Vision Form" first examines the ambiguous, often indeterminate dream taxonomies of Chaucer's heritage and demonstrates how his dream-poems reproduce and exploit the ambiguities of significance and interpretation associated with dreams. In the second part of this chapter, dedicated to the analogously complex issue of *fin' amors*, Minnis considers "the implications of the conventions of courtly love for the construction of gender" (p. 60). Responding to the spate of recent analyses—singled out are those of R. Howard Bloch, Maud Ellmann, and Elaine Tuttle Hansen—that depict courtly love as a "patriarchal conspiracy" (p. 67), Minnis argues that such judgments, while obviously valid in part, ultimately constitute totalizing oversimplifications. Power relations in Chaucer's world were not fixed or immutable; at particular moments, in specific situations, a poet such as Chaucer could use the conventions of courtly love to raise "gender games . . . to the level of an alternative art . . . which opens up fresh possibilities for the production of fiction and the business of living" (p. 69).

The chapter on *BD* is organized around the poem's "negotiations between art and life, conventional discourses and emotional integrity" (p. 73). Most important to Minnis is the "strategy of deference" (p. 130)—of the narrator to the Man in Black, and by extension of Chaucer to John of Gaunt—which underlies Chaucer's adaptation of the dialogue between a bereaved lady and an abandoned knight in Machaut's *Jugement dou Roy de Behaingne*. The deference of the poet to his noble patrons is a feature of Machaut's and Froissart's *dits*, but their blend of flattery and claimed intimacy has been metamorphosed by

Chaucer into a more subtle, if no less status-marked, relationship that establishes (through dialogue) the depth of the Man in Black's grief over the loss of his "goode faire White"—a sensitivity (whether historically real or poetically constructed) characteristic of true nobility, and well beyond anything the lovesick narrator shows himself capable of feeling at the beginning of the poem. By means of the "strategy of deference," Chaucer can offer both consolation and praise to John of Gaunt on the occasion of his wife's death.

Minnis's interpretation, like all others of this enigmatic poem, raises questions. Why, for example, if the narrator is suffering from unrequited love, does Chaucer suppress the lines from the opening of Froissart's *Paradys d'Amours* (the basis for the opening lines of *BD*) that clearly announce that fact (cf. pp. 104–5)? It is at least as readily deduced from the poem's structure that the narrator is suffering from a bereavement paralleled first by Alcyone's, then by the Man in Black's; the figure he meets in his dream is thus (whoever else he may represent) a personification of his own sorrow (cf. *BD* 597: "for y am sorwe, and sorwe ys y"). And left untouched by Minnis's reading of *BD* is the poet-audience relationship so carefully constructed in the poem—an important place of intersection between Chaucer's poetic concerns and his anatomy of grief and melancholy.

More successful, I think, is the chapter on *HF*, of which the single most intriguing suggestion is that the poem "just might have been composed after *Troilus and Criseyde*, the two works forming a "creative engagement" with Italian literature, during which Chaucer moves away from the *roman antique* and Boccaccio "to confront the *Comedy* (of Dante) and all it implied for vernacular poetics" (p. 171). Minnis's discussion aligns him with the critical tradition—perhaps best represented by John Fyler's chapter in *Chaucer and Ovid* (1979)—that sees *HF* as a comic poem which seriously calls into question the truth and authority of poetry, thus setting itself in parodic opposition to Dante's celebration of the vernacular and of himself as a poet whose authority equals that of the ancients. (As Minnis puts it, "In sharp opposition to Dante, Chaucer seems to have found it difficult to make or imply a claim for the high status of his own art in the vernacular" [p. 248].)

The key to the poem, in this reading, is that in adapting to his purposes the descriptions of Fame and its workings in Virgil, Ovid, and Boethius, Chaucer creates a fickle goddess "who can create or destroy reputations. And writers are her agents in this process . . . *makeres* of fame" (p. 190). Ultimately, "*HF* implies that poetry is an art of lying. . . . The poets are liars, the lovers who [*sic*] poets write about are liars—and fame itself may be a pack of lies, or at best a mixture of truth and fiction. . . ." Since "the *auctoritas* of the revered Latin poets seems so shaky . . . the *House of Fame* can be said to record Chaucer's crisis of authority" (p. 236).

Minnis approaches *PF* as a debate poem built on contrasts, rather than one organized around a unifying theme, or "certeyn thing" (*PF* 20; oddly, Minnis doesn't consider this crucially ambiguous line). As in *HF*, "the univocal pronouncements of men of great authority do not rule the roost; the bird parliament counters with a cacophony of conflicting voices" (p. 253). Authoritative texts (Cicero's *Somnium scipionis*, Alan of Lille's *De planctu naturae*, Boccaccio's *Teseida*) are treated with a disrespectful freedom; the overall effect of this poetic strategy is to establish *PF* as "a performance text, a work meant to open rather than close debate" (p. 312), i.e., inconclusive in itself (as often happens in medieval debate poems), but inviting "active participation," rather than "passive consumption," by its audience(s) (p. 292). By presenting a spectrum of ideas about love—philosophical, procreative, courtly, erotic—the poem avoids totalizing formulations about human desire (of the kind read into the poem by Robertsonians and others), even though, as Minnis admits, "the sociopolitical, as opposed to the intellectual, assumptions which underpin the poem are incapable of much negotiation" (pp. 301–2), given the privileged audience for which it appears to have been exclusively intended.

For Minnis, *LGW* shares with *PF* the status of a poem designed to create debate among members of its audience, this time with respect to gender construction and politics. The upside-down world of the tales, in which all women are virtuous and all men cruel deceivers and seducers, places gender orthodoxies (and the "structural anti-feminism" [p. 427] of late medieval European civilization that underlies them) under scrutiny, but in a carnivalesque way that would potentially stimulate a variety of viewpoints and, at least *in potentia*, open a space within ideological formulations where potential reassessment, and even social and political change, could be considered.

Building on Paul Strohm's analysis of Chaucer's social placement at a point of intersection between "horizontal"—or associational—and "vertical"—or hierarchical—social models (see pp. 292–93), Minnis finds it possible to conceive an (even if temporary) openness of response by the poet's audience to the representation of gender roles and responsibilities in *LGW*; he also asks us to consider the situation of women, some of them powerful, in Chaucer's audience who might get a pleasant frisson from *LGW*'s representation of them as morally (though by no means politically) "on top," even as men laughed at the extremes to which the poem appears to take profeminist arguments and representations.

Given the breadth of reference and depth of learning constantly demonstrated throughout this book, it seems almost ungrateful to speak of omissions. Nonetheless, there are a few puzzling gaps, of which the least explicable, to this reader, is the absence of reference to John H. Fisher's research and hypothesizing on the cultural dynamic underlying the rise of English as a literary language in Chaucer's lifetime. Puzzling for different reasons are the apparent attribution of the entire text of the *Roman de la rose* to Jean de Meun (as on p. 128), and the discussion of rhyme royal that seems to suggest it is written in six- instead of seven-line stanzas (p. 262). Of the relatively few typographical errors, only those involving names suggest culpable carelessness: C. K. Zacker (for Zacher; pp. 166, 541) and—*mirabile lectu*—Alan Leviathan (for Levitan; pp. 227, 548).

*Oxford Guides to Chaucer: The Shorter Poems* should prove the most indispensable of the three volumes in the series; no other volume known to me offers so much information and analysis of Chaucer's poetic oeuvre outside the *Tales* and the *Troilus*. Students and scholars alike will also find it the liveliest of the three: the author's voice, opinions, and quite engaging literary allusions and wordplay make this a good critical read as well as a first-rate reference book and vademecum.

Robert W. Hanning
Columbia University

Lynette R. Muir. *The Biblical Drama of Medieval Europe.* Cambridge: Cambridge University Press, 1995. Pp. xxiii, 320. $60.00.

Muir's book has the ambitious aim of providing "a comprehensive picture of European medieval biblical drama" (p. xiv). The phrase is significant. Muir adopts a pan-European perspective into which she draws an impressive range of local and national studies of drama that fully justifies the term "comprehensive." Moreover, she recognizes no strict limits of time or genre for "medieval," a word that remains undefined.

279

She claims to include all texts composed before 1500 (excluding some unpublished material) and references to all plays with "medieval links" or "in the medieval tradition" from the post-1500 period (p. xiv). And she limits her study by subject matter to "biblical" drama, and more precisely to the *adaptation* of the biblical source-material in those plays. This is not a book that significantly explores dramatic effect or the interaction of different modes of drama.

Rather, Muir's "overall purpose is to encourage and facilitate detached and comparative critical investigation of the plays, not to provide it" (p. xiii). She offers no definition of "drama" and claims no critical agenda. Her book thus avoids the shortcomings of those pioneer encyclopedic scholars of early drama—Chambers, Cohen, Creizenach, D'Ancona—whose vast knowledge was suffused with subjective judgment, critical condescension, and a desire to endorse a monolithic model of dramatic origins. Yet some concealed definition of "drama" compatible with their evolutionary approach can be detected when Muir distinguishes between "simple" and "more elaborate" plays (p. 46) or speaks of the plays "bursting out of their liturgical bonds" (p. 28), or refers to their "representational" function (p. 2), the need for an "audience" (p. 4), or rubrics for "gestures" and "roles" (p. 19).

The book is organized in two parts. The first part—a miracle of compression in only fifty-seven pages—presents medieval theatre from the standpoint of its organizers and performers, following the familiar track from liturgy to drama and then looking at who performed the plays, where they were performed, and how they were paid for. This overview reveals clearly the catalytic effect of specific ceremonies and symbols for dramatic development. In particular, Muir stresses the importance of Italian lay-productions for the establishment of Corpus Christi drama—a useful counterbalance to the liturgical emphasis of critics such as Kolve—and provocatively suggests that the skeptical German priest in the earliest Corpus Christi play, from Orieste, might be intended as a challenge to the Liege-based origins of the Feast. Her account is spiced with curious incidental detail—the oldest paper manuscript in France, the place of Constantine's proclamation as emperor, the first woman play-director, etc. (though the occasional error enters— Chester's Corpus Christi play was transferred not to Midsummer but to Whitsun [p. 38]).

The second part, a further 113 pages, is organized in terms of biblical history, like a mystery cycle, beginning with Creation and ending with Doomsday. Woolf's study of the English cycles provides the model-framework, and the reader is referred to her for the English drama. Within each episode the "core material" is described from the Bible and other relevant sources, plays utilizing it are briefly indicated, and significant variations in the adaptation or utilization of the material are characterized. The strains of organizing a wide range of material within a short space are evident in the repeated vagueness of introductory phrases such as "a few plays," "in several plays," "a few references" (cf. pp. 105–8), and the account threatens to become a generalized listing. Detail seems to have merely intrinsic value. The strange miracles related by the Magi in Eger 63, for example, are described at some length (p. 105), but we gain little sense of how these narratives bear upon the total dramatic effect of the play. The discussion of the treatment of the Jews in the different countries of Europe, which adds welcome depth to "Lazarus," is a rare example of the potential for greater comparative depth. A concluding chapter traces the survival and modern revival of such plays in Europe.

The generalized discussion is underpinned by a further 130 pages, which provide a useful appendix on the liturgical context; extensive and informative footnotes; and bibliographies of plays cited, performance records, and critical studies, which provide valuable points for future work. There are also three "distribution" maps. Those footnotes supply the detail and the critical edge that the discussion lacks. Two examples from this wealth of information must suffice. Note 47 on page 188 elaborates informedly upon the involvement of the craft guilds of Seville in the city's Corpus Christi play, an exceptional situation in Spain that is explained in terms of the city's peculiar economic development. And in note 6 on page 189, Muir writes as the authority on the Anglo-Norman *Jeu d'Adam*, speculating about the travels of the lost original with an Anglo-Norman aristocrat journeying in English-held France. In the notes, too, we find a refreshing and personal alertness to the text that is often lost in the discussion. Note 3 on page 259, for example, describes with amusement the way Peter's promised *dos motz* are expanded into a 440-line speech and comments upon the way the presentation of "speaking with tongues" is handled. It is this detailed apparatus that transforms the book from a generalized survey into an invaluable scholarly reference work.

This dual function may be connected with the envisaged readership. As so often with medieval drama books, the target audience is said to be twofold—"scholars working in the field" and a lay-readership, specifically those who may have witnessed a modern revival of a medieval play (p. xiii). The discussion seems addressed to the latter, providing a "reader-friendly" guide to the subject, whereas the main interest for the scholar lies in the specifics of the notes and apparatus. The chapters are short and punctuated by subsections, sometimes shorter than a page, that break the text into "manageable" units. The biblical narratives are paraphrased for an audience not versed in the subject. The approach is, as promised, a data-centered survey that offers no model of comparative method for the student reader to follow; but it is executed with evident enthusiasm and energy and is indeed a tour de force that the general reader can enjoy.

And for the specialist the book is impressive in its range and learning. I am left with profound admiration for Muir's knowledge, powers of assimilation, and sheer courage in attempting this enterprise. She has done us a considerable service in revealing the wealth of material now available. This is a book that all who work in medieval drama should have on their shelves for reference, and one that should encourage all for whom "medieval theatre" still means "medieval *English* theatre" to widen their horizons.

DAVID MILLS
University of Liverpool

RICHARD G. NEWHAUSER and JOHN A. ALFORD, eds. *Literature and Religion in the Later Middle Ages: Philological Studies in Honor of Siegfried Wenzel*. Medieval and Renaissance Texts and Studies, vol. 118. Binghamton: Medieval and Renaissance Texts and Studies, 1995. Pp. ix, 414. $25.00.

This collection of seventeen essays offers its readers a satisfying repast of several courses, ranging from literary studies of Chaucer and Langland through historical studies of religious writers and their works to editions of selected pastoral and devotional texts. The broad guiding principle behind the volume, as the editors observe, is one that has consistently marked Professor Wenzel's scholarly practice: the "philologi-

cal orientation" (p. 1), centered always on "the text in its historical surroundings" (p. 2).

The editors have clustered the essays under five authorial and generic
headings: Chaucer (four essays, by Theo Stemmler, Piero Boitani,
Edward B. Irving, Jr., and Albert E. Hartung); Langland (three, by
Ralph Hanna III, John A. Alford, and Joan Heiges Blythe); pastoral lit-
erature (four, by Joseph Goering, A. G. Rigg, A. I. Doyle, Christina von
Nolcken); Scripture and homiletics (four, by A. J. Minnis, Kent Emery,
Jr., D. L. D'Avray, David Anderson); and lyric poetry (two, by Karl
Reichl, Richard Newhauser).

In "Chaucer's Ballade 'To Rosemounde'—A Parody?" Stemmler takes
a skeptical look at the longstanding critical claim that the short poem
"To Rosemounde" was written in a humorous vein, and answers his title
question with a decided negative, by comparing evidence cited in earlier interpretations with usage in various nonparodic English love-
poetry. Boitani and Irving offer interpretive readings of *The Nun's
Priest's Tale* and *The Knight's Tale*, respectively. Hartung's essay, "'The
Parson's Tale' and Chaucer's Penance," may be the most provocative
within the Chaucer section: he identifies passages (mainly sexual in content) in *The Parson's Tale* that show a particular "intensity of response"
(p. 68) to the tale's sources and suggests that this intensity may reflect
some specific personal concern with the issues raised in those passages.

In the Langland section, Alford argues for a specific source and compositional method for Conscience's dinner party in *Piers Plowman* B,
namely Hugh of St. Cher's commentary on Proverbs 23 and the concord-
ing scriptural cross-references common to biblical exegesis. Blythe
surveys the whole span of the poem for its treatments of sins of the tongue,
placing them in the context of the penitential tradition to suggest that
"language-related failure in *Piers Plowman* is not language's fault"
(p. 119). Perhaps the most interesting of these essays is Hanna's "Robert
the Ruyflare and His Companions," which explores the implications of a
complex pattern of B to C revisions in the confession of the sins and finds
in those revisions a convincing weave of intertextual, thematic, structural,
and aesthetic motives and effects. Hanna discovers a recurrent phenomenon of doubling in the C revisions surrounding Covetyse's confession
(Robert the Ruyflare and ȝeuan-ȝelde-aȝeyn, references by Repentance to
clerical profits among friars and parish priests, Covetyse's own "second"
confession drawn in from B.13); he reads that doubling as a poetic analogue of the frustrating transformation of genuine repentance into a

repetitive running in place generated in many ways by the very discourses of penitence that drive the whole confession scene.

Of the ten remaining essays, several perform the essential scholarly service of making primary texts available through editions and commentaries on hitherto unpublished works. Doyle edits a short, rather charming devotional work in "'Lectulus noster floridus': An Allegory of the Penitent Soul," introducing the Middle English text with concise, informative descriptions of the seven manuscripts in which the piece occurs. Rigg edits about a quarter of a 946-line Latin poem on the causes and effects of sin, "De motu et pena peccandi," with summaries of the sections omitted for reasons of space. Reichl describes the manuscript setting of seven English, Latin, and French lyrics in MS Digby 2 (a manuscript probably written by Franciscans in Oxford, and consisting mainly of computistical, philosophical, and logical texts). Newhauser edits and translates a short Latin allegory on spiritual armaments, in which is integrally embedded a variant of a Middle English death lyric, "Strong It Is to Flitte"; his introduction to the edition also situates the text in its manuscript context, a miscellany of preaching aids and other religious texts with what he plausibly suggests is a likely Franciscan provenance for the manuscript.

With longer primary texts, of course, scholarly writers limited to a single chapter can hardly provide full new editions as a means of making those texts more available to readers. They can, however, still introduce readers to the contents of those texts and, where known or inferrable, to the texts' authors. Such introductions are given by Goering, Minnis, Emery, D'Avray, and Anderson. Goering reviews the contents of the popular pastoral summa "Qui bene presunt" and then mounts a detailed argument for identifying its author (most commonly known as Richard of Wetheringsett) as Richard of Leicester, chancellor of Cambridge University and Lincoln Cathedral, who near the end of his life served as archbishop of Canterbury (1229–1231). Emery examines an intriguing group of sixteenth-century *collectaria* compiled and revised by the Benedictine monk Trudo of Gembloux, who continues the medieval practice of excerpting and organizing materials from many authorities into encyclopedic surveys of spiritual and secular learning. In "Medium and Message: Henry of Ghent on Scriptural Style," Minnis gives a detailed summary of Henry's position on questions of "sacred stylistics"—the simplicity or complexity of discourse appropriate in exegetical and theological exposition to all manner of audiences. Many of

Henry's views mirror Augustine's, as laid out in *De doctrina christiana*, but Minnis concludes with a brief but tantalizing discussion of ways in which Henry's position, which stresses the fundamental unity of Scripture beneath its stylistic diversity, reacts against twelfth- and thirteenth-century trends that tended to secularize Scripture by positing greater autonomy for its human authors.

D'Avray and Anderson both turn their attention to sermon collections by Italian preachers, though with rather different goals and methods. D'Avray uses a highly philosophical sermon from a thirteenth-century collection by the Franciscan Servasanto da Faenza as a counterexample to the hypothesis that Minorite preaching was characterized by "imaginative vividness," in contrast to a presumed "philosophical sophistication" among Dominican preachers (p. 266). Anderson's essay, "'Dominus Ludovicus' in the Sermons of Jacobus of Viterbo," connects a sermon collection with the specific historical context that can be deduced for it: Naples from 1303 to 1307. Of particular interest are two memorial sermons on the second son of Charles II, Louis of Anjou (d. 1297), who gave up his secular inheritance to enter the Franciscan Order ca. 1294–1296 and who was canonized in 1317. These sermons help illuminate the interrelations between the papacy, the Neapolitan church, and the Angevin court, as well as shedding light on early and hitherto obscure stages of the process that led up to Louis's canonization.

One of the most stimulating essays in the whole collection focuses neither on a single text nor a single author's works, but on the style of a whole community of writers, the Wycliffites. In "A 'Certain Sameness' and Our Response to It in English Wycliffite Texts," von Nolcken reads the frequent sameness of vocabulary, tendency to generalize rather than particularize arguments, and confidence of assertion as a consequence of the "realist vision" (p. 206) that the Wycliffites inherited from Wyclif himself. She suggests that modern readers need to recognize that such seemingly "tiresome" stylistic features—to use F. D. Matthew's term— probably reflect a deliberate and ideological choice by Wycliffite writers.

The collective richness of the essays in *Literature and Religion in the Later Middle Ages* can be seen not only in their individual content but also in the number of different threads that bind them in various mutually illuminating combinations. Besides the generic, authorial, and formal relationships implied by the editors' groupings of the essays and by the groupings used in this review, some of these essays (Reichl, D'Avray, Newhauser) can be clustered around the vexed issue of the extent of Franciscan influence in medieval devotional and pastoral literature. Several essays intersect in illustrating the competing medieval impulses toward univocality or multivocality of authoritative discourse (Minnis, von Nolcken, Hanna, Emery); additional linkages between the volume's chapters can be found with little difficulty. This richness demonstrates the continuing creative force of the scholarship to which Professor Wenzel has contributed so influentially and makes the volume a fitting tribute to those contributions.

M. Teresa Tavormina
Michigan State University

W. F. H. Nicolaisen, ed. *Oral Tradition in the Middle Ages.* Medieval and Renaissance Texts and Studies, vol. 112. Binghamton: Medieval and Renaissance Texts and Studies, 1995. Pp. vi, 231. $24.00.

The twelve essays in this collection were selected from those presented at the Twenty-Second Annual Conference of the Center for Medieval and Early Renaissance Studies held at Binghamton, New York, in 1988. The conference's theme, now the title of the volume, was chosen in connection with the centennial of the American Folklore Society, celebrated in the same year. Its editor describes the collection as intended to provide "a sampling of the vast scope of current studies in oral tradition" (p. 2), and indeed its range extends to works in Old and Middle English, Old French, Middle Irish, Hebrew, Greek, medieval Latin, Serbo-Croatian, and Old Norse-Icelandic. Nicolaisen's brief introduction points to a few of the most basic questions and best-known scholarly works in the lively area in which folklore methodologies intersect with other means of discovering and evaluating the evidence that remains for medieval oral traditions.

*Oral Tradition in the Middle Ages* inherits its structure from the conference: four "plenary papers" and eight "sectional papers." Two of the plenary papers, those by the late Albert B. Lord and by John Miles Foley, range widely over various literatures—ancient, medieval, and modern—in pursuit of continuities between oral compositions and the written literatures that survive from the Middle Ages. Lord's piece is typical of his later work in moving away from the search for evidence of spontaneous composition in performance toward a better understanding of the stylistic choices made by medieval writers influenced by oral traditions. Foley takes a more emphatic step in the same direction, arguing that such texts, which he calls "oral-derived," are ill served by aesthetic criteria that take account only of the norms of textuality and neglect ways of meaning that are unique to oral traditions. His argument, more fully developed in *Immanent Art* (1991), is that oral-derived works encode and express meaning metonymically—they use established traditional structures (formulas, themes) to convey a wealth of associations carried over from previous contexts in which their audiences have encountered them. Carl Lindahl's essay cautions against simplistic equations between "written" and "elite" on the one hand, and "oral" and "folk" on the other, and uses late medieval romance as a medium through which to seek "a culturally variegated view of medieval oral artistry" (p. 59). His essay shows the advantages of marking out the common ground between elite and folk performance styles and labeling the overlap "neutral" instead of "elite" (p. 65), thus offering a welcome corrective both to the exaggerated binarism "elite versus folk," and to the distorting tendency to see non-elite art forms only as corruptions of elite ones. Joseph Falaky Nagy's piece on the Irish *Acallam na Senórach* ("Colloquy of the Ancients") offers another promising means of illuminating the oral and literary backgrounds to a written work of complex cultural origins. Like many medieval texts, the *Acallam* claims to record oral materials otherwise in danger of vanishing, and Nagy shows the resultant tension between the norms of written composition and those of the oral art forms that the work purports to transmit. Nagy's reading of this internal tension as dynamic and artistically productive affirms the central argument of Aron Gurevich's undervalued *Medieval Popular Culture* (1988).

A very brief account of the materials and methods of each will have to suffice to convey the interest and variety of the eight sectional papers. Saul Levin traces the movement toward increased textualization of Jewish religious traditions under the influence of Muslim rule. Gail Ivy Berlin's "case studies" of memorization in Anglo-Saxon England include both monastic and lay settings, and she offers some suggestive distinctions between the methods of memorization and the standards of accuracy employed in her sampling. Jeremy Downes uses the two contrastive accounts in *Beowulf* of the swimming match with Breca to argue that, in oral settings, notions of truth emphasize fidelity to universal laws over verisimilitude. John Lindow's concise and elegant piece concerns the representation of oral performance in the Old Norse *Íslendinga þættir*, a corpus of texts that often features as hero an Icelandic poet who performs his verse for the king. In a study of the founding legends of Worcester Cathedral Priory, Mary Lynn Rampolla demonstrates that the account of the conversion of the cathedral from secular to monastic life (ca. 960–979) was altered by its early twelfth-century transmitters to suit their current needs and interests. Nancy Freeman Regalado's essay on François Villon's *Testament* shows a writer making brilliantly innovative use of oral syntactic and discursive practices. Two remaining pieces may tell us more about oral traditions and folk culture in the early modern period than in the Middle Ages. Samuel Kinser's richly documented taxonomy of wildmen in festivals, particularly Carnival, spans the period 1300–1550, but, as so often happens, the majority of the evidence comes toward the end of this period. Esha Niyogi De's Bakhtinian reading of the Revesby Mummer's play treats a work not recorded until 1779, in a performance tradition itself only scantily attested before the seventeenth century.

In addition to the volume under review (1995), two other collections concerned with medieval oral traditions have appeared within the last five years: *Vox Intexta: Orality and Textuality in the Middle Ages* (ed. A. N. Doane and Carol Braun Pasternack, 1991) and *Oral Poetics In Middle English Poetry* (ed. Mark C. Amodio, 1994). The three complement one another admirably, with very little overlap in their substance or even among their contributors. *Vox Intexta* seeks to break new theoretical ground by relating oral theory to the various modes of postmodern criticism (p. xi), while Amodio's selections pursue matters of style, structure, and genre in pursuit of a poetics for written works of oral ancestry. To the emphasis on theory in Doane and Pasternack and on literary criticism in Amodio, *Oral Tradition in the Middle Ages* adds an important third emphasis, on the methods of folklore scholarship: identifying, collecting, classifying, contextualizing, and interpreting traditional materials. As Nicolaisen reminds us, "it is the *folklorists* who have for almost two centuries now not only recognized the existence of such a phenomenon as oral tradition but have also found it to be something worth studying for its own sake" (p. 3).

NANCY MASON BRADBURY
Smith College

JOHN F. PLUMMER III, ed. *The Summoner's Tale. A Variorum Edition of the Works of Geoffrey Chaucer, Vol. 2*, The Canterbury Tales, Part 7. Norman and London: University of Oklahoma Press, 1995. Pp. xxviii, 242. $47.50.

John Plummer's very welcome and useful contribution to the emerging *Variorum* enterprise offers Chaucerians an encouraging perspective on the relationship of scholarship to literary reception. While many of Chaucer's well-admired tales have enjoyed their acclaim with or without the informing apparatus of modern scholarship, *The Summoner's Tale*, as this *Variorum* edition suggests, owes a larger portion of its received admiration to relatively recent research. As Plummer observes, the uncomfortable ambivalence that the tale has generated in readers because of its sordidness and triviality on the one hand and its narrative artistry on the other has been "assuaged . . . by the discovery in recent years that *The Summoner's Prologue and Tale* is saturated with allusions to contemporary theological-political issues" (p. 3). The concentration of such material—given all the more emphasis in a variorum format—has prompted an increasingly favorable and more sophisticated reception for *The Summoner's Tale*. Plummer's survey of the criticism attests especially to a growing appreciation for Chaucer's purposeful fusions of the sacred and the sordid, for his marshalling of realistic detail toward deft characterization, and for intricate thematic dynamics that override the scurrility of the surface narrative. Of course, some Chaucerians remain reluctant in their appreciation; and generally, Plummer concludes, "those who have seen *The Summoner's Prologue and Tale* as particularly appropriate to the Summoner as narrator have found least in it to praise, while those who have seen it as sophisticated have either tacitly or explicitly assigned its artistry to Chaucer" (p. 31).

Plummer's survey of the criticism includes some predictable points of focus: sources and analogues (including a fascinating tour of procto-scatological iconography), the relationship of the tale to other tales, the appropriateness of tale to teller, and the like. Other focuses are more eclectically chosen to represent the criticism on its own terms. Among the most valuable segments are those on irony, social issues, authorial intention (serious or comic), and Chaucer's attitude toward exegesis. One obvious shortcoming is the paltry five-line discussion of the date of *The Summoner's Tale*. The date, Professor Plummer notes, "has not been the object of serious study" (p. 16), and that situation will not be improved upon by this edition. Here, surely, the editor ought to step forward, if only to offer a foundation for further study.

With the exceptions cited above, the editor's own assessments of the criticism are exceedingly rare. Plummer presents the spectrum of critical approaches in persistently neutral terms. Readers may find themselves ambivalent about such a strategy. On the one hand, a variorum edition should reflect a high level of objectivity; on the other hand, of course, many variorum readers look to the editor as an authority in a privileged position to indicate, if only in passing, the most significant strengths and weaknesses of the scholarship. Overall, however, the editor has aptly selected his materials to represent accurately the range of published criticism and to serve efficiently the needs of scholarly readers.

As might be expected, the textual commentary summarizes some of the more salient features of the manuscript tradition, focusing on the ten base manuscripts selected for the *Variorum* project, with careful and cautious attention to the more comprehensive work of Manly and Rickert. Perhaps the most significant issue of the manuscript tradition is the evidence that the Ellesmere MS, after sharing an exemplar with Hengwrt, shifts at about line 1991, roughly halfway through the tale, to a new exemplar. (Ellesmere contains three times as many unique variants as Hengwrt in the last half of the tale.) Plummer's carefully weighed reassessment of the problem ends disappointingly, however, when he leaves the issue as one that "needs to be addressed in another forum" (p. 68). What better forum, one might ask, than the *Variorum* to press toward some conclusions on this subject, especially since the more numerous Ellesmere variants would further support the *Variorum* editors' election of Hengwrt as the principal manuscript authority? Nevertheless, if the textual commentary disappoints in this respect, it compensates elsewhere, particularly in its generous coverage of the printed editions prior to Skeat. The review of Urry's eighteenth-century edition is recommended to those readers who can find humor in the record of a convicted text molester, while the review of Tyrwhitt is recommended to the righteous who would redress such deviance.

The text of the tale itself is based on sound editorial assumptions and carefully prepared from the Hengwrt MS, which is very clean and unproblematic in *The Summoner's Prologue and Tale*. Very conservatively edited like others in the *Variorum* series, Plummer's text admits into Hengwrt only five emendations (all minor), three on the basis of scribal error and two on the basis of "overwhelming manuscript evidence" (p. 62). Plummer's conservative approach precludes emendation on the basis of meter; moreover, "the regularity of Chaucer's meter . . . has been for some years a matter of dispute" (p. 64). The present text rejects fifty-two variants appearing in other modern editions—among those readings, some forty adopted by *The Riverside Chaucer*. Regarding Plummer's minimal emendations, one can only object at the level of personal quibble: the rejected Hengwrt reading at line 2287 seems not only metrically but stylistically superior to the editor's emendation; and a reader might favor, for instance, the *Riverside* readings at 1721 and 2134 if only for metrical reasons. Punctuation, the editor claims, is "quite light" (pp. 97–98)—though not without semicolons. But one editor's "light" is another editor's "moderate." In any case, Plummer's text is a reliable resource that Chaucerians can confidently employ.

On the whole, this edition is fine and careful work, of particular value for its excellent text and for its coverage of the criticism in its introduction as well as in the explanatory notes. Nevertheless, one might wish that this 1995 edition were more attentive to current scholarship by at least a year or two. Plummer provides comprehensive coverage of the scholarship through the *SAC* bibliography for 1986 (published in *SAC*, 1988), although his own bibliography and commentary include an additional twenty-one publications from 1987 to 1990, as well as three *Variorum* installments from 1990 to 1993. If the real problem is publication lag-time, it is a difficulty too general for any specific criticism to be registered, but it is an issue that needs to be addressed at a time when academic presses are becoming increasingly vulnerable to pragmatic scrutiny. In the long run, a dated bibliography in the *Variorum* may be of relatively little consequence; in the short run, however, academic scholars need to make the most of their published forums, especially bibliographic forums. On general principles, but also with a sense of gratitude for Professor Plummer's important contribution to Chaucer studies, I would wish for greater promptness in our discipline. The subjects of medieval studies will always be old, but the same need not be true of our commentary upon medieval subjects.

WILLIAM KAMOWSKI
Montana State University-Billings

RICHARD REX. *"The Sins of Madame Eglentyne" and Other Essays on Chaucer*. Newark: University of Delaware Press; London: Associated University Presses, 1995. Pp. 201. $35.00.

The title of this book suggests that the nine essays it contains are not all necessarily concerned with Chaucer's Prioress, whose character and narrative are so problematic in any discussion of *The Canterbury Tales*. In fact, however, virtually all the essays deal with problems raised by her description in the *General Prologue* and the tale she tells. The brief second essay, "Chaucer's Censured Ballads," does not, but both the equally brief fifth chapter, "'Grey' Eyes and the Medieval Ideal of Feminine Beauty," and the longer and more important leadoff essay, "Chaucer and the Jews," are, if indirectly, clearly focused on Madame Eglentyne. The other chapter headings specifically point to questions about her: "Pastiche as Irony in the Prioress's Prologue and Tale," "Wild Horses, Justice, and Charity in the Prioress's Tale," "Why the Prioress's Gauds Are Green," "Why the Prioress Sings through Her Nose," "Madame Eglentyne and the Bankside Brothels," and, in last place, the title essay, "The Sins of Madame Eglentyne."

As the acknowledgments page reveals, of these nine essays four appear in revised form from publication as journal papers, the leadoff essay included. Thus over half the textual material appears for the first time. The Works Cited section is rich, comprising well over 500 primary and secondary items, of which no less than thirty are unpublished dissertations. All in all, within the relatively brief compass of a 200-page book Rex makes available a comprehensive archive on that eternally ambiguous figure, Chaucer's Prioress, and on the problematic of anti-Semitism on her part and, by extension, on Chaucer's. That is not all there is to say about Madame Eglentyne, of course, and Rex covers most of the other questions raised by her depiction and her narration—her presumed vanity, her physical appearance, her manner of singing, her beads—and all this with very little overlapping. His presentation in this series of studies emphasizes the widely held interpretation of the Prioress as one of Chaucer's most complex creations.

This presentation accords with and even extends the disparaging school of Prioress criticism. His work sustains the older attitudes of, for instance, Schoeck, Bronson, Donaldson, Robertson, and others, is more or less against Ridley's attempt at a balanced view, and decidedly runs counter to that defensive and even favorable school of Prioress criticism represented by Madeleva, Lowes, Coghill, Brewer, and, in an extreme way, by Coulton, whose judgment it was that "Chaucer loved the Prioress."[1] Few if any of these old-fashioned views are dealt with, and wisely so. It is, however, somewhat surprising to find a fair number of omissions that in fact focus in an important way on the crucial question of why and how Chaucer makes her deal so harshly with the Jews who live in her pungently described ghetto.

In discussing this question, Rex naturally refers to the origins of the Prioress's bigotry, namely the ritual murder blood libel that Schoeck dealt with so vigorously. Rex could, perhaps, have pointed out with equal vigor that in the Prioress the poet has depicted a woman of no mean sagacity, who takes care in her narrative not to ascribe to the Jews the motiveless blood lust typically found in such legends and which were specifically forbidden by papal rulings. This latter point was emphasized by Edward Synan in his classic work *The Popes and the Jews in the Middle Ages* (New York: Macmillan, 1965), one of the rather surprising omissions from the Works Cited in this book.[2] The problem here is that Madame Eglentyne had other analogues to follow, hardly less anti-Semitic in purport but somewhat more merciful in resolution. Mirk's *Festial* is a case in point. This contemporary work is mentioned in the Works Cited, but not John Bromyard's *Summa praedicantium*. Rex seems to have depended on Owst's highly selective extracts from that contemporary work,[3] but had he consulted the original text, even in the defective Venice 1586 edition, he would have found, *s.v.* "Maria," a natural enough locus, an account of a similar Jewish atrocity and the consequences of the Virgin's intervention, all of which bears closely on the version chosen by the Prioress. The Bromyard analogue is peripherally mentioned in Beverly Boyd's Variorum edition of *The Prioress's Tale* (1987), a key work also not cited by Rex. While it had not yet been issued at the time of his original essay in *MLQ* (1984), it could have been referred to in this 1995 collection. Moreover, on the subject of the blood libel, one would also expect to find some direct use made of J. W. F. Hill's *Medieval Lincoln* (Cambridge: Cambridge University Press, 1948), if only for the reason that Chaucer has seen fit to make the

---

[1] G. G. Coulton, *Chaucer and His England*, 8th ed. (London: Methuen, 1950), p. 156.

[2] Other standard authorities on the history of the Jews in the Middle Ages, not listed in the Works Cited, are Salo Wittmayer Baron, Cecil Roth, and J. R. Marcus.

[3] The probable date of *Summa praedicantium* was definitely set by Leonard E. Boyle as 1348; *Speculum* 48 (1973): 533–37.

Prioress refer particularly, if confusedly, to that terrible event. Still another version of the blood libel, in this case drawn from twentieth-century bigotry, would also have been appropriate to Rex's discussion, although perhaps not available at the time: Elisabeth Orsten's account of a *modern* parallel, described in *Florilegium* 11 (1992).

Of course, the evidence, even in its incomplete state in Rex's book, only serves to problematize the question still farther—why has Chaucer seen fit to make the Prioress take the hardest possible line in her narration? If we reject—as who will not?—the possibility that Chaucer himself was a hard-liner, why has he gone out of his way to depict Madame Eglentyne as such? Is it to force the audience to see the Prioress as a hypocrite of the worst sort—proclaiming her devotion to the Virgin, traditionally a fount of mercy and compassion, yet reveling in vengeance upon those she hates? It is tempting, in such considerations, to fall back on the obvious, in particular the citing of *GP* 133–35 in conjunction with Matthew 23:25. One of the features of Rex's crisply written, succinctly argued book is that he steers clear of stating the obvious.

One last quibble, or perhaps commendation. The author of this excellent book is very sparing in his secondary references. Yet can one easily escape a sense of absence in discovering, in a book about a fictive account of a fourteenth-century prioress, the absence of any citation to Eileen Power's 1922 classic, *Medieval English Nunneries?*

DOUGLAS WURTELE
Carleton University

A. V. C. SCHMIDT, ed. Piers Plowman: *A Parallel-Text Edition of the A, B, C, and Z Versions*. Vol. I. Text. London and New York: Longman, 1995. Pp. xv, 762. $199.95.

This is a welcome book. Recent study of *Piers Plowman* has often emphasized moving beyond the individual versions of the poem and considering the work (i.e., Langland's imaginative life) as a single developing whole. We have been hampered in this pursuit by the absence of any modern equivalent to Skeat's great parallel-text edition of 1886,[1] a de-

---

[1] Walter W. Skeat, ed., *The Vision of William Concerning Piers the Plowman in Three Parallel Texts*, 2 vols. (London: Oxford University Press, 1886).

ficiency Schmidt and Longman now seek to remedy. We can, of course, no longer rely upon Schmidt's self-avowed model, for Skeat's work has become passé because of the narrowness of his evidentiary basis for presenting the poem and because of the development of more powerful editorial tools for studying the textual tradition (an advance due to the work of R. W. Chambers and his students, in the main of George Kane).[2]

Thus, all students of Langland must be in the debt of editor and publisher. Once again, as previously for B. A. Windeatt's opulent *Troilus and Criseyde*, medievalists owe Longman profuse thanks. *A Parallel-Text Edition* represents an extraordinary risk venture by a commercial publisher—a central (and very lengthy) text promulgated in a form subjected to scholarly scrutiny and accompanied by a substantial variant apparatus. And the book has been handsomely produced, with legible type and ample margins.

Yet in terms of scholarly scrutiny, of Schmidt's work as an editor, this may eventually prove an unwelcome book. At this time, one cannot offer a definitive reading, quite simply because describing this volume as "sparse in explanation" is generous. The book is precisely what the title promises, text and collations only. Even though providing it here would not have substantially increased the size of a very large volume, "A full account of editorial procedure will be found in Volume II, Introduction" (p. xiii). Indeed, even page [xv], the only information offered to guide a reader in using the volume, has the look of an afterthought. It occurs on the otherwise unused last leaf of the sixteen-page front matter—and is unpaginated and not typeset in the normal format. Moreover, even with the information provided, I find Schmidt's collation frequently impossible to follow.

One's skepticism about the staying power of Schmidt's editorial work begins with the gross contents of the volume. Unlike Skeat, Schmidt presents *Piers* in four parallel versions, including the infamous "Z Text." It remains uncertain why anyone should believe this an authorial text (as edited A, B, or C might claim to be); certainly, no one other than Schmidt and the authors of the Z theory seems yet convinced that it is

---

[2] The standard editions resulting from Chambers's initiative are George Kane, ed., *Piers Plowman: The A Version* (London: Athlone, 1960); Kane and E. Talbot Donaldson, *Piers Plowman: The B Version* (London: Athlone, 1975); George Russell's companion C Version has been on the edge of completion for nearly three decades, but has yet to appear. As a stopgap, one falls back on Derek Pearsall's diplomatic *Piers Plowman by William Langland: An Edition of the C-text* (London: Arnold, 1978).

Langland's.[3] Again, the appendix, on page 743, presents two bits of text, a single EAMH[3] intrusion of B lines into the A confession of Glutton and the lines on Hophni and Phineas from the Ilchester (C Version) prologue; neither has any particular evidence to offer about the activity of the author, and I do not understand why they uniquely are provided. Finally, on page 449, Schmidt's italics apparently ask the reader to take A.12.99ff. as the work of John But, while preserving the remainder of the passus as authorial. It is unclear to me how Schmidt might believe most of this passus authorial, had he read Anne Middleton's trenchant demonstration of the extent of But's work.[4]

In trying to assess further the quality of Schmidt's editorial service, I examine a sample passage, and that only tentatively; for this purpose, I choose Glutton's confession (pp. 218–29: A.5.146–214, B.5.297–385, C.6.349–440).[5] Schmidt provides, so far as I can see, a sequence of what I'd call $O^1$ texts. He reproduces the archetype or last common ancestor of all surviving copies (which is not necessarily identical to Langlandian holograph). One gathers, at least on the basis of Schmidt's identification of "familial groups," their recurrence in his collations, and his procedures in his earlier student B Version,[6] that the text has been constructed by traditional stemmatic techniques. For example, in the B Version, the two MSS R and F[7] have a weight equal to the remaining fourteen witnesses collated because they represent an independent line of descent from the archetype.

This choice is variously successful as a procedure, depending on the situation. In the case of the A Version, Kane's edition presents an $O^1$ text also,[8] although not one predicated on stemmatic recension. Nonetheless, the Schmidt and Kane texts are nearly identical for portions I

---

[3] See my *Pursuing History* (Stanford: Stanford University Press, 1996), pp. 195–202; and *Yearbook of Langland Studies* 9 (1995): 183–90. On the Ilchester prologue, mentioned in the next sentence, see *Pursuing History*, pp. 204–14 (209–11 for Hophni and Phineas).

[4] "Making a Good End: John But as a Reader of *Piers Plowman*," in Edward Donald Kennedy, Ronald Waldron, and Joseph S. Wittig, eds., *Middle English Studies Presented to George Kane* (Woodbridge: D. S. Brewer, 1988), pp. 243–66.

[5] I choose this passage on the basis of having rather arbitrarily run a trial of a B version edition on this piece of the poem, an effort which received welcome suggestions and encouragement from Anne Middleton, Hoyt Duggan, and Derek Pearsall.

[6] *William Langland, The Vision of Piers Plowman: A Complete Edition of the B-Text* (London: Dent, Everyman, 1978 and 1987), pp. xxxv–ix (in both editions).

[7] And rather frequently, R alone, since F is prone to stimulating, but archetypally irrelevant, participatory poetics.

[8] See *Pursuing History*, p. 296 n. 31, and the discussion to which it refers, p. 80.

survey. Important variations would include several pointing to Schmidt's inversion of one of Kane and Donaldson's favored procedures, printing an A text that accords with the B Version (the earlier editors too often made B accord with A). Such readings occur at line 159, "wariner" (Kane "waffrer"), and in supplying line 167 (not in Kane). The two editors make differing choices between attested B-verses at line 178.

With B, I find Schmidt's text often superior to Kane and Donaldson's, more proximate to what I would print than to what appears in the Athlone edition. This is largely the result of Schmidt's staying resolutely within the B tradition, rather than following Kane and Donaldson in rejecting the B archetype in favor of the readings of Kane's A Version.[9] But when an erroneous reading of the B archetype may be bracketed between agreeing authorial A and C readings,[10] Schmidt often doesn't hesitate to emend it, e.g., the supply of B.5.328, perhaps lost when the archetypal B scribe returned to his copy after transcribing line 327 and confused "-selue" (line 327) with "werse" (line 328), resuming his transcription at the head of line 329.

Schmidt's superiority to Kane and Donaldson in B isn't universal, however. For example, his predecessors follow the B archetype where Schmidt implausibly emends it at B.5.378 (the fussy, intruded "it"). They correctly identify the archetypal reading where Schmidt fails to at B.5.370, 382, and 383, all minor readings. And they correctly reject the archetype (omitting "and halidome") where Schmidt would defend it at B.5.370.

The C Version seems to me much more problematic, for Schmidt as editor and for me as reviewer. A complete collation of C manuscripts has never been published, and thus no past scholarly edition to guide Schmidt exists. In this portion of C, copies split into two large families (*p* and *i*, the latter Schmidt's *x*). Thus, in this textual tradition, recension should usually allow an editor to construct the archetype through free choice between two competing variants. Lacking a collation, I can only assess Schmidt's performance by comparing Skeat's text (based on a *p* copy, Huntington Library MS HM 137) and Pearsall's (based on an *x*, Huntington Library MS HM 143), and on that basis, I rather more frequently than elsewhere find Schmidt's choices here uncompelling.

---

[9] A major point raised by Robert Adams, "Editing *Piers Plowman* B: The Imperative of an Intermittently Critical Edition," *Studies in Bibliography* 45 (1992): 31–68.

[10] A solution proposed by Kane and Donaldson; see *The B Version*, pp. 76–83.

For example, Schmidt prints C.6.436 as the painful "Of al my luyther lyf in al my lyf-tyme." His collation shows that he retains *x* "lyf[1]" and rejects the more persuasive *pP²* reading "lyuyng." But Schmidt fails to notice that contamination from the second half-line pervades the first. Not only has "lyuyng" been assimilated to "lyf-," but the first "al" of the line represents a scribal supply, an echo of the correct second one.[11]

A further problem, common to all three texts, is that Schmidt seems to have edited with some kind of metrical theory. He notes, for example, "a few cases where another MS spelling is preferred [to the base manuscript] as possibly more authentic or as providing superior metre for the line" (p. xiii). And appendix 2 (pp. 761–62) lists spellings adjusted for metrical purposes, but these are all in the unproblematic line-final position.

Schmidt's metrical theory clearly does not accord with the substantial agreements of the two leading students of alliterative verse, Hoyt Duggan and Thomas Cable.[12] Thus, Schmidt prints a fairly large number of lines capable of easy metrical correction in the same ametrical form of past editions. For example, to deal only with the B Version, one should correct at least the following: in line 311, "Hugh" is disyllabic (cf. C.6.364 "Hewe"); in 312, omit "and"[13]; in 342, omit "a²" (although archetypal in all three versions); in 343, read "ruggebon[e]"; in 354, follow Kane and Donaldson and drop "a²"; in 356, read "Hert[e]fordshire"; in 376, omit "þat."

And occasionally Schmidt nods rather badly over metrical matters. For example, at B.5.321, he follows R "And to þe newe feire." But this reading, in spite of its recurrence in C, destroys the metrical (and authorial) line transmitted elsewhere, "And at þe newe feire." Metricality

---

[11] Although this is perhaps the archetypal reading, since both Skeat and Pearsall print two *al*'s.

[12] Among Duggan's many useful publications on the subject, most relevant are "Notes Toward a Theory of Langland's Meter," *Yearbook of Langland Studies* 1 (1987): 41–70, and "Langland's Dialect and Final -*e*," *Studies in the Age of Chaucer* 12 (1990): 157–91; see also "The Authenticity of the Z-Text of *Piers Plowman*: Further Notes on Metrical Evidence," *Medium Ævum* 56 (1987): 25–45. And see Thomas Cable, *The English Alliterative Tradition* (Philadelphia: University of Pennsylvania Press, 1991).

[13] This "and" depends, at least partially, upon the reversal of lines 312 and 313 in the B archetype, with loss of the actual consecutive grammatical sense. Langland hoped he was describing "a priest pressed 'mid prostitutes a pair,'" a reading clarified only by the overemphatic punctuation: "Clarice of Cokkeslane; þe Clerk of þe chirche, / Sire Piers of Pridie; and Pernele of Flaunders."

here depends upon the elided form "N'at," in "slant alliteration" with "newe" and "nempned."[14]

So I am troubled by the texts Schmidt reconstructs. But I remain happy to have at least a usable text from which to teach and consider the poem as the developing entity it is. We may eventually, once Schmidt fully reveals his views of textual matters in volume 2, resume/continue quoting from some other source. But then *A Parallel-Text Edition* will fulfill its designs and come to more closely resemble our now discardable copies of Skeat's volume 1—in the more plausible readings from other editors and our own wits with which we annotate its inviting margins.

RALPH HANNA III
University of California, Riverside

M. C. SEYMOUR. *A Catalogue of Chaucer Manuscripts, Volume 1: Works Before the* Canterbury Tales. Hants, UK: Scolar Press and Brookfield, VT: Ashgate Publishing, 1995. Pp. x, 171. $67.95.

Given an academic market that prefers big ideas and brilliant aperçus, one feels compelled to applaud scholars who still choose to do the "foundational" work that must precede any study of material culture. Their labor is tedious, literal, and not highly regarded, but absolutely essential. M. C. Seymour is just such a scholar, and his *Catalogue of Chaucer Manuscripts* ought to be commended, both for the effort that went into it and for the information—new and old, descriptive and bibliographical—that it provides. It must, of course, be evaluated too—first by

---

[14] The "to" of C.6.376 reflects accidental coincidence with R in either Langland's (scribal) copy-text for or the archetype of C, in the first case aided by inattention to a passage that the author knew he was not extensively revising in the C Version. A further example: at B.5.363, Kane and Donaldson reject the archetype while Schmidt (like the B scribes) misidentifies an alliterative pattern. The reading of only Hm among the B MSS, "spak," corresponds to A.5.206, C.6.419. The "warp" of the remaining copies from which Schmidt constructs the common ancestor probably is not archetypal, but the result of several coincident substitutions of an alliterative set-phrase. (It may especially appeal to a modern editor because we know, as Langland very probably didn't, "þe fyrst word þat he warp, 'Wher is,' he seyde / 'þe gouernour of þis gyng?'" [*Gawain and the Green Knight* 224–25]). In fact, "was" carries the second rhyming stave of Langland's line.

assessing how well its goals have been met. Unfortunately the catalogue lacks a clear statement of aims. The preface (p. vii) does refer to a "need . . . to examine the primary evidence behind some major textual problems . . . glossed over" elsewhere, but Seymour does not identify those problems here or adduce them in any systematic way in the catalogue. Nor does he indicate how codicological description will help to solve textual cruces. One is left then to determine for oneself what the utility of the book may be.

There are several facets of utility that may be considered: efficiency, accuracy, objectivity, and fullness of information. Seymour's presentation of information is for the most part neat and compact. He arranges the catalogue in chapters on each of Chaucer's works, except for the short poems (the omission of lyrics is not explained) and for *CT* (to be dealt with in a second volume). These are put in a sequence that reflects the presumed chronology of composition. The efficiency of this arrangement is compromised only in the cases of manuscripts that contain more than one Chaucerian work. Codicological and paleographic descriptions of *BD*, *HF*, *Anel*, *PF*, and *LGW* contain some redundancies and occasional instances in which data appropriate to one work appears in the discussion of another work. For example, on page 4 there is no need to describe the placement of *BD* in Fairfax 16; the cross-reference to pages 85–87, where the contents of the manuscript are fully listed, is sufficient (the list also corrects a typographical error in the rubric on page 4, which indicates that *BD* begins on fol. 137 [properly 130]). Again, the discussion of the scribe on page 4 is not only repeated at page 87 but elaborated and made more precise. The same is true for the discussion of the scribes of Tanner 346; on page 5 the statement is misleading, on page 84 there is greater accuracy of presentation. And why bother to point out that in Bodley 638 *BD* is more spaciously set out than is *LGW* (so is *PF*, which comes between the other two poems, but this is not noted)?

It is not always easy to determine how much information to include when space is limited. But by eliminating redundancy and random observation Seymour could have made room for fuller details. For example, he notes (p. 4) that Bodley 638 reverses lines 787–88 of *BD*, but he fails to mention that the scribe corrected this error by adding in the margin, twice, the conventional *b* and *a* markers. Similarly, his records of a leaf missing from the text of *PF* and of a leaf missing from the text of *BD* fail to indicate that these are conjoint leaves. Again, he states

(p. 20) that Scribe 6 of CUL Ff. 1.6 wrote the first part of *PF*, but says nothing about the scribe(s) of the remainder of the *PF* text.

Sometimes one gets the impression that this catalogue was put together in haste, and that some information is obtained at second hand. There are occasional transcription errors. For example, the title of *PF* in Trinity College MS R.3.19 reads *followeth* (not *-ith*) and the *et c.* at the end is clearly added in a later hand, though Seymour gives no indication of this (p. 23). Similar errors occur in transcriptions from Pepys 2006 (on pp. 134–35). Seymour (p. 14) states that the text of *HF* in Bodley 638 has no marginalia, which is an impression one might get from glancing at "Corrections and Annotations" in Pamela Robinson's introduction to the facsimile edition; but the facsimile pages and Robinson's "Layout and Presentation of the Texts" reveal that there are over a dozen Latin glosses accompanying the text and other, late marginalia as well. One notes too that Seymour's report of the collation of *Rom* manuscript "GLASGOW, Hunterian Museum MS V 3 7 (409)" (the current designation, I am told, is Glasgow Univ. Library, Hunter 409) follows the erroneous report in Young and Aitken's *Catalogue of Manuscripts in the Hunterian Museum* (1908); in fact quire 10 does not want leaf 6, and quire 20 does want leaf 3. Seymour's report of missing lines also needs correction: the manuscript lacks line 380 but not lines 7375–76.

Another glitch in the report of line numbers occurs in the description of Harley 7333 (p. 21), which is said to lack line 874 of *MerT* (actually the lacuna begins with line 875) and lines 1–78 of *FrT*. The oddity here is that Seymour cites the alternative line numbers from Skeat's edition (those that Skeat puts in parentheses) instead of the continuous numbering of the tale groups (E 2119 and D 1299–1376). By so doing, he neglects the absence of *FrP* (1–34 or E 1265–98) from Harley 7333. Seymour (p. x) expressly chooses to use Skeat's century-old edition as his standard for line references but does not explain why.

Another idiosyncracy is Seymour's tendency, in remarks introducing some of the sections, to make sweeping judgments or criticisms. For example, Seymour does not believe that Chaucer left works unfinished (see discussions of *LGW* and *Astr* on pages 81 and 101). He dismisses as "wholly silly" the suggestion that Chaucer "abandoned" *HF* (p.11), and in this connection he reports with sadness the bibliographical naiveté of George Kane and Derek Pearsall (!). "The general opinion," he adds, "is that the poem is moving to a dénouement in line 2158"—but he does not supply bibliography to validate that assessment. Nor does he support the assertion that copies of *TC* and *PF* originally "included musical notation with the songs" (p. 58). Seymour, one senses, knows that a catalogue is not the place to push a thesis but cannot resist introducing a few personal favorites.

Seymour includes other material that is perplexing. Why quote "Chaucer's Words on his Books and Scribes" (appendix A) or offer a treatment of Chaucer's portraits (appendix B) when simple references to the passages and to Pearsall's extended treatment of portraits (duly noted) would have sufficed? One wishes that Seymour had provided instead an index of Chaucer's short poems that appear in manuscripts described in the catalogue. Indeed, a listing of the nine available facsimiles of manuscripts described in the catalogue would have been helpful. Given that their introductory descriptions, more elaborate than Seymour's, would have to be consulted in any serious pursuit of information about those manuscripts, a greater service may have been rendered if Seymour had recorded only corrections and additions to those descriptions and made more space available for fuller treatment of other manuscripts and other works, such as the lyrics. I would hope that Seymour's planned volume on *The Canterbury Tales* recapitulate as little as possible of Manly and Rickert's very full descriptions of *CT* manuscripts, and simply augment the data and highlight the corrections and points of divergent interpretation. As for the present volume, scholars should use it as a starting point and always double-check the facts.

DANIEL J. RANSOM
University of Oklahoma

JAMES SIMPSON. *Sciences and the Self in Medieval Poetry: Alan of Lille's* Anticlaudianus *and John Gower's* Confessio Amantis. Cambridge Studies in Medieval Literature, vol. 25. Cambridge: Cambridge University Press, 1995. Pp. 321. $59.95.

At the beginning of this flawed and repetitive but nevertheless welcome new study of "science" in two significant medieval scholastic poems, Simpson explains that by "science" he means "the entire range of academic disciplines available to a given writer" (p. 1), that is, the old

Germanic concept of *Wissenschaft*, knowledge, or what in the Middle Ages was more conventionally known as the liberal arts and philosophy. Accordingly, he turns to the origin of scientific information in "the academic works of trained philosophers" (p. 1), specifically Plato, for twelfth-century Alan of Lille in the *Anticlaudianus*, and Aristotle, for fourteenth-century John Gower in the *Confessio Amantis*. In nine chapters (including an introduction and conclusion), Simpson details the form, allegorical structure, and philosophical idea of the *Anticlaudianus* and *Confessio*, based on an "Aristotelian division" of what he terms the scientific hierarchy, into *theoria* and *practica*, and focused on readings of both as commentaries on these "sciences." Three chapters are keyed to each psychological allegory, with a culminating, seventh, chapter on the aesthetics of "information." By "psychological allegory" Simpson means that "Movement through the sciences, from ethics, to politics, and to cosmology, is premised on the capacities and desires of the soul itself (i.e., a psychology)" (p. 14). Further, both poems reenact their information of the soul by simultaneously engaging the reader into self-knowledge through interpretation. That is, each work involves a hero who is a model for the reader.

Central to the study is Simpson's contention that both poems "reveal the ways in which an ethics is dependent on a politics, which in turn is dependent on a cosmology" (p. 12). Simpson is arguing for a medieval "reader-response theory" that recognizes the exceptionally political context of each poem: "Alan's politics are Platonic, Virgilian, elitist, and rooted in the practice of the highest of the soul's faculties (the intelligence); Gower's politics are Aristotelian, Ovidian, much less strictly elitist, and rooted much 'lower down' in the soul, at the point where the imagination and physical desire meet" (p. 16).

"Information" (*informatio*) becomes, then, an artistic as well as scientific (moral, educational, philosophical) process that implies becoming rather than being, and appears in both of these medieval works to designate the form of what Simpson anachronistically and perhaps misleadingly describes by a term common to writing of the nineteenth century, Bildungsroman, the journey toward human perfection (pp. 7, 13). The three chapters on the *Anticlaudianus* delineate the outer and inner form, or its information, that is, the Aristotelian division of sciences (or the arts) mirrored in the actual *ascensus mentis ad Deum* in the creation of the New Man, which prompts us, according to Simpson, to read the narrative as if it were a theological artifact (chapter 2). His "Preposterous

Interpretation of the *Anticlaudianus*" (chapter 3) explains the apparent asynchronicity of beginning with Fronesis-Prudentia's ascent through the spheres by means of the chariot of the seven liberal arts guided by Ratio, to obtain a soul from God (and his agent Noys), and ending with the creation of the Novus Homo on earth, through God's agent Natura, at which time the *iuvenis* is crowned with *intellectus*. In the fourth chapter, on "Alan's Philosopher-King," the hero of the poem is revealed to be the reader.

In chapter 5, moving from the problem of the "incoherence" of the *Anticlaudianus* to the Ovidian "disunity" of the *Confessio*, Simpson traces the analogous position of the narrative as a figure for the education of the soul, or the reader, processed by means of ironic Genius as a "Moralized Ovid," a *praeceptor amoris* who draws from the *Ars amatoria* and also the *Remedia amoris*, in relation to Amans as an Ovidian lover, in both figures of whom the reader shares. In chapter 6, Simpson explains that Genius serves as the soul's imagination, Amans as its will, a bond most obvious in book 3. In chapter 7, Gower presents a *Remedia amoris* for Amans by means of Genius's discourse on philosophy, and in particular, the Aristotelian schema of ethics, economics, and politics. Chapter 8 compares the imaging poetics of Alan and Gower by means of the use of metaphor and painting in *De planctu Naturae* and the imagination in the Genius of the *Confessio*. The conclusion compares the political positions of the two poets in relation to their poems' psychology.

The novelty of Simpson's overarching argument about the role of the arts in the education of the soul in the *Anticlaudianus* and *Confessio* is, however, less than he imagines, given its dependence on previous scholarship. A more precise contextualization of Simpson's argument at the beginning, rather than in scattered notes, and in it how he planned to extend or elaborate on what others have already published, would have been most helpful and appropriate. Simpson's ideas about the literary journey-narrative as a reflection of the figurative meaning, the process of the education of the soul as if a work of artistry, are informed by the studies of Richard H. Green ("Alan of Lille's *Anticlaudianus: Ascensus Mentis in Deum*," *Annuale Mediaevale* 8 [1967]: 3–16) and Chance ("The Artist as Epic Hero in Alan of Lille's *Anticlaudianus*," *Mittellateinisches Jahrbuch* 18 [1983]: 238–47) on the arts and the function and imagery of the artist in *Anticlaudianus*, and of Linda Marshall ("The Identity of the 'New Man' in the *Anticlaudianus* of Alan de Lille," *Viator* 10 [1979]: 77–99) on the relationship between politics and philosophy in the work. And preceding and informing Simpson's general concept of Alanian Platonic poetics is Winthrop Wetherbee's in *Platonism and Poetry in the Twelfth Century: The Literary Influence of the School of Chartres* (1972), the latter of which Simpson modifies by establishing for it a Boethian conduit itself Neoplatonic in nature. For Gower, specifically grounding Simpson's argument is also the idea of Genius as an artifex "enforming" classical tales and also the new self of Amans, uniting body and soul, in a role analogous to that of Natura in generating the individual in Alan's *De planctu Naturae*, in the framing work of Chance Nitzsche's chapter on Gower in *Genius Figure in Antiquity and the Middle Ages* (1975), and the politicization of the education of Amans, defined by the relationship between ethics and politics, microcosm and macrocosm, in Russell Peck's *Kingship and Common Profit in Gower's 'Confessio Amantis'* (1978) and A. J. Minnis's "John Gower, *Sapiens* in Ethics and Politics," *Medium Ævum* 49 (1980): 214–15.

While the specific elaborations in the developmental chapters approach the two poems from a much more detailed excursus on the nature of the arts than have previous works of scholarship, their arguments also reveal caesuras of rather surprising breadth. Most representative is Simpson's insistence on substituting "science" (*scientia*) for knowledge (*ars*), a rhetorical sleight of hand that does not really work in the twelfth century. Limited to the idea of expertness, skill, and knowledge, *scientia* often referred to a very practical branch of knowledge associated with what we would call engineering and not with the *artes*, the theory of any art or science, just as "information" (*informatio*) in the twelfth century refers less to a body of discrete knowledge than to representation, an idea, or conception (as *informo* denoted the giving of form to a thing—its in-formation). And of course "science" cannot include what was meant in the twelfth century by *sapientia*—wisdom, but also theology. By moving back and forth between the modern denotation and the medieval, Simpson unnecessarily misleads his reader. He also asks if the chariot of Fronesis-Prudentia is the "chariot of the soul" (p. 65), as if unaware that the seven liberal arts (or handmaidens) who construct this chariot (described between 2.305 and 4.70—nearly two books of the seven) are guided for Fronesis-Prudentia by Ratio, Reason, and the five horses of the senses (Sheridan, ed., p. 120 n. 17). Other, similar elisions in and misreadings of the text include the incorrect association, in Alan's poesis, of metaphor and painting as figure with the art of rhetoric (which Alan denigrates in *De planctu Naturae*) instead of with the art of grammar (p. 239); the etymological and psychological misreading of

Gower's Genius as the faculty of the imagination (passim, but esp. chapter 8, pp. 252–63; "imagination" in the sense in which we understand it was not so understood by scholars in the Middle Ages; *ingenium*, which comes the closest, actually refers to memory); the interpretation of Amans as a king in book 7 of the *Confessio* (pp. 280–81) when he has already been identified as representing the faculty of the will.

Overall, Simpson's narrowly focused reading and his inability to consider influential what lies outside his own argument—that is, the earlier Latin literary and philosophical tradition that shaped Alan's own works—seriously undermines his argument whenever he attempts to read either of the learned poems under discussion *in vacuo*. (Simpson does admit that, like Abelard, he might be accused of "twisting the sense of the texts" to fit an argument [p. 92], but once this possibility is mentioned it is apparently enough to ignore its danger.) Most exemplary of such flaws is the interpretation in chapter 3 ("Preposterous Interpretation of the *Anticlaudianus*"), one less preposterous than ill founded: Simpson argues simplistically that the poem should be read backward, so that the creation of the Novus Homo at work's end (books 6–9) would be *followed*, in the reader's mind, by the New Man's education in the seven liberal arts and theology at the work's *beginning* (books 1–5). Here Simpson misunderstands the Bernardian definition of the natural (philosophical) order of a poem (as opposed to its artificial or integumental, narrative order) and therefore (indeed, preposterously) claims that the natural order of the *Anticlaudianus* actually begins in midpoem (6.428–65), at the point that the literal creation of the New Man by Nature (a literal descent to Nature, so to speak) occurs (p. 79). Clearly, the journey of Fronesis-Prudentia in *Anticlaudianus* to obtain the human soul from Noys, God's agent, in the first six books is also reflective of the natural order—Simpson does not seem to understand twelfth-century concepts of Natura as Anima Mundi, World Soul. That is, it is necessary first to fetch the soul from its celestial origins, just as second must occur the construction of the body and the temperamental endowments of the human virtues and attributes, within the macrocosmic equivalent of the earthly world where physical making (and corporal generation and conception) takes place.

More plausible would be the possibility that in beginning with an ascent through the heavens to God and ending with a descent back to earth Alan is merely following the allegorical and cosmogonic narrative patterns of birth and generation established earlier in the Middle Ages. It is damaging to Simpson's argument to ignore the profound literary influence of seminal Latin antecedents, given Alan's awareness of Bernard's commentary on Martianus (as well as on the *Aeneid*), Alan's much-documented indebtedness to Bernard in general, and Alan's use of Fronesis-Prudentia, taken from Martianus, as one of the central characters of the *Anticlaudianus*. Further, most fabulous philosophical tracts trace the journey of the immortal soul from the originary spheres into the corporal body on earth, for example, Macrobius's commentary on the *Somnium Scipionis*, twelfth-century scholar Bernard Silvestris's *Cosmographia* (*Megacosmus et Microcosmus*) ["Mentem de caelo, corpus trahet ex elementis, / Ut terras habitet corpore, mente polum," "he will draw his mind (*mens*) from the heavens (*caelum*, firmament), his body from the elements, / So that he may inhabit the earth with his body, the poles (heavens) with his mind" (2.10.15–16)]; and Bernard's commentary on Martianus Capella's *De nuptiis Philologiae et Mercurii*. In the latter, in a similar *ascensus mentis ad Deum* portrayed in the first two, framing, books, the god Mercury ascends through the heavens with Apollo in his search for a bride, then returns to earth to marry the mortal Philology, whose mother is Fronesis, after which his bride is then granted immortality. The remaining seven books on the seven liberal arts—Philology's handmaidens—illustrate the process of education to which the mortal soul should adhere. The hero is the reader in *all* of these cosmogonic and pedagogic journey allegories.

Despite these flaws in contextualization and reading, Simpson will no doubt with this study regenerate contemporary scholarly interest in the twelfth-century scholastic tradition and its influence by drawing attention to its correspondence with contemporary literary theory, especially in regard to subjectivity and the self. His attention to these two works in a book that synthesizes the past twenty-five years of scholarship on them—given their lack of previous comparison in this scholarship—should attract new readers. Also significant is Simpson's revision of "humanism" (in line with the recent work of other medieval scholars) to refer to the twelfth to fourteenth centuries (rather than the later period of the Italian Renaissance) and thereby support a most necessary and long overdue redefinition of the cultural history of the Middle Ages.

JANE CHANCE
Rice University

JEFFREY L. SINGMAN and WILL MCLEAN. *Daily Life in Chaucer's England*. Daily Life Through History Series. London and Westport, Conn.: Greenwood Press, 1995. Pp. xii, 252. $45.00.

From its title, this book seems a potential new option for recommended reading in advanced undergraduate or graduate classes covering either the works of Chaucer and/or his late medieval contemporaries. With its extratextual focus on the material culture of Chaucer's England, it might provide a substitute for or companion to other collections of predominantly written source materials from the period, like Robert P. Miller's *Chaucer: Sources and Backgrounds*, which concentrates on literary and patristic texts, or Alcuin Blamires's *Woman Defamed and Woman Defended*, which is perhaps too gender-limited to be an all-purpose, supplementary classroom text. In their introduction, Singman and McLean themselves distinguish their book from the many others already written about daily life in Chaucer's England, which merely "tell you what kinds of clothes people wore, what kinds of games they played, or what kinds of songs they sang" (p. xi). By including "actual patterns for medieval clothes, rules for medieval games, and music for medieval songs" (p. xi), their book, they argue, is the first to be written from the perspective of "living history," that is, the attempt "to recreate materially some aspect of the past" which "in its most comprehensive form . . . tries to recreate an entire historical milieu" (p. x) and "encourages a hands-on approach to the past" (p. xi). That is not only a tall order, but in terms of the physical limitations of modern classrooms and recent experiments at many urban colleges and universities in "distance learning," such an approach may be, practically speaking, untenable.

The authors also acknowledge that the present volume is "a revised and expanded version of *The Chaucerian Handbook*, . . . a manual for Chaucerian living history published by the University Medieval and Renaissance Society of Toronto in February 1991 for its 'Tabard Inn' living history event" (p. viii). Not surprisingly, this book includes, in appendix A, advice about how a group might organize such an event and suggests that readers consult the local chapter of the Society for Creative Anachronism (SCA) (p. 222). Indeed, *Daily Life in Chaucer's England* resembles nothing so much as guides to "living in the current Middle Ages," such as *The Known World Handbook*, published for its members by the SCA. Ironically, such "popular" handbooks (and now that organization's current Internet web resources) may cover a broader spectrum of topics about medieval life than does Singman's and McLean's book in its chapters: Historical Background to Chaucer's England; Chaucer's World; The Course of Life; Cycles of Time; The Living Environment; Clothing and Accessories; Arms and Armor; Food and Drink; Entertainments. In addition to the patterns, musical lyrics, recipes and game rules included in *Daily Life in Chaucer's England*, SCA handbooks also provide illustrations of and bibliography about medieval heraldry, calligraphy, herbalism, needlework, manuscript illumination, beer-making, jousting and tournament rules, archery, and armor-making, to name only a few aspects of medieval life offered for reasonably authentic contemporary emulation.

Since its "hands-on" approach does not sufficiently improve on SCA support materials, the crucial criterion for evaluation of *Daily Life in Chaucer's England* is its "quality of scholarship," which its authors, maintaining that they held to a "high standard of fidelity to the sources" (p. xi), claim is its other major distinction. In fact, the book's chief drawback is its dearth of scholarly documentation, averaging eleven footnotes per chapter over nine chapters, and none at all for its skimpy first chapter, which promises to cover in seven pages the "Historical Background to Chaucer's England." Some footnotes do provide cata- logues of additional bibliographical items, often more recently pub- lished, which are not listed in the volume's official bibliography of pri- mary and secondary sources, novels about the period, audiovisual materials, and sources of its illustrations. This inconsistent placement of cited documentation of (or recommended further research about) life in late medieval England sometimes necessitates cumbersome cross- searches. While undergraduates might feel secure trusting Singman and McLean at their word and citing them as evidence, graduate stu- dents would find the scholarly support for the assertions made not only insufficient, but difficult to corroborate. This is a shame, because in some respects this book provides fascinating and potentially illuminat- ing information about the lives of Chaucer's contemporaries, many of whom mirror the very classes and professions he represents in his works.

At the same time, the identification of the book's focus as "Chaucer's" England is misleading. The authors make little or no direct connection between their account of the daily lives of generic knights, monks, fri- ars, yeomen, franklins, etc., and either the pilgrim-portraits of *The General Prologue* or characters in the *Tales*. This is puzzling, especially where, for example, in an otherwise excellent discussion of arms and armor, they describe the tendency for a knight's "shining" armor to rust, yet fail to connect this to Chaucer's description of the pilgrim Knight's tunic, which is "besmotered" by his rusty mail (p. 153). In the same section, while vividly describing an array of large and small medieval weapons, they fail to note how many of these very items are carried by the various pilgrims. The "Arms and Armor" chapter might, however, splendidly inform a classroom discussion of the "arming of the warrior" scenes in *Sir Gawain and the Green Knight*.

In sum, this book is an inconsistent mix of hits and misses. Scattered throughout the volume are useful and illuminating charts. Table 2.1, "The Social Hierarchy" (p. 23), which arranges the traditional three estates across a grid equating a priest or master of arts from the first estate with a squire from the second estate and a lesser merchant from the third estate, indicates a social parity that belies Chaucer's arrangement of representatives of these same groups in his *Prologue*. The chapter "Cycles of Time," covering the canonical hours, the agricultural calendar year, and the liturgical calendar of feasts, is informative but has little demonstrable connection to Chaucer's works. The patterns for costumes (whose authentic sources are actually Scandinavian, not English) give a sense of the construction of medieval garments; however, realizing them from a small line drawing to their ultimate "fabrication" would probably challenge even the most skilled home sewer. The recipes add little or nothing to the collections of medieval recipes by Lorna Sass, Sharon Butler, and Constance Hieatt. This book will be appreciated best by enthusiasts of the Middle Ages. Its academic usefulness is questionable and, at $45.00, it is beyond the acceptable price range for a recommended text in a Chaucer course.

LORRAINE STOCK
University of Houston

SUSAN L. SMITH. *The Power of Women: A Topos in Medieval Art and Literature*. Philadelphia: University of Pennsylvania Press, 1995. Pp. xv, 294. $44.95.

*The Power of Women: A Topos in Medieval Art and Literature* is a powerful and fascinating study of the literary and visual representation of a rarely examined medieval topos. Like a number of conventions of recent interest, the Power of Women topos is so familiar a motif to scholars of medieval art and literature that its meaning has been taken for granted. In revealing the manifold significations of this topos, Smith provides a wealth of information about medieval culture. The topos is "the representational practice of bringing together at least two, but usually more, well-known figures from the Bible, ancient history, or romance to exemplify a cluster of interrelated themes that include the wiles of women, the power of love, and the trials of marriage" (p. 2). Examining how the topos was used to make different sorts of commentaries in a variety of contexts, Smith demonstrates how its meaning continually shifted throughout the Middle Ages.

The book covers a wide temporal, geographical, and disciplinary range, encompassing a large swath of literary, theological, rhetorical, artistic, and social history. A work of careful and deeply thoughtful scholarship, it abounds in detailed analysis, broad-ranging commentary, and critical insight. The chapters are organized logically and pleasingly: Smith begins with the rhetorical foundations of the topos, moves to an analysis of its place in literary and narrative traditions and then shifts to a discussion of the topos in the visual arts from its emergence on the margins of manuscripts to its uses in such divergent contexts as cathedral decoration and secular luxury items.

One general concern of the book is the place of tradition in the medieval arts. Since most medieval artistry relied on, imitated, parodied, or otherwise made variations on rhetorical and iconographical conventions, this topic is relevant to any study of representational art in the period. In particular, Smith examines how literary and visual artists, while keeping within a tradition that was known and familiar, manipulated and commented on the idea of the Power of Women, expressing a variety of points of view as well as their own originality in the process.

The first three chapters are taken up by the literary and rhetorical traditions into which the topos fits, including a skillful summary of the place of paradigm and exemplum in classical and medieval rhetoric. Literary scholars may find the survey of the rhetorical traditions of the Middle Ages to be a nicely executed review, although it may perhaps be too sketchy for readers new to the subject. Smith centers on the twelfth through fourteenth centuries in Latin, French, and English sources, but ranges freely before and beyond where appropriate. In literary texts, the topos operated "to bring to bear the authority of history on the issue of women and power" (p. 2). No matter what its context, the topos functioned to warn that no man, however superior his mental, physical, and moral endowments, can resist women's wiles.

In taking up other forms of the argument by example, Smith surveys the *ars rhetorica* and *praedicandi*, invoking the larger subject of the uses of authority. The more general discussion of the power structures of medieval society opens up the question of how such rhetorical devices reflect the attempt by social and religious institutions to maintain hegemony and control public behavior. Smith links the emergence of the Power of Women topos in particular with social and political movements of the middle of the twelfth century to the end of the fourteenth, when "developments that made it advantageous to the patriarchal power structure to set new limits on the customary rights and powers that had devolved upon women in the earlier Middle Ages focused new attention on the power of women" (p. 19). In setting up these associations, Smith documents the larger implications of her subject.

A wide-ranging survey of the different uses to which the topos was put finds its way up to Lydgate, turning a retrospective glance back to classical precursors, through the troubadours and trouvères, the *Romance of the Rose*, Christine de Pizan's works, and Middle English literature, including Chaucer. While the author does not dwell on each example for long, her explanations are precise and careful. Literary scholars, for whom many of the examples will be familiar, will find to their satisfaction that Smith pinpoints all the major stops along the way; as they read, they will doubtless acquire a more ramified view of the shades of meanings that are applicable to the convention: "By 1300, the Power of Women *topos* in verbal form might be voiced by a preacher holding forth from the pulpit against the sin of lust, by a lyric poet pleading for a lady's love, or by a fictional character in a romance defending himself, or herself, for loving not wisely but too well" (p. 140).

If the first chapters provide large-ranging surveys, the third and fourth introduce and analyze one image—the mounted Aristotle—first in narrative and then in iconographical form. The image, depicting Aristotle being ridden by the emperor Alexander's beautiful mistress, Phyllis, surfaced originally not in Aristotle's own age or region, but in Western Europe at the beginning of the thirteenth century. Its best-known versions are recorded in sermons by the Dominican Jacques de Vitry, and in the vernacular poem "Lai d'Aristote" by the northern French poet Henry D'Andeli. In contrasting the visual with the verbal rhetoric of persuasion, Smith examines the particular resonances that it carried as a visual image and that set it apart from the exemplary use of Aristotle in texts. In narrative, the ride is presented as part of a sequence of events, but the visual mounted Aristotle focuses attention "on Aristotle's metaphorical transformation from man to beast and on the perilous instability of the body and its desires which lies beneath the image's surface piquancy" (p. 105).

Here as elsewhere, Smith demonstrates wide-ranging expertise, delving into the connections between orality, literacy, and visual art. She weaves together literary, rhetorical, artistic, historical, theological, and sociological dimensions. The mounted Aristotle, she asserts, detached from its textual moorings, became "common cultural property, possessing the quality of existing 'outside' both the discourses of individual speakers and the fabrications of individual artists, the quality that gives the example its supposedly objective status and thus its claim to truth" (p. 110). The focus on marginal images in manuscripts does not prevent her ranging over related artistic subjects to offer background on the equestrian ruler portrait (which represented dominion and power since medieval times), on bestiality, on the metamorphoses in which men are turned to beasts, and on the symbology of horses.

Smith dwells on the philosophical, social, and theological ramifications of the mounted Aristotle image: the "triumph of passion over reason, figured in the image of woman as rider and man as horse, is represented as taking place in the act of sex and moreover, in a deviant act of sex, since the position of 'woman on top' not only gives the woman the active, controlling role reserved to men, but constitutes a position forbidden in canon law as sinful and perverse" (p. 120). This leads to a piquant aside on the "scold's bridle" of late medieval satire, which could be placed over women's heads to hold their tongues: "To medieval moralists, the bridle in the hand of a woman like the Wife [of Bath], disobedient, quarrelsome, lustful, was their worst nightmare: the triumph of the beast" (p. 121).

The reader may wonder whether Smith spends too inordinate an amount of time on the mounted Aristotle image, but she outlines the crucial purpose and central place this image has by explaining that "no other visual image of the Power of Women imbues the reversal of normative gender hierarchy with as profound implications for the fate of the human—more properly speaking, the male—soul" (p. 113). The topos inverts the gender hierarchy by placing the man, woman's proper ruler, in a position of subjection, and simultaneously comparing his condition to a beast's, thereby also

reversing the proper relation between human and beast that in the Middle Ages further signified the relations between spirit and flesh, reason and passion. . . . Male : female::husband : wife::human : beast::mind : body::spirit : flesh. . . . As sinner, the position of the mounted man is tragic; as henpecked husband, it is ludicrous; as the passive sexual partner dominated by the 'woman on top,' it undermines his masculinity in the most intimate of power relations between the sexes. (pp. 113, 121)

The latter half of the book analyzes a series of forty-eight black-and-white illustrations, figuring the mounted Aristotle and related motifs. The images are from manuscript illuminations, cathedral façades (i.e., the Rouen pinnacles), reliefs on capitals (i.e., the late fourteenth-century capital from the nave of St. Pierre, Caen), misericords, carvings in cathedrals, sculptures, reliefs on caskets and boxes of various kinds (i.e., the Bargello casket), embroideries (i.e., the Malterer embroidery), mirror cases, and even a fourteenth-century leather shoe.

As with the literary exemplars, there is no monolithic "iconography" of the mounted Aristotle: the diversity of the images and their ever-changing contexts is eloquent evidence of the inventiveness of many artists who exploited opportunities to make new statements using traditional material (p. 131). On a casket cover, for instance, the image refers to a very different set of expectations than on a church façade. Smith brings to life what the shifting experience may have been like for the medieval viewer, who became familiar with the Power of Women topos in one context, and then saw it emerge in divergent contexts, framed in unique and varying ways.

In the case of secular luxury items, such as ivory caskets, the topos of the power of women is transformed into a love-offering by a man to a woman—as a token of the lover's love, fealty, service, and submission. In exchange for her body, for her affairs being transferred to her husband by her father, for her dowry, she is offered "a symbolic representation of her power" which in the civil or secular laws of marriage was no power at all:

Only in the temporally limited rituals of betrothal and marriage, which marked a woman's transition from virgin to wife, and again in the equally circumscribed rituals surrounding childbirth, which marked the second major transition in her life from wife to mother, did social practice sanction the representation of women as possessing power over men, acknowledging their real power in matters of sexuality and reproduction, power that is institutionally contained and controlled within the patriarchal family structure. (pp. 183–84)

Smith shows a solid and strong command of the literary and visual material in its social contexts as well as the relevant scholarship. Written with little hype and self-congratulation, the book is filled with useful facts and information and perceptive observations. For the most part, the prose is precise and clear. Occasionally, particularly in the review of the rhetorical tradition, there are passages that are overly jargon-ridden and infelicitous, but as soon as the author picks up momentum that obstacle vanishes. The solid and interesting endnotes furnish a substantial scholarly supplement to an already learned text. The conclusion, a short chapter on the topos in the fifteenth century and beyond, presents a view of the future of the medieval topos in the Renaissance rather than a summing up of what has already been covered. For the medievalist-reader such a chapter holds less interest than the bulk of this otherwise masterful study.

GALE SIGAL
Wake Forest University

MARTIN M. STEVENS and DANIEL WOODWARD, eds. *The Ellesmere Chaucer: Essays in Interpretation*. San Marino, Ca.: Huntington Library Press, 1995. Pp. xvi, 363. $75.00.

This lavishly produced volume is, in format, elegance of layout, and in range and depth of contents, a worthy companion to the *New Ellesmere Chaucer Facsimile* (Tokyo and San Marino: Huntington Library and Yushudo Publishing, 1995) it is designed to accompany. Like the facsimile itself, it is an exemplar of the publisher's art. It is appropriate therefore that it should begin with a detailed account, by Daniel Woodward, of the making of the facsimile. This introduction should be required reading for anyone who still believes that the making of a facsimile, of any kind, is a purely objective and "scientific" activity, removed from any editorial judgment. No doubt the makers of the 1911

Manchester Press facsimile thought they were achieving an exactly faithful facsimile: in the hindsight of eighty years, their decisions tell us more about their own editorial values (as Ralph Hanna's excellent introduction to the 1989 Brewer reprint shows) than they do about the manuscript itself.

Similarly, one can expect that a scholar of the next century might examine the facsimile, and this volume, for insight into the editorial values of the last decade of this century. On page 8, Woodward declares that a principal aim of the facsimile was to achieve "some of the overall *effect* of the manuscript" (his emphasis). As the later pages make clear, the emphasis is on physical effect: on the presentation in the facsimile of the manuscript as physical artifact. Thus, the facsimile is printed on sheets of paper in the same quiring as the original, with some copies having pages trimmed to the edges of each sheet. So, too, Woodward asserts that the facsimile is much better presented in printed hard copy than on a computer screen. The Ellesmere manuscript is a codex, and best understood as a physical artifact.

This emphasis on the manuscript as object is in harmony with the movement in medieval textual studies in the last decades toward the study of manuscripts as objects of cultural history in their own right: as the product of the workshops that prepare the parchment and bind the finished folios, of the teams of scribes, illustrators, and supervisors who write and ornament the pages; and as the possession of those who commission, sell, keep, and reuse the finished manuscript. (Outside medieval studies, Jerome McGann's work on "bibliographic codes" has reminded textual critics of the importance of the physical instantiation of the text.) Fundamental advances have been made in this work by many of the contributors to this volume, and the essays by Parkes on the planning and construction of Ellesmere, by Doyle on its scribe, by Scott on its illumination, and by David on its owners, are both timely summaries of years of work and contributions of new knowledge. One regrets here that the editors were not able to include the full version of Antony Cains's report on the bindings of the Ellesmere Chaucer, or Ralph Hanna's and Tony Edwards's discussion of the manuscript's Rotheley and De Vere connections, contained in the special number of the *Huntington Library Quarterly* (58:1 [1996]) edited by Seth Lerer. Both of these supplement material in this present volume in interesting directions: the parallel offered by Hanna and Edwards between the reactions of the De Veres to their loss of power, memorialized in the Rotheley poem contained in Ellesmere, and of Chaucer to his loss of political power, is pregnant with possibility.

It is consistent with the emphasis of this volume on Ellesmere as artifact that these essays are among the most satisfying in the volume. The essays of Doyle and Parkes are rich in exact detail, concerning the identity and characteristics of the Ellesmere scribe and the making of the manuscript. Scott's painstaking analysis of the illuminators notably shifts the likely date of the manuscript earlier, and brings it rather closer to Chaucer's death, "in a period beginning in or just after 1400 and ending no later than 1405" (p. 106). One should not make too much of this as a means of reinforcing the authority of Ellesmere. An early date is no guarantee of a good text, as is shown by the example of the notoriously unreliable Harleian 7334 and Corpus 198, both contemporary with or earlier than Ellesmere. All these essays benefit from the generous space and opportunity for ample pictorial illustration given by the editors to present familiar arguments in rare detail.

Some of the essays that do not center so closely on the manuscript itself as object, by comparison, appear less focused. Gaylord's essay on pictorial images of poets in contemporary manuscripts has interesting material about Gower portraits, and gives useful context for students of the Ellesmere Chaucer portrait. Bowden's essay leaves Ellesmere behind altogether to illustrate handsomely visual presentations of Chaucer in printed editions up to 1809. However, Emmerson concentrates on the miniatures in Ellesmere itself and argues, convincingly, for the complexity of text-image relationships in Ellesmere, as further evidence of the creative care behind the making of the manuscript. Pearsall usefully summarizes the context of Ellesmere within contemporary literary manuscripts, and reminds us that there is no evidence (much as we might wish it) to link Thomas Chaucer with Ellesmere. However, Kendrick's essay on the context of *The Canterbury Tales* in contemporary translations seems to have very little connection with Ellesmere or the other essays in this volume, and might have appeared better elsewhere.

Study of the manuscript as book has its strengths, as many of the essays in this volume show. But it has weaknesses too, and to this reader the three essays on aspects of the text, by Blake, Hanna, and Cooper, are less satisfying, and for the most part only restate positions elsewhere elaborated. It should be emphasized, however, that Blake does not say in this essay (as Cooper asserts he does, p. 259 n. 10) "that any portion of text that does not appear in Hengwrt cannot be authentic." Indeed, to this reviewer's knowledge, Blake has never asserted this. What he says is rather more challenging: if one accepts that Hengwrt has the best text (and this has been common ground among most scholars for the last fifty years; it is not seriously disputed by Hanna in his article) then one must start from the presumption that what is not in Hengwrt needs justification if it is to be accepted as by Chaucer. To put it another way: the fact that Ellesmere is the most splendid and carefully produced of early *Canterbury Tales* manuscripts does not mean automatically that it has the best tale-order or the best text. One has to argue these things. Indeed, that the Ellesmere order can be argued is well shown by Cooper, whose article presents the case for the Ellesmere fragment 4 and 5 ordering lucidly and convincingly: one does not have to accept that Hengwrt is "right" in every detail. Hanna's article is a curious performance. It attempts to assess Ellesmere by a survey of the possible manuscript sources available to its production team, and that team's use of it. The method is certainly well-conceived, but in this short space Hanna is able to base the analysis on just five manuscripts, making no use of the possibly crucial "independent" manuscripts such as Christ Church, Bodley 686, Additional 35286 manuscripts and Caxton's second edition. From his analysis, Hanna agrees that word-by-word Hengwrt gives the best text—in the first half of *The Wife of Bath's Prologue*, markedly so—but arrives at a rather odd conclusion: that "any editing [sc. in Ellesmere] that occurred is likely to have rendered the text more Chaucerian, not less." One may wonder just what this means. More "Chaucerian" than what? Than Hengwrt? This can hardly be so, given Hanna's admission that Hengwrt has a better word-by-word text than Ellesmere. Hanna's statement is taken up by Martin Stevens in his foreword, and is there transformed into an ever stranger assertion (p. 22): this amounts to a "redefinition of authorship," as Chaucer is constructed for us by the Ellesmere editorial team, and then further reconstructed by the many modern editions built on Ellesmere. Stevens comments that "this is the Chaucer that the twentieth century knows." Certainly: and it is possible that the twentieth century knows the wrong Chaucer, and that it is time it had a Chaucer based on sounder textual foundations.

Finally, one must note the presence of an excellent essay on the language of Ellesmere by Jeremy Smith, which in its understated way reveals rather nakedly the relative imperfections of the Ellesmere text compared to Hengwrt. One regrets the absence of an essay on the glosses in Ellesmere: a surprising omission, given their prominence in the manuscript and the recent work that has been done on them. One fears too that the concentration on Ellesmere alone may lead the reader to undervalue the importance of the other eighty-plus surviving manuscripts of *The Canterbury Tales*, some of them at least as splendid, or as textually important, as Ellesmere. But there is much here to absorb the reader.

PETER ROBINSON
De Montfort University, Leicester


M. TERESA TAVORMINA. *Kindly Similitude: Marriage and Family in* Piers Plowman. Piers Plowman Studies, vol. 11. Cambridge: D. S. Brewer, 1995. Pp. xix, 262. $71.00.

Perhaps the only happy and secure time to have been a reader of Langland's *Piers Plowman* was the period immediately following the publication of Skeat's heroic two-volume edition in 1886. The three versions had been clearly sorted out; A, B, and C were printed in a parallel-text format; the poet's biography was outlined with a fair amount of conviction; and generous annotations illuminated the myriad details of the poem's contents. Since then, critical security has had a rough time. Much of the scholarly energy of the last hundred years has been marshalled to undermine Skeat's confidence in the singleness of authorship, the number and dating of the poem's three distinct versions, the reliability of the manuscripts to preserve authentic readings, and most recently the sequence of the canonic versions—A, B, and then C, or B, C, and then A?

Not surprisingly, scholarly inquiry has tended to produce scholarly responses to these perplexities. We look down into the deep well of the past and see our own faces reflected at the bottom. Langland has been transformed into an Oxford-trained clergyman and *Piers* has become a theological text primarily concerned with the knotty issues of semi-Pelagianism, Cistercian spirituality, the Ockhamist skepticism of the *Moderni*, and so forth. However, it is worth remembering that one of the earliest documented owners of the poem, the London rector William Palmere, decided in 1400 to bequeath his copy to Agnes Eggesfeld, presumably a laywoman of his acquaintance. What was there about *Piers*,

we might ask, that would have qualified this woman to take possession—and act as a capable reader—of such a text if she was not schooled
in semi-Pelagianism, Cistercian spirituality, and the Ockhamist skepticism of the *Moderni?*

Tess Tavormina's *Marriage and Family in* Piers Plowman goes far toward answering this question by exposing in learned detail the homely
images in the poem, images that a fourteenth-century woman would
readily have understood—and understood with an immediacy and an
urgency that has eluded the many commentators (myself included) who
have busied themselves among the dustier shelves of the *PL.* Piers and
Will are both family men, after all. Nobody has ever accused Langland
of writing a sexy poem, but Tavormina demonstrates that *Piers* is in-
tensely concerned with nearly every aspect of matrimony at all levels of
society, from aristocrat to peasant, without ever losing sight of the fact
that the poet struggles with a single spiritual imperative: "How I may
saue my soule þat seint art yholden."

With great industry and erudition, she deploys a series of close readings of the most prominent passages, with special attention upon the
marriage of Meed (B.2–4), Wit's speech (B.9) and the Tree of Charity
(C.18). Constantly alert to revisions made from A to B and from B to
C, she offers scrupulous accounts of each passage in terms of social,
legal, and economic backgrounds. Then she advances to an interpretation in terms of the allegory, often moving back to the literal image to
demonstrate how the spiritual meaning bestows some comment, almost
invariably corrective, upon the contemporary practice of wedlock.
Though Langland is not always the clearest of thinkers, the distinction
between the literal and spiritual was already blurred. Marriage was not
only a biological and social necessity, after all; it was also a spiritual
state. It was the only sacrament instituted before the Fall and therefore
was understood as contributing ideally to the spiritual repair of
mankind. It was therefore the foundational expression of a "kindly
similitude," the natural likeness that medieval thinkers read as a sign
of deeper ontological relationships.

The marriage of Lady Meed affords a prime example in which, according to Tavormina's thorough analysis, the practice of forced betrothal serves as an allegory for the unholy union of Reward with
Falsehood. But the significance of financial corruption is then made to
turn back upon the original image, becoming a caustic critique of the

traffic in women. The problem arises, as it often does, when Langland loses his grip on the image while widening the scope of his moral satire. Contradictions creep in, especially as he revises from one version to the next, and the result is a deterioration of the literal sense for which Langland is justly notorious. Tavormina takes pains to chart the course of this deterioration, and for these exacting efforts she deserves high marks.

Described as a starting point for future considerations, "A Kind Familiarity" moves the discussion toward a stimulating conclusion by engaging with a wide range of issues relating to the human life-cycle: childhood, sibling affections, parental governance, and familial affection in old age. Some readers will find the discussion of "sexuality" (pp. 176–87) surprisingly innocent of the provocative initiatives by theorists such as Foucault and Sedgwick, though the former does make a brief cameo appearance on page 185, note 27. Indeed, the twenty-page bibliography does not include any of the names that might be expected—Judith Butler, Elaine Showalter, Toril Moi, or Julia Kristeva—not to mention any of the medievalists who have engaged in various forms of gender criticism, such as Carolyn Dinshaw, Elaine Tuttle Hansen, Susan Schibanoff, and Gail McMurray Gibson. Though Langland would seem no less alert than Chaucer to the economic dimension of matrimony and the ways in which the domestic power struggle enacted between husband and wife functions as a trope for larger social contests, feminist criticism has not shaped the course or predetermined the outcome of Tavormina's painstaking examination of marriage in *Piers*. Nobody will complain that this book is overtheorized.

Brewer's Piers Plowman Studies, under the series editor James Simpson, has produced an exceptionally handsome text with the extensive notes located where they belong, at the bottom of the page. The scholarly documentation is nothing short of awe-inspiring. It would be no exaggeration to say that the book has independent value for the exhaustive survey of Langland criticism and for the equally full citation of studies relating to medieval marriage and family life.

JOHN M. BOWERS
University of Nevada, Las Vegas

M. Teresa Tavormina and R. F. Yeager, eds. *The Endless Knot: Essays on Old and Middle English in Honor of Marie Borroff.* Cambridge: D. S. Brewer, 1995. Pp. ix, 252. $81.00.

This anthology of fifteen elegant essays by Marie Borroff's students and friends is an appropriate tribute upon the retirement of one of the fine medievalists of our time. Several of the essays acknowledge their origin in Professor Borroff's own scholarship or in remarks in her lectures or papers prepared for her seminars. The names of the participants bespeak the distinction of Professor Borroff's affinity. Would that we could all call upon the influence of a Yale to enhance our efforts with our students.

The essays that impress me most are Sherry Reames, "Artistry, Decorum, and Purpose in Three Middle English Retellings of the Cecelia Legend," and R. F. Yeager, "Ben Jonson's *English Grammar* and John Gower's Reception in the Seventeenth Century." Reames's essay, which grows out of her continuing study of the St. Cecelia legend cited in her footnotes, is the most impressive scholarly contribution in the volume in its familiarity with manuscripts, texts, and previous criticism. Her discussion of the significance for date and method of composition and possible political implications of the discovery of two sources for Chaucer's *Second Nun's Tale* is genuinely important.

Yeager's essay is interesting to me for the light it throws on the continuing standardization of English in the seventeenth century. I do not think that grammars and dictionaries had much effect on the process of standardization until the advent of general education for upward mobility in the eighteenth century, but Jonson's *Grammar* shows a prescience for cultivating English as a medium independent of Latin, and his more than 150 illustrative quotations from Gower, Chaucer, Lydgate, Cheke, Fox, Jewell, Norton, More, Lambert, Ascham, Lord Berners, and the King James Bible (p. 229) established the precedence of the bureaucratic/literary establishment that has controlled the standardization of the language since the fifteenth century.

Eric Stanley's introductory essay on the survival of dual pronouns in Old English is very interesting, although I wish that he had used the term "direct address" instead of "direct speech" for the locutions in which the dual forms survive. Melissa Furrow's comparison of the deferential uses of Latin tags by Gower and Langland with the derisive uses by Chaucer illustrates another reason for Chaucer's superior popularity. Teresa Tavormina has found fascinating associations between the names of John and Aleyn in Chaucer's *Miller's Tale* and John Aleyn, a clerk in Edward III's Chapel Royal. Solar Hall in Cambridge was King's Hall, a branch of the Chapel Royal to which choristers of the Chapel might be sent for further education. John Aleyn was a clerk of the Chapel Royal, a musician of some consequence, and, like Chaucer, employed in various errands for the King and Queen. In a motet possibly by John Aleyn there is a "Flos Oxonie miratur Nicholaus, qui vocatur Vade Famelico." This Nicholaus became Prior of St. Frideswide's Priory in Oxford, and Tavormina recounts several interesting events that occurred during his administration. She wishes that there were more certainty and significance about the names and associations, but the essay reveals again the extent to which Chaucer's poems were addressed to a familiar audience now lost to us.

Mary Carruthers has an interesting essay on the purpose of sense imagery in Prudentius and the *Pearl*. She has informative things to say about education in the era of memory. Elizabeth Kirk has a sensitive reading of healing mourning in *Pearl*. Warren Ginsberg discusses the arrangement of details in Chaucer's *Wife of Bath's Prologue and Tale* as conventionally "relational" rather than postmodernly "associational." John Burrow cites Chaucer's allusions to his "elvishness" as evidence of his reticence and abstraction. Traugott Lawler gives a very close reading of Conscience's dinner in *Piers Plowman* B.13.

Fred Robinson prints eight letters by the Anglo-Saxonist Elizabeth Elstob that point up the plight of an educated woman without resources in the eighteenth century. Elstob had to support herself as a governess, and her letters might well have been written by Jane Eyre. Ralph Hanna reclassifies the alliterative poems upon the basis of the frequency of "heteromorphic" lines. He finds alliteration the least distinctive feature of these poems (p. 50). Perhaps he should find a new name for this body of verse. Elizabeth Archibald analyzes Chaucer's *Man of Law's Tale* as a family romance, with many comparisons to other accused queens. Stephen Barney provides a study of the prosody of *Piers Plowman* that will be comprehensible only to those who share his identification of "lifts" and "dips." H. Marshall Leicester provides a very Yale in-group discussion of religious feeling in *The Canterbury Tales* that discerns piety only in *The Canon's Yeoman's Tale*. Anne Higgins re-presents Alicie de

Cestre, a washerwoman in the royal household, and searches again for some connection with Alceste in the *Prologue* to Chaucer's *Legend of Good Women*.

JOHN H. FISHER
Emeritus, University of Tennessee

THORLAC TURVILLE-PETRE. *England the Nation: Language, Literature, and National Identity, 1290–1340*. Oxford: Clarendon Press, 1996. Pp. vii, 241. $65.00.

In the course of a series of lectures on patriotism and nationalism delivered, with dark appropriateness, in Leiden in February, 1940, Johan Huizinga pointed out that it is "not difficult to demonstrate the untenability of the notion that national antitheses were alien to the Middle Ages and that national consciousness is a product of the modern period."[1] That the news has still not reached many of our nonmedievalist colleagues is unsurprising but unfortunate, for the Middle Ages provides unusually interesting evidence for the formation of the idea of the nation. Since at least the ninth century, medieval Europeans were possessed of (and at times by) a sense of what Susan Reynolds calls "regnal solidarity."[2] The elements that went toward creating such a feeling included a common territory, a common language, a sense of being an identifiable *gens* or *populus* (with a specific descent myth, shared *mores*, and a common history), habits of loyalty to a prestigious monarchy (regardless of attitudes toward the current king), and an awareness of other, easily identifiable *nationes* that could be defined, at least for a while, as different from one's own. To this basic substratum of national feeling were added the lineaments of statehood: a centralized government defined by a more or less extensive administrative, financial, and judicial bureaucracy; a common law; and some institutional means, such as a parliament, by which the *populus* or *communa*—the community

[1] "Patriotism and Nationalism in European History," in Johan Huizinga, *Men and Ideas: History, the Middle Ages, the Renaissance*, trans. James S. Holmes and Hans van Marle (New York: Meridian Books, 1959 [1940]), p. 117.
[2] Susan Reynolds, *Kingdoms and Communities in Western Europe, 900–1300* (Oxford: Clarendon Press, 1984), p. 262.

of the realm—could represent itself to its king and itself.[3] Finally, those in authority generated the symbolics of nationhood, which included national saints, festal celebrations of royal and national import, the identification of the king with his people, national sanctuaries, and hallowed heraldic and military symbols like France's oriflamme, lilies, and white cross.[4]

Given England's extraordinary history of large-scale migration, foreign conquest, and monarchical supersession, none of these processes was easily accomplished. That they were accomplished at all is an index of people's desire to belong to national and cultural communities, a tribalism we have reason these days to deplore but one that seems virtually coextensive with being human. In his very interesting book, Thorlac Turville-Petre throws light upon a small but crucial aspect of this process: the way in which writers in the fifty years before the Hundred Years' War identified themselves as speaking, in English, for and to a nation of which they were themselves a part. He is concerned above all with the role of language in the development of national consciousness, and he shows with learning and clarity both the way English writers constructed a unified nation in defiance of the facts and the strategies they used to exploit difference in the service of sameness.

Turville-Petre's archive is a collection of texts of which, for the most part, there are few to read and even fewer to love. These include Robert of Gloucester's *Chronicle* (completed after 1297); the *Short Metrical Chronicle* (various redactions between 1307 and 1340); Robert Mannyng of Brunne's *Handlyng Synne* (ca. 1332) and *Story of England* (completed in 1338); the *Cursor Mundi* (three versions, ca. 1300–1350); the *Anglo-Norman Brut* (compiled ca. 1272); the *South English Legendary* (some six redactions, ca. 1300–1400); the *Northern Homilies* (ca. 1300–1350); *Havelok the Dane*; and some of the texts found in four manuscripts: the Auchinleck manuscript (*Guy of Warwick, Sir Beues of Hamtoun, King Richard, Roland and Vernagu, Otuel a Kniȝt, Of Arthour and of Merlin, Þe King of Tars, Seynt Margaret, Seynt Katerine*, and *Þe Simonie*); Harley 913 (*Pers of Bermingham, Satire on the Townfolk, The Walling of*

---

[3] Bernard Guenée, *States and Rulers in Later Medieval Europe*, trans. Juliet Vale (Oxford: Basil Blackwell, 1985 [1971]), pp. 49–65; Joseph R. Strayer, *The Medieval Origins of the Modern State* (Princeton: Princeton University Press, 1970).

[4] See Colette Beaune, *The Birth of an Ideology: Myths and Symbols of Nation in Late-Medieval France*, trans. Susan Ross Huston, ed. Frederic L. Cheyette (Berkeley: University of California Press, 1991 [1985]).

*New Ross*, *The Land of Cockaygne*, *The Song on the Times*, and *Earth*); Add. 46919 (William Herebert's manuscript, ca. 1330); and Harley 2253 (compiled in the late 1330s).

With a deft and tactful hand, Turville-Petre shows how this unpromising material can reveal the way in which the contemporary criteria of nationhood—territory, people, and language—were met, despite the fact that all three were contradicted by the facts: the borders of the territory were contested by the Scots and Welsh, the "racial" makeup of the people was heterogenous, and until the last quarter of the fourteenth century the country was trilingual. But as Turville-Petre demonstrates, "What is significantly new in this period is the conviction that national sentiment is most properly expressed in English, and that the people of England, those who are the backbone of the nation, are 'þo þat in þus land won / Þat þe Latyn no Frankys cone'—'those who live in this country who know neither Latin or French'"—a citation from Mannyng's *Chronicle*.

After this introductory chapter, Turville-Petre shows that clerical authors like Mannyng (in both his *Chronicle* and *Handlyng Synne*), the compiler of *Cursor Mundi*, and the author of the *South English Legendary* constructed their audience as fellow members of the English nation. They are *lered*, their audience *lewed*, but *lewed* was not a stigma—rather, a word that "came to denote one who valued English in preference to Latin or French." And all of these works stress their relevance to a specifically English audience. He then turns to the vernacular chronicles written by Robert of Gloucester and Robert Mannyng, showing in detail the strategies by which they deal with both the "racial" heterogeneity of the people living in England and the unpleasant facts of Saxon treachery and Norman conquest. For myself, the most compelling part of this chapter is the discussion of the "Norman yoke" argument that surfaces repeatedly in these texts, and its affiliation with class tensions and an emergent myth of "native English freedom." It was neither the seventeenth nor the nineteenth century that invented this model of political formation, but the thirteenth; and its early emergence helps to explain some of the forms assumed by political tensions in the later fourteenth century, especially the complaints about Richard II's "Frenchified" court.

Chapter 4 discusses the Auchinleck manuscript, showing the relevance of its texts to contemporary conditions, its stress upon English heroes, and the way it promotes the ideology of the crusade as a specifically English enterprise. Next comes an account of *Havelok* to show that it expresses a Lincolnshire regionalism that defines itself in relation to the nation, and a fascinating account of the tortuous means by which the Anglo-Irish—as witnessed by MS Harley 913—sought to found their colonialist society upon a largely unreciprocated loyalty to the homeland while simultaneously coping with deep internal divisions and the constant threat of assimilation. The book concludes with an account of two trilingual manuscripts, William Herebert's collection in MS Add. 46919 and the famous MS Harley 2253. Turville-Petre's argument is that Herebert's careful sequestration of the three languages, and his use of each, reveal a lack of any linguistic nationalism, while the Harley compiler carefully organized his manuscript to set the formalized conventions of Anglo-Norman poetry against the emotionally direct and hence more powerful expressiveness of native writing. But the designations "French elegance and English plainness" are familiar national stereotypes: according to Froissart, when John of Gaunt was negotiating a truce with Philip of Burgundy in 1394 he worried that he would be hoodwinked because French was (in Lord Berners' translation) "full of subtyle wordes, and cloked perswacions . . . which Englysshemen use nat in their language, for their speche and entent is playne."[5] The plainspoken Englishman versus the linguistically wily Frenchman: this opposition probably has as much to do with the Common Market's *euro* as it does with Harley 2253. "Nationalism is a childhood disease," Albert Einstein is reported to have said, "the measles of mankind." But will we ever get over it?

In sum, this is a fine book, limiting itself to an argument capable of demonstration, full of instruction, unpretentious in its style, clear in its exposition, and blessedly free of the unpleasant moralism that seems to creep into most academic discussions these days, including this one.

One final comment. The price—$65.00—is an outrage. Is it not time for academic authors to forgo the prestige provided by venerable presses like Oxford and Cambridge in preference to less well known publishers who will make their books available at prices that their fellow academics will be willing to pay? Self-interest alone argues for it. If scholars

---

[5] For this citation, and further examples of linguistic stereotyping, see Lee Patterson, "Making Identities in Fifteenth-Century England: Henry V and John Lydgate," in *New Historical Literary Study: Essays on Reproducing Texts, Representing History*, eds. Jeffrey N. Cox and Larry J. Reynolds (Princeton: Princeton University Press, 1993), pp. 69–107, quotation from p. 83.

want their books read, and their university libraries to continue to acquire books, then they must resist the cachet of a label in favor of more colleague-friendly presses.

LEE PATTERSON
Yale University

RICHARD J. UTZ, ed. *Literary Nominalism and the Theory of Rereading Late Medieval Texts: A New Research Paradigm.* Medieval Studies, vol. 5. Lewiston, N.Y., and Queenston, Ontario: Edwin Mellen Press, 1995. Pp. 256. $90.00.

This volume is a collection of essays dealing with what the editor, Richard J. Utz, derivatively calls "a paradigm shift," after the phrase made famous, if not bromidic, by the contemporary philosopher Thomas S. Kuhn. As recent scholarship of the late medieval period has moved nominalism from the margins to the center of philosophical and theological attention, so literary criticism—in quasi-vassalage—has come to reexamine the literature of the period according to the dictates of the new paradigm. Although Chaucer has been the focus of most of these nominalist reconsiderations—even in this volume seven of the ten essays focus on Chaucerian themes—Professor Utz has editorially extended the paradigm to include three extra-Chaucerian essays: Jay Ruud's on Julian of Norwich's *Revelations of Divine Love*, which argues for a correspondence of concerns therein between mysticism and nominalism; Michael Randall's on Jean Molinet's *Chappellet des Dames*, which places the poem in a shifting fifteenth-century "episteme" from the realist/analogical to the nominalist/anti-analogical; and J. Stephen Russell's on *Sir Gawain and the Green Knight*, of which more anon.

In his own lead-off essay, Utz is extremely helpful to readers who are still trying to "negotiate" the shift, not only by bibliographically surveying its movers and shakers but also by cueing the uninitiated into understanding some of its presuppositions: that, for example, Augustinianism and Thomism had by Chaucer's time given way to nominalism as the philosophical or theological underpinning of literary texts. Despite the paucity of references to specific nominalists in the literature of the time, Utz argues that since fourteenth-century thinkers—like the Dominican Robert Holcot—"attempted to spread nominalist thought in a more popular mode among 'lewed' non-specialists" (p. 14), they could not but have influenced the *literati* as well. Even Chaucer's friend Ralph Strode, who since Israel Gollancz's well-known 1898 *DNB* article had been considered a Thomist, finds himself conscripted into the nominalist camp here and therefore serves as a convenient *point d'appui* for nominalist readings of Chaucer's works. Utz's arguments for Strode's nominalism are, by his own admission, not incontrovertible, but compelling nonetheless. Compelling too is his reading of the narrator's leap *to* faith in the Epilogue of *Troilus and Criseyde*, not merely as another illustration of the *contemptus mundi* tradition but as a narrative strategy that "resembles the academic fideism of [Chaucer's] coeval nominalist counterparts" (p. 19).

Notwithstanding his own preference for nominalist readings, Utz has sought to recruit a few recalcitrant voices in his symposium. Edgar Laird, for example, takes issue with those who would write off *The Knight's Tale* as a kind of Boethianism *manqué* by placing it in the tradition of universals signified by the "scientific ontology" of Albumasar, Grosseteste, and Wyclif. He thus supports Peggy Knapp's idea that *The Canterbury Tales* moves from the intelligible world of *The Knight's Tale* to the world of sensibles in *The Miller's Tale*. And John Micheal Crafton argues that by being drawn to *both* sides of the nominalist controversy, Chaucer consumes both his Augustinian and nominalist precursors. Having confronted realist themes in *The Book of the Duchess*, he abandons allegory for nominalism in the other dream visions, but is finally disillusioned by it. *Troilus and Criseyde* continues the dialectic and *The Canterbury Tales* perfects it.

Grover Furr enters the lists by considering the problem of future contingents—considered by many the dominant nominalist theme of Ricardian literature—in his article on *The Nun's Priest's Tale*. Although the Nun's Priest seems to be agreeing with Chauntecleer that what "God forwoot moost needes bee," Furr contends that the subsequent allusion to the great philosophical dispute over simple or conditional necessity (line 3236ff.) renders Chaucer's own position deliberately indeterminate and complicates the determinist/realist/allegorical readings that have conventionally described the intention of the tale.

In the best-written essay of the collection, Joseph Grossi agrees with John Micheal Crafton that Chaucer's art escapes the easy polarization of naive realism or radical nominalism, particularly when these categories have been used to subsume the Clerk's and Wife's narratives. Grossi argues that the Clerk's "tendentious storytelling" serves not only as Chaucer's *respondeo* to the Wife's nominalism but also as his critique of the "excessive naiveté of the Clerk's Realism" (p. 167). But beyond critiquing both the "atomistic particularity" of the one and the "ordered universality" of the other, Chaucer seems to be anagogically proposing in *The Clerk's Tale* that "the mysticality of ideal human conduct and worship" that responds to the "ahistorical divine mystery" hovering over "historical fortune" (p. 176) is common to both realism and nominalism.

Although Utz does, as he promises in his acknowledgments, include proponents of various epistemological stripes in his collection, he affords pride of place to strong nominalist readings by rounding off his choices with two essays on Chaucer's dream visions, traditionally the most fertile territory for nominalist "semiosis" in the canon. In the first, Kathryn L. Lynch examines the dream vision of *The House of Fame* from the labyrinthine perspective of terminist logic and convincingly concludes that the peculiar crush of singular details in the poem renders it unamenable to universals, that is, to any traditional cognitive process of abstraction from particulars. Accordingly, because the poem's main interest lies in what W. H. Auden has called the uncategorizable "eachness of things," Fame's palace, to cite one example among many, becomes "the domain of multiplicity" (p. 201) and Fame herself sports as many "eyen . . . as fetheres upon foules" and as many "eres / And tonges as on bestes heres" (line 1381ff.). The troublesome conclusion for Lynch, especially without benefit of closure in this poem, is that, in such a world of the Many, the One has been made inaccessible to the human mind.

Universals suffer a less worrisome and more gleeful kind of deconstruction in Hugo Keiper's essay—the finale of this collection—on *The Parliament of Fowls*. The question that the poem asks— "What is this thing called love?" (with my apologies to Cole Porter)—Keiper answers with a kind of polysyllabic *brio* that announces his postmodern partialities: e.g., "heteroglossic multiplicity of voices and points of view that are not hierarchized nor privileged in any way—which, in effect, could be termed a marked 'enfranchizement' of subjectivity and individual perspective" (p. 214). The only certainty in the poem, then, is that there is no fixed reality called love and that, in fact, the *only* reality is perspective, avian though it may be. This kind of relativism places Chaucer, at least in the dream poems, in a posture that is not only militantly nominalist but even postmodern, which to a critic like Keiper puts Geoffrey in quite agreeable company. Keiper concludes his essay with the hope that criticism may one day draw an ineradicable line between those texts that fall under the separate dominions of realism (like *Pearl*) and of nominalism (like Chaucer's dream poems).

When we observe nominalist critics like Hugo Keiper claiming a realist identity for a poem like *Pearl* and J. Stephen Russell claiming a nominalist identity for a poem like *Sir Gawain and the Green Knight* (can they both be right about two poems presumably written by the same poet?), we may suspect that the boundaries of the new paradigm are being stretched, if not violated. The danger with paradigm shifts, of course, is that the cartographers of the shift invariably overstate their case, as we saw with the Robertsonians who, despite their valuable contributions to Chaucer scholarship decades ago, seemed ready to anathematize anyone who did not see medieval literature through their Augustinian bifocals of *caritas* and *cupiditas*. The new paradigm occasionally overstates its case in bifocal ways too, as Crafton and Grossi intimate in their essays, by demarcating realist from nominalist literature according to oversimplified philosophical distinctions. Notwithstanding the valuable contributions of J. Stephen Russell to nominalist criticism elsewhere, for example, he stretches nominalist parameters to the breaking point in his essay on *Sir Gawain and the Green Knight* when he interprets Gawain's acceptance of the "magical" sash as an instance of misplaced confidence in philosophical realism. Russell's contention that "Arthur and then Gawain fail the test and lose the game *because they are realists*" (p. 61) endows the philosophical polarities of realism and nominalism with an antithetical thematic significance that fails, it seems to me, to surface credibly from the narrative. To assert, moreover, that Arthur's knight invested the merely literal thing, the sash, "with invisible essences or identities," similar to the way in which "the realist Thomas Aquinas saw phenomena as 'participating' in the identities of their essences" (p. 78), not only loads the narrative with an insupportable philosophical cargo but even does some violence to our understanding of the "isms" themselves. Certainly, any easy identification of Thomas with realism, as we observe happening in other essays as well, ignores the considerable differences that obtain between realism and *moderate* realism. To collapse moderate realism into realism and then place it in polar hostility to nominalism is simply to forget that for Aquinas, as for Ockham, knowledge begins with, and is utterly dependent on, the particular. It is true that universals for Aquinas exist *ante rem* in the mind of God, as they do not for Ockham, but human knowledge is no more privy to that transcendence for Aquinas than it is for Ockham. If we accepted only half of the Thomistic dictum—that essence precedes existence in the ontological order—we would be correct in calling Aquinas a realist and making our narrative judgments therefrom; but we must recall the other half—that existence precedes essence in the *psychological* order—and it is the psychological order with which epistemology and poetry are concerned. Accordingly, to read Gawain's acceptance of the magical sash as "the last best evidence of his philosophical realism" and then to leap to Aquinas's complicity in that identification is not only to claim too much for philosophy's role in *Gawain* but also to blur complex epistemological distinctions upon which that narrative criticism would seem to depend.

Another idea that I suspect will fail to inspire approbation among many readers of this volume is the one that assumes Boethius to be a "strong determinist" in the matter of future contingents [Furr on *The Nun's Priest's Tale*, p. 139]. Although Boethius in the *Consolation* agrees with the determinists that "all the things God sees as present will undoubtedly come to pass" because they do so according to the necessity of their natures, he nevertheless insists (in book 5) that human beings can will actions according to "the absolute freedom of their own natures." Therefore, when God foreknows human acts (and the word "*foreknow*" is itself an anthropomorphic concession to the human understanding of time which God's eternity transcends), He knows that they do *not* happen through necessity but as a consequence of their own freedom. This position is at some distance from a free-wheeling nominalist understanding of future contingents, but it is also equally distant from a determinism that denies freedom of the will.

All obligatory caveats aside, however, this volume does offer a competent balance of theory and practice about nominalist criticism of late medieval texts that will lead its catechumens and devotees, and perhaps even the merely curious, through the labyrinth of the new paradigm with a strong Ariadnean thread.

RODNEY DELASANTA
Providence College

WILLIAM VANTUONO, ed. and trans. Pearl: *An Edition with Verse Translation*. Notre Dame and London: University of Notre Dame Press, 1995. Pp. xxxiv, 255. $29.95 cloth, $15.95 paper.

Reinforcing his position as the preeminent contemporary editor of the *Pearl* poems, Vantuono now furnishes readers with an edition of *Pearl* as well as a verse translation on pages facing the text. Employing a conservative Middle English text (twelve emendations) reproduced from volume 1 of *The Pearl Poems: An Omnibus Edition* (1984), Vantuono offers a carefully framed translation, one arranged to reflect the original's complex web of refrain words and concatenations. Explanatory notes—ranging from glosses for individual words to extensive textual commentary—are supplied at the bottom of each page of this edition. Such notes, Vantuono contends, serve as guideposts to "the literal sense of the Middle English vocabulary" (p. xxxii) whenever he coins translations that alter the original words' denotations. As Vantuono freely admits, however, the intricate patterning of *Pearl*'s word play could not always be echoed in the translation, notably in his rendition of the link-word *date* (p. xxxiii).

Apart from these features—the true heart of his book—the editor-translator provides a fully documented introduction (pp. xiii–xxx); extensive variorum commentary (pp. 95–166) that appraises *Pearl* scholarship "through the early 1990s" (p. xi); detailed appendices (pp. 167–80) on *Pearl*'s verse form, dialect, language, and sources; several bibliographies (pp. 185–215); and a full glossary (pp. 217–55).

The introduction, a painstaking review of the progress of *Pearl* criticism, charts the history of the British Library's Cotton Nero manuscript as well as its dating, dialect, and illustrations. After discussing the ordering of the four Cotton Nero works, Vantuono explores the thicket of scholarly argument (Huchown or Ralph Strode up to John de Mascy of Sale) about the *Pearl*-poet's identity and audience. Then, highlighting the multivalent nature of *Pearl*—at once a fusion of elegy, *consolatio*, dream allegory, and theological tract (p. xxiii)—the editor justly claims that *Pearl* employs "no single theme, and yet the multiple concepts merge and unify in one great vision" (p. xxiv). Vantuono's analysis concludes with an examination of both the poem's "triple-three structure" (p. xxvii) and symmetrical design, particularly the import of the vineyard parable, numerical patterns, and circularity.

The elaborate variorum commentary, however, enriches the critical terrain cultivated in the introduction. Keyed to individual words, lines, or passages, such annotations unearth the conventions (rhetorical, lapidary, *amour courtois*), motifs (*noli me tangere*), and imagery (vegetative, apocalyptic, liturgical) at the core of *Pearl*. Furthermore, the extensive commentary section discloses the critical history of glosses for key words in *Pearl*, identifies important symbols (crowns, flowers, animals, glass, water), and unveils the ties between diction in *Pearl* and similar phraseology in the other Cotton Nero works.

Vantuono's attention to scholarly comprehensiveness is reflected further in his appendices. The most illuminating appendix ("Poetic Mastery in *Pearl*"), for instance, reveals the crucial roles of 101 and $12 \times 12$ in the poem's structure, discusses the work's musical qualities, and elucidates *Pearl*'s refrains, link words, and concatenations. Of particular interest to students and scholars of *Pearl* is the editor's classification of medieval verse patterns, an exercise substantiated by scansions of individual lines from *Pearl*. Demonstrating clearly that *Pearl* is rooted in the Old English syllabic tradition, Vantuono then argues (p. 174) that *Pearl*'s rhythms are analogous to those found in the other Cotton Nero poems. The remaining appendices, however, focus on dialect, language, and the numerous source materials (literary, artistic, liturgical, and Vulgate) for *Pearl*.

The editor's comprehensive bibliographies represent the scholarly moorings for his introduction, variorum commentary, and appendices. Targeting *Pearl* criticism through the early 1990s, presumably 1991 or 1992, Vantuono supplies 425 entries in the first bibliography. Inasmuch as Vantuono's primary goal is to produce the first *Pearl* edition combining a sound Middle English text, graceful verse translation, and thorough scholarly commentary, bibliographical lacunae are unavoidable. Accordingly, a number of items should be appended to his first bibliography. Such references include Sarah Stanbury's article (*ChauR*, 1987); Paul F. Reichardt's article (*Manuscripta*, 1992); R. A. Shoaf's article (*TSLL*, 1990); Michael J. Bennett's *Community, Class and Careerism* (1983), especially pp. 192–235; Ann W. Astell's *The Song of Songs in the Middle Ages* (1990), particularly pp. 119–35; Eugene Vance's essay in *Poetics*, ed. Boitani and Torti (1991), pp. 131–47; and A. C. Spearing's *Readings in Medieval Poetry* (1987), notably pp. 195–215. Vantuono's second bibliography—consisting of eighty-eight entries— includes helpful reference tools, especially Bibles, concordances, dictionaries, grammar texts, ancillary texts and translations, and "Yearly Bibliographies and Other Bibliographical Listings."

Finally, the editor's superb glossary provides relevant information "for every form of every word" (p. 217) in *Pearl*. Such data is anchored further by the "literal meanings [of words], line numbers, grammatical elements, and etymological derivatives [*OED, MED*]" (p. xi).

In general, Vantuono succeeds admirably in his editorial purposes, for he has crafted a book suitable for students and scholars alike. Such an edition, then, both illuminates *Pearl*'s rich vision world and complements Vantuono's earlier work, *Sir Gawain and the Green Knight: A Dual-Language Version* (1991).

ROBERT J. BLANCH
Northeastern University

ANGELA JANE WEISL. *Conquering the Reign of Femeny: Gender and Genre in Chaucer's Romance.* Chaucer Studies, vol. 22. Cambridge: D. S. Brewer, 1995. Pp. ix, 133. $53.00.

This provocative little volume begins with an image from Italo Calvino's *Invisible Cities* in which several men simultaneously dream of a long-haired naked woman vanishing through an unknown city into the darkness. Failing to locate the city, they construct one of their own, with mazes to trap the vision should she reappear. This image, Angela Jane Weisl tells us, embodies the romance genre in that its essential content of male desire, the action of pursuing the woman, and the method of execution through entrapping labyrinths recapitulate the romance. It is a haunting metaphor.

Insights in the twenty-page introduction, which this reader found more evocative than the somewhat repetitive readings of four individual romances, are quite creative. Weisl's thesis is that Chaucer pushes "boundaries [the glass ceiling that defines roles, positions, and possibilities], testing the genre's limits . . . to show both its confines and its potential" (p. 3). Since romance defines the nature and behavior of heroines (who cannot be ugly Loathly Ladies, self-motivated, independent young Alisons, or gregariously assertive old Alisons), it contains them. Feminine confinement, such as that of the coerced, unwilling Emelye, then, symbolizes the genre. In upsetting her gendered role, Criseyde flaunts tradition, upsetting both the genre and her tale, which can no longer support a standard romance ending.

Although these ideas seem intriguing, many romances defy the "confined-woman" schema—*Parzival, Amis and Amiloun* (with one very dominant Belisaunt and another domineering wife), *Sir Gawain and the Green Knight* (whose two women wield much power), and the alliterative *Morte Arthure* (with no primary woman) come to mind. Eventually Weisl acknowledges exceptions, that "many poems that are generally . . . lays or romances are not really about romantic love at all" (p. 8), seemingly contradicting herself. Classifying is hazardous, as Susan Crane has noted, but perhaps limiting the thesis to certain types of romances might have ameliorated the problem. Several evocative issues tease us, but remain unclarified. How, for example, is Boccaccio a source for Chaucer's methodology as much as for plot? How do Chaucer's romances, transformed into self-referential narratives, tell us as much about narrative as they do about love? Some claims seem controversial or contradictory. For example, Weisl states, "Chaucer, strikingly, cannot end two of his romances" (p. 5), discounting those who insist *The Squire's Tale* and *Tale of Sir Thopas* are in fact ended precisely at the right, intended moment. Since some romances contain didactic elements, the author posits a reverse mimesis—life imitating art. But from Horace or before, the ends of poetry have always been to teach and entertain, so how does romance differ? Certain statements appear self-evident or unremarkable, such as Chaucer's attitude to romance: "The genre is problematic for him; he continually challenges, expands, and tests the limits of the romance by shifting its contexts and altering its conventions" (p. 2). Does his policy differ for other genres, equally manipulated for the new creative spark they elicit? Is not his genius that he regularly transgresses, defies boundaries, violates generic expectations, and to successful, not deconstructive, ends?

Weisl believes that although women are necessary to the genre, their space and roles are restricted. Yet she admits: "The woman's role can be greater than [inspiring and perfecting the male hero], however. Her adventures can form a substantial part of the narratives and . . . [quoting Schmidt and Jacobs] 'determine the progress of the hero but also affect the tone and colouring of the whole work'" (p. 16). These adventures appear to defy restriction and break through genre conventions, which Weisl elsewhere implies is impossible. Further, she argues: "The romance is also, finally, a male genre, since the knight's 'getting' of the woman then requires her submission and rescinding of her power over him" (p. 35). Do all women submit? Has Laudine rescinded or the Loathly Lady submitted? Is not the romance genre traditionally the most female-gendered of them all—conceived, commissioned, purchased, read, and promulgated by women? Do women not play the greatest role within romance, controlling the narrative, obtaining their ends, satisfying their needs, and finally claiming happiness? I do not posit total autonomy for women, given the cultural milieu, but certainly more impact than Weisl concedes. If the genre is so oppressive and constraining, why have women created it in this model, accepted, imbibed, supported, and rehearsed it? Are they masochistic, or oblivious?

Further, Calvino's city, and hence romance, is said to be "built around the woman who is both the narrative's center and confined by it, and who by her objectification is inherently marginal to it" (p. 2). How can a narrative center be marginal, regardless of objectification? Nevertheless, the idea of generic boundaries for some classes of romances is intriguing, as are notions of self-referentiality (which might be expanded), the move from epic community or lyric solipsism to romance individuality, the power relationships of romance men and women, and interior and exterior spaces in the genre. The foregoing fragmented description derives from the introduction, itself rich with ideas, but not logically inevitable in its presentation.

Chapter 1, "Walls with Windows and Rooms with Doors: The Gendered and Genred Spaces of *Troilus and Criseyde*," opposes public and private, epic and romance, masculinization and feminization. Its thesis is that "Criseyde and the spaces she inhabits represent both the romance genre and its inherent feminization, in opposition to the masculine, epic world of the war that threatens it . . . [as well as] the romance's coercion of the feminine; within the poem, these 'feminized' spaces are questioned; they contain the woman but do not protect her, for these spaces are ultimately male-centered and male-defined" (p. 21). Does the author mean "questionable" here? Weisl sees Chaucer employing the usual amatory topos of female power over men, but in the *Troilus*, he "exposes these romance topoi to show just how coercive they are. These seemingly powerful [female] positions are smoke screens for the men who control both the women and the text" (p. 24). Undoubtedly the men of this romance are the power wielders. But Criseyde is not without power over Troilus. And I question certain statements that seem to draw unwarranted conclusions from the text. For instance, "Criseyde is symbolically raped by the eagle in her dream and is threatened by the possibility of actual rape in the Greek camp" (p. 26). The actual lines describing the eagle read:

> . . . an egle, fethered whit as bon,
> Under hire brest his longe clawes sette,
> And out hire herte he rente, and that anon,
> And dide his herte into hire brest to gon—
> Of which she nought agroos, ne nothyng smerte—
> And forth he fleigh, with herte left for herte. (2.926–31)

Without Weisl's gloss as "a violent sexual assault" (p. 33), I would have seen this exchange of hearts as a symbol of romantic love, heralded by the nightingale who sings her to sleep, especially given the narrator's claim that she felt neither fright nor pain. Such an emotional state— lacking affect—makes a rape, even a symbolic one, rather dubious. The author comments that because "the violence of the dream goes unquestioned [Is it really there to question?] and is thematically linked to the consummation scene which follows" (p. 34 n. 12) [suggesting a love act rather than a rape?], "structures which make romance a romance" (p. 33) are overturned. Notably, "Criseyde sings a lay of love, her alba after the consummation" (p. 34), which appears to undercut the notion of her brutalization. My own reading here finds the tone amatory, and the genre typically romance. Similarly, at the Greek camp, "Ful sorwfully [Criseyde] sighte, and seyde Allas! . . . And forth she rit ful sorwfully a pas" (5.58, 61). Having searched in vain for any threat or suggestion of violation, I feel a stronger sense of loss than of fear for her safety in Criseyde's words and gestures. This does not deny her social subordination and vulnerability—clearly a cliché by now. A reminder of her habitation in domestic, interior, protected spaces such as closets or gardens, and the public intrusion into them, is apt. Weisl's metaphor of walls is also legitimate. But I would qualify this statement: "The inner city that is Criseyde is invaded by male power and male political agendae" (p. 28). Certainly male power. But is it male political agenda (don't the males have a war to fight?) or sexual desire? Some would perhaps find the sexual also "political."

Yet another dubious statement bears consideration: "Just as Pandarus intrudes on the feminine world, so, too, does romance, coopting it and making it a part of a masculine system of desire" (p. 37). How does the feminine romance "coopt" the feminine world? And surely they are in two metaphysical planes of reality. Similarly, saying "Pandarus . . . can create the spaces of romance, but . . . subverts them by entering them himself" (p. 38) precludes plot movement. Further, does not the feminine world contain a system of desire, given that women have both sexual, economic, and political desire quite as much as men? Finally, one questions this reasoning: "For women, the romance is inescapable; its patterns are finally fixed to require their ultimate sacrifice of the autonomy that Criseyde knows she will abandon by loving Troilus" (pp. 40–41). Has not her sin been seen as *keeping* that autonomy, and abandoning *Troilus*?

Weisl's structural evaluation of the romance is useful: "In the first three books of the poem, the movement is inward toward the enclosed love space; in the last two it moves outward toward the Greek camp and the eighth sphere" (p. 44). Equally sound is the comment that "Diomede's directness suggests that they are in a different generic world from that of the poem's first three books; this is no longer the space of romance. There is no assumption of female power here. . . . Diomede's courtship, so nasty, brutish, and short, becomes an ironic parody of courtly romance" (p. 45). I take issue with the conclusion, however, which contends, "It requires the reader to question whether the romance version was, in fact, any different" (p. 45). Perhaps it shows precisely the great difference between the courtship and romance.

Chapter 2, "Like Father, Unlike Son: Order, Control, and Woman's Position in the *Knight's* and *Squire's Tale*," posits: "For the Knight, romance is a dark, intrusive force that must be controlled; left alone, its private desires would wreak havoc on the public world. The Squire takes a brighter view of the romance: he is charmed by its courtly elegance and gentle subject matter" (p. 51). Weisl claims that Palamon and Arcite's confrontation symbolizes the genre conflict: ". . . the masculine world of the epic is subservient to the imperatives of love inherent to the romance" (p. 56). Erotic competition between, or conjoining of two men over a woman "makes primary the relationship between these men, eroticizing it as well" (p. 57). The epic world cannot accommodate the eroticized, ideal woman, however. "Yet Emilye fares no better in the romance world where she is objectified, unaware of the competition for her favors; in neither world is her will very important" (p. 59). Weisl rightly notes that Theseus begins in an epic mode, and returns to it, imposing a political, nonerotic marriage on Emelye and Palamon. "Emily the Amazon, whose voice enters the tale only once, resists the romance, but finally, the romance conquers her. In a contest of determination, the genre wins" (p. 61). This kind of personification is a bit puzzling: is it not the creating Knight, standing in front of Chaucer, who orchestrates, rather than the genre? The tale *might* have ended differently without losing its generic characteristics had the teller so chosen.

Contrasts between the tales, order vs. chaos, historical setting vs. exotic fantasy, unified vs. episodic, and controlled vs. uncontrolled language reveal degrees of competence. Weisl finds the Squire's Canacee playing the "wrong role"—in an "authoritative, creative position of viewer . . . discovering the truth of romance femininity and the romance plot" (p. 64), and finally building a mewe to exclude men. But perhaps this is only the "wrong role" if one holds such a conception of romance boundaries as the author has posited. However, Weisl rightly shows Chaucer inverting the stereotypical romance icons of bird, secret, private language, magic ring, May garden, beautiful woman: the discourse is between two women, Canacee and the female falcon, lamenting love's dangers; it parallels the discourse between two men, Palamon and Arcite, lamenting love's absence. "In the *Knight's Tale*, the romance is created between Palamon and Arcite without Emelye; in the *Squire's Tale*, the romance is undone by Canacee and the falcon with no men present" (p. 64). I agree that the mewe is a place where women are separate from men and erotic love, but I do not see why "it physically manifests her inability to enter the standard romance plot" (p. 67), which plot presumably Weisl would not accept. If the genre is so oppressive to women, I should think deviation from it would be heralded as victory. Rather, the author maintains, "By having Canacee fail to fulfill her role as the compliant heroine the way Emilye does . . . Chaucer arrests the romance's narrative movement" (p. 68). Could he not choose to further it in another fashion? Perhaps the narrative movement *is* complete. Does Canacee really "remain the cause of the tale's stasis, of its inability to go," or is she the means to break generic convention, free heroines from a single course of action, and establish a new, open paradigm? The chapter ends with the Franklin's courtly interruption, "telling a far more successful example of the genre himself, an example that suggests the value of a different kind to [*sic*] story and a different kind of teller" (p. 69). Unfortunately the expectation raised to hear of his tale next is unfulfilled.

Chapter 3, "The Absent Woman: Generic Stasis in the *Tale of Sir Thopas*," claims, "While the romance must both centralize and marginalize woman, while she must be its center and its ultimate goal despite being denied any subjectivity (and even while being derided), it cannot work as a narrative without her. By making *Sir Thopas* fail to go, Chaucer elucidates the inevitable connection of gender and genre in the romance" (p. 71). Thus lacking a woman, the romance makes power and gender matters of size instead. Similarly lacking a woman, this chapter spends four of its fourteen pages summarizing previous critical opinion. Yet the role Weisl assigns to romance women is distinctly major: "The woman stands for the narrative itself[,] . . . the source of the narrative even when she is not actually in it[,] . . . either the motivator or its ultimate goal, without whom there is no story[,] . . . the motivating force in much of courtly romance" (p. 75). It is difficult to perceive this role as marginal.

Weisl, pointing to the role of the female replacement, notes that "the entire story is affected with giantism, a narrative Sir Oliphant" (p. 80). She argues that lacking a female to propel the action "is the means by which Chaucer comments on the feminization of the genre. . . . [T]he gap created between the essential feminization of romance and the lack of women in the tale informs the poem to the point that Thopas, ostensibly the venturesome hero, begins to become domesticated by his genre. Without a lady to serve, he starts to sound distinctly like one" (p. 81). But the androgynous, presexual child has difficulty in "romance's sexualized context . . . [for] he is the immature undeveloped male whose fantasy lover is equally unfeminine in any 'real' sense" (p. 81). These insights into Chaucer's convention-breaking enhance our appreciation of this elusive poem. Linking Thopas with the "sexually ambiguous Pardoner" because he finds a masculine giant instead of a lady elf-queen seems speculative, however. Weisl maintains that "it is the romance's duty to assert heterosexual love and desire; by removing the lady and making the hero sexually ambiguous, the genre fails in its task" (p. 82). Is not Weisl imposing the designations and boundaries on the genre which she claims are its characteristics? Her statement that "Thopas is a narcissus in search of the unobtainable—himself" (p. 83) sounds provocative, but lacks evidence or explanation. The author concludes that "romance can marginalize the woman, but it cannot work once she is taken out of the story entirely. Finally, the woman stands for the romance text itself, the focus and locus of masculine narrative desire" (p. 84).

Chapter 4, "Public Authority and Private Power in Chaucer's Two Breton Lais," notes that lais accept powerful, often female otherworld figures. Here, "interior space [unlike exterior space of masculine power such as epics] becomes the locus for female concerns and feminine desire . . . [where] women hold a kind of power" (p. 87). However, "masculine fear of feminine desire, subjectivity and power" consigns women to locked towers or confined psychic situations. In *The Wife of Bath's Tale*, Alison deconstructs "the values of knighthood, exposing masculine violence and showing its implications for women" (p. 95). Despite Arthur's masculine court and the friar's male world, "women demand their own kind of justice" (p. 97) and retain their authority. But the claim that the Loathly Lady "must speak 'like a man' to make [the knight] stop thinking 'like a man'" (p. 101) is unclear; I should think the opposite true.

Weisl believes "the Wife's privacy . . . is the only real locus of power she has. . . . By showing that this privacy is unsustainable . . . Chaucer uses the *Wife of Bath's Tale* to expose a feminine problem without offering a feminist solution" (pp. 103, 104). Ironically I find her power in her very self-revelation, and see no "feminine problem." Although much of this tale's discussion is derivative, the author interestingly notes the traditional inversion: a male damsel-in-distress finds a female rescuer, albeit an ugly one. Weisl concludes that "ideologies, then, also inform an author's choice of genre; the lai can reflect its author's ideologies of genre—and the genre's own irrepressible ideologies" (p. 92); this seems to undermine the point of her book—that gender controls genre, that "Chaucer's complex set of responses to the [romance] genre revolve around gender" (p. 2). Weisl suggests that *"The Franklin's Tale*, in its analysis of *gentilesse*, shows . . . the extent to which romance itself is a male game that disenfranchises its female characters . . . ultimately about the way men's treatment of women forces them into subservience" (p. 105). Yet, according to Weisl, the Franklin "takes literally the courtly topos of the superior, powerful woman and tries to impose it, out of context, on marriage, which traditionally demands a different hierarchy altogether" (p. 106). Similarly, "By reversing the standard order of the lai, which should end in marriage . . . the Franklin ends up with a romance that undercuts itself, making its own terms impossible" (p. 106). Since Weisl decries female confinement by generic boundaries, one would assume such independent boundary-breaking would be heralded instead of disparaged. It is unclear why "the conventions of the romance subvert the radical reformulations that both

Dorigen and the Franklin attempt to create" (p. 106). The author rightly sees Dorigen transformed from powerful private romance heroine to powerless public wife, a commodity of male exchange. She concludes: "The genre cannot accommodate women's sovereignty except in the very private context of love service; once tested outside the romance garden, it collapses and patriarchal authority reasserts itself. . . . The genre is finally about men and their desires."

Weisl's epilogue finds that subtly undercut happy endings mark the romances. *The Knight's Tale* marriage was not desired by the bride, the Wife's old woman accedes to her husband's desires, the *Franklin's Tale* marriage has been refigured without equality, and no romance resolution ends *Troilus and Criseyde*. The author concludes, "By problematizing, rather than solving, the initial questions they pose, these endings leave the reader dissatisfied [because of] Chaucer's use of the romance as a gendered genre. . . . Romance, as a genre, despite its room for expansion and examination, ultimately constrains its characters and defines the worlds in which they live while at the same time being constrained by them" (p. 120). I find that very problematizing to be a virtue, adding dimension and complexity to Chaucer's work.

This volume successfully resists most distracting jargon, preferring metaphysical realities, and is willing to be speculative and creative. Its drawback is that some claims cannot be tied down to the Chaucerian texts it purports to interpret, remaining nebulous speculations without concrete evidence. Too often one feels the author is fitting the text to the thesis rather than vice versa. Metaphors and images, especially of the romance genre (e.g., "the love affair becomes a spatial representation of the genre" [p. 42]), take on a life of their own, with little connection to the texts. Nonetheless, many suggestions possess merit, whether or not they can be taken to the extent Weisl contends. Rarely does she succumb to the pitfall of some overzealous promoters whose agendas exceed the provable or credible, hence undercutting their arguments. Usually Weisl is clear, if repetitive. Metaphors such as this liven the text: "Romance is a kind of literary wait at the airport for a lover; while the end result is inevitable, the delay of his or her arrival creates anxiety and anticipation, the visceral excitement inherent in such situations, particularly when the guest is the last person off the plane" (p. 5).

Given the number of people who have read the text (noted in the acknowledgments), as well as final editors, its numerous grammatical infelicities are surprising: at least a dozen misspellings, unnecessary apostrophes, the repeated "different than" instead of "different from" and "like" instead of "such as" constructions, omission of words or accent marks, misquotation of three titles and three dates ("19483" twice and "19647"), and ambiguous sentences. Some stylistic infelicities could be avoided, as could the use of semicolons before dependent clauses. Though minor, these forty-two solecisms in a volume of 130 pages appear excessive. They become intrusive because of their frequency and the confusion they generate, seriously detracting from the work's credibility. A three-page index fails to include much of what readers might want to locate, and although criticism to support these ideas is moderately comprehensive, one searches in vain for the edition of *Sir Degaré* used for three quotations. Careful proofreading would have prevented a number of errors that distract from the issues and undercut the larger argument. Surprisingly, colloquialisms such as "buttinski," "rattle its cage," "coopted," and "plays fast and loose" have slipped past this British press.

Notwithstanding these technical drawbacks, this slim little volume offers fresh, insightful perspectives and challenging assessments that open up Chaucer's four romances in new ways. Weisl's exploration considerably contributes to our understanding of medieval gender attitudes and the romance genre as well as Chaucerian romance texts.

JEAN E. JOST
Bradley University

# BOOKS RECEIVED

Aers, David, and Lynn Staley. *The Powers of the Holy: Religion, Politics, and Gender in Late Medieval English Culture*. University Park: Pennsylvania State University Press, 1996. Pp. 310. $45.00 cloth, $19.95 paper.

Andersson, Theodore M., and Stephen A. Barney, eds. *Contradictions: From* Beowulf *to* Chaucer. *Selected Studies of Larry D. Benson*. Brookfield, Vt.: Ashgate Publishing, 1995. Pp. xxiii, 322. $84.95.

Astell, Ann W. *Chaucer and the Universe of Learning*. Ithaca, N.Y., and London: Cornell University Press, 1996. Pp. xvi, 254. $35.00.

Barratt, Alexandra, ed. *The Seven Psalms: A Commentary on the Penitential Psalms Translated from French into English by Dame Eleanor Hull*. Early English Text Society, vol. 307. Oxford: Oxford University Press, 1995. Pp. xl, 326. $65.00.

Batt, Catherine, ed. *Essays on Thomas Hoccleve*. Westfield Publications in Medieval Studies, vol. 10. London: Centre for Medieval and Renaissance Studies, Queen Mary and Westfield College, University of London; Turnhout: Brepols, 1996. Pp. ix, 130. N.p.

Besserman, Lawrence, ed. *The Challenge of Periodization: Old Paradigms and New Perspectives*. Garland Reference Library of the Humanities, vol. 1938. New York and London: Garland Publishing, 1996. Pp. xxiv, 244. $46.00.

Boffey, Julia, and Pamela King, eds. *London and Europe in the Later Middle Ages*. Westfield Publications in Medieval Studies, vol. 9. London: Centre for Medieval and Renaissance Studies, Queen Mary and Westfield College, University of London, 1995. Pp. vi, 258. N.p.

Brewer, Derek, ed. *Medieval Comic Tales*. 2d ed. Cambridge: D. S. Brewer, 1996. Pp. xxxiv, 190. £35.00.

Burrow, J. A., and Thorlac Turville-Petre. *A Book of Middle English.* 2d ed. Oxford: Blackwell, 1996. Pp. xii, 373. $59.95 cloth, $22.95 paper.

Cazelles, Brigitte. *The Unholy Grail: A Social Reading of Chrétien de Troyes's* Conte du Graal. *Figurae*: Reading Medieval Culture Series. Stanford: Stanford University Press, 1996. Pp. 325. $42.50.

Chance, Jane, ed. *Gender and Text in the Later Middle Ages.* Gainesville: University Press of Florida, 1996. Pp. xv, 342. $59.95.

Coleman, Joyce. *Public Reading and the Reading Public in Late Medieval England and France.* Cambridge Studies in Medieval Literature, vol. 26. Cambridge: Cambridge University Press, 1996. Pp. xiv, 250. $59.95.

Cooper, Helen. *The Canterbury Tales.* Oxford Guides to Chaucer. 2d ed. Oxford: Oxford University Press, 1996. Pp. xii, 439. $22.00 paper.

Copeland, Rita, ed. *Criticism and Dissent in the Middle Ages.* Cambridge: Cambridge University Press, 1996. Pp. xii, 332. $59.95.

Cowgill, Kent. *The Cranberry Trail: Misfits, Dreamers and Drifters on the Heartland Road.* Rochester, Minn.: Lone Oak Press, 1995. Pp. 208. $11.95 paper.

Dante Alighieri. *De Vulgari Eloquentia.* Ed. and trans. Steven Botterill. Cambridge Medieval Classics, vol. 5. Cambridge: Cambridge University Press, 1996. Pp. xxix, 105. $59.95.

———. *Inferno: The Divine Comedy*, vol. 1. Ed. and trans. Robert M. Durling. Intro. and notes by Ronald L. Martinez and Robert Durling. Oxford and New York: Oxford University Press, 1996. Pp. xviii, 654. $39.95.

———. *Monarchia.* Ed. and trans. Prue Shaw. Cambridge Medieval Classics, vol. 4. Cambridge: Cambridge University Press, 1995. Pp. xlvi, 186. $54.95.

Davis, Craig R. Beowulf *and the Demise of Germanic Legend in England.* Albert Bates Lord Studies in Oral Tradition, vol. 17. New York and London: Garland Publishing, 1996. Pp. xvii, 237. $36.00.

Dean, James M., ed. *Medieval English Political Writings.* TEAMS: Middle English Texts Series. Kalamazoo, Mich.: Medieval Institute Publications, 1996. Pp. xxv, 270. $14.00 paper.

Earp, Lawrence. *Guillaume de Machaut: A Guide to Research.* Garland Composer Resource Manuals Series. New York and London: Garland Publishing, 1995. Pp. xix, 669. $95.00.

Eckhardt, Caroline D., ed. Castleford's Chronicle *or* The Boke of Brut. 2 vols. Early English Text Society, vol. 305. Oxford: Oxford University Press, 1995. Pp. xvi, 1065. $125.00.

Edwards, Huw M. *Dafydd ap Gwilym: Influences and Analogues.* Oxford Modern Languages and Literature Monographs. Oxford: Clarendon Press, 1996. Pp. xiii, 300. $70.00.

Farrell, Thomas J., ed. *Bakhtin and Medieval Voices.* Gainesville: University of Florida Press, 1995. Pp. xi, 240. $49.95.

Ferster, Judith. *Fictions of Advice: The Literature and Politics of Counsel in Late Medieval England.* Middle Ages Series. Philadelphia: University of Pennsylvania Press, 1996. Pp. xii, 216. $32.95.

Findlen, Paula. *Possessing Nature: Museums, Collecting, and Scientific Culture in Early Modern Italy.* Studies on the History of Society and Culture, vol. 20. Berkeley, Los Angeles, and London: University of California Press, 1994. Pp. xvii, 449. $18.95 paper.

Flores, Nona C., ed. *Animals in the Middle Ages: A Book of Essays.* Garland Medieval Casebooks, vol. 13. New York and London: Garland Publishing, 1996. Pp. xvii, 206. $31.00.

Fowler, David C. *The Life and Times of John Trevisa, Medieval Scholar.* Seattle and London: University of Washington Press, 1995. Pp. xiv, 281. $40.00.

Gradon, Pamela, and Anne Hudson, eds. *English Wycliffite Sermons*, vol. 4. Oxford: Clarendon Press, 1996. Pp. xv, 333. $110.00.

————. *English Wycliffite Sermons*, vol. 5. Oxford: Clarendon Press, 1996. Pp. xiii, 443. $125.00.

Grimbert, Joan Tasker, ed. *Tristan and Isolde: A Casebook*. Arthurian Characters and Themes, vol. 2. New York and London: Garland Publishing, 1996. Pp. cxviii, 520. $60.00.

Hanawalt, Barbara A., and David Wallace, eds. *Bodies and Disciplines: Intersections of Literature and History in Fifteenth-Century England*. Medieval Cultures Series, vol. 9. Minneapolis and London: University of Minnesota Press, 1996. Pp. xii, 242. $19.95 paper.

Hanna, Ralph, III. *Pursuing History: Middle English Manuscripts and Their Texts. Figurae*: Reading Medieval Culture Series. Stanford: Stanford University Press, 1996. Pp. x, 362. $39.50.

Hart, Jonathan, ed. *Reading the Renaissance: Culture, Poetics, and Drama*. Garland Studies in the Renaissance, vol. 4. New York and London: Garland Publishing, 1996. Pp. 290. $44.00.

Hassig, Debra. *Medieval Bestiaries: Text, Image, Ideology*. Res Monographs on Anthropology and Aesthetics. Cambridge: Cambridge University Press, 1995. Pp. xx, 300. $90.00.

Hieatt, Constance B., Brenda Hosington, and Sharon Butler. *Pleyn Delit: Medieval Cookery for Modern Cooks*. 2d ed. Toronto, Buffalo, and London: University of Toronto Press, 1996. Pp. xxviii, 172. $17.95 paper.

Hirsh, John C. *The Boundaries of Faith: The Development and Transmission of Medieval Spirituality*. Studies in the History of Christian Thought, vol. 67. Leiden: E. J. Brill, 1996. Pp. xii, 189. $97.00.

Hudson, Harriet, ed. *Four Middle English Romances:* Sir Isumbras, Octavian, Sir Eglamour of Artois, Sir Tryamour. TEAMS: Middle English Texts Series. Kalamazoo, Mich.: Medieval Institute Publications, 1996. Pp. 241. $13.00 paper.

Huemer, Frances. *Rubens and the Roman Circle: Studies of the First Decade.* Garland Studies in the Renaissance, vol. 5. New York and London: Garland Publishing, 1996. Pp. xxi, 255. $70.00.

Hunt, Tony. *Villon's Last Will: Language and Authority in the* Testament. Oxford: Clarendon Press, 1996. Pp.166. $55.00.

Itnyre, Cathy Jorgensen, ed. *Medieval Family Roles: A Book of Essays.* Garland Medieval Casebooks, vol. 15. New York and London: Garland Publishing, 1996. Pp. xiv, 248. $35.00.

Jackson, Peter, ed. *Words, Names and History: Selected Writings of Cecily Clark.* Cambridge: D. S. Brewer, 1995. Pp. xxviii, 448. $53.00.

Kanno, Masahiko. *Studies in Chaucer's Words: A Contextual and Semantic Approach.* Eihōsha, Japan, 1996. Pp. ix, 226. N.p.

Kennedy, Edward Donald, ed. *King Arthur: A Casebook.* Arthurian Characters and Themes, vol. 1. New York and London: Garland Publishing, 1996. Pp. lvi, 311. $45.00.

The Knight of the Two Swords: *A Thirteenth-Century Arthurian Romance.* Trans. Ross G. Arthur and Noel L. Corbett. Gainesville: University Press of Florida, 1996. Pp. xvii, 188. $39.95.

Lacy, Norris J., ed. *The New Arthurian Encyclopedia.* Garland Reference Library of the Humanities, vol. 931. Updated paperback edition. New York and London: Garland Publishing, 1996. Pp. xxxviii, 615. $29.95 paper.

Larrington, Carolyne. *Women and Writing in Medieval Europe: A Sourcebook.* London and New York: Routledge, 1995. Pp. xiv, 277. $17.95 paper.

Le Saux, Françoise H. M., ed. *The Formation of Culture in Medieval Britain: Celtic, Latin, and Norman Influences on English Music, Literature, History, and Art.* Lewiston, Queenston, and Lampeter: Edwin Mellen Press, 1995. Pp. xiv, 197. $89.95.

Lerer, Seth, ed. *Literary History and the Challenge of Philology: The Legacy of Erich Auerbach. Figurae:* Reading Medieval Culture Series. Stanford: Stanford University Press, 1996. Pp. xii, 301. $45.00.

————, ed. *Reading From the Margins: Textual Studies, Chaucer, and Medieval Literature*. Simultaneously published as *Huntington Library Quarterly* vol. 58. no.1. San Marino, Calif.: Huntington Library, 1996. Pp. vii, 160. $12.00 paper.

Lester, G. A. *The Language of Old and Middle English Poetry*. The Language of Literature Series. New York: St. Martin's Press, 1996. Pp. vii, 182. $39.95.

McCash, June Hall, ed. *The Cultural Patronage of Medieval Women*. Athens and London: University of Georgia Press, 1996. Pp. xix, 402. $60.00 cloth, $25.00 paper.

Noel, William. *The Harley Psalter*. Cambridge Studies in Palaeography and Codicology, vol. 4. Cambridge: Cambridge University Press, 1995. Pp. xvi, 231. $64.95.

Osberg, Richard H., ed. *The Poems of Lawrence Minot, 1333–1352*. TEAMS: Middle English Texts Series. Kalamazoo, Mich.: Medieval Institute Publications, 1996. Pp. vii, 148. $12.00 paper.

Parsons, John Carmi, and Bonnie Wheeler, eds. *Medieval Mothering*. The New Middle Ages Series. New York and London: Garland Publishing, 1996. Pp. xvii, 384. $60.00.

Pasternack, Carol Braun. *The Textuality of Old English Poetry*. Cambridge Studies in Anglo-Saxon England, vol. 13. Cambridge: Cambridge University Press, 1995. Pp. xii, 219. $59.95.

Psaki, Regina, ed. and trans. *Jean Renart*: The Romance of the Rose or of Guillaume de Dole. Garland Library of Medieval Literature, vol. 92A. New York and London: Garland Publishing, 1996. Pp. xli, 280. $48.00.

Reynolds, Susan. *Medieval Reading: Grammar, Rhetoric and the Classical Text*. Cambridge Studies in Medieval Literature, vol. 27. Cambridge: Cambridge University Press, 1996. Pp. xvi, 255. $54.95.

Richmond, Velma Bourgeois. *The Legend of Guy of Warwick*. Garland Studies in Medieval Literature, vol. 14. New York and London: Garland Publishing, 1996. Pp. xv, 551. $95.00.

Richter, Michael. *Studies in Medieval Language and Culture*. Dublin and Portland, Ore.: Four Courts Press, 1995. Pp. 227. $49.50.

Rosenthal, Joel T. *Old Age in Late Medieval England*. Middle Ages Series. Philadelphia: University of Pennsylvania Press, 1996. Pp. xv, 260. $39.95.

Sadowski, Piotr. *The Knight on His Quest: Symbolic Patterns of Transition in* Sir Gawain and the Green Knight. Newark, Del.: University of Delaware Press, 1996. Pp. 289. $37.50.

Scattergood, John. *Reading the Past: Essays on Medieval and Renaissance Literature*. Dublin: Four Courts Press, 1996. Pp. 310. $49.50.

Scully, D. Eleanor, and Terence Scully. *Early French Cookery: Sources, History, Original Recipes and Modern Adaptations*. Ann Arbor: University of Michigan Press, 1995. Pp. xi, 377. $29.95.

Seymour, M. C., gen. ed. *Authors of the Middle Ages: English Writers of the Late Middle Ages*, vol. 3, nos. 7–11. William Caxton, Reginald Pecock, Robert Henryson, William Dunbar, John Capgrave. Brookfield, Vt.: Variorum, Ashgate Publishing, 1996. Pp. vi, 256. $67.95.

Shillingsburg, Peter L. *Scholarly Editing in the Computer Age: Theory and Practice*. 3d ed. Editorial Theory and Literary Criticism Series. Ann Arbor: University of Michigan Press, 1996. Pp. xvi, 187. $42.50 cloth, $17.95 paper.

Sigal, Gale. *Erotic Dawn-Songs of the Middle Ages: Voicing the Lyric Lady*. Gainesville: University Press of Florida, 1996. Pp. xii, 241. $49.95.

Smith, Lesley, and Jane H. M. Taylor, eds. *Women, the Book and the Worldly*. Selected Proceedings of the St. Hilda's Conference, 1993. Vol. 2. Cambridge: D. S. Brewer, 1995. Pp. xiv, 193. $53.00.

Smyth, Alfred P. *King Alfred the Great*. Oxford: Oxford University Press, 1995. Pp. xxv, 744. $35.00.

Stock, Brian. *Augustine the Reader: Meditation, Self-Knowledge, and the Ethics of Interpretation*. Cambridge, Mass., and London: Harvard University Press, 1996. Pp. x, 463. $39.95.

Szarmach, Paul E., ed. *Holy Men and Holy Women: Old English Prose Saints' Lives and Their Contexts*. SUNY Series in Medieval Studies. Albany: State University of New York Press, 1996. Pp. xvii, 390. $24.95 paper.

Taylor, Paul Beekman. *Chaucer's Chain of Love*. Madison, Wis., and Teaneck, N.J.: Fairleigh Dickinson University Press, 1996. Pp. 215. $35.00.

Tinkle, Teresa. *Medieval Venuses and Cupids: Sexuality, Hermeneutics, and English Poetry. Figurae*: Reading Medieval Culture Series. Stanford: Stanford University Press, 1996. Pp. xiii, 294. $39.50.

Tolan, John Victor, ed. *Medieval Christian Perceptions of Islam: A Book of Essays*. Garland Reference Library of the Humanities, vol. 1768. Garland Medieval Casebooks, vol. 10. New York and London: Garland Publishing, 1996. Pp. xxi, 414. $60.00.

Wiethaus, Ulrike. *Ecstatic Transformation: Transpersonal Psychology in the Work of Mechtild of Magdeburg*. Syracuse: Syracuse University Press, 1996. Pp. 195. $16.95 paper.

Wright, Laura. *Sources of London English: Medieval Thames Vocabulary*. Oxford: Clarendon Press, 1996. Pp. x, 245. $55.00.

# An Annotated Chaucer Bibliography
## 1995

Compiled and edited by Mark Allen and Bege K. Bowers

Regular contributors:

Bruce W. Hozeski, *Ball State University* (Indiana)
George Nicholas, *Benedictine College* (Kansas)
Martha S. Waller, *Butler University* (Indiana)
Marilyn Sutton, *California State University at Dominguez Hills*
Larry L. Bronson, *Central Michigan University*
Glending Olson, *Cleveland State University* (Ohio)
Jesús Luis Serrano Reyes (*Córdoba*)
Winthrop Wetherbee, *Cornell University*
Elizabeth Dobbs, *Grinnell College* (Iowa)
Masatoshi Kawasaki, *Komazawa University* (Tokyo, Japan)
William Schipper, *Memorial University* (Newfoundland, Canada)
Daniel J. Pinti, *New Mexico State University*
Erik Kooper, *Rijksuniversiteit te Utrecht*
Amy Goodwin, *Randolph-Macon College* (Virginia)
Cindy L. Vitto, *Rowan College of New Jersey*
Richard H. Osberg, *Santa Clara University* (California)
Margaret Connolly, *University College, Cork* (Ireland)
Juliette Dor, *Université de Liège* (Belgium)
Mary Flowers Braswell and Elaine Whitaker, *University of Alabama at Birmingham*
Denise Stodola, *University of Missouri, Columbia*
Cynthia Gravlee, *University of Montevallo* (Alabama)
Gregory M. Sadlek, *University of Nebraska at Omaha*
Cynthia Ho, *University of North Carolina, Asheville*
Richard J. Utz, *University of Northern Iowa*
Thomas Hahn, *University of Rochester* (New York)
Rebecca Beal, *University of Scranton* (Pennsylvania)

Stanley R. Hauer, *University of Southern Mississippi*
Mark Allen, Gail Jones, and Connie Sabo-Risley, *University of Texas at San Antonio*
Andrew Lynch, *University of Western Australia*
Brian A. Shaw, *University of Western Ontario*
Joyce T. Lionarons, *Ursinus College* (Pennsylvania)
John M. Crafton, *West Georgia College*
Robert Correale, *Wright State University* (Ohio)
Bege K. Bowers, *Youngstown State University* (Ohio)

Ad hoc contributions were made by the following: D. Thomas Hanks (*Baylor University*); Mara Amster (*University of Rochester*); Brian Maloney (*University of Scranton*); Elizabeth Scala (*University of Texas at Austin*); William Buhrman, Judith Hurst, Cynthia Klekar, Miyo Tonegawa, and Arturo Vasquez II (*University of Texas at San Antonio*); Susan M. Wojnar (*Youngstown State University*); and Celeste Van Vloten (*University of Guelph*).

The bibliographers acknowledge with gratitude the MLA typesimulation provided by Terence Ford, Director, Center for Bibliographical Services of the MLA; postage from the University of Texas at San Antonio Division of English, Classics, and Philosophy; and assistance from the library staff, especially Susan McCray, at the John Peace Library, University of Texas at San Antonio.

This bibliography continues the bibliographies published since 1975 in previous volumes of *Studies in the Age of Chaucer*. Bibliographical information up to 1975 can be found in Eleanor P. Hammond, *Chaucer: A Bibliographic Manual* (1908; reprint, New York: Peter Smith, 1933); D. D. Griffith, *Bibliography of Chaucer, 1908–53* (Seattle: University of Washington Press, 1955); William R. Crawford, *Bibliography of Chaucer, 1954–63* (Seattle: University of Washington Press, 1967); and Lorrayne Y. Baird, *Bibliography of Chaucer, 1964–73* (Boston: G. K. Hall, 1977). See also Lorrayne Y. Baird-Lange and Hildegard Schnuttgen, *Bibliography of Chaucer, 1974–1985* (Hamden, Conn.: Shoe String Press, 1988).

Additions and corrections to this bibliography should be sent to Mark Allen, Bibliographic Division, New Chaucer Society, Division of English, Classics, and Philosophy, University of Texas at San Antonio, San Antonio, Texas 78249–0643 (FAX: 210-458-5366; E-MAIL: MALLEN@LONESTAR.JPL.UTSA.EDU). An electronic version of this bibliography (1975–95) is available via the New Chaucer Society webpage (http://www.cohums.ohio-state.edu/chaucer) or via TELNET connection (UTSAIBM.UTSA.EDU; type "library" at the applications prompt, and "cho chau" at the request for a database). Authors are urged to send annotations for articles, reviews, and books that have been or might be overlooked.

# Classifications

357

# Abbreviations of Chaucer's Works

| | |
|---|---|
| *ABC* | *An ABC* |
| *Adam* | *Adam Scriveyn* |
| *Anel* | *Anelida and Arcite* |
| *Astr* | *A Treatise on the Astrolabe* |
| *Bal Compl* | *A Balade of Complaint* |
| *BD* | *The Book of the Duchess* |
| *Bo* | *Boece* |
| *Buk* | *The Envoy to Bukton* |
| *CkT, CkP, Rv–CkL* | *The Cook's Tale, The Cook's Prologue, Reeve–Cook Link* |
| *ClT, ClP, Cl–MerL* | *The Clerk's Tale, The Clerk's Prologue, Clerk–Merchant Link* |
| *Compl d'Am* | *Complaynt d'Amours* |
| *CT* | *The Canterbury Tales* |
| *CYT, CYP* | *The Canon's Yeoman's Tale, The Canon's Yeoman's Prologue* |
| *Equat* | *The Equatorie of the Planetis* |
| *For* | *Fortune* |
| *Form Age* | *The Former Age* |
| *FranT, FranP* | *The Franklin's Tale, The Franklin's Prologue* |
| *FrT, FrP, Fr–SumL* | *The Friar's Tale, The Friar's Prologue, Friar–Summoner Link* |
| *Gent* | *Gentilesse* |
| *GP* | *The General Prologue* |
| *HF* | *The House of Fame* |
| *KnT, Kn–MilL* | *The Knight's Tale, Knight–Miller Link* |
| *Lady* | *A Complaint to His Lady* |
| *LGW, LGWP* | *The Legend of Good Women, The Legend of Good Women Prologue* |
| *ManT, ManP* | *The Manciple's Tale, The Manciple's Prologue* |
| *Mars* | *The Complaint of Mars* |
| *Mel, Mel–MkL* | *The Tale of Melibee, Melibee–Monk Link* |
| *MercB* | *Merciles Beaute* |
| *MerT, MerE–SqH* | *The Merchant's Tale, Merchant Endlink–Squire Headlink* |

| | |
|---|---|
| *MilT, MilP, Mil–RvL* | *The Miller's Tale, The Miller's Prologue, Miller–Reeve Link* |
| *MkT, MkP, Mk–NPL* | *The Monk's Tale, The Monk's Prologue, Monk–Nun's Priest Link* |
| *MLT, MLH, MLP, MLE* | *The Man of Law's Tale, Man of Law Headlink, The Man of Law's Prologue, Man of Law Endlink* |
| *NPT, NPP, NPE* | *The Nun's Priest's Tale, The Nun's Priest's Prologue, Nun's Priest's Endlink* |
| *PardT, PardP* | *The Pardoner's Tale, The Pardoner's Prologue* |
| *ParsT, ParsP* | *The Parson's Tale, The Parson's Prologue* |
| *PF* | *The Parliament of Fowls* |
| *PhyT, Phy–PardL* | *The Physician's Tale, Physician–Pardoner Link* |
| *Pity* | *The Complaint unto Pity* |
| *Prov* | *Proverbs* |
| *PrT, PrP, Pr–ThL* | *The Prioress's Tale, The Prioress's Prologue, Prioress–Thopas Link* |
| *Purse* | *The Complaint of Chaucer to His Purse* |
| *Ret* | *Chaucer's Retraction {Retractation}* |
| *Rom* | *The Romaunt of the Rose* |
| *Ros* | *To Rosemounde* |
| *RvT, RvP* | *The Reeve's Tale, The Reeve's Prologue* |
| *Scog* | *The Envoy to Scogan* |
| *ShT, Sh–PrL* | *The Shipman's Tale, Shipman–Prioress Link* |
| *SNT, SNP, SN–CYL* | *The Second Nun's Tale, The Second Nun's Prologue, Second Nun–Canon's Yeoman Link* |
| *SqT, SqH, Sq–FranL* | *The Squire's Tale, Squire Headlink, Squire–Franklin Link* |
| *Sted* | *Lak of Stedfastnesse* |
| *SumT, SumP* | *The Summoner's Tale, The Summoner's Prologue* |
| *TC* | *Troilus and Criseyde* |
| *Th, Th–MelL* | *The Tale of Sir Thopas, Sir Thopas–Melibee Link* |
| *Truth* | *Truth* |
| *Ven* | *The Complaint of Venus* |
| *WBT, WBP, WB–FrL* | *The Wife of Bath's Tale, The Wife of Bath's Prologue, Wife of Bath–Friar Link* |
| *Wom Nob* | *Womanly Noblesse* |
| *Wom Unc* | *Against Women Unconstant* |

# Periodical Abbreviations

| | |
|---|---|
| *Anglia* | *Anglia: Zeitschrift für Englische Philologie* |
| *ANQ* | *A Quarterly Journal of Short Articles, Notes, and Reviews* |
| *Archiv* | *Archiv für das Studium der Neueren Sprachen und Literaturen* |
| *BAM* | *Bulletin des Anglicistes Médiévistes* |
| *BJRL* | *Bulletin of the John Rylands University Library of Manchester* |
| *C&L* | *Christianity and Literature* |
| *CEA* | *CEA Critic: An Official Journal of the College English Association* |
| *ChauR* | *Chaucer Review* |
| *Cithara* | *Cithara: Essays in the Judaeo-Christian Tradition* |
| *CMat* | *Critical Matrix: The Princeton Journal of Women, Gender, and Culture* |
| *Comitatus* | *Comitatus: A Journal of Medieval and Renaissance Studies* |
| *CR* | *Critical Review* |
| *DAI* | *Dissertation Abstracts International* |
| *DownR* | *Downside Review: A Quarterly of Catholic Thought* |
| *ÉA* | *Études Anglaises: Grand-Bretagne, Etats-Unis* |
| *EHR* | *English Historical Review* |
| *ELN* | *English Language Notes* |
| *ELR* | *English Literary Renaissance* |
| *English* | *English: The Journal of the English Association (Leicester, England)* |
| *ES* | *English Studies* |
| *ESA* | *English Studies in Africa: A Journal of the Humanities* |
| *Exemplaria* | *Exemplaria: A Journal of Theory in Medieval and Renaissance Studies* |
| *FMLS* | *Forum for Modern Language Studies* |

| | |
|---|---|
| *FR* | *French Review: Journal of the American Association of Teachers of French* |
| *JEGP* | *Journal of English and Germanic Philology* |
| *JELL* | *Journal of English Language and Literature* |
| *JEP* | *Journal of Evolutionary Psychology* |
| *JMRS* | *Journal of Medieval and Renaissance Studies* |
| *JRMMRA* | *Journal of the Rocky Mountain Medieval and Renaissance Association* |
| *Library* | *The Library: The Transactions of the Bibliographical Society* |
| *LJGG* | *Literaturwissenschaftliches Jahrbuch im Auftrage der Görres-Gesellschaft* |
| *MA* | *Le Moyen Age: Revue d'Histoire et de Philologie* |
| *MÆ* | *Medium Ævum* |
| *M&H* | *Medievalia et Humanistica: Studies in Medieval and Renaissance Culture* |
| *MedPers* | *Medieval Perspectives* |
| *MLN* | *Modern Language Notes* |
| *MLS* | *Modern Language Studies* |
| *Mosaic* | *Mosaic: A Journal for the Interdisciplinary Study of Literature* |
| *MP* | *Modern Philology: A Journal Devoted to Research in Medieval and Modern Literature* |
| *MS* | *Mediaeval Studies* (Toronto, Canada) |
| *N&Q* | *Notes and Queries* |
| *Neophil* | *Neophilologus* (Dordrecht, Netherlands) |
| *NM* | *Neuphilologische Mitteilungen* |
| *NOWELE* | *NOWELE: North-Western European Language Evolution* |
| *OT* | *Oral Tradition* |
| *PCP* | *Pacific Coast Philology* |
| *PQ* | *Philological Quarterly* |
| *PMLA* | *Publications of the Modern Language Association* |
| *RES* | *Review of English Studies* |
| *RMSt* | *Reading Medieval Studies* |
| *RR* | *Romanic Review* |
| *SAC* | *Studies in the Age of Chaucer* |
| *SEL* | *Studies in English Literature, 1500–1900* |

| | |
|---|---|
| *SELIM* | *SELIM: Journal of the Spanish Society for Mediaeval English Language and Literature* |
| *SHR* | *Southern Humanities Review* |
| *SiM* | *Studies in Medievalism* |
| *SN* | *Studia Neophilologica: A Journal of Germanic and Romance Languages and Literature* (Uppsala, Sweden) |
| *SoAR* | *South Atlantic Review* |
| *Speculum* | *Speculum: A Journal of Medieval Studies* |
| *SSF* | *Studies in Short Fiction* |
| *Text* | *Text: Transactions of the Society for Textual Scholarship* |
| *TLS* | *Times Literary Supplement* (London, England) |
| *UTQ* | *University of Toronto Quarterly: A Canadian Journal of the Humanities* |
| *WS* | *Women's Studies: An Interdisciplinary Journal* |
| *YES* | *Yearbook of English Studies* |
| *YJC* | *Yale Journal of Criticism: Interpretation in the Humanities* |
| *YLS* | *Yearbook of Langland Studies* |
| *YWES* | *Year's Work in English Studies* |

# Bibliographical Citations
# and Annotations

## Bibliographies, Reports, and References

1. Allen, Mark, and Bege K. Bowers. "An Annotated Chaucer Bibliography, 1993." *SAC* 17 (1995): 287–362. Continuation of *SAC* annual bibliography (since 1975); based on 1993 *MLA Bibliography* listings, contributions from an international bibliographic team, and independent research. A total of 340 items, including reviews.

2. Allen, Valerie, and Margaret Connolly. "Middle English: Chaucer." *YWES* 74 (1993): 143–68. A discursive bibliography of Chaucerian scholarship and research in 1993; divided into four categories: general, *CT*, *TC*, and other works.

3. Ashby, Cristina, Geoff Couldrey, Susan Dickson, et al., developers. *Chaucer: Life and Times CD-ROM*. Woodbridge, Conn., and Reading: Primary Source Media, 1995. 1 compact disk; user's guide, 23 pp. A "comprehensive interactive resource for both students and teachers," providing hypertext-linked, point-and-click access to Chaucer's works (*The Riverside Chaucer*) and accompanying glossary, introductions to the works and seventeen previously published essays, translations of major works (by Nevill Coghill and Brian Stone), and "audio clips" (read by John Burrow). Also provides more than 200 images of manuscripts and pertinent sites, a biography of Chaucer with social history and time line, a map of pilgrim routes to Canterbury linked to commentary, and "thematic routes" through the works (topics: authority, chivalry-courtly love, dreams, marriage, language, and religion). Users can create customized thematic routes and annotate them with oral or written notes. Texts are searchable by word and phrase; image searches are also possible. Information can be downloaded. Minimum computer requirements: 4 MB free RAM, 386 SX/33 processor, Windows 3.1, CD-ROM drive.

4. Earp, Lawrence. *Guillaume de Machaut: A Guide to Research*. Garland Composer Resource Manuals, no. 36. Garland Reference

Library of the Humanities, no. 996. New York and London: Garland, 1995. xx, 669 pp. A guide to secondary sources on Machaut's life, music, and literature, plus his influence on later traditions. The general index enables users to track discussions of Machaut's influence on Chaucer, both generally and with reference to individual works.

5. Jimura, Akiyuki, Yoshiyuki Nakao, and Masatsugu Matsuo, eds. *A Comprehensive List of Textual Comparison Between Blake's and Robinson's Editions of* The Canterbury Tales. Okayama, Japan: University Education Press, 1995. xv, 520 pp. A line-by-line comparison of N. F. Blake's and F. N. Robinson's editions of *CT*. Includes an alphabetized word-pairs index.

6. Oizumi, Akio, and Hiroshi Yonekura; programmed by Kunihiro Miki. *A Rhyme Concordance to the Poetical Works of Geoffrey Chaucer*. 2 vols. A Complete Concordance to the Works of Geoffrey Chaucer, XI-XII. Supplement Series, I-II. Hildesheim, Zürich, and New York: Olms-Weidmann, 1994. A computer-generated, alphabetical concordance of rhymes in Chaucer's poetry, based on *The Riverside Chaucer*, arranged by rhyme elements (e.g., *-aas, -aat, -abbe*) within individual works. Includes for each work, in addition to the basic concordance, lists of rhyme-element frequency and rhyme-word frequency, a rhyme-word index, and lists of rhyme schemes and rhyme structures (i.e., combinations of vowels and consonants). Volume 1 includes *CT*, *BD*, *HF*, *Anel*, and *PF*; volume 2, *TC*, *LGW*, short poems, and apocrypha or questionable works.

7. Seymour, M. C. *A Catalogue of Chaucer Manuscripts: Volume I, Works Before the* Canterbury Tales. Hants; Brookfield, Vt.: Scolar Press, 1995. x, 171 pp. Describes eighty-eight manuscripts and fragments that include "all known copies of Chaucer's work," except *CT* and "a few stray lyrics and short poems." Excludes *Equat* and apocrypha, although these, along with portraits of Chaucer, are discussed in appendices. These descriptions are arranged in the supposed chronological order of the works, and they are cross-referenced to avoid duplication. Descriptions include reports of physical features, collation, contents, scribal hands, marginalia, decoration, and history.

See also no. 133.

## Recordings and Films

8. *The Clerk's Tale.* Occasional Readings, no. 15. Provo, Utah: Chaucer Studio, 1995. Audiocassette; 72 min. Dir. T. L. Burton. Recorded at the University of Adelaide. Read by Tom Burton.

9. Graham, Kenneth W. *The Secular and Religious Worlds of Chaucer's* Canterbury Tales. Videotape; approx. 53 min. Guelph: Videolit (University of Guelph), 1995. Videotape discussion of *GP*, with footage from Cleves Abbey, Canterbury Cathedral, Lavenham, the Pilgrim's Way, and other sites. Assesses the Knight, Squire, Prioress, Clerk, and Parson to introduce Chaucer's larger vision of religious and secular values in *CT*.

10. *The Knight's Tale.* Occasional Readings, no. 13. Provo, Utah: Chaucer Studio, 1995. Two audiocassettes; 62, 79 min. Dir. Alan T. Gaylord. Recorded at Dartmouth College. Read by Alan T. Gaylord.

11. *The Man of Law's Tale.* Occasional Readings, no. 14. Provo, Utah: Chaucer Studio, 1995. Audiocassette; 74 min. Dir. T. L. Burton. Recorded at University of Adelaide. Read by Tom Burton.

12. *The Nun's Priest's Tale.* NCS Readings, no. 10. Provo, Utah: Chaucer Studio, 1995. Audiocassette; 38 min. Dir. Paul R. Thomas. Recorded at the Ninth International Congress of the New Chaucer Society, Trinity College, Dublin. Readers include Paul R. Thomas, D. Thomas Hanks, Jr., Peter G. Beidler, Jane Chance, Mary Hamel, and Beverly Kennedy.

13. *The Wife of Bath's Tale.* NCS Readings, no. 9. Provo, Utah: Chaucer Studio, 1995. Audiocassette; 80 min. Dir. Paul R. Thomas. Recorded at the Ninth International Congress of the New Chaucer Society, Trinity College, Dublin. Readers include Mary Hamel, D. Thomas Hanks, Jr., Peter G. Beidler, Paul R. Thomas, Beverly Kennedy, and Jane Chance. Includes *WBPT*.

See also no. 3.

## Chaucer's Life

14. Carruthers, Leo. "Chaucer's In-laws: Who Was Who in the Wars of the Roses." In Roger Lejosne and Dominique Sipière, eds. *Mariages à la mode anglo-saxonne*. Amiens: Sterne, 1995, pp. 40–50;

includes genealogical table. Examines Chaucer's involvement with the royal family and shows how one of his descendants became heir to the throne in 1484. Table of succession from Edward I to Henry VIII includes families of De Bohun, Holland, Mortimer, Beaufort, Tudor, Neville, De la Pole, and Chaucer.

15. Galván Reula, Fernando. "Medieval English Literature: A Spanish Approach." In *Actas del Primer Congreso Internacional de S.E.L.I.M.* Oviedo: Universidad de Oviedo, 1989, pp. 98–111. Considers Chaucer's knowledge of Spain in light of medieval Spanish-English relations. The Pedro-of-Spain stanzas of *MkT* and historical evidence suggest that Chaucer had direct contact with Spain in the 1360s, perhaps as an important envoy of the English royal family.

16. Pearsall, Derek. "Chaucer's Tomb: The Politics of Reburial." *MÆ* 64 (1995): 51–73. Reburial is always a political act. Richard II had started having his faithful servants buried in Westminster Abbey, and Chaucer may have become an Abbey tenant in 1399 to be buried there. When he died, he was buried outside St. Benedict's chapel, as Caxton tells us. In 1556, Nicholas Brigham had Chaucer's remains moved to the south transept and had an inscription placed against its east wall. Pearsall explains the political implications of this removal, especially as "part of this larger programme of counter-reformation, a move to reappropriate England's greatest poet to the traditional faith."

See also no. 3.

## Facsimiles, Editions, and Translations

17. Archibald, Diana C. "Beauty, Unity, and the Ideal: Wholeness and Heterogeneity in the Kelmscott *Chaucer*." *SiM* 7 (1995): 169–80. William Morris's attempt to produce the ideal book "fails to match form with content." The harmonious presentation of his Kelmscott *Chaucer* disguises the diversity of tales and conceals unresolved problems of text and structure. The choice and character of Edward Burne-Jones's illustrations (those for *KnT* are discussed in detail) give a misleading impression of "frozen sanctity."

18. Cowen, Janet, and George Kane, eds. *Geoffrey Chaucer: The Legend of Good Women.* Medieval Texts and Studies, no. 16. East Lansing, Mich.: Colleagues Press, 1995. xii, 344 pp. An edition of *LGW* that

provides variants and textual commentary. The copy text for *LGWP* is Bodleian Library MS Tanner 346 ("Prologue I," or F-version), while Cambridge University Library MS Gg.4.27 is here edited separately ("Prologue II," or G-version). A complete list of variants accompanies the eclectic text. The introduction includes a description and classification of the manuscripts and analysis of the variants as they relate to emendation. The introduction also discusses the grammar of Chaucer's final -*e*, the text of *LGW* in Gg.4.27, past editorial treatments of *LGWP*, and a justification of the copy text.

19. Crépin, André. "Geoffrey Chaucer." In *Premières mutations: De Pétrarque à Chaucer, 1304–1400*. Volume 5 in Jean-Claude Polet, gen. ed. *Patrimoine littéraire européen*. Bruxelles: De Boeck Université, 1995, pp. 646–58. The twelve-volume *Patrimoine littéraire européen* surveys major European authors and works from the early roots of European literature to the present, providing for each an introduction, a short bibliography, and extracts in French translation—some reprinted, others published here for the first time. Texts from Chaucer are *Anelida et Arcite* (trans. Emile Legouis); *Troilus et Criseyde* ("La nuit d'amour," by Jean-Robert Simon, and "Palinodie," by Florence Bourgne); *La ballade de bon conseil* (by A. Koszul); and *Les contes de Cantorbery* ("Prologue general," by Le Chevalier de Chatelain, and "La bourgeoise de Bath," by Juliette Dor).

20. Dane, Joseph A. "On 'Correctness': A Note on Some Press Variants in Thynne's 1532 Edition of Chaucer." *Library*, ser. 6, 17 (1995): 156–67. Dane argues on the basis of two copies of Thynne's edition that one cannot properly speak of them as "corrected" or "uncorrected." Parts of the books are corrected or uncorrected, but the distribution of variants between the two copies indicates that the notion of correctness or uncorrectness does not apply to the book as a whole.

21. Edwards, A. S. G. "Chaucer from Manuscript to Print: The Social Text and the Critical Text." *Mosaic* 28:4 (1995): 1–12. Edwards surveys pre-twentieth-century editions of Chaucer to see how their editorial goals anticipate and differ from those of the "modern critical edition." Print technology enforced a "single monolithic conception of text" that differs from the variations among manuscripts; however, modern technology can encompass the variant forms of manuscripts. Scholars need to assess relations between textual and contextual approaches to medieval literature.

22. Havely, Nicholas R., ed. *Chaucer: The House of Fame*. Durham Medieval Texts, no. 11. Durham, N.C.: Durham Medieval Texts,

Department of English, 1994. viii, 216 pp. An edition of *HF* based on a collation of all five witnesses (three manuscripts plus editions of Caxton and Thynne), with a substantial, though incomplete, set of variants. Bodleian MS Fairfax 16 is the base text and the exemplar for spelling. The introduction includes descriptions of the witnesses and discussions of fate, language, versification, "intertextualities," "poetics," and Chaucer's use of the grotesque. The text is lightly glossed, and the volume includes a glossary, an index of proper names, and fifty-three pages of explanatory notes.

23. Plummer, John F., III, ed. *The Summoner's Tale. A Variorum Edition of the Works of Geoffrey Chaucer*. Vol. 2, *The Canterbury Tales*, Part 7. Norman and London: University of Oklahoma Press, 1995. xxviii, 242 pp. Edition of *SumT*, based on the Hengwrt manuscript. Collates nine additional manuscripts and the major editions from Caxton to *The Riverside Chaucer*. Spelling is lightly modernized, and punctuation is introduced. Notes, critical commentary, and textual commentary are based on a comprehensive survey of significant scholarship from 1635 to 1986. The critical commentary addresses sources and analogues, date, adaptations, and critical approaches; the textual commentary includes descriptions of the witnesses to the text and discussion of textual tradition, glosses, and the place of *SumT* in *CT*.

24. Santoyo, Julio César. "Mone/Manuel Pérez del Río, primer traductor de 'Los cuentos de Canterbury.'" In Antonio León Sendra, María C. Casares Trillo, and María M. Rivas Carmona, eds. *Second International Conference of the Spanish Society for Medieval Language and Literature* (*SAC* 19 [1997], no. 123), pp. 149–55. Brief biography of the first translator of *CT* into Spanish (ca. 1920).

25. Stevens, Martin. "The Ellesmere Chaucer: Essays in Interpretation." In Martin Stevens and Daniel Woodward, eds. *The Ellesmere Chaucer: Essays in Interpretation* (*SAC* 19 [1997], no. 26), pp. 15–28; 2 b&w illus. Describes the inadequacy of the 1911 facsimile of Ellesmere and introduces a new facsimile—"as accurate a photographic copy of the original as modern technology allows." Surveying the contents of the volume accompanying the new facsimile, Stevens suggests (among other observations) that a "redefinition of authorship" emerges when one views the original Ellesmere "production team" as having constructed a Chaucerian voice composed of Chaucer's own work and of its redaction by these early editors.

26. Stevens, Martin, and Daniel Woodward, eds. *The Ellesmere Chaucer: Essays in Interpretation*. San Marino, Calif.: Huntington Library; Tokyo: Yushodo, 1995. xvi, 363 pp.; 57 b&w illus. The frontispiece is the first page of the Ellesmere MS (reduced, in color) followed by two foldout pages of full-size, color MS portraits of the twenty-three tale-tellers of *CT*. Fourteen essays are "designed to provide the most up-to-date scholarly description of the manuscript and to explore the editorial and critical issues that define its place in Chaucer studies." Also includes two introductions by the editors and a summary of the report by Anthony G. Cains, director of the "1994–95 conservation phase of the Ellesmere Chaucer facsimile project." See nos. 25, 28–31, 33, 34, 36, 39–42, 127, 138, 140, 148, 160, and 258.

27. Wickham, D. E. "An Early Editor of Chaucer Reidentified." *N&Q* 240 (1995): 428. Adds a possible detail to the life of Thomas Speght.

28. Woodward, Daniel. "The New Ellesmere Chaucer Facsimile." In Martin Stevens and Daniel Woodward, eds. *The Ellesmere Chaucer: Essays in Interpretation* (*SAC* 19 [1997], no. 26), pp. 1–13. Describes the new facsimile of Ellesmere and the project that led to its production and the accompanying volume. The facsimile was produced in three forms, and some copies of the bound version have trimmed margins that do not match the original exactly.

29. Woodward, Daniel, and Maria Fredericks. "Summary of Anthony G. Cains's Report on the Preparation of the Ellesmere Manuscript for the New Facsimile, the Repair (and History of Repair) of the Manuscript, and Its Rebinding." In Martin Stevens and Daniel Woodward, eds. *The Ellesmere Chaucer: Essays in Interpretation* (*SAC* 19 [1997], no. 26), pp. 29–39; 3 b&w figs.; 8 b&w photos. Summarizes the operations and observations attendant upon restoring, photographing, and rebinding Ellesmere during preparation of the new facsimile. Considers conservation necessary for the photography, new discoveries concerning the history of the manuscript and of its two bindings, repairs made during the present rebinding, and the process of rebinding the manuscript in an "early fifteenth-century-English-style."

30. Woodward, Daniel, and Martin Stevens, eds. *The* Canterbury Tales *by Geoffrey Chaucer: The New Ellesmere Chaucer Facsimile* (of Huntington Library MS EL 26.C.9). San Marino, Calif.: Huntington Library; Tokyo: Yushodo, 1995. xvi, 464 pp. A full-size, full-color facsimile of the Ellesmere manuscript of *CT*, published in three forms and

250 copies. Copies 1–50 are bound in oak boards fully covered by tawed calf; copies 51–150, in boards and quarter brown leather; and copies 151–250, boxed rather than bound, presented in folded but unsewn gatherings. The facsimile reproduces—as exactly as contemporary technology permits—the text, illuminations, wrinkles, smears, scribbles, holes, rules, prick markings, etc. of all pages, with one minor exception: the gold leaf over gesso in the original illustrations lies flat in the facsimile. The letters of the text are clear and easily readable. See the companion volume of essays, *SAC* 19 [1997], no. 26.

See also nos. 3, 76, 198.

## Manuscripts and Textual Studies

31. Blake, N. F. "The Ellesmere Text in the Light of the Hengwrt Manuscript." In Martin Stevens and Daniel Woodward, eds. *The Ellesmere Chaucer: Essays in Interpretation* (*SAC* 19 [1997], no. 26), pp. 205–24. Since the text of the Ellesmere manuscript is highly edited, Hengwrt is superior to it and should be used as the basis for standard editions of *CT*. Accepting the thesis that Hengwrt is "the earliest extant manuscript," Blake argues that the Ellesmere ordering of *CT* was developed from Hengwrt. He assumes "that the Hg scribe had access to Chaucer's drafts," and thus argues that any material not included in Hengwrt (e.g., *CYT*) should be regarded as spurious until it can be proved genuine.

32. Burnley, David. "Scribes and Hypertext." *YES* 25 (1995): 41–62. Comments on scribal habits reflected in late-medieval English manuscripts and assesses the utility of electronic hypertext to record variations, using examples from Chaucer and other Middle English authors. Medieval scribal practice may be the closest available analogue to hypertext composition.

33. David, Alfred. "The Ownership and Use of the Ellesmere Manuscript." In Martin Stevens and Daniel Woodward, eds. *The Ellesmere Chaucer: Essays in Interpretation* (*SAC* 19 [1997], no. 26), pp. 307–26. Traces the ownership of Ellesmere from (speculatively) Thomas Chaucer and the de Vere family to Henry E. Huntington. Includes commentary on the relations of Ellesmere to Hengwrt and on the problematic nature of Chaucer's original "text" as it has been presented in printed editions.

34. Doyle, A. I. "The Copyist of the Ellesmere *Canterbury Tales*." In Martin Stevens and Daniel Woodward, eds. *The Ellesmere Chaucer: Essays in Interpretation* (*SAC* 19 [1997], no. 26), pp. 49–67; 7 b&w figs. Paleographic analysis of the five manuscripts or fragments attributable to the Ellesmere scribe: Ellesmere itself; the Hengwrt manuscript, except for "a few lines"; twenty-four folios of a copy of Gower's *Confessio Amantis*; a fragment of a leaf of *TC*; and a leaf from *PrP* and *PrT*. The attribution of the latter remains questionable.

35. Griffiths, Jeremy. "New Light on the Provenance of a Copy of *The Canterbury Tales*, John Rylands MS Eng. 113." *BJRL* 77 (1995): 25–30. Notes the existence of a nineteenth-century transcript of the Rylands manuscript made by William James Pynwell, now Schoyn Collection MS 1580, and the implications that the transcript may have for the provenance of the Rylands manuscript.

36. Hanna, Ralph, III. "(The) Editing (of) the Ellesmere Text." In Martin Stevens and Daniel Woodward, eds. *The Ellesmere Chaucer: Essays in Interpretation* (*SAC* 19 [1997], no. 26), pp. 225–43. Ellesmere was not edited in a modern sense; i.e., it was not revised or corrected for such matters as metrical regularity. Having compared approximately 6,000 lines of Ellesmere with parallel lines in six other manuscripts nearly contemporary with Ellesmere, Hanna concludes that "any editing that occurred is likely to have rendered the text more Chaucerian, not less. El provides a more faithful version of the poem than is found in the scribe's primary archetypes."

37. Moorman, Charles. *The Statistical Determination of Affiliation in the Landmark Manuscripts of* The Canterbury Tales. Lewiston, N.Y.; Queenston, Ontario; Lampeter, Wales: Edwin Mellen, 1993. xii, 209 pp. Statistical analyses, including charted data, of variant readings of *CT* in (1) a given single tale in pairs of manuscripts, and (2) paired tales in single manuscripts. Linear and multiple correlation tests, cluster analysis, and factor analysis are applied to the manuscripts published within ten years of Chaucer's death, with Hengwrt serving as base text. The conclusions drawn include (1) the likelihood that, late in Chaucer's lifetime, Hengwrt was produced from Chaucer's originals; (2) archetypes of extant manuscript groups were commercially produced shortly after Chaucer's death; and (3) independent manuscripts other than Hengwrt were produced by noncommercial scribes.

38. Mosser, Daniel W. "Reading and Editing the *Canterbury Tales*: Past, Present, and Future?" *Text* 7 (1994): 201–32. Demonstrates the

"openness" and "dynamic character" of the *CT* text by detailing how early scribes and editors dealt with various lacunae left by Chaucer. Describes how some apocryphal materials and various links between tales are presented in manuscripts, arguing that while traditional editions cannot reflect them, such materials can and should be made available through hypertext.

39. Parkes, M. B. "The Planning and Construction of the Ellesmere Manuscript." In Martin Stevens and Daniel Woodward, eds. *The Ellesmere Chaucer: Essays in Interpretation* (SAC 19 [1997], no. 26), pp. 41–47. Codicologically, Ellesmere was constructed by methods commonly used for fifteenth-century English books, including techniques by which "the scribe and the artists accommodated their work so precisely to the format predetermined by the size and number of leaves" and made a good fit for all elements of the book. Parkes discusses preparation of the skins for the pages, plus "practices of the scribe" in accommodating the text, the marginalia, and the illustrations.

40. Pearsall, Derek. "The Ellesmere Chaucer and Contemporary English Literary Manuscripts." In Martin Stevens and Daniel Woodward, eds. *The Ellesmere Chaucer: Essays in Interpretation* (SAC 19 [1997], no. 26), pp. 263–80. Situates the Ellesmere manuscript in the scribal production of "literary" manuscripts in London from 1400 to 1450–1475, i.e., manuscripts of "Chaucer, Gower, Langland, Walton, Hoccleve, and Lydgate (in verse), Trevisa and Nicholas Love—and . . . *Mandeville's Travels*." Scribal production in London grew because of the expansion of English over French, "the general increase in literacy," the vogue for translations, and—with Chaucer and Gower—the presence of "vernacular poetry in quantity of a prestigious kind, capable of attracting paying customers."

41. Scott, Kathleen L. "An Hours and Psalter by Two Ellesmere Illuminators." In Martin Stevens and Daniel Woodward, eds. *The Ellesmere Chaucer: Essays in Interpretation* (SAC 19 [1997], no. 26), pp. 87–119; 7 b&w illus.; 6 full-page. Bodleian Library MS Hatton 4, a combined hours and psalter, contains borders created by two Ellesmere limners. Comparison of the borders in the two manuscripts shows "the methodology of using borderwork as a codicological tool"; strengthens "the existing case for locating the limners in London"; and suggests a date for Ellesmere of 1400–1405.

42. Smith, Jeremy J. "The Language of the Ellesmere Manuscript." In Martin Stevens and Daniel Woodward, eds. *The Ellesmere Chaucer:*

*Essays in Interpretation* (*SAC* 19 [1997], no. 26), pp. 69–86. Argues for the superiority of Hengwrt over Ellesmere on metrical and dialectical grounds. Hengwrt, which better reflects both the Northernisms of *RvT* and Chaucer's admittedly difficult-to-ascertain metrical goals, should be the basis for modern editions of *CT*. Hengwrt's superiority results from the fact that it "was a makeshift volume assembled in some haste, whereas the Ellesmere manuscript was more carefully planned and executed." Since Ellesmere is more heavily edited, Hengwrt more accurately represents "the authorial original."

See also nos. 3, 7, 21, 26, 30, 138, 140, 184, 194, 198, 276, 305.

## Sources, Analogues, and Literary Relations

43. Alford, John A. "Langland's Learning." *YLS* 9 (1995): 1–8. Alford avers that comparisons with Chaucer have falsely made Langland appear unlearned. There are no specific references to Chaucer's works.

44. Herold, Christine. "Chaucer's Tragic Muse: The Paganization of Christian Tragedy." *DAI* 55 (1995): 2382A. Discusses the differences and similarities between classical Greek ideas and late Roman and medieval Christian concepts of tragedy, focusing on Lucias Annaeus Seneca and his influence on the works of Chaucer, Jean de Meun, and Boccaccio.

45. Serrano Reyes, Jesús L. *Didactismo y moralismo en Geoffrey Chaucer y Don Juan Manuel: Un estudio comparativo textual*. Córdoba: Universidad de Córdoba, 1995. 432 pp. Microfilm publication of Serrano Reyes's dissertation, which argues that there are analogous relationships between *CT* and *El Conde Lucanor* and that Chaucer was influenced by the Spanish work.

46. Tejera Llano, Dionisia. "'So Is Flesh' or 'El Amor Loco del Mundo' in G. Chaucer and Juan Ruiz." In Antonio León Sendra, María C. Casares Trillo, and María M. Rivas Carmona, eds. *Second International Conference of the Spanish Society for Medieval Language and Literature* (*SAC* 19 [1997], no. 123), pp. 197–206. Perhaps because of their proximity in time (fifty years apart), Chaucer and the "Arcipreste de Hita" present love in similar ways. Both depict lovers' laments, the pleasures of the flesh, nuns willing to have love affairs, and so forth.

47. Wheeler, Bonnie. "Grammar, Genre, and Gender in Geoffrey Chaucer and Murasaki Shikibu." *Poetica* (Tokyo) 44 (1995): 13–22.

Chaucer and Murasaki Shikibu, author of *Genji Monogatari*, share a number of literary features: a commitment to vernacular expression, grammatically and stylistically open texts, celebration of generic variety, and preoccupation with the female gender and its relations with power.

See also nos. 88, 132, 151, 158, 167, 169, 177, 188, 191, 196, 200, 202, 204, 229, 230, 234, 236, 247, 271, 290, 297, 301, 305, 308–10.

## Chaucer's Influence and Later Allusion

48. Alfano, Christine Lynn. "Under the Influence: Drink, Discourse, and Narrative in Victorian Britain." *DAI* 56 (1995): 2244A. The popular tradition of conviviality in Merrie Olde England stretches back through Shakespeare to Chaucer. With the rise of the temperance movement and the spread of literacy, both didactic hacks and serious novelists reversed the given view.

49. Beidler, Peter G. "William Cartwright, Washington Irving, and the 'Truth': A Shadow Allusion to Chaucer's *Canon's Yeoman's Tale*." *ChauR* 29 (1995): 434–39. The "Rip Van Winkle" epigraph on keeping one's word until one dies (meaning that one will *not* keep one's word) is taken from a passage spoken by an old man to a widow in search of a husband in Cartwright's comedy, *The Ordinary*. Cartwright, in turn, borrows from *CYT*, in which the dishonest canon swears his eternal fidelity to the gullible and greedy priest. Irving probably did not know that the allusion came from Chaucer.

50. Boswell, Jackson Campbell, and Sylvia Wallace Holton. "References to the *Canterbury Tales*." *ChauR* 29 (1995): 311–36. Listings of references to Chaucer and his work published 1475–1640, updating Caroline Spurgeon's *Five Hundred Years of Chaucer Criticism and Allusion, 1357–1900*.

51. Bowden, Betsy. "*Chaucer New Painted* (1623): Three Hundred Proverbs in Performance Context." *OT* 10 (1995): 304–58. William Painter's frame-narrative proverb collection reflects the general influence of *CT* and perhaps the more specific influence of *Mel*. Bowden traces a brief history of collections of proverbs for performance and edits Painter's 1153-line poem from a unique octavo in the Huntington Library.

52. Braekman, Martine. "A Chaucerian 'Courtly Love Aunter' by Henry Howard, Earl of Surrey." *Neophil* 79 (1995): 675–87. Howard's "Complaint of a diyng louer refused vpon his ladies iniust mistaking of his writyng," a poem of eighty-two lines first published in *Tottel's Miscellany* (1557) and here reprinted, is a "refreshingly renewed" late example of a courtly love "aunter" influenced by *BD* and *TC*.

53. Carlson, David R. "Chaucer, Humanism, and Printing: Conditions of Authorship in Fifteenth-Century England." *UTQ* 64:2 (1995): 274–88. Inferences about Chaucer's court life and patronage provided literary successors with a model for the profitability of writing poetry, which—along with the increase in the number of Italian humanists and the advent of printing—fostered the viability of literary professionalism in fifteenth-century England.

54. Farvolden, Pamela Laura. "A Critical Edition of John Lydgate's *Fabula duorum mercatorum*." *DAI* 55 (1995): 1965A. The inadequacies of the two previous editions of Lydgate's *Fabula* call for this full treatment, based on all manuscripts and annotated with references to related works, including *KnT*.

55. Hamilton, A. C. "The Renaissance of the Study of the English Literary Renaissance." *ELR* 25 (1995): 372–87. In arguing that a genuine study of Renaissance works is impossible without examining their literary and historical context, Hamilton briefly cites Chaucer's importance in the formation of the English canon that initiated the English literary Renaissance.

56. Haydock, Nicholas A. "Remaking Chaucer: Influence and Interpretation in Late Medieval Literature." *DAI* 56 (1995): 1348A. The works of Chaucer's contemporaries (Clanvowe, Lydgate, Dunbar) and later admirers (e.g., Henryson) show varying responses, especially to *HF* and *PF*. Analysis of *HF* as printed by Caxton reveals how change in context influenced the text.

57. Holland, Peter. "Theseus' Shadows in *A Midsummer Night's Dream*." *Shakespeare Survey* 47 (1994): 139–51. Examines various possible sources for Shakespeare's play, including *KnT*, arguing that such sources must be considered in light of the audience's perception. Focuses on the character and tradition of Theseus.

58. Ryan, Francis X., SJ. "Sir Thomas More's Use of Chaucer." *SEL* 35 (1995): 1–17. Explores More's likely knowledge of Chaucer by examining the former's references and allusions to Chaucer, his quotations of the earlier poet, and their uses of similar proverbs. Includes a

developed examination of relations between More's *History of Richard III* and *ClT*.

59. Spearing, A. C. "The Poetic Subject from Chaucer to Spenser." In David G. Allen and Robert A. White, eds. *Subjects on the World's Stage: Essays on British Literature of the Middle Ages and the Renaissance* (*SAC* 19 [1997], no. 75), pp. 13–37. In the development of the literary subjective "I," Chaucer's work—especially *KnT* with its images of prison and mirrors that become images for the exploration of subjectivity—greatly influenced subsequent writers from Hoccleve to Spenser.

See also nos. 160, 222, 255, 285, 309, 316, 318.

## Style and Versification

60. Benson, Larry D. "The Beginnings of Chaucer's English Style." In Theodore M. Andersson and Stephen A. Barney, eds. *Contradictions: From* Beowulf *to* Chaucer (*SAC* 19 [1997], no. 78), pp. 243–65. Surveys the lyric and romance traditions of England and France that most likely influenced Chaucer's early writing, commenting on how *Rom*, *ABC*, and *BD* reflect the possible sources and development of Chaucer's colloquial English style.

61. Bice, Deborah Marie. "Preceptive Portraiture: Chaucerian and Spenserian *Effictio.*" *DAI* 56 (1995): 2230A. Not mere ornament, the *effictio*, or physical and spiritual portrait, had become a fixed literary convention by the time of Geoffrey of Vinsauf. Bice analyzes Chaucerian characters from *GP*, *KnT*, *NPT*, and *MilT*, as well as from *Sir Gawain and the Green Knight* and Spenser.

62. Bormann, Sally. "End-rhyme and Alliteration Sonotations in Chaucer, Gower, Langland and the 'Gawain'-poet." *DAI* 56 (1995): 199A. "Sonotations" (generated by sound patterns that affect both denotation and connotation) appear in rhymed and alliterative verse. Poets balance the structural and sensuous qualities of sound with sense, and aesthetic qualities with didactic ones.

63. Chickering, Howell. "Comic Meter and Rhyme in the *Miller's Tale.*" *Chaucer Yearbook* 2 (1995): 17–47. Surveys critical commentary on Chaucer's prosody, noting its subordination to commentary on his narrative art. Exemplifies Chaucer's prosodic virtuosity by demonstrating the colloquial ease that underlies *MilT* and examining specific in-

stances of comic manipulation of meter, rhyme, and couplet in the tale. Examines passages in unpunctuated form.

64. Guthrie, Steve. "Dialogics and Prosody in Chaucer." In Thomas J. Farrell, ed. *Bakhtin and Medieval Voices* (*SAC* 19 [1997], no. 94), pp. 94–108. Contrasts the prosodic polyglossia of Chaucer's verse with the less various rhythms of Gower's verse. Welding French and English rhythms, Chaucer avoided the dullness that Gower did not escape, achieving a poetic style characterized by rhythmic syncopation, phonological complexity, controlled tempo, and cumulative rhythms. Guthrie examines the relation of prosody to theme in *BD*.

## Language and Word Studies

65. Akbari, Suzanne Conklin. "Theories of Vision and the Development of Late Medieval Allegory." *DAI* 56 (1995): 919A. Medieval optical theory recognized two types of mirrors, one aiding vision and the other inverting images. Language can operate likewise, as shown by various works, including Chaucer's dream visions, his *Mel*, and *MerT*.

66. Blake, N. F. "Speech and Writing: An Historical Overview." *YES* 25 (1995): 6–21. Surveys interrelations between speech and writing in the history of English, drawing on *KnT* and *RvT* to illustrate features of late medieval lexis and syntax. Features of *KnT* may reflect "oral residue," while dialect features of *RvT* are better seen as matters of style.

67. Breeze, Andrew. "Chaucer's 'Malkin' and Dafydd ap Gwilym's 'Mald y Cwd.'" *N&Q* 240 (1995): 159–60. Deterioration in the name Malkin, which came to mean "member of the lower classes, slut," can be paralleled by the Welsh "Mald."

68. Burrow, J. A. "Elvish Chaucer." In M. Teresa Tavormina and R. F. Yeager, eds. *The Endless Knot: Essays on Old and Middle English in Honor of Marie Borroff* (*SAC* 19 [1997], no. 128), pp. 105–11. Explores connotations of "elvyssh" in *Pr–ThL* as an aspect of "Chaucer's poetic self-representations" in *CT* and in *HF*, suggesting that they indicate characteristic reserve.

69. Furrow, Melissa M. "Latin and Affect." In M. Teresa Tavormina and R. F. Yeager, eds. *The Endless Knot: Essays on Old and Middle English in Honor of Marie Borroff* (*SAC* 19 [1997], no. 128), pp. 29–41. By exploring the uses of Latin quotations in the works of Langland and

Chaucer, Furrow indicates late Middle English readers' facility with Latin. Langland "drew deeply on the potential poetic power in familiar Latin biblical texts," while in Chaucer's *CT* Latin "always occurs with some taint of suspicion or ridicule attached to it," especially in *GP*, *SumT*, *PardP*, and *PrT*.

70. Leicester, H. Marshall. "Piety and Resistance: A Note on the Representation of Religious Feeling in the *Canterbury Tales*." In M. Teresa Tavormina and R. F. Yeager, eds. *The Endless Knot: Essays on Old and Middle English in Honor of Marie Borroff* (*SAC* 19 [1997], no. 128), pp. 151–60. Leicester explores nuances of "pietee" and "pietas," distinguishes between institutional and affective piety, and asserts that texts cannot be pious but can only represent piety. *CYPT* is religious insofar as it represents the Yeoman's "hunger to discover spirit behind the masks of matter."

71. Nakao, Yoshiyuki. "A Semantic Note on the Middle English Phrase *As He/She That*." *NOWELE* 25 (1995): 25–48. The phrase "as he/she that," a calque from French *com cil/cele qui*, developed polysemic use in Chaucer's day. The article includes a chart of occurrences of the English phrase from ca. 1000 to Caxton, indicating Chaucer's uses by work and recording heavy use of the phrase in Gower's *Confessio Amantis*.

72. Rex, Richard. "'Grey' Eyes and the Medieval Ideal of Feminine Beauty." In Richard Rex. *"The Sins of Madame Eglentyne" and Other Essays on Chaucer* (*SAC* 19 [1997], no. 118), pp. 54–60. When applied to eyes in Middle English literature, the adjective "grey" is best seen as synonymous with "bright" and "clear."

73. Stein, Gabriele. "Chaucer and Lydgate in Palsgrave's *Lesclarcissement*." In Braj B. Kachru and Henry Kahane, eds. *Cultures, Ideologies, and the Dictionary: Studies in Honor of Ladislav Zgusta*. Tübingen: Niemeyer, 1995, pp. 127–39. Examines citations of Chaucer and Lydgate in John Palsgrave's *Lesclarcissement de la langue francoyse* (1530) as indications of the dictionary-maker's efforts to record "special language use," i.e., dialectical use and varying registers.

74. Sugakawa, Seizo. "The Evolution of an English Color Word and Its Connotations." *Dokkyo Gaigaku Eigo Kenkyu* 41 (1993): 178–96 (in Japanese). Examines the word "red," its connotations, and the evolution of related color words such as "crimson" and "peach" from Old English through 1900, focusing on Shakespeare and Chaucer.

See also nos. 42, 121, 142, 144, 148, 161, 216, 217, 232, 304, 306, 312, 314.

## Background and General Criticism

75. Allen, David G., and Robert A. White, eds. *Subjects on the World's Stage: Essays on British Literature of the Middle Ages and the Renaissance*. Newark: University of Delaware Press, 1995. 319 pp. Contains three essays on Chaucerian topics; see nos. 59, 243, and 304.

76. Arn, Mary-Jo, ed. *"Fortunes Stabilnes": Charles of Orleans's English Book of Love*. Medieval & Renaissance Texts & Studies, no. 138. Binghamton, N.Y.: Medieval & Renaissance Texts & Studies, 1994. xiii, 624 pp. The introduction to this critical edition addresses cultural, historical, syntactic, and metrical aspects pertinent to Chaucer's works as well as to those of Charles of Orleans.

77. ———, ed. *Medieval Food and Drink*. ACTA, no. 21. Binghamton, N.Y.: Center for Medieval and Early Renaissance Studies, 1995. iv, 140 pp. Nine essays on medieval food and drink, including their representation in medieval art and poetry.

78. Benson, Larry D. *Contradictions: From* Beowulf *to* Chaucer: *Selected Studies of Larry D. Benson*. Theodore M. Andersson and Stephen A. Barney, eds. Aldershot, Hants: Scolar; Brookfield, Vt.: Ashgate, 1995. xxiii, 322 pp. Includes thirteen essays by Benson, all but one reprinted from earlier publications. For the essays that pertain to Chaucer, see *SAC* 5 (1983), no. 121; *SAC* 6 (1994), no. 162; *SAC* 9 (1987), no. 54; *SAC* 10 (1988), no. 218; *SAC* 16 (1994), no. 265; and *SAC* 19 (1997), nos. 60 and 79.

79. ———. "Courtly Love and Chivalry in the Later Middle Ages." In Robert Yeager, ed. *Fifteenth-Century Studies: Recent Essays* (*SAC* 8 [1986], no. 30), pp. 237–57; reprinted in Theodore M. Andersson and Stephen A. Barney, eds. *Contradictions: From* Beowulf *to* Chaucer (*SAC* 19 [1997], no.78), pp. 294–313. Though there may never have been a "doctrine" of courtly love, late medieval literature reflects conventions that may be called courtly. Drawing examples from a number of literary works (including *TC*, *Rom*, *BD*, and *LGW*) and various historical records, Benson argues that medieval ceremonialism and gentle speech indicate internalization of courtly ideals drawn from romance tradition.

80. Bertolet, Craig E. "The Rise of London Literature: Chaucer, Gower, Langland and the Poetics of the City in Late Medieval English Poetry." *DAI* 56 (1995): 1766A. Certain qualities of fourteenth-century London created a cultural atmosphere in which a new kind of poetry flourished, emphasizing urban community and its values. Chaucer adapts urban poetry to debate with a wide variety of voices,

depicts moral book-balancing, and shows how some characters imperil the community.

81. Blanco, Karen Keiner. "Of 'Briddes and Beestes': Chaucer's Use of Animal Imagery as a Means of Audience Influence in Four Major Poetic Works." *DAI* 56 (1995): 920A. Writing for an audience that knew animals and animal lore well (from physical interaction, folklore, and religious tradition), Chaucer appealed to, influenced, and manipulated this lore in *HF*, *PF*, *NPT*, and *TC*.

82. Bowers, John M. "Chaste Marriage: Fashion and Texts at the Court of Richard II." *PCP* 30 (1995): 15–26. Chaucer exposes the Ricardian practice of chaste marriage "for what perhaps it really was: sexual hypocrisy posing as virtuous Christian abstinence." The false romantic passion and comic fusion of the clerkly and courtly in male characters such as Absolon in *MilT* and the Pardoner in *PardT* undercut such hypocrisy.

83. Burlin, Robert B. "Middle English Romance: The Structure of Genre." *ChauR* 30 (1995): 1–14. Burlin proposes a structuralist model for the medieval romance, adopting a Saussurean paradigm of intersecting axes: the "paradigmatic axis furnished with the test and courtly codes and the syntagmatic axis with the quest and the test." Includes discussions of *TC* and *KnT*.

84. Busse, Wilhelm G. "Träume sind Schäume." In Rudolf Hiestand, ed. *Traum und Träumen: Inhalt, Darstellungen, Funktionem einer Lebenserfahrung in Mittelalter und Renaissance*. Studia humaniora, no. 24. Düsseldorf: Droste, 1994, pp. 43–67. Places Chaucer's presentations of dreams in *TC*, *PF*, *HF*, and *NPT* in the context of the development of Western attitudes toward the validity of dreams.

85. Chance, Jane. *The Mythographic Chaucer: The Fabulation of Sexual Politics*. Minneapolis and London: University of Minnesota Press, 1995. xxix, 378 pp. Examines Chaucer's astrological and mythological allusions in light of medieval mythographic commentaries, arguing that such analysis discloses "embarrassing secrets." Assesses *MLP* and *ManT* as indicators of Chaucer's concern with poetic disguise and explores aspects of love and gender in *BD*, *LGW*, *HF*, and *PF*. While the surface love story in *TC* shields darker concerns of gender and family, *CT* also contains social, sexual, and political depths implicit in its mythographic allusions and patterns. Includes discussion of *KnT*, *WBPT*, *MerT*, *FranT*, *PhyT*, *PardPT*, and *Ret*.

86. Ciccone, Nancy Ferguson. "Loose Ends: Practical Reason and Inner Debate in Medieval Romance." *DAI* 55 (1995): 2820A. Since sec-

ular narratives treat behavior, twelfth-century scholars regarded them as practical philosophy. Thus, internal debate and decision-making in both French and English romance are often based on theology and philosophy. Among the works, Ciccone analyzes *FranT*, *Mel*, and *TC*.

87. Coleman, Joyce. "Interactive Parchment: The Theory and Practice of Medieval English Aurality." *YES* 25 (1995): 63–79. Argues that aural reading—the reading aloud of a written text—lasted much longer in English tradition than is normally assumed. Coleman surveys theoretical approaches to the relations between orality and literacy and adduces evidence from Chaucer and others that "public reading pleased and stimulated audiences into the late fifteenth century."

88. Crépin, André. "Le code amoureux d'après le *Confessio Amantis* de Gower et le *Troilus* de Chaucer." In Danielle Buschinger and Wolfgang Spiewok, eds. *La "fin'amor" dans la culture féodale*. Actes du colloque du Centre d'Études Médiévales de l'Université de Picardie Jules Verne, Amiens, mars 1991. WODAN ser., no. 36. Greifswald: Reineke, 1994, pp. 67–72. Compares and contrasts courtly love in Gower's *Confessio Amantis* and Chaucer's *TC*.

89. Dalrymple, R. "The Literary Use of Religious Formulae in Certain Middle English Romances." *MÆ* 64 (1995): 250–63. Isolates various religious formulae that are "more than merc line-fillers" in Middle English romances; they are significant in the vows and prayers.

90. Donnelly, Colleen. "Chaucer's Sense of an Ending." *JRMMRA* 11 (1990): 19–32. Chaucer's "open-endedness" and "lack of an ending" relate to the fact that he was writing in a "time of crisis" (the Black Death, the corruption of the church). He sought to confront conditions of his time through pluralism, and his lack of closure reflects the instability of the era. Donnelly examines *HF*, *BD*, and *PF* in detail and comments on *CT* and *TC*.

91. Dor, Juliette. "The Wheat and the Chaff: Early Chaucer Scholarship in France." In Danielle Buschinger and Wolfgang Spiewok, eds. *Études de linguistique et de littérature en l'honneur d'André Crépin*. Greifswalder Beiträge zum Mittelalter, no. 5. WODAN ser., no. 20. Greifswald: Reineke, 1993, pp. 123–33. Surveys nineteenth- and early twentieth-century French Chaucer criticism, from early appropriations of Chaucer into French literary tradition to recognition of his importance in anticipating the Renaissance.

92. East, W. G. "'Goddes Pryvetee.'" *DownR* 112 (1994): 164–69. Chaucer's work contains an "astonishing range of interest in every aspect of the Christian religion," including mystical contemplation.

Examples of Chaucer's knowledge of this type of religion are found in
*HF*, *MilT*, and *SumT*.

93. Fanego Lema, Teresa, ed. *Papers from the IVth International
Conference of the Spanish Society for Medieval Language and Literature.*
Cursos e congresos, no.74. Santiago de Compostela: Universidad de
Santiago de Compostela, 1993. 336 pp. Thirty literary and linguistic
essays from the SELIM IV conference (September 1991), on topics ranging from *Beowulf* to Robin Hood and including discussions of lyrics,
drama, dream visions, and various individual works and themes. For essays that pertain to Chaucer, see nos. 105, 131, 141, 157, 161, 193,
219, 249, and 265.

94. Farrell, Thomas J., ed. *Bakhtin and Medieval Voices.* Gainesville:
University Press of Florida, 1995. xii, 240 pp. Eleven essays by various
authors, including three on Chaucer. Each essay applies the critical theory of Mikhail Bakhtin to one or more works of medieval literature. For
essays that pertain to Chaucer, see nos. 64, 190, and 212.

95. Fernández Nistal, Purificación, and José Mª Bravo Gazalo, eds.
*Proceedings of the VIth International Conference of the Spanish Society for
Medieval English Language and Literature.* Linguistica y filologia, no. 22.
Valladolid: Universidad de Valladolid, 1995. 396 pp. Includes four es-
says that pertain to Chaucer. See nos. 201, 236, 311, and 319.

96. Hadden, Barney Craig. "Social Limitations on Chaucer's
Knowledge of Scripture: Quoting and Cribbing from the Bible in 'The
Canterbury Tales.'" *DAI* 55 (1995): 3519A. Defines the extent of the
laity's knowledge of the Bible in late fourteenth-century England.
Chaucer knew relatively little Scripture, apparently never having read
the Bible through. *ParsT* is almost certainly an early work.

97. Hagstrum, Jean H. *Esteem Enlivened by Desire: The Couple from
Homer to Shakespeare.* Chicago and London: University of Chicago Press,
1992. xvi, 518 pp. A historical assessment of representations of heterosexual love and marriage in the art, myth, and religion of the Western
world, concentrating on differing ways in which esteem and desire have
been aligned, rationalized, and sanctified. A brief section (pp. 264–74)
explores how Chaucer confronts pagan, orthodox Christian, courtly, and
Chartrian views of love and sexuality. The section focuses on *KnT*, *TC*,
*PF*, *FranT*, *WBP*, and *WBT*. The Wife, not the Franklin, represents
Chaucer's views.

98. Heffernan, James A. W. *Museum of Words: The Poetics of
Ekphrasis from Homer to Ashbery.* Chicago and London: University of

Chicago Press, 1993. xii, 249 pp. Surveys "how painting and sculpture have been represented by poets ranging from Homer's time to our own," focusing on Homer, Ovid, Virgil, Dante, Chaucer and Gower, Spenser and Shakespeare, Wordsworth, Keats, Shelley, Byron, Browning, Auden, William Carlos Williams, and John Ashbery. Recurrent topics include the tensions between silent and verbal representation, the gendering of ekphrasis, and the enduring nature of the device. Heffernan briefly treats the ekphrasis at the beginning of *HF* and examines at greater length the temples of Venus in *KnT*. See also no. 352.

99. Henningfeld, Diane Andrews. "Contextualizing Rape: Sexual Violence in Middle English Literature." *DAI* 55 (1995): 1945A. Medieval anatomical, religious, and legal ideas about rape appear in medical texts, religious rules, saints' legends, romances, and *WBT*. These works reveal cultural attitudes toward rape and women in general.

100. Iglesias-Rabade, Luis. "Multi-lingual Education in England 1200–1500." *SN* 67 (1995): 185–95. Reviews the language used in schools and universities. French was the usual language of instruction until 1350, and perhaps later in universities. The author examines the role of the friars, Wyclif, and the Lollards in the increasing use of English and the growth of literacy.

101. Jurkowski, Maureen. "New Light on John Purvey." *EHR* 110 (1995): 1180–90. Prints the inventory of books found in Purvey's residence upon his arrest in 1414, which were assessed at £12-18s-8d, and analyzes what the titles and their value imply.

102. Kawasaki, Masatoshi. *Chaucer's Literary World: "Game" and Its Topography*. Tokyo: Nan'Un-Do Press, 1995. 422 pp. (in Japanese). Examines the topoi of "game" v. "ernest" and "authority" v. "experience" in Chaucer's works, considering the influence of medieval rhetorical tradition on the poet's imagination.

103. Klassen, Norman. *Chaucer on Love, Knowledge and Sight*. Chaucer Studies, no. 21. Cambridge: D. S. Brewer, 1995. xi, 225 pp. Examines Chaucer's views on knowing and loving as they are connected and opposed through sight imagery. Surveys in individual chapters the philosophical and literary backgrounds of such connection and opposition and assesses their roles in the tradition of medieval love poetry. In Chaucer's works, the interrelations among love, knowledge, and sight are particularly self-reflexive, here examined in *BD*, *HF*, *PF*, *LGW*, and, most extensively, *TC*. *KnT*, *MerT*, and *SNT* receive the most attention among the tales of *CT*.

104. Kuczynski, Michael P. *Prophetic Song: The Psalms as Moral Discourse in Late Medieval England*. Philadelphia: University of Pennsylvania Press, 1995. xxx, 292 pp. Studies the influence of the book of Psalms on moral discourse in late medieval England. Surveys the tradition of psalms commentary from St. Augustine to Richard Rolle's English *Psalter*, describes how psalms were used to encourage contrition in religious literature, and assesses the use of psalms for social and political complaint. Gives significant attention to Lollard texts, William Langland, John Lydgate, and miscellaneous works of verse and prose and makes brief references to Chaucer's Parson and Monk.

105. Lazaro Lafuente, Luis Alberto. "Modern Features in Chaucer." In Teresa Fanego Lema, ed. *Papers from the IVth International Conference of the Spanish Society for Medieval Language and Literature* (*SAC* 19 [1997], no. 93), pp. 175–82. Outlines the aspects of Chaucer's works that are usually regarded as characteristic of twentieth-century British modernism: innovation and convention-breaking, fusion of genres, colloquial idioms, metrical license, dramatic monologue, poetic self-consciousness, and a number of specific themes, including the complexity of personal relations, continuity with European culture, and continuity with the past.

106. Leyser, Henrietta. *Medieval Women: A Social History of Women in England, 450–1500*. London: Weidenfeld and Nicolson, 1995. xi, 337 pp.; 15 b&w illus. Surveys the legal, literary, and social status of women in medieval England, concentrating on the twelfth century and later. An opening section on Anglo-Saxon women explores evidence from archeology and law, as well as from history, saints' lives, and other literature. The second section assesses the impact of the Norman Conquest on women in England, while the third breaks the discussion of English women in the high and later Middle Ages into separate chapters on marriage and motherhood, work, and widowhood. The fourth section assesses various issues of women's religious status and outlook, as well as their literary interest and depictions. The book includes fifty pages of source material translated into modern English and briefly discusses Chaucer's Wife of Bath in light of *Sir Gawain and the Green Knight* and Christine de Pizan.

107. Lynch, Andrew, and Philippa Maddern, eds. *Venus and Mars*. Nedlands: University of Western Australia Press, 1995. viii, 214 pp. Includes one essay that pertains to Chaucer; see no. 223.

108.   Mann, Jill. "Chaucer and Atheism." The Presidential Address. Ninth International Congress of the New Chaucer Society, 23–27 July 1994, Trinity College, Dublin. *SAC* 17 (1995): 5–19. Examines how a twentieth-century atheist can read and respond to Chaucer, suggesting that a form of "dialogism" can mediate between the present and the past and can enable us to recognize that Chaucer is essentially more humanistic than, for example, Dante.

109.   McHardy, A. K. "The Churchmen of Chaucer's London: The Seculars." *Medieval Prosopography* 16 (1995): 57–87. Examination of tax records gives a picture of the distribution of clerical personnel in London around 1380. The majority of more than 800 seculars were unbeneficed chaplains, many coming from outside the city. Other categories include clerks, beneficed parochial clergy, beneficed chantry chaplains, and the most elite group, the canons of St. Paul's and the chapel of St. Martin-le-Grand.

110.   Mehl, Dieter. "Buch, Autor, und Leser bei Chaucer und Lawrence." *Archiv* 232 (1995): 253–70. Contrasts the life of Chaucer with that of D. H. Lawrence, focusing on their corresponding views about books, authors, and authorship.

111.   Minnis, A. J. "From Medieval to Renaissance? Chaucer's Position on Past Gentility." *Proceedings of the British Academy* 72 (1986): 205–46. Discusses whether Chaucer is a medieval or a Renaissance poet, examining Chaucer's attitudes toward his world and the process by which Chaucer was inspired. Minnis defines Chaucer as a "medieval 'classicizer'" and a "poet of the past."

112.   ———, with V. J. Scattergood and J. J. Smith. *The Shorter Poems*. Oxford Guides to Chaucer. Oxford: Clarendon; New York: Oxford University Press, 1995. xiii, 578 pp. Describes critical approaches to Chaucer's poetry (except *CT* and *TC*) and the crucial issues they have disclosed. Prefatory chapters by Minnis assess the social and cultural contexts of poetry in the late fourteenth century and the formal and thematic issues of the love vision and courtly love. Subsequent chapters on *BD*, *HF*, *PF*, and *LGW* (also by Minnis) summarize critical opinion on date, style and rhetoric, structure, sources, genre, and interpretive themes in the respective works. In a chapter on *ABC*, Chaucer's complaints, his lyrics, and his begging poems, Scattergood considers questions of canonicity and literary tradition, as well as interpretive approaches. The volume includes an appendix, by Smith, on

Chaucer's language, including spelling, pronunciation, prosody, vocabulary, and verbal play.

113. Mulvihill, John Francis. "Titling the Poem." *DAI* 56 (1995): 1345A. Ancient and medieval poems often received no titles from their authors. With commercial dissemination, editors provided titles to attract readers, as with poems by Chaucer, Wyatt, Shakespeare, and Dickinson. Authorial titles tend to orient readers by grounding the poem in actuality or by extending it to abstraction.

114. Newhauser, Richard G., and John A. Alford, eds. *Literature and Religion in the Later Middle Ages: Philological Studies in Honor of Siegfried Wenzel*. Medieval & Renaissance Texts and Studies, no. 118. Binghamton, N.Y.: Medieval & Renaissance Texts & Studies, 1995. ix, 414 pp. Includes seventeen essays on Chaucer, *Piers Plowman*, pastoral literature, Scripture and homilies, and lyric poetry; a dedicatory introduction; and a list of Wenzel's publications. For essays that pertain to Chaucer, see nos. 171, 262, 277, and 322.

115. Nicolaisen, W. F. H., ed. *Oral Tradition in the Middle Ages*. Medieval & Renaissance Texts & Studies, no. 112. Binghamton, N.Y.: Medieval & Renaissance Texts & Studies, 1995. vi, 231 pp. Four plenary papers and eight sectional papers from the Twenty-Second Annual Conference, Center for Medieval and Early Renaissance Studies, State University of New York at Binghamton, 21–22 October 1988. The papers examine aspects of oral tradition for their own sake and investigate the characteristics of preliterature or nonliterate cultural features and their effects on the literate culture, i.e., on the manuscript tradition and its contents. The third plenary paper, by Carl Lindahl, discusses romance elements in *CT*. See no. 150.

116. Ožbot, Martina. "Chaucer—A Medieval Writer?" *Acta Neophilologica* 26 (1993): 17–26. Although there is little doubt that Chaucer is a medieval poet, his emphasis on the real world in *CT* and his use of temporal and reality-based allusions point to a Renaissance influence. These influences suggest that "Chaucer cannot be identified with the society he lived in, as he surpassed the principles on which it was based."

117. Patton, Celeste A. "Chaucer's Poetics of the Female Body." *DAI* 56 (1995): 545A. In medieval literature, the human (especially the female) body is treated ambivalently—as ideal, as erotic, and as grotesque, as with Chaucer's Pardoner ("feminized male grotesque") and characters in *BD*, *LGW*, *KnT*, *MLT*, *PrT*, *ClT*, and *SNT*.

118. Rex, Richard. *"The Sins of Madame Eglentyne" and Other Essays on Chaucer*. Newark, N.J.: University of Delaware Press; London: Associated University Presses, 1995. 201 pp. An anthology of nine essays by Rex, four of which pertain to *PrT*, revised from previous publications (see *SAC* 9 [1987], no. 201; *SAC* 10 [1988], nos. 194 and 195; and *SAC* 12 [1990], no. 189). For the new essays, see nos. 72, 252–54, and 323.

119. Ronquist, Eyvind C. "Rhetoric and Early Modern Skepticism and Pragmatism." *Canadian Journal of Rhetorical Studies* 5 (1995): 49–75. Assesses brief passages from Langland and Chaucer as indications of late fourteenth-century protopragmatism—or reliance on experience and rhetorical argument as epistemological modes. The variegated opinions, unstable exempla, and inconclusive proverbs offered by the two authors connect them with Cicero in the past and Montaigne in the future.

120. Santano Moreno, Bernardo, Adrian R. Birtwhistle, and Luis G. Girón Echevarría, eds. *Papers from the VIIth International Conference of SELIM*. Cáceres: Universidad de Extremadura, 1995. Includes five essays that pertain to Chaucer; see nos. 152, 195, 244, 291, and 299.

121. Saul, Nigel. "Richard II and the Vocabulary of Kingship." *EHR* 110 (1995): 854–77. In 1397, Richard II's rule became more tyrannical, a fact reflected, some chroniclers report, in more elaborate forms of address that were more appropriate for God than for a king. Saul examines common petitions and letters for evidence of this change and analyzes the reason for it. Some of the new forms were influenced by Continental usage.

122. Scala, Elizabeth Doreen. "Absent Narratives: Medieval Literature and Textual Repression." *DAI* 56 (1995): 187A. Later medieval literature (as represented by Chaucer and others) demonstrates "cultural anxiety," manifested through marginal glosses, commentary, and illumination that make each manuscript unique, unlike modern printings.

123. Sendra, Antonio León, María C. Casares Trillo, and María M. Rivas Carmona, eds. *Second International Conference of the Spanish Society for Medieval Language and Literature*. Córdoba: Universidad de Córdoba, 1993. For individual essays that pertain to Chaucer, see nos. 24, 46, 302, 307, 313, and 318.

124. Singman, Jeffrey L., and Will McLean. *Daily Life in Chaucer's England*. Daily Life Through History Series. Westport, Conn., and

London: Greenwood, 1995. xiv, 252 pp; illus. Presents the social history of late fourteenth-century England so readers may duplicate medieval food, clothing, entertainment, etc. The volume sketches in general terms the social context of Chaucerian England and offers practical instruction on how to re-create its details and atmosphere. Mentions Chaucer's works when they support individual practices. Includes numerous line drawings modeled on medieval artifacts and manuscript illuminations.

125. Strohm, Paul. "Chaucer's Lollard Joke: History and Textual Unconscious." The Biennial Chaucer Lecture. Ninth International Congress of the New Chaucer Society, 23–27 July 1994, Trinity College, Dublin. *SAC* 17 (1995): 23–42. Reads Chaucer's reference to cooks' turning "substaunce to accident" (*PardT* 538–40) as a joke about Lollard attitudes toward the Eucharist. Employing Freudian psychology of jokes and New Historicist evaluation of Lollard views and views of Lollards, Strohm uses the reference to disclose the "unconscious" of the text—a metaphor for its many layers of meaning.

126. Takada, Yasunari. "Chaucer's Use of Neoplatonic Traditions." In Anna Baldwin and Sarah Hutton, eds. *Platonism and the English Imagination*. Cambridge: Cambridge University Press, 1994, pp. 45–51. Chaucer's treatment of Neoplatonic concerns with love, ascent to heaven, and nature is characterized "by obliqueness, a sense of humour and even irony." Takada assesses love and ascent in *TC* and nature in *PF*.

127. Takamiya, Toshiyuki. "Chaucer Studies in Japan: A Personal View." In Martin Stevens and Daniel Woodward, eds. *The Ellesmere Chaucer: Essays in Interpretation* (*SAC* 19 [1997], no. 26), pp. 327–35. Summarizes the development of Chaucerian studies in Japan, noting major Japanese scholars of Chaucer, the founding of the Centre for Medieval English Studies at the University of Tokyo, the inception of *Poetica: An International Journal of Linguistic-Literary Studies*, and the formation of the Japan Society for Medieval English Studies. Japanese scholars have concentrated on "philological or linguistic approaches to Chaucer and the making of concordances."

128. Tavormina, M. Teresa, and R. F. Yeager, eds. *The Endless Knot: Essays on Old and Middle English in Honor of Marie Borroff*. Cambridge: D. S. Brewer, 1995. x, 252 pp. Sixteen essays by different authors, one on the Old English dual pronoun, thirteen on Middle English (Chaucer, Langland, and the *Pearl*-poet), one on the reception of Gower by Ben Jonson, and one on the scholar Elizabeth Elstob (1683–1756). For the

eight essays that pertain to Chaucer, see nos. 68–70, 162, 185, 187, 273, and 295.

129. Utz, Richard J. "Negotiating the Paradigm: Literary Nominalism and the Theory and Practice of Rereading Late Medieval Texts." In Richard J. Utz, ed. *Literary Nominalism and the Theory of Rereading Late Medieval Texts: A New Research Paradigm* (*SAC* 19 [1997], no. 130), pp. 1–30. Surveys the critical application of nominalism to medieval literary texts, suggesting three main approaches: nominalist text as source, as coeval philosophical substratum, and as historical corroboration of modern perceptions. Postulates Chaucer's knowledge of nominalism via Ralph Strode and public *disputationes* and reads the epilogue of *TC* as a problem-solving device similar to nominalist leaps of faith.

130. ————, ed. *Literary Nominalism and the Theory of Rereading Late Medieval Texts: A New Research Paradigm*. Medieval Studies, no. 5. Lewiston, N.Y.; Queenston, Ont.; Lampeter, Wales: Edwin Mellen, 1995. viii, 256 pp. Ten essays address correspondences between late medieval nominalism and literature, including Julian of Norwich, *Sir Gawain and the Green Knight*, Jean Molinet, and Chaucer. For essays that pertain to Chaucer, see nos. 129, 139, 173, 215, 264, 287, and 300.

131. Valdés Miyares, Rubén. "Structural Unity and Mystical Unity in Later Medieval English Narrative." In Teresa Fanego Lema, ed. *Papers from the IVth International Conference of the Spanish Society for Medieval Language and Literature* (*SAC* 19 [1997], no. 93), pp. 305–13. Mutual concern with mystical wholeness and unity in Chaucer, Langland, and Malory derives from literary and intellectual tradition rather than from the authors' philosophical acceptance of such an ideal. The ideal is unattainable in their works, thereby reflecting the nominalistic challenge to Neoplatonic tradition. Truth is the goal of their protagonists, but the protagonists fail to achieve this goal on earth.

132. Weisl, Angela Jane. *Conquering the Reign of Femeny: Gender and Genre in Chaucer's Romances*. Chaucer Studies, no. 22. Cambridge: D. S. Brewer, 1995. ix, 133 pp. Explores the relation of gender and the genre of romance in Chaucer's *CT*, especially the mutually defining and delimiting power of the two categories. Women conform to the particular roles romance carves out for them, while the genre is simultaneously limited by these restricted female roles. Defined by a uniquely "vague set of generic criteria," romance mimes the position of women in the romances themselves. Chaucer questions the role and position of women

and tests the limits of romance, a form that appears to be coterminous with femininity itself. Weisl considers *TC*, *KnT* and *SqT*, *Th*, and *FrT* and *WBT*, comparing them with their sources and analogues to demonstrate Chaucer's understanding of romance and his critique of its limitations.

133. Whitaker, Muriel, ed. *Sovereign Lady: Essays on Women in Middle English Literature*. Garland Medieval Casebooks, no. 11. Garland Reference Library of the Humanities, no. 1876. New York and London: Garland, 1995. xviii, 220 pp. Nine essays by various authors, addressing topics such as Julian of Norwich, Margery Kempe, the *Ancrene Riwle*, the Paston daughters, Malory's Guinevere, and several works by Chaucer. Includes a selective annotated bibliography of studies about women and medieval literature. For essays that pertain to Chaucer, see nos. 167, 222, 225, and 269.

134. Wilkins, Nigel. *Music in the Age of Chaucer.* 2d ed., with *Chaucer Songs*. Chaucer Studies, no. 1. Cambridge: D. S. Brewer, 1995. xiv, 210 pp. Combines in one volume Wilkins' two previously published works, *Music in the Age of Chaucer* (1979) and *Chaucer Songs* (1980).

See also nos. 136, 168.

### *The Canterbury Tales*—General

135. Blake, Norman F. "The Canterbury Tales Project." *Archiv* 232 (1995): 126–37. A report on the history and goals of the *Canterbury Tales* Project.

136. Boenig, Robert. *Chaucer and the Mystics:* The Canterbury Tales *and the Genre of Devotional Prose*. Lewisburg, Penn.: Bucknell University Press, 1995. 231 pp. Similarities between Chaucer and the Middle English mystics do not imply a conscious intention on his part either to imitate the mystics or to parody them ironically. Chaucer may or may not have known the works of Pseudo-Dionysius, Margery Kempe, Richard Rolle, and Julian of Norwich, but these mystics were part of the cultural, social, and political circumscriptions that helped shape his texts. *CT* shares specific ideas, topoi, and motifs with the large body of Middle English mystical and devotional treatises. In addition, the mystics' doubts about the valency of language may partially explain

Chaucer's persistent fragmentation and his tendency toward simultaneous affirmation and denial, as demonstrated by Chaunticleer's mistranslation of his Latin tag in *NPT* and by the spiritual erasure of a series of tales in *Ret*.

137. Conrad, Peter. *To Be Continued: Four Stories and Their Survival.* Oxford: Clarendon Press, 1995. 207 pp. Chaucer's pilgrims in *CT* do not reach the martyr's shrine in the cathedral, Langland's pilgrims in *Piers Plowman* do not attain any of his even remoter visionary goals, and Spenser's Arthur in *The Faerie Queene* falls short of his ideal destination at the court of Gloriana. The four essays in Conrad's book discuss the unfinished state of *CT*, *Romeo and Juliet*, *Lear*, and *Prometheus* and analyze various modern continuations of these works. For Chaucer, twentieth-century writers such as Eliot, Burroughs, Murray, Chesterton, Powell, Pasolini, and Jarusch propose several answers. Their continuations variously declare that the pilgrims did not deserve to arrive at their sacred destination; that they might have arrived after all, received the blessings denied by Chaucer, and departed once more to save the civilized world; or that their arrival is a calamity that has given them power to bolster dogma and to destroy our secular civilization by medievalizing the modern world.

138. Cooper, Helen. "The Order of the Tales in the Ellesmere Manuscript." In Martin Stevens and Daniel Woodward, eds. *The Ellesmere Chaucer: Essays in Interpretation* (*SAC* 19 [1997], no. 26), pp. 245–61. The manuscripts and internal evidence of *CT* indicate that those who "put the various exemplars of the tales, links, and fragments in order for Ellesmere did not have any manuscript consensus to work from, and indeed, they have helped create such consensus as there is. But they do seem to have made the fullest use of whatever evidence was available to them, and the end result is more likely than any other order to represent Chaucer's own scheme."

139. Crafton, John Micheal. "Emptying the Vessel: Chaucer's Humanistic Critique of Nominalism." In Richard J. Utz, ed. *Literary Nominalism and the Theory of Rereading Late Medieval Texts: A New Research Paradigm* (*SAC* 19 [1997], no. 130), pp. 117–34. Chaucer's works reflect a pattern of concern with the realist-nominalist issues of language. Early on, Chaucer critiques realism, and, later on, nominalism, while *TC* and especially *CT* pose the two views in dialogic debate. Fragment 6 (*PhyT* and *PardT*) represents the opposed extremes and

then undermines them, exemplifying how Chaucer struggled with his predecessors and anticipated the Renaissance.

140. Emmerson, Richard K. "Text and Image in the Ellesmere Portraits of the Tale Tellers." In Martin Stevens and Daniel Woodward, eds. *The Ellesmere Chaucer: Essays in Interpretation* (*SAC* 19 [1997], no. 26), pp. 143–70. The twenty-three portraits in the Ellesmere manuscript are not closely related to Chaucer's text. Only eight of the portraits show "striking features" described in *GP*, and even these eight show details not derived from the text. The portrait artists derived their paintings not from a study of the *GP* but from a team supervisor's general directions. The miniatures mark the beginnings of each tale, serving as visual incipits, part of the *ordinatio* of the manuscript.

141. Fernández García, Alfonso, and Gabriela García Teruel. "Narrative Structures Generated by the Theme of Deception in Medieval European Short Stories." In Teresa Fanego Lema, ed. *Papers from the IVth International Conference of the Spanish Society for Medieval Language and Literature* (*SAC* 19 [1997], no. 93), pp. 113–24. Examines narrative structures in *Disciplina clericalis*, *Sendebar*, *Calila e Dimna*, *CT*, *Decameron*, *Aubereé et Le Prêtre et Alison*, and *Dame Siriz*, using Bremond's sequential analysis to explore event-linking and deception, and Barthes's analysis to study initial elements and their expansions in these works.

142. Fields, Peter John. "Craft in 'The Canterbury Tales': Rhetoric and Survival." *DAI* 55 (1995): 2821A. Chaucer's use of the word "craft" and its derivations in *CT* indicate a difference between individuals and the world they want to control. For Chaucer's speakers, the craft of knowledge and social customs is not enough. For survival of the self, they must depend on rhetorical craft as well.

143. Grudin, Michaela Paasche. "Discourse and the Problem of Closure in the *Canterbury Tales*." *PMLA* 107 (1992): 1157–67. *CT* "shows a surprising array" of ways in which Chaucer "ignores, skirts, transcends, or even anticipates structural closure," engaging his readers in the "dialogic processes of discourse itself." Grudin surveys the techniques of open-endedness in *CT*, arguing that they result from Chaucer's imitations of oral tradition and that they invite us to read the work as a "drama of the reception of discourse" and an assertion of an open epistemology.

144. Hallissy, Margaret. *A Companion to Chaucer's* Canterbury Tales. Westport, Conn., and London: Greenwood, 1995. xiv, 333 pp. Intended

as a "do-it-yourself course" for first-time readers of *CT*, the companion is organized in a series of separate chapters devoted to *GP* and to most tales, although the Links, *CkT* and *SqT*, *Th*, *Mel*, *MkT*, and *ParsT* are consigned to appendices. The discussions include basic descriptive and critical information, though a brief annotated bibliography, suggested for "Further Reading," accompanies each section. Key passages are given in Middle English with modern translation. Also includes brief sections on Chaucer's world and his language.

145. Irwin, Bonnie D. "What's in a Frame? The Medieval Textualization of Traditional Storytelling." *OT* 10 (1995): 27–53. Describes the frame tale as a device of an "oral/literate continuum" that enabled medieval authors to draw on both traditions and to produce a flexible form. Authors such as Chaucer in *CT* and Boccaccio in *Decameron* capitalize on the open-ended potential of oral and literate rhetorical forms, their competing time frames, and their variety of narrator-audience dynamics.

146. Jacobs, Kathryn. "Rewriting the Marital Contract: Adultery in the *Canterbury Tales*." *ChauR* 29 (1995): 337–47. Analyzes *MerT*, *MilT*, *ShT*, and *FrT* in light of the twofold nature of the English medieval marriage contract: personal duties and business responsibilities. In those marriages concerned with property alone, adultery exposes the lack of reciprocity. In those concerned with spousal interactions, adultery may restore the intent of the marriage bonds.

147. Kaylor, Noel Harold. "The Orientation of Chaucer's *Canterbury Tales*." *MedPers* 10 (1995–96): 133–47. Chaucer's allusions to the East (e.g., to Turkey, Syria, and India) refer, on the one hand, to a practical knowledge of geography and, on the other—with ecclesiastical use of the *mappae mundi* in mind—to a symbolic spiritual goal, a reorientation in which East is upward.

148. Kendrick, Laura. "The *Canterbury Tales* in the Context of Contemporary Vernacular Translations and Compilations." In Martin Stevens and Daniel Woodward, eds. *The Ellesmere Chaucer: Essays in Interpretation* (*SAC* 19 [1997], no. 26), pp. 281–305. Surveys French compilations to argue that *CT* "appears to burlesque the uniformly high-minded French prose compilations . . . actively encouraged by the Valois princes in the second half of the fourteenth century." The narrator's apology for using the pilgrims' own words indicates that, in a time of French translations and compilations, English was a suspect innovation. Chaucer and his contemporaries "almost surely" saw Chaucer as a translator and compiler of others' works.

149. Laskaya, Anne. *Chaucer's Approach to Gender in the* Canterbury Tales. Chaucer Studies, no. 23. Cambridge: D. S. Brewer, 1995. 224 pp. *CT* resists the dominant medieval gender discourses that it inscribes. Competition between Chaucer's male narrators and characters both reveals and challenges masculine stereotypes of the hero, the lover, and the intellectual. Tales of masculine spirituality question behavioral norms. *ParsT* addresses the social conflicts of the frame-narrative by inviting men to "repudiate the competitiveness of the world." Women who compete with men are "rebellious"; "obedient" women are pitied as outcasts and victims, but "the narrators perceive this condition as 'acceptable.'" The female narrators are wrapped within layers of male discourse, but, especially in *WBPT*, this layering helps to set up an ultimately liberating blurring of gender boundaries.

150. Lindahl, Carl. "The Oral Undertones of Late Medieval Romance." In W. F. H. Nicolaisen, ed. *Oral Tradition in the Middle Ages* (*SAC* 19 [1997], no. 115), pp. 59–75. As a cultural mirror and cultural battleground, romance seems to blend voices from all ranges of society: secular and sacred, rural and urban, rich and poor. As a festive processional storytelling contest, Chaucer's *CT* successfully imitates the play styles of the major social factions of his day. The two opposing styles of acting and speaking—the gentil and the churl—are not only apparent throughout *CT* but also found everywhere in the records of actual medieval festivals. Chaucer's bold setting of these styles against each other is a structuring principle of his poem.

151. Pérez Gállego, Cándido. "¿Cómo funcionan los *Cuentos de Canterbury?*" In Cándido Pérez Gállego. *Circuitos Narrativos*. Serie Crítica, no. 3. Zaragoza: Universidad de Zaragoza, Facultad de Filosofia y Letras, Departamento de Lengua y Literatura Inglesas, 1975, pp. 153–201. Introduction to *CT* that surveys major concerns of the work, including narrative technique, character development, comedy, setting, major themes, reader involvement, and sources and analogues. Considers *CT* in light of works by Boccaccio, the *Gawain*-poet, Shakespeare, Lawrence Sterne, Dickens, Arthur Miller, Bertold Brecht, and Dostoevski.

152. Ridley, Florence. "Chaucerian Strategies: Effects and Causes." In Bernardo Santano Moreno, Adrian R. Birtwhistle, and Luis G. Girón Echevarría, eds. *Papers from the VIIth International Conference of SELIM* (*SAC* 19 [1997], no. 120), pp. 239–56. Assesses Chaucer's methods of drawing audiences into a mutually creative process by confronting

them with questions. By repetition, Chaucer ensures that responses to such questions lead ultimately to comprehension of the overall moral message of *CT*.

153. Sanchez Escribano, F. Javier. "Los Maridos en *The Canterbury Tales*." *Cuadernos de Investigación Filológica* 5 (1979): 129–44. Summarizes the literary and social position of women in Chaucer's time and discusses the various marital relationships in *CT*. Assesses *MilT*, *WBPT*, *ClT*, *MerT*, *FranT*, *ShT*, and *ManT*, observing how the works focus on one or more of the following: adultery, authority, battle of the sexes, patience, age differences in marriage, and the dangers of jealousy.

154. Serrano Reyes, Jesús L. "The Host's Ideolect." *SELIM* 4 (1994): 20–47. Describes the Host's speech habits, assessing how they characterize him and how his various forms of address depict him as pilgrim, master of ceremonies, philosopher, etc.

155. Taavitsainen, Irma. "Narrative Patterns of Affect in Four Genres of the *Canterbury Tales*." *ChauR* 30 (1995): 191–210. Chaucer uses interjections and exclamations as a means of audience involvement, promoting dramatic suspense in his works. Certain words are so closely associated with certain genres that when Chaucer uses them in another context, they echo the original text. Chaucer often manipulates this technique for comic or ironic effect.

156. Taylor, Paul Beekman. "Time in the *Canterbury Tales*." *Exemplaria* 7 (1995): 371–93. The time of the Canterbury pilgrimage imitates the time and eternity of the cosmos. In the poem, time acts as a measurable, conceptual principle for men, but it is embodied as a perceptual force in women such as the hag in *WBT* and Griselda in *ClT*.

157. Vila de la Cruz, Maria Purificación. "Education and Social Aspects of Children's Education in English Medieval Society (14th Century)." In Teresa Fanego Lema, ed. *Papers from the IVth International Conference of the Spanish Society for Medieval Language and Literature* (SAC 19 [1997], no. 93), pp. 319–23. Tallies instances of Chaucer's attention to childhood education in *CT*.

158. Watson, Michael. "Genre, Convention, Parody, and the 'Middle Flight': *Heike Monogatari* and Chaucer." *Poetica* (Tokyo) 44 (1995): 23–40. Despite the difficulties of comparing literature cross-culturally, *CT* and the *Heike Monogatari* are similar in their "middle" styles, their adaptability to parody, and their capacious allusions to "native and foreign literary studies."

159. Wauhkonen, Rhonda L. "'Reading from Within': Nicholas of Lyra, the *Sensus iteralis* and the Structural Logic of 'The Canterbury Tales.'" *DAI* 56 (1995): 1349A. Considers the Hebraic and patristic in the philosophical and English background of Chaucer's poem.

See also nos. 5, 19, 24–26, 28–31, 33–42, 45, 50, 51, 69, 85, 103, 160, 165, 192, 212, 258, 278.

## CT—The General Prologue

160. Bowden, Betsy. "Visual Portraits of the Canterbury Pilgrims, 1484(?) to 1809." In Martin Stevens and Daniel Woodward, eds. *The Ellesmere Chaucer: Essays in Interpretation* (*SAC* 19 [1997], no. 26), pp. 171–204; 17 b&w illus. Surveys pilgrim portraits, ranging from Caxton's woodcuts to Blake's 1809 (1810?) engraving of *Chaucer's Canterbury Pilgrims*, exploring "earlier readers' understandings of Chaucer's text [in order] to begin to distinguish those perceptions that remain constant across time from those limited to a given sociohistorical context." Includes historical analysis of such details as background and clothing, plus interpretation of pilgrim-riders' abilities to manage their horses and equine attitudes toward one another or toward the actions of their riders.

161. Downing, Angela. "Theme and Topic in the *General Prologue*." In Teresa Fanego Lema, ed. *Papers from the IVth International Conference of the Spanish Society for Medieval Language and Literature* (*SAC* 19 [1997], no. 93), pp. 55–76. Linguistic analysis of Chaucer's syntactical techniques in *GP*. Examines Chaucer's methods of introducing and delaying information, suggesting that he may seem familiar to modern readers because his strategies are the same as those used in modern speech.

162. Ginsberg, Warren. "Chaucer's Disposition." In M. Teresa Tavormina and R. F. Yeager, eds. *The Endless Knot: Essays on Old and Middle English in Honor of Marie Borroff* (*SAC* 19 [1997], no. 128), pp. 129–40. Examines *GP* sketches of the Wife of Bath, the Miller, and the Franklin to exemplify how Chaucer's arrangements of details can best be understood relationally. We perceive the "dispositions" of the characters as functions of the interplay among the "ends" to which the details of the sketches refer.

163. Mertens-Fonck, Paule. "*The Canterbury Tales*: New Proposals of Interpretation." In *Atti della Accademia Peloritana dei Pericolanti Classe di Lettere, Filosofia e Belle Arti* 69 (1995): 1–29. The systematic inconsistencies between numbers in *GP* (number of pilgrims "announced" v. number found by reader, number of tales "promised" v. actual number, number of potential narrators v. number of tales told) seem to proceed from a poetic strategy inspired by the nominalist theory of knowledge, designed to invite the reader to a critical reappraisal.

164. Sato, Tsutoma. "Chaucer's Narrative Typology in the 'General Prologue' to the *Canterbury Tales*." *Dokkyo Gaigaku Eigo Kenkyu* 41 (1993): 10–39 (in Japanese, with English abstract). Analyzes the rhetorical shift between the third-person presentational voice of the first eighteen lines of *GP* and the following first-person voice of the involved narrator. The passage exploits a new paradigm of narration and validates the theories of Saussure and Genette.

165. Yesufu, Abdul R. "The Spring Motif and the Subversion of Guaranteed Meaning in Chaucer's *The Canterbury Tales*." *ESA* 38:2 (1995): 1–15. Examines Chaucer's uses of the "reverdie" of spring and allusions to the season especially in *GP* and elsewhere in *CT*. Chaucer deconstructs the traditional connotations of springtime imagery, suggesting that spring distracts humanity from spiritual pursuits.

See also nos. 9, 61, 69, 140, 249, 252–54, 269.

### CT—The Knight and His Tale

166. Chewning, Susannah Mary. "'Wommen . . . Folwen Alle the Favour of Fortune': A Semiotic Reading of Chaucer's *Knight's Tale*." In Robert S. Corrington and John Deely, eds. *Semiotics 1993*. New York: Peter Lang, pp. 373–79. Explores Emily's moments of speech and silence in *KnT* to argue that, at the end of the narrative, she is "the perfect example of the silent signifier," lacking any personal meaning beyond what is inscribed by the prevailing courtly attitudes.

167. Farvolden, Pamela. "'Love Can No Frenship': Erotic Triangles in Chaucer's 'Knight's Tale' and Lydgate's *Fabula duorum mercatorum*." In Muriel Whitaker, ed. *Sovereign Lady: Essays on Women in Middle English Literature* (SAC 19 [1997], no. 133), pp. 21–45. In *KnT*, courtly love

seems antithetical to brotherhood in arms, but the eventual disposal of Emelye reinstates male friendship. Lydgate offers a related, more explicit model of supposedly benign homosocial exchange.

168. Gellrich, Jesse M. *Discourse and Dominion in the Fourteenth Century: Oral Contexts of Writing in Philosophy, Politics, and Poetry.* Princeton, N.J.: Princeton University Press, 1995. xiv, 304 pp. Examines the ways oral tradition continues to influence writing in late medieval literature, considering works of Ockham and Wyclif, chronicles of the reigns of Edward III and Richard II, *Sir Gawain and the Green Knight*, and *KnT*. In *KnT*, Chaucer poses relations between political domination and metalinguistic discourse, issues important during the minority of Richard II. The conflict between spoken and written modes in *KnT* is self-reflexive, and it critiques contemporary political dominion in which power resulted from the displacement of voice.

169. Gambera, Disa. "Disarming Women: Gender and Poetic Authority from the 'Thebaid' to the 'Knight's Tale.'" *DAI* 55 (1995): 3505A. Women furnish the "crucial means" for authors to adapt the Theban tradition to their own poetic vision. Statius shows women as criticizing epic history; the *Roman de Thèbes*, Dante's *Purgatorio*, and Boccaccio's *Teseida* impose differing emphases; and *KnT*, more nearly like the epic history of Statius, shows women as sustaining losses and sacrifices.

170. Hodges, Laura F. "Costume Rhetoric in the Knight's Portrait: Chaucer's Every-Knight and his Bismotered Gypon." *ChauR* 29 (1995): 274–302. The multilayered details of the Knight's clothing represent both a realistic fourteenth-century knight, who might well have looked grimy and disheveled, and a symbolic knight, whose profession of chivalry in the fourteenth century was far from ideal. Chaucer's choice of conflicting particulars complicates the portrait of this pilgrim.

171. Irving, Edward B., Jr. "Heroic Worlds: 'The Knight's Tale' and 'Beowulf.'" In Richard G. Newhauser and John A. Alford, eds. *Literature and Religion in the Later Middle Ages: Philological Studies in Honor of Siegfried Wenzel* (*SAC* 19 [1997], no. 114), pp. 43–59. A comparison of *Beowulf* and *KnT* reveals that the latter has epic elements such as death, mortality, and the struggle with the chaos inherent in an epic universe. These parallel themes "help us to better see a dark traditional dimension in Chaucer."

172. Klitgård, Ebbe. *Chaucer's Narrative Voice in* The Knight's Tale. Copenhagen: Museum Tusculanum Press, 1995. 111 pp. Emphasizes the stylistic and rhetorical innovation of Chaucer's narrative voice, ar-

guing that it can be perceived behind his various narrators and implied authors. Comparing and contrasting the voice of *KnT* with that of Chaucer's other works and those of contemporary romances, Klitgård examines how Chaucer achieves a paradoxical distance from and closeness to his material in *KnT* and leaves the poem without thematic resolution. Chaucer's voice can be perceived despite the various and shifting registers and narrative postures of *KnT*.

173.    Laird, Edgar. "Cosmic Law and Literary Character in Chaucer's *Knight's Tale*." In Richard J. Utz, ed. *Literary Nominalism and the Theory of Rereading Late Medieval Texts: A New Research Paradigm* (*SAC* 19 [1997], no. 130), pp. 101–15. *KnT* "participates in a tradition antagonistic to the new nominalism," based on a "scientific ontology consonant with Boethianism" and understandable in light of the truth-theories of Albumasar, Robert Grosseteste, and John Wyclif.

See also nos. 10, 17, 54, 57, 59, 61, 66, 83, 85, 97, 98, 103, 117, 132, 320.

## CT—The Miller and His Tale

174.    Coletes Blanco, Agustín. "An Atypical 'Fabliau': Genre and Expression in *The Miller's Tale*." *Cuadernos de Filología Inglesa* 2 (1986): 63–81. *MilT* is a typical fabliau in form and content, but it goes beyond the conventions of the genre in its links with the rest of *CT*, its metafictive deep structure, and its riches of lexicon and parody.

175.    Jones, Lowanne E. "The Phallic Leek." In Rupert T. Pickens, ed. *Studies in Honor of Hans-Erich Keller: Medieval French and Occitan Literature and Romance Linguistics*. Kalamazoo, Mich.: Medieval Institute Publications, Western Michigan University, 1993, pp. 419–26. Jones explores the use of the leek as a phallic symbol in works by Chaucer, Shakespeare, Boccaccio, and Rabelais. Chaucer's use of the leek as metaphor represents sexual prowess in *MilT* and virility in old age in *MerT*.

176.    Lomperis, Linda. "Bodies That Matter in the Court of Late Medieval England and in Chaucer's *Miller's Tale*." *RR* 86 (1995): 243–64. In *MilT*, identity is a matter of theatrical impersonation, encouraging the audience to recognize that Alisoun is depicted as a man playing a woman. This cross-gendering capitalizes on contemporary

fashion and homosexuality in the court of Richard II to suggest that Nicholas and Alisoun engage in homosexual relations and that Absolon recognizes Alisoun's true gender at the moment of the misdirected kiss. Through *MilT*, Chaucer critiques the self-fashioning nature of Richard's court.

177. Morey, James H. "The 'Cultour' in the *Miller's Tale*: Alison as Iseult." *ChauR* 29 (1995): 373–81. In *MilT*, the coulter was chosen by Chaucer for its etymological and judicial significance and because it parallels a scene from *Tristan and Iseult*—the trial by ordeal. Nicholas, John, and Alisoun provide comic equivalents of Tristan (the trickster), Mark (the unsuitable husband), and Iseult (the love object).

178. Royle, Nicholas. "'The Miller's Tale' in Chaucer's Time." In Bill Readings and Bennet Schaber, eds. *Postmodern Across the Ages: Essays for a Postmodernity That Wasn't Born Yesterday*. Syracuse, N.Y.: Syracuse University Press, 1993, pp. 63–71. Impressionistic commentary on the levels of narration in *MilT*, its self-conscious concern with auditory and visual perspective, its mockery of the Bible, and the process of its humor. The reader's point of view is that of a panopticon that turns out to be deceptive.

179. Rudat, Wolfgang E. H. "Gender-Crossing in the *Miller's Tale*—and a New Chaucerian Crux." *JEP* 16 (1995): 134–46. Thomas W. Ross's *Variorum Edition* of *MilT* creates new possibilities for interpreting the misdirected kiss. Through multivalent language, *MilT* explores gender-crossing as well as gender power struggles. Actions in the window scene suggest not only sexual impotence but also "psychological castration."

180. Walls, Kathryn. "The Significance of *Arca* and *Goddes pryvetee* in *The Miller's Tale*." *N&Q* 240 (1995): 24–26. Suggests that an "ark" is a hiding place and that this provides another dimension to *pryvetee* in *MilT*.

See also nos. 61, 63, 82, 92, 146, 153, 162, 182, 185, 259.

## CT—The Reeve and His Tale

181. Campbell, Bruce. "The Livestock of Chaucer's Reeve: Fact or Fiction?" In Edwin Brezette De Windt, ed. *The Salt of Common Life:*

*Individuality and Choice in the Medieval Town, Countryside, and Church: Essays Presented to J. Ambrose Raftis*. Studies in Medieval Culture, no. 36. Kalamazoo, Mich.: Medieval Institute Publications, Western Michigan University, 1995, pp. 271–305. Extant manorial accounts representing over two hundred different demesnes in Norfolk (from the period 1250 to 1449) suggest that Oswald the Reeve's dwelling and husbandry were based on a specific landscape and rural economy that would have been recognizable to many in Chaucer's audience.

182. Justman, Stewart. "*The Reeve's Tale* and the Honor of Men." *SSF* 32 (1995): 21–27. Explores relations among cuckoldry, charivari, and notions of masculine honor in *MilT* and *RvT* to argue that the pretensions to honor in *RvT* are debunked and that traditional notions of honor are themselves questioned.

183. Smith, Charles R. "Chaucer's Reeve and St. Paul's Old Man." *ChauR* 30 (1995): 101–6. The Reeve's four burning coals ("Avauntyng, liying, anger, covetise" [line 3884]) are taken from the description of the spiritual old man in Ephesians 4:22–28. They serve to characterize not only the Reeve but also the four main characters in the tale, who, however young, are spiritually old men as well.

184. Stanley, E. G. "Francis Burton: Old Chaucer's *Reeve's Tale* 'Put into Better Englishe.'" *N&Q* 240 (1995): 271–78. Identifies and edits from Bodleian Library MS Add. A.267 Francis Burton's version of *RvT*, in quatrains, from the early seventeenth century.

185. Tavormina, M. Teresa. "'Lo, Swilk a Complyn': Musical Topicality in the Reeve's and Miller's Tales." In M. Teresa Tavormina and R. F. Yeager, eds. *The Endless Knot: Essays on Old and Middle English in Honor of Marie Borroff* (*SAC* 19 [1997], no. 128), pp. 141–50. The names of the students in *RvT* recall the court musician John Aleyn, contemporary of Chaucer and composer of the motet *Sub arturo plebs*. The self-conscious Englishness of the motet—plus its inclusion of the name Nicholas—correlates in intriguing ways with musical allusions in *RvT* and *MilT*.

186. Woods, William F. "The Logic of Deprivation in the *Reeve's Tale*." *ChauR* 30 (1995): 150–63. *RvT* is a social allegory reflecting economic and social practices. Symkyn upsets the balance of trade by reducing supply, thus increasing demand. Balance is eventually restored.

See also nos. 42, 66.

## CT—The Man of Law and His Tale

187.   Archibald, Elizabeth. "Contextualizing Chaucer's Constance: Romance Modes and Family Values." In M. Teresa Tavormina and R. F. Yeager, eds. *The Endless Knot: Essays on Old and Middle English in Honor of Marie Borroff* (SAC 19 [1997], no. 128), pp. 161–75. Considers *MLT* "in the context of other Middle English family romances," a genre in which "members of a nuclear family are separated and then reunited after various adventures." Unlike most other examples of the genre, *MLT* and *Emaré* contain heroines who are central to their plots, and only in *MLT* is the ending more religious than celebratory. In *MLT*, Chaucer "casts doubt on the conventional, patriarchal construction of family values."

188.   Beidler, Peter G. "Chaucer's Request for Money in the Man of Law's Prologue." *Chaucer Yearbook* 2 (1995): 1–15. Compares *MLP* to its source in Innocent III's *De miseria condicionis humane* and to *Purse* to argue that *MLP* was originally written for Chaucer to read before a group of merchants to ask for payment.

189.   George, J.-A. "Repentance and Retribution: The Use of the Book of Daniel in Old and Middle English Texts." *BJRL* 77 (1995): 177–92. Mentions how the Susannah story was used in *MLT*.

190.   Jordan, Robert M. "Heteroglossia and Chaucer's Man of Law's Tale." In Thomas J. Farrell, ed. *Bakhtin and Medieval Voices* (SAC 19 [1997], no. 94), pp. 81–93. Examines the "ideological markers" that indicate the various "languages" of *MLT*, arguing that they cannot be resolved into unity by recourse to a supposed personality of the teller. *MLT* comprises several literary languages, and unlike the postmedieval novels examined by Mikhail Bakhtin, it does not include social or professional languages.

191.   Scala, Elizabeth. "Canacee and the Chaucer Canon: Incest and Other Unnarratables." *ChauR* 30 (1996): 15–39. *SqT* and *MLT* are alike in that both tell and do not tell the story of incest. *MLT* tells the story it dismisses, and *SqT* dismisses—with its curious method of storytelling—the story it tells. Both tales show Chaucer's fascination with narrative technique.

See also nos. 11, 85, 117, 208.

## CT—The Wife of Bath and Her Tale

192. Arfin, William. "Chaucerian Choice: Formal and Thematic Considerations in the *Wife of Bath's Tale*." *CR* 35 (1995): 64–80. Arfin considers *WBT* as a *demande*, written toward the end of the composition of *CT* as Chaucer's comment on "the collection as a whole" or on the "nature of literature in general" in his work-in-progress. In discussing ethics and choice, the article makes passing references to the Pardoner, *MLT*, *FranT*, *ParsT*, and *Ret*.

193. Doñabeita Fernandez, María Louisa. "Alas! Alas! Unhappy Wife of Bath: A Close Reading of the Wife of Bath's Prologue." In Teresa Fanego Lema, ed. *Papers from the IVth International Conference of the Spanish Society for Medieval Language and Literature* (SAC 19 [1997], no. 93), pp. 43–53. A deconstructive-psychoanalytical reading of *WBP* that examines the gaps left in the Wife's discourse, exploring implications of rape, sexual economics, and prostitution. Doñabeita Fernandez reads Bath as a complex sign rather than a simple geographical reference.

194. Eadie, John. "The Wife of Bath's Non-Hengwrt Lines: Chaucerian Revision or Editorial Meddling?" *NM* 96 (1995): 169–76. Four passages (3.575–84, 609–12, 619–26, and 717–20), absent from the majority of manuscripts of *WBP*, are present in most modern editions. They seem to reflect not Chaucer's own revisionary impulse but the work of later editors who wished to bring *WBP* into line with conventional medieval attitudes toward women.

195. Giménez Bon, Margarita. "A Good Wif Was Ther of Biside Bath." In Bernardo Santano Moreno, Adrian R. Birtwhistle, and Luis G. Girón Echevarría, eds. *Papers from the VIIth International Conference of SELIM* (SAC 19 [1997], no. 120), pp. 101–6. Analyzes the medieval features of the characterization in Éilis Ní Dhuibhne's *The Wife of Bath* (Dublin, 1989).

196. Ho, Cynthia. "Old 'Wives' and Their Sources: The Wife of Bath, *The Romance of the Rose*, *Genji Monogatari*, and *Ise Monogatari*." *Poetica* (Tokyo) 44 (1995): 1–12. Comments on differences and similarities among these characters: the Wife of Bath as depicted in *WBP*, La Vieille of *Roman de la Rose*, and old women who take young lovers in two medieval Japanese narratives.

197. Hopenwasser, Nanda. "The Wife of Bath as Storyteller: 'Al Is for to Selle' or Is It? Idealism and Spiritual Growth as Evidenced in the

*Wife of Bath's Tale."* *MedPers* 10 (1995–96): 101–15. The Wife is "the female shaman" who creates *WBT* as an initiation rite into manhood. Like Margery Kempe and St. Bridget of Sweden, the Wife uses "preaching and teaching to heal the ills of her society through the performative action of storytelling."

198. Kennedy, Beverly. "The Variant Passages in the Wife of Bath's Prologue and the Textual Transmission of *The Canterbury Tales*: The 'Great Tradition' Revisited." In Lesley Smith and Jane H. M. Taylor, eds. *Women, the Book and the Worldly: Selected Proceedings of the St. Hilda's Conference, 1993, Volume II.* Cambridge: D. S. Brewer, 1995, pp. 85–101. Documents the manuscript evidence of the authenticity of six passages in *WBP* (lines 44a–f, 575–84, 605–8, 609–12, 619–26, 717–20) and surveys justifications for their inclusion in various editions. Attributes the continued inclusion of these questionable passages to editorial conservatism and modern refusal to distinguish between repeated remarriage (evident throughout *WBP*) and sexual promiscuity (evident only in the passages).

199. Lee, Brian S. "Exploitation and Excommunication in *The Wife of Bath's Tale.*" *PQ* 74 (1995): 17–35. The rape victim in *WBT* quickly vanishes from the text because she is "excommunicated," or denied access to the privileges of the knight who exploits her. Only when society assimilates such marginalized others can the rapist himself be subjected to excommunication, which in this tale is only temporary and is occasioned by the victim's symbolic "reappearance" via the hag and the transformed wife. Lee compares the circumstances of this rape to the events in other works, including *PhyT*, *FranT*, and *LGW* (Lucrece).

200. Lucas, Angela M. "The Knight in Chaucer's *Wife of Bath's Tale.*" *Poetica* (Tokyo) 35 (1992): 29–40. Compares the knights in *Weddynge of Sir Gawen and Dame Ragnell* and *Tale of Florent* with the knight in *WBT* to show that Alison is an antifeminist character. The interaction between Alison and the knight demonstrates a "battle of the sexes" that portrays women making generous sacrifices to unworthy men.

201. Manzanas Calvo, Ana M. "From Experience to Authority: The Authentication of the Self in *The Book of Margery Kempe* and *The Wife of Bath's Prologue.*" In Purificación Fernández Nistal and José Mª Bravo Gazalo, eds. *Proceedings of the VIth International Conference of the Spanish Society for Medieval English Language and Literature* (SAC 19 [1997], no. 95), pp. 223–30. Margery Kempe and Alison of Bath represent a basic

conflict: as representatives of the nascent bourgeoisie, they seek to inscribe themselves in a tradition that, since they are women, silences them.

202. Olson, Glending. "The Marital Dilemma in *The Wife of Bath's Tale*: An Unnoticed Analogue and Its Chaucerian Court Context." *ELN* 33:1 (1995): 1–7. A ballade by Eustache Deschamps poses a *demande d'amour* similar to that of the Loathly Lady in *WBT*, wherein a courtier is required to render judgment on a question of love.

203. Saunders, Corrine J. "Women Displaced: Rape and Romance in Chaucer's *Wife of Bath's Tale*." *Arthurian Literature* 16 (1995): 115–31. Assesses the rape in *WBT* in light of rape as an "episodic unit" in medieval romance and in light of medieval law. In both the romance and the legal contexts, rape is ambiguous, and *WBT* reflects this ambiguity, affirming patriarchal values while exploring the possibility for educating men about female desire for action against rape.

204. Vasta, Edward. "Chaucer, Gower, and the Unknown Minstrel: The Literary Liberation of the Loathly Lady." *Exemplaria* 7 (1995): 395–418. Compares *WBT*, Gower's *Tale of Florent*, and *Weddynge of Sir Gawen and Dame Ragnell* in light of Bakhtin's theory of carnival. Both Gower (thoroughly) and Chaucer (ambiguously) assimilate the Lady into official culture, while the *Weddynge* liberates both Lady and culture from that culture's repressive forces.

205. Weil, Susanne. "Freedom Through Association? Chaucer's Psychology of Argumentation in *The Wife of Bath's Prologue*." *PCP* 30 (1995): 27–41. Associative thinking in *WBP* may have drawn on the model of Aristotelian psychology and argumentation as understood in Chaucer's day. As a consequence, the Wife of Bath's voice remains more real to a modern audience than does the debate she represents.

See also nos. 13, 85, 97, 99, 132, 149, 153, 156, 162, 215, 240, 311.

## *CT*—The Friar and His Tale

206. Miller, Clarence H. "The Devil's Bow and Arrows: Another Clue to the Identity of the Yeoman in Chaucer's *Friar's Tale*." *ChauR* 30 (1995): 211–14. It was commonly assumed in the Middle Ages that the devil carried arrows and shot them at his human prey. That the Friar's

"yeoman" bears arrows "brighte and kene" (line 1381) is yet another clue that escapes the stupid summoner.

See also nos. 132, 146.

## CT—The Summoner and His Tale

207. Cox, Catherine S. "'Grope Wel Bihynde': The Subversive Erotics of Chaucer's Summoner." *Exemplaria* 7 (1995): 145–77. Through the trope of "groping," *SumT* reveals a narrative erotics that simultaneously privileges and destabilizes heterosexual orthodoxy.

208. Holford-Strevens, Leofranc. "*Quid iuris questio.*" *N&Q* 240 (1995): 164–65. In light of a passage in a Bibliothèque Nationale Paris manuscript, the sense of the phrase *quid iuris questio* in *GP* is "The question arises of what is the law (upon these facts)."

209. Pulsiano, Phillip. "The Twelve-Spoked Wheel of the *Summoner's Tale.*" *ChauR* 29 (1995): 382–89. The ending of *SumT* parodies the "division of the winds," a problem for the medieval natural sciences that Chaucer notes in *Astr*. Manuscript illustrations on the four cardinal and eight secondary winds took the form of a wheel with spokes. Chaucer uses this configuration in *SumT* both farcically and literally.

See also nos. 23, 69, 92.

## CT—The Clerk and His Tale

210. Carruthers, Leo. "The Medieval Student: Chaucer's Poor Clerk of Oxford." In Roger Lejosne, ed. *Educations anglo-saxonnes de l'an mil à nos jours*, vol. 2. Amiens: Sterne, 1995, pp. 13–24.

211. Chickering, Howell. "Form and Interpretation in the *Envoy* to the *Clerk's Tale.*" *ChauR* 29 (1995): 352–72. A close reading of the Envoy to *ClT* underscores Chaucer's brilliant ambiguity and makes the assigning of it to a single speaker impossible. Chaucer works with multiple strategies within *ClT* and ends it with a variety of interpretations as well.

212. Farrell, Thomas J. "The Chronotopes of Monology in Chaucer's Clerk's Tale." In Thomas J. Farrell, ed. *Bakhtin and Medieval Voices (SAC 19 [1997], no. 94),* pp. 141–57. Assesses the utility of applying

Bakhtinian analysis to Chaucer's works and examines the monologia of *ClT* in light of the *Tale*'s intersections of "Ecclesiastes time" and figural time. The characters of *ClT*, especially Griselda, act in anticipation that Providence will "compensate or balance the alternating times" of their lives; Chaucer modifies this "chronotope" with figural imagery. The Envoy to *ClT* reminds us that the various voices of *CT* are not in dialogue but juxtaposed, exemplifying Bakhtin's "First Stylistic Line" of the novel.

213. Georgianna, Linda. "*The Clerk's Tale* and the Grammar of Assent." *Speculum* 70 (1995): 793–821. Griselda's assent to Walter's wishes, which goes beyond the patience or concealment that he demands, represents complete identification or unity of will. In the theological terms of Rudolph Otto, her assent is not "moral" but "numinous." The absoluteness of her assent therefore defies political or moral explanation.

214. Grinnell, Natalie. "Griselda Speaks: The Scriptural Challenge to Patriarchal Authority in 'The Clerk's Tale.'" *CMat* 9:1 (1995): 79–94. Scriptural allusions in *ClT* challenge the patriarchal views traditionally found in it.

215. Grossi, Joseph L., Jr. "The Clerk vs. the Wife of Bath: Nominalism, Carnival, and Chaucer's Last Laugh." In Richard J. Utz, ed. *Literary Nominalism and the Theory of Rereading Late Medieval Texts: A New Research Paradigm (SAC* 19 [1997], no. 130), pp. 147–78. Reads *ClT* as a realist's attack on nominalism, with Walter depicting an unfree deity, and Griselda, rampant fideism. Chaucer moderates the Clerk's realism at the end of the *Tale* and in the Envoy.

216. Jimura, Akiyuki. "Chaucer's Use of 'un'-Words in 'The Clerk's Tale.'" In Masuo Umeda, ed. *Perspectives on Words: Essays on English Language and Literature.* Tokyo: Eihōsha, 1995, pp. 47–54. Explores the use of "unsad," "untrewe," and "undiscreet" in *ClT*, relating these words to their stems—"sad," "trewe," and "discreet"—and to Chaucer's characterization of Griselda.

217. ———. "Negative Expressions in 'The Clerk's Tale.'" *Bulletin of the Faculty of School Education* (Hiroshima University) 17 (1995): 1–9. An investigation of the relationship between negatives and negative expressions, content, and characterization in *ClT*. Includes frequency tables for *ClT* and other works by Chaucer.

218. Moon, Hi Kyung. "Chaucer's *Clerk's Tale*: A Disrupted Exemplum." *JELL* 40 (1994): 643–55. Chaucer's sympathy toward

women is questionable, given the context of *ClT* and Walter's dominance over Griselda. This uncertainty is perpetuated by the double narrative of *CT*, which presents the *Tale* through the voice of a fictional storyteller as well as the voice of the author. It is difficult to realize Chaucer's view on feminism, since he allows Griselda to maintain her identity while placing her in a submissive and passive role.

219. Olivares Merino, Eugenio. "*The Clerk's Tale*: Griselda's Virtue as Both Disruptive and Necessary." In Teresa Fanego Lema, ed. *Papers from the IVth International Conference of the Spanish Society for Medieval Language and Literature* (*SAC* 19 [1997], no. 93), pp. 223–31. Compares and contrasts Griselda of *ClT* with the biblical Job to show that her morality is unorthodox and that she can be seen as a usurper of male roles.

220. Sprung, Andrew. "'If It Youre Wille Be': Coercion and Compliance in Chaucer's *Clerk's Tale*." *Exemplaria* 7 (1995): 345–69. The relationship between Walter and Griselda partially reenacts the paradigm of a child's ego development. While Walter's inordinate tyranny is fueled by Griselda's inordinate compliance, an alternative model of domination is shown by the Clerk's own ordinate exercise of authority and his submission in his relations with the other pilgrims.

221. Van Dyck, Carolynn. "The Clerk's and Franklin's Subjected Subjects." *SAC* 17 (1995): 45–68. Griselda and Dorigen embody more coherent subjectivities than do their counterparts in analogous tales, although neither becomes a true agent in the outcome of her plot. In his efforts to include women in the category "mankind," Chaucer intrudes the "heavily gendered subissues" of marital sovereignty and female chastity into plots that traditionally focus on obedience and *gentilesse*. As a result, he "forcefully disrupts the semiotic order that subsumes individual agency under universal ideas."

222. Whitaker, Muriel. "The Artists' Ideal Griselda." In Muriel Whitaker, ed. *Sovereign Lady: Essays on Women in Middle English Literature* (*SAC* 19 [1997], no. 133), pp. 85–114; 6 b&w plates. Iconographic imagery in *ClT* indicates Griselda's exemplary physical, moral, and spiritual beauty. British paintings, from 1721 onward, have created various Griseldas—betrayed, patient, virginal, and sexually victimized. Sculptors have idealized her beyond recognition.

See also nos. 8, 58, 117, 153, 156.

## CT—The Merchant and His Tale

223. Dove, Mary. "'Swiche Olde Lewed Wordes': Books about Medieval Love, Medieval Books about Love and the Medieval Book of Love." In Andrew Lynch and Philippa Maddern, eds. *Venus and Mars* (*SAC* 19 [1997], no. 107), pp. 11–33. Intertextual references in *MerT* invite recourse to medieval commentators on the Song of Solomon. The glosses on Solomon suggest views of medieval marriage and sexuality different from those of either C. S. Lewis or Michel Foucault. They provide a complex idea of Aristotelian "causes" of love, resisting the opposition of "literal" sexuality to "spiritual" sense that D. W. Robertson and David Aers have, in different ways, applied to Chaucer.

224. Edwards, Robert R. "Some Pious Talk about Marriage: Two Speeches from the *Canterbury Tales*." In Robert R. Edwards and Vickie Ziegler, eds. *Matrons and Marginal Women in Medieval Society*. Woodbridge, Suffolk: Boydell Press, 1995, pp. 111–27. Examines the encomium on marriage in *MerT* and the speech on marital values in *FranT*. In their structural placements and their relations with their sources, the speeches do not so much critique or assert specific views on marriage as represent doctrine against which the actions of the *Tales* are posed. The speeches are theory; the tales are practice.

225. Everest, Carol. "'Paradys or Helle': Pleasure and Procreation in Chaucer's 'Merchant's Tale.'" In Muriel Whitaker, ed. *Sovereign Lady: Essays on Women in Middle English Literature* (*SAC* 19 [1997], no. 133), pp. 63–84. The traditional Galenic idea that conception requires female orgasm indicates that May is not pregnant by January. However, implicit and symbolic references to seed and fruit suggest that Damian has impregnated her.

226. Everest, Carol A. "Pears and Pregnancy in Chaucer's 'Merchant's Tale.'" In Melitta Weiss Adamson, ed. *Food in the Middle Ages: A Book of Essays*. New York and London: Garland, 1995, pp. 161–75. May's request for pears in *MerT* indicates that she is pregnant, since medieval texts align the condition with a desire for unripe fruit. Moreover, medieval medical treatises recommend pears for the treatment of stomach disorders, "especially the nausea due to pregnancy."

227. Heffernan, Carol Falvo. "Contraception and the Pear Tree Episode of Chaucer's *Merchant's Tale*." *JEGP* 94 (1995): 31–41. Medieval contraceptive information includes mention of pears in

discussion of techniques for preventing conception, so May's desire for a pear in *MerT* may indicate that she wants to deny January's foolish desire for offspring.

228. Hussey, S. S. "Comedy for the Cognoscenti: Chaucer's *Merchant's Tale*." In Elizabeth Maslen, ed. *Comedy: Essays in Honour of Peter Dixon by Friends and Colleagues*. London: Queen Mary and Westfield College, University of London, 1993, pp. 1–13. The comedy of *MerT* is brought out through Chaucer's manipulation of various literary sources and styles. For readers to appreciate fully the comedy of *MerT*, they must be familiar with Chaucer's works, as well as the literary context from which they derive.

See also nos. 65, 85, 103, 146, 153, 175.

## CT—The Squire and His Tale

229. Crépin, André. "L'exotisme dans le Conte de l'Ecuyer des *Canterbury Tales*." In Danielle Buschinger and Wolfgang Spiewok, eds. *Nouveaux mondes et mondes nouveaux au Moyen Age*. Actes du colloque du Centre d'Études Médiévales de l'Université de Picardie Jules Verne, Amiens, mars 1992. Greifswalder Beiträge zum Mittelalter, no. 37. WODAN ser., no. 20. Greifswald: Reineke, 1994, pp. 29–34. Explores the foreign, exotic elements of *SqT*, commenting on its setting, its inclusion of marvelous objects, and its relations with other literature set in the Orient.

230. Lynch, Kathryn L. "East Meets West in Chaucer's Squire's and Franklin's Tales." *Speculum* 70 (1995): 530–51. Explores the possible oriental analogues of *SqT*. The *Tale* exhibits an open-ended narrative that contrasts with the Western emphasis on closure, resolution, and rhetorical discipline in *FranT*.

See also nos. 132, 191.

## CT—The Franklin and His Tale

231. Parry, Joseph Douglas. "Narrative Mobility in Layamon, Malory, Chaucer, and Spenser." *DAI* 56 (1995): 945A. Among the nar-

rative techniques employed to achieve authorial purposes, Chaucer's characterization of Dorigen in *FranT* shows her postponing her ultimately necessary conformity with male ideologies by contemplating authoritative tales based on those very ideologies.

232. Pearsall, Derek. "*The Franklin's Tale*, Line 1469: Forms of Address in Chaucer." *SAC* 17 (1995): 69–78. Surveys the use of the vocative, "thou" and "you" forms, and other "unadorned" forms of address in Chaucer's works to argue that in *FranT* Arveragus adopts an authoritative tone in sending Dorigen to meet Aurelius to fulfill her promise.

233. Scott, Anne. "'Considerynge the Beste on Every Syde': Ethics, Empathy, and Epistemology in the *Franklin's Tale*." *ChauR* 29 (1995): 390–415. Much of the ambivalence of *FranT* comes from the various ways the characters perceive the world and the ways they act on these perceptions. By analyzing the different perspectives, we can identify with the "moral" behaviors of the characters and discern the "model for human relationships" that they supply.

234. Stevenson, Barbara. "West Meets East: Geoffrey Chaucer's 'Franklin's Tale' and the Japanese 'Captain of Naruto.'" *Poetica* (Tokyo) 44 (1995): 41–52. Advocates a multicultural approach to literature by comparing *FranT* to a thirteenth-century Japanese narrative of the Emperor Gosaga. Unlike Aurelius, Gosaga does not release his beloved from her promise, and comparison of the tales highlights how the two works reflect different aspects of feudal societies and medieval cultures.

See also nos. 85, 86, 97, 153, 162, 199, 221, 224, 230.

## CT—The Physician and His Tale

235. Collette, Carolyn P. "'Peyntyng with Greet Cost': Virginia as Image in the *Physician's Tale*." *Chaucer Yearbook* 2 (1995): 49–62. Compares the description of Virginia in *PhyT* with Wycliffite or Lollard materials to argue that Virginia is cast as a perfect image rather than a false one—a reflection of contemporary concern with images, their uses, and their abuses.

236. Sendra, Antonio R. León, and Francisco J. García de Quesada. "The *Physician's Tale*." In Purificación Fernández Nistal and José Mª Bravo Gazalo, eds. *Proceedings of the VIth International Conference of the*

*Spanish Society for Medieval English Language and Literature* (*SAC* 19 [1997], no. 95), pp. 207–16. Assesses the Physician as a skillful practitioner and comments on *PhyT*, audience response to the tale, sources, arrangement of materials, and Chaucer's message.

237. Whitaker, Elaine E. "John of Arderne and Chaucer's Physician." *ANQ* 8:1 (1995): 3–8. John of Arderne's contemporary treatise *Fistula in Ano* is a manual for the medieval physician. Comparison with it indicates that "Chaucer's physician commits malpractice."

See also nos. 85, 139, 199.

## *CT*—The Pardoner and His Tale

238. Braswell, Mary Flowers. "Chaucer's Palimpsest: Judas Iscariot and *The Pardoner's Tale*." *ChauR* 29 (1995): 303–10. Certain details of *PardT*, a story of "brotherhood and betrayal," suggest old stories of Judas Iscariot, the consummate betrayer. The theme of avarice, the inability to die, the oak tree, the treasure up the "croked wey," and the "last supper" all have parallels in art, architecture, and apocryphal texts concerning Judas.

239. Copeland, Rita. "The Pardoner's Body and the Disciplining of Rhetoric." In Sarah Kay and Miri Rubin, eds. *Framing Medieval Bodies*. Manchester and New York: Manchester University Press, 1994, pp. 138–59. Explores the roles of sexuality and gender in the institutional history of rhetoric and argues that the Pardoner's ambiguity dramatizes a double sense of rhetoric, both as an academic discipline and as a regulated body of practice.

240. Dinshaw, Carolyn. "Chaucer's Queer Touches/A Queer Touches Chaucer." *Exemplaria* 7 (1995): 75–92. Both *PardT* and the Pardoner's interruption of the Wife in *WBT* are "touches of the queer" that temporarily denaturalize heterosexual subjectivity, revealing its performative nature. "Heteronormativity" is reinscribed in the romance discourse of *WBT* and in the Host's silencing of the Pardoner after his *Tale*.

241. Gross, Gregory W. "Trade Secrets: Chaucer, the Pardoner, the Critics." *MLS* 25:4 (1995): 1–36. Characterizing the critics as essentialist, Gross traces views of the Pardoner's sexuality, beginning with Kittredge's and Curry's interests in secrecy and moral scapegoating.

After establishing the medieval relationship of idolatry and sodomy, Gross concludes that the Pardoner makes "unnatural," "unproductive" use of both his sexuality and his knowledge of rhetoric.

242. ———. "Secrecy and Confession in Late Medieval Narrative: Gender, Sexuality, and the Rhetorical Subject." *DAI* 55 (1995): 1945A. Secrecy about sex cuts across genres and develops its own forms of rhetoric, as seen in works from Petrarch's *Secretum* through the *Roman de Silence*, Margery Kempe, *PardP* and *PardT*.

243. Johnson, Bruce A. "The Moral Landscape of the *Pardoner's Tale*." In David G. Allen and Robert A. White, eds. *Subjects on the World's Stage: Essays on British Literature of the Middle Ages and the Renaissance* (*SAC* 19 [1997], no. 75), pp. 54–61. The geographic references in *PardT*, of which the stile is the central figure, represent a loosely symbolic, "moral" landscape that adds to the moral tone of the tale.

244. Manzanas Calvo, Ana M. "The Economics of Salvation in *The Book of Margery Kempe* and *The Pardoner's Prologue*." In Bernardo Santano Moreno, Adrian R. Birtwhistle, and Luis G. Girón Echevarría, eds. *Papers from the VIIth International Conference of SELIM* (*SAC* 19 [1997], no. 120), pp. 175–85. Key figures of the premodernity and precapitalism of the fourteenth and fifteenth centuries, the Pardoner and Margery Kempe exemplify inverted values. Despite their spiritual differences, each conceives of salvation and spiritual reward in economic terms.

245. Marsi, Heather. "Carnival Laughter in the *Pardoner's Tale*." *MedPers* 10 (1995–96): 148–56. Mikhail Bakhtin's theory of carnival and a comparison with fifteenth-century drama suggest that pilgrims' laughter is ambivalent and arises from engagement with paradox. The Pardoner's "quete" invites simultaneous complicity and disdain.

246. Ruud, Jay. "*The Pardoner's Tale* and the Parody of the Resurrection." In Bruce E. Brandt, ed. *Proceedings of the Third Dakotas Conference on Earlier British Literature*. Brookings, S.D.: English Department, South Dakota State University, 1995, pp. 35–44. Discusses the Old Man in *PardT* as a parody of the Resurrection, rather than simply interpreting him allegorically. Looks at the Old Man in the context of the Resurrection, the imagery of the oak tree, and the rioters.

See also nos. 69, 82, 85, 125, 139.

## CT—The Shipman and His Tale

247. Winnick, R. H. "Luke 12 and Chaucer's *Shipman's Tale.*" *ChauR* 30 (1995): 164–90. A likely source of inspiration for *ShT* is the scriptural text from Luke, where interrelated sins parallel those of Chaucer's characters and where images and phrases are analogous to Chaucer's. The biblical text (not a lost French fabliau) as source provides the moral commentary on retributive justice believed missing from *ShT*, thus supplying outside the text what the *Tale* itself is essentially about.

See also nos. 146, 153, 260.

## CT—The Prioress and Her Tale

248. Adams, Robert. "Chaucer's 'Newe Rachel' and the Theological Roots of Medieval Anti-Semitism." *BJRL* 77 (1995): 9–18. Questions whether *PrT* is an exercise in dramatic irony in which the Prioress's anti-Semitism is exposed to ridicule. The mother in the *Tale* is called "this newe Rachel," but Rachel was a Jewish mother lamenting the massacre of Jewish babies by a Gentile ruler. If this is an ironic reference, it could imply that Chaucer was attacking the whole exegetical system of interpreting the Bible.

249. De la Torre Moreno, Maria José. "The Contradictions of Madame Eglentyne: Why She Would Become a Nun." In Teresa Fanego Lema, ed. *Papers from the IVth International Conference of the Spanish Society for Medieval Language and Literature* (SAC 19 [1997], no. 93), pp. 293–303. Examines the *GP* sketch of the Prioress for evidence that she is poorly matched with her vocation, a mismatch especially evident in her attractiveness, coquetry, and "zest for life." *PrT* shows "more reference to praise than to love," indication that the Prioress's understanding of Christian values is simplistic. The article hypothesizes why such a woman may have entered a convent.

250. Narin van Court, Elisa. "*The Siege of Jerusalem* and Augustinian Historians: Writing about Jews in Fourteenth-Century England." *ChauR* 29 (1995): 227–48. *The Siege of Jerusalem* is not simply another anti-Semitic text but instead one that responds humanely to the Jewish plight. Evidence indicates that this poem was written by an Augustinian canon at Bolton Priory, where there was regard for the doctrine of toleration.

251. Paley, Karen Surman. "The Assassination of the 'Litel Clergeon': A Post-colonial Reading of the Prioress's Tale." *Diversity* 3 (Summer 1995): 39–65. Asserting the impossibility of a neutral approach and citing her Jewish ancestry, Paley considers *PrT* in its historical context. Chaucer's uncharacteristic omission of a tale to balance the Prioress's— i.e., his omission of a Jewish tale—is a disservice to the reader.

252. Rex, Richard. "Madame Eglentyne and the Bankside Brothels." In Richard Rex. *"The Sins of Madame Eglentyne" and Other Essays on Chaucer* (*SAC* 19 [1997], no. 118), pp. 78–94. Argues that the name Eglentyne ("rose") connoted sexual dalliance to Chaucer's audience. Fourteenth-century property records indicated affiliations between property owned by the priory at Stratford-at-Bow and the Bankside brothel, the Rose.

253. ———. "The Sins of Madame Eglentyne." In Richard Rex. *"The Sins of Madame Eglentyne" and Other Essays on Chaucer* (*SAC* 19 [1997], no. 118), pp. 95–129. Examines historical and literary backgrounds of details in the *GP* sketch of the Prioress to argue that Chaucer leads us to judge her harshly. In her dress, mannerisms, and actions, the Prioress "is characterized by false piety and hypocrisy, and she fails signally to practice charity." Chaucer exposes her with "biting satire."

254. ———. "Why the Prioress Sings Through Her Nose." In Richard Rex. *"The Sins of Madame Eglentyne" and Other Essays on Chaucer* (*SAC* 19 [1997], no. 118), pp. 69–77. Identifies a medieval tradition in which singing through the nose is a "sign of weak faith and lack of devotion," contributing to the satire of the Prioress in her *GP* sketch.

See also nos. 69, 117, 118, 321.


## CT—*The Tale of Sir Thopas*

See nos. 68, 132.


## CT—*The Tale of Melibee*

255. Anderson, Judith H. "Prudence and Her Silence: Spenser's Use of Chaucer's *Melibee*." *ELH* 62 (1995): 29–46. Spenser's account of

Melibee in *The Faerie Queene* 6 reveals affinities with Chaucer's *Mel*, as well as significant differences from it. Both honey-drinkers tend to be complacent, and both suffer. Spenser's Melibee (whose wife is silent) talks in proverbs but lacks prudence; Chaucer's is married to Prudence, who speaks in proverbs. Both narrators reflect difficult times, with Spenser's undergoing personal and literal loss.

256. Collette, Carolyn P. "Heeding the Counsel of Prudence: A Context for the *Melibee*." *ChauR* 29 (1995): 416–33. The concept of prudence was well known in the Middle Ages and was often seen as a specifically feminine virtue in medieval French texts. Drawing from those texts, Chaucer also underscores the feminine, making *Mel* a story for "real women living complicated lives" who are trying to find their own voices.

257. Dauby, Hélène. "Clercs et femmes au Moyen Age." In Danielle Buschinger and Wolfgang Spiewok, eds. *Études de linguistique et de littérature en l'honneur d'André Crépin*. Greifswalder Beiträge zum Mittelalter, no. 5. WODAN ser., no. 20. Greifswald: Reineke, 1993, pp. 107–12. *Mel* capitalizes on a pattern of attention to women earlier in *CT*, reflecting Chaucer's own concern with female rights of speech and self-expression.

258. Gaylord, Alan T. "Portrait of a Poet." In Martin Stevens and Daniel Woodward, eds. *The Ellesmere Chaucer: Essays in Interpretation* (*SAC* 19 [1997], no. 26), pp. 121–42; 10 b&w illus. Similarities between Thomas Hoccleve's portrait of Chaucer in *Regement of Princes* and the Ellesmere portrait do not confirm speculations that the artists were drawing from life. Rather, similarities in subject matter between *Regement* and *Mel*, where the Ellesmere portrait appears, indicate that the figure is an icon of good counsel, a major theme of *Mel*.

See also nos. 51, 65, 86.

## CT—The Monk and His Tale

259. Biscoglio, Frances. "'Unspun' Heroes: Iconography of the Spinning Woman in the Middle Ages." *JMRS* 25 (1995): 163–77. While the iconography of the spinning woman is generally considered to represent domestic virtue, it can also demonstrate either a model of misaligned femininity, as exemplified by Cenobia in *MkT* (lines

2373–74), or an instance of role reversal—a mark of opprobrium within the male domain—as evidenced by Absolon in *MilT* (lines 3774–75).

260. Pardee, Sheila. "Sympathy for the Monastery: Monks and Their Stereotypes in *The Canterbury Tales*." *JRMMRA* 14 (1993): 65–79. Chaucer's portrayal of the Monk and of the monk in *ShT* is complex and sympathetic. Contemporary expectations about monks are clear in the Host's reactions to the Monk. Daun John fits the stereotype but may be motivated by a desire to chastise gently the wife and husband.

See also nos. 15, 104.

## *CT*—The Nun's Priest and His Tale

261. Bidard, Josseline. "Reynard the Fox as Anti-Hero." In Leo Carruthers, ed. *Heroes and Heroines in Medieval English Literature: A Festschrift Presented to André Crépin on the Occasion of His Sixty-Fifth Birthday* (*SAC* 18 [1996], no. 81), pp. 119–23. In medieval beast fables, including *NPT*, the fox is a figure of vice. Neither his basic animalism nor his comic villainy qualifies him as an antihero, but his consistent distortion of truth does.

262. Boitani, Piero. "'My Tale Is of a Cock' or, The Problems of Literal Interpretation." In Richard G. Newhauser and John A. Alford, eds. *Literature and Religion in the Later Middle Ages: Philological Studies in Honor of Siegfried Wenzel* (*SAC* 19 [1997], no. 114), pp. 25–42. The cock of *NPT*, through correct Latin quotations and their English mistranslations, provides three literal interpretations of Scripture. By placing the ideological meaning of *NPT* within the gap between these interpretations—and thus providing a puzzle of determining the correct literal meaning—Chaucer shows his awareness of the pain and pleasure of writing in an "ideological age" and yet, ultimately, "justifies the letter by itself, and *forces* us to *stay* within it."

263. Chapin, Arthur. "Morality Ovidized: Sententiousness and the Aphoristic Moment in the *Nun's Priest's Tale*." *YJC* 8:1 (1995): 7–33. Compares the comic treatment of sententiousness in *NPT* with modern philosophical uses of aphorism. Both are "Menippean" in their contrasts of high and low discourse, and both ask us to perceive their points rather than to understand conceptually.

264. Furr, Grover C. "Nominalism in the *Nun's Priest's Tale*: A Preliminary Study." In Richard J. Utz, ed. *Literary Nominalism and the Theory of Rereading Late Medieval Texts: A New Research Paradigm* (*SAC* 19 [1997], no. 130), pp. 135–46. Examines the theme of free will in *NPT* in light of the "nominalist-Augustinian debate of the fourteenth century," arguing that Chaucer's position reflects contemporary indeterminacy.

265. López-Peláez Casellas, Jesús. "Flattery, Women and Tragicomedy in *The Nun's Priest's Tale*." In Teresa Fanego Lema, ed. *Papers from the IVth International Conference of the Spanish Society for Medieval Language and Literature* (*SAC* 19 [1997], no. 93), pp. 183–92. Examines the interconnections of theme and genre in *NPT*, maintaining that rhetoric links the "fictive manner" and "fictive matter" of the tale.

266. Vander Weele, Michael, with Deb Powell. "'Fruyt' and 'Chaf' Revisited, or What's Cooking in Chaucer's Kitchen?" *CEA* 57:3 (1995): 39–50. The "fruyt" and "chaf" passage of *NPT* places the reading of the *Tale* in an ethical context, complemented by Plato's *Gorgias*, with "fruyt" and "chaf" representing true and false counsel.

See also nos. 12, 61, 81, 84, 136.


## CT—The Second Nun and Her Tale

267. Connolly, Thomas. *Mourning into Joy: Music, Raphael, and Saint Cecilia*. New Haven, Conn., and London: Yale University Press, 1994. xvi, 365 pp. Studies the history and hagiography of St. Cecilia, plus her status as patron saint of music. Examines the iconography of the saint, especially as depicted in Raphael's altar piece, arguing that it reflects the "mourning-into-joy" motif that expresses the "soul's passages between vice and virtue as a flux of the contrary passions of joy and sadness." Summarizes the iconographic contrasts between *SNT* and *CYT* and examines Chaucer's Cecilia in opposition to idleness, explaining her "work" as a figure of spiritual change.

268. Cowgill, Bruce Kent. "Sweetness and Sweat: The Extraordinary Emanations in Fragment Eight of the *Canterbury Tales*." *PQ* 74 (1995): 343–57. By emphasizing the contrast between excessive sweat in *CYT* and its absence in *SNT*, Chaucer indicates the disjunction be-

tween carnal and spiritual. In addition, Cecilia's "bath of flambes" suggests the purifying water of baptism as opposed to the "watres corosif" of *CYT*. Finally, Chaucer capitalizes on the similitude of "sweten" (to sweat) and "sweten" (to sweeten), wordplay also used in *Form Age*.

269. Filax, Elaine. "A Female I-deal: Chaucer's Second Nun." In Muriel Whitaker, ed. *Sovereign Lady: Essays on Women in Middle English Literature* (*SAC* 19 [1997], no. 133), pp. 133–56. *SNT* reflects a Marian-driven ideal of virginal power, "mayde and martyr," while *SNP* stresses Mary as mediatrix, "Mayde and Mooder." The absent, female-gendered body of the Second Nun, undescribed in *GP*, bears witness to the bodies of female spiritual heroines.

270. Kennedy, Thomas C. "The Translator's Voice in the Second Nun's *Invocacio*: Gender, Influence, and Textuality." *M&H*, n.s., 22 (1995): 95–110. Chaucer's translative and appropriative practice in *SNP* is characterized by "a limited personal perspective transcended by an authoritative source," plus a movement from abstraction (particularly in Dante) to concreteness.

271. Pelen, Marc M. "Idleness and Alchemy in Fragment VIII(G) of Chaucer's *Canterbury Tales*: Oppositions in Themes and Images from the *Roman de la Rose*." *FMLS* 31 (1995): 193–214. Chaucer's mode of composition of *SNT* and *CYT* owes much to the structure of the *Roman de la Rose*, in which the theme of contradictions and contraries plays a major role. The correspondence goes beyond the specific similarities in image and subject that have long been noted between the two works.

272. Pigg, Daniel F. "Constructing a Voice for Chaucer's Second Nun: Martyrdom as Institutional Discourse." *Æstel* 3 (1995): 81–95. The Second Nun's voice is undefined by Chaucer, yet it is intriguing since it probes the nature of "agency, voice, and reappropriation." The voice of the Nun becomes more clear as her character develops, and the *Tale* "becomes a product of the voice."

273. Reames, Sherry D. "Artistry, Decorum, and Purpose in Three Middle English Retellings of the Cecilia Legend." In M. Teresa Tavormina and R. F. Yeager, eds. *The Endless Knot: Essays on Old and Middle English in Honor of Marie Borroff* (*SAC* 19 [1997], no. 128), pp. 177–99. Retellings of the Cecilia legend exemplify the range and flexibility of Middle English hagiography. The *Northern Homily Cycle* "presents Cecilia as a model of ladylike behavior"; the *South English Legendary* "makes her quite bold and transgressive." Chaucer treads a

middle ground in *SNT*, presenting his heroine in a restrained fashion that effects a "satiric commentary on a contemporary ruler or rulers whom he saw as re-enacting the sins" of ancient Roman persecutors.

See also nos. 103, 117, 321.

### *CT*—The Canon's Yeoman and His Tale

See nos. 31, 49, 70, 267, 268, 271.

### *CT*—The Manciple and His Tale

274. Chaganti, Seeta. "A Thai Analogue to *The Manciple's Tale*." *N&Q* 240 (1995): 26–27. Discusses a Thai analogue to *ManT*, similar in structure and moral.

275. Kanno, Masahiko. "*The Manciple's Tale*: The Manciple's Warning." In Nobuyuki Yuasa et al., eds. *Essays on Language and Literature in Honour of Michio Kawai* (*SAC* 17 [1995], no. 127), pp. 29–36. As the Manciple uses his tale to warn the Cook not to accuse him, so Chaucer uses *ManT* to warn his audience to be careful of the stories they tell.

See also nos. 85, 153.

### *CT*—The Parson and His Tale

276. Bourgne, Florence. "Corpus chaucérien et corporéité des vertus. Le MS. Cambridge Gg 4.27(1)." In Marie-Claire Rouyer, ed. *Le corps dans tous ses états*. Bordeaux: Presses Universitaires de Bordeaux, 1995, pp. 69–79. Although the manuscript is a typical instance of *compilatio* and unification (e.g., punctuation of *ParsT*), the virtues portrayed to illustrate *ParsT* do not belong to a typical iconographic program. After identifying the three virtues with two saints (Charité and Abstinence with Elizabeth, Chasteté with Margaret), Bourgne reevaluates the possible provenance of the Chaucerian collection, arguing in favor of a tie with Jacqueline de Hainaut.

277. Hartung, Albert E. "'The Parson's Tale' and Chaucer's Penance." In Richard G. Newhauser and John A. Alford, eds. *Literature*

*and Religion in the Later Middle Ages: Philological Studies in Honor of Siegfried Wenzel* (SAC 19 [1997], no. 114), pp. 61–80. A psychoanalytic reading shows that *ParsT* and *Ret* belonged originally to a separate document that was later added to *CT* through *ParsP*.

278. Heinrichs, Katherine. "Tropological Woman in Chaucer: Literary Elaborations of an Exegetical Tradition." *ES* 76 (1995): 209–14. Allusions to the Fall appear in at least half of the tales in *CT*, but a full tropological reading occurs only in *ParsT* (line 330), where the allegory explains that "the image of God in man guarantees our ability to rise after a fall."

279. Jost, Jean E. "The *Parson's Tale*: Ending 'Thilke Parfit Glorious Pilgrymage That Highte Jerusalem Celestial.'" *Proceedings of the Medieval Association of the Midwest* 3 (1995): 94–109. *ParsT* critiques both the tales in *CT* and life, as well as concluding *CT*. The tales and the Parson's meditation work together in a "problem-solution relationship." The tales present betrayals and sins through a variety of voices and genres, while *ParsT* creates a new tone to remedy and exonerate the betrayals in the tales and in life.

280. Tamaki, Atsuko, and Tadahiro Ikegami. "The Influence of Handbooks to the Inquisition." *Seijo Bungei* 152 (1995): 21–40. Examines the source of *ParsT* and concludes that the *Tale* was strongly influenced by Frère Laurent's *Summe le Roy* (1279).

See also nos. 96, 104, 149.

## *CT—Chaucer's Retraction*

281. Lares, Jameela. "Chaucer's *Retractions*: A 'Verray Parfit Penitance.'" *Cithara* 34:1 (1994): 18–33. Comparison with the ending of *TC* shows that Chaucer's *Ret* is not a literary device but rather an absolute statement of repentance.

See also nos. 85, 136, 277, 301.

## *Anelida and Arcite*

See nos. 19, 112.

## A Treatise on the Astrolabe

See no. 209.

## The Book of the Duchess

282. Bardavío, José M. "Chaucer: En torno a cuatro Poenas Mayores." *Estudios de Filología Inglesa* 3 (1977): 5–17. Assesses the relations between the dreamer and the narrator in *BD, PF, HF,* and *LGW.*

283. Ellis, Steve. "The Death of *The Book of the Duchess.*" *ChauR* 29 (1995): 249–58. *BD* should be given Chaucer's own title (*LGW* 418): *The Death of Blanche.* Chaucer's title is more fitting for a poem of anti-consolation that emphasizes "death's power over the loveliest visions of youth and happiness."

284. Heffernan, Carol Falvo. *The Melancholy Muse: Chaucer, Shakespeare, and Early Medicine.* Pittsburgh, Penn.: Duquesne University Press, 1995. xiv, 185 pp. Summarizes medieval and Renaissance attitudes toward melancholy as a medical disorder and examines literary uses of melancholy in *BD, TC,* and Shakespeare's *As You Like It* and *Hamlet. BD* reflects Chaucer's close familiarity with medical scholarship on melancholy and the related disease of lovesickness, from which the narrator of the poem and the Black Knight suffer. Heffernan's analysis of *TC* (a revision of her essay in *Neophil* 74 [1990]: 294–309) also addresses "hereos," or lovesickness, and the way it is "an integral part of the imaginative structure" of the poem.

See also nos. 52, 60, 64, 65, 79, 85, 90, 103, 112, 117, 300, 319.

## The House of Fame

285. Erzgräber, Willi. "Chaucer zwischen Mittelalter und Neuzeit." *LJGG* 36 (1995): 27–46. Although securely grounded in medieval moral and theological conventions, Chaucer anticipates modernist concepts of literature, as is evident in his individualism and psychological realism, his ironic crossings of medieval narrative and philosophical boundaries, and his playful skepticism toward oral and written traditions. Erzgräber compares *HF* with James Joyce's *Ulysses.*

286. León Sendra, Antonio. "Chaucer y la fama." *Estudios Ingleses de la Universidad Complatense* 2 (1994): 91–100. Commentary on *HF* as a self-conscious narrative that confronts questions of human knowledge and individual behavior.

287. Lynch, Kathryn L. "The Logic of the Dream Vision in Chaucer's *House of Fame*." In Richard J. Utz, ed. *Literary Nominalism and the Theory of Rereading Late Medieval Texts: A New Research Paradigm* (*SAC* 19 [1997], no. 130), pp. 179–203. Through the Eagle's arguments and Fame's arbitrary inferences and syllogisms, *HF* satirizes the logical analysis of language. This discrediting of late medieval dialectic is a new use of the dream-vision genre, which traditionally celebrates reason and analytic science.

288. Park, Elaine Virginia Verbicky. "The Rhetoric of Antecedence: Latin in Middle English Poetry." *DAI* 55 (1995): 1946A. Medieval English literature often incorporates Latin in any form, from close translation to radical reduction and including wordplay and allusion. Interplay of medieval English and Latin is examined in a variety of works, including *HF*.

289. Russell, J. Stephen. "Is London Burning? A Chaucerian Allusion to the Rising of 1381." *ChauR* 30 (1995): 107–9. *HF* 2.935–49 contains references to the uprising of 1381, the attack on the Temple, and the burning of the Savoy. Watling Street was the route the peasants took, and the young "Pheton," the "sonnes sone" (of Edward III), refers to Richard II. These references provide a *terminus a quo* for *HF*, placing it much later than previously suggested.

290. Schembri, Anthony M. "Chaucer's 'House of Fame' and Saint Augustine." *Augustinian Panorama* 5–7 (1988–90): 14–55. *HF* contains the elements of allegory: dialectical form with at least two speakers, episodes associated with a "deeper and hidden meaning," and a mixture of the serious and comic. Though most critics look at French and Italian influences on the poem, it also echoes Augustinian teachings and concepts, which permeated the world of Chaucer and his readers.

291. Valdés Miyares, Rubén. "Chaucer in the House of History: 'Moo Tydynges.'" In Bernardo Santano Moreno, Adrian R. Birtwhistle, and Luis G. Girón Echevarría, eds. *Papers from the VIIth International Conference of SELIM* (*SAC* 19 [1997], no. 120), pp. 351–59. Chaucer is an "accommodated deconstructionist" rather than a politically committed one. Nonetheless, *HF* goes beyond mere textual play to historical reference, and Chaucer wavers in the uneasy

contradiction between the formal presence of authority and its empty meaning.

See also nos. 22, 56, 65, 68, 81, 84, 85, 90, 92, 98, 103, 112, 282, 292, 300.

### The Legend of Good Women

292. Baswell, Christopher. *Virgil in Medieval England: Figuring the Aeneid from the Twelfth Century to Chaucer.* Cambridge: Cambridge University Press, 1995. xvii, 438 pp.; illus. Traces the evolution of Virgil's authority during the Middle Ages as stimulated by translations of his works and marginalia in his manuscripts. Examines various types of access to Virgil and suggests that there are three main approaches to Virgilian material: allegorical, pedagogical, and via romance. Chapter 6 focuses on the interaction among the three approaches within Chaucer's *HF* and *LGW*. Like the medieval treatment of Virgilian materials, Chaucer's treatment of the Matter of Troy also undergoes an evolution, apparent in his treatment of authority in *LGW*, where he asserts his own authority among the *auctores*—Virgil and Ovid—in order to challenge any author's claim to such an authoritative status.

293. Gould, Cynthia Marie. "Penitential Fictions, the Trial of Courtly Love, and the Emancipation of Story in the 'Legend of Good Women' and the 'Confessio Amantis.'" *DAI* 55 (1995): 2403A. Penitential fictions in Chaucer's *LGW* and Gower's *Confessio Amantis* critique the amorous code in courtly literature. In *LGW*, Chaucer uses Christian martyrdom to depict his heroine's amorous self-sacrifice as futile.

294. Hanrahan, Michael. "Traitors and Lovers: The Politics of Love in Chaucer's 'Legend of Good Women,' Gower's 'Confessio Amantis,' and Usk's 'Testament of Love.'" *DAI* 56 (1995): 2248A. Richard II's reign produced political upheaval that redefined treason not only politically but also as reflected in literary depictions of love. In *LGWP*, Alceste blunts Cupid's accusation of treason but sets up the absurd notion that "all men are traitors."

295. Higgins, Anne. "Alceste the Washerwoman." In M. Teresa Tavormina and R. F. Yeager, eds. *The Endless Knot: Essays on Old and Middle English in Honor of Marie Borroff* (SAC 19 [1997], no. 128), pp. 13–27. One key to recognizing the parody of hagiography in *LGW*

is the identification of Alceste as Alice de Cestre in *LGWP*. Alice was a washerwoman of the royal household—perhaps a prostitute—and the double identity of Alceste-Alice establishes a "flexible morality" for the poem, "a model of moral relativism and tolerance."

296. Laird, Judith. "Good Women and *Bonnes Dames*: Virtuous Females in Chaucer and Christine De Pizan." *ChauR* 30 (1995): 58–70. In *LGW*, Chaucer asks, "Can women be faithful in love?" Christine asks, "Does virtue recognize gender?" Chaucer's "good women" are judged according to their relationships with men; Christine's are considered as separate beings.

297. Phillips, Helen. "Chaucer and Jean Le Fèvre." *Archiv* 232 (1995): 23–36. Argues that *LGW* was inspired by Jean Le Fèvre's *Lamentations de Matheolus* (1371–72?) and Livre de Leësce (1373 or 1380–87).

298. ———. "Literary Allusion in Chaucer's Ballade, "Hyd, Absalon, Thy Gilte Tresses Clere.'" *ChauR* 30 (1995): 134–49. Chaucer's catalog of women in *LGWP* contains attributes specifically chosen to reflect both the themes of the work itself and allusions to other literary works on the respective characters. Chaucer thus demonstrates his knowledge of previous treatments of the themes in earlier writers and books.

See also nos. 18, 65, 79, 85, 103, 112, 117, 199, 282.

### The Parliament of Fowls

299. Gutierréz Arranz, José M. "The Classical and Modern Concept of Nature in Geoffrey Chaucer's 'The Parliament of Fowls.'" In Bernardo Santano Moreno, Adrian R. Birtwhistle, and Luis G. Girón Echevarría, eds. *Papers from the VIIth International Conference of SELIM* (*SAC* 19 [1997], no. 120), pp. 141–48. In *PF*, Chaucer's Nature fulfills a double role: a divinity who presides over weddings (classical) and a mediatrix for the Christian deity (early modern).

300. Keiper, Hugo. "'I Wot Myself Best How Y Stonde': Literary Nominalism, Open Textual Form and the Enfranchisement of Individual Perspective in Chaucer's Dream Visions." In Richard J. Utz, ed. *Literary Nominalism and the Theory of Rereading Late Medieval Texts: A New Research Paradigm* (*SAC* 19 [1997], no. 130), pp. 205–34. Aligns

nominalism with "open" literary forms; realism, with "closed" ones. Demonstrates the fundamental, formal open-endedness of *BD*, *HF*, and, especially, *PF*, arguing that the poems exemplify a kind of "literary nominalism" that obliquely reflects contemporary philosophical discourse.

See also nos. 56, 65, 81, 84, 85, 90, 97, 103, 112, 126, 282.

### *Troilus and Criseyde*

301. Crépin, André. "Liturgy as a Common Source for Chaucer and Deschamps." *BAM* 48 (1995): 23–43. The liturgy is omnipresent in the texts of medieval writers, including lay writers, although its influence is often indirect. Deschamps, Chaucer, and their fellow poets were proud of their pagan learning and eager to display it, although Chaucer felt some remorse; hence, his palinode at the end of *TC* and his *Ret* at the end of *CT*. The conclusion of *TC* unites elements from Dante and the liturgy.

302. Doñabeita, María L. "Criseyde and Diomede: A Study of *Troilus and Criseyde*." In Antonio León Sendra, María C. Casares Trillo, and María M. Rivas Carmona, eds. *Second International Conference of the Spanish Society for Medieval Language and Literature* (*SAC* 19 [1997], no. 123), pp. 36–43. Criseyde rejects the values of courtly love that Troilus embraces. In her relation with Diomede, Criseyde rejects courtly love and its attachment to death in favor of a life-affirming love.

303. Edwards, A. S. G. "Chaucer's *Troilus and Criseyde* IV.588." *Expl* 53 (1995): 66. By altering the proverb in *TC* 4.588 from "day" to "nyght," Chaucer ironically foreshadows the beginning of Troilus's period of unrest.

304. Farrell, Thomas J. "The *Fyn* of the *Troilus*." In David G. Allen and Robert A. White, eds. *Subjects on the World's Stage: Essays on British Literature of the Middle Ages and the Renaissance* (*SAC* 19 [1997], no. 75), pp. 38–53. Uses of the word *fyn* by Criseyde, Pandarus, and the narrator invite the reader to consider the teleology of the various parts of the work.

305. Hardman, Phillipa. "Chaucer's Articulation of the Narrative in *Troilus*: The Manuscript Evidence." *ChauR* 30 (1995): 111–33. A comparison of the manuscripts of *TC* with those of Boccaccio's *Filostrato* indicates that Chaucer's narrative divisions correspond to the summary rubrics in the earlier work, even if he did not retain Boccaccio's internal subdivisions.

306. Jimura, Akiyuki. "The Language of Criseyde in Chaucer's *Troilus and Criseyde* (III)." *Bulletin of the Faculty of School Education* (Hiroshima University) 16 (1994): 1–8. A sociolinguistic exploration of Criseyde's grammar, literacy, pronunciation, and verbosity, considered in relation to the vocabulary and syntax of fourteenth-century upper-class women. Includes word-count tables.

307. León Sendra, Antonio R. "Criseyde and Her Lovers." In Antonio León Sendra, María C. Casares Trillo, and María M. Rivas Carmona, eds. *Second International Conference of the Spanish Society for Medieval Language and Literature* (SAC 19 [1997], no. 123), pp. 114–25. Examines a series of passages that characterize Criseyde's relations with her lovers.

308. Milliken, Roberta. "Neither 'Clere Laude' Nor 'Sklaundre': Chaucer's Translation of Criseyde." *WS* 24 (1995): 191–204. In *TC*, Chaucer amplified traits in Criseyde that Boccaccio emphasized less in *Filostrato*. Criseyde's social isolation, fearfulness, awareness of her social rank, and vulnerability both make her a more fully realized character than Boccaccio's Criseida and make her betrayal of Troilus more understandable.

309. Park, Yoon-hee. "Rewriting Woman Evil? Antifeminism and Its Hermeneutic Problems in Four Criseida Stories." *DAI* 56 (1995): 1796A. Chaucer's *TC* responds to antifeminist treatment of the Criseida character, especially Boccaccio's; Henryson's version replies to Chaucer. Shakespeare's Cressida offers a different antifeminist view, recast without basic change by Dryden. Criseyde continues to fascinate through her varying images.

310. Schembri, A. M. "Love, Pity and Reason in the *Troilus*: Chaucer's Debt to Dante." *Journal of Anglo-Italian Studies* 2 (1992): 1–35. Influenced by Dante, Chaucer transforms romance into "a vehicle for philosophic exposition." *TC* mixes passion and innocence, the real and the ideal, the courtly and the Christian.

311. Shaw, Patricia. "Representations and Functions of Widowhood in Middle English Writings." In Purificación Fernández Nistal and José Mª Bravo Gazalo, eds. *Proceedings of the VIth International Conference of the Spanish Society for Medieval English Language and Literature* (SAC 19 [1997], no. 95), pp. 31–40. Compares the roles and functions of Criseyde and the Wife of Bath as two of the most outstanding female characters in Middle English literature. As the Wife goes from one husband to another, so Criseyde's acceptance of Troilus as a lover may suggest that she will go from one lover to another.

312. Silver, Marcia H. "Chaucer's Lexicon of Love: A Study of Thematically Significant Words in 'Troilus and Criseyde.'" *DAI* 56 (1995): 1798A. *TC* shows Chaucer's ambivalence about the language of courtly love; he uses it denotatively with romantic meaning yet reveals its duplicity through Troilus's idealism, Diomede's cynicism, Pandarus's manipulativeness, and Criseyde's combined sincerity and irony. The narrator, unable to handle Criseyde's betrayal, continues to feel sympathy for her.

313. Sola Buil, Ricardo J. *"Troilus and Criseyde*: A Pragmatic Approach." In Antonio León Sendra, María C. Casares Trillo, and María M. Rivas Carmona, eds. *Second International Conference of the Spanish Society for Medieval Language and Literature (SAC* 19 [1997], no. 123), pp. 180–90. Examines Chaucer's narratorial intrusions in *TC*, arguing that they both lead the reader to assimilate abrupt shifts in sensibility and perspective and move the reader from objective observation to subjective response.

314. Spillenger, Paul. "The Metamorphosis of *Musorno*: A Note on Chaucer's Translation of *Filostrato* I, 54 in *Troilus* I, 526–32." *ChauR* 29 (1995): 348–51. The "byjaped fol," to whom Chaucer refers in *TC* 1.526–32, is not a specific person but rather a mistranslation of Boccaccio's word "musorno," which Chaucer took to refer to a well-known person—a particular "fool"—rather than to the foolish quality of a person.

315. Steinberg, Diane Vanner. "'We Do Usen Here No Wommen for to Selle': Embodiment of Social Practices in *Troilus and Criseyde.*" *ChauR* 29 (1995): 259–73. The two distinct "social spaces" within the poem—the city of Troy and the Greek camp—represent the varying attitudes of the characters inhabiting them, particularly their attitudes concerning women. When Criseyde is given over to Diomede, however, the "courtly" Trojans come to espouse the Greek tendency to view women as objects to be exchanged.

316. Stiller, Nikki. *The Figure of Cressida in British and American Literature: Transformation of a Literary Type.* Lewiston, N.Y.: Edwin Mellen, 1990. 193 pp. Chapter 2, "Civilization and Its Ambivalence," explores how Chaucer's rendering of Criseyde has set the stage for all subsequent British and American portrayals of her.

317. Utz, Richard J. "Medievalism as Modernism: Alfred Andersch's Nominalist Littérature Engagée." *SiM* 6 (1993): 76–91. Compares the consciously nominalistic modern poetics of German realist Andersch to Chaucer's nominalist mentality as evident in the anti-deterministic mood in *TC*.

318. Valdés Miyares, Rubén. "From Chaucer's Troilus to Henryson's Cresseid: Problems of Interpretation in *The Testament of Cresseid*." In Antonio León Sendra, María C. Casares Trillo, and María M. Rivas Carmona, eds. *Second International Conference of the Spanish Society for Medieval Language and Literature* (*SAC* 19 [1997], no. 123), pp. 207–16. While Chaucer approached *TC* as a "historial" poet, Henryson wrote as a "literary" poet, relying less than Chaucer on rhetorical ornamentation and more on his own invention. Both authors are poets of "doctryne."

319. Vila de la Cruz, Purificación. "The Fight of Feelings in the *Book of the Duchess* and *Troilus and Criseyde*." In Purificación Fernández Nistal and José Mª Bravo Gazalo, eds. *Proceedings of the VIth International Conference of the Spanish Society for Medieval English Language and Literature* (*SAC* 19 [1997], no. 95), pp. 385–91. Explores different aspects of the love felt by Criseyde in light of the emotions expressed in *BD*. As a pragmatist, Criseyde thinks she will not suffer love's pains. Her feelings lack heroic grandeur.

320. Wetherbee, Winthrop. "Chivalry under Siege in Ricardian Romance." In Ivy A. Corfis and Michael Wolfe, eds. *The Medieval City under Siege*. Woodbridge, Suffolk: Boydell Press, 1995, pp. 207–23. Surveys how chivalry is promoted or assumed in various medieval romances and argues that it is critiqued in *TC*, *KnT*, and *Sir Gawain and the Green Knight*. *TC* shows the "chivalric ideal suspended in a state of blind and seemingly helpless complicity in its own betrayal"; in *KnT*, the temple of Mars reveals the realities of late medieval warfare to be in tension with courtly ideals.

See also nos. 19, 52, 79, 81, 83–86, 88, 97, 103, 126, 129, 132, 139, 281, 284.

## Lyrics and Short Poems

See no. 112.

## *An ABC*

321. Boyd, Beverly. "Chaucer's Moments in the 'Kneeling World.'" In Anne Clark Bartlett, Thomas H. Bestul, Janet Goebel, and William F. Pollard, eds. *Vox Mystica: Essays on Medieval Mysticism in Honor of Professor Valerie M. Lagorio*. Rochester, N.Y., and Cambridge: D. S.

Brewer, 1995, pp. 99–105. Traces a strain of Marian mysticism in Chaucer's works, including *ABC* and several aspects of *SNT* and *PrT*.

See also no. 60.

## The Former Age

See no. 268.

## The Complaint of Chaucer to His Purse

See no. 188.

## To Rosemounde

322. Stemmler, Theo. "Chaucer's Ballade 'To Rosemounde'—a Parody?" In Richard G. Newhauser and John A. Alford, eds. *Literature and Religion in the Later Middle Ages: Philological Studies in Honor of Siegfried Wenzel* (SAC 19 [1997], no. 114), pp. 11–23. Disagreeing throughout with Joerg Fichte and Edmund Reiss, Stemmler uses literature contemporary with Chaucer to show that *Ros* is a "seriously meant love-lyric." It is not a parody.

## Chaucerian Apocrypha

323. Rex, Richard. "Chaucer's Censured Ballads." In Richard Rex. *"The Sins of Madame Eglentyne" and Other Essays on Chaucer* (SAC 19 [1997], no. 118), pp. 27–33. Assesses the textual history and canonicity of two ballads of a manuscript owned by John Shirley, now British Museum Additional MS 16165. The two ballads have not received serious consideration, because they have been omitted from Chaucer's canon—one of them apparently because of its obscene content.

See also no. 38.

## The Romaunt of the Rose

See nos. 60, 79.

## Book Reviews

324. Andrew, Malcolm, Charles Moorman, and Daniel J. Ransom, eds., with the assistance of Lynne Hunt Levy. *The General Prologue* (*SAC* 17 [1995], no. 11). Rev. A. S. G. Edwards, *SAC* 17 (1995): 157–60; Walter Scheps, *ANQ* 8:1 (1995): 48–55; E. G. Stanley, *N&Q* 240 (1995): 82–84.

325. Arden, Heather M. The Roman de la Rose: *An Annotated Bibliography* (*SAC* 18 [1996], no. 33). Rev. Jillian Hill, *MÆ* 64 (1995): 143–44.

326. Astell, Ann W. *Job, Boethius, and Epic Truth* (*SAC* 18 [1996], no. 72). Rev. Lawrence Besserman, *SAC* 17 (1995): 160–63.

327. Barney, Stephen A. *Studies in* Troilus: *Chaucer's Text, Meter, and Diction* (*SAC* 17 [1995], no. 21). Rev. Malcolm Andrew, *ES* 76 (1995): 479–80; Leo Carruthers, *ÉA* 48 (1995): 90; A. S. G. Edwards, *Speculum* 70 (1995): 875–77; James R. Sprouse, *SAC* 17 (1995): 163–67.

328. Beal, F., and Jeremy Griffiths, eds. *English Manuscript Studies, 1100–1700* (*SAC* 16 [1994], nos. 265–66). Rev. E. G. Stanley, *N&Q* 240 (1995): 230–32.

329. Benson, C. David, and Elizabeth Robertson, eds. *Chaucer's Religious Tales* (*SAC* 14 [1992], no. 130). Rev. Vincent DiMarco, *Anglia* 113 (1995): 396–400.

330. Benson, Larry D. *A Glossarial Concordance to the* Riverside Chaucer (*SAC* 17 [1995], no. 2). Rev. Joseph S. Wittig, *Speculum* 70 (1995): 341–43.

331. Biscoglio, Frances Minetti. *The Wives of the* Canterbury Tales *and the Tradition of the Valiant Woman of Proverbs 31:10–31* (*SAC* 17 [1995], no. 128). Rev. Paul T. Piehler, *C&L* 43 (1993): 105–6.

332. Blake, Norman, and Peter Robinson, eds. *The* Canterbury Tales *Project: Occasional Papers, Volume I* (*SAC* 17 [1995], no. 23). Rev. Tim William Machan, *SAC* 17 (1995): 175–78.

333. Blamires, Alcuin, ed., with Karen Pratt and C. W. Marx. *Woman Defamed and Woman Defended: An Anthology of Medieval Texts*

(*SAC* 16 [1994], no. 68). Rev. Stephen F. Trantner, *Anglia* 113 (1995): 245–47.

334. Burnley, David, and Matsuji Tajima. *The Language of Middle English Literature* (*SAC* 18 [1996], no. 4). Rev. Helmut Gneuss, *Anglia* 113 (1995): 518–19.

335. Chamberlain, David, ed. *New Readings of Late Medieval Love Poems* (*SAC* 17 [1995], no. 274). Rev. Julia Boffey, *N&Q* 240 (1995): 474.

336. Crane, Susan. *Gender and Romance in Chaucer's* Canterbury Tales (*SAC* 18 [1996], no. 139). Rev. David Aers, *MÆ* 53 (1995): 316–18; Laurel Amtower, *Æstel* 3 (1995): 97–105; Allen J. Frantzen, *SAC* 17 (1995): 185–89.

337. Dean, James M., and Christian Zacher, eds. *The Idea of Medieval Literature: New Essays on Chaucer and Medieval Culture in Honor of Donald R. Howard* (*SAC* 16 [1994], no.79). Rev. Joerg O. Fichte, *Anglia* 113 (1995): 400–4.

338. Delany, Sheila. *Chaucer's* House of Fame: *The Poetics of Skeptical Fideism* (*SAC* 18 [1996], no. 261). Rev. Richard J. Utz, *Carmina Philosophiae* 3 (1994): 87–90.

339. ———. *The Naked Text: Chaucer's* Legend of Good Women (*SAC* 18 [1995], no. 265). Rev. William A. Quinn, *SAC* 17 (1995): 192–95.

340. Dillon, Janette. *Geoffrey Chaucer* (*SAC* 17 [1995], no. 84). Rev. Peter G. Beidler, *SAC* 17 (1995): 195–98; Derek Pearsall, *YES* 25 (1995): 247–50.

341. Doob, Penelope Reed. *The Idea of the Labyrinth from Classical Antiquity Through the Middle Ages* (*SAC* 14 [1992], no. 74). Rev. Jeanette Beer, *FR* 68 (1995): 520–21.

342. Dor, Juliette, ed. *A Wyf Ther Was: Essays in Honour of Paule Mertens-Fonck* (*SAC* 16 [1994], no. 83). Rev. Françoise Le Saux, *MA* 101 (1995): 349–50; Patricia Shaw, *Archiv* 232 (1995): 193–96.

343. Ecker, Ronald L., and Eugene Crook, trans. The Canterbury Tales *by Geoffrey Chaucer* (*SAC* 17 [1995], no. 13). Rev. Malcolm Andrew, *ES* 76 (1995): 480–81.

344. Edwards, Robert R., ed. *Art and Context in Late Medieval English Narrative: Essays in Honor of Robert Worth Frank, Jr.* (*SAC* 18 [1996], no. 85). Rev. Jerome Mandel, *Arthuriana* 5:3 (1995): 113–17.

345. Emmerson, Richard K., and Ronald B. Herzman. *The Apocalyptic Imagination in Medieval Literature* (*SAC* 16 [1994], no. 137).

Rev. Kevin Madigan, *Church History* 64 (1995): 466–68; H. L. Spencer, *RES*, n.s., 46 (1995): 391–92.

346. Fisher, John H. *The Importance of Chaucer* (*SAC* 16 [1994], no. 35). Rev. Beryl Rowland, *ELN* 32:2 (1995): 76–81.

347. Frese, Dolores Warwick. *An Ars Legendi for Chaucer's Canterbury Tales: A Reconstructive Reading* (*SAC* 15 [1993], no. 150). Rev. Charles R. Smith, *JRMMRA* 14 (1993): 154–55.

348. Goodman, Anthony. *John of Gaunt: The Exercise of Princely Power in Fourteenth-Century England* (*SAC* 17 [1995], no. 92). Rev. André Leguai, *MA* 101 (1995): 349–50.

349. Hallissy, Margaret. *Clean Maids, True Wives, Steadfast Widows: Chaucer's Women and Medieval Codes of Conduct* (*SAC* 17 [1995], no. 93). Rev. Barbara Nolan, *Speculum* 70 (1995): 627–29; Dhira B. Mahoney, *SAC* 17 (1995): 210–14.

350. Hanawalt, Barbara A., ed. *Chaucer's England: Literature in Historical Context* (*SAC* 16 [1994], no. 89). Rev. Elaine Tuttle Hansen, *Journal of British Studies* 33 (1994): 204–10.

351. Hansen, Elaine Tuttle. *Chaucer and the Fictions of Gender* (*SAC* 16 [1994], no. 90). Rev. Catherine S. Cox, *SoAR* 58:1 (1993): 124–26; Mary F. Wack, *MP* 92 (1995): 501–5.

352. Heffernan, James A. W. *Museum of Words: The Poetics of Ekphrasis from Homer to Ashbery* (*SAC* 19 [1997], no. 98). Rev. Richard Macksey, *MLN* 110 (1995): 1010–15.

353. Hill, John M. *Chaucerian Belief: The Poetics of Reverence and Delight* (*SAC* 15 [1993], no. 108). Rev. Dolores Warwick Frese, *Chaucer Yearbook* 2 (1995): 172–79; Katharine S. Gittes, *JRMMRA* 14 (1993): 155–57.

354. Hill, Ordelle G. *The Manor, the Plowman, and the Shepherd: Agrarian Themes and Imagery in Late Medieval and Early Renaissance English Literature* (*SAC* 18 [1996], no. 92). Rev. John C. Hirsh, *MÆ* 64 (1995): 315–16.

355. Hines, John. *The Fabliau in English* (*SAC* 17 [1995], no. 130). Rev. Glending Olson, *SAC* 17 (1995): 214–17.

356. Jager, Eric. *The Tempter's Voice: Language and the Fall in Medieval Literature* (*SAC* 18 [1996], no. 208). Rev. David Lawton, *SAC* 17 (1995): 217–20.

357. Justice, Steven. *Writing and Rebellion: England in 1381* (*SAC* 18 [1996], no. 95). Rev. Curtis Gruenler, *Comitatus* 26 (1995): 118–24; Derek Pearsall, *MÆ* 64 (1995): 319–21.

358. Keenan, Hugh T., ed. *Typology and English Medieval Literature* (*SAC* 16 [1994], no. 96). Rev. Edward Wilson, *RES*, n.s., 46 (1995): 252–53.

359. Kelly, Henry Ansgar. *Ideas and Forms of Tragedy from Aristotle to the Middle Ages* (*SAC* 18 [1996], no. 98). Rev. Renate Haas, *SAC* 17 (1995): 220–22.

360. Kindrick, Robert L. *Henryson and the Medieval Arts of Rhetoric* (*SAC* 18 [1996], no. 50). Rev. George D. Gopen, *SAC* 17 (1995): 223–26.

361. Kinney, Clare Regan. *Strategies of Poetic Narrative: Chaucer, Spenser, Milton, Eliot* (*SAC* 16 [1994], no. 97). Rev. Jeremy Tambling, *YES* 25 (1995): 231–32.

362. Kiser, Lisa J. *Truth and Textuality in Chaucer's Poetry* (*SAC* 15 [1993], no. 113). Rev. Katharine S. Gittes, *JRMMRA* 14 (1993): 155–57.

363. Kruger, Steven F. *Dreaming in the Middle Ages* (*SAC* 16 [1994], no. 101). Rev. Michael Uebel, *SoAR* 58:4 (1993): 135–38.

364. Lancashire, Ian, ed. *Computer-based Chaucer Studies* (*SAC* 17 [1995], no. 101). Rev. Hoyt N. Duggan, *SAC* 17 (1995): 226–29.

365. Lerer, Seth. *Chaucer and His Readers: Imagining the Author in Late-Medieval England* (*SAC* 17 [1995], no. 50). Rev. N. F. Blake, *ES* 76 (1995): 96–98; Leo Carruthers, *ÉA* 48 (1995): 89–90; R. James Goldstein, *SHR* 29 (1995): 392–97; Glending Olson, *ANQ* 8:3 (1995): 45–47; Derek Pearsall, *YES* 25 (1995): 247–50; Karen A. Winstead, *SAC* 17 (1995): 229–34.

366. Mandel, Jerome. *Geoffrey Chaucer: Building the Fragments of the Canterbury Tales* (*SAC* 16 [1994], no. 147). Rev. Helen Cooper, *RES*, n.s., 46 (1995): 398–99; Richard J. Utz, *Anglia* 113 (1995): 251–54.

367. Margherita, Gayle. *The Romance of Origins: Language and Sexual Difference in Middle English Literature* (*SAC* 18 [1996], no. 108). Rev. Alcuin Blamires, *MÆ* 64 (1995): 313–14.

368. Meale, Carol M., ed. *Readings in Medieval English Romance* (*SAC* 18 [1996], no. 109). Rev. Corrine J. Saunders, *N&Q* 240 (1995): 473–74.

369. ———, ed. *Women and Literature in Britain, 1150–1500* (*SAC* 17 [1995], no. 105). Rev. Nicholas Watson, *SAC* 17 (1995): 236–41.

370. Minnis, A. J., ed. *Chaucer's* Boece *and the Medieval Tradition of Boethius* (*SAC* 17 [1995], no. 220). Rev. N. F. Blake, *ES* 76 (1995): 98–99; Susan Yager, *C&L* 43 (1993): 106–8.

371. ————, and Charlotte Brewer, eds. *Crux and Controversy in Middle English Textual Criticism* (*SAC* 16 [1994], no. 17). Rev. John Fankis, *RES*, n.s., 46 (1995): 393–95.

372. Neuse, Richard. *Chaucer's Dante: Allegory and Epic Theater in The Canterbury Tales* (*SAC* 15 [1993], no. 158). Rev. Robert Watson, *Chaucer Yearbook* 2 (1995): 180–90.

373. Ní Cuilleanáin, Eiléan, and J. D. Pheifer, eds. *Noble and Joyous Histories: English Romances, 1375–1650* (*SAC* 17 [1995], no. 108). Rev. Mary Hamel, *SAC* 17 (1995): 245–48.

374. Nolan, Barbara. *Chaucer and the Tradition of the Roman Antique* (*SAC* 16 [1994], no. 30). Rev. Donald C. Baker, *ELN* 33:1 (1995): 76–78; J. D. Burnley, *RES*, n.s., 46 (1995): 397–98; Nick Havely, *YES* 25 (1995): 250–51; Lesley Johnson, *FR* 69 (1995): 324–25; Dieter Mehl, *Archiv* 232 (1995): 196–201.

375. Owen, Charles A., Jr. *The Manuscripts of The Canterbury Tales* (*SAC* 15 [1993], no. 28). Rev. A. I. Doyle, *RES*, n.s., 46 (1995): 68–70.

376. Patterson, Lee. *Chaucer and the Subject of History* (*SAC* 15 [1993], no. 124). Rev. Elaine Tuttle Hansen, *Journal of British Studies* 33 (1994): 204–10; Scott D. Troyan, *Chaucer Yearbook* 2 (1995): 191–95.

377. Pearsall, Derek. *The Canterbury Tales* (*SAC* 9 [1987], no. 123). Rev. Helen Cooper, *RES*, n.s., 46 (1995): 67–68; David J. Williams, *RMSt* 21 (1995): 114–15.

378. ————. *The Life of Geoffrey Chaucer: A Critical Biography* (*SAC* 16 [1994], no. 5). Rev. Michael Alexander, *English* 42 (1993): 88–91.

379. Purdon, Liam O., and Cindy L. Vitto, eds. *The Rusted Hauberk: Feudal Ideals of Order and Their Decline* (*SAC* 18 [1996], no. 118). Rev. Thomas H. Bestul, *SAC* 17 (1995): 248–50.

380. Rand Schmidt, Kari Anne. *The Authorship of The Equatorie of the Planetis* (*SAC* 17 [1995], no. 233). Rev. Stephen Partridge, *SAC* 17 (1995): 254–57; P. R. Robinson, *MÆ* 64 (1995): 129–30.

381. Richmond, Velma Bourgeois. *Geoffrey Chaucer* (*SAC* 16 [1994], no. 112). Rev. John Micheal Crafton, *SoAR* 58:4 (1993): 138–40.

382. Rooney, Anne. *Hunting in Middle English Literature* (*SAC* 17 [1995], no. 111). Rev. J. D. Burnley, *RES*, n.s., 46 (1995): 551–52.

383. Rudat, Wolfgang E. H. *Earnest Exuberance in Chaucer's Poetics: Textual Games in the Canterbury Tales* (*SAC* 17 [1995], no. 137). Rev. Susanna Greer Fein, *SAC* 17 (1995): 251–54.

384. Rudd, Niall. *The Classical Tradition in Operation: Chaucer/Virgil, Shakespeare/Plautus, Pope/Horace, Tennyson/Lucretius, Pound/Propertius* (*SAC* 18 [1996], no. 37). Rev. Don Fowler, *TLS*, Apr. 14, 1995, p. 10.

385. Scanlon, Larry. *Narrative, Authority, and Power: The Medieval Exemplum and the Chaucerian Tradition* (*SAC* 18 [1996], no. 120). Rev. Seth Lerer, *Speculum* 70 (1995): 960–62; N. Mortimer, *MÆ* 64 (1995): 318–19.

386. Shoaf, R. A., ed., with the assistance of Catherine S. Cox. *Chaucer's* Troilus and Criseyde: *"Subgit to Alle Poesye": Essays in Criticism* (*SAC* 16 [1994], no. 309). Rev. David Anderson, *Anglia* 113 (1995): 249–51.

387. Spearing, A. C. *The Medieval Poet as Voyeur: Looking and Listening in Medieval Love-Narratives* (*SAC* 17 [1995], no. 117). Rev. Dieter Mehl, *Anglia* 113 (1995): 390–94; Edward Wilson, *RES*, n.s., 46 (1995): 548–50.

388. Spencer, H. Leith. *English Preaching in the Late Middle Ages* (*SAC* 17 [1995], no. 118). Rev. Leo Carruthers, *ÉA* 48 (1995): 215–16; J. Catto, *MÆ* 64 (1995): 128; Thomas J. Heffernan, *SAC* 17 (1995): 258–63.

389. Stillinger, Thomas C. *The Song of Troilus: Lyric Authority in the Medieval Book* (*SAC* 16 [1994], no. 314). Rev. Regina Psaki, *Chaucer Yearbook* 2 (1995): 206–10; Myra Stokes, *RES*, n.s., 46 (1995): 390–91.

390. Stone, Gregory B. *The Death of the Troubadour: The Late Medieval Resistance to the Renaissance* (*SAC* 17 [1996], no. 259). Rev. Daniel Rubey, *SAC* 17 (1995): 263–67.

391. Strohm, Paul. *Hochon's Arrow: The Social Imagination of Fourteenth-Century Texts* (*SAC* 16 [1994], no. 119). Rev. Robert S. Sturges, *Arthuriana* 5:3 (1995): 135–37.

392. Takamiya, Toshiyuki, and Richard Beadle, eds. *Chaucer to Shakespeare: Essays in Honour of Shinsuke Ando* (*SAC* 16 [1994], no. 120). Rev. Patrick J. Gallacher, *Anglia* 113 (1995): 254–56.

393. Taylor, Robert A., James F. Burke, Patricia J. Eberle, Ian Lancashire, and Brian S. Merrilees, eds. *The Centre and Its Compass: Studies in Medieval Literature in Honour of John Leyerle* (*SAC* 17 [1995], no. 121). Rev. Julia Boffey, *SAC* 17 (1995): 268–71.

394. Utz, Richard J. *Literarischer Nominalismus im Spätmittelalter: Eine Untersuchung zur Sprache, Charakterzeichnung und Struktur in Geoffrey Chaucers* Troilus and Criseyde (*SAC* 14 [1992], no. 271). Rev. Paule Mertens-Fonck, *MA* 101 (1995): 315–20.

395. Wimsatt, James I. *Chaucer and His French Contemporaries: Natural Music in the Fourteenth Century* (*SAC* 15 [1993], no. 45). Rev. William Calin, *Chaucer Yearbook* 2 (1995): 211–14.

396. Windeatt, Barry. *Troilus and Criseyde* (Oxford Guides to Chaucer) (*SAC* 16 [1994], no. 320). Rev. Donald C. Baker, *ELN* 33:1 (1995): 74–76; John M. Fyler, *YES* 25 (1995): 251–52; Myra Stokes, *RES*, n.s., 46 (1995): 252–53.

397. Yeager, R. F., ed. *Chaucer and Gower: Difference, Mutuality, Exchange* (*SAC* 15 [1993], no. 47). Rev. H. L. Spencer, *RES*, n.s., 46 (1995): 252–53.

# Author Index—Bibliography

# Index